TAKING SIDES

Clashing Views on

Political Issues

FIFTEENTH EDITION

Selected, Edited, and with Introductions by

George McKenna
City College, City University of New York

and

Stanley Feingold
City College, City University of New York

McGraw Hill **Contemporary Learning Series**

A Division of The McGraw-Hill Companies

In memory of Hillman M. Bishop and Samuel Hendel, masters of an art often neglected by college teachers: teaching.

Photo Acknowledgment
Cover image: DoD photo by Petty officer
1st Class Shane T. McCoy, U.S. Navy

Cover Acknowledgment
Maggie Lytle

Manufactured in the United States of America

Fifteenth Edition

123456789DOCDOC9876

Library of Congress Cataloging-in-Publication Data
Main entry under title:
Taking sides: clashing views on political issues/selected, edited, and with introductions by George McKenna and Stanley Feingold.—15th ed.
Includes bibliographical references and index.
1. United States—Politics and government—1945–. I. McKenna, George, *comp.*
II. Feingold, Stanley, *comp.*
320'.973
0-07-351505-1
978-0-07-351505-2
ISSN: 1080-580X

Preface

Dialogue means two people talking to the same issue. This is not as easy as it sounds. Play back the next debate between the talking heads you see on television. Listen to them try to persuade each other—actually, the TV audience—of the truth of their own views and of the irrationality of their opponents' views.

What is likely to happen? At the outset, they will probably fail to define the issue with enough clarity and objectivity to make it clear exactly what it is that they are disputing. As the philosopher Alasdair MacIntyre has put it, the most passionate pro and con arguments are often "incommensurable"—they sail past each other because the two sides are talking about different things. As arguments proceed, both sides tend to employ vague, emotion-laden terms without spelling out the uses to which the terms are put. When the heat is on, they may resort to shouting epithets at one another, and the hoped-for meeting of minds will give way to the scoring of political points and the reinforcement of existing prejudices. For example, when the discussion of affirmative action comes down to both sides accusing the other of "racism," or when the controversy over abortion degenerates into taunts and name-calling, then no one really listens and learns from the other side.

It is our conviction that people *can* learn from the other side, no matter how sharply opposed it is to their own cherished viewpoint. Sometimes, after listening to others, we change our view entirely. But in most cases, we either incorporate some elements of the opposing view—thus making our own richer—or else learn how to answer the objections to our viewpoint. Either way, we gain from the experience. For these reasons we believe that encouraging dialogue between opposed positions is the most certain way of enhancing public understanding.

The purpose of this 15th edition of *Taking Sides* is to continue to work toward the revival of political dialogue in America. As we have done in the past 14 editions, we examine leading issues in American politics from the perspective of sharply opposed points of view. We have tried to select authors who argue their points vigorously but in such a way as to enhance our understanding of the issue.

We hope that the reader who confronts lively and thoughtful statements on vital issues will be stimulated to ask some of the critical questions about American politics. What are the highest-priority issues with which government must deal today? What positions should be taken on these issues? What should be the attitude of Americans toward their government? Our conviction is that a healthy, stable democracy requires a citizenry that considers these questions and participates, however indirectly, in answering them. The alternative is apathy, passivity, and, sooner or later, the rule of tyrants.

Plan of the book   Each issue has an issue *introduction*, which sets the stage for the debate as it is argued in the YES and NO selections. Each issue concludes with a *postscript* that makes some final observations and points the way to other questions related to the issue. In reading the issue and forming your own opinions you should not feel confined to adopt one or the other of the positions presented. There are positions in between the given views or totally outside them, and the *suggestions for further reading* that appear in each issue postscript should help you find resources to continue your study of the subject. We have also provided relevant Internet site addresses (URLs) on the *On the Internet* page that accompanies each part opener. At the back of the book is a listing of all the *contributors to this volume,* which will give you information on the political scientists and commentators whose views are debated here.

Changes to this edition   Over the 30 years *Taking Sides* has undergone extensive changes and improvements, and we are particularly proud of this 15th edition. We present nine new issues, more than ever before, and we have adopted other new selections, revising fully half the book. The new issues are: "Should Americans Believe in a Unique American 'Mission'"? (Issue 1), "Is Democracy the Answer to Global Terrorism?" (Issue 2), "Should the Electoral College be Abolished?" (Issue 3), "Should American Adopt Public Financing of Political Campaigns?" (Issue 5), "Should the Courts Seek the 'Original Meaning' of the Constitution?" (Issue 7), "May the President Wiretap Without a Warrant to Protect National Security" (Issue 8), "Stopping Illegal Immigration: Should Border Security Come First?" (Issue 16), "Does the War in Iraq Help the War Against Terrorism?" (Issue 18), and "Is the Use of Torture Against Terrorist Suspects Ever Justified?" (Issue 19). In addition, we have changed one of the selections in Issue 4 ("Do the News Media Have a Liberal Bias?"), and both of the selections in Issue 10 ("Does Affirmative Action Advance Racial Equality").

We worked hard on what we hope will be a truly memorable 15th edition, and we think you will like the result. Let us know what you think by writing to us in care of McGraw-Hill Contemporary Learning Series, 2460 Kerper Blvd., Dubuque, IA 52001 or e-mailing us at GMcK1320@aol.com or Stanleyfeingold@mindspring.com. Suggestions for further improvements are most welcome!

A word to the instructor   An *Instructor's Manual With Test Questions* (multiple-choice and essay) is available through the publisher for the instructor using *Taking Sides* in the classroom. A general guidebook, *Using Taking Sides in the Classroom,* which discusses methods and techniques for integrating the pro-con approach into any classroom setting, is also available. An online version of *Using Taking Sides in the Classroom* and a correspondence service for *Taking Sides* adopters can be found at http://www.mhcls.com/usingts/.

Taking Sides: Clashing Views on Political Issues is only one title in the Taking Sides series. If you are interested in seeing the table of contents for any of the other titles, please visit the Taking Sides Web site at http://www.mhcls.com/takingsides/.

Acknowledgments   We are grateful to Laura McKenna for her help and suggestions in preparing this edition. Thanks also to the reference departments of City College's Morris Raphael Cohen Library and the public library of Tenafly, New Jersey—especially to Agnes Kolben.

We also appreciate the spontaneous letters from instructors and students who wrote to us with comments and observations. Many thanks to Larry Loeppke and Jill Peter for their able editorial assistance. Needless to say, the responsibility for any errors of fact or judgment rests with us.

George McKenna
Stanley Feingold

Contents In Brief

Contents

PART 1   DEMOCRACY AND THE AMERICAN POLITICAL PROCESS   1

Issue 1.   Should Americans Believe in a Unique American "Mission"?   2

YES: **Wilfred M. McClay,** from "The Founding of Nations," *First Things* (March 2006)   4

NO: **Howard Zinn,** from "The Power and the Glory: Myths of American Exceptionalism," *Boston Review* (Summer 2005)   13

Humanities professor Wilfred M. McClay argues that America's "myth," its founding narrative, helps to sustain and hold together a diverse people. Historian Howard Zinn is convinced that America's myth of "exceptionalism" has served as a justification for lawlessness, brutality, and imperialism.

Issue 2.   Is Democracy the Answer to Global Terrorism?   22

YES: **George W. Bush,** from Speech at National Defense University (March 8, 2005)   24

NO: **F. Gregory Gause III,** from "Can Democracy Stop Terrorism?" *Foreign Affairs* (September/October 2005)   29

President George W. Bush argues that the best antidote to terrorism is the tolerance and hope generated by democracy. Political scientist Gregory Gause contends that there is no relationship between terrorism emanating from a country and the extent to which democracy is enjoyed by its citizens.

Issue 3.   Should the Electoral College Be Abolished?   38

YES: **George C. Edwards III,** from *Why the Electoral College Is Bad for America* (Yale University Press, 2004)   40

NO: **Gary L. Gregg,** from "The Electoral College Is Good for America," *National Review Online* (October 25–27, 2004)   45

University Professor George C. Edwards III believes that the Electoral College method of election violates the democratic principle of majority election and has resulted in the election of candidates with fewer votes than their leading opponent. Leadership Institute Director Gary L. Gregg maintains that the Electoral College system has succeeded in moderating and stabilizing American politics, and its abolition would risk the creation of radical parties and the election of minority presidents.

Supreme Court Justice Antonin Scalia rejects the notion of a "living Constitution," arguing that the judges must try to understand what the framers meant at the time. Supreme Court Justice Stephen Breyer contends that in finding the meaning of the Constitution, judges cannot neglect to consider the probable consequences of different interpretations.

Former federal prosecutor Andrew C. McCarthy supports the National Security Agency program of surveillance without a warrant as an effective means of protecting national security that employs the inherent power of the president to protect the country against subversion. Former vice president Al Gore views the warrantless wiretapping of American citizens as a brazen violation of the Constitution and of specific acts of Congress that have spelled out the circumstances under which a president may receive judicial permission to wiretap or otherwise invade the privacy of citizens.

Essayist Robert W. Lee argues that capital punishment is the only fair way for society to respond to certain heinous crimes. Law professor Eric M. Freedman contends that the death penalty does not reduce crime but does reduce public safety and carries the risk of innocent people being executed.

Political scientist Glenn Loury argues that the prudent use of "race-sighted" policies is essential to reducing the deleterious effects of race stigmatization, especially the sense of "racial otherness," which still remain in America. Economist Walter Williams argues that the use of racial preferences sets up a zero-sum game that reverses the gains of the civil rights movement, penalizes innocent people, and ends up harming those they are intended to help.

Daniel Pipes, director of the Middle East Forum, argues that "heightened scrutiny" of Muslims and Middle Eastern–looking people is justified because, while not all Muslims are Islamic extremists, all Islamic extremists are Muslims. Law professor David A. Harris opposes profiling people of Middle Eastern appearance because, like racial profiling, it compromises civil liberties and actually damages our intelligence efforts.

Legal philosopher Robert P. George asserts that, since each of us was a human being from conception, abortion is a form of homicide and should be banned. Writer Mary Gordon maintains that having an abortion is a moral choice that women are capable of making for themselves, that aborting a fetus is not killing a person, and that antiabortionists fail to understand female sexuality.

Wall Street Journal editorial writer Amity Shlaes maintains that the federal income tax is too high, too complex, and biased against high-income earners who invest in economic growth. Economist Paul Krugman believes that the Bush tax cuts increase economic inequality, contribute to a huge budget deficit, and endanger the future of Medicare and Social Security.

Editor and author Jeff Madrick maintains that the striking recent increase in income and wealth inequality reflects increasing inequality of opportunity and threatens the civil and political rights of less wealthy Americans. American Enterprise Institute president Christopher C. DeMuth asserts that Americans have achieved an impressive level of wealth and equality and that a changing economy ensures even more opportunities.

forces the least productive companies to reduce their output or shut down, resulting in better goods at lower prices. David Morris, vice president of the Institute for Local Self-Reliance, argues that free trade is unnecessary because gains in efficiency do not require large-scale multinational enterprises and that it is undesirable because it widens the standard-of-living gap between rich and poor nations.

Introduction

Labels and Alignments in American Politics

George McKenna and Stanley Feingold

Like a giant tidal wave crashing ashore, the September 11, 2001, attacks on the United States seemed to wash away some of America's most recognizable political landmarks. Suddenly, America's competing political parties, interest groups, and ideologies—whose outlines had been prominent in congressional debates, political campaigns, and media talk shows—seemed irrelevant. In the face of these murderous attacks, who cared about petty political differences? In the most remarkable display of national unity since Pearl Harbor, Congress, with only one dissent, voted to authorize President George W. Bush to use "all necessary and appropriate force" against those he considered responsible for the attacks and even those nations harboring them. On September 20th some of Bush's harshest congressional critics were on their feet cheering his dramatic speech before a special joint session of Congress. As the Republican president left the chamber, he approached the Democratic Senate majority leader, Tom Daschle, and in a moment the two were locked in a fervent embrace. The act symbolized the embrace of all Americans at that moment. Democrats, Republicans, liberals, conservatives, moderates, radicals—none of these labels seemed to matter anymore: all Americans were in the trenches together.

But even the mightiest tidal wave must recede at some point. When it does, some of the features of the old landscape may start to reappear. Something like this happened in the American political landscape between the fall of 2001 and September of 2006. It happened gradually, almost imperceptively, at first, but it started picking up speed in 2004. The presidential contest of that year was unusually bitter, with Democrats and Republicans exchanging heated charges on virtually every controversial topic, from how terrorist suspects should to be treated to whether we were winning or losing in Iraq. Democrats charged that the war had been cooked up by "neoconservative" White House advisors even before Bush came into office, and Republicans charged that the voting record of the Democratic nominee, Senator John Kerry, showed his indifference to the nation's defense and his excessive liberalism. Bush's reelection, together with Republican gains in both houses, ensured that, for the next two years at least, Republicans would be in charge of all three branches of the federal government. Undaunted, Democrats built alliances with some congressional Republicans on issues such as immigration and support for the filibuster. Conservative Republicans were annoyed by Republican defections from what they considered to be Republican orthodoxy. Some of them called the defectors RINOs, Republicans in Name Only, tagging them "liberals," though the defectors preferred to be called "moderates." Sensing an opportunity, the Democrats hoped to split the ranks of the Republicans and recapture control of at least one house of Congress in the 2006 elections. Touting America's tradition of "pluralism," they said it was dangerous for one party to maintain control of all three branches of government, for it tended to pull the nation toward ideological "extremism."

Some deplore this reemergence of "partisan wrangling." We regard it as the inevitable expression of political differences. Americans vote for different political parties because, however loosely, American parties help to give expression to competing ideologies embraced by Americans. In this introduction we shall attempt to explore these ideologies, put some labels on them—labels such as *liberal, conservative, moderate, extremist,* and *pluralist*—and see how they fit the issue positions presented in this book. We have sought to do our labeling gently and tentatively, not only because Americans generally shy away from political labels but also because, as we shall see, the meanings of some of these terms appear to have shifted over the past two and a half centuries.

Liberals Versus Conservatives: An Overview

Let us examine, very briefly, the historical evolution of the terms *liberalism* and *conservatism.* By examining the roots of these terms, we can see how these philosophies have adapted themselves to changing times. In that way, we can avoid using the terms rigidly, without reference to the particular contexts in which liberalism and conservatism have operated over the past two centuries.

Classical Liberalism

The classical root of the term *liberalism* is the Latin word *libertas,* meaning "liberty" or "freedom." In the early nineteenth century, liberals dedicated themselves to freeing individuals from all unnecessary and oppressive obligations to authority—whether the authority came from the church or the state. They opposed the licensing and censorship of the press, the punishment of heresy, the establishment of religion, and any attempt to dictate orthodoxy in matters of opinion. In economics, liberals opposed state monopolies and other constraints upon competition between private businesses. At this point in its development, liberalism defined freedom primarily in terms of freedom *from.* It appropriated the French term *laissez-faire,* which literally means "leave to be." Leave people alone! That was the spirit of liberalism in its early days. It wanted government to stay out of people's lives and to play a modest role in general. Thomas Jefferson summed up this concept when he said, "I am no friend of energetic government. It is always oppressive."

Despite their suspicion of government, classical liberals invested high hopes in the political process. By and large, they were great believers in democracy. They believed in widening suffrage to include every white male, and some of them were prepared to enfranchise women and blacks as well. Although liberals occasionally worried about "the tyranny of the majority," they were more prepared to trust the masses than to trust a permanent, entrenched elite. Liberal social policy was dedicated to fulfilling human potential and was based on the assumption that this often-hidden potential is enormous. Human beings, liberals argued, were basically good and reasonable. Evil and irrationality were believed to be caused by "outside" influences; they were the result of a bad social environment. A liberal commonwealth, therefore, was one that would remove the hindrances to the full flowering of the human personality.

The basic vision of liberalism has not changed since the nineteenth century. What has changed is the way it is applied to modern society. In that respect, liberalism has changed dramatically. Today, instead of regarding government with suspicion, liberals welcome government as an instrument to serve the people. The change in philosophy began in the latter years of the nineteenth century, when businesses—once small, independent operations—began to grow into giant structures that overwhelmed individuals and sometimes even overshadowed the state in power and wealth. At that time, liberals began reconsidering their commitment to the *laissez-faire* philosophy. If the state can be an oppressor, asked liberals, can't big business also oppress people? By then, many were convinced that commercial and industrial monopolies were crushing the souls and bodies of the working classes. The state, formerly the villain, now was viewed by liberals as a potential savior. The concept of freedom was transformed into something more than a negative freedom *from;* the term began to take on a positive meaning. It meant "realizing one's full potential." Toward this end, liberals believed, the state could prove to be a valuable instrument. It could educate children, protect the health and safety of workers, help people through hard times, promote a healthy economy, and—when necessary—force business to act more humanely and responsibly. Thus was born the movement that culminated in New Deal liberalism.

New Deal Liberalism

In the United States, the argument in favor of state intervention did not win an enduring majority constituency until after the Great Depression of the 1930s began to be felt deeply. The disastrous effects of a depression that left a quarter of the workforce unemployed opened the way to a new administration—and a promise. "I pledge you, I pledge myself," Franklin D. Roosevelt said when accepting the Democratic nomination in 1932, "to a new deal for the American people." Roosevelt's New Deal was an attempt to effect relief and recovery from the Depression; it employed a variety of means, including welfare programs, public works, and business regulation—most of which involved government intervention in the economy. The New Deal liberalism relied on government to liberate people from poverty, oppression, and economic exploitation. At the same time, the New Dealers claimed to be as zealous as the classical liberals in defending political and civil liberties.

The common element in *laissez-faire* liberalism and welfare-state liberalism is their dedication to the goal of realizing the full potential of each individual. Some still questioned whether this is best done by minimizing state involvement or whether it sometimes requires an activist state. The New Dealers took the latter view, though they prided themselves on begin pragmatic and experimental about their activism. During the heyday of the New Deal, a wide variety of programs were tried and—if found wanting—abandoned. All decent means should be tried, they believed, even if it meant dilution of ideological purity. The Roosevelt administration, for example, denounced bankers and businessmen in campaign rhetoric but worked very closely with them while trying to extricate the nation from the Depression. This set a pattern of pragmatism that New Dealers from Harry Truman to Lyndon Johnson emulated.

Progressive Liberalism

Progressive liberalism emerged in the late 1960s and early 1970s as a more militant and uncompromising movement than the New Deal had ever been. Its roots go back to the New Left student movement of the early 1960s. New Left students went to the South to participate in civil rights demonstrations, and many of them were bloodied in confrontations with southern police; by the mid-1960s they were confronting the authorities in the North over issues like poverty and the Vietnam War. By the end of the decade, the New Left had fragmented into a variety of factions and had lost much of its vitality, but a somewhat more respectable version of it appeared as the New Politics movement. Many New Politics crusaders were former New Leftists who had traded their jeans for coats and ties; they tried to work within the system instead of always confronting it. Even so, they retained some of the spirit of the New Left. The civil rights slogan "Freedom Now" expressed the mood of the New Politics. The young university graduates who filled its ranks had come from an environment where "nonnegotiable" demands were issued to college deans by leaders of sit-in protests. There was more than youthful arrogance in the New Politics movement, however; there was a pervasive belief that America had lost, had compromised away, much of its idealism. The New Politics liberals sought to recover some of that spirit by linking up with an older tradition of militant reform, which went back to the time of the Revolution. These new liberals saw themselves as the authentic heirs of Thomas Paine and Henry David Thoreau, of the abolitionists, the radical populists, the suffragettes, and the great progressive reformers of the early twentieth century.

While New Deal liberals concentrated almost exclusively on bread-and-butter issues such as unemployment and poverty, the New Politics liberals introduced what came to be known as social issues into the political arena. These included: the repeal of laws against abortion, the liberalization of laws against homosexuality and pornography, the establishment of affirmative action programs to ensure increased hiring of minorities and women, and the passage of the Equal Rights Amendment. In foreign policy, too, New Politics liberals departed from the New Deal agenda. Because they had keener memories of the unpopular and (for them) unjustified war in Vietnam than of World War II, they became doves, in contrast to the general hawkishness of the New Dealers. They were skeptical of any claim that the United States must be the leader of the free world or, indeed, that it had any special mission in the world; some were convinced that America was already in decline and must learn to adjust accordingly. The real danger, they argued, came not from the Soviet Union but from the mad pace of America's arms race with the Soviets, which, as they saw it, could bankrupt the country, starve its social programs, and culminate in a nuclear Armageddon.

New Politics liberals were heavily represented at the 1972 Democratic national convention, which nominated South Dakota senator George McGovern for president. By the 1980s the New Politics movement was no longer new, and many of its adherents preferred to be called progressives. By this time their critics had another name for them: radicals. The critics saw their positions as inimical to the interests of the United States, destructive of the family, and fundamentally at odds with the views of most Americans. The adversaries of the progressives were not only conservatives but many New Deal liberals, who openly scorned the McGovernites.

This split still exists within the Democratic party, though it is now more skillfully managed by party leaders. In 1988 the Democrats paired Michael Dukakis, whose Massachusetts supporters were generally on the progressive side of the party, with New Dealer Lloyd Bentsen as the presidential and vice-presidential candidates, respectively. In 1992 the Democrats won the presidency with Arkansas governor Bill Clinton, whose record as governor seemed to put him in the moderate-to-conservative camp, and Tennessee senator Albert Gore, whose position on environmental issues could probably be considered quite liberal but whose general image was middle-of-the-road. Both candidates had moved toward liberal positions on the issues of gay rights and abortion. By 1994 Clinton was perceived by many Americans as being "too liberal," which some speculate may have been a factor in the defeat of Democrats in the congressional elections that year. Clinton immediately sought to shake off that perception, positioning himself as a "moderate" between extremes and casting the Republicans as an "extremist" party. (These two terms will be examined presently.)

Conservatism

Like liberalism, conservatism has undergone historical transformation in America. Just as early liberals (represented by Thomas Jefferson) espoused less government, early conservatives (whose earliest leaders were Alexander Hamilton and John Adams) urged government support of economic enterprise and government intervention on behalf of certain groups. But today, in reaction to the growth of the welfare state, conservatives argue strongly that more government means more unjustified interference in citizens' lives, more bureaucratic regulation of private conduct, more inhibiting control of economic enterprise, more material advantage for the less energetic and less able at the expense of those who are prepared to work harder and better, and, of course, more taxes—taxes that will be taken from those who have earned money and given to those who have not.

Contemporary conservatives are not always opposed to state intervention. They may support larger military expenditures in order to protect society against foreign enemies. They may also allow for some intrusion into private life in order to protect society against internal subversion and would pursue criminal prosecution zealously in order to protect society against domestic violence. The fact is that few conservatives, and perhaps fewer liberals, are absolute with respect to their views about the power of the state. Both are quite prepared to use the state in order to further *their* purposes. It is true that activist presidents such as Franklin Roosevelt and John Kennedy were likely to be classified as liberals. However,

Richard Nixon was also an activist, and, although he does not easily fit any classification, he was far closer to conservatism than to liberalism. It is too easy to identify liberalism with statism and conservatism with antistatism: it is important to remember that it was liberal Jefferson who counseled against "energetic government" and conservative Alexander Hamilton who designed bold powers for the new central government and wrote, "Energy in the executive is a leading character in the definition of good government."

For a time, a movement calling itself *inconsiderations* occupied a kind of intermediate position between New Deal liberalism and conservatism. Composed for the most part of former New Deal Democrats and drawn largely from academic and publishing circles, neoconservatives supported most of the New Deal programs of federal assistance and regulation, but they felt that state intervention had gotten out of hand during the 1960s. In foreign policy, too, they worried about the directions in which the United States was going. In sharp disagreement with progressive liberals, they wanted a tougher stance toward the Soviet Union, fearing that the quest for detente was leading the nation to unilateral disarmament. After the disappearance of the Soviet Union, neoconcervatism itself disappeared—at least as a distinctive strain of conservatism—and most former neoconservatives either resisted all labels or considered themselves simply to be conservatives.

The Religious Right

A more enduring category within the conservative movement is what is often referred to as "the religious right." Termed "the new right" when it first appeared more than 20 years, ago, the religious right is composed of conservative Christians who are concerned not so much about high taxes and government spending as they are about the decline of traditional Judeo-Christian morality, a decline that they attribute in part to certain unwise government policies and judicial decisions. They oppose many of the recent judicial decisions on sociocultural issues such as abortion, school prayer, pornography, and gay rights, and they have been outspoken critics of the Clinton administration, citing everything from President Clinton's views on gays in the military to his sexual behavior while in the White House.

Spokesmen for progressive liberalism and the religious right stand as polar opposites: The former regard abortion as a woman's right; the latter see it as legalized murder. The former tend to regard homosexuality as a lifestyle that needs protection against discrimination; the latter are more likely to see it as a perversion. The former have made an issue of their support for the Equal Rights Amendment; the latter includes large numbers of women who fought against the amendment because they believed it threatened their role identity. The list of issues could go on. The religious right and the progressive liberals are like positive and negative photographs of America's moral landscape. Sociologist James Davison Hunter uses the term *culture wars* to characterize the struggles between these contrary visions of America. For all the differences between progressive liberalism and the religious right, however, their styles are very similar. They are heavily laced with moralistic prose; they tend to equate compromise with selling out; and they claim to represent the best, most authentic traditions of America.

This is not to denigrate either movement, for the kinds of issues they address are indeed moral issues, which do not generally admit much compromise. These issues cannot simply be finessed or ignored, despite the efforts of conventional politicians to do so. They must be aired and fought over which is why we include some of them, such as abortion (Issue 12), in this volume.

Neoconservatism

The term "neoconservatism" came into use in the early 1970s as a designation for former New Deal Democrats who had became alarmed by what they saw as the drift of their party's foreign policy toward appeasing Communists. When Senator George McGovern, the party's presidential nominee in 1972, stated that he would "crawl to Hanoi on my knees" to secure peace in Vietnam, he seemed to them to exemplify this new tendency. They were, then, "hawks" in foreign policy, which they insisted was the historic stance of their party; they regarded themselves as the true heirs of liberal presidents such as Truman and Kennedy and liberal Senators such as Henry ("Scoop") Jackson of Washington State. On domestic policy, they were still largely liberal, except for their reactions to three new liberal planks added by the "progressives": gay rights, which neoconservatives tended to regard as a distortion of civil rights; abortion, which to some degree or another went against the grain of their moral sensibilities; and affirmative action, which some compared to the "quota system" once used to keep down the number of Jews admitted to elite universities. In fact, a number of prominent neoconservatives were Jews, including Norman Podhoretz, Midge Decter, Gertrude Himmelfarb, and Irving Kristol (though others, such as Michael Novak and Daniel Patrick Moynihan, were Roman Catholics, and one, Richard John Neuhaus, was a Lutheran pastor who later converted to Catholicism and became a priest). The term "neoconservative" seemed headed for oblivion in the 1980s, when some leading neoconservatives dropped the "neo" part and classified themselves as conservatives, period. By the time the Soviet Union collapsed in 1991, it appeared that the term was no longer needed–the Cold War with "world Communism" was over. But the rise of Islamic terrorism in the 1990s, aimed at the West in general and the United States in particular, brought back alarms analogous to those of the Cold War period, with global terrorism now taking the place of world Communism. So, too, was the concern that liberal foreign policy might not be tough enough for the fight against these new, ruthless enemies of Western democracy. The concern was ratcheted up considerably after the events of 9/11, and now a new generation of neoconservatives was in the spotlight— some of its members literally the children of an earlier "neo" generation. They included Bill Kristol, John Podhoretz, Dauglas Feith, Paul Wolfowitz, Richard Perle, David Brooks, and (though he was old enough to overlap with the previous generation), Bill Bennett.

Radicals, Reactionaries, and Moderates

The label *reactionary* is almost an insult, and the label *radical* is worn with pride by only a few zealots on the banks of the political mainstream. A reactionary is not a conserver but a backward-mover, dedicated to turning the clock back to better times. Most people suspect that reactionaries would restore us to a time that never was, except in political myth. For many, the repeal of industrialism or universal education (or the entire twentieth century itself) is not a practical, let alone desirable, political program.

Radicalism (literally meaning "from the roots" or "going to the foundation") implies a fundamental reconstruction of the social order. Taken in that sense, it is possible to speak of right-wing radicalism as well as left-wing radicalism—radicalism that would restore or inaugurate a new hierarchical society as well as radicalism that calls for nothing less than an egalitarian society. The term is sometimes used in both of these senses, but most often the word *radicalism* is reserved to characterize more liberal change. While the liberal would effect change through conventional democratic processes, the radical is likely to be skeptical about the ability of the established machinery to bring about the needed change and might be prepared to sacrifice "a little" liberty to bring about a great deal more equality.

Moderate is a highly coveted label in America. Its meaning is not precise, but it carries the connotations of sensible, balanced, and practical. A moderate person is not without principles, but he or she does not allow principles to harden into dogma. The opposite of moderate is *extremist,* a label most American political leaders eschew. Yet there have been notable exceptions. When Arizona senator Barry Goldwater, a conservative Republican, was nominated for president in 1964, he declared, "Extremism in defense of liberty is no vice! . . . Moderation in the pursuit of justice is no virtue!" This open embrace of extremism did not help his electoral chances; Goldwater was overwhelmingly defeated. At about the same time, however, another American political leader also embraced a kind of extremism, and with better results. In a famous letter written from a jail cell in Birmingham, Alabama, the Reverend Martin Luther King, Jr., replied to the charge that he was an extremist not by denying it but by distinguishing between different kinds of extremists. The question, he wrote, "is not whether we will be extremist but what kind of extremist will we be. Will we be extremists for hate, or will we be extremists for love?" King aligned himself with the love extremists, in which category he also placed Jesus, St. Paul, and Thomas Jefferson, among others. It was an adroit use of a label that is usually anathema in America.

Pluralism

The principle of pluralism espouses diversity in a society containing many interest groups and in a government containing competing units of power. This implies the widest expression of competing ideas, and in this way, pluralism is in sympathy with an important element of liberalism. However, as James Madison and Alexander Hamilton pointed out when they analyzed the sources of pluralism in their *Federalist* commentaries on the Constitution, this philosophy springs from a profoundly pessimistic view of human nature, and in this respect it more closely resembles conservatism. Madison, possibly the single most influential member of the convention that wrote the Constitution, hoped that in a large and varied nation, no single interest group could control the government. Even if there were a majority interest, it would be unlikely to capture all of the national agencies of government—the House of Representatives, the Senate, the presidency, and the federal judiciary—each of which was chosen in a different way by a different constituency for a different term of office. Moreover, to make certain that no one branch exercised excessive power, each was equipped with "checks and balances" that enabled any agency of national government to curb the powers of the others. The clearest statement of Madison's, and the Constitution's, theory can be found in the 51st paper of the *Federalist:*

> It may be a reflection on human nature that such devices should be necessary to control the abuses of government. But what is government itself, but the greatest of all reflections on human nature? If men were angels, no government would be necessary.

This pluralist position may be analyzed from different perspectives. It is conservative insofar as it rejects simple majority rule; yet it is liberal insofar as it rejects rule by a single elite. It is conservative in its pessimistic appraisal of human nature; yet pluralism's pessimism is also a kind of egalitarianism, holding as it does that no one can be trusted with power and that majority interests no less than minority interests will use power for selfish ends. It is possible to suggest that in America pluralism represents an alternative to both liberalism and conservatism. Pluralism is antimajoritarian and antielitist and combines some elements of both.

Some Applications

Despite our effort to define the principal alignments in American politics, some policy decisions do not fit neatly into these categories. Readers will reach their own conclusions, but we suggest some alignments here in order to demonstrate the variety of viewpoints.

In Issue 1, concerning the notion of a unique American "mission," Howard Zinn expresses a view common among New Politics liberals: skepticism of any claim that the United States must be the leader of the free world or, indeed, that it has ever had any special mission in the world. Wilfred McClay's view that the "myth" of America is a noble one is still shared today by many New Deal liberals, but it is embraced more conspicuously by conservatives. In Issue 3, on the Electoral College, George Edwards argues a position on the Electoral College long shared by liberals: that it is an elitist institution, a relic of a bygone era, which serves no good purpose today. Gary L. Gregg sounds familiar conservative themes in arguing that the system "works," that it promotes order and stability, and that none better has been found. In Issue 5 Mark Green favors taxpayer funding of political campaigns, based upon the progressive liberal argument that our democratic system needs not just an honest ballot count but a playing field leveled through the elimination of money as a factor in elections; John Samples adopts the conservative view that taxpayers should not be forced to fund the electoral campaigns of politicians.

The Tenth Amendment states that all powers not delegated to the federal government nor denied to the states "are reserved to the States respectively, or to the people." Yet the federal government passes laws affecting many entities *within* states, from businesses to educational institutions. How can it do that? One of the main "hooks" for federal power within states is the constitutional clause authorizing Congress to regulate commerce "among the several states." The Supreme Court has interpreted the commerce clause to mean that any entity within a state that substantially "affects" interstate commerce can be regulated by the federal government. But how close should the "effect" be? Conservatives insist that the effects on interstate commerce must be quite direct and tangible, while liberals would give Congress more leeway in regulating "instrastate" activities. This liberal/conservative dichotomy is crisply illustrated in the majority opinion versus one of the dissents in the Supreme Court case of *United States v. Lopez* (1995), both of which we present in Issue 6. The immediate question is whether or not the federal government has the authority to ban handguns from the vicinity of public schools, but the larger issue is whether or not the federal government can regulate activities within a state that do not directly and tangibly affect interstate commerce. Liberals say yes, conservatives say no.

In Issue 7, on courts seeking the "original meaning" of the Constitution, Supreme Court Justice Stephen Breyer believes that constitutional interpretation must reflect what he believes to be the democratic trajectory of the Constitution, a long-held liberal position, while his colleague on the bench, Justice Antonin Scalia, takes a position long argued by conservatives when he insists that the Constitution, unlike statutes, was not meant to be changed, except by amendment. Warrantless wiretapping by the president, covered in Issue 8, also taps into liberal/conservative dichotomies. Andrew McCarthy insists, as do many conservatives, that it is necessary, long practiced by presidents during wartime, and authorized by the president's wartime powers, while former Vice President Al Gore takes the liberal position that it violates essential liberties.

Affirmative action (Issue 10) has become a litmus test of the newer brand of progressive liberalism. The progressives say that it is not enough for the laws of society to be color-blind or gender-blind; they must now reach out to remedy the ills caused by racism and sexism. New Deal liberals, along with conservatives and libertarians, generally oppose affirmative action. One major dispute between liberals and conservatives concerns liberalism itself: whether or not it pervades news coverage in the media. In Issue 4, Bernard Goldberg, a former CBS reporter, takes a position often held by conservatives when he argues that it does. Robert Kennedy argues that, taken as a whole, the media are actually conservative.

The death penalty is another issue dividing liberals and conservatives. Robert Lee's defense of the death penalty (Issue 9) is a classic conservative argument. Like other conservatives. Lee is skeptical of the possibilities of human perfection, and he therefore regards retribution—giving a murderer what he or she "deserves" instead of attempting some sort of "rehabilitation"—as a legitimate goal of punishment. Issue 14, on whether or not the gap between the rich and the poor is increasing, points up another disagreement between liberals and conservatives. Most liberals would agree with Jeff Madrick that socioeconomic inequality is increasing and that this undermines the basic tenets of American democracy. Christopher DeMuth, representing the conservative viewpoint, maintains that Americans are becoming more equal and that virtually all people benefit from increased prosperity because it takes place in a free market. Then there is the battle over taxes, the hardiest perennial of all the issues that divide liberals and conservatives. Issue 13 features Amity Shales, who advances the conservative argument that "the greedy hand" of government is taking too much from taxpayers, versus Paul Krugman, who rejects the idea that the pretax money was "theirs," in any meaningful sense, in the first place.

Immigration, explored in Issue 16, is another issue that can sharply separate liberals from conservatives. For good historical reasons American liberals have generally welcomed immigration. The ranks of New Deal liberalism were filled by immigrants, first from Ireland, later from Southern and Eastern Europe; more recent immigrants from Latin America have been friendly to the economic program of New Deal liberalism. In recent years conservatives have also courted immigrants, realizing that many Latinos actually lean toward the conservative side of certain social issues, such as those raised by homosexuality and abortion. But the sticking point for conservatives is illegal immigration. Emphasizing their law and order credentials, conservatives, like Mark Krikorian, oppose anything resembling amnesty for undocumented aliens while liberals—in this case Frank Sharry—are more inclined to favor at least a roadway to amnesty. Issue 19, on torture, also divides many liberals and conservatives. Few conservatives would say that they condone torture, but many take Charles Krauthammer's position that the protection put in place by the Geneva Accords of 1947 were never meant to include terrorists; liberals generally agree with Andrew Sullivan's position that there can never be any authorization to use painful or degrading methods to extract information from prisoners, even information pertaining to a "ticking time bomb."

This book contains a few arguments that are not easy to categorize. Issue 12, on whether or not abortion should be restricted, is one such issue. The pro-choice position, as argued by Mary Gordon, is not a traditional liberal position. Less than a generation ago legalized abortion was opposed by liberals such as Senator Edward Kennedy (D-Massachusetts) and the Reverend Jesse Jackson, and even recently some liberals, such as the late Pennsylvania governor Robert Casey and columnist Nat Hentoff, have opposed it. Nevertheless, most liberals now adopt some version of Gordon's pro-choice views. Opposing Gordon is Robert George, whose argument here might be endorsed by liberals like Hentoff. Issue 18, on the war in Iraq and the war on terrorism, is also hard to classify. Many liberals initially favored a hard line against Saddam Hussein, endorsing economic sanctions, no-fly zones, bombing strikes, and "regime change" in Iraq in the 1990s, and later, in 2002, authorizing the president to undertake hostilities. But Robert Jervis nevertheless speaks for many liberals today in deploring what he regards as Bush's reckless unilateralism. J. R. Dunn is more in tune with conservatives in his belief that success in Iraq will lead to a healthy domino effect throughout the Middle East, thwarting the designs of the terrorists.

Issue 2, President George bush argues that democracy will help greatly in the war on terror by bringing about peaceful and orderly change through the ballot. Bush, of course, is a self-described conservative, yet this has always been a liberal idea. (It has earned Bush criticism from some key advisors from his father's administration—and perhaps, privately, from the father himself.) At any rate, it is Gregory Gause who sounds conservative in warning that the sudden installation of democracy in countries that are not socially ready for it can lead to disaster, though perhaps many liberals share that view.

Obviously one's position on the issues in this book will be directed by circumstances. However, we would like to think that the essays in this book are durable enough to last through several seasons of events and controversies. We can be certain that the issues will survive. The search for coherence and consistency in the use of political labels underlines the options open to us and reveals their consequences. The result must be more mature judgments about what is best for America. That, of course, is the ultimate aim of public debate and decision making and it transcends all labels and categories.

On the Internet . . .

In addition to the Internet sites listed below, type in key words, such as "democracy," "political campaigns," and "media bias," to find other listings.

The Federal Web Locator

Use this handy site as a launching pad for the Web sites of U.S. federal agencies, departments, and organizations. It is well organized and easy to use for informational and research purposes.

http://www.infoctr.edu/fwl/

The Library of Congress

Examine this Web site to learn about the extensive resource tools, library services/resources, exhibitions, and databases available through the Library of Congress in many different subfields of government studies.

http://www.loc.gov

U.S. Founding Documents

Through this Emory University site you can view scanned originals of the Declaration of Independence, the Constitution, and the Bill of Rights. The transcribed texts are also available, as are the *Federalist Papers.*

http://www.law.emory.edu/FEDERAL/

Hoover Institution Public Policy Inquiry: Campaign Finance

Use this Stanford University sjte to explore the history of campaign finance as well as the current reforms and proposals for future change.

http://www.campaignfinancesite.org

Poynter.org

This research site of the Poynter Institute. a school for journalists, provides extensive links to information and resources about the media, including media ethics and reportage techniques. Many bibliographies and Web sites are included.

http://www.poynter.org/research/index.htm

Freedom House

Founded over sixty years ago by Eleanor Roosevelt, Wendell Wike, and others concerned about the suppression of democracy in the world, Freedom House charts the progress and retrogression of freedom in the nations of the world. You can view its annual "map of freedom" to see which countries it lists each year as "free" (in green), "partly free" (in yellow) and "not free" (in blue).

http://www.freedomhouse.org

Democracy and the American Political Process

*D*emocracy *is derived from two Greek words, demos and kratia, which mean, respectively, "people" and "rule." The prerequisites for rule by the people include free speech and other vital liberties, a well-informed citizenry, a variety of available points of view, and an equal counting of votes. Does America's electoral and campaign system meet these prerequisites? Some analysts of democracy would go further and include among the prerequisites a people's belief in their nation and its unique "mission." But is that necessary? And does it pose its own dangers? In this section we address these and related issues.*

- Should Americans Believe in a Unique American "Mission"?

- Is Democracy the Answer to Global Terrorism?

- Should the Electoral College Be Abolished?

- Do the Media Have a Liberal Bias?

- Should America Adopt Public Financing of Political Campaigns?

ISSUE 1

Should Americans Believe in a Unique American "Mission"?

YES: Wilfred M. McClay, from "The Founding of Nations," *First Things* (March 2006)

NO: Howard Zinn, from "The Power and the Glory: Myths of American Exceptionalism," *Boston Review* (Summer 2005)

ISSUE SUMMARY

YES: Humanities professor Wilfred M. McClay argues that America's "myth," its founding narrative, helps to sustain and hold together a diverse people.

NO: Historian Howard Zinn is convinced that America's myth of "exceptionalism" has served as a justification for lawlessness, brutality, and imperialism.

Take a dollar from your wallet and look at the back of it. On the left side, above an unfinished pyramid with a detached eye on top, are the words "Annuit Coeptis," Latin for, "He has favored our endeavors." The "He" is God.

Since the time of the Puritans, Americans have often thought of themselves collectively as a people whose endeavors are favored by God. "We shall be as a city upon a hill, the eyes of all people are upon us," said Puritan leader John Winthrop aboard the *Arbella*, the Puritans' flagship, as it left for the New World in 1630. Later in that century another Puritan, the Rev. Samuel Danforth, famously spoke of New England's divinely assigned "errand into the wilderness." By the eighteenth century, the role of New England had become the role of America: God had led his people to establish a new social order, a light to the nations. "Your forefathers," John Jay told New Yorkers in 1776, "came to America under the auspices of Divine Providence." For Patrick Henry, the American Revolution "was the grand operation, which seemed to be assigned by the Deity to the men of this age in our country." In his First Inaugural Address, George Washington saw an "invisible hand" directing the people of the United States. "Every step they have taken seems to have been distinguished by some token of providential agency." Even the most secular-minded founders thought of their nation in providential terms. Thomas Jefferson paid homage to the "Being . . . who led our fathers, as Israel of old, from their native land and planted them in a country flowing with all the necessaries and comforts of life; who has covered our infancy with His providence and our riper years with his wisdom and power." At the Constitutional Convention in Philadelphia, Benjamin Franklin declared that "God governs in the affairs of men," adding: "And if a sparrow cannot fall to the ground without his notice, is it probable that an empire cannot rise without his aid?"

Throughout the nineteenth and twentieth centuries, this notion of America as "a people set apart" was a perennial feature of American public discourse. Its most eloquent expression came in the speeches of Abraham Lincoln. Perhaps in deference to biblical literalists, Lincoln did not call Americans a "chosen people" (a name limited to the Jews in the Bible), but he came close: he said Americans were God's "almost chosen people." In other speeches, particularly in his Second Inaugural Address, he stressed the role of Divine Providence in directing the course of American history. Frederick Douglas, the black abolitionist leader, called the Second Inaugural "more like a sermon than a state paper."

So it has gone, down through the nation's history. Herbert Croly, the influential Progressive writer in the early twentieth century, called on Americans to realize "the promise of American life." In 1936 Franklin Roosevelt told a newer generation of Americans that they had a "rendezvous with destiny." John F. Kennedy proclaimed that "God's work must truly be our own." Martin Luther King, in his prophetic "I Have a Dream" speech identified his dream with the God-given promises of America. Ronald Reagan, paraphrasing John Winthrop's speech of 1630, saw America as a "shining city on a hill."

All of this sounds inspiring, and no doubt it did help inspire many worthy reforms, from the abolition of slavery in the 1860s to the landmark civil rights laws a century later. But is there a darker side to it? To its critics, American "exceptionalism" is a dangerous notion. They remind us that other nations, too, such as the ancient Romans, the Dutch, the Spanish, the British, and the Germans, have at various times boasted of themselves as an exceptional people, and that this has led them down the path to chauvinism, imperialism, and even genocide. To them, the invocation, "God bless America" sounds like hubris, as if God is being asked to bless whatever it is that America decides to do. Such a spirit lay behind "Manifest Destiny," a slogan from the mid-nineteenth century that was used to justify American expansion into territory claimed by Mexico, and in the 1890s American imperialists justified American expansion into Cuba and the Philippines in nearly similar language. From Indian removal at home to imperial adventures abroad, there have been few dark episodes in American history that have not found defenders ready to put them in terms of American exceptionalism.

In the selections that follow, humanities professor Wilfred M. McClay looks at the brighter side of American providentialism, while historian Howard Zinn argues that what he calls "American exceptionalism" is a dangerous idea because it has served as a justification for lawlessness, brutality, and imperialism.

YES

Wilfred M. McClay

The Founding of Nations

Did the United States really have a beginning that can be called its "Founding"? Can any society, for that matter, be said to have a founding moment in its past that ought to be regarded as a source of guidance and support?

Much of the intellectual culture of our time stands resolutely opposed to the idea of a founding as a unique moment in secular time that has a certain magisterial authority over what comes after it. The cult of ancestors, in its many forms, is always one of the chief objects of modernity's deconstructive energies. Kant's famous command, *Sapere Aude*—"Dare to Reason," the battle cry of the Enlightenment—always ends up being deployed against arguments claiming traditional authority.

Foundings, in this view, are fairy tales that cannot be taken seriously—indeed, that it is dangerous to take seriously, since modern nation-states have used them as tools of cultural hegemony. One has a moral obligation to peek behind the curtain, and one ought to have a strong presupposition about what one will find there. There is a settled assumption in the West, particularly among the educated, that every founding was in reality a blood-soaked moment, involving the enslavement or exploitation of some for the benefit of others. Foundational myths are merely attempts to prettify this horror. Our ancestors were not the noble heroes of epic. They were the primal horde or the Oedipal usurpers, and their authority derived ultimately from their successful monopolization of violence—and then their subsequent monopolization of the way the story would be told.

The perfect expression of this view is Theodor Adorno's dictum, "There is no monument of civilization that is not at the same time a monument of barbarism." Every achievement of culture involves an elaborate concealment of the less-than-licit means that went into its making. Property is theft, in Proudhon's famous phrase, which means that legitimacy is nothing more than the preeminent force, and our systems of law are the ways that the stolen money is laundered and turned into Carnegie libraries and Vanderbilt universities and other carved Corinthian pillars of society. From this point of view, the credulous souls who speak of the American founding are merely trying to retail a heroic myth about the Founding Fathers, a group of youthful and idealistic patriarchs who somehow reached up into the heavens and pulled down a Constitution for all time.

Admittedly, American filiopietism about the Founding can get out of hand. On the ceiling of the rotunda of the United States Capitol building—the inside of

From *First Things*, March 2006, pp. 33–39. Copyright © 2006 by Institute on Religion and Public Life. Reprinted by permission.

the dome which, in its external aspect, is arguably the single most recognizable symbol of American democracy—there is painted a fresco called "The Apotheosis of George Washington." It is as if the Sistine Chapel were transposed into an American key. The first president sits in glory, flanked by the Goddess of Liberty and the winged figure Fame sounding a victorious trumpet and holding aloft a palm frond. The thirteen female figures in a semi-circle around Washington represent the thirteen original states. On the outer ring stand six allegorical groups representing classical images of agriculture, arts and sciences, commerce, war, mechanics, and seafaring. This figure of a deified Washington, painted significantly enough in the year 1865, reflects a vision that appealed powerfully to the American public. But it is actually a rather disturbing image, and it cries out for debunking.

Still, debunking is a blunt instrument of limited value, despite the modern prejudice in its favor. To the question "What is a man?" André Malraux once gave the quintessential modern debunking answer: "A miserable little pile of secrets." That answer is too true to dismiss—but not quite true enough to embrace. And it is, in its way, the exact opposite number to the saccharin image of a deified and perfected George Washington dwelling in the clouds atop the Capitol dome. Such a conflict between grand moral oversimplifications impoverishes our thinking and sets us a false standard of greatness—one that is too easily debunked and leaves us too easily defrauded. . . .

When we speak of American national identity, one of the chief points at issue arises out of the tension between *creed* and *culture*. This is a tension between, on the one hand, the idea of the United States as a nation built on the foundation of self-evident, rational, and universally applicable propositions about human nature and human society; and, on the other hand, the idea of the United States as a very unusual, historically specific and contingent entity, underwritten by a long, intricately evolved, and very particular legacy of English law, language, and customs, Greco-Roman cultural antecedents, and Judeo-Christian sacred texts and theological and moral teachings, without whose presences the nation's flourishing would not be possible.

All this makes a profound tension, with much to be said for both sides. And the side one comes down on will say a lot about one's stance on an immense number of issues, such as immigration, education, citizenship, cultural assimilation, multiculturalism, pluralism, the role of religion in public life, the prospects for democratizing the Middle East, and on and on.

Yet any understanding of American identity that entirely excluded either creed or culture would be seriously deficient. Any view of American life that failed to acknowledge its powerful strains of universalism, idealism, and crusading zeal would be describing a different country from the America that happens to exist. And any view of America as simply a bundle of abstract normative ideas about freedom and democracy and self-government that can flourish just as easily in any cultural and historical soil, including a multilingual, post-religious, or post-national one, takes too much for granted and will be in for a rude awakening.

⌘

The antagonism of creed and culture is better understood not as a statement of alternatives but as an antinomy, one of those perpetual oppositions that can never be resolved. In fact, the two halves of the opposition often reinforce each other. The creed needs the support of the culture—and the culture, in turn, is imbued with respect for the creed. For the creed to be successful, it must be able to presume the presence of all kinds of cultural inducements—toward civility, restraint, deferred gratification, nonviolence, loyalty, procedural fairness, impersonal neutrality, compassion, respect for elders, and the like. These traits are not magically called into being by the mere invocation of the Declaration of Independence. Nor are they sustainable for long without the support of strong and deeply rooted social and cultural institutions that are devoted to the formation of character, most notably the traditional family and traditional religious institutions. But by the same token, the American culture is unimaginable apart from the influence of the American creed: from the sense of pride and moral responsibility Americans derive from being, as Walter Berns has argued, a carrier of universal values—a vanguard people.

❧

Forcing a choice between creed and culture is not the way to resolve the problem of cultural restoration. Clearly both can plausibly claim a place in the American Founding. What seems more urgent is the repair of some background assumptions about our relation to the past. It is a natural enough impulse to look back in times of turbulence and uncertainty. And it is especially natural, even obligatory, for a republican form of government to do so, since republics come into being at particular moments in secular time, through self-conscious acts of public deliberation. Indeed, philosophers from Aristotle on have insisted that republics *must* periodically recur to their first principles, in order to adjust and renew themselves through a fresh encounter with their initiating vision.

A constitutional republic like the United States is uniquely grounded in its foundational moment, its time of creation. And a founding is not merely the instant that the ball started rolling. Instead, it is a moment that presumes a certain authority over all the moments that will follow—and to speak of a founding is to presume that such moments in time are possible. It most closely resembles the moment that one takes an oath or makes a promise. One could even say that a constitutional founding is a kind of covenant, a meta-promise entered into with the understanding that it has a uniquely powerful claim on the future. It requires of us a willingness to be constantly looking back to our initiating promises and goals, in much the same way that we would chart progress or regress in our individual lives by reference to a master list of resolutions.

Republicanism means self-government, and so republican liberty does not mean living without restraint. It means, rather, living in accordance with a law that you have dictated to yourself. Hence the especially strong need of republics to recur to their founding principles and their founding narratives, in a never-ending process of self-adjustment. There should be a constant interplay between founding ideals and current realities, a tennis ball bouncing back and forth between the two.

And for that to happen, there need to be two things in place. First, founding principles must be sufficiently fixed to give us genuine guidance, to *teach* us something. Of course, we celebrate the fact that our Constitution was created with a built-in openness to amendment. But the fact that such ideals are open to amendment is perhaps the least valuable thing about them. A founding, like a promise or a vow, means nothing if its chief glory is its adaptability. The analogy of a successful marriage, which is also, in a sense, a *res publica* that must periodically recur to first principles, and whose flourishing depends upon the ability to distinguish first principles from passing circumstances, is actually a fairly good guide to these things.

⋰⊙⋱

Second, there needs to be a sense of connection to the past, a reflex for looking backward, and cultivating that ought to be one of the chief uses of the formal study of history. Unfortunately, the fostering of a vital sense of connection to the past is not one of the goals of historical study as it is now taught and practiced in this country. The meticulous contextualization of past events and ideas, arising out of a sophisticated understanding of the past's particularities and discontinuities with the present, is one of the great achievements of modern historiography. But we need to recognize that this achievement comes at a high cost when it emphasizes the *pastness* of the past—when it makes the past completely unavailable to us, separated from us by an impassable chasm of contextual difference.

In the case of the American Founding, a century-long assault has taken place among historians, and the sense of connection is even more tenuous. The standard scholarly accounts insist this heated series of eighteenth-century debates—among flawed, unheroic, and self-interested white men—offers nothing to which we should grant any abiding authority. That was then, and this is now.

The insistence on the pastness of the past imprisons us in the present. It makes our present antiseptically cut off from anything that might really nourish, surprise, or challenge it. It erodes our sense of being part of a common enterprise with humankind. An emphasis on scholarly precision has dovetailed effortlessly with what might be called the debunking imperative, which generally aims to discredit any use of the past to justify or support something in the present, and is therefore one of the few gestures likely to win universal approbation among historians. It is professionally safest to be a critic and extremely dangerous to be too affirmative.

Scholarly responsibility thus seems to demand the deconstruction of the American Founding into its constituent elements, thereby divesting it of any claim to unity or any heroic or mythic dimensions, deserving of our admiration or reverence. There was no coherence to what they did, and looking backward to divine what they meant by what they were doing makes no sense. The Founders and Framers, after all, fought among themselves. They produced a document that was a compromise, that waffled on important issues, that remains hopelessly bound to the eighteenth century and inadequate to our contemporary problems, etc. And so—in much the same manner as the source criticism of the Bible, which challenges the authority of Scripture by understanding the text as a compilation of haphazardly generated redactions—the Constitution is seen as a concatenation of disparate elements, a mere political deal meant to be superseded by other political deals, and withal an instrument of the powerful. The last thing in the world you would want to do is treat it as a document with any intrinsic moral authority. Every text is merely a pretext. This is the kind of explanation one has learned to expect from the historical guild.

•◦◉◦•

In this connection, it is amusing to see the extent to which historians, who are pleased to regard the Constitution as a hopelessly outdated relic of a bygone era, are themselves still crude nineteenth-century positivists at heart. They still pride themselves on their ability to puncture myths, relying on a shallow positivistic understanding of a myth as a more or less organized form of falsehood, rather than seeing myth as a structure of meaning, a manner of giving a manageable shape to the cosmos, and to one's own experience of the world, a shape that expresses cultural ideals and shared sentiments, and that guides us through the darkness of life's many perils and unanswerable questions by providing us with what Plato called a "likely story."

To be sure, there are good things to be said of a critical approach to history, and there are myths aplenty that richly deserve to be punctured. I am glad, for example, that we know beyond a shadow of a doubt that Washington, D.C., in the Kennedy years had very little in common with the legendary Camelot, aside from the ubiquity of adulterous liaisons in both places. That kind of ground-clearing is important, and we are better off without that kind of propagandistic myth. We might even be better off without the Apotheosis of George Washington sitting atop the Capitol dome.

But ground-clearing by itself is not enough. And to think otherwise is to mistake an ancillary activity for the main thing itself—as if agriculture were nothing more than the application of insecticides and weedkillers. History as debunking is ultimately an empty and fruitless undertaking, which fails to address the reasons we humans try to narrate and understand our pasts. It fails to take into account the ways in which a nation's morale, cohesion, and strength derive from a sense of connection to its past. And it fails to acknowledge how much a healthy sense of the future—including the economic and cultural preconditions for a critical historiography to ply its trade—depends on a mythic sense of the nation. The human need to encompass life within the framework of myth is not merely a longing for pleasing illusion. Myths reflect a fundamental human need for a larger shape to our collective aspirations. And it is an illusion to think that we can so ignore that need, and so cauterize our souls, that we will never again be troubled by it.

Indeed, the debunking imperative operates on the basis of its own myth. It presumes the existence of a solid and orderly substratum, a rock-solid reality lying just beneath the illusory surfaces, waiting to be revealed in all its direct and unfeigned honesty when the facades and artifices and false divisions are all stripped away. There is a remarkable complacency and naiveté about such a view. The near-universal presumption that the demise of the nation-state and the rise of international governance would be very good things has everything, except a shred of evidence, to support it. And as for the debunking of bourgeois morality that still passes for sophistication in some quarters and has been the stock-in-trade of Western intellectuals for almost two centuries now—well, this has always been a form of moral free-riding, like the radical posturing of adolescents who always know they can call Mom when they get into trouble.

✧

One residue of the debunking heritage is the curious assumption that narratives of foundings are mere fairy tales—prettified, antiseptic flights of fancy, or wish-fulfillment fantasies, telling of superlative heroes and maidens acting nobly and virtuously to bring forth the status quo or its antecedents. I think it's fair to say that foundational narratives, including creation myths, tend to be conservative in character, in the sense that they tend to provide historical and moral support for existing regimes and social arrangements. It's hard to imagine them being any other way. But the part about their being prettifying fairy tales is demonstrably wrong. In fact, one could say that the most amazing feature of the great foundational myths is their moral complexity.

One need not even consider the appalling creation myths of Greek antiquity, such as the story of Kronos, who castrated his father Ouranos with a sickle given him by his mother, and then, in order to protect himself against the same dismal fate, swallowed his own children until his youngest child, Zeus, also aided by his mother, was able to overthrow him and assume primacy among the gods.

Consider instead the great Biblical stories of the Pentateuch, foundational texts not only for the Jewish people but for the entire family of monotheistic Abrahamic religious faiths—which is to say, those faiths that have been most constitutive of Western civilization. These Biblical texts are anything but tracts of unrelieved patriotism. In fact, one would be justified in seeing them as an exercise in collective self-humiliation. They are replete with the disreputable deeds of their imperfect and dissembling patriarchs, who pawn off their wives as sisters, deceive their fathers, cheat their brothers, murder, and commit incest—together with tales of an incorrigibly feckless people, the people of Israel, sheep-like fools who manage to forget every theophany and divine favor shown them, and prove unable and unwilling to follow the law that has been given to them.

The narrative does not blink at those things. It is itself the harshest critic of the things it describes, and every one of its human heroes is presented as deeply flawed. But what holds all this together is not the greatness of the heroes but the enduring quality of God's successive covenants with them and with His people. The God of the Hebrew Bible makes promises and keeps them, operating through covenants and laws that superintend and take precedence over the force of passing events. In that sense, the complexity of the Biblical account registers, in a remarkably accurate way, the same set of moral directives regarding the authority of the past—and the elements of pain and suffering and shame in that past—that goes into the making of any durable founding. The Passover seder, which is also the template for the Christian gospel story, is not a story of heroic triumph but of deliverance from slavery by a promise-keeping Deity. . . .

Perhaps the most interesting question about these foundational stories is why they are so complex. And the answer is surely to be found in the complexity of the mythic dimension itself, the ways in which it can register and mirror and instruct a civilization, precisely by virtue of its being a rich and truthful narrative that is widely shared. This quality can be neglected in an overly politicized or rationalized age, which wants to see the play of tangible and measurable material interests or causes always at the bottom of things. And it certainly eludes a culture that has ceased to understand the human necessity of looking backward.

⋅⟨⊙⟩⋅

Human knowledge about human affairs always has a reflexive quality about it. It is never a matter of the tree falling unheard and unwitnessed in the forest. There is always someone listening and watching, always a feedback effect—and most prophecies tend to be either self-fulfilled or self-averted. The best social scientists understand this perfectly well (after all, they were the ones who gave us the term "self-fulfilling prophecy"), but they give us such knowledge in a vocabulary and form that are often all but self-subverting. Who, after all, wants to embrace a myth while *calling* it a myth?

But to do so may be preferable to the alternative of nineteenth-century positivism, so long as we are able to proceed with a capacious understanding of "myth," as something more than a mere tall tale, something that can be both life-giving and true. In this connection, there may be particular value in revisiting Ernest Renan's celebrated 1882 essay "What is a Nation?", a rich evocation of the nation's mythic dimension. For Renan, a nation was fundamentally "a soul, a spiritual principle," constituted not only by "present-day consent" but also by the residuum of the past, "the possession in common of a rich legacy of memories" which form in the citizen "the will to perpetuate the value of the heritage that one has received in an undivided form." He declared:

> The nation, like the individual, is the culmination of a long past of endeavors, sacrifice, and devotion. Of all cults, that of the ancestors is the most legitimate, for the ancestors have made us what we are. A heroic past, great men, glory (by which I understand genuine glory), this is the social capital upon which one bases a national idea. To have common glories in the past and to have a common will in the present, to have performed great deeds together, to wish to perform still more—these are the essential conditions for being a people. . . . A nation is therefore a large-scale solidarity, constituted by the feeling of the sacrifices that one has made in the past and of those that one is prepared to make in the future.

Renan strongly opposed the then-fashionable view that nations should be understood as entities united by racial or linguistic or geographical or religious or material factors. None of those factors were sufficient to account for the emergence of this "spiritual principle." Active consent had to be a part of it. But it was insufficient without the presence of the past—the past in which that consent was embedded and through which it found meaning.

The ballast of the past, and our intimate connection to it, is similarly indispensable to the sense of American national identity. It forms a strain in our identity that is in some respects far less articulate (and less frequently articulated) than the universalistic principles that some writers have emphasized, precisely because it seems to conflict with American assertions of universalism, and its intellectual basis is less well-defined. But it is every bit as powerful, if not more so, and just as indispensable. And it is a very *particular* force. Our nation's particular triumphs, sacrifices, and sufferings—and our memories of those things—draw and hold us together, precisely because they are the sacrifices and sufferings, not of all humanity, but of us in particular.

No one has spoken of American national identity with greater mastery than Abraham Lincoln. In his 1838 speech on "The Perpetuation of Our Political Institutions," delivered to the Young Men's Lyceum of Springfield, Illinois, Lincoln responded to the then-raging violence directed at blacks and abolitionists in Southern and border states with an admonition that could have come from Toynbee: "If destruction be our lot, we must ourselves be its author and finisher. As a nation of freemen, we must live through all time, or die by suicide." The danger he most feared was that rampant lawlessness would dissolve the "attachment of the People" to their government. And the answer he provides to this danger is remarkable for the way it touches on the same themes that Renan recounts:

> Let every American, every lover of liberty, every well wisher to his posterity, swear by the blood of the Revolution, never to violate in the least particular, the laws of the country; and never to tolerate their violation by others. As the patriots of seventy-six did to the support of the Declaration of Independence, so to the support of the Constitution and Laws, let every American pledge his life, his property, and his sacred honor;—let every man remember that to violate the law, is to trample on the blood of his father, and to tear the character of his own, and his children's liberty. Let reverence for the laws, be breathed by every American mother, to the lisping babe, that prattles on her lap—let it be taught in schools, in seminaries, and in colleges;—let it be written in Primmers, spelling books, and in Almanacs;—let it be preached from the pulpit, proclaimed in legislative halls, and enforced in courts of justice. And, in short, let it become the political religion of the nation; and let the old and the young, the rich and the poor, the grave and the gay, of all sexes and tongues, and colors and conditions, sacrifice unceasingly upon its altars.

The excerpt shows Lincoln's remarkable ability to intertwine the past and the present, and evoke a sense of connection between them. The speech performs the classic republican move, back to the founding origins, connecting the public order explicitly with something so primal as a son's love of, and respect for, his father. Obedience to the law and reverence for the Constitution—these are directly connected with memory, the reverence owed to the sufferings of the patriot generation, and the blood of one's own father. Such words gesture toward his even more famous invocation of "the mystic chords of memory" in his First Inaugural Address, chords "stretching from every battlefield and patriot grave to every living heart and hearthstone all over this broad land," chords that provide the music of the Union. He performs a similar move of memorial linkage in the Gettysburg Address, beginning with the Founding Fathers and ending with a rededication and recommitment, drawn from knowledge of the "honored dead" who hallowed the ground with their sacrifice.

It is pointless to ask whether such a vision of the Union reflects an "objective" reality. The mythic reality on which such rhetoric depends, and which it helps to create and sustain, is powerful in its own right, too compelling to be dismissed or deconstructed into the language of "state formation" or "cultural hegemony." You could say that the antiseptic scholarly language offers insights that Lincoln cannot give us, and you would be right. But you could also say that Lincoln's reverent and hortatory language offers insights that the antiseptic scholars cannot provide, and you would be equally right. The real question is which language tells us more, and for what purposes.

A belief in the particularly instructive and sustaining qualities of the American Founding does not depend on a belief in the moral perfection of the Founders themselves, or the presumption that they were completely pure and disinterested regarding the measures they sought, or that they were invariably wise or prudent or far-sighted, or that they agreed in all important things, or that the Constitution they created is perfect in every way. The stories that we tell ourselves about ourselves, in order to remember who we are, should not neglect to tell us the ways we have fallen short and the ways we have suffered, both needfully and needlessly, by necessity or by chance.

We should not try to edit out those stories' strange moral complexity, because it is there for a reason. Indeed, it is precisely our encounter with the surprise of their strangeness that reminds us of how much we have yet to learn from them.

The Power and the Glory: Myths of American Exceptionalism

The notion of American exceptionalism—that the United States alone has the right, whether by divine sanction or moral obligation, to bring civilization, or democracy, or liberty to the rest of the world, by violence if necessary—is not new. It started as early as 1630 in the Massachusetts Bay Colony when Governor John Winthrop uttered the words that centuries later would be quoted by Ronald Reagan. Winthrop called the Massachusetts Bay Colony a "city upon a hill." Reagan embellished a little, calling it a "shining city on a hill."

The idea of a city on a hill is heartwarming. It suggests what George Bush has spoken of: that the United States is a beacon of liberty and democracy. People can look to us and learn from and emulate us.

In reality, we have never been just a city on a hill. A few years after Governor Winthrop uttered his famous words, the people in the city on a hill moved out to massacre the Pequot Indians. Here's a description by William Bradford, an early settler, of Captain John Mason's attack on a Pequot village.

> Those that escaped the fire were slain with the sword, some hewed to pieces, others run through with their rapiers, so as they were quickly dispatched and very few escaped. It was conceived that they thus destroyed about 400 at this time. It was a fearful sight to see them thus frying in the fire and the streams of blood quenching the same, and horrible was the stink and scent thereof; but the victory seemed a sweet sacrifice, and they gave the praise thereof to God, who had wrought so wonderfully for them, thus to enclose their enemies in their hands and give them so speedy a victory over so proud and insulting an enemy.

The kind of massacre described by Bradford occurs again and again as Americans march west to the Pacific and south to the Gulf of Mexico. (In fact our celebrated war of liberation, the American Revolution, was disastrous for the Indians. Colonists had been restrained from encroaching on the Indian territory by the British and the boundary set up in their Proclamation of 1763. American independence wiped out that boundary.)

Expanding into another territory, occupying that territory, and dealing harshly with people who resist occupation has been a persistent fact of American history from the first settlements to the present day. And this was often accompanied from very early on with a particular form of American exceptionalism: the idea that American expansion is divinely ordained. On the eve of the war with Mexico in the middle of the 19th century, just after the United States annexed Texas, the editor and writer John O'Sullivan coined the famous phrase "manifest destiny." He said it was "the fulfillment of our manifest destiny to overspread the continent allotted by Providence for the free development of our yearly multiplying millions." At the beginning of the 20th century, when the United States invaded the Philippines, President McKinley said that the decision to take the Philippines came to him one night when he got down on his knees and prayed, and God told him to take the Philippines.

Invoking God has been a habit for American presidents throughout the nation's history, but George W. Bush has made a specialty of it. For an article in the Israeli newspaper *Ha'aretz*, the reporter talked with Palestinian leaders who had met with Bush. One of them reported that Bush told him, "God told me to strike at al Qaeda. And I struck them. And then he instructed me to strike at Saddam, which I did. And now I am determined to solve the problem in the Middle East." It's hard to know if the quote is authentic, especially because it is so literate. But it certainly is consistent with Bush's oft-expressed claims. A more credible story comes from a Bush supporter, Richard Lamb, the president of the Ethics and Religious Liberty Commission of the Southern Baptist Convention, who says that during the election campaign Bush told him, "I believe God wants me to be president. But if that doesn't happen, that's okay."

Divine ordination is a very dangerous idea, especially when combined with military power (the United States has 10,000 nuclear weapons, with military bases in a hundred different countries and warships on every sea). With God's approval, you need no human standard of morality. Anyone today who claims the support of God might be embarrassed to recall that the Nazi storm troopers had inscribed on their belts, "Gott mit uns" ("God with us").

Not every American leader claimed divine sanction, but the idea persisted that the United States was uniquely justified in using its power to expand throughout the world. In 1945, at the end of World War II, Henry Luce, the owner of a vast chain of media enterprises—*Time, Life, Fortune*— declared that this would be "the American Century," that victory in the war gave the United States the right "to exert upon the world the full impact of our influence, for such purposes as we see fit and by such means as we see fit."

This confident prophecy was acted out all through the rest of the 20th century. Almost immediately after World War II the United States penetrated the oil regions of the Middle East by special arrangement with Saudi Arabia. It established military bases in Japan, Korea, the Philippines, and a number of Pacific islands. In the next decades it orchestrated right-wing coups in Iran, Guatemala, and Chile, and gave military aid to various dictatorships in the Caribbean. In an attempt to establish a foothold in Southeast Asia it invaded Vietnam and bombed Laos and Cambodia.

The existence of the Soviet Union, even with its acquisition of nuclear weapons, did not block this expansion. In fact, the exaggerated threat of "world communism" gave the United States a powerful justification for expanding all over the globe, and soon it had military bases in a hundred countries. Presumably, only the United States stood in the way of the Soviet conquest of the world.

Can we believe that it was the existence of the Soviet Union that brought about the aggressive militarism of the United States? If so, how do we explain all the violent expansion before 1917? A hundred years before the Bolshevik Revolution, American armies were annihilating Indian tribes, clearing the great expanse of the West in an early example of what we now call "ethnic cleansing." And with the continent conquered, the nation began to look overseas.

On the eve of the 20th century, as American armies moved into Cuba and the Philippines, American exceptionalism did not always mean that the United States wanted to go it alone. The nation was willing—indeed, eager—to join the small group of Western imperial powers that it would one day supersede. Senator Henry Cabot Lodge wrote at the time, "The great nations are rapidly absorbing for their future expansion, and their present defense all the waste places of the earth. . . . As one of the great nations of the world the United States must not fall out of the line of march." Surely, the nationalistic spirit in other countries has often led them to see their expansion as uniquely moral, but this country has carried the claim farthest.

American exceptionalism was never more clearly expressed than by Secretary of War Elihu Root, who in 1899 declared, "The American soldier is different from all other soldiers of all other countries since the world began. He is the advance guard of liberty and justice, of law and order, and of peace and happiness." At the time he was saying this, American soldiers in the Philippines were starting a bloodbath which would take the lives of 600,000 Filipinos.

The idea that America is different because its military actions are for the benefit of others becomes particularly persuasive when it is put forth by leaders presumed to be liberals, or progressives. For instance, Woodrow Wilson, always high on the list of "liberal" presidents, labeled both by scholars and the popular culture as an "idealist," was ruthless in his use of military power against weaker nations. He sent the navy to bombard and occupy the Mexican port of Vera Cruz in 1914 because the Mexicans had arrested some American sailors. He sent the marines into Haiti in 1915, and when the Haitians resisted, thousands were killed.

The following year American marines occupied the Dominican Republic. The occupations of Haiti and the Dominican Republic lasted many years. And Wilson, who had been elected in 1916 saying, "There is such a thing as a nation being too proud to fight," soon sent young Americans into the slaughterhouse of the European war.

Theodore Roosevelt was considered a "progressive" and indeed ran for president on the Progressive Party ticket in 1912. But he was a lover of war and a supporter of the conquest of the Philippines—he had congratulated the general who wiped out a Filipino village of 600 people in 1906. He had promulgated the 1904 "Roosevelt Corollary" to the Monroe Doctrine, which justified the occupation of small countries in the Caribbean as bringing them "stability."

During the Cold War, many American "liberals" became caught up in a kind of hysteria about the Soviet expansion, which was certainly real in Eastern Europe but was greatly exaggerated as a threat to western Europe and the

United States. During the period of McCarthyism the Senate's quintessential liberal, Hubert Humphrey, proposed detention camps for suspected subversives who in times of "national emergency" could be held without trial.

After the disintegration of the Soviet Union and the end of the Cold War, terrorism replaced communism as the justification for expansion. Terrorism was real, but its threat was magnified to the point of hysteria, permitting excessive military action abroad and the curtailment of civil liberties at home.

The idea of American exceptionalism persisted as the first President Bush declared, extending Henry Luce's prediction, that the nation was about to embark on a "new American Century." Though the Soviet Union was gone, the policy of military intervention abroad did not end. The elder Bush invaded Panama and then went to war against Iraq.

The terrible attacks of September 11 gave a new impetus to the idea that the United States was uniquely responsible for the security of the world, defending us all against terrorism as it once did against communism. President George W. Bush carried the idea of American exceptionalism to its limits by putting forth in his national-security strategy the principles of unilateral war.

This was a repudiation of the United Nations charter, which is based on the idea that security is a collective matter, and that war could only be justified in self-defense. We might note that the Bush doctrine also violates the principles laid out at Nuremberg, when Nazi leaders were convicted and hanged for aggressive war, preventive war, far from self-defense.

Bush's national-security strategy and its bold statement that the United States is uniquely responsible for peace and democracy in the world has been shocking to many Americans.

But it is not really a dramatic departure from the historical practice of the United States, which for a long time has acted as an aggressor, bombing and invading other countries (Vietnam, Cambodia, Laos, Grenada, Panama, Iraq) and insisting on maintaining nuclear and non-nuclear supremacy. Unilateral military action, under the guise of prevention, is a familiar part of American foreign policy.

Sometimes bombings and invasions have been cloaked as international action by bringing in the United Nations, as in Korea, or NATO, as in Serbia, but basically our wars have been American enterprises. It was Bill Clinton's secretary of state, Madeleine Albright, who said at one point, "If possible we will act in the world multilaterally, but if necessary, we will act unilaterally." Henry Kissinger, hearing this, responded with his customary solemnity that this principle "should not be universalized." Exceptionalism was never clearer.

Some liberals in this country, opposed to Bush, nevertheless are closer to his principles on foreign affairs than they want to acknowledge. It is clear that 9/11 had a powerful psychological effect on everybody in America, and for certain liberal intellectuals a kind of hysterical reaction has distorted their ability to think clearly about our nation's role in the world.

In a recent issue of the liberal magazine *The American Prospect,* the editors write, "Today Islamist terrorists with global reach pose the greatest immediate threat to our lives and liberties. . . . When facing a substantial, immediate, and provable threat, the United States has both the right and the obligation to strike preemptively and, if need be, unilaterally against terrorists or states that support them."

Preemptively and, if need be, unilaterally; and against "states that support" terrorists, not just terrorists themselves. Those are large steps in the direction of the Bush doctrine, though the editors do qualify their support for preemption by adding that the threat must be "substantial, immediate, and provable." But when intellectuals endorse abstract principles, even with qualifications, they need to keep in mind that the principles will be applied by the people who run the U.S. government. This is all the more important to keep in mind when the abstract principle is about the use of violence by the state—in fact, about preemptively initiating the use of violence.

There may be an acceptable case for initiating military action in the face of an immediate threat, but only if the action is limited and focused directly on the threatening party—just as we might accept the squelching of someone falsely shouting "fire" in a crowded theater if that really were the situation and not some guy distributing anti-war leaflets on the street. But accepting action not just against "terrorists" (can we identify them as we do the person shouting "fire"?) but against "states that support them" invites unfocused and indiscriminate violence, as in Afghanistan, where our government killed at least 3,000 civilians in a claimed pursuit of terrorists.

It seems that the idea of American exceptionalism is pervasive across the political spectrum.

The idea is not challenged because the history of American expansion in the world is not a history that is taught very much in our educational system. A couple of years ago Bush addressed the Philippine National Assembly and said, "America is proud of its part in the great story of the Filipino people. Together our soldiers liberated the Philippines from colonial rule." The president apparently never learned the story of the bloody conquest of the Philippines.

And when the Mexican ambassador to the UN said something undiplomatic about how the United States has been treating Mexico as its "backyard" he was immediately reprimanded by then-Secretary of State Colin Powell. Powell, denying the accusation, said, "We have too much of a history that we have gone through together." (Had he not learned about the Mexican War or the military forays into Mexico?) The ambassador was soon removed from his post.

The major newspapers, television news shows, and radio talk shows appear not to know history, or prefer to forget it. There was an outpouring of praise for Bush's second inaugural speech in the press, including the so-called liberal press (*The Washington Post, The New York Times*). The editorial writers eagerly embraced Bush's words about spreading liberty in the world, as if they were ignorant of the history of such claims, as if the past two years' worth of news from Iraq were meaningless.

Only a couple of days before Bush uttered those words about spreading liberty in the world, *The New York Times* published a photo of a crouching, bleeding Iraqi girl. She was screaming. Her parents, taking her somewhere in their car, had just been shot to death by nervous American soldiers.

One of the consequences of American exceptionalism is that the U.S. government considers itself exempt from legal and moral standards accepted by other nations in the world. There is a long list of such self-exemptions: the refusal to sign the Kyoto Treaty regulating the pollution of the environment, the refusal to strengthen the convention on biological weapons. The United States has failed to join the hundred-plus nations that have agreed to ban land mines, in spite of the appalling statistics about amputations performed on children mutilated by those mines. It refuses to ban the use of napalm and cluster bombs. It insists that it must not be subject, as are other countries, to the jurisdiction of the International Criminal Court.

What is the answer to the insistence on American exceptionalism? Those of us in the United States and in the world who do not accept it must declare forcibly that the ethical norms concerning peace and human rights should be observed. It should be understood that the children of Iraq, of China, and of Africa, children everywhere in the world, have the same right to life as American children.

These are fundamental moral principles. If our government doesn't uphold them, the citizenry must. At certain times in recent history, imperial powers—the British in India and East Africa, the Belgians in the Congo, the French in Algeria, the Dutch and French in Southeast Asia, the Portuguese in Angola—have reluctantly surrendered their possessions and swallowed their pride when they were forced to by massive resistance.

Fortunately, there are people all over the world who believe that human beings everywhere deserve the same rights to life and liberty. On February 15, 2003, on the eve of the invasion of Iraq, more than ten million people in more than 60 countries around the world demonstrated against that war.

There is a growing refusal to accept U.S. domination and the idea of American exceptionalism. Recently, when the State Department issued its annual report listing countries guilty of torture and other human-rights abuses, there were indignant responses from around the world commenting on the absence of the United States from that list. A Turkish newspaper said, "There's not even mention of the incidents in Abu Ghraib prison, no mention of Guantánamo." A newspaper in Sydney pointed out that the United States sends suspects—people who have not been tried or found guilty of anything— to prisons in Morocco, Egypt, Libya, and Uzbekistan, countries that the State Department itself says use torture.

Here in the United States, despite the media's failure to report it, there is a growing resistance to the war in Iraq. Public-opinion polls show that at least half the citizenry no longer believe in the war. Perhaps most significant is that among the armed forces, and families of those in the armed forces, there is more and more opposition to it.

After the horrors of the first World War, Albert Einstein said, "Wars will stop when men refuse to fight." We are now seeing the refusal of soldiers to fight, the refusal of families to let their loved ones go to war, the insistence of the parents of high-school kids that recruiters stay away from their schools. These incidents, occurring more and more frequently, may finally, as happened in the case of Vietnam, make it impossible for the government to continue the war, and it will come to an end.

The true heroes of our history are those Americans who refused to accept that we have a special claim to morality and the right to exert our force on the rest of the world. I think of William Lloyd Garrison, the abolitionist. On the masthead of his antislavery newspaper, *The Liberator*, were the words, "My country is the world. My countrymen are mankind."

POSTSCRIPT

Should Americans Believe in a Unique American "Mission"?

It is difficult to find much agreement between the overall views of Howard Zinn and Wilfred McClay, though both seem to share some underlying moral premises. Both would agree, for example, that it is wrong to mistreat prisoners, to massacre civilians, and to start wars without provocation, but they launch their moral arguments from very different locations. Zinn's moral premises seem to come from the eighteenth-century Enlightenment. Though claiming universal validity, its reach was limited both in time and place; it was never fully accepted outside of Western Europe and parts of North America, nor is it accepted today in large parts of the world. McClay's point of view seems to be built upon a more openly particularistic foundation: the providential foundation of America. He is no less ready than Zinn to acknowledge America's moral deviations, but he would see them as not only wrong but, in the deepest sense, un-American.

Howard Zinn's *People's History of the United States: 1492 to Present* (Harper Perennial Modern Classics, 2005) presents a more sweeping presentation of his argument here, while Stephen H. Webb make the case for a doctrine of providence in *American Providence: A Nation With a Mission* (Continuum, 2004). James H. Hutson's edited *The Founders on Religion: A Book of Quotations* (Princeton, 2005) served as the source for the quotations from the founders presented in the Introduction to this issue. Alexis de Tocqueville is credited with inventing the term "American exceptionalism," and in his classic *Democracy in America* (Knopf, 1951) he seemed to endorse the idea by stating his belief that "the people of the United States [are] that portion of the English people who are commissioned to explore the forests of the new world." Seymour Martin Lipset's *American Exceptionalism: A Double-Edged Sword* (Norton, 1997) thinks America is different not so much because of its founding narrative but because, unlike Europe, it was "born modern," with a distinct creed. But Michael Lind, in *The Next American Nation* (Free Press, 1996) thinks that "the American nation is defined by language and culture," not political creed. "Even if the federal government were abolished tomorrow, the American culture nation would endure." Samuel P. Huntington's *Who Are We?* (Simon & Schuster, 2004) highlights America's uniqueness among industrial nations today, especially in terms of its highly charged mixture of piety and patriotism. In *Hellfire Nation*, James A. Morone (Yale, 2004) finds both good and bad effects following from America's belief in its "mission"—on the one hand, utopian and reformist impulses, which he likes, and on the other hand, Victorian censoriousness, which he doesn't like.

In the 1960s the former Socialist candidate for President, Norman Thomas, admonished an angry crowd of antiwar demonstrators not to burn the flag but to wash it. Thomas was one of many critics of American policies who would insist that they love America more, not less, because they can acknowledge how far their country sometimes falls short of achieving its professed goals of "liberty and justice for all."

ISSUE 2

Is Democracy the Answer to Global Terrorism?

YES: George W. Bush, from Speech at National Defense University (March 8, 2005)

NO: F. Gregory Gause III, from "Can Democracy Stop Terrorism?" *Foreign Affairs* (September/October 2005)

ISSUE SUMMARY

YES: President George W. Bush argues that the best antidote to terrorism is the tolerance and hope generated by democracy.

NO: Political scientist Gregory Gause contends that there is no relationship between terrorism emanating from a country and the extent to which democracy is enjoyed by its citizens.

The Greek philosopher Plato characterized democracy as "an agreeable form of anarchy with plenty of variety and an equality of a peculiar kind for equals and unequals alike." Plato was contemptuous of Greek democracy because it gave equal power to citizens regardless of their intelligence, knowledge, or moral character. Until relatively recent times—in considering the merits of democracy—political thinkers have largely echoed the founder of Western philosophy. Medieval thinkers, though wary of unchecked rule by secular elites, were at least as opposed to direct rule by the people, and even during the Enlightenment Period of the eighteenth century, most major political thinkers were decidedly cool to democracy. In *The Federalist #10,* on the best kind of government for countering the dangers of a majority "faction," James Madison briefly considered what he called "pure democracy"—government by direct vote of the people. Such a governing system, he wrote, would be the worst means of controlling a majority faction because "there is nothing to check the inducements to sacrifice the weaker party or an obnoxious individual."

These concerns were still being voiced in America in the early years of the nineteenth century. But with the broadening of the suffrage, the term "democracy" acquired a more positive connotation, and by the time of Andrew Jackson's election in 1828 it was surrounded with a romantic aura.

By the end of the nineteenth century hardly anyone of importance in America questioned the ideal of democracy. If the predominant sentiment pointed anywhere, it was toward extending it. Domestically, leaders of the Progressive period sought to bring the big corporations to heel, making them more responsive to public needs and demands. Then, cautiously at first, American leaders began asking aloud whether democracy might be expanded abroad, to places still ruled by autocrats and dynastic regimes.

The question gained greater force with the outbreak of World War I in Europe, which many Americans blamed on the autocratic regimes ruling Germany and the other Central Powers. When President Woodrow Wilson finally asked Congress to declare war on them in 1917, he couched his appeal in democratic terms. "We have no quarrel with the German people," he said, "for our quarrel is only with the narrow circle of autocrats ruling Germany." Their removal was essential to the restoration of world peace, for "self-governed nations do not fill their neighbor states with spies or set the course of intrigue," permitting them to "strike and make conquest." Aggressive acts of this kind can be planned only within the narrow circles of unelected elites. "They are happily impossible where public opinion commands and insists upon full information concerning all the nation's affairs." America was to go to war, then, as a champion of the rights of mankind. Free peoples do not commit terrorist acts or aggression upon others, and so "the world must be made safe for democracy."

President George W. Bush has approached the war on terror with a somewhat similar rationale. In his Second Inaugural Address, Bush said, "The best hope for peace in the world is the expansion of freedom in the world." The theory is that terrorist groups win support from young idealists frustrated by their inability to bring about change in their countries. The classic case is Saudi Arabia, from which seventeen of the nineteen 9/11 hijackers came. There the ruling elite, stifling democracy but anxious to guard against revolution, tries to redirect the rage of militants by sponsoring Islamic clerics who turn it against the West. The belief is that we can "dry up the swamp" by encouraging the spread of democracy throughout the Middle East. If people can change their countries' policies by peaceful means they are less likely to heed the siren calls of terrorist groups.

In recent years Americans of both political parties have endorsed some version of the "dry up the swamp" theory, among them Massachusetts Senator John Kerry, Morton Halperin, President Clinton's chief State Department policy planner, and *New York Times* columnist Thomas Friedman. But it has remained for President Bush to attempt putting the theory to work. Besides seeking to establish a democratic government in Iraq, he has supported Palestinian elections and elections in Lebanon, prodded the Saudis and the Egyptians to allow greater democracy, and joined those who insisted on new elections in Ukraine in the wake of the rigged elections there.

In the following selections, President Bush spells out his theory that "the best antidote to terrorism is the tolerance and hope kindled in free societies," while political science professor F. Gregory Gause contends that there is no relationship between terrorism emanating from a country and the degree of freedom enjoyed by its citizens. He thinks that the better way to fight terror is to encourage secular, nationalist, and liberal organizations to compete with the Islamists.

YES

George W. Bush

President Discusses War on Terror

We meet at a time of great consequence for the security of our nation, a time when the defense of freedom requires the advance of freedom, a time with echoes in our history.

Twice in six decades, a sudden attack on the United States launched our country into a global conflict, and began a period of serious reflection on America's place in the world. The bombing of Pearl Harbor taught America that unopposed tyranny, even on far-away continents, could draw our country into a struggle for our own survival. And our reflection on that lesson led us to help build peaceful democracies in the ruins of tyranny, to unite free nations in the NATO Alliance, and to establish a firm commitment to peace in the Pacific that continues to this day.

The attacks of September the 11th, 2001 also revealed the outlines of a new world. In one way, that assault was the culmination of decades of escalating violence—from the killing of U.S. Marines in Beirut, to the bombing at the World Trade Center, to the attacks on American embassies in Africa, to the attacks on the USS Cole. In another way, September the 11th provided a warning of future dangers—of terror networks aided by outlaw regimes, and ideologies that incite the murder of the innocent, and biological and chemical and nuclear weapons that multiply destructive power.

Like an earlier generation, America is answering new dangers with firm resolve. No matter how long it takes, no matter how difficult the task, we will fight the enemy, and lift the shadow of fear, and lead free nations to victory.

Like an earlier generation, America is pursuing a clear strategy with our allies to achieve victory. Our immediate strategy is to eliminate terrorist threats abroad, so we do not have to face them here at home. The theory here is straightforward: terrorists are less likely to endanger our security if they are worried about their own security. When terrorists spend their days struggling to avoid death or capture, they are less capable of arming and training to commit new attacks. We will keep the terrorists on the run, until they have nowhere left to hide.

In three and a half years, the United States and our allies have waged a campaign of global scale—from the mountains of Afghanistan, to the border regions of Pakistan, to the Horn of Africa, to the islands of the Philippines, to the plains of North Central Iraq. The al Qaeda terror network that attacked

From a Speech at the National Defense University, March 8, 2005.

our country still has leaders, but many of its top commanders have been removed. There are still governments that sponsor and harbor terrorists, but their number has declined. There are still regimes seeking weapons of mass destruction—but no longer without attention and without consequence. Our country is still the target of terrorists who want to kill many, and intimidate us all. We will stay on the offensive against them, until the fight is won.

. . . The advance of hope in the Middle East requires new thinking in the region. By now it should be clear that authoritarian rule is not the wave of the future; it is the last gasp of a discredited past. It should be clear that free nations escape stagnation, and grow stronger with time, because they encourage the creativity and enterprise of their people. It should be clear that economic progress requires political modernization, including honest representative government and the rule of law. And it should be clear that no society can advance with only half of its talent and energy—and that demands the full participation of women.

The advance of hope in the Middle East also requires new thinking in the capitals of great democracies—including Washington, D.C. By now it should be clear that decades of excusing and accommodating tyranny, in the pursuit of stability, have only led to injustice and instability and tragedy. It should be clear that the advance of democracy leads to peace, because governments that respect the rights of their people also respect the rights of their neighbors. It should be clear that the best antidote to radicalism and terror is the tolerance and hope kindled in free societies. And our duty is now clear: For the sake of our long-term security, all free nations must stand with the forces of democracy and justice that have begun to transform the Middle East.

Encouraging democracy in that region is a generational commitment. It's also a difficult commitment, demanding patience and resolve—when the headlines are good and when the headlines aren't so good. Freedom has determined enemies, who show no mercy for the innocent, and no respect for the rules of warfare. Many societies in the region struggle with poverty and illiteracy, many rulers in the region have longstanding habits of control; many people in the region have deeply ingrained habits of fear.

For all these reasons, the chances of democratic progress in the broader Middle East have seemed frozen in place for decades. Yet at last, clearly and suddenly, the thaw has begun. The people of Afghanistan have embraced free government, after suffering under one of the most backward tyrannies on earth. The voters in Iraq defied threats of murder, and have set their country on a path to full democracy. The people of the Palestinian Territories cast their ballots against violence and corruption of the past. And any who doubt the appeal of freedom in the Middle East can look to Lebanon, where the Lebanese people are demanding a free and independent nation. In the words of one Lebanese observer, "Democracy is knocking at the door of this country and, if it's successful in Lebanon, it is going to ring the doors of every Arab regime."

Across the Middle East, a critical mass of events is taking that region in a hopeful new direction. Historic changes have many causes, yet these changes have one factor in common. A businessman in Beirut recently said, "We have removed the mask of fear. We're not afraid anymore." Pervasive fear is the foundation of every dictatorial regime—the prop that holds up all power not based on consent. And when the regime of fear is broken, and the people find their courage and find their voice, democracy is their goal, and tyrants, themselves, have reason to fear.

History is moving quickly, and leaders in the Middle East have important choices to make. The world community, including Russia and Germany and France and Saudi Arabia and the United States has presented the Syrian government with one of those choices—to end its nearly 30-year occupation of Lebanon, or become even more isolated from the world. The Lebanese people have heard the speech by the Syrian president. They've seen these delaying tactics and half-measures before. The time has come for Syria to fully implement Security Council Resolution 1559. All Syrian military forces and intelligence personnel must withdraw before the Lebanese elections, for those elections to be free and fair.

The elections in Lebanon must be fully and carefully monitored by international observers. The Lebanese people have the right to determine their future, free from domination by a foreign power. The Lebanese people have the right to choose their own parliament this spring, free of intimidation. And that new government will have the help of the international community in building sound political, economic, and military institutions, so the great nation of Lebanon can move forward in security and freedom.

Today I have a message for the people of Lebanon: All the world is witnessing your great movement of conscience. Lebanon's future belongs in your hands, and by your courage, Lebanon's future will be in your hands. The American people are on your side. Millions across the earth are on your side. The momentum of freedom is on your side, and freedom will prevail in Lebanon.

America and other nations are also aware that the recent terrorist attack in Tel Aviv was conducted by a radical Palestinian group headquartered in Damascus. Syria, as well as Iran, has a long history of supporting terrorist groups determined to sow division and chaos in the Middle East, and there is every possibility they will try this strategy again. The time has come for Syria and Iran to stop using murder as a tool of policy, and to end all support for terrorism.

In spite of attacks by extremists, the world is seeing hopeful progress in the Israel-Palestinian conflict. There is only one outcome that will end the tyranny, danger, violence and hopelessness, and meet the aspirations of all people in the region: We seek two democratic states, Israel and Palestine, living side-by-side in peace and security.

And that goal is within reach, if all the parties meet their responsibilities and if terrorism is brought to an end. Arab states must end incitement in their own media, cut off public and private funding for terrorism, stop their support for extremist education, and establish normal relations with Israel. Israel must freeze settlement activity, help the Palestinians build a thriving economy, and ensure that a new Palestinian state is truly viable, with contiguous territory on the West Bank. Palestinian leaders must fight corruption, encourage free enterprise, rest true authority with the people, and actively confront terrorist groups.

The bombing in Tel Aviv is a reminder that the fight against terrorists is critical to the search for peace and for Palestinian statehood. In an interview last week, Palestinian President Abbas strongly condemned the terrorist attack in Tel Aviv, declaring, "Ending violence and security chaos is first and foremost a Palestinian interest." He went on to say, "We cannot build the foundations of a state without the rule of law and public order."

President Abbas is correct. And so the United States will help the Palestinian Authority build the security services that current peace and future statehood require: security forces which are effective, responsive to civilian control, and dedicated to fighting terror and upholding the rule of law. We will coordinate with the government of Israel, with neighbors such as Egypt and Jordan, and with other donors to ensure that Palestinians get the training and equipment they need. The United States is determined to help the parties remove obstacles to progress and move forward in practical ways, so we can seize this moment for peace in the Holy Land.

In other parts of the Middle East, we're seeing small but welcome steps. Saudi Arabia's recent municipal elections were the beginning of reform that may allow greater participation in the future. Egypt has now—has now the prospect of competitive, multi-party elections for President in September. Like all free elections, these require freedom of assembly, multiple candidates, free access by those candidates to the media, and the right to form political parties. Each country in the Middle East will take a different path of reform. And every nation that starts on that journey can know that America will walk at its side.

Progress in the Middle East is threatened by weapons of mass destruction and their proliferation. Today, Great Britain, France, and Germany are involved in a difficult negotiation with Iran aimed at stopping its nuclear weapons program. We want our allies to succeed, because we share the view that Iran's acquisition of nuclear weapons would be destabilizing and threatening to all of Iran's neighbors. The Iranian regime should listen to the concerns of the world, and listen to the voice of the Iranian people, who long for their liberty and want their country to be a respected member of the international community. We look forward to the day when Iran joins in the hopeful changes taking place across the region. We look forward to the day when the Iranian people are free.

Iran and other nations have an example in Iraq. The recent elections have begun a process of debate and coalition building unique in Iraqi history, and inspiring to see. Iraq's leaders are forming a government that will oversee the next—and critical—stage in Iraq's political transition: the writing of a permanent constitution. This process must take place without external influence. The shape of Iraq's democracy must be determined by the Iraqis, themselves.

Iraq's democracy, in the long run, must also be defended by Iraqis, themselves. Our goal is to help Iraqi security forces move toward self-reliance, and they are making daily progress. Iraqi forces were the main providers of security at about 5,000 polling places in the January elections. Our coalition is providing equipment and training to the new Iraqi military, yet they bring a spirit all of their own.

Last month, when soldiers of the U.S. 7th Cavalry Regiment were on combat patrol north of Baghdad, one of their Humvees fell into a canal, and Iraqi troops came to their rescue—plunging into the water again and again, until the last American was recovered. The Army colonel in charge of the unit said, "When I saw those Iraqis in the water, fighting to save their American brothers, I saw a glimpse of the future of this country." One of the Iraqi soldiers commented, "These people have come a hundred—10,000 miles to help my country. They've left their families and their children. If we can give them something back, just a little, we can show our thanks." America is proud to defend freedom in Iraq, and proud to stand with the brave Iraqis as they defend their own freedom.

Three and a half years ago, the United States mourned our dead, gathered our resolve, and accepted a mission. We made a decision to stop threats to the American people before they arrive on our shores, and we have acted on that decision. We're also determined to seek and support the growth of democratic movements and institutions in every nation and culture, with the ultimate goal of ending tyranny in our world.

This objective will not be achieved easily, or all at once, or primarily by force of arms. We know that freedom, by definition, must be chosen, and that the democratic institutions of other nations will not look like our own. Yet we also know that our security increasingly depends on the hope and progress of other nations now simmering in despair and resentment. And that hope and progress is found only in the advance of freedom.

This advance is a consistent theme of American strategy—from the Fourteen Points, to the Four Freedoms, to the Marshall Plan, to the Reagan Doctrine. Yet the success of this approach does not depend on grand strategy alone. We are confident that the desire for freedom, even when repressed for generations, is present in every human heart. And that desire can emerge with sudden power to change the course of history.

Americans, of all people, should not be surprised by freedom's power. A nation founded on the universal claim of individual rights should not be surprised when other people claim those rights. Those who place their hope in freedom may be attacked and challenged, but they will not ultimately be disappointed, because freedom is the design of humanity and freedom is the direction of history.

In our time, America has been attacked. America has been challenged. Yet the uncertainty, and sorrow, and sacrifice of these years have not been in vain. Millions have gained their liberty; and millions more have gained the hope of liberty that will not be denied. The trumpet of freedom has been sounded, and that trumpet never calls retreat.

Before history is written in books, it is written in courage—the courage of honorable soldiers; the courage of oppressed peoples; the courage of free nations in difficult tasks. Our generation is fortunate to live in a time of courage. And we are proud to serve in freedom's cause.

May God bless you all.

F. Gregory Gause III  **NO**

Can Democracy Stop Terrorism?

What Freedom Brings

The United States is engaged in what President George W. Bush has called a "generational challenge" to instill democracy in the Arab world. The Bush administration and its defenders contend that this push for Arab democracy will not only spread American values but also improve U.S. security. As democracy grows in the Arab world, the thinking goes, the region will stop generating anti-American terrorism. Promoting democracy in the Middle East is therefore not merely consistent with U.S. security goals; it is necessary to achieve them.

But this begs a fundamental question: Is it true that the more democratic a country becomes, the less likely it is to produce terrorists and terrorist groups? In other words, is the security rationale for promoting democracy in the Arab world based on a sound premise? Unfortunately, the answer appears to be no. Although what is known about terrorism is admittedly incomplete, the data available do not show a strong relationship between democracy and an absence of or a reduction in terrorism. Terrorism appears to stem from factors much more specific than regime type. Nor is it likely that democratization would end the current campaign against the United States. Al Qaeda and like-minded groups are not fighting for democracy in the Muslim world; they are fighting to impose their vision of an Islamic state. Nor is there any evidence that democracy in the Arab world would "drain the swamp," eliminating soft support for terrorist organizations among the Arab public and reducing the number of potential recruits for them.

Even if democracy were achieved in the Middle East, what kind of governments would it produce? Would they cooperate with the United States on important policy objectives besides curbing terrorism, such as advancing the Arab-Israeli peace process, maintaining security in the Persian Gulf, and ensuring steady supplies of oil? No one can predict the course a new democracy will take, but based on public opinion surveys and recent elections in the Arab world, the advent of democracy there seems likely to produce new Islamist governments that would be much less willing to cooperate with the United States than are the current authoritarian rulers.

The answers to these questions should give Washington pause. The Bush administration's democracy initiative can be defended as an effort to spread

Reprinted by permission of *Foreign Affairs,* September/October 2005, pp. 62–76. Copyright © 2005 by the Council on Foreign Relations, Inc.

American democratic values at any cost, or as a long-term gamble that even if Islamists do come to power, the realities of governance will moderate them or the public will grow disillusioned with them. The emphasis on electoral democracy will not, however, serve immediate U.S. interests either in the war on terrorism or in other important Middle East policies.

It is thus time to rethink the U.S. emphasis on democracy promotion in the Arab world. Rather than push for quick elections, the United States should instead focus its energy on encouraging the development of secular, nationalist, and liberal political organizations that could compete on an equal footing with Islamist parties. Only by doing so can Washington help ensure that when elections finally do occur, the results are more in line with U.S. interests.

The Missing Link

President Bush has been clear about why he thinks promoting democracy in the Arab world is central to U.S. interests. "Our strategy to keep the peace in the longer term," Bush said in a speech in March 2005,

> is to help change the conditions that give rise to extremism and terror, especially in the broader Middle East. Parts of that region have been caught for generations in a cycle of tyranny and despair and radicalism. When a dictatorship controls the political life of a country, responsible opposition cannot develop, and dissent is driven underground and toward the extreme. And to draw attention away from their social and economic failures, dictators place blame on other countries and other races, and stir the hatred that leads to violence. This status quo of despotism and anger cannot be ignored or appeased, kept in a box or bought off.

. . . The numbers published by the U.S. government do not bear out claims of a close link between terrorism and authoritarianism either. Between 2000 and 2003, according to the State Department's annual "Patterns of Global Terrorism" report, 269 major terrorist incidents around the world occurred in countries classified as "free" by Freedom House, 119 occurred in "partly free" countries, and 138 occurred in "not free" countries. (This count excludes both terrorist attacks by Palestinians on Israel, which would increase the number of attacks in democracies even more, and the September 11, 2001, attacks on the United States, which originated in other countries.) This is not to argue that free countries are more likely to produce terrorists than other countries. Rather, these numbers simply indicate that there is no relationship between the incidence of terrorism in a given country and the degree of freedom enjoyed by its citizens. They certainly do not indicate that democracies are substantially less susceptible to terrorism than are other forms of government.

Terrorism, of course, is not distributed randomly. According to official U.S. government data, the vast majority of terrorist incidents occurred in only a few countries. Indeed, half of all the terrorist incidents in "not free" countries in 2003 took place in just two countries: Iraq and Afghanistan. It seems that democratization did little to discourage terrorists from operating there and may even have encouraged terrorism.

As for the "free" countries, terrorist incidents in India accounted for fully 75 percent of the total. It is fair to assume that groups based in Pakistan carried out a number of those attacks, particularly in Kashmir, but clearly not all the perpetrators were foreigners. A significant number of terrorist events in India took place far from Kashmir, reflecting other local grievances against the central government. And as strong and vibrant as Indian democracy is, both a sitting prime minister and a former prime minister have been assassinated— Indira Gandhi and her son, Rajiv Gandhi, respectively. If democracy reduced the prospects for terrorism, India's numbers would not be so high.

Comparing India, the world's most populous democracy, and China, the world's most populous authoritarian state, highlights the difficulty of assuming that democracy can solve the terrorism problem. For 2000–2003, the "Patterns of Global Terrorism" report indicates 203 international terrorist attacks in India and none in China. A list of terrorist incidents between 1976 and 2004, compiled by the National Memorial Institute for the Prevention of Terrorism, shows more than 400 in India and only 18 in China. Even if China underreports such incidents by a factor of ten, it still endures substantially fewer terrorist attacks than India. If the relationship between authoritarianism and terrorism were as strong as the Bush administration implies, the discrepancy between the number of terrorist incidents in China and the number in India would run the other way. . . .

There is, in other words, no solid empirical evidence for a strong link between democracy, or any other regime type, and terrorism, in either a positive or a negative direction. In her highly praised post-September 11 study of religious militants, *Terror in the Name of God,* Jessica Stern argues that "democratization is not necessarily the best way to fight Islamic extremism," because the transition to democracy "has been found to be an especially vulnerable period for states across the board." Terrorism springs from sources other than the form of government of a state. There is no reason to believe that a more democratic Arab world will, simply by virtue of being more democratic, generate fewer terrorists.

Flawed

There are also logical problems with the argument supporting the U.S. push for democracy as part of the war on terrorism. Underlying the assertion that democracy will reduce terrorism is the belief that, able to participate openly in competitive politics and have their voices heard in the public square, potential terrorists and terrorist sympathizers would not need to resort to violence to achieve their goals. Even if they lost in one round of elections, the confidence that they could win in the future would inhibit the temptation to resort to extra-democratic means. The habits of democracy would ameliorate extremism and focus the anger of the Arab publics at their own governments, not at the United States.

Well, maybe. But it is just as logical to assume that terrorists, who rarely represent political agendas that could mobilize electoral majorities, would reject the very principles of majority rule and minority rights on which liberal democracy is based. If they could not achieve their goals through democratic politics, why would they privilege the democratic process over those goals? It seems more likely that, having been mobilized to participate in the demo-cratic process by a burning desire to achieve particular goals—a desire so strong that they were willing to commit acts of violence against defenseless civilians to realize it—terrorists and potential terrorists would attack democ-racy if it did not produce their desired results. Respect for the nascent Iraqi democracy, despite a very successful election in January 2005, has not stopped Iraqi and foreign terrorists from their campaign against the new political order.

Terrorist organizations are not mass-based organizations. They are small and secretive. They are not organized or based on democratic principles. They revolve around strong leaders and a cluster of committed followers who are willing to take actions from which the vast majority of people, even those who might support their political agenda, would rightly shrink. It seems unlikely that simply being out voted would deflect them from their path.

The United States' major foe in the war on terrorism, al Qaeda, certainly would not close up shop if every Muslim country in the world were to become a democracy. Osama bin Laden has been very clear about democracy: he does not like it. His political model is the early Muslim caliphate. In his view, the Taliban regime in Afghanistan came the closest in modern times to that model. In an October 2003 "message to Iraqis," bin Laden castigated those in the Arab world who are "calling for a peaceful democratic solution in dealing with apostate governments or with Jewish and crusader invaders instead of fighting in the name of God." He referred to democracy as "this deviant and misleading practice" and "the faith of the ignorant." Bin Laden's ally in Iraq, Abu Musab al-Zarqawi, reacted to the January 2005 Iraqi election even more directly: "The legislator who must be obeyed in a democracy is man, and not God. . . . That is the very essence of heresy and polytheism and error, as it contradicts the bases of the faith and monotheism, and because it makes the weak, ignorant man God's partner in His most central divine prerogative—namely, ruling and legislating."

Al Qaeda's leaders distrust democracy, and not just on ideological grounds: they know they could not come to power through free elections. There is no reason to believe that a move toward more democracy in Arab states would deflect them from their course. And there is no reason to believe that they could not recruit followers in more democratic Arab states— especially if those states continued to have good relations with the United States, made peace with Israel, and generally behaved in ways acceptable to Washington. Al Qaeda objects to the U.S. agenda in the Middle East as much as, if not more than, democracy. If, as Washington hopes, a democratic Mid-dle East continued to accept a major U.S. role in the region and cooperate with U.S. goals, it is foolish to think that democracy would end Arab anti-Americanism and dry up passive support, funding sources, and recruiting channels for al Qaeda.

When it works, liberal democracy is the best form of government. But there is no evidence that it reduces or prevents terrorism. The fundamental assumption of the Bush administration's push for democracy in the Arab world is seriously flawed.

Angry Voices

It is highly unlikely that democratically elected Arab governments would be as cooperative with the United States as the current authoritarian regimes. To the extent that public opinion can be measured in these countries, research shows that Arabs strongly support democracy. When they have a chance to vote in real elections, they generally turn out in percentages far greater than Americans do in their elections. But many Arabs hold negative views of the United States. If Arab governments were democratically elected and more representative of public opinion, they would thus be more anti-American. Further democratization in the Middle East would, for the foreseeable future, most likely generate Islamist governments less inclined to cooperate with the United States on important U.S. policy goals, including military basing rights in the region, peace with Israel, and the war on terrorism. . . .

The problem with promoting democracy in the Arab world is not that Arabs do not like democracy; it is that Washington probably would not like the governments Arab democracy would produce. Assuming that democratic Arab governments would better represent the opinions of their people than do the current Arab regimes, democratization of the Arab world should produce more anti-U.S. foreign policies. In a February–March 2003 poll conducted in six Arab countries by Zogby International and the Anwar Sadat Chair for Peace and Development at the University of Maryland, overwhelming majorities of those surveyed held either a very unfavorable or a somewhat unfavorable attitude toward the United States. The Lebanese viewed the United States most favorably, with 32 percent of respondents holding a very favorable or a somewhat favorable view of the United States. Only 4 percent of Saudi respondents said the same.

The war in Iraq—which was imminent or ongoing as the poll was conducted—surely affected these numbers. But these statistics are not that different from those gathered by less comprehensive polls conducted both before and after the war. In a Gallup poll in early 2002, strong majorities of those surveyed in Jordan (62 percent) and Saudi Arabia (64 percent) rated the United States unfavorably. Only in Lebanon did positive views of the United States roughly balance negative views. In a Zogby International poll conducted in seven Arab countries at about the same time, unfavorable ratings of the United States ranged from 48 percent in Kuwait to 61 percent in Jordan, 76 percent in Egypt, and 87 percent in Saudi Arabia and the UAE. One year after the war began, a Pew Global Attitudes poll showed that 93 percent of Jordanians and 68 percent of Moroccans had a negative attitude toward the United States. . . .

The trend is clear: Islamists of various hues score well in free elections. In countries where a governing party dominates or where the king opposes political Islam, Islamists run second and form the opposition. Only in Morocco, where more secular, leftist parties have a long history and an established presence, and in Lebanon, where the Christian-Muslim dynamic determines electoral politics, did organized non-Islamist political blocs, independent of the government, compete with Islamist forces. The pattern does not look like it is about to change. According to the 2004 Zogby International-Sadat Chair poll, pluralities of those surveyed in Jordan, Saudi Arabia, and the UAE said the clergy should play a greater role in their political systems. Fifty percent of Egyptians polled said the clerics should not dictate the political system, but as many as 47 percent supported a greater role for them. Only in Morocco and Lebanon did anticlerical sentiment dominate pro-clerical feelings—51 percent to 33 percent in Morocco and 50 percent to 28 percent in Lebanon. The more democratic the Arab world gets, the more likely it is that Islamists will come to power. Even if those Islamists come to accept the rules of democracy and reject political violence, they are unlikely to support U.S. foreign policy goals in the region.

The Long Haul

The Bush administration's push for democracy in the Arab world is unlikely to have much effect on anti-American terrorism emanating from there; it could in fact help bring to power governments much less cooperative on a whole range of issues—including the war on terrorism—than the current regimes. Unfortunately, there is no good alternative at this point to working with the authoritarian Arab governments that are willing to work with the United States.

If Washington insists on promoting democracy in the Arab world, it should learn from the various electoral experiences in the region. Where there are strongly rooted non-Islamist parties, as in Morocco, the Islamists have a harder time dominating the field. The same is true in non-Arab Turkey, where the Islamist political party has moderated its message over time to contend with the power of the secular army and with well-established, more secular parties. Likewise, the diverse confessional mix of voters in Lebanon will probably prevent Hezbollah and other Islamists from dominating elections there. Conversely, where non-Islamist political forces have been suppressed, as in Saudi Arabia and Bahrain, Islamist parties and candidates can command the political field. Washington should take no comfort from the success of ruling parties in Algeria, Egypt, and Yemen over Islamist challengers: once stripped of their patronage and security apparatus, ruling parties do not fare very well in democratic transitional elections.

The United States must focus on pushing Arab governments to make political space for liberal, secular, leftist, nationalist, and other non-Islamist parties to set down roots and mobilize voters. Washington should support those groups that are more likely to accept U.S. foreign policy and emulate U.S. political values. The most effective way to demonstrate that support is to openly pressure Arab regimes when they obstruct the political activity of more liberal groups—as the administration did with Egypt after the jailing of the liberal reformers Saad Eddin Ibrahim and Ayman Nour, and as it should do with Saudi Arabia regarding the May sentencing of peaceful political activists to long prison terms. But Washington will also need to drop its focus on prompt elections in Arab countries where no strong, organized alternative to Islamist parties exists—even at the risk of disappointing Arab liberals by being more cautious about their electoral prospects than they are.

Administration officials, including President Bush, have often stated that the transition to democracy in the Arab world will be difficult and that Americans should not expect quick results. Yet whenever the Bush administration publicly defends democratization, it cites a familiar litany of Muslim-world elections—those in Afghanistan, Iraq, Lebanon, the Palestinian territories, and Saudi Arabia as evidence that the policy is working. It will take years, however, for non-Islamist political forces to be ready to compete for power in these elections, and it is doubtful that this or any other U.S. administration will have the patience to see the process through. If it cannot show that patience, Washington must realize that its democratization policy will lead to Islamist domination of Arab politics.

It is not only the focus on elections that is troubling in the administration's democracy initiative in the Arab world. Also problematic is the unjustified confidence that Washington has in its ability to predict, and even direct, the course of politics in other countries. No administration official would sign on, at least not in public, to the naive view that Arab democracy will produce governments that will always cooperate with the United States. Yet Washington's democracy advocates seem to assume that Arab democratic transitions, like the recent democratic transitions in eastern Europe, Latin America, and East Asia, will lead to regimes that support, or at least do not impede, the broad range of U.S. foreign policy interests. They do not appreciate that in those regimes, liberalism prevailed because its great ideological competitor, communism, was thoroughly discredited, whereas the Arab world offers a real ideological alternative to liberal democracy: the movement that claims as its motto "Islam is the solution." Washington's hubris should have been crushed in Iraq, where even the presence of 140,000 American troops has not allowed politics to proceed according to the U.S. plan. Yet the Bush administration displays little of the humility or the patience that such a daunting task demands. If the United States really does see the democracy-promotion initiative in the Arab world as a "generational challenge," the entire nation will have to learn these traits.

POSTSCRIPT

Is Democracy the Answer
to Global Terrorism?

Al Qaeda's leaders, Gause notes, "distrust democracy, and not just on ideological grounds: they know they could not come to power through free elections." On its face, this seems to bolster President Bush's theory of democracy as a means of fighting terror. But what Gause is getting at is that, if a pro-American or pro-Israeli regime comes to power in any Islamic country, even if it does so through democratic means, al Qaeda will have no trouble recruiting new members there. This may well be true, but the question is whether democracy may finally marginalize al Qaeda once the people realize how opposed to self-rule al Qaeda really is.

In *The Future of Freedom* (Norton, 2003), Fareed Zakaria argues that unrestrained democracy threatens vital liberties and goes so far as to suggest that "what we need in politics today is not more democracy but less." In a *New Republic* essay entitled, "The Ungreat Washed," (July 7 & 14, 2001), Robert Kagan contends that in today's world, democracy is the only practical means of protecting vital liberties. In the same vein, see Michael McFaul, "The Liberty Doctrine," *Policy Review*, April 2002. Arguing the other side is Robert D. Kaplan ("Was Democracy Just a Moment?," *Atlantic Monthly*, December 1997) who insists that not all nations enjoy conditions that allow democracy to thrive, and that some are better off without it. Morton H. Halperin's *The Democratic Advantage: How Democracies Promote Peace* (Routledge, 2004) makes the case that democracy promotes industrial development and the reduction of poverty in third-world countries. Reuel Marc Gerecht (*The Islamic Paradox*, AEI Press, 2004) agrees with the critics of democratization that democracy will probably bring even more clerical domination and anti-American rhetoric to the Middle East, but that it is actually the "least dangerous option for the United States." Political scientist Samuel P. Huntington is not so sure about that. Within the space of a few years, Huntington changed his position from a positive view of the spread of democracy, in *The Third Wave: Democratization in the Late Twentieth Century* (University of Oklahoma Press, 1991), to a negative outlook in *The Clash of Civilizations and the Remaking of the World Order* (Simon & Schuster, 1996).

One difficulty in the theory of democracy as a means of fighting terror is the possibility that a democratic election could actually bring a terrorist group to power. That this is more than hypothetical was demonstrated in the Palestinian elections of February, 2006, in which Hamas, a known terrorist group, captured control of the Palestinian Authority. Those who cling to their trust in the democratic process believe that this new power may, in time, make Hamas more mature and responsible. Henceforth, its performance in ministering to the day-to-day needs of the Palestinian people—jobs, health care, garbage collection, and so on—will be measured and judged by the people themselves, and it will be rejected by them if it fails. This will leave little time for plotting terrorism. Or so it is hoped. For now, at least, it remains a hope rather than a demonstrable fact.

ISSUE 3

Should the Electoral College Be Abolished?

YES: George C. Edwards III, from *Why the Electoral College Is Bad for America* (Yale University Press, 2004)

NO: Gary L. Gregg, from "The Electoral College Is Good for America," *National Review Online* (October 25–27, 2004)

ISSUE SUMMARY

YES: University Professor George C. Edwards III believes that the Electoral College method of election violates the democratic principle of majority election and has resulted in the election of candidates with fewer votes than their leading opponent.

NO: Leadership Institute Director Gary L. Gregg maintains that the Electoral College system has succeeded in moderating and stabilizing American politics, and its abolition would risk the creation of radical parties and the election of minority presidents.

Whenever they first learn about it, Americans have difficulty grasping the fact that the President of the United States is elected not directly by the people but by electors whose names they do not know. When voters go to the polls on Election Day—the first Tuesday after the first Monday in November every four years (the next presidential election will be on November 4, 2008)—they choose between two competing slates of electors in their state or the District of Columbia. Although the electors cast their votes a little more than a month later, the American people usually know who won shortly after the voting booths close on Election Day.

The presidential election of 2000 was decided 36 days after Election Day, and only when a 5–4 decision of the U.S. Supreme Court had the effect of ending the recount of votes in Florida, giving George W. Bush that state's electoral votes and victory, despite the fact that Al Gore had a half-million vote national plurality. In three previous elections (1824, 1876 and 1888), the newly elected president had fewer votes than his opponent.

The framers of the Constitution imagined that a number of public-spirited citizens—perhaps political elders who had retired from public office—would be chosen in each state to constitute the Electoral College. The Electoral College is not a college and never meets as a single entity, but it greatly influences the character of the parties, the nominating process, and the outcome of the presidential election. Here is how it works: Each state has a number of electoral votes equal to its membership in the two houses of Congress. Because all states have two senators and at least one representative, the smallest number of electoral votes a state may have is three. There are 50 states (and, therefore, 100 senators), the size of the House of Representatives has been limited to 435 by law, and a constitutional amendment has given the District of Columbia 3 electoral votes, resulting in a total of 538 electoral votes. A majority of 270 is necessary for election. The authors of the Constitution did not anticipate political parties or modern communications, and they believed that many candidates would receive votes in each election. If no candidate received an electoral majority, the president would be chosen by the House of Representatives (with each state casting but one vote) from among the five leading candidates.

The design of the Framers did not function as they had intended for long. Political parties quickly developed, ensuring broad national support for their candidates. The states gradually moved to the popular election of the electors. The composition of the voting population increased with the abolition of property qualifications and the extension of the ballot to African Americans, women, and young adults of 18. Soon all the electors in each state were elected with the understanding that they would cast their votes for the candidates who had received the most votes in that state. (Most electors were bound by party and precedent, not by law, and a small number of so-called faithless electors have ignored the voters' choice.)

The existence of the Electoral College usually undermines third parties, which are unlikely to win electoral votes, although some minor parties have sought to win the electoral vote of one or two states in order to prevent a majority and thereby obtain bargaining power in choosing the next president. Also, the electoral vote usually exaggerates the popular strength of the majority party, but in a close election it can result in the election of a candidate who received fewer popular votes than his opponent. That, of course, is what happened for the fourth time in 2000.

Critics argue that the electors are, at best, an anachronism and, at worst, capable of distorting or even altering the result of an election. In defense of the Electoral College, its supporters point out that a straight popular election would encourage minor party candidates, making the election of a plurality president, possibly even one with a relatively small percentage of the vote, likely.

Opposing positions are argued here by George C. Edwards III and Gary L. Gregg, both scholars with a special interest in the way in which Americans elect their president.

YES

George C. Edwards III

Why the Electoral College
Is Bad for America?

Perhaps the most important—and overlooked—legacy of the 2000 presidential election is demonstrating the critical role of the electoral college. It was the electoral college, not the Supreme Court's decision in *Bush v. Gore*, that actually determined the outcome of the election. If we selected presidents like we select governors, senators, representatives, and virtually every elected official in the United States, Al Gore would have been elected president—no matter which chads were counted in Florida.

The runner-up in the popular votes winning the presidency raises yet again the question of the electoral college mechanism for selecting the president. Should the candidate receiving the most votes win the election? Supporters of the electoral college saw no problem in the outcome of the Bush–Gore race. Those wishing to reform the electoral college saw another side of the story of the 2000 election, however. They viewed the outcome of the election as violating central tenets of democracy—political equality and majority (or at least plurality) rule. . . .

Two aspects of the debate over the electoral college are especially striking. First, the issues are rarely joined. Reformers argue that the electoral college violates political equality, one of the most fundamental tenets of democracy. Given the prominence of the principle of equality in American life and the country's commitment to democracy, one might anticipate that supporters of the electoral college would respond with principled arguments in kind. But they rarely do. Instead, they typically simply dismiss such concerns, sweeping them aside to focus on what they see as the advantages of the electoral college.

The second striking aspect of the debate over the electoral college is the nature of the discussion. Supporters argue, often passionately—sometimes hysterically—that the electoral college has a wide range of advantages for the American polity. These benefits, they contend, include protecting the interests of small states and strategically placed minorities, preserving federalism, encouraging the two-party system, and protecting against voter fraud. These assertions certainly deal with important issues and require careful examination, especially when on their face many of the claims seem to be quite mistaken.

It is disconcerting, then, to find that supporters of the electoral college are extraordinarily insouciant about their claims on its behalf and virtually never marshal data systematically or rigorously evaluate supposed benefits. Nor do they cite relevant literature. Instead, they make assertions. Yet there are ways to test claims. For example, do candidates really pay attention to small states? We can find out. Is the electoral college really a fundamental pillar of federalism? Let us examine the federal system and see. Is the winner-take-all system in the electoral college the critical institutional underpinning of the two-party system? Researchers have been studying party systems for years. . . .

The electoral college is an extraordinarily complex system for electing a president, one that has the potential to undo the people's will at many points in the long journey from the selection of electors to counting their votes in Congress. Faithless electors may fail to vote as the people who elected them wish. Congress may find it difficult to choose justly between competing slates of electors. What is more significant, the electoral college violates political equality, favoring some citizens over others depending solely on the state in which they live. The unit rule, the allocation of electoral votes among the states, the differences in voter turnout among states, and the size of the House make the aggregation of votes for president inherently unjust.

Virtually no one is willing to defend the electoral college's provisions for contingent elections of the president and vice president. These provisions: blatantly violate political equality, directly disenfranchise hundreds of thousands of Americans, have the potential to grossly misrepresent the wishes of the public, make the president dependent on Congress, give a few individuals extraordinary power to select the president, enable the selection of a president and vice president from different parties, and fail to deal with a tie for third in the electoral college.

For two centuries, supporters of the electoral college have built their arguments on a series of faulty premises. We cannot justify the electoral college as a result of the framers' coherent design based on clear political principles. The founders did not articulate a theory to justify political inequality. Instead, the electoral college was a jerry-rigged improvisation formulated in a desperate effort to reach a compromise that would allow the Constitutional Convention to adjourn and take the entire Constitution to the people.

We have also seen that the electoral college does not protect important interests that would be overlooked or harmed under a system of direct election of the president. States—including states with small populations—do not embody coherent, unified interests and communities, and they have little need for protection. Even if they did, the electoral college does not provide it. Contrary to the claims of its supporters, candidates do not pay attention to small states. The electoral college actually distorts the campaign so that candidates ignore many large and most small states and devote most of their attention of competitive states.

Similarly, blacks and other minorities do not benefit from the electoral college because they are not well positioned to determine the outcomes in states. As a result, the electoral college system actually discourages attention to minority interests. Rather than protecting the interests of states and minorities, the electoral college weakens incentives for voter participation in states that are safe for a candidate and similarly weakens the incentive for either the majority or minority party to attempt to persuade citizens to support them and to go to the polls.

Neither is the electoral college a bastion of federalism. It is not based on federative principles and is not essential for the continuance of a healthy federal system. Direct election of the president would not diminish the role of state and local parties and officials or the nominating conventions, and national standards for elections are already in place and not to be feared.

The electoral college also contributes little to maintaining the cohesion of the American polity by protecting it from alleged harms of direct election of the president. It does not contain the results of fraud and accidental circumstances within states. Instead, it magnifies their consequences for the outcome nationally. . . .

Direct election of the president would not diminish benefits from the electoral college that . . . do not exist. Those who worry that direct election would change the nature of campaigns are correct. It would. Candidates would actually have to do what advocates of the electoral college say they want candidates to do. They would have to take their case to the entire nation—instead of focusing on a few battleground states as they do now. Incentives for personal visits would remain the same—but these visits would be more dispersed around the nation. *Since candidates' campaign appearances are virtually always before party enthusiasts, they have little to do with generating voter interest anyway.* And how could a nationwide campaign generate less voter interest than a campaign that ignores approximately two-thirds of the country? Similarly, there is no reason to be concerned that a national campaign would force candidates to rely more on technology. In the twenty-first century, candidates rely almost entirely on television and direct mail—under the electoral college—to reach voters. It is true that it would cost more to campaign across the nation than in only a few battleground states. We actually spend very little on the general election for president, much less than one dollar per eligible voter. Surely the richest nation in the world can afford a bit more to select its chief executive.

The only potential disadvantage of direct election of the president is the proposal for a runoff between the top two candidates if no candidate receives, in the most common proposal, at least 40 percent of the popular vote on the first ballot. The runoff has some potential to fragment the party system. A runoff at the end of an already lengthy campaign would also place added burdens on the presidential candidates and especially on their depleted campaign treasuries. It would require a more rapid count and certification of ballots, including the resolution of disputes, than would otherwise be necessary. It is possible that a runoff would also result in a considerable vote drop-off from the initial ballot. By definition, a second ballot would delay the selection of the winner.

These costs of a runoff raise the question: Is it possible to institute direct election of the president without a runoff? . . .

Would a runoff enhance the prospects of selecting the candidate most preferred by the public? If the most preferred candidate got the most votes and more than 40 percent of the vote on the first ballot, no runoff would be necessary. Since the beginning of popular voting in presidential elections, only one candidate, Abraham Lincoln, received less than 40 percent. He received 39.8 percent of the vote even though he was not on the ballot in ten states—a situation unlikely to recur. (It is rare for a winning gubernatorial candidate to receive less than 45 percent of the vote. Even in the chaotic circumstances of the California recall election of 2003, with more than one hundred candidates on the ballot, the winner received 49 percent of the vote. Similarly, in the days of the one-party South, it was typical for the primary to produce a *majority* on the first ballot.) A runoff thus seems unnecessary.

In addition, there is no need to force artificially a majority vote for a candidate for the winner to govern. . . . Plurality winners are among the strongest presidents in U.S. history. Almost all elected offices in the United States are filled by plurality election, so why should the presidency differ? . . .

At the core of the democratic process is the view that "all votes must be counted as equal." In an election for a national officeholder, each voter has a right to expect that he or she will stand in the same relation to the national official as every other voter. Given its advantages for the polity, the United States should adopt direct election of the president.

Yet there is no question that instituting direct election of the president will be difficult. Change will require amending the Constitution, a complex and time-consuming task. Although the public and many states and organizations support direct election, there are obstacles to change. Principal among them are officials who believe that their states or the members of their organizations (such as racial minorities) benefit from the electoral college. We now know that these officials are wrong. They have reached their conclusions on the basis of faulty premises.

Defense of or opposition to the electoral college has traditionally not been a partisan issue. Over the years, Richard Nixon, Gerald Ford, Jimmy Carter, Robert Taft, Hubert Humphrey, Robert Dole, the American Bar Association, the League of Women Voters, the U.S. Chamber of Commerce, and the AFL-CIO have supported abolishing the electoral college and directly electing the president. Another obstacle to reform at present, however, could be the stake some Republicans may feel they have in the electoral college because George W. Bush won the presidency in 2000 although he received fewer votes than his opponent.

Before Election Day, Republicans were actually much more concerned about the opposite scenario in which Bush would win the popular vote but lose the electoral vote, and the Bush campaign apparently prepared contingency plans in case this happened. CNN analyst Jeff Greenfield reported that "at least two conservative commentators were specifically briefed by the Bush campaign shortly before taking to the airwaves about the line of attack to be taken in the event that Bush would up losing the Electoral count despite a popular vote lead." Similarly, the *New York Daily News* reported before the election that the Bush campaign had prepared talking points about the essential unfairness of the electoral college and intended to run advertisements, encourage a massive talk radio operation, and mobilize local business leaders and the clergy against acceptance of a Gore victory if Bush won the popular vote. The goal was to convince electors that they should cast their votes for the popular vote winner and not the winner in the electoral college.

It would not be unprecedented for a political party to abandon a principled stance in favor of what it perceives to be political gain. In the case of the electoral college, however, there need not be a conflict between principle and pragmatism. The best evidence is that neither party has a lock on the electoral college. If the Republicans had such a lock, Bill Clinton would not have won the presidency. Our political history shows that party strength in various states ebbs and flows. Reliance on institutional arrangements to advantage a party is likely to backfire. Republicans successfully appeal to voters around the country and do not need to rely on an antidemocratic relic of the eighteenth century to achieve power.

Understanding the flawed foundations of the electoral college is the critical first step on the road to reforming the system of presidential selection. The culmination of this effort should be giving Americans the right to directly elect the presidents who serve them.

Gary L. Gregg  **NO**

The Electoral College Is Good for America

T he quadrennial attack on the electoral college has begun once again. The bumper stickers have come out and the trite calls for a "fairer" system have begun to populate op-ed pages and Internet chat rooms around the nation. Not too long ago we dodged a bullet aimed at the heart of our political system when proposals by Senators Hillary Clinton and Arlen Specter to abolish the electoral college fizzled and drifted off into the ether.

Why did the electoral college survive electing a president who failed to win a majority of the popular vote? Quite simply, we learned from 2000 that no matter what the drawbacks of the current system, it is imminently better than the alternative.

The electoral-college system serves to focus our political battles into state-by-state contests for the most votes. In 2000, the post-election battle centered on Florida and stayed there because the electoral college worked to give the winner of the Sunshine State the presidency. If a national plurality were allowed to choose the president, and the election were as close as it was in 2000, Gore and Bush being separated by less than one half of one percent, how would the post-election contest have been different?

Without the electoral college, Bush and Gore would have both realized that either of them could demand recounts and mount challenges against ballots in every precinct, in every county, in every state of the Union with the real hope of finding enough votes that the election could have been overturned. Thousands of lawyers would tie up hundreds of courts around the nation with little hope of any clean or clear conclusion. Rather than *Bush* v. *Gore*, we likely would have had hundreds of lawsuits winding their way to the Supreme Court.

In 2000 the electoral college saved us from a national nightmare much worse than that which we suffered. Even with the electoral college, Kerry is said to have lined up 10,000 lawyers ready to mount legal challenges to the vote. Abolishing the electoral college would dismantle the firewalls protecting us all from a quadrennial national nightmare that would turn over our elections to lawyers and judges.

The alternative to the electoral college is a national nightmare of hanging chads and clever lawyers from the Carolinas to California.

In *Federalist Paper #68,* Alexander Hamilton wrote that the constitutional system for electing presidents "is almost the only part of the system, of any consequence, which has escaped without severe censure or which has received the slightest mark of approbation from its opponents." Such a situation would not last long. Starting almost immediately, challenges were raised to the electoral college method of selecting the president and they have continued throughout American history. Opponents today worship at the altar of an abstraction called "one man, one vote" and a desire to nationalize all of our politics. Nothing short of a national referendum will suffice for these critics.

Those agitating for the abolition of the electoral college fail to see that the system has evolved and developed with the evolution of American politics. As our politics has democratized, so has the college. Democracy now reigns supreme in every state as the candidate with the most votes in each state gets the electoral votes of that state. It s 50 little democracies, not the unfair and undemocratic system critics contend.

Our electoral-college system is not just a neutral way of counting votes, however. It has real and tangible consequences for our political system that we ignore at our own peril. The former Democratic senator from New York, Daniel Patrick Moynihan said it most persuasively when he searched the globe for a more stable political system than our own and, finding none, traced the roots of our political prosperity to the salutary effects of the electoral college.

We start with the simple fact that the system works. It has never failed to give us a president and it has almost always produced decisive outcomes that have served the political system. As Walter Berns has argued, instead of arguing about "inputs," we should be arguing about "outputs." Opponents of the electoral college have the burden of proof. If they can t show an alternative system can produce better presidents in a more clear and decisive manner, the current system should not be amended to serve an abstract goal of letting a "national voice" be heard.

In most elections, the system has served to exaggerate the margin of victory, thereby adding stability to our system. In 1980 Ronald Reagan won just 50.7 percent of the popular vote but won an electoral-college landslide with more than 90 percent of the electoral vote. In 1992, Bill Clinton only won 43 percent of the popular vote but won 70 percent of the electoral-college votes.

The electoral-college system has moderated and stabilized our political system. The "unit rule" whereby the plurality winner of the votes in each state get all the electoral votes of that state combined with the demand that a successful candidate achieve an absolute majority serve to support a broad and moderate two-party system. Radical third-party candidates are discouraged by the current system. If they cannot hope to win actual electoral votes, they cannot hope to have a meaningful influence on the election outcome.

Do I often wish my party was more pure and principled? Absolutely. But I do not pine for purity at the cost of a radicalization of our system.

John Kerry recently went goose hunting in Ohio and posed for the cameras in his camouflage coat, a shotgun tucked under his arm. His website sports more pictures of him shooting, talking with veterans, and standing in the pulpit of churches. *One picture* is creatively cropped to perfectly center the name "Christ" behind Kerry's head. The battle for the presidency has now settled into rural areas in states like Ohio, Pennsylvania, Wisconsin, Minnesota, and Colorado. And, it's all because of the electoral college.

Take a look at the results of the 2000 election and it becomes radically clear that the electoral college that produced the Bush victory is having an important and salutary impact on our political system. It's the electoral college that keeps the values of traditional America relevant in the 21st century and the electoral college that helps rural America balance the immense cultural, economic, and social power of urban centers.

Abolishing the electoral college would mean transferring near complete political power to metropolitan areas who are already producing the candidates and funding them as well. Al Gore demonstrated in 2000 that the national popular vote can be won by appealing to a narrow band of the electorate heavily secular, single, and concentrated in cities.

In 2000, Al Gore won the vote in major cities 71 percent to 26 percent for George Bush. Alternatively, Bush won rural communities 59 percent to 37 percent. These are very large margins showing a drastic difference in the geographic centers of the divided electorate.

In 2000 we discovered, though the media didn't focus on it, that the much discussed "gender gap" was really a marriage gap with Bush overwhelmingly winning the votes of married people and Gore solidly winning the votes of unmarried people. For instance, Gore bested Bush among unmarried women by more than 30 percent while Bush actually won the vote among married women.

Among gun owners, Bush won by more than 25 percent. Among people with children in the home, Bush bested Gore by 7 percent. Among those who attend church at least weekly, Bush beat Gore by more than 20 percent. On the other hand, among those that never attend a house of worship, Gore beat Bush by almost 30 percent.

Partisan Democrats and cultural liberals have come to understand these vast differences in the electorate and it is a chief reason they wish to abolish the electoral college. With its slight benefit to smaller, more rural states, the electoral college forces candidates to appeal beyond a secular urban base to win the presidency.

John Sperling, the billionaire founder of Phoenix University, and those that have collaborated with him to produce the book *The Great Divide* have demonstrated this in their argument to abolish the electoral college so that Democratic candidates can dedicate themselves to a regime of thoroughgoing secular liberalism without having to try to appeal to the backward rednecks in rural America. Their language is stark, offensive, and demonstrates the radicalization of our politics that would come with an abolition of the electoral college. If you want to see what our future would look like with the abolition of the Electoral College, take a look at Sperling's book.

The electoral college is a democratic way of electing presidents that has produced good and moderate candidates in the past and gives some voice to the men and women who serve in the military, raise our families, and keep our communities of faith vibrant entities. Without it, you would see what Sperling calls "Retro" America ignored by candidates that could win the presidency while ignoring the entire middle of the nation.

Our politics would be radicalized as even more power came into the hands of a metropolitan elite who distain the cultures and values of middle America.

Removing the electoral college would instantly have the effect of empowering radical elements of both left and right and encouraging them to run and thereby become influential in our electoral system. Two parties on the right would naturally face off against two parties on the left. The result would be a splitting of the national vote with the more extreme fringes having the potential power to control the electoral outcome.

In such a system, are we willing to let the president be decided by 40 percent of the vote? 35 percent? 30 percent? Unless we are willing to allow our president to be selected by as few as 30 percent of the voters, any attempt to nationalize our elections with a direct popular vote will have to include a provision for a run-off election. Are there any among us that really want to move to a national run-off for president?

The electoral college also serves to give us more diverse and moderate campaigns and candidates than would a national and direct popular vote.

Al Gore won the popular vote in 2000 by wracking up massive majorities in major cities and urban counties while losing almost everywhere else in the nation. Gore won just 677 counties compared to Bush's 2,434. Gore won the popular vote but could fly from Pittsburgh to Los Angeles without ever passing over a county he was able to win.

A direct national popular vote would encourage candidates to settle down into major metropolitan areas with the aim of maximizing voter turnout in those areas. In such a situation, what candidate would ever again visit West Virginia, Missouri, Nevada, New Mexico, or Colorado? Would it be good for America to have candidates running on platforms that ignore rural values and interests in the service of wracking up majorities in urban areas? The current system puts a premium on spreading votes around urban and rural areas in a variety of states.

That diversity is good for America and serves as a stabilizing force in our democracy.

POSTSCRIPT

Should the Electoral College Be Abolished?

Although there is no serious prospect that the Electoral College will be abolished or altered in the near future, the issue has long engaged those who consider the consequences of the American electoral system. Is it democratic? How does it affect the choice of presidential candidates, the course of presidential election campaigns, and the conduct of presidents in office? The selections by George C. Edwards III and Gary L. Gregg provide two diametrically opposed perspectives.

Other possibilities might also be examined. The electoral vote might be divided in each state proportionate to the vote each candidate received. That would not eliminate the possibility that a president would be elected with fewer votes than his opponent. Such a division would have resulted in the election of Richard Nixon over John Kennedy in 1960, as well as the election of other minority presidents. One electoral vote could be allocated to each congressional district in a state, with two votes given to the candidate with a statewide plurality. As a matter of fact, two small states (Maine and Nebraska), each of which has four electoral votes, allow for the possibility that a different candidate may win each of the state's two congressional districts.

Direct popular election would eliminate the possibility of victory for a candidate with fewer votes than an opponent: John Quincy Adams had fewer votes than Andrew Jackson in 1824, Rutherford B. Hayes had fewer votes than Samuel Tilden in 1876, Benjamin Harrison had fewer votes than Grover Cleveland in 1888, and George W. Bush had fewer votes than Al Gore in 2000, but received electoral majorities and were elected president. Proponents of abolishing the Electoral College cite these elections in support of reform. They also argue that a popular election would encourage greater participation. In recent presidential elections, the turnout has varied from less than half to little more than 55 percent of the potential electorate. The case for reform is made by Jack N. Rakove, "Electoral Fallacies," in *Political Science Quarterly,* Spring 2004.

Opposed to direct election is the conviction that the existing system reflects the federal character of the Constitution and the belief that popular election would encourage more parties to nominate candidates, increasing the likelihood that the winning candidate would win with an even smaller percentage of the vote, thus fragmenting political divisions. This and other arguments in support of the constitutional system are made in Tara Ross's, *Enlightened Democracy: The Case for Electoral College* (Los Angeles: World Ahead Publishing, 2004).

Fuller treatments of the philosophical and political positions for and against the Electoral College can be found in Judith A. Best, *The Choice of the*

People?: Debating the Electoral College (Rowman and Littlefield, 1996), and Lawrence D. Longley and Neal R. Peirce, *The Electoral College Primer 2000* (Yale University Press, 1999). Best's book is a long essay commending the rational relationship between the Electoral College and the principle of federalism. Longley and Peirce conclude that the Electoral College results in distorting debate in the election campaign, risks the influence of faithless electors who do not cast their ballots for the winning candidate in their state, and creates a bias in favor of sectional parties and candidates.

ISSUE 4

Do the Media Have a Liberal Bias?

YES: Bernard Goldberg, from *Arrogance: Rescuing America from the Media Elite* (Warner Books, 2003)

NO: Robert F. Kennedy Jr., from *Crimes Against Nature* (Harper Collins, 2005)

ISSUE SUMMARY

YES: Former CBS reporter Bernard Goldberg argues that liberal bias is pervasive in news reporting, the result not of a conspiracy but of a mind-set among media elites acquired from the homogeneous social circles in which they live and work.

NO: Environmentalist and political activist Robert F. Kennedy Jr. believes that conservative bias, fostered by conservative foundations, media owners, and talk radio commentators, has stifled investigative reporting and misinformed millions of Americans.

The First Amendment to the United States Constitution asserts that "Congress shall make no law . . . a bridging the freedom of speech, or of the press." Although the Framers of the Constitution and later Presidents sometimes sought to curtail what they deemed to be excesses of press freedom, they invariably paid lip service to the view that the press should be free. Throughout American history, thoughtful Americans have acknowledged that the right of people to voice their views, even views opposed to the official policies of the government, is indispensable in a free society.

But how is that freedom to be exercised and how is it to be protected? In the twentieth century, the printed word exploded in a torrent of newspapers, periodicals, and books. Then came, almost in successive generations, the inventions of motion pictures, radio, and television, making it possible for a single voice or point of view to reach millions of people. For many years after the enactment of the Federal Communications Act in 1934, the Federal Communications Commission sought to diversify media ownership by granting radio and television licenses to groups other than the owners of a region's leading newspapers.

That is no longer the case. It is now commonplace for a single corporation to own the sole daily newspaper and the leading radio and television station in a town or city. Liberal critics deplore the fact that five corporations—General Electric, The News Corporation, Time Warner, Viacom, and the Walt Disney Company—own the four leading television broadcast channel networks, as well as many other broadcast and cable television systems. They also own major motion picture studios, radio stations, book publishers, magazines, and newspapers throughout the world. One company, Clear Channel Communications, owns more than 100 radio stations, which dominate the audience share in 100 of 112 major markets.

Conservative critics respond that, despite conservative ownership, what the media broadcast and print has a liberal bias. A three-year study by a University of California political scientist and University of Missouri economist concluded in 2005 that eighteen of twenty major media outlets were more liberal, and only two were more conservative, than the average American voter.

The study contradicts some popular assumptions and raises some interesting questions. *The Wall Street Journal*, whose editorial pages are generally acknowledged to be among the most conservative, had the most liberal news pages. Why does this conservative newspaper support such liberal news coverage? The same 2005 analysis concluded that the "News Hour With Jim Lehrer" on public television was the most centrist (that is, least biased) of the surveyed news sources. Why is the leading PBS news program more balanced than news programs supported by conservative corporations?

Political bias in newspaper, radio, and television news reporting is difficult to analyze, but conservatives believe that a liberal slant is widespread in the choice of news stories and the manner in which they are reported. Liberals counter that most of the more subjective commentary on talk radio is conservative, to which conservatives reply that a distinction should be made between what is clearly the presentation of a commentator's opinion and what purports to be an objective reporting of the news. These critics often cite unbiased studies that demonstrate that journalists tend to be decidedly more liberal than the general population and this influences their reporting. Liberals respond that newspaper editorial policy is more evenly divided. The controversy raises, but does not resolve, such questions as to why journalists are more liberal and whether that preference is reflected in the news stories they cover.

Bernard Goldberg spent many years in television news, and his account stresses his claim that liberal bias, masquerading as objective news reporting, condemns conservative views as immoral and politically incorrect. Robert Kennedy Jr. is equally convinced that the mass media reflect a conservative bias that misinforms the public and keeps millions of Americans ignorant of important political facts.

YES

Bernard Goldberg

Arrogance: Rescuing America from the Media Elite

Introduction

So I'm sitting in a very nice conference room in the very nice Time & Life Building, high above bustling West Fiftieth Street in Manhattan, for my first meeting on this book. There are about ten big shots from Warner Books sitting around a very nice long table waiting to hear what I have in mind, which basically is to use my earlier book *Bias* as a jumping-off point to examine the powerful behind-the-scenes forces that have turned too many American newsrooms into bastions of political correctness; to examine those forces and see why they generate bias in the news and how they sustain it; and to tell the media elites, who are too arrogant to see for themselves, the ways they'd better change if they want to stay relevant. Because if they don't, they'll cease to be serious players in the national conversation and become the journalistic equivalent of the leisure suit—harmless enough but hopelessly out of date.

But as I'm sitting there I'm not thinking about any of that. To be perfectly honest, what I am thinking is, before *Bias* caught on with so many Americans, before it became such a hit, no one in the liberal, highbrow book business would have thrown water on me if I were on fire. None of them would have dirtied their hands on a book that would have dismayed their smart, sensitive liberal friends. Before *Bias* I would have been the skunk at their garden party. *But now they can't wait to hear what I think?*

But about fourteen seconds in, I am brought back to earth when one of the participants informs me that a friend of his thinks the whole idea of liberal bias is bogus.

I smile the kind of insincere smile I detest in others and look at the guy, wondering if I'm also looking at his "friend." I'm also wondering if everyone else in the room also thinks that bias in the news is just the stuff of right-wing paranoia. I am in Manhattan, after all, the belly of the beast.

And besides, Manhattan is one of those trendy places where the new hot media chic thing is not only to dismiss the notion of liberal bias in the news, but actually to say, with a straight face, that the real problem is . . . *conservative bias!*

This is so jaw-droppingly bizarre you almost don't know how to respond. It reminds me of a movie I saw way back in the sixties called *A Guide for the Married Man.* In one scene, Joey Bishop plays a guy caught by his wife red-handed in bed with a beautiful woman. As the wife goes nuts, demanding to know what the hell is going on, Joey and the woman get out of bed and calmly put on their clothes. He then casually straightens up the bed and quietly responds to his wife, who by now has smoke coming out of her ears, "What bed? What girl?" After the woman leaves, Joey settles in his lounge chair and reads the paper, pausing long enough to ask his wife if she shouldn't be in the kitchen preparing dinner!

Joey's mantra in such situations is simple: Deny! Deny! Deny! And in this scene his denials are so matter-of-fact and so nonchalant that by the time the other woman leaves the bedroom, leaving just Joey and his wife, her head is spinning and she's so bamboozled that she's seriously beginning to doubt what she just saw with her own two eyes. She's actually beginning to believe him when he says there was no other woman in the room!

Just think of Joey Bishop as the media elite and think of his wife as *you*—the American news-consuming public.

You have caught them red-handed over and over again with their biases exposed, and all they do is Deny! Deny! Deny! Only now the media have become even more brazen. Simply denying isn't good enough anymore. Now they're not content looking you in the eye and calmly saying, "What bias?" Now they're just as calmly turning truth on its head, saying the real problem is *conservative bias.*

What's next? They look up from their paper and ask why you're not in the kitchen preparing dinner?

❧

Having been on the inside for as long as I have, twenty-eight years as a CBS News correspondent, I should have known it would be just a matter of time before they would stop playing defense and go on the offensive. Given their arrogance, I should have known that sooner or later they would say, "*We* don't have a bias problem—and if you think we do, then that proves that *you're* the one with the bias problem." Never mind that millions of Americans scream about liberal bias in the media; all the journalists can say is "You're the one with the bias!" The emperors of alleged objectivity have been naked for quite some time now, and sadly, they're the only ones who haven't noticed. Or as Andrew Sullivan, the very perceptive observer of all things American, so elegantly puts it, "Only those elite armies of condescension keep marching on, their privates swinging in the breeze."

But to deny liberal bias, the elites not only have had to brush off their own viewers, they also have had to paint their critics as wild-eyed ideologues—and then completely misrepresent what they say. For example, on March 4, 2003, this is how Nicholas Kristoff began his column in the *New York Times:* "Claims that the news media form a vast liberal conspiracy strike me as utterly unconvincing." Well, they strike *me* as utterly unconvincing, too. Exactly who, Nick, is making those "claims"? Got any names? Because I travel all over the country and speak about bias in the media, and I haven't met one serious conservative—not one—who believes that a "vast liberal conspiracy" controls the news. And for what it's worth, I write on page four of the introduction to *Bias* that "It is important to know, too, that there isn't a well-orchestrated, vast left-wing conspiracy in America's newsrooms." What I and many others do believe, and what I think is fairly obvious, is that the majority of journalists in big newsrooms slant leftward in their personal politics, especially on issues like abortion, affirmative action, gay rights, and gun control; and so in their professional role they tend to assume those positions are reasonable and morally correct. Bias in the news stems from *that*—not from some straw man conspiracy concocted by liberals in the supposedly objective, mainstream media.

Yet the idea that socially liberal reporters might actually take a liberal tack in their reporting is a proposition too many journalists on the Left refuse even to consider. Better to cast conservatives as a bunch of loonies who see conspiracies under every bed, around every corner, behind every tree and, most important of all, in every newsroom.

In fact, right on the heels of the Kristoff column, the conspiracy thing pops up again in—surprise, surprise—the *New York Times*. This time in a book review: "The notion that a vast left-wing conspiracy controls America's airwaves and newsprint [is] . . . routinely promoted as gospel on the right."

Wrong again! But they are right about one thing: There is plenty of paranoid talk about a "vast left-wing conspiracy" in the newsroom. The problem is, the paranoids dreaming it up aren't conservatives—*they're liberals!*

And the uncomfortable truth—uncomfortable for ideologues on the Left, anyway—is that there now exists "a huge body of literature—including at least 100 books and research monographs—documenting a widespread left-wing bias in the news," according to Ted Smith III of Virginia Commonwealth University, who has done extensive research into the subject. And much of the evidence comes *not* from conservatives with axes to grind but straight from the journalists themselves, who in survey after survey have identified themselves as liberal on all the big, important social issues of our time.

Despite the overwhelming evidence, despite all the examples of bias that were documented in my book and others, despite the surveys that show that large numbers of Americans consider the elite media too liberal, *despite all of that,* the elites remain in denial. Why? Well, for starters, as I say, a lot them truly don't understand what the fuss is all about, since they honestly believe that their views on all sorts of divisive issues are not really controversial—or even liberal. After all, their liberal friends in Manhattan and Georgetown share those same views, which practically by definition make them moderate and mainstream. So, the thinking goes, it is all those Middle Americans who take the opposing view on, say, guns or gay marriage who are out of the mainstream, the ones who are "fringe." Journalists don't usually use the word—not in public anyway—but those supposedly not-too-sophisticated "fringe" Americans are smart enough to pick up on the condescension. . . .

Deny! Deny! Deny! By now it's not only their mantra, it's practically official newsroom policy. In one way or another Dan Rather, Peter Jennings, and Tom Brokaw have all dismissed the very idea of liberal bias in the news. Rather has called it a "myth" and a "canard" and has actually said that "Most reporters don't know whether they're Republican or Democrat." Jennings thinks that "It's just essential to make the point that we are largely in the center, without particular axes to grind, without ideologies which are represented in our daily coverage." Ditto Brokaw, Couric, Lauer, Stahl, Wallace, and Bradley. The list, as they say, goes on and on.

But as strategies go, this new wrinkle—*"There is no liberal bias in the news, but there is a conservative bias"*—is far better. This is what you say if you're a media liberal who is not only tired of playing defense but wants to put his critics on the defensive for a change. This is what you say if you're trapped in a corner, and you don't know what else to do and you think you're fighting for your life. . . .

❦

This seems like a good place to state the obvious: Yes, Republicans do indeed have friends in some conservative places like talk radio, Fox News, and the *Washington Times,* whom I'm sure they use to get their talking points out. But what Al Gore and his pals in the media forget to mention is that Democrats also have friends, in some very powerful *liberal* places, and the Democrats use them to get *their* talking points out. Places like major newspapers in every big city in the country, big-circulation mainstream news magazines, television networks with their millions and millions of viewers—all very large platforms that journalists use, intentionally or not, to frame the national debate on all sorts of big important issues, in the process creating "conventional" and "mainstream" points of view. *That* is what media power is really about.

The fact is, Rush Limbaugh, Fox News, and the *Washington Times* might not even exist if weren't for the routine (and the generally *unconscious*) liberal tilt of the mainstream media. Liberal journalists may indeed try to keep their biases in check (as they keep telling us), but—mainly because they don't even recognize that their liberal views are liberal—they often don't succeed. As I once told Bill O'Reilly, he should send a case of champagne to Rather, Brokaw, and Jennings with a nice little note that reads, "Thanks a lot, guys, for sending over all those viewers." . . .

❦

"Well, what about all those media outlets with right-wing point of view?" the guy in the conference room wants to know, repeating what his friend (who doesn't think there's a liberal bias in the news) told him. "There's Bill O'Reilly; there's talk radio; there are a bunch of conservative syndicated columnists . . ."

I'm not sure if he or anyone else in the room notices that my eyes are rolling around my head in lazy circles. I have heard this one about 40 million times.

I find it both tiresome and disingenuous when liberals say, "Stop your whining about liberal bias; you've got plenty of conservatives in the media." Of course there's a conservative media. There's Rush Limbaugh and Sean Hannity and George Will and Robert Novak and Cal Thomas and Fred Barnes and Bill Buckley. But let's not forget that just about every editorial writer and columnist at the big powerful mainstream news outlets like the *New York Times, Los Angeles Times, Washington Post,* and *Boston Globe* are *liberals!* So conservatives have clout in the world of opinion and liberals have clout in the world of opinion. Wonderful! But, fundamentally, that's not the point. The point is that opinion is one thing and news is another. So telling me that there are all those conservative commentators out there and that I should stop my whining doesn't make me feel even the slightest bit better about the liberal bias of supposedly objective *news* reporters. News reporters are supposed to play it straight. It's that simple!

But even beyond that, in the media world, power and influence come from numbers. So consider these: The evening newscasts on ABC, CBS, NBC, and PBS total about 35 million viewers a night compared to *Special Report* with Brit Hume—Fox's evening newscast—which (right before the war in Iraq) was averaging about 1.3 million viewers. (Over an entire twenty-four-hour news cycle, Fox averaged about 1.058 million viewers; again, that's just before the war began.) Yes, it's true that Brit Hume brings certain conservative sensibilities to his newscast, but then Dan Rather brings certain liberal sensibilities to his. So, let's review: 35 million for the supposedly mainstream, nonliberal, nonbiased media, and just over a million for conservative Fox News. I repeat my earlier question: And we're supposed to fret about *conservative* influence on the news?

Of course, part of what *really* bothers so many liberals—though you can bet very few have actually thought about it this way—is that there even exists a more conservative alternative to the mainstream news outlets. Liberals, you see, had the playing field to themselves for so many years, controlling the rules of the game, that to them it had come to seem the natural order of things. It's ironic, isn't it, that liberals, who are always telling us that they're for change, that they're against the status quo, that *that* is what largely defines liberalism and (of course) makes liberals better, don't really mean it when the change doesn't quite suit them, when it means they will have a little competition—irreverent, edgy competition at that—to contend with. That's when they embrace the status quo with everything they've got and pine for the good old days, the days before those annoying *outsiders* got into the act, when the Big Three networks had to compete only with themselves. So while many Americans are encouraged that there's now some genuine diversity out there, many liberals regard this news as distressing—even *disorienting*, especially since ratings at the old news networks have been dropping for years while the upstart Fox News has been coming on strong, picking up new viewers just about every month since it went on the air in October 1996.

❧

"Then what about the mainstream media's treatment of Clinton? You can't possibly think they went easy on him, can you?" is what liberals always ask.

It's a fair question. And the answer is, no, they didn't go easy on Clinton. The truth is, reporters will go after any politician—liberal or conservative—if the story is big enough and the politician is powerful enough. Still, all things being equal, there's no question the media elites salivate more when they're going after Republicans and conservatives—even the elites would admit to that, I think, after a few drinks.

But the entire premise of the question is wrong, because party politics is not primarily what liberal bias is about. What media bias is mainly about are the fundamental assumptions and beliefs and values that are the stuff of everyday life. The reason so many Americans who are pro-life or anti-affirmative action or who support gun rights detest the mainstream media is that day after day they fail to see in the media any respect for their views. What they see is a mainstream media seeming to legitimize one side (the one media elites agree with) as valid and moral, while seeking to cast the other side as narrow, small-minded, and bigoted. Even the editor of the liberal *Los Angeles Times* noticed that. On May 22, 2003, John Carroll wrote a scathing memo to his staff about political bias in the paper, singling out what he considered a liberally biased page-one story on abortion. "I'm concerned about the perception," he wrote, "and the occasional reality that the *Times* is a liberal, 'politically correct' newspaper. Generally speaking, this is an inaccurate view, but occasionally we prove our critics right. . . . The reason I'm sending this note to all section editors is that I want everyone to understand how serious I am about purging all political bias from our coverage. We may happen to live in a political atmosphere that is suffused with liberal values (and is unreflective of the nation as a whole), but we are not going to push a liberal agenda in the news pages of the *Times*."

Three cheers for John Carroll of the *Los Angeles Times!* The only part I'd take issue with is where he says, "generally speaking, [it] is an inaccurate view" to think the *Los Angeles Times* is a "liberal, 'politically correct' newspaper." No, generally speaking, it's quite an accurate view to believe the *Times* "is a liberal, 'politically correct' newspaper." And then there's the only "*occasionally* we prove our critics right." I don't think so. But I don't want to quibble. And besides, I understand he's got to live with these people. . . .

Even the good guys give you reason to despair. In early 2003, David Shaw of the *Los Angeles Times,* who is one of the top media writers in the country, came up with an earth-shaking theory. There is no significant liberal bias in the news, he told us, but there *is* another kind of bias, one that is far more dangerous. "We're biased in favor of bad news, rather than good news. We're biased in favor of conflict rather than harmony. Increasingly we're biased in favor of sensationalism, scandal, celebrities and violence as opposed to serious, insightful coverage of important issues of the day."

There's a scoop, huh? Anyone who has tuned into *48 Hours, 20/20,* or *Dateline* for two or three seconds knows all of that. But now we're being told that just because there's a bias toward crap in the news—which there most certainly is—we need to worry far more about that than "about any ideological infiltration" in the news, as David Shaw puts it. Sorry, David, I can walk and chew gum at the same time. And I can worry about two kinds of bias at the same time, too, because, despite what you seem to think, *both* exist.

But I don't want to make this point, or any of the others, simply to people who already know it. Which is why one of the things I'm hoping this book will do is reach beyond the traditional conservative "ghetto" to reasonable and well-intentioned people across the political spectrum—to people with an open mind, no matter what their politics. To be sure, in today's highly polarized world, that will not be easy. Too often we talk right past each other in our culture—and no one, liberal or conservative, has clean hands on this one. Still, it seems to me that liberals—the very people who take such pride in seeing themselves as civil and open-minded—have, in a sad kind of way, become precisely what they accuse conservatives of: being close-minded and nasty. Many liberals these days—and ironically, especially the elites who think of themselves as worldly and sophisticated—are even narrower and more provincial than they imagine the rest of America to be. How can this be? It's easy when you live in a bubble, surrounded by others who think the same way about almost everything.

Yes, it's true that many conservatives also spend too much time in their own bubble, surrounded by like-minded souls who are always agreeing with one another. But here's the difference: Liberal culture in America is pervasive. You get it in movies and you hear it in music and you read it in magazines and you watch it on TV, in sitcoms and dramas as well as on the news. In America, unless you live in a cave, it's nearly impossible *not* to be exposed to liberal attitudes and assumptions on all sorts of issues ranging from guns to gay rights. Liberals, on the other hand, if they avoid just a couple of spots on the radio and TV dial—and especially if they live in liberal ghettoes like Beverly Hills or the Upper West Side of Manhattan—can pretty much stay clear of conservative attitudes and assumptions *and even conservative people,* secure in the knowledge that they're not really missing anything worth knowing.

Examples of this are not hard to come by, but some, like the following, are just amazingly telling. On February 6, 2003, while America was deeply divided on whether we should go to war with Iraq, veteran *Washington Post* columnist Mary McGrory wrote these remarkable words: "Among people I know, nobody was for the war." Imagine that. What a single-minded little world she must live in where, among all the people she knows, nobody—absolutely *nobody*—thought that invading Iraq was a good idea.

They live in a world, these bubble people, that is reassuringly uncomplicated and blissfully unchallenged by new ideas. As far as many liberals are concerned, all that's necessary to know is that different ideas can be dangerous ideas, embraced by the narrow-minded and intolerant, a threat to everything that good and decent people (like themselves) believe in.

In fact, the only reason so many smart liberals are convinced there is no liberal bias in the news in the first place is that this is what they keep hearing from the mainstream media they rely on for so much of their information. Since almost no one in these liberal circles ever risks exposure to another point of view, they truly don't understand why so many Middle Americans are so upset with Big Media. Yet what I have often found is that when liberals, for whatever reason, actually do come face-to-face with some of these scary ideas, they surprise themselves by how much they agree with them. . . .

A Final Word

George Orwell, the British essayist and author of *Animal Farm* and *1984,* once wrote about how societies censor themselves. "At any given moment there is a sort of all-pervading orthodoxy, a general tacit agreement not to discuss large and uncomfortable facts." He might just as well have been talking about the orthodoxies and the agreements that pervade America's most elite newsrooms.

Fair-minded reporters see and hear things all the time that they know just aren't right, large and uncomfortable facts they tacitly agree not to discuss. It doesn't take a genius to understand that certain issues aren't covered with equal respect for all points of view. The American people know that powerful assumptions about right and wrong, good guys and bad guys, influence and often distort the way certain stories are handled.

One of the most telling examples is how the media cover the abortion story. Every poll shows that Americans are sharply divided on the issue, regarding it as deeply troubling ethically and morally, and that while a majority support the right to legal abortion in the first trimester, large segments of the population favor important restrictions on the procedure.

But in many newsrooms—including the most powerful news organizations—such doubts are almost never heard. Those on the pro-life side are assumed to be fanatics, religious and otherwise. They are anti-women. They are the enemy.

And while it is almost never expressed explicitly, a rare revealing slip was Dan Rather's question to a U.S. senator, wondering if he thought Supreme Court Justice David Souter's views were "antiabortion or anti–women's rights, whichever way you want to put it," as if the two were one and the same. But even when it's not so blatant, those on the other side can read between the lines, and they are justly offended. As *New York Times* science writer Gina Kolata told an interviewer, "Anybody who reads the *New York Times* who doesn't think the *New York Times* is pro-choice, they are out of their minds. . . . We send messages all the time about what we think."

But the fact is, there are many, many journalists more troubled by the prevailing atmosphere than they let on. Some actually differ with newsroom sentiment on the most controversial issues of the day; others just recognize the crucial importance of a lively ongoing debate. But either way, they are more silent about their feelings than they should be.

That is the nature of peer pressure. Everyone understands that it's good for your career if you're a team player. No one wants to be seen as a trouble-maker—or worse, as a right-wing crazy.

That has to change. Reporters need to start standing up to newsroom orthodoxies, not merely because it's right, but also because it's good policy. An ongoing civil conversation in the newsroom about contentious issues, challenging pat assumptions and unexamined beliefs, by its very nature will start to open minds. Inevitably it will make for fuller, fairer coverage of the news.

The next time a *Washington Post* reporter writes that the pope at times "speaks with the voice of a conservative crank" because he won't budge on issues like abortion and birth control, someone in the newsroom needs to say that using language like that is not just wrong—it's also deeply offensive.

When an ABC News reporter offers the view that while, since September 11, *terrorist* has come to mean *Islamic and foreign,* "many believe we have as much to fear from a homegrown group of antiabortion crusaders," someone in the newsroom needs to stand up and say, "Really? You *really* believe many Americans think antiabortion crusaders pose as big a threat to Americans as Osama bin Laden?"

And if Dan Rather repeats that the Republican Congressional agenda will "demolish or damage government programs, many of them designed to help children and the poor," someone needs to stand up and say, "You know, Dan, that kind of language is way over the top and offends a lot of people who aren't even Republicans."

I'm not saying there will never be consequences. Some of the biggest names in journalism are also some of the biggest bullies. They confuse even mild dissent with disloyalty. But reporters like to pride themselves on their guts. Ask a reporter to name his or her favorite movie, and the chances are good you'll hear *High Noon* or *To Kill a Mockingbird*—movies built around brave figures risking everything on principle. That's why they're so quick to condemn cops who won't speak up against other cops who step out of line, and doctors who won't speak out against other doctors; and priests who overlook wrongdoing in their ranks.

They're right—principle matters. Fairness matters. Standing up for those things is how character is defined.

Many journalists, of course, have shown remarkable courage covering wars and insurrections. It's now time for many more to be brave enough to stand up in their own newsrooms and say, "I think this is wrong. Let's talk about it." . . .

 **NO**

The Disinformation Society

Many Democratic voters marveled at the election results. George W. Bush, they argued, has transformed a projected $5.6 trillion, 10-year Bill Clinton surplus into a projected $1.4 trillion deficit—a $7 trillion shift in wealth from our national treasury into the pockets of the wealthiest Americans, particularly the president's corporate paymasters. Any discerning observer, they argued, must acknowledge that the White House has repeatedly lied to the American people about critical policy issues—Medicare, education, the environment, the budget implications of its tax breaks, and the war in Iraq—with catastrophic results.

President Bush has opened our national lands and sacred places to the lowest bidder and launched a jihad against the American environment and public health to enrich his corporate sponsors. He has mired us in a costly, humiliating war that has killed more than 1,520 American soldiers and maimed 11,300. He has made America the target of Islamic hatred, caused thousands of new terrorists to be recruited to al-Qaeda, isolated us in the world, and drained our treasury of the funds necessary to rebuild Afghanistan and to finance our own vital homeland-security needs. He has shattered our traditional alliances and failed to protect vulnerable terrorist targets at home-chemical plants, nuclear facilities, air-cargo carriers, and ports. He has disgraced our nation and empowered tyrants with the unpunished excesses at Guantánamo and Abu Ghraib. These baffled Democrats were hard-pressed to believe that their fellow Americans would give a man like this a second term.

To explain the president's victory, political pundits posited a vast "values gap" between red states and blue states. They attributed the president's success in the polls, despite his tragic job failures, to the rise of religious fundamentalism. Heartland Americans, they suggested, are the soldiers in a new American Taliban, willing to vote against their own economic interests to promote "morality" issues that they see as the critical high ground in a life-or-death culture war.

I believe, however, that the Democrats lost the presidential contest not because of a philosophical chasm between red and blue states but due to an information deficit caused by a breakdown in our national media. Traditional broadcast networks have abandoned their former obligation to advance democracy and promote the public interest by informing the public about both sides of issues relevant to those goals. To attract viewers and advertising revenues, they entertain rather than inform. This threat to the flow of information, vital to democracy's survival, has been compounded in recent years by the growing power of right-wing media that twist the news and deliberately deceive the public to advance their radical agenda.

According to an October 2004 survey by the Program on International Policy Attitudes (PIPA), a joint program of the Center on Policy Attitudes, in Washington, D.C., and the Center for International and Security Studies at the University of Maryland:

- Seventy-two percent of Bush supporters believed Iraq had weapons of mass destruction (or a major program for developing them), versus 26 percent of Kerry voters. A seven-month search by 1,500 investigators led by David Kay, working for the C.I.A., found no such weapons.
- Seventy-five percent of Bush supporters believed that Iraq was providing substantial support to al-Qaeda, a view held by 30 percent of Kerry supporters. *The 9/11 Commission Report* concluded that there was no terrorist alliance between Iraq and al-Qaeda.
- Eighty-two percent of Bush supporters erroneously believed either that the rest of the world felt better about the U.S. thanks to its invasion of Iraq or that views were evenly divided. Eighty-six percent of Kerry supporters accurately understood that a majority of the world felt worse about our country.
- Most Bush supporters believed the Iraq war had strong support in the Islamic world. Kerry's supporters accurately estimated the low level of support in Islamic countries. Even Turkey, the most Westernized Islamic country, was 87 percent against the invasion.
- Most significant, the majority of Bush voters agreed with Kerry supporters that if Iraq did not have W.M.D. and was not providing assistance to al-Qaeda the U.S. should not have gone to war. Furthermore, most Bush supporters, according to PIPA, favored the Kyoto Protocol to fight global warming, the Mine Ban Treaty to ban land mines, and strong labor and environmental standards in trade agreements, and wrongly believed that their candidate favored these things. In other words, the values and principles were the same. Bush voters made their choice based on bad information.

It's no mystery where the false beliefs are coming from. Both Bush and Kerry supporters overwhelmingly believe that the Bush administration at the time of the 2004 U.S. election was telling the American people that Iraq had W.M.D. and that Saddam Hussein had strong links to al-Qaeda. The White House's false message was carried by right-wing media in bed with the administration. Prior to the election, Fox News reporters, for example, regularly made unsubstantiated claims about Iraq's W.M.D. Fox anchor Brit Hume, on his newscast in July 2004, announced that W.M.D. had actually been found. Sean Hannity repeatedly suggested without factual support that the phantom weapons had been moved to Syria and would soon be found. An October 2003 survey by PIPA showed that people who watch Fox News are disproportionately afflicted with the same misinformation evidenced by the 2004 PIPA report. The earlier study probed for the source of public misinformation about the Iraq war that might account for the common misperceptions that Saddam Hussein had been involved in the 9/11 attacks, that he supported al-Qaeda, that W.M.D. had been found, and that world opinion favored the U.S. invasion. The study discovered that "the extent of Americans' misperceptions vary significantly depending on their source of news. Those who receive most of their news from Fox News are more likely than average to have misperceptions."

Unfortunately for John Kerry, many Americans now do get their information from Fox—according to Nielsen Media Research, in February, Fox was the cable news leader, with an average of 1.57 million prime-time viewers, nearly 2.5 times CNN's average viewership in the same time slot—and from Fox's similarly biased cable colleagues, CNBC and MSNBC. Millions more tune to the Sinclair Broadcast Group—one of the nation's largest TV franchises. After 9/11, Sinclair forced its stations to broadcast spots pledging support for President Bush, and actively censored unfavorable coverage of the Iraq war—blacking out Ted Koppel's *Nightline* when it ran the names of the U.S. war dead. It retreated from its pre-election proposal to strong-arm its 62 TV stations into pre-empting their prime-time programming to air an erroneous and blatantly biased documentary about John Kerry's war record only when its stock dropped 17 percent due to Wall Street fears of sponsor boycotts and investor worries that Sinclair was putting its right-wing ideology ahead of shareholder profits.

Americans are also getting huge amounts of misinformation from talk radio, which is thoroughly dominated by the extreme right. A Gallup Poll conducted in December 2002 discovered that 22 percent of Americans receive their daily news from talkradio programs. An estimated 15 million people listen to Rush Limbaugh alone, and on the top 45 AM radio stations in the country, listeners encounter 310 hours of conservative talk for every 5 hours of liberal talk. According to the nonprofit Democracy Radio, Inc., 90 percent of all political talk-radio programming is conservative, while only 10 percent is progressive. All the leading talk-show hosts are right-wing radicals—Rush Limbaugh, Sean Hannity, Michael Savage, Oliver North, G. Gordon Liddy, Bill O'Reilly, and Michael Reagan—and the same applies to local talk radio.

Alas, while the right-wing media are deliberately misleading the American people, the traditional corporately owned media—CBS, NBC, ABC, and CNN—are doing little to remedy those wrong impressions. They are, instead, focusing on expanding viewership by hawking irrelevant stories that appeal to our prurient interest in sex and celebrity gossip. None of the three major networks gave gavel-to-gavel coverage of the party conventions or more than an hour in prime time, opting instead to entertain the public with semi-pornographic reality shows. "We're about to elect a president of the United States at a time when we have young people dying in our name overseas, we just had a report from the 9/11 commission which says we are not safe as a nation, and one of these two groups of people is going to run our country," commented PBS newsman Jim Lehrer, in disgust at the lack of convention coverage. CBS anchor Dan Rather said that "I argued the conventions were part of the dance of democracy. I found myself increasingly like the Mohicans, forced farther and farther back into the wilderness and eventually eliminated."

The broadcast reporters participating in the presidential debates were apparently so uninterested in real issues that they neglected to ask the candidates a single question about the president's environmental record. CBS anchor Bob Schieffer, who M.C.'d the final debate, asked no questions about the environment, focusing instead on abortion, gay marriage, and the personal faith of the candidates, an agenda that could have been dictated by Karl Rove.

Where is that dreaded but impossible-to-find "liberal bias" that supposedly infects the American press? The erroneous impression that the American media have a liberal bias is itself a mark of the triumph of the right-wing propaganda machine.

⋅◈⋅

The Republican Noise Machine: Right-Wing Media and How It Corrupts Democracy, by David Brock—the president and C.E.O. of Media Matters for America, a watchdog group that documents misinformation in the right-wing media—traces the history of the "liberal bias" notion back to the Barry Goldwater presidential campaign, in 1964, in which aggrieved conservatives railed against Walter Cronkite and the "Eastern Liberal Press" at the Republican National Convention. In response to Spiro Agnew's 1969 attack on the networks as insufficiently supportive of Nixon's policies in Vietnam, conservatives formed an organization called Accuracy in Media, whose purpose was to discredit the media by tagging it as "liberal," and to market that idea with clever catchphrases. Polluter-funded foundations, including the Adolph Coors Foundation and the so-called four sisters—the Lynde and Harry Bradley Foundation, the John M. Olin Foundation, Richard Mellon Scaife's foundations, and the Smith Richardson Foundation—all of which funded the anti-environmental movement, spent hundreds of millions of dollars to perpetuate the big lie of liberal bias, to convince the conservative base that it should not believe the mainstream, to create a market for right-wing media, and to intimidate and discipline the mainstream press into being more accommodating to conservatism.

According to Brock, right-wing groups such as the Heritage Foundation and Scaife's Landmark Legal Foundation helped persuade Ronald Reagan and his Federal Communications Commission, in 1987, to eliminate the Fairness Doctrine—the F.C.C.'s 1949 rule which dictated that broadcasters provide equal time to both sides of controversial public questions. It was a "godsend for conservatives," according to religious-right pioneer and Moral Majority co-founder Richard Viguerie, opening up talk radio to one-sided, right-wing broadcasters. (Rush Limbaugh nationally launched his talk show the following year.) Radical ideologues, faced with Niagara-size flows of money from the Adolph Coors Foundation, the four sisters, and others, set up magazines and newspapers and cultivated a generation of young pundits, writers, and propagandists, giving them lucrative sinecures inside right-wing think tanks, now numbering more than 500, from which they bombard the media with carefully honed messages justifying corporate profit taking.

Brock himself was one of the young stars recruited to this movement, working in turn for the Heritage Foundation, the Reverend Sun Myung

Moon's *Washington Times,* and Scaife's *American Spectator.* "If you look at this history," Brock told me recently, "you will find that the conservative movement has in many ways purchased the debate. You have conservative media outlets day after day that are intentionally misinforming the public." Brock, who admits to participating in the deliberate deception while he was a so-called journalist on the right-wing payroll, worries that the right-wing media are systematically feeding the public "false and wrong information. It's a really significant problem for democracy.

"We're in a situation," continues Brock, "where you have 'red facts' and 'blue facts.' And I think the conservatives intentionally have done that to try to confuse and neutralize accurate information that may not serve the conservative agenda."

The consolidation of media ownership and its conservative drift are growing ever more severe. Following the election, Clear Channel, the biggest owner of radio stations in the country, announced that Fox News will now supply its news feed to many of the company's 1,240 stations, further amplifying the distorted drumbeat of right-wing propaganda that most Americans now take for news.

Sadly enough, right-wing radio and cable are increasingly driving the discussion in mainstream broadcasting as well. At a Harvard University symposium the day before the Democratic convention, three network anchors and a CNN anchor straightforwardly discussed the effects that right-wing broadcasters, conservative money, and organized pressure have on the networks. And in February 2005, Pat Mitchell announced her resignation as president of PBS, hounded from office by right-wing critics who felt her conciliatory efforts to conservatize the network—canceling a cartoon episode with a lesbian couple and adding talk shows by such right-wingers as Tucker Carlson and Paul Gigot—did not go far enough fast enough.

Furthermore, Fox's rating success has exerted irresistible gravities that have pulled its competitors' programming to starboard. In the days leading up to the Iraq war, MSNBC fired one of television's last liberal voices, Phil Donahue, who hosted its highest-rated show; an internal memo revealed that Donahue presented "a difficult public face for NBC in a time of war." CBS's post-election decision to retire Dan Rather, a lightning rod for rightwing wrath, coincided with Tom Brokaw's retirement from NBC. He was replaced by Brian Williams, who has said, "I think Rush [Limbaugh] has actually yet to get the credit he is due." According to NBC president Jeff Zucker, "No one understands this NASCAR nation more than Brian."

Conservative noise on cable and talk radio also has an echo effect on the rest of the media. One of the conservative talking points in the last election was that terrorists supported the candidacy of John Kerry. According to Media Matters, this pearl originated on Limbaugh's radio show in March 2004 and repeatedly surfaced in mainstream news. In May, CNN's Kelli Arena reported "speculation that al-Qaeda believes it has a better chance of winning in Iraq if John Kerry is in the White House"; in June it migrated to Dick Morris's *New York Post* column. Chris Matthews mentioned it in a July edition of *Hardball.* In September, Bill Schneider, CNN's senior political analyst, declared that al-Qaeda "would very much like to defeat President Bush," signaling that Limbaugh's contrivance was now embedded firmly in the national consciousness.

That "echo effect" is not random. Brock shows in his book how the cues by which mainstream news directors decide what is important to cover are no longer being suggested by *The New York Times* and other responsible media outlets, but rather by the "shadowy" participants of a Washington, D.C., meeting convened by Grover Norquist's Americans for Tax Reform, an anti-government organization that seeks to prevent federal regulation of business.

Every Wednesday morning the leaders of 80 conservative organizations meet in Washington in Norquist's boardroom. This radical cabal formulates policy with the Republican National Committee and the White House, developing talking points that go out to the conservative media via a sophisticated fax tree. Soon, millions of Americans are hearing the same message from cable news commentators and thousands of talk jocks across America. Their precisely crafted message and language then percolate through the mainstream media to form the underlying assumptions of our national debate.

This meeting has now grown to include more than 120 participants, including industry lobbyists and representatives of conservative media outlets such as *The Washington Times* and the *National Review*. According to Brock, columnist Bob Novak sends a researcher. *The Wall Street Journal's* Peggy Noonan may attend in person. The lockstep coordination among right-wing political operatives and the press is new in American politics.

A typical meeting might focus on a new tax proposal released by President Bush. Following conference calls throughout the week, the decision will be made to call the plan "bold." Over the next 10 days, radio and cable will reiterate that it's "bold, bold, bold." The result, according to Brock, is that "people come to think that there must be something 'bold' about this plan."

This highly integrated network has given the right frightening power to disseminate its propaganda and has dramatically changed the way Americans get their information and formulate policy. In *The Republican Noise Machine*, Brock alleges routine fraud and systematically dishonest practices by his former employer the Reverend Sun Myung Moon's *Washington Times*, which is the primary propaganda organ for Moon's agenda to establish America as a Fascist theocracy. The paper doesn't reach more than a hundred thousand subscribers, but its articles are read on the air by Rush Limbaugh, reaching 15 million people, and are posted on Matt Drudge's Web site, to reach another 7 million people, and its writers regularly appear on *The O'Reilly Factor*, before another 2 million. Network TV talk-show producers and bookers use those appearances as a tip sheet for picking the subject matter and guests for their own shows. And so the capacity of the conservative movement to disseminate propaganda has increased exponentially.

This right-wing propaganda machine can quickly and indelibly brand Democratic candidates unfavorably—John Kerry as a flip-flopper, Al Gore as a liar. The machine is so powerful that it was able to orchestrate Clinton's impeachment despite the private and trivial nature of his "crime"—a lie about an extramarital tryst—when compared with President Bush's calamitous lies about Iraq, the budget, Medicare, education, and the environment. During the

2000 campaign, A1 Gore was smeared as a liar—a charge that was completely false—by rightwing pundits such as gambling addict Bill Bennett and prescription-painkiller abuser Rush Limbaugh, both of whom the right wing has sold as moral paradigms. Meanwhile, George Bush's chronic problems with the truth during the three presidential debates that year were barely mentioned in the media, as Brock has noted. Americans accepted this negative characterization of Gore, and when they emerged from the voting booths in 2000, they told pollsters that Bush won their vote on "trust."

In the 2004 campaign, the so-called Swift Boat Veterans for Truth launched dishonest attacks which, amplified and repeated by the right-wing media, helped torpedo John Kerry's presidential ambitions. No matter who the Democratic nominee was, this machinery had the capacity to discredit and destroy him.

Meanwhile, there is a palpable absence of strong progressive voices on TV, unless one counts HBO's Bill Maher and Comedy Central's Jon Stewart—both comedians—or Fox's meek foil, Alan Colmes, who plays the ever losing Washington Generals to Scan Hannity's Harlem Globetrotters. There are no liberal equivalents to counterbalance Joe Scarborough, John Stossel, Bill O'Reilly, and Lawrence Kudlow. Brock points to the systematic structural imbalance in the panels that are featured across all of cable and on the networks' Sunday shows. Programs like *Meet the Press* and Chris Matthews's *Hardball* invariably pit conservative ideologues such as William Safire, Robert Novak, and Pat Buchanan against neutral, nonaligned reporters such as Andrea Mitchell, the diplomatic correspondent for NBC News, or *Los Angeles Times* reporter Ronald Brownstein in a rigged fight that leaves an empty chair for a strong progressive point of view.

There is still relevant information in the print media. But even that has been shamefully twisted by the pressures of the right. Both *The New York Times* and *The Washington Post,* which jumped on Scaife's bandwagon to lead the mainstream press in the Clinton-impeachment frenzy, have been forced to issue *mea culpas* for failing to ask the tough questions during the run-up to Bush's Iraq war.

Furthermore, America's newspapers, like most other media outlets, are owned predominantly by Republican conservatives. Newspapers endorsed Bush by two to one in the 2000 election. According to a recent survey, the op-ed columnists who appear in the most newspapers are conservatives Cal Thomas and George Will. Republican-owned newspapers often reprint misinformation from the right. And red-state journalists, whatever their personal political sympathies, are unlikely to offend their editors by spending inordinate energy exposing right-wing lies.

Print journalism is a victim of the same consolidation by a few large, profit-driven corporations that has affected the broadcasters. Today, a shrinking pool of owners—guided by big business rather than journalistic values—forces news executives to cut costs and seek the largest audience. The consolidation has led to demands on news organizations to return profits at rates never before expected of them. Last summer, just a few months after winning five Pulitzer Prizes, the *Los Angeles Times* was asked by its parent company to drop 60 newsroom positions.

The pressure for bottomline news leaves little incentive for investment in investigative reporting. Costcutting has liquidated news staffs, leaving reporters little time to research stories. According to an Ohio University study, the number of investigative reporters was cut almost in half between 1980 and 1995.

During the debate over the Radio Act of 1927, an early forerunner of the Fairness Doctrine, Texas congressman Luther Johnson warned Americans against the corporate and ideological consolidation of the national press that has now come to pass. "American thought and American politics will be largely at the mercy of those who operate these stations," he said. "For publicity is the most powerful weapon that can be wielded in a republic . . . and when a single selfish group is permitted to either tacitly or otherwise acquire ownership and dominate these broadcasting stations throughout the country, then woe be to those who dare to differ with them. It will be impossible to compete with them in reaching the ears of the American people."

The news isn't entirely bleak. Progressive voices are prevalent on the Internet, which is disproportionately utilized by the younger age groups that will exercise increasing influence in public affairs each year. The success of Air America Radio, the progressive network whose best-known host is Al Franken, offers great cause for optimism. Despite a shoestring budget and financial chaos at its inception, Air America has grown in one year to include 50 stations, from which it is accessible to half the American people. Most encouraging, a recent study shows that Air America personalities as a group rank second in popularity to Rush Limbaugh. Last fall in San Diego, a traditional Republican bastion, Air America was reported to be the No. 1 radio station among listeners 18 to 49 years old. But progressive activists need also to find a voice on television, and there the outlook is dark.

If there is a market for progressive voices, as the Air America experience suggests, why don't the big corporate owners leap in? A top industry executive recently told me that he was dead certain that there would be a large audience for a progressive TV news network to counterbalance the right-wing cable shows. "But," he said, "the corporate owners will never touch it. Multi-nationals, like Viacom, Disney, and General Electric, that rely on government business, contracts, and goodwill are not going to risk offending the Republicans who now control every branch of government."

This executive had recently spoken to Viacom chairman Sumner Redstone (a lifelong Democrat) about the corporation's open support of the Bush administration. "I said, 'Sumner, what about our children and what about our country?' He replied, 'Viacom is my life. I've got to do what's best for the company. I need to buy more stations, and the Republicans are going to let me do it. It's in the company's interest to support Republicans.'"

When veteran television journalist and former CBS news analyst Bill Moyers resigned as host of PBS's *Now* in December, he observed, "I think my peers in commercial television are talented and devoted journalists, but they've chosen to work in a corporate mainstream that trims their talent to fit the corporate nature of American life. And you do not get rewarded for telling the hard truths about America in a profit-seeking environment." Moyers called the decline in American journalism "the biggest story of our time." He added, "We have an ideological press that's interested in the election of Republicans, and a mainstream press that's interested in the bottom line. Therefore, we don't have a vigilant, independent press whose interest is the American people."

Moyers has elsewhere commented that "the quality of journalism and the quality of democracy are inextricably joined." By diminishing the capacity for voters to make rational choices, the breakdown of the American press is threatening not just our environment but our democracy.

POSTSCRIPT

Do the Media Have a Liberal Bias?

The importance of freedom of the press was expressed by Thomas Jefferson in 1787, when he wrote: "Were it left to me to decide whether we should have a government without newspapers, or newspapers without a government, I should not hesitate a moment to prefer the latter." Twenty years later, he seemed to adopt an opposite opinion, observing: "The man who never looks into a newspaper is better informed than he who reads them; inasmuch as he knows nothing is nearer to truth than he whose mind is filled with falsehood and errors." Like other presidents and political commentators, Jefferson was sometimes pleased and sometimes peeved by press reporting and commentary.

Bernard Goldberg's *Bias: A CBS Insider Exposes How the Media Distort the News* (Regnery, 2002) struck a responsive chord with many readers, leading to the sequel from which the preceding essay has been taken. Ann Coulter has gone farther than Goldberg in sharply criticizing both the influence of liberalism in the media and in the government in *Slander: Liberal Lies About the American Right* (Random House, 2002). Sean Hannity, a conservative television commentator, has written *Let Freedom Ring: Winning the War of Liberty over Liberalism* (Regan Books, 2002).

Goldberg's accusation of liberal media bias led Eric Alterman, a columnist for *The Nation,* a liberal weekly, to write *What Liberal Media?: The Truth About Bias and the News* (Basic Books, 2003). Alterman maintains that there is a conservative bias in the mass media. Naming the names of frequent television commentators who have a conservative perspective, he argues that not one of the prominent liberals writing for newspapers and opinion magazines enjoys a prominent position in television. Robert McChesney, in *The Problem of the Media: U.S. Communication Politics in the Twenty-First Century* (Monthly Review Press, 2004), believes that corporate concentration of ownership limits diversity and the expression of unorthodox ideas.

Robert F. Kennedy Jr. believes that, as a result of one-sided conservative reporting by the news media, the American people have been misinformed about the policies of the Bush Administration in the war in Iraq, the response to terrorism, the environment, and a host of other issues.

Whichever side is right, perhaps the issue of media bias is becoming less important. David T. Z. Mindich, in *Tuned Out: Why Americans Under 40 Don't Follow the News* (Oxford University Press, 2004), states that while more than 70 percent of older Americans read a newspaper every day, fewer than 20 percent of younger Americans do. Mindich writes that "America is facing the greatest exodus of informed citizenship in its history."

Press critic A. J. Liebling is credited with having first said that "freedom of the press belongs to those who have one." The fascinating possibility exists that, in a world in which anyone with a computer and access to the Internet can circulate political (or other) opinion to as wide an audience as wants to receive it, freedom of the press has become a widely-held reality. The popularity of some Internet bloggers suggests that this is a growing audience. What this will mean for the wider dissemination of news and opinion, and whether it will render irrelevant the issue of media bias, remains to be seen.

ISSUE 5

Should America Adopt Public Financing of Political Campaigns?

YES: Mark Green, from *Selling Out: How Big Corporate Money Buys Elections, Rams Through Legislation, and Betrays Our Democracy* (Regan Books, 2002)

NO: John Samples, from "Taxpayer Financing of Campaigns," in John Samples, ed., *Welfare for Politicians? Taxpayer Financing of Campaigns* (Cato Institute, 2005)

ISSUE SUMMARY

YES: Political activist and author Mark Green sums up his thesis in the subtitle of his book, a work that urges adoption of public financing of election campaigns in order to make politics more honest and to reduce the dependency of elected officials on selfish interests.

NO: Cato Institute director and political scientist John Samples opposes public financing of candidates for public office because it does not achieve any of the goals of its advocates and it forces voters to underwrite the financing of candidates they do not support.

$\mathbf{A}$pproximately \$4 billion was spent on the 2004 presidential and congressional elections, nearly \$1 billion more than in the election four years earlier. It was the most expensive election in American history, but it will almost certainly be exceeded in 2008. Internet advertising has been added on to print, radio, television, and live campaigning, resulting not in altering how the money is spent but in adding to it.

This has occurred despite the efforts of Congress to regulate and restrict campaign expenditures. In 2000, Congress established disclosure requirements for nonparty political groups known as Section 527 organizations, which were not required to register with the Federal Elections Commission because their principle purpose was alleged to be something other than influencing federal elections. In 2002, the first important revision of federal campaign finance law in more, than two decades, the Bipartisan Campaign Reform Act was adopted. The following year, the U.S. Supreme Court upheld its major provisions: the elimination of party soft money and the regulation of candidate-specific issue advertising. Nevertheless, the presidential candidacies of President George W. Bush and Senator John Kerry inspired vaster contributions and expenditures in accordance with—and sometimes in circumvention of—the law.

What is wrong with this increased spending? A great deal, say those who believe that rampant spending on political campaigns discourages less prosperous citizens from seeking elective office, diverts office-holders from doing their jobs to seeking contributions and bending their convictions to conform to those of their contributors, exaggerates the political influence of special interests, and discourages would-be voters who conclude that money matters more than their votes.

Soft money is money that is contributed not to individual campaigns but to political parties, ostensibly for the purpose of "party-building" activities, such as get-out-the-vote drives. The Federal Election Commission (FEC), an agency created in 1974, began allowing this practice in 1978, and within a decade fundraisers in both parties began to realize its usefulness as a way around existing contribution limits. Under then-existing law, "hard money" contributions (funds contributed directly to the campaigns of particular candidates) were limited to $1,000 per person for each candidate; the assumption was that no candidate can be "bought" for a mere $1,000. But unlimited soft money allowed wealthy donors and interest groups to contribute huge sums to the parties at dinners, coffees and other such gatherings—thus subtly (or not-so-subtly) reminding them of who was buttering their bread. Another concern of those who supported the new law was what they saw as the misuse of "issue advocacy" during campaigns. Interest groups had been able to get around the legal limits on contributions by pouring millions of unregulated dollars into "attack" ads that did not explicitly ask people to vote for or against a candidate. Instead, they said something like "Call Senator Smith and tell him to stop supporting polluters."

The new law sought to plug these loopholes and to bring the existing system of federal campaign finance regulation up-to-date. Among its major provisions are the following:

- A ban on soft money contributions to the national political parties.
- An increase in hard money contribution limits. For example, limits to individual candidates were increased from $1,000 to $2,000 per candidate per election. The increase was meant to take inflation into account.
- Restrictions on the ability of corporations, labor unions, and other interest groups to run "issue ads" featuring the names or likenesses of candidates within 60 days of a general election and 30 days of a primary election.

Some critics of existing campaign finance methods believe that the recent changes do not go far enough. Mark Green, in the selection that follows, concludes that nothing less than public financing of campaigns and elections will serve the public interest and further democracy. Critics of public financing maintain that these changes in the law are contrary to democracy because they use public tax money to support views that many citizens oppose. One of these critics, John Samples, argues that the changes would have a negative effect on voter participation and would limit competition.

YES

Mark Green

Change, for Good

The evidence . . . makes it clear: our campaign finance system is broken, citizens of all persuasions want change, and successful alternatives exist.

The alibis of apologists—change helps incumbents; money is speech; money doesn't buy votes—are shallow and unpersuasive. So now the defenders of the status quo have shifted to political and free-market arguments. Voters don't really care, they say; or, as Mitch McConnell argued in 2000, they assert that no candidate has ever been elected or defeated on the issue of campaign reform, and thus it can be safely ignored. Yet McConnell's Senate nemesis, John McCain, made campaign finance reform the heart and soul of his electrifying 2000 presidential campaign. Only by vastly outspending McCain did George W. Bush squeak by him in a tight primary battle that was supposed to be a coronation—and not before soft money became a dinner-table conversation staple. That same year, Maria Cantwell believes, making campaign finance reform a centerpiece of her Washington State U.S. Senate race was a major reason for her squeaker of a victory.

Senators McCain and Cantwell ran against what big money buy for special interests—tax breaks and loopholes for big corporation weakened environmental regulations for manufacturers, and price protections for durg companies. But they also ran against what those purchases cost Americans: higher taxes, more pollution, and expensive health care, respectively.

To be successful, a pro-democracy movement like campaign finance reform cannot be merely an abstract, good-government ideal. It must be tied to the issues that Americans care most about: affordable child care, education, health care, and housing; a clean environment and safe streets; and tax rates that are fair. Do we want children with lower rates of asthma? Then we need campaign finance reform. Do we want enough funds for smaller class sizes and qualified, well-paid teachers? Then we need campaign finance reform. Do we want senior to have access to lifesaving medicine? Then we need campaign finance reform. Do we want to keep guns out of the hands of kids and crimlnals? Then we need campaign finance reform. . . .

Both Republicans and Democrats came to agree that the problem with welfare was not necessarily the result of bad people but of a very bad system that—by paying more if a recipient had no work and no husband—discouraged employment and marriage. Ditto campaign finance. The sin is the *system*. How else can we explain how such provably honorable people as John Glenn, Alan Cranston, and John McCain felt it necessary to go to bat for the likes of a big, sleazy contributor like Charles Keating?

A comprehensive campaign finance reform program is ideally suited to achieve the conservative goals on which our economy and society are built—competition, efficiency, accountability, open markets, and market integrity. Specifically, four reforms would restore our electoral democracy by elevating voters over donors: spending limits, public financing, a restructured enforcement agency, and free broadcast time and mailings.

Limits on campaign spending are an integral part of restoring our democracy; Congress understood this fact when it included expenditure limits in the 1971 and 1974 campaign finance laws. Furthermore, the experience of the last quarter century has taught us that without caps on campaign spending to complement contribution limits, money will always find ways back into the system. But as long as *Buckley v. Valeo* remains the law, the courts are likely to strike down any attempts to place limits on campaign spending.

The Court in *Buckley* concluded that expenditures did not raise the problem of corruption in the same way contributions did. The Court's conclusion is based on two critical errors: (1) subjecting expenditure limits to a higher standard than contribution limits, and (2) considering only the anticorruption rationale while dismissing the other interests.

Why should campaign expenditures be entitled to much greater constitutional protection than campaign contributions? Neither expenditures nor contributions actually are speech; both merely facilitate expressive activities. And the argument that contributions pose a greater danger of quid pro quo corruption than expenditures seems ridiculous on its face: Are we really to believe that a $2000 contribution to a candidate will create a greater sense of obligation than millions of dollars in independent expenditures for that candidate?

And what makes preventing quid pro quo corruption so much more important than any other governmental interest? Of course, it is unacceptable for public officials to sell votes, access, or influence to the highest bidder. Why? Not because of the quid pro quo–ness of it all; we exchange money for goods and services all the time in our daily lives. Rather, it is because the sale of our government undermines the most fundamental principles of our democracy: competitive elections, effective government, and—most important of all—the guarantee that our public officials answer to their true constituents, not a handful of wealthy benefactors. Quid pro quo arrangements are surely egregious violations of these democratic norms, but they are not the only ones. . . .

Until *Buckley* falls and a spending cap is found constitutional, funding limits can only be encouraged by offering public funds to candidates who voluntarily accept them. Only spending limits can end the arms race for campaign cash and reduce the power of war chests that incumbents build to scare off competition. And only the combination of spending limits and public funds can level the political playing field.

Spending limits that are set too high tend to favor incumbents, because few others can raise the resources to compete with them. Limits that are set too low, however, also favor incumbents, since challengers need to spend enough to overcome the natural advantages that accrue to incumbents through years of constituent service, free media, and use of the franking privilege. So the porridge must not be too hot or too cold. When weighing these two considerations, a third must also be taken into account: incumbents and the well-connected will not voluntarily join a public financing program if they feel its spending limits are significantly below what they could otherwise raise. If limits are too low, so too will be participation rates, and the program's purposes will be seriously compromised.

Of these three considerations, two point toward higher spending limits, which suggests that it is better to err on the side of caution. The average House winner spent $842,245 in 2000; the average candidate who challenged an incumbent spent just $143,685. In 1988, only 22 House campaigns hit the million-dollar mark; in 2000, the number reached 176. To control costs without discouraging participation or diminishing a challenger's ability to compete, House candidates should be held to inflation-adjusted spending limits of $900,000–$450,000 each for the primary and general election. A strong argument may be made that a $900,000 limit, which memorializes a level of spending that is about the current average, does not do enough to suppress campaign spending. But to undercut opponents who will use inadequate spending limits as an excuse to oppose reform, and to ensure that challengers can spend at significant levels, it is in the reform coalition's best interests to support limits around the current average cost of a winning campaign. By definition, this amount can't be too low or too high if it's the average amount it takes to win.

Senate candidates should be able to spend $1 million, plus fifty cents for each voting-age person in the state—which would come to about $8 million (for the primary and general election combined) in New York State, $7 million in Florida, $5 million in Ohio and Pennsylvania, and $2 million in Arkansas— or about one-fourth to one-half of what's recently been spent in these states. But in comparison to House contests, Senate races have higher profiles and receive significantly more media attention, making it harder for incumbents to dominate. Consequently, spending limits lower than current averages will protect challengers from the war chests that Senate incumbents can build over six years, and still ensure—because of free media coverage—that challengers will have ample opportunity to get their message out.

For instance, in Michigan's 2000 Senate race Debbie Stabenow spent $8 million in her victory over incumbent Senator Spencer Abraham, who spent $14.5 million. Under the spending-limit formula just outlined, both candidates would have been held to about $5 million. Similarly, in Pennsylvania, a $5 million limit would have helped challenger Ron Klink, who was outspent by nearly $10 million in his losing 2000 campaign against incumbent Senator Rick Santorum.

Separate limits for the primary and general election ensure that the winner of a hard-fought primary will not be placed at a disadvantage by facing a general-election opponent who suffered no primary challenge. To ensure equity, of course, candidates without primary election opponents should be allowed to spend up to the limit in the primary election period, although no public funds should be given to candidates without serious opponents, whether in primary or general elections.

A bonus provision   Again, so long as *Buckley* is the constitutional standard, legislation cannot prevent the super-rich from spending tens of millions of dollars on their campaigns. We can, however, help their opponents by eliminating the spending limit. It is unfair to keep a lid on a non-rich candidate when his or her opponent effectively says the sky's the limit. . . .

The airwaves belong to us, the public. We provide broadcasters with federal licenses—for free—on the condition that they agree to serve "the public interest, convenience, and necessity." They have not lived up to their end of the bargain.

How have they gotten away with it? (You'll never guess.) The powerful broadcast industry vehemently opposes reforms affecting their bottom lines. The industry gave $6.8 million to candidates and parties in the presidential election year of 2000, with half coming in soft money. Their annual largesse has allowed them to skirt their public duty, and then some: despite a thirty-year-old law designed to hold down campaign ad rates, broadcasters routinely gouge candidates. When the Senate included a provision in McCain-Feingold to close the loophole that allows for such price gouging, the industry went on the attack, showering both parties with hard and soft money. Their efforts paid off: the House stripped the provision from Shays-Meehan and the loophole remains.

Why is the broadcast industry unwilling to live up to its public service obligations? In the 2000 elections, broadcasters pulled down revenue from political commercials that approached $1 billion. Reducing that revenue would mean cutting into profit margins that average between 30 and 50 percent. So it makes perfect business sense for the industry to invest a relatively minute amount in contributions to candidates and parties, because the payoff is astronomical. Dan O'Connor, the general sales manager of WSYT-TV in Syracuse, New York, put it this way: Ad buyers for candidates "call you up and say, 'Can you clear $40,000 [in TV ad time] next week?' It's like, 'What? Am I dreaming? Of course I can clear that!' And they send you a check in the mail overnight. It's like Santa Claus came to town. It's a beautiful thing."

Paul Taylor, executive director of the Alliance for Better Campaigns, a nonpartisan group that advocates for free airtime, sums up the scam this way: "Let's follow the bouncing ball. Our government gives broadcasters free licenses to operate on the public airwaves on the condition that they serve the public interest. During the campaign season, broadcasters turn around and sell access to these airwaves to candidates at inflated prices. Meanwhile, many candidates sell access to the government in order to raise special-interest money to purchase access to the airwaves. It's a wonderful arrangement for the broadcasters, who reap windfall profits from political campaigns. It's a good system for incumbents, who prosper in the big-dollar, high-ante political culture of paid speech. But it's a lousy deal for the rest of us."

Walter Cronkite, the iconic American newsman, is chairman of the Alliance for Better Campaigns. According to Cronkite, "In the land of free speech, we've permitted a system of 'paid speech' to take hold during the political campaigns on the one medium we all own—our broadcast airwaves. It's long past time to turn that around. Free airtime would help free our democracy from the grip of the special interests." That's the way it is, and even Senator Mitch McConnell, the self-described Darth Vader of campaign finance reform, agrees that the broadcasters are not giving the public a fair shake. And for the rest of the world, this is a no-brainer. "America is almost alone among the Atlantic democracies in declining to provide political parties free prime time on television during elections," writes historian Arthur Schlesinger Jr. "[If it did so], it could do much both to bring inordinate campaign costs under control and revitalize the political parties."

It's time for electronic consumers to negotiate a better deal with those we give free licenses to. Cronkite's alliance is pushing an innovative and market-based proposal-first discussed in a 1982 monograph from the Democracy Project, Independent Expenditures in Congressional Campaigns: The Electronic Solution-that would provide free broadcast vouchers to candidates and parties. Here's how it would work: Qualifying candidates who win their parties' nominations would receive vouchers for use in their general election campaigns. Candidates, particularly those from urban areas who don't find it cost-effective to advertise on television or radio, could trade their vouchers to their party in exchange for funds to pay for direct mail or other forms of communication. Parties, in turn, could use the vouchers themselves or give them to other candidates. The system creates a market for broadcast vouchers that, because of pricing incentives, ensures their efficient distribution.

A comprehensive campaign finance reform program should provide candidates with a right of access to the public airwaves. Until then, the alliance's voucher proposal should be restricted to those candidates who accept spending limits. Whether vouchers were used for airtime or exchanged for party monies for direct mail, candidates would report them as expenditures. Under such a system, spending limits would retain their integrity. The value of the vouchers should be set at $250,000 for House candidates and vary by population for Senate candidates, with candidates in midsize states receiving up to $2.5 million in vouchers. As in public financing, candidates should be required to reach contribution thresholds to qualify for vouchers.

One might argue that vouchers would simply encourage the proliferation of slickly produced thirty-second advertisements. Yet the reality, for better or worse, is that political commercials are part of elections in America, and there's little chance that will change. The voucher proposal bows to that reality, but it also offers hope: candidates who accept the vouchers should be required to feature their own voices in at least 50 percent of all their ads—whether paid for by vouchers, private contributions, or public funds. There is a growing public distaste for anonymous negative advertising, and candidates, given free access to the airwaves, should be held accountable for their ads.

And there are other ways to promote civic discourse. Cronkite's alliance has put forth a complement to its voucher proposal, called "Voters' Time," that would require broadcasters to air a minimum of two hours a week of candidate discussion in the month preceding every election. At least half of the programs would have to be aired in prime time or drive time, and the formats—debates, interviews, town hall meetings—would be of the broadcasters' choosing. A voters' time requirement is necessary, because broadcasters are airing less and less campaign news and candidate discourse.

In the 2000 election campaign, despite the closest presidential election in a generation, ABC, CBS, and NBC devoted 28 percent less time to campaign coverage than in 1988. In a nationwide survey conducted two days prior to the 2000 elections, more than half the population could not answer basic questions about Bush's and Gore's positions on the issues. There are many factors contributing to that result, but two of them—the domination of election by big money interests, and the unwillingness of the broadcast industry to be a part of the solution—can be cured.

Mandating free airtime for candidates and candidate discussion would appropriately hold broadcasters to a minimal standard of what it means, under the Federal Communications Commission Act, to serve "the public interest, convenience, and necessity." But this will require a committed Congress standing up to an unusually powerful industry, one that gives big contributions and confers access to voters via the airwaves.

At a minimum, two other useful methods of encouraging civic discourse and facilitating candidate communication should be part of any reform bill. First, candidates who accept public funds should be required to debate. Kentucky, New Jersey, Los Angeles, and New York City all require dabates of publicly funded candidates. Especially when the public has invested its money in public campaigns, it deserves to see the candidates in public face-to-face meetings. In March 2000, Al Gore proposed that he and George W. Bush eliminate campaign television advertisements and instead hold issue debates twice a week until the elections. Bush declined, but a CBS News poll showed that voters responded positively, with 65 percent calling it a "good idea."

Second, cities like New York and Seattle mail a voters' guide to registered voters before elections. The guides include candidate statements and biographical information, as well as information on voting. New York City's guide costs fifty cents a copy to publish and mail, a bargain by any standard. The federal government should do the same. Or it could create and promote a Web-based guide to serve as a clearing-house for candidate and election information. Before voting, citizens could log on to the site, read statements for federal candidates, and find out information about their polling stations. In the age of information technology, demology, democracy should not be left behind.

John Samples  **NO**

Taxpayer Financing of Campaigns

Candidates and parties need money to fight election campaigns. In the United States, this money comes largely from individuals and groups, not the government, that is, the taxpayers. Some critics decry such private financing of politics. They argue that private donations advance special interests and corrupt politics and government. Some of them argue that government should ban private campaign contributions in favor of public financing. Since public funding comes from everyone, they reason, it actually comes from no one, thereby precluding the influence of private interests on public affairs. That argument has found few converts at the national level. States and cities have been more willing to experiment with taxpayer support for campaigns . . . .

Proponents claim government financing of campaigns servers the public interest in three ways: it advances the integrity of elections and lawmaking, promotes political equality, and fosters electoral competitiveness.

Corruption

The Supreme Court held in *Buckley v. Valeo* that the government has a compelling interest in preventing corruption or the appearance of corruption in campaigns and policymaking, an interest that may outweigh the First Amendment rights implicated in contributing to a political campaign. Allegations of corruption thus increase the probability that a law regulating campaign finance will pass constitutional muster.

Advocates of government financing claim the current system of largely private financing of campaigns fosters corruption (or its appearance) in several ways. They say campaign contributions buy favors from elected officials, the quid-pro-quo corruption noted in *Buckley*. Others say contributors receive favorable action on policies that attract little public attention and debate. Advocates also say private money fosters more subtle forms of favoritism; for example, members of Congress may allocate their time and effort in committees to help contributors. If private money corrupts, the advocates conclude, the private financing system should be abolished in favor of government financing.

In their contribution to this volume, Jeffrey Milyo and David Primo summarize the academic studies of Congress and campaign contributions, almost all of which provide little evidence to support allegations of corruption. Having surveyed the field, even Andrew Geddis, a supporter of government financing, concludes, "One obstacle is that various studies have failed to produce the sort of evidence of a strong correlation between campaign donations and a representative's public actions needed to back up suspicions of general quid pro quo understandings." Should we not have strong evidence to uproot our current system of campaign finance, especially when money is tied to the exercise of free speech?

If corruption involves using public power for private ends, government financing itself provides an example of corruption; after all, the program takes money from everyone and gives it to particular interests. One might counter with Richard Briffault's argument that government financing cannot be corrupt because tax revenue "comes from everyone, and thus, from no one in particular." But that leaves out an important part of the story. Tax money used to finance campaigns may come from everyone, but it goes predominantly, and is designed to go predominantly, to particular interests and groups within the American polity. Government subsidies for ethanol are no less corrupt because everyone pays for them and neither are government subsidies to particular candidates.

Equality

Some Americans contribute to political campaigns, but most do not. For advocates of government financing, these differences create intolerable inequalities that are "in sharp tension with the one person-one vote principle enshrined in our civic culture and our constitutional law. Public funding is necessary to bring our campaign finance system more in line with our central value of political equality." Similarly, Public Campaign, a leading organization advocating taxpayer financing, argues that private financing "violates the rights of all citizens to equal and meaningful participation in the democratic process." The principle of one person-one vote means "one man's vote in a congressional election is to be worth as much as another's" because assigning different weights to different votes in various House districts would violate Article 1, § 2 of the Constitution. The principle applies to state elections because of the equal protection clause of the 14th Amendment. Is one person-one vote thus "our central value of political equality"? A look at American institutions suggests otherwise.

The representation of states in the U.S. Senate assigns different weights to different votes in different states. Because the Electoral College also recognizes state representation, the election of the president also accords greater weight to votes in small states compared with those in large states. Moreover, the Supreme Court has not subjected judicial elections to the principle of one person-one vote.

One person-one vote applies only to voting. No American has a right to "equal and meaningful participation in the democratic process" if that means the whole of political life. In particular, the rights of association and speech set out in the First Amendment have been explicitly protected from government efforts to compel "equal . . . participation." In *Buckley*, the Supreme Court noted that federal election law sought to equalize the influence of individuals and groups over the outcome of elections. The justices demurred:

> But the concept that government may restrict the speech of some elements of our society in order to enhance the relative voice of others is wholly foreign to the First Amendment, which was designed "to secure 'the widest possible dissemination of information from diverse and antagonistic sources,'" and "to assure unfettered interchange of ideas for the bringing about of political and social changes desired by the people."

Far from being "our central value of political equality," equal participation remains "wholly foreign to the First Amendment."

Moreover, even if the government financed all campaigns, we would not have equal participation in elections. Proponents of government financing focus on one source of political inequality: money. They ignore all other sources of inequality such as a talent for speaking, the ability to write, good looks, media ownership and access, organizational ability, and so on. The proponents do not propose to restrain the many nonmonetary sources of influence perhaps because such talents are often found among the proponents of government financing of campaigns. The leveling impulse, they imply, should not restrict such political talents; only people with money should be excluded from political influence. Sometimes in public policy what is not regulated tells you more about a piece of legislation than what is covered. So it is with government financing of campaigns. . . .

Proponents of government financing argue that public subsidies will enable new candidates to run who would otherwise be excluded from the race. They argue the candidates who now obtain funding reflect the investment and consumption preferences of wealthy and conservative individuals. They believe contributions reproduce the inequalities of wealth in the economy and lead to a government that is unrepresentative of America. This argument depends crucially on the stereotypical image of "fat cat" contributors devoted to conservative causes. Large donors may be unrepresentative of the United States as a whole—they do have more money than the average American—but that does not mean they hold vastly different political views than most Americans. In fact, a recent study indicates large contributors often identify themselves as Democrats and as liberal on the issues. That should not be so surprising. In 1998, National Election Studies found that almost one-third of the richest Americans identified themselves as liberals.

Finally, we should be clear how extensive, intrusive, and dangerous a government financing system would be. Keep in mind that the goal of equalizing financial resources in an election requires extensive control and oversight of all electoral spending. The election authority must immediately know about all spending by privately financed candidates and every dollar laid out by any group participating in an election. Public Campaign's model legislation states that government-financed candidates must use a government-issued debit card that draws solely on funds in an account created by the government. Those who believe government usually acts benevolently will not worry about such extensive oversight and control of political activity. Those who expect abuses when government takes total control over anything—and especially over campaigns—will worry.

Competition

Over the past 40 years, the percentage of the vote an incumbent member of Congress receives simply for being an incumbent has risen from 2 percent to 6 or 7 percent. Similar increases in the advantages of incumbency have been observed in executive and legislature elections in the states. Advocates of government subsidies say the need to raise large sums to challenge an incumbent explains why incumbents are hard to challenge. Government financing, they say, would overcome this barrier to entry by giving challengers tax money leading to a more competitive system.

Much depends on who designs the system of government financing. Spending levels strongly influence the competitiveness of challengers to incumbents. If a challenger can spend enough to make his name and causes known, a government financing scheme might foster more competition. If legislatures enact the system, of course, incumbents will design and pass the law. They will be tempted to set spending limits low to favor their own reelections. For example, in 1997, Congress debated a government financing proposal that included spending caps: every challenger spending less than the proposed limits in Senate campaigns in 1994 and 1996 had lost; every incumbent spending less than the limits had won. Similarly, in the House, 3 percent of the challengers spending less than the proposed limits won in 1996, while 40 percent of the incumbents under the limits won.

Such legislative design issues may explain why government financing of campaigns has not *in fact* increased the competitiveness of elections. The leading study of government financing in the states concluded, "There is no evidence to support the claim that programs combining public funding with spending limits have leveled the playing field, countered the effects of incumbency, and made elections more competitive." Believing that government financing will increase competitiveness seems to be a triumph of hope over experience. . . .

Experience indicates that government financing tends to favor certain types of candidates. The political scientists Michael Malbin and Thomas Gais found sharp partisan differences in candidate participation. They studied gubernatorial elections in 11 states from 1993 to 1996 and found that 82 percent of Democratic candidates took taxpayer funding, while only 55 percent of Republican candidates participated. Their data on legislative elections in Minnesota and Wisconsin show a similar partisan divide. Malbin and Gais attribute these partisan variations to the libertarianism of Republicans: candidates who philosophically oppose government subsidies often do not accept them. In other words, government financing in practice provides an advantage to nonlibertarian candidates.

Full government financing of campaigns in Arizona and Maine tells a similar story. In the 2000 election in Arizona, 41 percent of Democratic candidates and 50 percent of Green Party candidates received public subsidies for their campaigns; 8 percent of Republicans accepted government money in the general election, while no candidates of the Libertarian Party took the subsidy. In Maine's 2000 election, 43.4 percent of democratic Party candidates chose government financing compared with 24 percent of Republicans.

Government financing of campaigns looks a lot like other political activity by individuals and groups that do not do well in private markets. Declining parts of the economy—say, small farmers and large steel mill owners—want government help to overcome their own mistakes or unfavorable economic changes. Similarly, candidates who have little appeal to voters and campaign contributors seek public subsidies (like farmers) and regulatory protections from competition (like steel mill owners).

Government subsidies for candidates, however, are crucially different from funding for ethanol. Government financing of campaigns takes money from taxpayers and gives it to a subset of all political candidates. For that reason, government financing seems either unnecessary or immoral. It is unnecessary if a taxpayer agrees with the candidate supported by the subsidy; the taxpayer may simply give the money directly to the candidate.

If, however, the taxpayer disagrees with the candidate, taxing him to support that candidate is immoral. An example will make clear the immorality of the policy. Imagine I had the power to force Nick Nyhart, the Executive Director of Public Campaign, to contribute to the Cato Institute, thereby supporting the writing and marketing of the very arguments against government financing you are reading right now. Such compulsion would strike most Americans as wrong. We think individuals should not be forced to support ideas that contravene their deepest commitments, whether those commitments are religious, social, or political. Government financing schemes, however, transfer money from taxpayers to political candidates and their campaigns. Inevitably they force liberals to support conservatives, Democrats to support Republicans, and vice versa.

Advocates of government financing of campaigns employ emotionally charged rhetoric at every turn. They implore us to "reform" the system to root out "corruption" and attain "clean elections." The reality of government financing belies this expansive rhetoric. Such proposals, especially the "clean elections" variant, simply transfer wealth from taxpayers to a preferred set of candidates and causes. That preferred set inevitably excludes candidates who believe forced transfers of wealth are immoral (such as Libertarians and Republican candidates with a libertarian outlook). Not surprisingly, government financing in the states has favored candidates of the left (such as Democrats and third parties like the Greens). For that reason, government financing of campaigns serves private goals through public means. Far from being a reform, government financing offers more "politics as usual," understood as the struggle to obtain special favors from government.

Those who wish to support the candidates and causes favored by government financing may do so now; they need only send their check to the candidate or cause they favor. Government financing forces all taxpayers to financially support candidates they would not otherwise support, candidates whose views they may find repugnant. On the question of government financing of campaigns, Thomas Jefferson should have the last word: "To compel a man to furnish contributions of money for the propagation of opinions which he disbelieves, is sinful and tyrannical."

POSTSCRIPT

Should America Adopt Public Financing of Political Campaigns?

There are four ways in which a country can limit the influence of money in elections: by limiting the amount of money individuals and groups may contribute to a candidate, by limiting the amount of money that can be spent by or on behalf of a candidate, by providing free access to media for candidates and political parties and restricting paid political advertisements, and by public financing of elections. Most established democracies—Great Britain and Western Europe, Canada, Australia, New Zealand, Israel, and Japan—use several of these methods; some employ them all. The United States alone employs only one—restricting contributions to candidates—and allows independent expenditures.

Critics of campaign finance reform, ranging from libertarians to the American Civil Liberties Union, maintain that the government in a free society should not restrict an individual who is prepared to put his money where his mouth is. Supporters of reform argue that every one of the other cited democracies has a much larger turnout of its citizens in national elections, and they believe that this is because citizens believe that the process is fairer when one candidate cannot vastly outspend another.

The Supreme Court decision in *Buckley v. Valeo* in 1976 came down largely on the side of critics of reform, concluding that money is speech, that candidates could not be restricted in their expenditures (although contributors to their campaigns could be restricted), and that independent expenditures (that is, by persons or groups other than the candidates and party) could not be restricted. That decision has been the focus of political debate ever since.

The first major revision of federal campaign finance law in several decades was adopted in 2002 and upheld by the Supreme Court the following year. It eliminated so-called "soft money" expenditures by the political parties that had not counted as campaign expenses because they did not expressly endorse a candidate. New campaign strategies were adopted by the parties, resulting in record expenditures in the 2004 presidential and congressional elections.

Diana Dwyre and Victoria A. Farrar-Myers followed the course of campaign finance reform through Congress in *Legislative Labyrinth: Congress and Campaign Finance Reform* (Congressional Quarterly Press, 2001). The authors explored the impact of the president, interest groups, and the media, as well as the roles of congressional sponsors and opponents, providing insight into how Congress grapples with an issue of paramount importance to its members.

Most studies do not attempt to achieve objectivity, and tend to support extreme positions, as the titles of two books suggest. Darrell M. West strongly supports public finance in *Checkbook Democracy: How Money Corrupts Political Campaigns* (Northeastern University Press, 2000). In total opposition to reform, Bradley Smith offers a vigorous critique in *Unfree Speech: The Folly of Campaign Finance Reform* (Princeton University Press, 2001), contending that all restrictions on campaign contributions should be eliminated. In *Sold to the Highest Bidder: The Presidency from Dwight D. Eisenhower to George W. Bush* (Prometheus Books, 2002), Daniel M. Friedenberg contends that "money controls the actions of both the executive and legislative branches of our government on the federal and state levels."

The most comprehensive overall examination of the role of money in elections is in *The New Campaign Finance Sourcebook*, by Anthony Corrado, Thomas E. Mann, Daniel R. Ortiz, and Trevor Potter (Brookings Institution, 2005). The authors conclude that campaign finance reform will always be a work in progress, dealing with but never resolving the inherent problems of money in politics.

On the Internet . . .

In addition to the Internet sites listed below, type in key words, such as "American federalism," "commerce power," "presidential appointments," and "government regulation," to find other listings.

U.S. House of Representatives

This page of the U.S. House of Representatives will lead you to information about current and past House members and agendas, the legislative process, and so on. You can learn about events on the House floor as they happen.

http://www.house.gov

The United States Senate

This page of the U.S. Senate will lead you to information about current and past Senate members and agendas, legislative activities, committees, and so on.

http://www.senate.gov

The White House

Visit the White House page for direct access to information about commonly requested federal services, the White House Briefing Room, and the presidents and vice presidents. The Virtual Library allows you to search White House documents, listen to speeches, and view photos.

http://www.whitehouse.gov/index.html

Supreme Court Collection

Open this Legal Information Institute (LII) site for current and historical Information about the Supreme Court. The LII archive contains many opinions issued since May 1990 as well as a collection of nearly 600 of the most historic decisions of the Court.

http://supct.law.cornell.edu/supct/index.html

National Security Agency

Find out more about the agency that has been at the center of controversy over the President's power to intercept telecommunications in and out of the country. In its home page it explains its many functions, relates its storied past in breaking the Japanese code during World War II, and boasts its continued role "in keeping the United States a step ahead of its enemies." It contains links to fourteen other federal agencies, including the C.I.A., the Defense Intelligence Agency, and the National Reconnaissance Office.

http://www.nsa.gov/about/index.cfm

PART 2

The Institutions of Government

*T*he Constitution creates a division of power between the national government and the states, and within the national government power is further divided between three branches: Congress, the President, and the federal courts, each of which can exercise checks upon the others. To what extent can any branch of government inhibit the exercise of power by the other branches? What dangers are there that a particular branch may abuse its legitimate powers, and are there means of countering that danger? These issues have existed since the beginning of our nation, and they are likely to continue.

- Is Congress Barred From Regulating Commerce Within a State?
- Should the Courts Seek the "Original Meaning" of the Constitution?
- May the President Wiretap Without a Warrant to Protect National Security?

ISSUE 6

Is Congress Barred from Regulating Commerce Within a State?

YES: William H. Rehnquist, from Majority Opinion, *United States v. Lopez,* U.S. Supreme Court (April 26, 1995)

NO: Stephen G. Breyer, from Dissenting Opinion, *United States v. Lopez,* U.S. Supreme Court (April 26, 1995)

ISSUE SUMMARY

YES: Supreme Court Chief Justice William H. Rehnquist argues that Congress cannot regulate activities within a state that are not economic and do not substantially affect commerce among the states.

NO: Supreme Court Justice Stephen G. Breyer upholds the right of Congress to regulate activities within a state if Congress has a rational basis for believing that it affects the exercise of congressional power.

Federalism—the division of power between the national government and the states—is a central principle of American government. It is evident in the country's name, the United States of America.

The 13 founding states, long separated as British colonies and later cherishing their hard-earned independence, found it necessary to join together for economic stability and military security, but they would not surrender all of their powers to an unknown and untested national government. Many expressed fear of centralized tyranny as well as the loss of state sovereignty.

To reduce those fears, the Framers of the Constitution sought to limit the action of the new government to defined powers. Article 1, Section 8, of the Constitution enumerates the powers granted to Congress, implicitly denying any other. The grants of national power were stated in very general terms to enable the new government to act in unforeseen circumstances. Recognizing that they could not anticipate how powers would be exercised, the Framers added that the national government could make all laws that were "necessary and proper" to execute its constitutional powers.

Even after the Constitution was ratified, the surviving fear of the proposed Constitution's critics that a too-powerful national government might undermine the powers of the states led to incorporation of the Tenth Amendment into the Bill of Rights. It states that powers not enumerated in the Constitution as belonging to the national government belong to the states and the people.

In the first important test of federalism, *McCulloch v. Maryland* (1819), Chief Justice John Marshall wrote, "If any one proposition could command the universal assent of mankind, we might expect it to be this—that the government of the Union, though limited in its powers, is supreme within its sphere of action." Forthright as that sounds, precisely what that sphere of action is has never been definitively decided.

For more than two centuries, the constitutional debate between the two levels of government has focused principally on Congress's powers to regulate commerce among the states and to tax and spend for the general welfare. The greatest challenges to states' rights developed when the national government, in the administrations of Presidents Woodrow Wilson and Franklin D. Roosevelt, began to regulate activities once thought to be wholly within the power of the states. The U.S. Supreme Court declared unconstitutional laws that they thought exceeded the bounds of national power.

The Supreme Court did an about-face in 1941 when it unanimously upheld a federal minimum wage law and reduced the Tenth Amendment to "a truism that all is retained which has not been surrendered." For more than 50 years, it appeared that the Supreme Court would sanction no limits on national power except those explicitly stated in the Constitution, as in the Bill of Rights.

In recent years a more conservative Court has reestablished some limits. In the 1990s it ruled that Congress cannot compel the states to enact and enforce legislation carrying out the will of Congress. More far-reaching is the Supreme Court's 1995 decision in *United States v. Lopez*. In 1990 Congress had outlawed the possession of guns in or near a school. In a five-to-four decision, the Supreme Court concluded that Congress cannot regulate within a state without demonstrating the substantial effect of the regulated activities on commerce among the states. In 2000 the same narrow majority declared unconstitutional a federal law that permitted victims of rape, domestic violence, and other crimes "motivated by gender" to seek remedies in federal courts. Chief Justice William H. Rehnquist declared that "the Constitution requires a distinction between what is truly national and what is truly local." In 2002 the same five-member majority again upheld the claims of a state against the federal government. The Eleventh Amendment forbids private parties to sue states in federal court, but the majority has now extended state "sovereign immunity" to cover proceedings before federal regulatory agencies.

In the following selections from *United States v. Lopez,* Chief Justice Rehnquist, in his majority opinion, concludes that the law barring guns within the vicinity of a school was too far removed from Congress's commerce power or any other valid national power. Associate Justice Stephen G. Breyer, dissenting with three other justices, argues that reducing the risk of violence in education is a valid exercise of congressional power.

YES

William H. Rehnquist

Majority Opinion

United States *v.* Lopez

Chief Justice Rehnquist delivered the opinion of the Court.

In the Gun-Free School Zones Act of 1990, Congress made it a federal offense "for any individual knowingly to possess a firearm at a place that the individual knows, or has reasonable cause to believe, is a school zone." The Act neither regulates a commercial activity nor contains a requirement that the possession be connected in any way to interstate commerce. We hold that the Act exceeds the authority of Congress "[t]o regulate Commerce . . . among the several States. . . ." U.S. Const., Art. I, § 8, cl. 3.

On March 10, 1992, respondent, who was then a 12th-grade student, arrived at Edison High School in San Antonio, Texas, carrying a concealed .38-caliber handgun and five bullets. Acting upon an anonymous tip, school authorities confronted respondent, who admitted that he was carrying the weapon. He was arrested and charged under Texas law with firearm possession on school premises. The next day, the state charges were dismissed after federal agents charged respondent by complaint with violating the Gun-Free School Zones Act of 1990. 18 U.S.C. § 922(q)(1)(A) (1988 ed., Supp. V).[1]

A federal grand jury indicted respondent on one count of knowing possession of a firearm at a school zone, in violation of § 922(q). Respondent moved to dismiss his federal indictment on the ground that § 922(q) "is unconstitutional as it is beyond the power of Congress to legislate control over our public schools." The District Court denied the motion, concluding that § 922(q) "is a constitutional exercise of Congress' well-defined power to regulate activities in and affecting commerce, and the 'business' of elementary, middle and high schools . . . affects interstate commerce." Respondent waived his right to a jury trial. The District Court conducted a bench trial, found him guilty of violating § 922(q), and sentenced him to six months' imprisonment and two years' supervised release.

On appeal, respondent challenged his conviction based on his claim that § 922(q) exceeded Congress' power to legislate under the Commerce Clause. The Court of Appeals for the Fifth Circuit agreed and reversed respondent's conviction. It held that, in light of what it characterized as insufficient congressional findings and legislative history, "section § 922(q), in the full reach of its terms, is invalid as beyond the power of Congress under the Commerce

From *United States v. Lopez*, 514 U.S. 549 (1995). Some notes, references, and case citations omitted.

Clause." Because of the importance of the issue, we granted certiorari, 511 U.S. 1029 (1994), and we now affirm.

We start with first principles. The Constitution creates a Federal Government of enumerated powers. See Art. I, § 8. As James Madison wrote, "The powers delegated by the proposed Constitution to the federal government are few and defined. Those which are to remain in the State governments are numerous and indefinite." The Federalist No. 45. . . .

The Constitution delegates to Congress the power "[t]o regulate Commerce with foreign Nations, and among the several States, and with the Indian Tribes." Art. I, § 8, cl. 3. The Court, through Chief Justice Marshall, first defined the nature of Congress' commerce power in *Gibbons v. Ogden*, 9 Wheat. 1, 189–190 (1824):

> "Commerce, undoubtedly, is traffic, but it is something more: it is intercourse. It describes the commercial intercourse between nations, and parts of nations, in all its branches, and is regulated by prescribing rules for carrying on that intercourse."

The commerce power "is the power to regulate; that is, to prescribe the rule by which commerce is to be governed. This power, like all others vested in Congress, is complete in itself, may be exercised to its utmost extent, and acknowledges no limitations, other than are prescribed in the constitution." *Id.*, at 196. The *Gibbons* Court, however, acknowledged that limitations on the commerce power are inherent in the very language of the Commerce Clause.

> "It is not intended to say that these words comprehend that commerce, which is completely internal, which is carried on between man and man in a State, or between different parts of the same State, and which does not extend to or affect other States. Such a power would be inconvenient, and is certainly unnecessary.
>
> "Comprehensive as the word 'among' is, it may very properly be restricted to that commerce which concerns more States than one. . . . The enumeration presupposes something not enumerated; and that something, if we regard the language, or the subject of the sentence, must be the exclusively internal commerce of a State." *Id.*, at 194–195.

For nearly a century thereafter, the Court's Commerce Clause decisions dealt but rarely with the extent of Congress' power, and almost entirely with the Commerce Clause as a limit on state legislation that discriminated against interstate commerce. Under this line of precedent, the Court held that certain categories of activity such as "production," "manufacturing," and "mining" were within the province of state governments, and thus were beyond the power of Congress under the Commerce Clause.

In 1887, Congress enacted the Interstate Commerce Act, and in 1890, Congress enacted the Sherman Antitrust Act. These laws ushered in a new era of federal regulation under the commerce power. When cases involving these laws first reached this Court, we imported from our negative Commerce Clause cases the approach that Congress could not regulate activities such as "production," "manufacturing," and "mining." Simultaneously, however, the

Court held that, where the interstate and intrastate aspects of commerce were so mingled together that full regulation of interstate commerce required incidental regulation of intrastate commerce, the Commerce Clause authorized such regulation.

In *A. L. A. Schecter Poultry Corp. v. United States,* 295 U.S. 495, 550 (1935), the Court struck down regulations that fixed the hours and wages of individuals employed by an intrastate business because the activity being regulated related to interstate commerce only indirectly. In doing so, the Court characterized the distinction between direct and indirect effects of intrastate transactions upon interstate commerce as "a fundamental one, essential to the maintenance of our constitutional system." Activities that affected interstate commerce directly were within Congress' power; activities that affected interstate commerce indirectly were beyond Congress' reach. The justification for this formal distinction was rooted in the fear that otherwise "there would be virtually no limit to the federal power and for all practical purposes we should have a completely centralized government."

Two years later, in the watershed case of *NLRB v. Jones & Laughlin Steel Corp.,* 301 U.S. 1 (1937), the Court upheld the National Labor Relations Act against a Commerce Clause challenge, and in the process, departed from the distinction between "direct" and "indirect" effects on interstate commerce. The Court held that intrastate activities that "have such a close and substantial relation to interstate commerce that their control is essential or appropriate to protect that commerce from burdens and obstructions" are within Congress' power to regulate.

In *United States v. Darby,* 312 U.S. 100 (1941), the Court upheld the Fair Labor Standards Act, stating:

> "The power of Congress over interstate commerce is not confined to the regulation of commerce among the states. It extends to those activities intrastate which so affect interstate commerce or the exercise of the power of Congress over it as to make regulation of them appropriate means to the attainment of a legitimate end, the exercise of the granted power of Congress to regulate interstate commerce."

In *Wickard v. Filburn,* the Court upheld the application of amendments to the Agricultural Adjustment Act of 1938 to the production and consumption of home-grown wheat. 317 U.S., at 128–129. The *Wickard* Court explicitly rejected earlier distinctions between direct and indirect effects on interstate commerce, stating:

> "[E]ven if appellee's activity be local and though it may not be regarded as commerce, it may still, whatever its nature, be reached by Congress if it exerts a substantial economic effect on interstate commerce, and this irrespective of whether such effect is what might at some earlier time have been defined as 'direct' or 'indirect.'" *Id.,* at 125.

The *Wickard* Court emphasized that although Filburn's own contribution to the demand for wheat may have been trivial by itself, that was not "enough to remove him from the scope of federal regulation where, as here, his contribution, taken together with that of many others similarly situated, is far from trivial."

Jones & Laughlin Steel, Darby, and *Wickard* ushered in an era of Commerce Clause jurisprudence that greatly expanded the previously defined authority of Congress under that Clause. In part, this was a recognition of the great changes that had occurred in the way business was carried on in this country. Enterprises that had once been local or at most regional in nature had become national in scope. But the doctrinal change also reflected a view that earlier Commerce Clause cases artificially had constrained the authority of Congress to regulate interstate commerce.

But even these modern-era precedents which have expanded congressional power under the Commerce Clause confirm that this power is subject to outer limits. In *Jones & Laughlin Steel,* the Court warned that the scope of the interstate commerce power "must be considered in the light of our dual system of government and may not be extended so as to embrace effects upon interstate commerce so indirect and remote that to embrace them, in view of our complex society, would effectually obliterate the distinction between what is national and what is local and create a completely centralized government." Since that time, the Court has heeded that warning and undertaken to decide whether a rational basis existed for concluding that a regulated activity sufficiently affected interstate commerce.

Similarly, in *Maryland v. Wirtz,* 392 U.S. 183 (1968), the Court reaffirmed that "the power to regulate commerce, though broad indeed, has limits" that "[t]he Court has ample power" to enforce. In response to the dissent's warnings that the Court was powerless to enforce the limitations on Congress' commerce powers because "[a]ll activities affecting commerce, even in the minutest degree, may be regulated and controlled by Congress," the *Wirtz* Court replied that the dissent had misread precedent as "[n]either here nor in *Wickard* has the Court declared that Congress may use a relatively trivial impact on commerce as an excuse for broad general regulation of state or private activities." Rather, "[t]he Court has said only that where *a general regulatory statute bears a substantial relation to commerce,* the *de minimis* character of individual instances arising under that statute is of no consequence." (emphasis added).

Consistent with this structure, we have identified three broad categories of activity that Congress may regulate under its commerce power. First, Congress may regulate the use of the channels of interstate commerce. Second, Congress is empowered to regulate and protect the instrumentalities of interstate commerce, or persons or things in interstate commerce, even though the threat may come only from intrastate activities. Finally, Congress' commerce authority includes the power to regulate those activities having a substantial relation to interstate commerce, *Jones & Laughlin Steel,* 301 U.S., at 37, i.e., those activities that substantially affect interstate commerce.

Within this final category, admittedly, our case law has not been clear whether an activity must "affect" or "substantially affect" interstate commerce in order to be within Congress' power to regulate it under the Commerce

Clause. We conclude, consistent with the great weight of our case law, that the proper test requires an analysis of whether the regulated activity "substantially affects" interstate commerce.

We now turn to consider the power of Congress, in the light of this framework, to enact § 922(q). The first two categories of authority may be quickly disposed of: § 922(q) is not a regulation of the use of the channels of interstate commerce, nor is it an attempt to prohibit the interstate transportation of a commodity through the channels of commerce; nor can § 922(q) be justified as a regulation by which Congress has sought to protect an instrumentality of interstate commerce or a thing in interstate commerce. Thus, if § 922(q) is to be sustained, it must be under the third category as a regulation of an activity that substantially affects interstate commerce.

First, we have upheld a wide variety of congressional Acts regulating intrastate economic activity where we have concluded that the activity substantially affected interstate commerce. Examples include the regulation of intrastate coal mining, intrastate extortionate credit transactions, restaurants utilizing substantial interstate supplies, inns and hotels catering to interstate guests, and production and consumption of home-grown wheat. These examples are by no means exhaustive, but the pattern is clear. Where economic activity substantially affects interstate commerce, legislation regulating that activity will be sustained.

Even *Wickard,* which is perhaps the most far reaching example of Commerce Clause authority over intrastate activity, involved economic activity in a way that the possession of a gun in a school zone does not. Roscoe Filburn operated a small farm in Ohio, on which, in the year involved, he raised 23 acres of wheat. It was his practice to sow winter wheat in the fall, and after harvesting it in July to sell a portion of the crop, to feed part of it to poultry and livestock on the farm, to use some in making flour for home consumption, and to keep the remainder for seeding future crops. The Secretary of Agriculture assessed a penalty against him under the Agricultural Adjustment Act of 1938 because he harvested about 12 acres more wheat than his allotment under the Act permitted. The Act was designed to regulate the volume of wheat moving in interstate and foreign commerce in order to avoid surpluses and shortages, and concomitant fluctuation in wheat prices, which had previously obtained. . . .

Section § 922(q) is a criminal statute that by its terms has nothing to do with "commerce" or any sort of economic enterprise, however broadly one might define those terms. Section § 922(q) is not an essential part of a larger regulation of economic activity, in which the regulatory scheme could be undercut unless the intrastate activity were regulated. It cannot, therefore, be sustained under our cases upholding regulations of activities that arise out of or are connected with a commercial transaction, which viewed in the aggregate, substantially affects interstate commerce.

. . . The Government argues that possession of a firearm in a school zone may result in violent crime and that violent crime can be expected to affect the functioning of the national economy in two ways. First, the costs of violent crime are substantial, and, through the mechanism of insurance, those costs are spread throughout the population. Second, violent crime reduces the willingness of individuals to travel to areas within the country that are perceived to be unsafe. The Government also argues that the presence of guns in schools poses a substantial threat to the educational process by threatening the learning environment. A handicapped educational process, in turn, will result in a less productive citizenry. That, in turn, would have an adverse effect on the Nation's economic well-being. As a result, the Government argues that Congress could rationally have concluded that § 922(q) substantially affects interstate commerce.

We pause to consider the implications of the Government's arguments. The Government admits, under its "costs of crime" reasoning, that Congress could regulate not only all violent crime, but all activities that might lead to violent crime, regardless of how tenuously they relate to interstate commerce. Similarly, under the Government's "national productivity" reasoning, Congress could regulate any activity that it found was related to the economic productivity of individual citizens: family law (including marriage, divorce, and child custody), for example. Under the theories that the Government presents in support of § 922(q), it is difficult to perceive any limitation on federal power, even in areas such as criminal law enforcement or education where States historically have been sovereign. Thus, if we were to accept the Government's arguments, we are hard-pressed to posit any activity by an individual that Congress is without power to regulate.

Although Justice Breyer argues that acceptance of the Government's rationales would not authorize a general federal police power, he is unable to identify any activity that the States may regulate but Congress may not. Justice Breyer posits that there might be some limitations on Congress' commerce power, such as family law or certain aspects of education. These suggested limitations, when viewed in light of the dissent's expansive analysis, are devoid of substance.

Justice Breyer focuses, for the most part, on the threat that firearm possession in and near schools poses to the educational process and the potential economic consequences flowing from that threat. Specifically, the dissent reasons that (1) gun-related violence is a serious problem; (2) that problem, in turn, has an adverse effect on classroom learning; and (3) that adverse effect on classroom learning, in turn, represents a substantial threat to trade and commerce. This analysis would be equally applicable, if not more so, to subjects such as family law and direct regulation of education.

For instance, if Congress can, pursuant to its Commerce Clause power, regulate activities that adversely affect the learning environment, then, *a fortiori*, it also can regulate the educational process directly. Congress could determine that a school's curriculum has a "significant" effect on the extent of classroom learning. As a result, Congress could mandate a federal curriculum for local elementary and secondary schools because what is taught in local schools has a significant "effect on classroom learning," and that, in turn, has a substantial effect on interstate commerce.

Justice Breyer rejects our reading of precedent and argues that "Congress . . . could rationally conclude that schools fall on the commercial side of the line." Justice Breyer's rationale lacks any real limits because, depending on the level of generality, any activity can be looked upon as commercial. Under the dissent's rationale, Congress could just as easily look at child rearing as "fall[ing] on the commercial side of the line" because it provides a "valuable service—namely, to equip [children] with the skills they need to survive in life and, more specifically, in the workplace." . . .

The possession of a gun in a local school zone is in no sense an economic activity that might, through repetition elsewhere, substantially affect any sort of interstate commerce. Respondent was a local student at a local school; there is no indication that he had recently moved in interstate commerce, and there is no requirement that his possession of the firearm have any concrete tie to interstate commerce.

To uphold the Government's contentions here, we would have to pile inference upon inference in a manner that would bid fair to convert congressional authority under the Commerce Clause to a general police power of the sort retained by the States. Admittedly, some of our prior cases have taken long steps down that road, giving great deference to congressional action. The broad language in these opinions has suggested the possibility of additional expansion, but we decline here to proceed any further. To do so would require us to conclude that the Constitution's enumeration of powers does not presuppose something not enumerated, and that there never will be a distinction between what is truly national and what is truly local. This we are unwilling to do.

Note

1.   The term "school zone" is defined as "in, or on the grounds of, a public, parochial or private school" or "within a distance of 1,000 feet from the grounds of a public, parochial or private school." § 921(a)(25).

Dissenting Opinion of Stephen G. Breyer

Justice Breyer, with whom Justice Stevens, Justice Souter, and Justice Ginsburg join, dissenting.

The issue in this case is whether the Commerce Clause authorizes Congress to enact a statute that makes it a crime to possess a gun in, or near, a school. 18 U.S.C. § 922(q)(1)(A) (1988 ed., Supp. V). In my view, the statute falls well within the scope of the commerce power as this Court has understood that power over the last half century.

I

In reaching this conclusion, I apply three basic principles of Commerce Clause interpretation. First, the power to "regulate Commerce . . . among the several States," U.S. Const., Art. I, § 8, cl. 3, encompasses the power to regulate local activities insofar as they significantly affect interstate commerce. As the majority points out, the Court, in describing how much of an effect the Clause requires, sometimes has used the word "substantial" and sometimes has not. . . . And, as the majority also recognizes . . . the question of degree (how *much* effect) requires an estimate of the "size" of the effect that no verbal formulation can capture with precision. I use the word "significant" because the word "substantial" implies a somewhat narrower power than recent precedent suggests. But to speak of "substantial effect" rather than "significant effect" would make no difference in this case.

Second, in determining whether a local activity will likely have a significant effect upon interstate commerce, a court must consider, not the effect of an individual act (a single instance of gun possession), but rather the cumulative effect of all similar instances (*i.e.,* the effect of all guns possessed in or near schools). As this Court put the matter almost 50 years ago:

> "[I]t is enough that the individual activity when multiplied into a general practice . . . contains a threat to the interstate economy that requires preventative regulation."

Third, the Constitution requires us to judge the connection between a regulated activity and interstate commerce, not directly, but at one remove. Courts must give Congress a degree of leeway in determining the existence of

From *United States v. Lopez,* 514 U.S. 549 (1995). Some references and case citations omitted.

a significant factual connection between the regulated activity and interstate commerce—both because the Constitution delegates the commerce power directly to Congress and because the determination requires an empirical judgment of a kind that a legislature is more likely than a court to make with accuracy. The traditional words "rational basis" capture this leeway. Thus, the specific question before us, as the Court recognizes, is not whether the "regulated activity sufficiently affected interstate commerce," but, rather, whether Congress could have had *a rational basis* for so concluding.

I recognize that we must judge this matter independently. "[S]imply because Congress may conclude that a particular activity substantially affects interstate commerce does not necessarily make it so." And, I also recognize that Congress did not write specific "interstate commerce" findings into the law under which Lopez was convicted. Nonetheless, as I have already noted, the matter that we review independently (*i.e.,* whether there is a "rational basis") already has considerable leeway built into it. And, the absence of findings, at most, deprives a statute of the benefit of some *extra* leeway. This extra deference, in principle, might change the result in a close case, though, in practice, it has not made a critical legal difference. It would seem particularly unfortunate to make the validity of the statute at hand turn on the presence or absence of findings. Because Congress did make findings (though not until after Lopez was prosecuted), doing so would appear to elevate form over substance. . . .

II

Applying these principles to the case at hand, we must ask whether Congress could have had a *rational basis* for finding a significant (or substantial) connection between gun-related school violence and interstate commerce. Or, to put the question in the language of the *explicit* finding that Congress made when it amended this law in 1994: Could Congress rationally have found that "violent crime in school zones," through its effect on the "quality of education," significantly (or substantially) affects "interstate" or "foreign commerce"? As long as one views the commerce connection, not as a "technical legal conception," but as "a practical one," the answer to this question must be yes. Numerous reports and studies—generated both inside and outside government—make clear that Congress could reasonably have found the empirical connection that its law, implicitly or explicitly, asserts.

For one thing, reports, hearings, and other readily available literature make clear that the problem of guns in and around schools is widespread and extremely serious. These materials report, for example, that four percent of American high school students (and six percent of inner-city high school students) carry a gun to school at least occasionally; that 12 percent of urban high school students have had guns fired at them; that 20 percent of those students have been threatened with guns; and that, in any 6-month period, several hundred thousand schoolchildren are victims of violent crimes in or near their schools. And, they report that this widespread violence in schools throughout the Nation significantly interferes with the quality of education in those schools. Based on reports such as these, Congress obviously could have thought that guns and learning are mutually exclusive. Congress could therefore have found a substantial educational problem—teachers unable to teach, students unable to learn—and concluded that guns near schools contribute substantially to the size and scope of that problem.

Having found that guns in schools significantly undermine the quality of education in our Nation's classrooms, Congress could also have found, given the effect of education upon interstate and foreign commerce, that gun-related violence in and around schools is a commercial, as well as a human, problem. Education, although far more than a matter of economics, has long been inextricably intertwined with the Nation's economy. When this Nation began, most workers received their education in the workplace, typically (like Benjamin Franklin) as apprentices. As late as the 1920's, many workers still received general education directly from their employers—from large corporations, such as General Electric, Ford, and Goodyear, which created schools within their firms to help both the worker and the firm. As public school enrollment grew in the early 20th century, the need for industry to teach basic educational skills diminished. But, the direct economic link between basic education and industrial productivity remained. Scholars estimate that nearly a quarter of America's economic growth in the early years of this century is traceable directly to increased schooling; that investment in "human capital" (through spending on education) exceeded investment in "physical capital" by a ratio of almost two to one); and that the economic returns to this investment in education exceeded the returns to conventional capital investment.

In recent years the link between secondary education and business has strengthened, becoming both more direct and more important. Scholars on the subject report that technological changes and innovations in management techniques have altered the nature of the workplace so that more jobs now demand greater educational skills. . . .

Increasing global competition also has made primary and secondary education economically more important. The portion of the American economy attributable to international trade nearly tripled between 1950 and 1980, and more than 70 percent of American-made goods now compete with imports. Yet, lagging worker productivity has contributed to negative trade balances and to real hourly compensation that has fallen below wages in 10 other industrialized nations. At least some significant part of this serious productivity problem is attributable to students who emerge from classrooms without the reading or mathematical skills necessary to compete with their European or Asian counterparts. . . .

Finally, there is evidence that, today more than ever, many firms base their location decisions upon the presence, or absence, of a work force with a basic education. . . . In light of this increased importance of education to individual firms, it is no surprise that half of the Nation's manufacturers have become involved with setting standards and shaping curricula for local schools, that 88 percent think this kind of involvement is important, that more than 20 States have recently passed educational reforms to attract new business, and that business magazines have begun to rank cities according to the quality of their schools.

The economic links I have just sketched seem fairly obvious. Why then is it not equally obvious, in light of those links, that a widespread, serious, and substantial physical threat to teaching and learning *also* substantially threatens the commerce to which that teaching and learning is inextricably tied? That is to say, guns in the hands of six percent of inner-city high school students and gun-related violence throughout a city's schools must threaten the trade and commerce that those schools support. The only question, then, is whether the latter threat is (to use the majority's terminology) "substantial." The evidence of (1) the *extent* of the gun-related violence problem, (2) the *extent* of the resulting negative effect on classroom learning, and (3) the *extent* of the consequent negative commercial effects, when taken together, indicate a threat to trade and commerce that is "substantial." At the very least, Congress could rationally have concluded that the links are "substantial." . . .

To hold this statute constitutional is not to "obliterate" the "distinction between what is national and what is local," nor is it to hold that the Commerce Clause permits the Federal Government to "regulate any activity that it found was related to the economic productivity of individual citizens," to regulate "marriage, divorce, and child custody," or to regulate any and all aspects of education. First, this statute is aimed at curbing a particularly acute threat to the educational process—the possession (and use) of life-threatening firearms in, or near, the classroom. The empirical evidence that I have discussed above unmistakably documents the special way in which guns and education are incompatible. This Court has previously recognized the singularly disruptive potential on interstate commerce that acts of violence may have. Second, the immediacy of the connection between education and the national economic well-being is documented by scholars and accepted by society at large in a way and to a degree that may not hold true for other social institutions. It must surely be the rare case, then, that a statute strikes at conduct that (when considered in the abstract) seems to removed from commerce, but which (practically speaking) has so significant an impact upon commerce.

In sum, a holding that the particular statute before us falls within the commerce power would not expand the scope of that Clause. Rather, it simply would apply pre-existing law to changing economic circumstances. It would recognize that, in today's economic world, gun-related violence near the classroom makes a significant difference to our economic, as well as our social, well-being. In accordance with well-accepted precedent, such a holding would permit Congress "to act in terms of economic . . . realities," would interpret the commerce power as "an affirmative power commensurate with the national needs," and would acknowledge that the "commerce clause does not operate so as to render the nation powerless to defend itself against economic forces that Congress decrees inimical or destructive of the national economy." . . .

IV

In sum, to find this legislation within the scope of the Commerce Clause would permit "Congress . . . to act in terms of economic . . . realities." It would interpret the Clause as this Court has traditionally interpreted it, with the exception of one wrong turn subsequently corrected. Upholding this legislation would do no more than simply recognize that Congress had a "rational basis" for finding a significant connection between guns in or near schools and (through their effect on education) the interstate and foreign commerce they threaten. For these reasons, I would reverse the judgment of the Court of Appeals. Respectfully, I dissent.

POSTSCRIPT

Is Congress Barred from Regulating Commerce Within a State?

The difference of views on today's divided Supreme Court may be defined (concededly too simply and neatly) in terms of whether the powers of the states are *reserved,* that is, secure against encroachment or abridgement by Congress or the president, or whether state powers are *residual,* that is, the powers that are left after upholding valid claims of national power.

On the one hand, the historical evidence leaves no doubt that the Constitution was designed to create a national government powerful enough to deal with areas that the states believed required unified action (such as commerce, coinage, and national defense) but not so powerful as to diminish the authority of the states in all other areas. The Constitution's authors went to some pains to define and confine the powers of the new central government.

States' rights theory is founded on a historical proposition: that the states were originally sovereign and that, in the act of forming a Union, they did not surrender their sovereignty. The states formed the nation, acting as states. Delegates to the Convention were chosen by existing states; none were selected by a popular process. They sat in convention as delegates of the states, voting as states, and always aware that the document they were composing would be referred back to the states for their approval. In fact, the Constitution was sent to the states for action by state conventions called by the state legislatures. The approval of nine states was necessary for the Constitution to go into effect, and it could not be made binding on states that had not given their approval. The opening words of the Preamble, "We the people," is a literary substitution for the enumeration of the states, because it would have been impossible and improper to anticipate which states would join the Union.

On the other hand, Chief Justice John Marshall has stated the logic of delegated national power: "Let the end be legitimate, let it be within the scope of the Constitution, and all means which are appropriate, which are plainly adapted to that end, which are not prohibited, but consistent with the letter and spirit of the Constitution, are constitutional." If Congress's exercise of power is valid, no matter how far it extends, the power of the states is reduced by that much.

The constitutional justification for a liberal interpretation of national power can be derived from the critical clauses that, first, allow breadth—the implied powers clause—and then give primacy—the supremacy clause—to the acts of the national government. The Framers deliberately designed a constitutional system in which national power would be explicitly set forth, partly to insure that the requisite power would exist and could be exercised, partly to guard against the assumption of power that was intended to remain within the authority of the states. Without regard to which was greater and which lesser, which more numerous and which less, federal power precedes state power, not in the history of the nation, but in the logic of the Constitution.

The impressive arguments on both sides have been echoed in numerous decisions of the Supreme Court, congressional hearings on proposed national legislation, and works of political scholarship. In *The Delicate Balance: Federalism, Interstate Commerce and Economic Freedom in the Technological Age* (Heritage Foundation, 1998), Adam D. Thierer seeks to redefine and defend federalism in the modern world. Edward B. McLean and other scholars deplore what they call *Derailing the Constitution: The Undermining of American Federalism* (Doubleday, 1997). In *Disunited States* (Basic Books, 1997), John D. Donahue expresses skepticism of the judicial movement toward reducing the exercise of national power.

The judicial shift in the direction of upholding state sovereignty that was marked in *United States v. Lopez* has been the subject of numerous law review articles. A variety of viewpoints are found in the essays by leading legal scholars in Martin Belsky, ed., *The Rehnquist Court: A Retrospective* (Oxford University Press, 2002). Thomas J. Conlan and François Vergniolle de Chantal, "The Rehnquist Court and Contemporary American Federalism," in *Political Science Quarterly*, 116:2 (2001), presents an excellent summary of what the authors describe as a continuing balancing act involving the opposing claims of national and state power. A briefer survey of the movement toward greater state sovereignty, can be found in "Federalism: Reconciling National Values with States' Rights and Local Control in the 21st Century," in the Spring 2001 edition of *Focus on Law Studies*, published by the Division for Public Education of the American Bar Association.

Since *Lopez* was decided, two members of the majority, Chief Justice William Rehnquist and Justice Sandra Day O'Connor, retired and were replaced by Chief Justice John Roberts and Justice Samuel Alito. Other changes in the future are likely to signal changes in the direction of the Supreme Court on federalism.

Despite the learned constitutional and historical arguments, one may harbor the suspicion that where one stands on the balance of power in American federalism often depends less on abstract theory than on practical considerations of public policy. Perhaps there is a more than a coincidental correspondence between positions on civil rights or national welfare legislation and the defense of either the principle of national supremacy or that of states' rights. As long as political differences exist as to whether we should have "more" or "less" national government, the constitutional debate will continue.

ISSUE 7

Should the Courts Seek the "Original Meaning" of the Constitution?

YES: Antonin Scalia, from Remarks at Woodrow Wilson International Center for Scholars (March 14, 2005)

NO: Stephen Breyer, from *Active Liberty: Interpreting Our Democratic Constitution* (Knopf, 2005)

ISSUE SUMMARY

YES: Supreme Court Justice Antonin Scalia rejects the notion of a "living Constitution," arguing that the judges must try to understand what the framers meant at the time.

NO: Supreme Court Justice Stephen Breyer contends that in finding the meaning of the Constitution, judges cannot neglect to consider the probable consequences of different interpretations.

On many matters the United States Constitution speaks with crystal clarity. In Article II, it says that "the Senate of the United States shall be composed of two Senators from each State." Even if it were desirable to have more than two Senators, or less, per state, there is no room for interpretation; "two" can only mean "two," and the only way of making it "one" or "three" is by constitutional amendment. (That process is itself clearly spelled out in Article V of the Constitution.) Other clauses, too, are defined in such a way as to put them beyond interpretative argument. Presidents Reagan and Clinton wanted very much to run again after their two terms, but there was no way either of them could get around the unambiguous words of the Twenty-Second amendment: "No person shall be elected to the office of President more than twice." The same clarity is found in many other provisions in the Constitution, such as the age requirements for Senators, representatives, and Presidents (Articles I and II); direct election of Senators (Amendment XVII); and both Prohibition and its repeal (Amendments XVIII and XXI).

But other clauses in the Constitution are not so clear-cut. The First Amendment states that "Congress shall make no law respecting an establishment of religion. . . ." What is an "establishment of religion"? The Constitution itself does not say. Some constitutional scholars take it to mean that the state may not single out any particular religion for state sponsorship or support; others interpret it to mean that the state may not aid any religions. Which interpretation is correct? And what method do we use to determine which is correct? The same questions have to be asked about other fuzzy-sounding phrases, such as "due process of law" (Article V and Amendment XIV), "cruel and unusual punishment" (Amendment VIII), and "commerce among the several states" (Article I). Down through the years, jurists and legal commentators have tried to devise guiding principles for interpreting these and other phrases that have been subjects of dispute in the courts.

One set of principles made headlines in the 1980s when federal Appeals Court judge Robert Bork was nominated to the Supreme Court by President Ronald Reagan. Bork was a champion of "originalism," interpreting the Constitution according to what he called the "original intent" of its framers. What the courts should do, Bork argued, is to go back to what the framers meant at the time they wrote the particular clauses in dispute. Since the effect of Bork's approach was to call into question some of the more recent decisions by the Court, such as those upholding affirmative action and abortion, his nomination provoked a tumultuous national debate, and in the end he failed to win Senate confirmation.

On its face, originalism seems to comport with common sense. In making a will, to take an analogy, people rightly expect that their will should be interpreted according to *their* intent, not what their heirs might want it to mean. The analogy, however, comes under serious strain when we consider that the Constitution is not, like a will, the product of one person, or even one generation. Its various clauses have been crafted over 220 years; they are the work of many people in various Congresses, and many, many more who ratified them in state conventions or legislatures. Each one of those people may have had a different idea of what those clauses meant. When we come to clauses like "establishment of religion" or "equal protection of the laws," how can we possibly determine what the "original intent" of these clauses was—or even if there was any single intent?

The reply of the originalists is that the goal of determining the framers' intent must be striven for even when it is not perfectly attained. Moreover, what are we going to put in its place? Surely we can't have judges simply making things up, slipping in their own personal policy preferences in place of the Constitution and statutes of the United States.

This is one of the arguments—what he calls the "killer argument"—advanced by Justice Antonin Scalia in the selections that follow. As if replying to him, Justice Stephen Breyer rises to Scalia's challenge by suggesting that in interpreting the Constitution judges should weigh the probable consequences of varying interpretations of disputed clauses in the Constitution.

YES

Antonin Scalia

Constitutional Interpretation

I am one of a small number of judges, small number of anybody:judges, professors, lawyers; who are known as originalists. Our manner of interpreting the Constitution is to begin with the text, and to give that text the meaning that it bore when it was adopted by the people. I'm not a strict constructionist, despite the introduction. I don't like the term "strict construction." I do not think the Constitution, or any text should be interpreted either strictly or sloppily; it should be interpreted reasonably. Many of my interpretations do not deserve the description "strict." I do believe, however, that you give the text the meaning it had when it was adopted.

This is such a minority position in modern academia and in modern legal circles that on occasion I'm asked when I've given a talk like this a question from the back of the room—"Justice Scalia, when did you first become an originalist?"—as though it is some kind of weird affliction that seizes some people—"When did you first start eating human flesh?"

Although it is a minority view now, the reality is that, not very long ago, originalism was orthodoxy. Everybody, at least purported to be an originalist. If you go back and read the commentaries on the Constitution by Joseph Story, he didn't think the Constitution evolved or changed. He said it means and will always mean what it meant when it was adopted.

Or consider the opinions of John Marshall in the Federal Bank case,[*] where he says, we must not, we must always remember it is a constitution we are expounding. And since it's a constitution, he says, you have to give its provisions expansive meaning so that they will accommodate events that you do not know of which will happen in the future.

Well, if it is a constitution that changes, you wouldn't have to give it an expansive meaning. You can give it whatever meaning you want and when future necessity arises, you simply change the meaning. But anyway, that is no longer the orthodoxy.

Oh, one other example about how not just the judges and scholars believed in originalism, but even the American people. Consider the Nineteenth Amendment, which is the amendment that gave women the vote. It was adopted by the American people in 1920. Why did we adopt a constitutional amendment for that purpose? The Equal Protection Clause existed in

---

McCulloch v. Maryland, 4 Wheat, 316 (1819). [*Eds.*]

From a Speech delivered at the Woodrow Wilson International Center for Scholars, March 14, 2005.

1920; it was adopted right after the Civil War. And you know that if that issue of the franchise for women came up today, we would not have to have a constitutional amendment. Someone would come to the Supreme Court and say, "Your Honors, in a democracy, what could be a greater denial of equal protection than denial of the franchise?" And the Court would say, "Yes! Even though it never meant it before, the Equal Protection Clause means that women have to have the vote." But that's not how the American people thought in 1920. In 1920, they looked at the Equal Protection Clause and said, "What does it mean?" Well, it clearly doesn't mean that you can't discriminate in the franchise—not only on the basis of sex, but on the basis of property ownership, on the basis of literacy. None of that is unconstitutional. And therefore, since it wasn't unconstitutional, and we wanted it to be, we did things the good old fashioned way and adopted an amendment.

Now, in asserting that originalism used to be orthodoxy, I do not mean to imply that judges did not distort the Constitution now and then, of course they did. We had willful judges then, and we will have willful judges until the end of time. But the difference is that prior to the last fifty years or so, prior to the advent of the "Living Constitution," judges did their distortions the good old fashioned way, the honest way—they lied about it. They said the Constitution means such and such, when it never meant such and such.

It's a big difference that you now no longer have to lie about it, because we are in the era of the evolving Constitution. And the judge can simply say, "Oh yes, the Constitution didn't used to mean that, but it does now." We are in the age in which not only judges, not only lawyers, but even school children have come to learn the Constitution changes. I have grammar school students come into the court now and then, and they recite very proudly what they have been taught: "The Constitution is a living document." You know, it morphs.

Well, let me first tell you how we got to the "Living Constitution." You don't have to be a lawyer to understand it. The road is not that complicated. Initially, the Court began giving terms in the text of the Constitution a meaning they didn't have when they were adopted. For example, the First Amendment, which forbids Congress to abridge the freedom of speech. What does the freedom of speech mean? Well, it clearly did not mean that Congress, or government could not impose any restrictions upon speech. Libel laws for example, were clearly Constitutional. Nobody thought the First Amendment was *carte blanche* to libel someone. But in the famous case of *New York Times v. Sullivan*, the Supreme Court said, "But the First Amendment does prevent you from suing for libel if you are a public figure and if the libel was not malicious." That is, the person, a member of the press or otherwise, thought that what the person said was true. Well, that had never been the law. I mean, it might be a good law. And some states could amend their libel law.

It's one thing for a states to amend its libel law and say, "We think that public figures shouldn't be able to sue." That's fine. But the courts have said that the First Amendment, which never meant this before, now means that if you are a public figure, that you can't sue for libel unless it's intentional, malicious. So that's one way to do it.

Another example is: the Constitution guarantees the right to be represented by counsel; that never meant the State had to pay for your counsel. But you can reinterpret it to mean that.

That was step one. Step two, I mean, that will only get you so far. There is no text in the Constitution that you could reinterpret to create a right to abortion, for example. So you need something else. The something else is called the doctrine of "Substantive Due Process." Only lawyers can walk around talking about substantive process, inasmuch as it's a contradiction in terms. If you referred to substantive process or procedural substance at a cocktail party, people would look at you funny. But lawyers talk this way all the time.

What substantive due process is, is quite simple, the Constitution has a Due Process Clause, which says that no person shall be deprived of life, liberty or property without due process of law. Now, what does this guarantee? Does it guarantee life, liberty or property? No, indeed! All three can be taken away. You can be fined, you can be incarcerated, you can even be executed, but not without due process of law. It's a procedural guarantee. But the Court said, and this goes way back, in the 1920s at least, in fact the first case to do it was Dred Scott. But it became more popular in the 1920s. The Court said there are some liberties that are so important, that no process will suffice to take them away. Hence, substantive due process.

Now, what liberties are they? The Court will tell you. Be patient. When the doctrine of substantive due process was initially announced, it was limited in this way, the Court said it embraces only those liberties that are fundamental to a democratic society and rooted in the traditions of the American people.

Then we come to step three. Step three: that limitation is eliminated. Within the last twenty years, we have found to be covered by Due Process the right to abortion, which was so little rooted in the traditions of the American people that it was criminal for two hundred years; the right to homosexual sodomy, which was so little rooted in the traditions of the American people that it was criminal for two hundred years.

So it is literally true, and I don't think this is an exaggeration, that the Court has essentially liberated itself from the text of the Constitution, from the text, and even from the traditions of the American people. It is up to the Court to say what is covered by substantive due process. What are the arguments usually made in favor of the Living Constitution? As the name of it suggests, it is a very attractive philosophy, and it's hard to talk people out of it: the notion that the Constitution grows. The major argument is the Constitution is a living organism, it has to grow with the society that it governs or it will become brittle and snap.

This is the equivalent of, an anthropomorphism equivalent to what you hear from your stock broker, when he tells you that the stock market is resting for an assault on the eleven-thousand level. The stock market panting at some base camp. The stock market is not a mountain climber and the Constitution is not a living organism for Pete's sake; it's a legal document, and like all legal documents, it says some things, and it doesn't say other things.

And if you think that the aficionados of the Living Constitution want to bring you flexibility, think again. My Constitution is a very flexible Constitution. You think the death penalty is a good idea: persuade your fellow citizens and adopt it. You think it's a bad idea: persuade them the other way and eliminate it. You want a right to abortion: create it the way most rights are created in a democratic society. Persuade your fellow citizens it's a good idea, and enact it. You want the opposite, persuade them the other way. That's flexibility. But to read either result into the Constitution is not to produce flexibility, it is to produce what a constitution is designed to produce: rigidity.

Abortion, for example, is offstage, it is off the democratic stage, it is no use debating it, it is unconstitutional. I mean prohibiting it is unconstitutional. I mean it's no use debating it anymore. Now and forever, coast to coast, I guess until we amend the constitution, which is a difficult thing. So, for whatever reason you might like the Living Constitution, don't like it because it provides flexibility.That's not the name of the game.

Some people also seem to like it because they think it's a good liberal thing. That somehow this is a conservative/liberal battle. And conservatives like the old-fashioned originalist Constitution and liberals ought to like the Living Constitution. That's not true either. The dividing line between those who believe in the Living Constitution and those who don't is not the dividing line between conservatives and liberals.

Conservatives are willing to grow the Constitution to cover their favorite causes just as liberals are. And the best example of that is two cases we announced some years ago on the same day, the same morning. One case was *Romer v. Evans*, in which the people of Colorado had enacted an amendment to the State Constitution by plebiscite, which said that neither the State, nor any subdivision of the State would add to the protected statuses against which private individuals cannot discriminate. The usual ones are: race, religion, age, sex, disability and so forth. Would not add sexual preference. Somebody thought that was a terrible idea, and since it was a terrible idea, it must be unconstitutional. Brought a lawsuit, it came to the Supreme Court. And the Supreme Court said, "Yes, it is unconstitutional." On the basis of. . .I don't know. The Sexual Preference Clause of the Bill of Rights, presumably. And the liberals loved it; and the conservatives gnashed their teeth.

The very next case we announced is a case called *BMW v. [Gore]*. Not the [Gore] you think; this is another [Gore]. Mr. Gore had bought a BMW, which is a car supposedly advertised at least as having a superb finish, baked seven times in ovens deep in the Alps, by dwarfs. And his BMW apparently had gotten scratched on the way over. They did not send it back to the Alps, they took a can of spray-paint and fixed it. And he found out about this and was furious, and he brought a lawsuit. He got his compensatory damages, a couple of hundred dollars, the difference between a car with a better paint job and a worse paint job. Plus, $2 million against BMW for punitive damages for being a bad actor, which is absurd of course, so it must be unconstitutional. BMW appealed to my court, and my court said, "Yes, it's unconstitutional." In violation of, I assume, the Excessive Damages Clause of the Bill of Rights. And if excessive punitive damages are unconstitutional, why aren't excessive compensatory damages unconstitutional? So you have a federal question whenever you get a judgment in a civil case. Well, that one the conservatives liked, because conservatives don't like punitive damages, and the liberals gnashed their teeth.

I dissented in both cases because I say, "A pox on both their houses." It has nothing to do with what your policy preferences are; it has to do with what you think the Constitution is.

Some people are in favor of the Living Constitution because they think it always leads to greater freedom. There's just nothing to lose. The evolving Constitution will always provide greater and greater freedom, more and more rights. Why would you think that? It's a two-way street. And indeed, under the aegis of the Living Constitution, some freedoms have been taken away. . . .

Well, I've talked about some of the false virtues of the Living Constitution, let me tell you what I consider its, principal, vices are. Surely the greatest, you should always begin with principal, its greatest vice is its illegitimacy. The only reason federal courts sit in judgment of the constitutionality of federal legislation is not because they are explicitly authorized to do so in the Constitution. Some modern constitutions give the constitutional court explicit authority to review German legislation or French legislation for its constitutionality. Our Constitution doesn't say anything like that. But John Marshall says in *Marbury v. Madison*: look, this is lawyers' work. What you have here is an apparent conflict between the Constitution and the statute. And, all the time, lawyers and judges have to reconcile these conflicts; they try to read the two to comport with each other. If they can't, it's judges' work to decide which ones prevail. When there are two statutes, the more recent one prevails. It implicitly repeals the older one. But when the Constitution is at issue, the Constitution prevails because it is a "superstatute." I mean, that's what Marshall says: it's judges' work.

If you believe, however, that the Constitution is not a legal text, like the texts involved when judges reconcile or decide which of two statutes prevail; if you think the Constitution is some exhortation to give effect to the most fundamental values of the society as those values change from year to year; if you think that it is meant to reflect, as some of the Supreme Court cases say, particularly those involving the Eighth Amendment, if you think it is simply meant to reflect the evolving standards of decency that mark the progress of a maturing society, if that is what you think it is, then why in the world would you have it interpreted by nine lawyers? What do I know about the evolving standards of decency of American society? I'm afraid to ask.

If that is what you think the Constitution is, then *Marbury v. Madison* is wrong. It shouldn't be up to the judges, it should be up to the legislature. We should have a system like the English. Whatever the legislature thinks is constitutional is constitutional. They know the evolving standards of American society, I don't. So in principle, it's incompatible with the legal regime that America has established.

Secondly, and this is the killer argument, I mean, it's the best debater's argument. They say in politics, you can't beat somebody with nobody, it's the same thing with principles of legal interpretation. If you don't believe in originalism, then you need some other principle of interpretation. Being a non-originalist is not enough. You see, I have my rules that confine me. I know what I'm looking for. When I find it, the original meaning of the Constitution, I am handcuffed. If I believe that the First Amendment meant when it was adopted that you are entitled to burn the American flag, I have to come out that way, even though I don't like to come out that way. When I find that the original meaning of the jury trial guarantee is that any additional time you spend in prison which depends upon a fact, must depend upon a fact found by a jury, once I find that's what the jury trial guarantee means, I am handcuffed. Though I'm a law-and-order type, I cannot do all the mean conservative things I would like to do to this society. You got me.

Now, if you're not going to control your judges that way, what other criterion are you going to place before them? What is the criterion that governs the living constitutional judge? What can you possibly use, besides original meaning? Think about that. Natural law? We all agree on that, don't we? The philosophy of John Rawls? That's easy. There really is nothing else. You either tell your judges, "Look, this is a law, like all laws, give it the meaning it had when it was adopted." Or, you tell your judges, "Govern us. You tell us whether people under eighteen, who committed their crimes when they were under eighteen, should be executed. You tell us whether there ought to be an unlimited right to abortion or a partial right to abortion. You make these decisions for us."

I have put this question, you know I speak at law schools with some frequency just to make trouble, and I put this question to the faculty all the time, or incite the students to ask their living constitutional professors. "OK professor, you are not an originalist, what is your criterion?" There is none other.

And finally, this is what I will conclude with, although it is not on a happy note, the worst thing about the Living Constitution is that it will destroy the Constitution. I was confirmed, close to nineteen years ago now, by a vote of nintieight to nothing. The two missing were Barry Goldwater and Jake Garn, so make it a hundred. I was known at that time to be, in my political and social views, fairly conservative. But still, I was known to be a good lawyer, an honest man, somebody who could read a text and give it its fair meaning, had judicial impartiality and so forth. And so I was unanimously confirmed.

Today, barely twenty years later, it is difficult to get someone confirmed to the Court of Appeals. What has happened? The American people have figured out what is going on. If we are selecting lawyers, if we are selecting people to read a text and give it the fair meaning it had when it was adopted, yes, the most important thing to do is to get a good lawyer. If on the other hand, we're picking people to draw out of their own conscience and experience, a new constitution, with all sorts of new values to govern our society, then we should not look principally for good lawyers. We should look principally for people who agree with us, the majority, as to whether there ought to be this right, that right, and the other right. We want to pick people that would write the new constitution that we would want.

And that is why you hear in the discourse on this subject, people talking about moderate, we want moderate judges. What is a moderate interpretation of the text? Halfway between what it really means and what you'd like it to mean? There is no such thing as a moderate interpretation of the text. Would you ask a lawyer, "Draw me a moderate contract?" The only way the word has any meaning is if you are looking for someone to write a law, to write a constitution, rather than to interpret one. The moderate judge is the one who will devise the new constitution that most people would approve of. So for example, we had a suicide case some terms ago, and the Court refused to hold that there is a constitutional right to assisted suicide. We said, "We're not yet ready to say that. Stay tuned, in a few years, the time may come, but we're not yet ready." And that was a moderate decision, because I think most people would not want—if we had gone, looked into that and created a national right to assisted suicide that would have been an immoderate and extremist decision.

I think the very terminology suggests where we have arrived: at the point of selecting people to write a constitution, rather than people to give us the fair meaning of one that has been democratically adopted. And when that happens, when the Senate interrogates nominees to the Supreme Court, or to the lower courts you know, "Judge so and so, do you think there is a right to this in the Constitution? You don't? Well, my constituents think there ought to be, and I'm not going to appoint to the court someone who is not going to find that." When we are in that mode, you realize, we have rendered the Constitution useless, because the Constitution will mean what the majority wants it to mean. The senators are representing the majority. And they will be selecting justices who will devise a constitution that the majority wants.

And that of course, deprives the Constitution of its principle utility. The Bill of Rights is devised to protect you and me against, who do you think? The majority. My most important function on the Supreme Court is to tell the majority to take a walk. And the notion that the justices ought to be selected because of the positions that they will take that are favored by the majority is a recipe for destruction of what we have had for two hundred years.

Stephen Breyer

 **NO**

Active Liberty: *Interpreting Our Democratic* Constitution (Knopf, 2005)

My discussion sees individual constitutional provisions as embodying certain basic purposes, often expressed in highly general terms. It sees the Constitution itself as a single document designed to further certain basic general purposes as a whole. It argues that an understanding of, and a focus upon, those general purposes will help a judge better to understand and to apply specific provisions. And it identifies consequences as an important yardstick to measure a given interpretation's faithfulness to these democratic purposes. In short, focus on purpose seeks to promote active liberty by insisting on interpretations, statutory as well as constitutional, that are consistent with the people's will. Focus on consequences, in turn, allows us to gauge whether and to what extent we have succeeded in facilitating workable outcomes which reflect that will.

Some lawyers, judges, and scholars, however, would caution strongly against the reliance upon purposes (particularly abstractly stated purposes) and assessment of consequences. They ask judges to focus primarily upon text, upon the Framers' original expectations, narrowly conceived, and upon historical tradition. They do not deny the occasional relevance of consequences or purposes (including such general purposes as democracy), but they believe that judges should use them sparingly in the interpretive endeavor. They ask judges who tend to find interpretive answers in those decision-making elements to rethink the problem to see whether language, history, tradition, and precedent by themselves will not yield an answer. They fear that, once judges become accustomed to justifying legal conclusions through appeal to real-world consequences, they will to often act subjectively and undemocratically, substituting an elite's views of good policy for sound law. They hope that language, history, tradition, and precedent will provide important safeguards against a judge's confusing his or her personal, undemocratic notion of what is good for that which the Constitution or statute demands. They tend also to emphasize the need for judicial opinions that set forth their legal conclusions in terms of rules that will guide other institutions, including lower courts.

This view, which I shall call "textualist" (in respect to statutes) or "originalist" (in respect to the Constitution) or "literalist" (shorthand for both), while logically consistent with emphasizing the Constitution's democratic objectives, is not hospitable to the kinds of arguments I have advanced. Nor is it easily reconciled with my illustrations. Why, then, does it not undercut my entire argument?

The answer, in my view, lies in the unsatisfactory nature of that interpretive approach. First, the more "originalist" judges cannot appeal to the Framers themselves in support of their interpretive views. The Framers did not say specifically what factors judges should take into account when they interpret statutes or the Constitution. This is obvious in the case of statutes. Why would the Framers have preferred (1) a system of interpretation that relies heavily on linguistic canons to (2) a system that seeks more directly to find the intent of the legislators who enacted the statute? It is close to obvious in respect to the Constitution. Why would the Farmers, who disagreed even about the necessity of *including* a Bill of Rights in the Constitution, who disagreed about the *content* of that Bill of Rights, nonetheless have agreed about *what school of interpretive thought* should prove dominant in interpreting that Bill of Rights in the centuries to come?

In respect to content, the Constitution itself says that the "enumeration" in the Constitution of some rights "shall not be construed to deny or disparage others retained by the people." Professor Bernard Bailyn concludes that the Framers added this language to make clear that "rights, like law itself, should never be fixed, frozen, that new dangers and needs will emerge, and that to respond to these dangers and needs, rights must be newly specified to protect the individual's integrity and inherent dignity." Given the open-ended nature of *content*, why should one expect to find fixed views about the nature of interpretive practice?

If, however, justification for the literalist's interpretive practices cannot be found in the Framers intentions, where can it be found—other than in an appeal to *consequences*, that is, in an appeal to the presumed beneficial consequences for the law or for the nation that will flow from adopting those practices? And that is just what we find argued. That is to say, literalist arguments often try to show that that approach will have favorable *results*, for example, that it will deter judges from substituting their own views about what is good for the public for those of Congress or for those embodied in the Constitution. They argue, in other words, that a more literal approach to interpretation will better control judicial subjectivity. Thus, while literalists eschew consideration of consequences case by case, their interpretive rationale is consequentialist in this important sense.

Second, I would ask whether it is true that judges who reject literalism necessarily open the door to subjectivity. They do not endorse subjectivity. And under their approach important safeguards of objectivity remain. For one thing, a judge who emphasizes consequences, no less than any other, is aware of the legal precedents, rules, standards, practices, and institutional understanding that a decision will affect. He or she also takes account of the way in which this system of legally related rules, institutions, and practices affects the world.

To be sure, a court focused on consequences may decide a case in a way that radically changes the law. But this is not always a bad thing. For example, after the late-nineteenth-century Court decided *Plessy v. Ferguson*, the case which permitted racial segregation that was, in principle, "separate but equal," it became apparent that segregation did not mean equality but not meant disrespect for members of a minority race and led to a segregated society that was totally unequal, a consequence directly contrary to the purpose and demands of the Fourteenth Amendment. The Court, in *Brown v. Board of Education* and later decisions, overruled *Plessy*, and the law changed in a way that profoundly affected the lives of many.

In any event, to focus upon consequences does not automatically invite frequent dramatic legal change. Judges, including those who look to consequences, understand the human need to plan in reliance upon law, the need for predictability, the need for stability. And they understand that too radical, too frequent legal change has, as a consequence, a tendency to undercut those important law-related human needs. Similarly, each judge's individual need to be consistent over time constrains subjectivity. As Justice O'Connor has explained, a constitutional judge's initial decisions leave "footprints" that the judge, in later decisions, will almost inevitably follow.

Moreover, to consider consequences is not to consider simply whether the consequences of a proposed decision are good or bad, in a particular judge's opinion. Rather, to emphasize consequences is to emphasize consequences related to the particular textual provision at issue. The judge must examine the consequences through the lens of the relevant constitutional value or purpose. The relevant values limit interpretive possibilities. If they are democratic values, they may well counsel modesty or restraint as well. And I believe that when a judge candidly acknowledges that, in addition to text, history, and precedent, consequences also guide his decision-making, he is more likely to be disciplined in emphasizing, for example, constitutionally relevant consequences rether than allowing his own subjectively held values to be outcome determinative. In all these ways, a focus on consequences will itself constrain subjectivity.

Here are examples of how these principles apply. The First Amendment says that "Congress shall make no law respecting an establishment of religion." I recently wrote (in dissent) that this clause prohibits government from providing vouchers to parents to help pay for the education of their children in parochial schools. The basic reason, in my view, is that the clause seeks to avoid among other things the "social conflict, potentially created when government becomes involved in religious education." Nineteenth- and twentieth-century immigration has produced a nation with fifty or more different religions. And that fact made the risk of "social conflict" far more serious after the Civil War and in twentieth-century America than the Framers, with their eighteenth-century experience, might have anticipated. The twentieth-century Supreme Court had held in applicable precedent that, given the changing nature of our society, in order to implement the basic value that the Framers wrote the clause to protect, it was necessary to interpret the clause more broadly than the Framers might have thought likely.

My opinion then turned to consequences. It said that voucher programs, if widely adopted, could provide billions of dollars to religious schools. At first blush, that may seem a fine idea. But will different religious groups become concerned about which groups are getting the money and how? What are the criteria? How are programs being implemented? Is a particular program biased against particular sects, say, because it forbids certain kinds of teaching? Are rival sects failing to live up to the relevant criteria, say, by teaching "civil disobedience" to "unjust laws"? How will claims for money, say, of one religious group against another, be adjudicated? In a society as religiously diverse as ours, I saw in the administration of huge grant programs for religious education the potential for religious strife. And that, it seemed to me, was the kind of problem the First Amendment's religion clauses seek to avoid.

The same constitutional concern—the need to avoid a "divisiveness based upon religion that promoters social conflict"—helped me determine whether the Establishment Clause forbade two public displays of the tables of the Ten Commandments, one inside a Kentucky state courthouse, the other on the grounds of the Texas State Capitol. It is well recognized that Establishment Clause does not allow the government to compel religious practices, to show favoritism among sects or between religion and non-religion, or to promote religion. Yet, at the same time, given the religious beliefs of most Americans, an absolutist approach that would purge all religious references from the public sphere could well promote the very kind of social conflict that the Establishment Clause seeks to avoid. Thus, I thought, the Establishment Clause cannot *automatically* forbid every public display of the Ten Commandments, despite the religious nature of its text. Rather, one must examine the context of the *particular* display to see whether, in that context, the tablets convey the kind of government-endorsed religious message that the Establishment Clause forbids.

The history of the Kentucky courthouse display convinced me and the other members of the Court's majority that the display sought to serve its sponsors' primarily religious objectives and that many of its viewers would understand it as reflecting that motivation. But the context of the Texas display differed significantly. A private civic (and primarily secular) organization had placed the tablets on the Capitol grounds as part of the organization's efforts to combat juvenile delinquency. Those grounds contained seventeen other monuments and twenty-one historical markers, none of which conveyed any religious message and all of which sought to illustrate the historical "ideals" of Texans. And the monument had stood for forty years without legal challenge. These circumstances strongly suggested that the public visiting the Capitol grounds had long considered the tablets' religious message as a secondary part of a broader moral and historical message reflecting a cultural heritage—a view of the display consistent with its promoters' basic objective.

It was particularly important that the Texas display stood uncontested for forty years. That fact indicated, as a practical matter of degree, that (unlike the Kentucky display) the Texas display was unlikely to prove socially divisive. Indeed, to require the display's removal itself would encourage disputes over the the removal of longstanding depictions of the Ten Commandments from public buildings across the nation, thereby creating the very kind of religiously based divisiveness that the Establishment Clause was designed to prevent. By way of contrast, the short and stormy history of the more contemporary Kentucky display revealed both religious motivation and consequent social controversy. Thus, in the two cases, which I called borderline cases, consideration of likely consequences—evaluated in light of the purposes or values embodied within the Establishment Clause—helped produce a legal result: The Clause allowed the Texas display, while it forbade the display in Kentucky.

I am not arguing here that I was right in any of these cases. I am arguing that my opinions sought to identify a critical value underlying the Religion Clauses. They considered how that value applied in modern-day America; they looked for consequences relevant to that value. And they sought to evaluate likely consequences in terms of that value. That is what I mean by an *interpretive approach* that emphasizes consequences. Under that approach language, precedent, constitutional values, and factual circumstances all constrain judicial subjectivity.

Third, "subjectivity" is a two-edged criticism, which the literalist himself cannot escape. The literalist's tools—language and structure, history and tradition—often fail to provide objective guidance in those truly difficult cases about which I have spoken. Will canons of interpretation provide objective answers? One canon tells the court to choose an interpretation that gives every statutory word a meaning. Another permits the court to ignore a word, treating it as surplus, if otherwise the construction is repugnant to the statute's purpose. Shall the court read the statute narrowly as in keeping with the common law or broadly as remedial in purpose? Canons to the left to them, canons to the right of them, which canons shall the judges choose to follow?

. . . Fourth, I do not believe that textualist or originalist methods of interpretation are more likely to produce clear, workable legal rules. But even were they to do so, the advantages of legal rules can be overstated. Rules must be interpreted and applied. Every law student whose class grade is borderline knows that the benefits that rules produce for cases that fall within the heartland are often lost in cases that arise at the boundaries.

. . . Fifth, textualist and originalist doctrines may themselves produce seriously harmful consequences—outweighing whatever risks of subjectivity or uncertainty are inherent in other approaches.

. . . Literalism has a tendency to undermine the Constitution's efforts to create a framework for democratic government—a government that, while protecting basic individual liberties, permits citizens to govern themselves, and to govern themselves effectively. Insofar as a more literal interpretive approach undermines this basic objective, it is inconsistent with the most fundamental original intention of the Framers themselves.

For any or all of these reasons, I hope that those strongly committed to textualist or literalist views—those whom I am almost bound not to convince—are fairly small in number. I hope to have convinced some of the rest that active liberty has an important role to play in constitutional (and statutory) interpretation.

That role, I repeat, does not involve radical change in current professional interpretive methods nor does it involve ignoring the protection the Constitution grants fundamental (negative) liberties. It takes Thomas Jefferson's statement as a statement of goals that the Constitution now seeks to fulfill: "[A]ll men are created equal." They are endowed by their Creator with certain "unalienable Rights." "[T]o secure these Rights, Governments are instituted among Men, *deriving their just powers from the consent of the governed.*" It underscores, emphasizes, or reemphasizes the final democratic part of the famous phrase. That reemphasis, I believe, has practical value when judges seek to assure fidelity, in our modern society, to these ancient and unchanging ideals.

POSTSCRIPT

Should The Courts Seek the "Original Meaning" of the Constitution?

Given their different methods of interpretation, certain cases might pose challenges for both Scalia and Breyer. For Scalia, the tough case would be *Brown v. Board of Education* (1954). Scalia is not about to defend racial segregation or seek to turn back the clock to Jim Crow days in the South. Yet, given his interpretative philosophy, how would he defend the *Brown* decision? The same Congress that passed the Fourteenth Amendment also required streetcars in the District of Columbia to be segregated, showing that the "original intent" of those legislators was certainly not to ban segregation. As for Breyer, if he is concerned about the social effects of any given interpretation, might he not want to reconsider his support for *Roe v. Wade* (1973), a decision that caused deep, bitter divisions in American society?

Ronald Dworkin also rises to Scalia's challenge to come up with a different interpretive approach if "originalism" doesn't work. Dworkin's approach is to lean toward interpretations that increase liberty and equality in America; those are his moral values and he frankly declares that they ought to be read into the Constitution. See his book, *Freedom's Law: The Moral Reading of the American Constitution* (Harvard University Press, 1996). In her book, *A Nation Under Lawyers* (Farrar, Straus, & Girouxs, 1994), Mary Ann Glendon warns of the perils of what she calls "romantic judging." Jamin Raskin's *Overruling Democracy: The Supreme Court Versus the American People* (Routledge, 2003) argues that it is actually the *conservatives* who have taken the most liberties in interpreting the Constitution, offering the decision in *Bush v. Gore* (2000) as the prime example. Phillip J. Cooper's *Battles on the Bench: Conflict Inside the Supreme Court* (University of Kansas Press, 1995) illuminates battles behind the scenes in the Court since John Marshall's time. Jeffrey A. Segal, et al., *The Supreme Court in the Legal System* (Cambridge University Press, 2005) is a comprehensive introduction to the Supreme Court and the lower federal courts.

In the past, sitting Supreme Court Justices have typically been reticent about making strong public statements outside the Court, especially on issues that might come before it. Today that appears to be changing. In a speech before the Federalist society in February of 2006, Justice Scalia continued to criticize those who say that the Constitution is "a living document." "You would have to be an idiot to believe that," he said. In another speech the following month he criticized the idea that detainees captured in the battlefield have full rights under the Constitution or international law, even though the Court was then considering the appeal of a man formerly detained without a jury trial on grounds of being an "enemy combatant." Justice Ruth Ginsberg, too, has not been hesitant to speak her mind outside the Court, decrying Republican efforts in Congress to ban the citation of foreign law in deciding cases. They "fuel the irrational fringe," she said in a February, 2006 speech in South Africa, and claimed that her life was threatened by "commandoes" who posted threats on the Internet. The line between the political and the judicial, never entirely definite, seems to be getting increasingly blurred.

ISSUE 8

May the President Wiretap Without a Warrant to Protect National Security?

YES: Andrew C. McCarthy, from "How to 'Connect the Dots'," *National Review* (January 30, 2006)

NO: Al Gore, from "Restoring the Rule of Law," From a Speech Presented to The American Constitution Society for Law and Policy and The Liberty Coalition (January 15, 2006)

ISSUE SUMMARY

YES: Former federal prosecutor Andrew C. McCarthy supports the National Security Agency program of surveillance without a warrant as an effective means of protecting national security that employs the inherent power of the president to protect the country against subversion.

NO: Former vice president Al Gore views the warrantless wiretapping of American citizens as a brazen violation of the Constitution and of specific acts of Congress that have spelled out the circumstances under which a president may receive judicial permission to wiretap or otherwise invade the privacy of citizens.

Americans overwhelmingly believe in the right to privacy. They subscribe to the old adage that a man's home is his castle (adding that a woman's home is hers). Yet the Constitution makes no explicit mention of a right to privacy. Controversy revolves not around the right to privacy but under what circumstances there are conflicting societal interests that would curtail it.

As it has on earlier occasions, privacy rights became a political issue when, shortly after the terrorist attack on September 11, 2001, on the World Trade Center in New York and the Pentagon in Washington, D.C., President Bush issued a secret executive order authorizing the National Security Agency to conduct warrantless electronic surveillance of telecommunications into and out of the United States of persons who might be linked to al Qaeda or other terrorist organizations. Some NSA surveillance involved persons in the United States.

The classified presidential authorization was made known to select members of the congressional leadership and intelligence committees, but was concealed from public knowledge until *The New York Times* reported it in December 2005, more than a year after it acquired information regarding it. (President Bush's administration had sought to have the newspaper not publish the article.)

The 1978 Foreign Intelligence Surveillance Act (FISA) had barred electronic surveillance of persons within the United States without the approval of a newly established Foreign Intelligence Surveillance Court. Before the public revelation of warrantless wiretapping, President Bush stated, with regard to domestic surveillance, "Constitutional guarantees are in place when it comes to doing what is necessary to protect our homeland, because we value the Constitution." He later maintained that warrantless surveillance was justified in dealing with international communications that threaten nation security, and that such surveillance was implicitly authorized by the 2001 congressional Authorization for Use of Military Force adopted days after 9/11. Supporting the president, some legal authorities argued that Congress cannot interfere with the means and methods the president uses to engage an enemy.

Critics of warrantless wiretapping hold that FISA established a clear and exclusive procedure for authorizing emergency wiretaps. They charge that such wiretaps by the president, when based upon the claim of "inherent authority," risk unauthorized government recording of the communications of a wholly domestic character.

Publication by the *Times* precipitated widespread public debate regarding the right to privacy and the legality of warrantless electronic surveillance of American citizens. Despite later revelations by the *Times* and the *Washington Post*, details of the extent of wiretapping or other secret interception of messages have not been revealed. Defending this silence, White House Press Secretary Scott McClellan said, "There's a reason we don't get into discussing ongoing intelligence activities, because it could compromise our efforts to prevent attacks from happening."

As for the success of warrantless wiretapping, General Michael Hayden, Principal Deputy Director for National Intelligence, stated, "The program has been successful in detecting and preventing attacks inside the United States." Along with administration officials, General Hayden has asserted, "Had this program been in effect prior to 9/11, it is my professional judgment that we would have detected some of the 9/11 Al Qaeda operatives in the United States, and we would have identified them as such."

Many members of both parties disagreed with the president's secret executive action. It is unlikely that all the facts regarding the extent of the program or what it achieved will be known for years, but the constitutional questions require answers.

Former federal prosecutor Andrew McCarthy defends secret surveillance as having been widely used (although sometimes abused) and wholly within the president's power. Former presidential candidate Al Gore believes that this activity is dangerous, unnecessary, and violates the rule of law.

YES

Andrew C. McCarthy

How to 'Connect the Dots'

Washington's scandal *du jour* involves a wartime surveillance program President Bush directed the National Security Agency to carry out after al-Qaeda killed nearly 3,000 Americans on September 11, 2001. The idea that there is anything truly scandalous about this program is absurd. But the outcry against it is valuable, highlighting as it does the mistaken assumption that criminal-justice solutions are applicable to national-security challenges.

The intelligence community has identified thousands of al-Qaeda operatives and sympathizers throughout the world. After Congress overwhelmingly authorized the use of military force immediately following the 9/11 attacks, the president, as part of the war effort, ordered the NSA to intercept the enemy's international communications, even if those communications went into and out of the United States and thus potentially involved American citizens. According to reports from the *New York Times*, which shamefully publicized leaks of the program's existence in mid-December 2005, as many as 7,000 suspected terrorists overseas are monitored at any one time, as are up to 500 suspects inside the U.S.

As is typical of such wartime operations, the NSA program was classified at the highest level of secret information. It was, nevertheless, completely different from the kind of rogue intelligence operations of which the Nixon era is emblematic (though by no means the only case). The Bush administration internally vetted the program, including at the Justice Department, to confirm its legal footing. It reviewed (and continues to review) the program every 45 days. It briefed the bipartisan leadership of Congress (including the intelligence committees) at least a dozen times. It informed the chief judge of the federal Foreign Intelligence Surveillance Court (FISC), the tribunal that oversees domestic national-security wiretapping. And it modified the program in mid-2004 in reaction to concerns raised by the chief judge, national-security officials, and government lawyers.

Far from being a pretextual use of war powers to spy on political opponents and policy dissenters, the NSA program has been dedicated to national security. More to the point, it has saved lives, helping break up at least one al-Qaeda conspiracy to attack New York City and Washington, D.C., in connection with which a plotter named Lyman Faris was sentenced to 20 years' imprisonment.

As potential scandal fodder, so unremarkable did the NSA program seem that the *Times* sat on the story for a year—and a year, it is worth noting, during which it transparently and assiduously sought to exploit any opportunity to discredit the administration and cast it as a mortal threat to civil liberties. The leak was not sprung until the eleventh hour of congressional negotiations over renewal of the Patriot Act—at which point it provided ammunition to those who would gut Patriot's crucial post-9/11 domesticsurveillance powers and simultaneously served as a marketing campaign for *Times* reporter James Risen, who just happened to be on the eve of publishing a book about, among other things, Bush's domestic "spying."

In fact, so obviously appropriate was wartime surveillance of the enemy that Rep. Jane Harman, the ranking Democrat on the House Intelligence Committee, issued a statement right after the *Times* exposed the program, saying: "I have been briefed since 2003 on a highly classified NSA foreign collection program that targeted Al-Qaeda. I believe the program is essential to US national security and that its disclosure has damaged critical intelligence capabilities." (With partisan "scandal" blowing in the wind, Harman changed her tune two weeks later, suddenly deciding that the "essential" program was probably illegal after all.)

⋙◉⋘

If President Bush's reelection is any indication, what most Americans will care about is that we are monitoring the enemy. Chances are they won't be overly interested in knowing whether that monitoring is done on the president's own constitutional authority or in accordance with a statutory scheme calling for judicial imprimatur. Nevertheless, the Left is already indulging in loose talk about impeachment. Even some Republican "moderates," such as Arlen Specter, say the domestic-spying allegations are troubling enough that hearings are warranted. So it's worth asking: What is all the fuss about?

At bottom, it is about a power grab that began nearly three decades ago. Ever since it became technologically possible to intercept wire communications, presidents have done so. All of them, going back to FDR, claimed that the powers granted to the chief executive under Article II of the Constitution allowed them to conduct such wiretapping for national-security purposes. Particularly in wartime, this power might be thought indisputable. The president is the commander in chief of the armed forces, and penetrating enemy communications is as much an incident of war-fighting as bombing enemy targets is.

But surveillance power has been abused—and notoriously by President Nixon, whose eavesdropping on political opponents was the basis of a draft article of impeachment. Watergate-era domestic-spying controversies dovetailed with important developments in the law of electronic surveillance. In 1967, the Supreme Court, in *Katz* v. *United States*, held that Fourth Amendment protection against unreasonable searches extended to electronic surveillance—meaning that eavesdropping without a judicial warrant was now presumptively unconstitutional. Congress followed by enacting a comprehensive scheme, known as "Title

III," that required law-enforcement agents to obtain a court warrant for probable cause of a crime before conducting electronic surveillance. Yet both *Katz* and Title III recognized inherent presidential authority to conduct *national-security* monitoring without being bound by the new warrant requirement.

The Supreme Court undertook to circumscribe this inherent authority in its 1972 *Keith* decision. It held that a judicial warrant was required for national-security surveillance if the target was a purely *domestic* threat—the Vietnam-era Court giving higher priority to the free-speech interests of "those suspected of unorthodoxy in their political beliefs" than to the safety of those who might be endangered by domestic terrorists. Still, the Court took pains to exempt from its ruling the "activities of *foreign* powers or their agents" (emphasis added).

The true power grab occurred in 1978, when Congress enacted the Foreign Intelligence Surveillance Act. FISA attempted to do in the national-security realm what Title III had done in law enforcement: erect a thorough-going legal regime for domestic eavesdropping. And therein lies the heart of the current dispute. If the president has inherent authority to conduct national-security wiretapping, it is a function of his constitutional warrant. It is not a function of Congress's having failed until 1978 to flex its own muscles. A constitutional power cannot be altered or limited by statute. Period.

But limiting presidential authority is precisely what FISA purports to do. It ostensibly prohibits national-security eavesdropping (and, since 1994, physical searches) unless the executive branch can satisfy a federal judge—one of eleven who sit on a specially created Foreign Intelligence Surveillance Court—that there is probable cause that the subject it seeks to monitor is an "agent of a foreign power" (generally either a spy or a member of a foreign terrorist organization).

FISA does not aim to restrict the power to eavesdrop on *all* conversations. Communications that are entirely foreign—in that they involve aliens communicating overseas, for example—are exempted, as are conversations that *unintentionally* capture "U.S. persons" (generally, American citizens and permanent resident aliens), as long as these communications are intercepted outside the U.S. But where it does apply, FISA holds that the president—the constitutional officer charged with the nation's security—is powerless to eavesdrop on an operative posing a threat to the United States unless a judge—who need not possess any national-security expertise—is persuaded that the operative is a genuine threat. One suspects that such a system would astonish the Founders.

◦◦◦

Does the NSA program violate FISA? That question is difficult to answer with certainty. The program remains highly classified, and many of its details are not publicly known, nor should they be. Much has been made of the fact that FISA approval is required to intercept calls into or out of the United States if an American is intentionally being targeted. But scant attention has been given to FISA's caveat that such conversations are protected only if their participants have a *reasonable expectation of privacy*. It is difficult to imagine that Americans who make or receive calls to war zones in, say, Afghanistan or Iraq, or to al-Qaeda operatives anywhere, can reasonably expect that no one is listening in.

Nevertheless, it would not be surprising to learn that at least some of the NSA monitoring transgresses the bounds of FISA. For example, the statute mandates—without qualification about the reasonable expectation of privacy— that the government seek a judicial warrant before eavesdropping on any international call to or from the U.S., if that call is intercepted *inside* our borders. A distinction based on where a call is intercepted made sense in 1978. Back then, if a conversation was intercepted inside our borders, its participants were almost certain to include at least one U.S. person. But modern technology has since blurred the distinction between foreign and domestic telephony. Packets of digital information are now routed through switches inside countries (including, predominately, the U.S.) where neither the sender nor the recipient of the call is located. The NSA has capitalized on this evolution, and is now able, from within the U.S., to seize calls between Tikrit and Kabul, or between Peshawar and Hamburg. If done without a warrant, those intercepts present no FISA problem, because all the speakers are overseas. But it's hard to believe that the NSA is using this technology *only* to acquire all-foreign calls, while intercepting calls between, say, New York and Hamburg only from locations *outside* the U.S.

Perhaps that is why the Bush administration's defense has been light on the abstruse details of FISA and heavy on the president's inherent Article II power—although carefully couched to avoid offending Congress and the FISC with suggestions that FISA is at least partly unconstitutional. Essentially, the administration argues that FISA is beneficial in ordinary times and for long-term investigations, but that it did not and cannot repeal the president's independent constitutional obligation to protect the country: an obligation that was explicitly reserved even by President Carter, who signed FISA; that has been claimed by every president since; and that is uniquely vital in a war against thousands of stateless, stealthy terrorists, in which both a "probable cause" requirement and a sclerotic bureaucracy for processing warrant applications would be dangerously impractical.

In advancing this argument, the administration finds much support in the one and only decision ever rendered by the Foreign Intelligence Court of Review—the appellate court created by FISA to review FISC decisions. That decision came in 2002, after a quarter-century of FISA experience. Tellingly, its context was a brazen effort by the FISC to reject the Patriot Act's dismantling of the "wall" that prevented intelligence agents and criminal investigators from pooling information. In overruling the FISC, the Court of Review observed that "all the other courts to have decided the issue [have] held that the President did have inherent authority to conduct warrantless searches to obtain foreign intelligence information." Notwithstanding FISA, the Court thus pronounced: "We take for granted that the President does have that authority."

The administration has also placed great stock in Congress's post-9/11 authorization of "all necessary and appropriate force" against those behind the terrorist attacks. While this resolution did not expressly mention penetrating enemy communications, neither did it explicitly include the detention of enemy combatants, which the Supreme Court, in its 2004 *Hamdi* decision, found implicit in the use-of-force authorization because it is a "fundamental incident of waging war." Capturing intelligence, of course, is as much a component of waging war as capturing operatives. Any other conclusion would lead to the absurdity of the president's having full discretion to kill terrorists but needing a judge's permission merely to eavesdrop on them.

FISA aside, the administration stresses that the NSA program fits comfortably within the Fourth Amendment. That Amendment proscribes *unreasonable* searches, not warrantless ones—and it is thus unsurprising that the Supreme Court has recognized numerous exceptions to the warrant requirement that are of far less moment than the imperative to protect the country from attack. Plainly, there is nothing unreasonable about intercepting potential enemy communications in wartime. Moreover, the courts have long held that searches conducted at the border are part of the sovereign right of self-protection, and thus require neither probable cause nor a warrant. Cross-border communications, which might well be triggers of terror plots, are no more deserving of constitutional protection.

⁕

Critics have made much of a lengthy analysis published on January 6, 2006, by the Congressional Research Service that casts doubt on the administration's core contentions. Media have treated the report as bearing special weight because the CRS is a nonpartisan entity. But that does not mean the CRS is *objective*. "The sole mission of CRS," it explains on its website, "is to serve the United States Congress." Yet the issue at stake is precisely a separation-of-powers dispute.

While the CRS study is an impressive compilation of the relevant law, it resorts to a fairly standard tactic for marginalizing executive power: reliance on the concurring opinion by Supreme Court Justice Robert Jackson in a 1952 case involving President Truman's failed effort to seize steel mills—a move Truman justified by referring to the exigencies of the Korean War. Jackson saw executive power as waxing or waning along a three-stage scale, depending on whether a president acted with the support, the indifference, or the opposition of Congress. On this theory, a statute like FISA could curb a president's inherent constitutional authority. The fatal problem with the Jackson construct, however, has always been that it makes Congress, not the Constitution, the master of presidential authority. It disregards the reality that the executive is a coequal branch whose powers exist whether Congress acts or not. But the CRS prefers Jackson's conveniently airy formula, which failed to command a Court majority, to relevant opinions that don't go Congress's way, such as that of the Foreign Intelligence Court of Review—which, unlike the Supreme Court, was actually considering FISA.

Frustrated by its inability to move public opinion, the Left is now emphasizing the large "volume of information harvested from telecommunication data and voice networks," as the *Times* breathlessly put it, "without court-approved warrants." But this is pure legerdemain. When we refer to "information" from "telecommunication data," we are talking about something that, legally, is worlds apart from the content of telephone calls or e-mail messages.

These data do not include the substance of what people privately say to one another in conversations, but rather comprise statistical facts about the use of telecommunications services (for example, what phone number called another number, the date and time of the call, how long it lasted, etc.). Court warrants have never been required for the acquisition of such information because, as the Supreme Court explained over a quarter-century ago in *Smith* v. *Maryland*, telecommunications data do not implicate the Fourth Amendment. All phone and e-mail users know this information is conveyed to and maintained by service providers, and no one expects it to be private.

Analyzing such data is clearly different from monitoring the calls and e-mails themselves. For our own protection, we should want the government to collect as many of these data as possible (since doing so affects no one's legitimate privacy interests) in order to develop investigative leads. That's how a country manages to go four years without a domestic terror attack.

Yet the Left's rage continues, despite the public's evident disinterest in the mind-numbingly technical nature of the dispute, and despite the obvious truth that the NSA program was a bona fide effort to protect the nation from harm, not to snoop on Americans—only a tiny fraction of whom were affected, and those with apparent good reason. The controversy is a disquieting barometer of elite commitment to the War on Terror. As recently as two years ago, when "connecting the dots" was all the rage, liberals ignored eight years of Clintonian nonfeasance and portrayed the Bush administration as asleep at the switch while terrorists ran amok. Now they ignore President Clinton's insistence on the very same executive surveillance power that the current administration claims and caricature Bush as the imperial president, shredding core protections of civil liberties by exaggerating the terror threat. Either way you slice it, national security becomes a game in which necessary decisions by responsible adults become political grist, and, if they get enough traction, phony scandals. What remains real, though, is the danger to Americans implicit in any system that can't tell a war from a crime.

Al Gore  **NO**

Restoring the Rule of Law

The Executive Branch of the government has been caught eavesdropping on huge numbers of American citizens and has brazenly declared that it has the unilateral right to continue without regard to the established law enacted by Congress to prevent such abuses.

It is imperative that respect for the rule of law be restored.

So, many of us have come here to Constitution Hall to sound an alarm and call upon our fellow citizens to put aside partisan differences and join with us in demanding that our Constitution be defended and preserved.

It is appropriate that we make this appeal on the day our nation has set aside to honor the life and legacy of Dr. Martin Luther King, Jr., who challenged America to breathe new life into our oldest values by extending its promise to all our people.

On this particular Martin Luther King Day, it is especially important to recall that for the last several years of his life. Dr. King was illegally wiretapped—one of hundreds of thousands of Americans whose private communications were intercepted by the U.S. government during this period.

The FBI privately called King the "most dangerous and effective negro leader in the country" and vowed to "take him off his pedestal." The government even attempted to destroy his marriage and blackmail him into committing suicide.

This campaign continued until Dr. King's murder. The discovery that the FBI conducted a long-running and extensive campaign of secret electronic surveillance designed to infiltrate the inner workings of the Southern Christian Leadership Conference, and to learn the most intimate details of Dr. King's life, helped to convince Congress to enact restrictions on wiretapping.

The result was the Foreign Intelligence and Surveillance Act (FISA), which was enacted expressly to ensure that foreign intelligence surveillance would be presented to an impartial judge to verify that there is a sufficient cause for the surveillance. I voted for that law during my first term in Congress and for almost thirty years the system has proven a workable and valued means of according a level of protection for private citizens, while permitting foreign surveillance to continue.

Yet, just one month ago, Americans awoke to the shocking news that in spite of this long settled law, the Executive Branch has been secretly spying on

From a speech by former Vice President Al Gore, "Restoring the Rule of Law," January 16, 2006. The event was co-sponsored by The American Constitution Society for Law and Policy and The Liberty Coalition. Reprinted by permission.

large numbers of Americans for the last four years and eavesdropping on "large volumes of telephone calls, e-mail messages, and other Internet traffic inside the United States." The New York Times reported that the President decided to launch this massive eavesdropping program "without search warrants or any new laws that would permit such domestic intelligence collection."

During tile period when this eavesdropping was still secret, the President went out of his way to reassure the American people on more than one occasion that, of course, judicial permission is required for any government spying on American citizens and that, of course, these constitutional safeguards were still in place.

But surprisingly, the President's soothing statements turned out to be false. Moreover, as soon as this massive domestic spying program was uncovered by the press, the President not only confirmed that the story was true, but also declared that he has no intention of bringing these wholesale invasions of privacy to an end.

At present, we still have much to learn about the NSA's domestic surveillance. What we do know about this pervasive wiretapping virtually compels the conclusion that the President of the United States has been breaking the law repeatedly and persistently.

A president who breaks the law is a threat to the very structure of our government. Our Founding Fathers were adamant that they had established a government of laws and not men. Indeed, they recognized that the structure of government they had enshrined in our Constitution—our system of checks and balances—was designed with a central purpose of ensuring that it would govern through the rule of law. As John Adams said: "The executive shall never exercise the legislative and judicial powers, or either of them, to the end that it may be a government of laws and not of men."

An executive who arrogates to himself the power to ignore the legitimate legislative directives of the Congress or to act free of the check of the judiciary becomes the central threat that the Founders sought to nullify in the Constitution— an all-powerful executive too reminiscent of the King from whom they had broken free. In the words of James Madison, "the accumulation of all powers, legislative, executive, and judiciary, in the same hands, whether of one, a few, or many, and whether hereditary, self-appointed, or elective, may justly be pronounced the very definition of tyranny."

Thomas Paine, whose pamphlet, "On Common Sense" ignited the American Revolution, succinctly described America's alternative. Here, he said, we intended to make certain that "the law is king."

Vigilant adherence to the rule of law strengthens our democracy and strengthens America. It ensures that those who govern us operate within our constitutional structure, which means that our democratic institutions play their indispensable role in shaping policy and determining the direction of our nation. It means that the people of this nation ultimately determine its course and not executive officials operating in secret without constraint.

The rule of law makes us stronger by ensuring that decisions will be tested, studied, reviewed and examined through the processes of government that are designed to improve policy. And the knowledge that they will be reviewed prevents over-reaching and checks the accretion of power.

A commitment to openness, truthfulness and accountability also helps our country avoid many serious mistakes. Recently, for example, we learned from recently classified declassified documents that the Gulf of Tonkin Resolution, which authorized the tragic Vietnam war, was actually based on false information. We now know that the decision by Congress to authorize the Iraq War, 38 years later, was also based on false information. America would have been better off knowing the truth and avoiding both of these colossal mistakes in our history. Following the rule and law makes us safer, not more vulnerable.

The President and I agree on one thing. The threat from terrorism is all too real. There is simply no question that we continue to face new challenges in the wake of the attack on September 11th and that we must be ever-vigilant in protecting our citizens from harm.

Where we disagree is that we have to break the law or sacrifice our system of government to protect Americans from terrorism. In fact, doing so makes us weaker and more vulnerable.

Once violated, the rule of law is in danger. Unless stopped, lawlessness grows. The greater the power of the executive grows, the more difficult it becomes for the other branches to perform their constitutional roles. As the executive acts outside its constitutionally prescribed role and is able to control access to information that would expose its actions, it becomes increasingly difficult for the other branches to police it. Once that ability is lost, democracy itself is threatened and we become a government of men and not laws.

The President's men have minced words about America's laws. The Attorney General openly conceded that the "kind of surveillance" we now know they have been conducting requires a court order unless authorized by statute. The Foreign Intelligence Surveillance Act self-evidently does not authorize what the NSA has been doing, and no one inside or outside the Administration claims that it does. Incredibly, the Administration claims instead that the surveillance was implicitly authorized when Congress voted to use force against those who attacked us on September 11th.

This argument just does not hold any water. Without getting into the legal intricacies, it faces a number of embarrassing facts. First, another admission by the Attorney General: he concedes that the Administration knew that the NSA project was prohibited by existing law and that they consulted with some members of Congress about changing the statute. Gonzalez says that they were told this probably would not be possible. So how can they now argue that the Authorization for the Use of Military Force somehow implicitly authorized it all along? Second, when the Authorization was being debated, the Administration did in fact seek to have language inserted in it that would have authorized them to use military force domestically—and the Congress did not agree. Senator Ted Stevens and Representative Jim McGovern, among others, made statements during the Authorization debate clearly restating that that Authorization did not operate domestically.

When President Bush failed to convince Congress to give him all the power he wanted when they passed the AUMF, he secretly assumed that power anyway, as if congressional authorization was a useless bother. But as Justice Frankfurter once wrote: "To find authority so explicitly withheld is not merely to disregard in a particular instance the clear will of Congress. It is to disrespect the whole legislative process and the constitutional division of authority between President and Congress."

This is precisely the "disrespect" for the law that the Supreme Court struck down in the steel seizure case.

It is this same disrespect for America's Constitution which has now brought our republic to the brink of a dangerous breach in the fabric of the Constitution. And the disrespect embodied in these apparent mass violations of the law is part of a larger pattern of seeming indifference to the Constitution that is deeply troubling to millions of Americans in both political parties. . . .

Whenever power is unchecked and unaccountable it almost inevitably leads to mistakes and abuses. In the absence of rigorous accountability, incompetence flourishes. Dishonesty is encouraged and rewarded.

Last week, for example, Vice President Cheney attempted to defend the Administration's eavesdropping on American citizens by saying that if it had conducted this program prior to 9/11, they would have found out the names of some of the hijackers.

Tragically, he apparently still doesn't know that the Administration did in fact have the names of at least 2 of the hijackers well before 9/11 and had available to them information that could have easily led to the identification of most of the other hijackers. And yet, because of incompetence in the handling of this information, it was never used to protect the American people.

It is often the case that an Executive Branch beguiled by the pursuit of unchecked power responds to its own mistakes by reflexively proposing that it be given still more power. Often, the request itself it used to mask accountability for mistakes in the use of power it already has.

Moreover, if the pattern of practice begun by this Administration is not challenged, it may well become a permanent part of the American system. Many conservatives have pointed out that granting unchecked power to this President means that the next President will have unchecked power as well. And the next President may be someone whose values and belief you do not trust. And this is why Republicans as well as Democrats should be concerned with what this President has done. If this President's attempt to dramatically expand executive power goes unquestioned, our Constitutional design of checks and balances will be lost. And the next President or some future President will be able, in the name of national security, to restrict our liberties in a way the framers never would have thought possible.

The same instinct to expand its power and to establish dominance characterizes the relationship between this Administration and the courts and the Congress.

In a properly functioning system, the Judicial Branch would serve as the constitutional umpire to ensure that the branches of government observed their proper spheres of authority, observed civil liberties and adhered to the rule of law. Unfortunately, the unilateral executive has tried hard to thwart the ability of the judiciary to call balls and strikes by keeping controversies out of its hands—notably those challenging its ability to detain individuals without legal process—by appointing judges who will be deferential to its exercise of power and by its support of assaults on the independence of the third branch.

The President's decision to ignore FISA was a direct assault on the power of the judges who sit on that court. Congress established the FISA court precisely to be a check on executive power to wiretap. Yet, to ensure that the court could not function as a check on executive power, the President simply did not take matters to it and did not let the court know that it was being bypassed. . . .

The Executive Branch, time and again, has co-opted Congress' role, and often Congress has been a willing accomplice in the surrender of its own power.

Look for example at the Congressional role in "overseeing" this massive four year eavesdropping campaign that on its face seemed so clearly to violate the Bill of Rights. The President says he informed Congress, but what he really means is that he talked with the chairman and ranking member of the House and Senate intelligence committees and the top leaders of the House and Senate. This small group, in turn, claimed that they were not given the full facts, though at least one of the intelligence committee leaders handwrote a letter of concern to VP Cheney and placed a copy in his own safe.

Though I sympathize with the awkward position in which these, men and women were placed, I cannot disagree with the Liberty Coalition when it says that Democrats as well as Republicans in the Congress must share the blame for not taking action to protest and seek to prevent what they consider a grossly unconstitutional program. . . .

Fear drives out reason. Fear suppresses the politics of discourse and opens the door to the politics of destruction. Justice Brandeis once wrote: "Men feared witches and burnt women:"

The founders of our country faced dire threats. If they failed in their endeavors, they would have been hung as traitors. The very existence of our country was at risk.

Yet, in the teeth of those dangers, they insisted on establishing the Bill of Rights.

Is our Congress today in more danger than were their predecessors when the British army was marching on the Capitol? Is the world more dangerous than when we faced an ideological enemy with tens of thousands of missiles poised to be launched against us and annihilate our country at a moment's notice? Is America in more danger now than when we faced worldwide fascism on the march—when our fathers fought and won two World Wars simultaneously?

It is simply an insult to those who came before us and sacrificed so much on our behalf to imply that we have more to be fearful of than they. Yet they faithfully protected our freedoms and now it is up to us to do the same. . . .

A special counsel should immediately be appointed by the Attorney General to remedy the obvious conflict of interest that prevents him from investigating what many believe are serious violations of law by the President. We have had a fresh demonstration of how an independent investigation by a special counsel with integrity can rebuild confidence in our system of justice. Patrick Fitzgerald has, by all accounts, shown neither fear nor favor in pursuing allegations that the Executive Branch has violated other laws.

Republican as well as Democratic members of Congress should support the bipartisan call of the Liberty Coalition for the appointment of a special counsel to pursue the criminal issues raised by warrantless wiretapping of Americans by the President.

Second, new whistleblower protections should immediately be established for members of the Executive Branch who report evidence of wrongdoing— especially where it involves the abuse of Executive Branch authority in the sensitive areas of national security.

Third, both Houses of Congress should hold comprehensive—and not just superficial—hearings into these serious allegations of criminal behavior on the part of the President. And, they should follow the evidence wherever it leads.

Fourth, the extensive new powers requested by the Executive Branch in its proposal to extend and enlarge the Patriot Act should, under no circumstances be granted, unless and until there are adequate and enforceable safeguards to protect the Constitution and the rights of the American people against the kinds of abuses that have so recently been revealed.

Fifth, any telecommunications company that has provided the government with access to private information concerning the communications of Americans without a proper warrant should immediately cease and desist their complicity in this apparently illegal invasion of the privacy of American citizens.

Freedom of communication is an essential prerequisite for the restoration of the health of our democracy.

It is particularly important that the freedom of the Internet be protected against either the encroachment of government or the efforts at control by large media conglomerates. The future of our democracy depends on it.

I mentioned that along with cause for concern, there is reason for hope. As I stand here today, I am filled with optimism that America is on the eve of a golden age in which the vitality of our democracy will be re-established and will flourish more vibrantly than ever. Indeed I can feel it in this hall.

As Dr. King once said, "Perhaps a new spirit is rising among us. If it is, let us trace its movements and pray that our own inner being may be sensitive to its guidance, for we are deeply in need of a new way beyond the darkness that seems so close around us."

POSTSCRIPT

May the President Wiretap Without a Warrant to Protect National Security?

The opposing positions of Andrew McCarthy and Al Gore raise several questions. Does the president have the inherent power to engage in secret surveillance or is that authority dependent upon an explicit delegation by Congress? Is there a difference between presidential interception of communications involving foreigners and those involving American citizens? Can national security curtail individual rights or is there no conflict between them?

These questions came to the fore after the December 2005 revelation of President Bush's creation of a warrantless wiretapping program in the National Security Agency. Testimony by Attorney General Alberto Gonzalez on February 6, 2006 before the U.S. Senate Committee on the Judiciary took the position that presidents have always employed enemy surveillance in support of the president's constitutional authority to protect the safety of all Americans. Gonzalez insists that the president must be capable of acting promptly, "rather than wait until it is too late." A group of scholars of constitutional law and former government officials rejected these arguments in an open letter to Congress addressed February 9, 2006, stating that domestic spying was explicitly prohibited by the Foreign Intelligence Surveillance Act.

Ellen Frankel Paul, Fred D. Miller, Jr., and Jeffrey Paul have edited *The Right to Privacy* (Cambridge University Press, 2000), a series of wide-ranging essays by philosophers and academic lawyers, examining various aspects of privacy, including its role in American constitutional law and the ways it influences public policy.

Privacy is the ability of an individual or group to keep their lives and personal affairs out of public view, or to stop information about themselves from becoming known to people other than those to whom they choose to give the information. Americans believe that a man's or woman's home is his or her castle, and it should not ordinarily be entered by others without permission.

Brief reflection will lead most Americans, except those firm libertarians who oppose all government action that impinges upon their lives, to conclude that there are trade-offs between privacy and liberty. The government needs to collect personal census information in order to determine appropriations for particular programs, and it needs to know the income of persons in order to assess income taxes, while individuals need to believe that this knowledge will not be widely circulated because it can be use in illegal and improper ways. Medical information is deemed to be private communication between physician and patient, yet moral issues arise, such as whether an

HIV-positive individual should reveal that condition before having relations with a prospective sexual partner. Similarly, the introduction of a universal identity card could have substantial social benefits, but it also raises the risks of unfair discrimination and identity theft.

Asked if the Bush administration was right or wrong in wiretapping conversations without a court order, the CNN/*USA Today*/Gallup poll showed a bare majority (50 to 46 percent) supported the president in January 2006, and a bare majority (50 to 47 percent) opposed the president the following month. The relationship and possible conflict between personal liberty and national security is not likely ever to be definitively resolved.

On the Internet . . .

In addition to the Internet sites listed below, type in key words, such as "capital punishment," "gun control," and "affirmative action," to find other listings.

New American Studies Web

This eclectic site provides links to a wealth of Internet resources for research in American studies, including agriculture and rural development, government, and race and ethnicity.

http://www.georgetown.edu/crossroads/asw/

Public Agenda Online

Public Agenda, a nonpartisan, nonprofit public opinion research and citizen education organization, provides links to policy options for issues ranging from abortion to Social Security.

http://www.publicagenda.org

NCPA Idea House

Through this site of the National Center for Policy Analysis, access discussions on an array of topics that are of major interest in the study of American government, from regulatory policy and privatization to economy and income.

http://www.ncpa.org/iss/

U.S. Immigration and Customs Enforcement

Created in 2003, this is the largest investigative branch of the Department of Homeland Security and targets illegal immigrants: the people, money, and materials that support terrorism and other criminal activities. The site contains some interesting information on child exploitation, counter-terrorism investigations, counter-narcotics efforts, and other topics.

http://www.ice.gov

Policy Library

This site provides a collection of documents on social and policy issues submitted by different research organizations all over the world.

http://www.policylibrary.com/US/index.html

PART 3

Social Change and Public Policy

*E*conomic and moral issues divide Americans. Americans appear to increasingly line up on one side or the other on issues as diverse as economic equality and opportunity, capital punishment and gun control laws, affirmative action and racial distinctions, abortion and gay marriage. Disagreement has spilled out of Congress and the state legislatures into the courts. These controversial issues generate intense emotions because they ask us to clarify our values and understand the consequences of the public policies America adopts in each of these areas.

- Is Capital Punishment Justified?
- Does Affirmative Action Advance Racial Equality?
- Is "Middle Eastern" Profiling Ever Justified?"
- Should Abortion Be Restricted?
- Are Tax Cuts Good for America?
- Is America Becoming More Unequal?
- Does the Patriot Act Abridge Essential Freedom?
- Stopping Illegal Immigration: Should Border Security Come First?

ISSUE 9

Is Capital Punishment Justified?

YES: Robert W. Lee, from "Deserving to Die," *The New American* (August 13, 1990)

NO: Eric M. Freedman, from "The Case Against the Death Penalty," *USA Today Magazine* (March 1997)

ISSUE SUMMARY

YES: Essayist Robert W. Lee argues that capital punishment is the only fair way for society to respond to certain heinous crimes.

NO: Law professor Eric M. Freedman contends that the death penalty does not reduce crime but does reduce public safety and carries the risk of innocent people being executed.

In 2005, 60 inmates in 16 states were executed, one more than in 2004. Lethal injection accounted for all of the executions. At the end of 2004, 36 states and the federal prison system held 3314 prisoners under sentence of death, 63 fewer than a year earlier. Although far fewer people are sentenced to death than commit murder, the issue of the death penalty remains highly divisive.

American public opinion continues to support capital punishment. A Harris Poll in 2004 concluded that 69 percent of the American people favored the death penalty, while only 22 percent opposed it. At the same time, 41 percent believed that it deterred murder, while 53 percent held that it did not have much effect, and 36 percent believed that there should be more executions, while 21 percent favored a decrease. The inescapable conclusion is that many Americans believe that, whatever its effect on murder, capital punishment is morally justified.

Capital punishment is an ancient penalty, but both the definition of a capital crime and the methods used to put convicted persons to death have changed dramatically. In eighteenth-century Massachusetts, for example, capital crimes included blasphemy and the worship of false gods. Slave states often imposed the death penalty upon blacks for crimes that were punished by only two or three years' imprisonment when committed by whites. It has been estimated that in the twentieth century approximately 10 percent of all legal executions have been for the crime of rape, 1 percent for all other crimes except murder (robbery, burglary, attempted murder, etc.), and nearly 90 percent for the commission of murder.

Long before the Supreme Court severely limited the use of the death penalty, executions in the United States were becoming increasingly rare. In the 1930s there were 1,667; the total for the 1950s was 717. In the 1960s the numbers fell even more dramatically. For example, seven persons were executed in 1965, one in 1966, and two in 1967.

Then came the Supreme Court case *Furman v. Georgia* (1972), which many thought—mistakenly—"abolished" capital punishment in America. Actually, only two members of the *Furman* majority thought that capital punishment *per se* violates the Eighth Amendment's injunction against "cruel and unusual punishment." The other three members of the majority took the view that capital punishment is unconstitutional only when applied in an arbitrary or racially discriminatory manner, as they believed it was in this case. The four dissenters in the *Furman* case were prepared to uphold capital punishment both in general and in this particular instance. Not surprisingly, then, with a slight change of Court personnel—and with a different case before the Court—a few years later, the majority vote went the other way.

In the latter case, *Gregg v. Georgia* (1976), the majority upheld capital punishment under certain circumstances. In his majority opinion in the case, Justice Potter Stewart noted that the law in question (a new Georgia capital punishment statute) went to some lengths to avoid arbitrary procedures in capital cases. For example, Georgia courts were not given complete discretion in handing out death sentences to convicted murderers but had to consult a series of guidelines spelling out "aggravating circumstances," such as if the murder had been committed by someone already convicted of murder, if the murder endangered the lives of bystanders, and if the murder was committed in the course of a major felony. These guidelines, Stewart said, together with other safeguards against arbitrariness included in the new statute, preserved it against Eighth Amendment challenges.

Although the Court has upheld the constitutionality of the death penalty, it can always be abolished by state legislatures. However, that seems unlikely to happen in many states. If anything, the opposite is occurring. Almost immediately after the *Furman* decision of 1972, state legislatures began enacting new death penalty statutes designed to meet the objections raised in the case. By the time of the *Gregg* decision, 35 new death penalty statutes had been enacted.

In response to the public mood, Congress has put its own death penalty provisions into federal legislation. In 1988 Congress sanctioned the death penalty for drug kingpins convicted of intentionally killing or ordering anyone's death. More recently, in the 1994 crime bill, Congress authorized the death penalty for dozens of existing or new federal crimes, such as treason or the murder of a federal law enforcement agent.

In the following selections, Robert W. Lee argues that capital punishment is an appropriate form of retribution for certain types of heinous offenses, while Eric M. Freedman asserts that the practice of capital punishment fails every practical and moral test that may be applied to it.

Deserving to Die

A key issue in the debate over capital punishment is whether or not it is an effective deterrent to violent crime. In at least one important respect, it unquestionably is: It simply cannot be contested that a killer, once executed, is forever deterred from killing again. The deterrent effect on others, however, depends largely on how swiftly and surely the penalty is applied. Since capital punishment has not been used with any consistency over the years, it is virtually impossible to evaluate its deterrent effect accurately. Abolitionists claim that a lack of significant difference between the murder rates for states with and without capital punishment proves that the death penalty does not deter. But the states with the death penalty on their books have used it so little over the years as to preclude any meaningful comparison between states. Through July 18, 1990 there had been 134 executions since 1976. Only 14 states (less than 40 percent of those that authorize the death penalty) were involved. Any punishment, including death, will cease to be an effective deterrent if it is recognized as mostly bluff. Due to costly delays and endless appeals, the death penalty has been largely turned into a paper tiger by the same crowd that calls for its abolition on the grounds that it is not an effective deterrent!

To allege that capital punishment, if imposed consistently and without undue delay, would not be a deterrent to crime is, in essence, to say that people are not afraid of dying. If so, as columnist Jenkin Lloyd Jones once observed, then warning signs reading "Slow Down," "Bridge Out," and "Danger—40,000 Volts" are futile relics of an age gone by when men feared death. To be sure, the death penalty could never become a 100-percent deterrent to heinous crime, because the fear of death varies among individuals. Some race automobiles, climb mountains, parachute jump, walk circus highwires, ride Brahma bulls in rodeos, and otherwise engage in endeavors that are more than normally hazardous. But, as author Bernard Cohen notes in his book *Law and Order*, "there are even more people who refrain from participating in these activities mainly because risking their lives is not to their taste."

Merit System

On occasion, circumstances *have* led to meaningful statistical evaluations of the death penalty's deterrent effect. In Utah, for instance, there have been three executions since the Supreme Court's 1976 ruling:

- Gary Gilmore faced a firing squad at the Utah State Prison on January 17, 1977. There had been 55 murders in the Beehive State during 1976 (4.5 per 100,000 population). During 1977, in the wake of the Gilmore execution, there were 44 murders (3.5 per 100,000), a 20 percent decrease.
- More than a decade later, on August 28, 1987, Pierre Dale Selby (one of the two infamous "hi-fi killers" who in 1974 forced five persons in an Ogden hi-fi shop to drink liquid drain cleaner, kicked a ballpoint pen into the ear of one, then killed three) was executed. During all of 1987, there were 54 murders (3.2 per 100,000). The count for January through August was 38 (a monthly average of 4.75). For September–December (in the aftermath of the Selby execution) there were 16 (4.0 per month, a nearly 16 percent decrease). For July and August there were six and seven murders, respectively. In September (the first month following Selby's demise) there were three.
- Arthur Gary Bishop, who sodomized and killed a number of young boys, was executed on June 10, 1988. For all of 1988 there were 47 murders (2.7 per 100,000, the fewest since 1977). During January–June, there were 26; for July–December (after the Bishop execution) the tally was 21 (a 19 percent difference).

In the wake of all three Utah executions, there have been notable decreases in both the number and the rate of murders within the state. To be sure, there are other variables that could have influenced the results, but the figures are there and abolitionists to date have tended simply to ignore them.

Deterrence should never be considered the *primary* reason for administering the death penalty. It would be both immoral and unjust to punish one man merely as an example to others. The basic consideration should be: Is the punishment deserved? If not, it should not be administered regardless of what its deterrent impact might be. After all, once deterrence supersedes justice as the basis for a criminal sanction, the guilt or innocence of the accused becomes largely irrelevant. Deterrence can be achieved as effectively by executing an innocent person as a guilty one (something that communists and other totalitarians discovered long ago). If a punishment administered to one person deters someone else from committing a crime, fine. But that result should be viewed as a bonus of justice properly applied, not as a reason for the punishment. The decisive consideration should be: Has the accused *earned* the penalty?

The Cost of Execution

The exorbitant financial expense of death penalty cases is regularly cited by abolitionists as a reason for abolishing capital punishment altogether. They prefer to ignore, however, the extent to which they themselves are responsible for the interminable legal maneuvers that run up the costs. . . .

As presently pursued, death-penalty prosecutions *are* outrageously expensive. But, again, the cost is primarily due to redundant appeals, time-consuming delays, bizarre court rulings, and legal histrionics by defense attorneys:

Willie Darden, who had already survived three death warrants, was scheduled to die in Florida's electric chair on September 4, 1985 for a murder he had committed in 1973. Darden's lawyer made a last-minute emergency appeal to the Supreme Court, which voted against postponing the execution until a formal appeal could be filed. So the attorney (in what he later described as "last-minute ingenuity") then requested that the emergency appeal be technically transformed into a formal appeal. Four Justices agreed (enough to force the full court to review the appeal) and the execution was stayed. After additional years of delay and expense, Darden was eventually put out of our misery on March 15, 1988.

Ronald Gene Simmons killed 14 members of his family during Christmas week in 1987. He was sentenced to death, said he was willing to die, and refused to appeal. But his scheduled March 16, 1989 execution was delayed when a fellow inmate, also on death row, persuaded the Supreme Court to block it (while Simmons was having what he expected to be his last meal) on the grounds that the execution could have repercussions for other death-row inmates. It took the Court until April 24th of [1990] to reject that challenge. Simmons was executed on June 25th.

Robert Alton Harris was convicted in California of the 1978 murders of two San Diego teenagers whose car he wanted for a bank robbery. Following a seemingly interminable series of appeals, he was at last sentenced to die on April 3rd of [1990]. Four days earlier, a 9th U.S. Circuit Court of Appeals judge stayed the execution, largely on the claim that Harris was brain-damaged and therefore may possibly have been unable to "premeditate" the murders (as required under California law for the death penalty). On April 10th, the *Washington Times* reported that the series of tests used to evaluate Harris's condition had been described by some experts as inaccurate and "a hoax."

The psychiatric game is being played for all it is worth. On May 14th, Harris's attorneys argued before the 9th Circuit Court that he should be spared the death penalty because he received "inadequate" psychiatric advice during his original trial. In 1985, the Supreme Court had ruled that a defendant has a constitutional right to "a competent psychiatrist who will conduct an appropriate examination." Harris had access to a licensed psychiatrist, but now argues that—since the recent (highly questionable) evaluations indicated brain damage and other alleged disorders that the original psychiatrist failed to detect (and which may have influenced the jury not to impose the death sentence)—a new trial (or at least a re-sentencing) is in order. If the courts buy this argument, hundreds (perhaps thousands) of cases could be reopened for psychiatric challenge.

On April 2, 1974 William Neal Moore shot and killed a man in Georgia. Following his arrest, he pleaded guilty to armed robbery and murder and was convicted and sentenced to death. On July 20, 1975 the Georgia Supreme Court denied his petition for review. On July 16, 1976 the U.S. Supreme Court denied his petition for review. On May 13, 1977 the Jefferson County Superior Court turned down a petition for a new sentencing hearing (the state Supreme Court affirmed the denial, and the U.S. Supreme

Court again denied a review). On March 30, 1978 a Tattnall County Superior Court judge held a hearing on a petition alleging sundry grounds for a writ of *habeas corpus,* but declined on July 13, 1978 to issue a writ. On October 17, 1978 the state Supreme Court declined to review that ruling. Moore petitioned the U.S. District Court for southern Georgia. After a delay of more than two years, a U.S. District Court judge granted the writ on April 29, 1981. After another two-year delay, the 11th U.S. Circuit Court of Appeals upheld the writ on June 23, 1983. On September 30, 1983 the Circuit Court reversed itself and ruled that the writ should be denied. On March 5, 1984 the Supreme Court rejected the case for the third time.

Moore's execution was set for May 24, 1984. On May 11, 1984 his attorneys filed a petition in Butts County Superior Court, but a writ was denied. The same petition was filed in the U.S. District Court for Georgia's Southern District on May 18th, but both a writ and a stay of execution were denied. Then, on May 23rd (the day before the scheduled execution) the 11th Circuit Court of Appeals granted a stay. On June 4, 1984 a three-judge panel of the Circuit Court voted to deny a writ. After another delay of more than three years, the Circuit Court voted 7 to 4 to override its three-judge panel and rule in Moore's favor. On April 18, 1988, the Supreme Court accepted the case. On April 17, 1989 it sent the case back to the 11th Circuit Court for review in light of new restrictions that the High Court had placed on *habeas corpus.* On September 28, 1989 the Circuit Court ruled 6 to 5 that Moore had abused the writ process. On December 18, 1989 Moore's attorneys again appealed to the Supreme Court.

Moore's case was described in detail in *Insight* magazine for February 12, 1990. By the end of [1989] his case had gone through 20 separate court reviews, involving some 118 state and federal judges. It had been to the Supreme Court and back four times. There had been a substantial turnover of his attorneys, creating an excuse for one team of lawyers to file a petition claiming that all of the prior attorneys had given ineffective representation. No wonder capital cases cost so much!

Meanwhile, the American Bar Association proposes to make matters even worse by requiring states (as summarized by *Insight*) "to appoint two lawyers for every stage of the proceeding, require them to have past death penalty experience and pay them at 'reasonable' rates to be set by the court."

During an address to the American Law Institute on May 16, 1990, Chief Justice Rehnquist asserted that the "system at present verges on the chaotic" and "cries out for reform." The time expended between sentencing and execution, he declared, "is consumed not by structured review . . . but in fits of frantic action followed by periods of inaction." He urged that death row inmates be given one chance to challenge their sentences in state courts, and one challenge in federal courts, period.

Lifetime to Escape

Is life imprisonment an adequate substitute for the death penalty? Presently, according to the polls, approximately three-fourths of the American people favor capital punishment. But abolitionists try to discount that figure by claiming that support for the death penalty weakens when life imprisonment without the possibility of parole is offered as an alternative. (At other times, abolitionists argue that parole is imperative to give "lifers" some hope for the future and deter their violent acts in prison.)

Life imprisonment is a flawed alternative to the death penalty, if for no other reason than that so many "lifers" escape. Many innocent persons have died at the hands of men previously convicted and imprisoned for murder, supposedly for "life." The ways in which flaws in our Justice system, combined with criminal ingenuity, have worked to allow "lifers" to escape include these recent examples:

- On June 10, 1977, James Earl Ray, who was serving a 99-year term for killing Dr. Martin Luther King Jr., escaped with six other inmates from the Brushy Mountain State Prison in Tennessee (he was captured three days later).
- Brothers Linwood and James Briley were executed in Virginia on October 12, 1984 and April 18, 1985, respectively. Linwood had murdered a disc jockey in 1979 during a crime spree. During the same spree, James raped and killed a woman (who was eight months pregnant) and killed her five-year-old son. On May 31, 1984, the Briley brothers organized and led an escape of five death-row inmates (the largest death-row breakout in U.S. history). They were at large for 19 days.
- On August 1, 1984 convicted murderers Wesley Allen Tuttle and Walter Wood, along with another inmate, escaped from the Utah State Prison. All were eventually apprehended. Wood subsequently sued the state for $2 million for violating his rights by allowing him to escape. In his complaint, he charged that, by allowing him to escape, prison officials had subjected him to several life-threatening situations: "Because of extreme fear of being shot to death, I was forced to swim several irrigation canals, attempt to swim a 'raging' Jordan River and expose myself to innumerable bites by many insects. At one point I heard a volley of shotgun blasts and this completed my anxiety."
- On April 3, 1988 three murderers serving life sentences without the chance of parole escaped from the maximum-security West Virginia Penitentiary. One, Bobby Stacy, had killed a Huntington police officer in 1981. At the time, he had been free on bail after having been arrested for shooting an Ohio patrolman.
- On November 21, 1988 Gonzalo Marrero, who had been convicted of two murders and sentenced to two life terms, escaped from New Jersey's Trenton state prison by burrowing through a three-foot-thick cell wall, then scaling a 20-foot outer wall with a makeshift ladder.
- In August 1989 Arthur Carroll, a self-proclaimed enforcer for an East Oakland street gang, was convicted of murdering a man. On September 28th, he was sentenced to serve 27-years-to-life in prison. On October 10th he was transferred to San Quentin prison. On October 25th he was set free after a paperwork snafu led officials to believe that he had served enough time. An all-points bulletin was promptly issued.
- On February 11, 1990 six convicts, including three murderers, escaped from their segregation cells in the maximum security Joliet Correctional

Center in Illinois by cutting through bars on their cells, breaking a window, and crossing a fence. In what may be the understatement of the year, a prison spokesman told reporters: "Obviously, this is a breach of security."

Clearly, life sentences do not adequately protect society, whereas the death penalty properly applied does so with certainty.

Equal Opportunity Execution

Abolitionists often cite statistics indicating that capital punishment has been administered in a discriminatory manner, so that the poor, the black, the friendless, etc., have suffered a disproportionate share of executions. Even if true, such discrimination would not be a valid reason for abandoning the death penalty unless it could be shown that it was responsible for the execution of *innocent* persons (which it has not been, to date). Most attempts to pin the "discrimination" label on capital convictions are similar to one conducted at Stanford University a few years ago, which found that murderers of white people (whether white or black) are more likely to be punished with death than are killers of black people (whether white or black). But the study also concluded that blacks who murdered whites were somewhat *less* likely to receive death sentences than were whites who killed whites.

Using such data, the ACLU attempted to halt the execution of Chester Lee Wicker in Texas on August 26, 1986. Wicker, who was white, had killed a white person. The ACLU contended that Texas unfairly imposes the death penalty because a white is more likely than a black to be sentenced to death for killing a white. The Supreme Court rejected the argument. On the other hand, the execution of Willie Darden in Florida attracted worldwide pleas for amnesty from sundry abolitionists who, ignoring the Stanford study, claimed that Darden had been "railroaded" because he was black and his victim was white.

All criminal laws—in all countries, throughout all human history—have tended to be administered in an imperfect and uneven manner. As a result, some elements in society have been able to evade justice more consistently than others. But why should the imperfect administration of justice persuade us to abandon any attempt to attain it?

The most flagrant example of discrimination in the administration of the death penalty does not involve race, income, or social status, but gender. Women commit around 13 percent of the murders in America, yet, from 1930 to June 30, 1990, only 33 of the 3991 executions (less than 1 percent) involved women. Only one of the 134 persons executed since 1976 (through July 18th [1990]) has been a woman (Velma Barfield in North Carolina on November 2, 1984). One state governor commuted the death sentence of a woman because "humanity does not apply to women the inexorable law that it does to men."

According to L. Kay Gillespie, professor of sociology at Weber State College in Utah, evidence indicates that women who cried during their trials had a better chance of getting away with murder and avoiding the death penalty. Perhaps the National Organization for Women can do something about this glaring example of sexist "inequality" and "injustice." In the meantime, we shall continue to support the death penalty despite the disproportionate number of men who have been required to pay a just penalty for their heinous crimes.

Forgive and Forget?

Another aspect of the death penalty debate is the extent to which justice should be tempered by mercy in the case of killers. After all, abolitionists argue, is it not the duty of Christians to forgive those who trespass against them? In Biblical terms, the most responsible sources to extend mercy and forgiveness are (1) God and (2) the victim of the injustice. In the case of murder, so far as *this* world is concerned, the victim is no longer here to extend mercy and forgiveness. Does the state or any other earthly party have the right or authority to intervene and tender mercy on behalf of a murder victim? In the anthology *Essays on the Death Penalty,* the Reverend E. L. H. Taylor clarifies the answer this way: "Now it is quite natural and proper for a man to forgive something you do to *him.* Thus if somebody cheats me out of $20.00 it is quite possible and reasonable for me to say, 'Well, I forgive him, we will say no more about it.' But what would you say if somebody had done you out of $20.00 and I said, 'That's all right. I forgive him on your behalf'?"

The point is simply that there is no way, in *this* life, for a murderer to be reconciled to his victim, and secure the victim's forgiveness. This leaves the civil authority with no other responsible alternative but to adopt *justice* as the standard for assigning punishment in such cases.

Author Bernard Cohen raises an interesting point: ". . . if it is allowable to deprive a would-be murderer of his life, in order to forestall his attack, why is it wrong to take away his life after he has successfully carried out his dastardly business?" Does anyone question the right of an individual to kill an assailant should it be necessary to preserve his or her life or that of a loved one?

Happily, however, both scripture and our legal system uphold the morality and legality of taking the life of an assailant, if necessary, *before* he kills us. How, then, can it be deemed immoral for civil authority to take his life *after* he kills us?

Intolerant Victims?

Sometimes those who defend the death penalty are portrayed as being "intolerant." But isn't one of our real problems today that Americans are *too tolerant* of evil? Are we not accepting acts of violence, cruelty, lying, and immorality with all too little righteous indignation? Such indignation is not, as some would have us believe, a form of "hatred." In *Reflections on the Psalms,* C. S. Lewis discussed the supposed spirit of "hatred" that some critics claimed to see in parts of the Psalms: "Such hatreds are the kind of thing that cruelty and injustice, by a sort of natural law, produce. . . . Not to perceive it at all—not even to be tempted to resentment—to accept it as the most ordinary thing in the world— argues a terrifying insensibility. Thus the absence of anger, especially that sort of anger which we call indignation, can, in my opinion, be a most alarming symptom."

When mass murderer Ted Bundy was executed in Florida on January 24, 1989, a crowd of some 2000 spectators gathered across from the prison to cheer and celebrate. Many liberal commentators were appalled. Some contended that it was a spectacle on a par with Bundy's own callous disrespect for human life. One headline read: "Exhibition witnessed outside prison was more revolting than execution." What nonsense! As C. S. Lewis observed in his commentary on the Psalms: "If the Jews cursed more bitterly than the Pagans this was, I think, at least in part because they took right and wrong more seriously." It is long past time for us all to being taking right and wrong more seriously. . . .

Seeds of Anarchy

As we have seen, most discussions of the death penalty tend to focus on whether it should exist for murder or be abolished altogether. The issue should be reframed so that the question instead becomes whether or not it should be imposed for certain terrible crimes in addition to murder (such as habitual law-breaking, clearly proven cases of rape, and monstrous child abuse).

In 1953 the renowned British jurist Lord Denning asserted: "Punishment is the way in which society expresses its denunciation of wrongdoing; and in order to maintain respect of law, it is essential that the punishment for grave crimes shall adequately reflect the revulsion felt by a great majority of citizens for them." Nineteen years later, U.S. Supreme Court Justice Potter Stewart noted (while nevertheless concurring in the Court's 1972 opinion that temporarily banned capital punishment) that the "instinct for retribution is part of the nature of man and channeling that instinct in the administration of criminal justice serves an important purpose in promoting the stability of a society governed by law. When people begin to believe that organized society is unwilling or unable to impose upon criminal offenders the punishment they 'deserve,' then there are sown the seeds of anarchy—of self-help, vigilante justice, and lynch law."

To protect the innocent and transfer the fear and burden of crime to the criminal element where it belongs, we must demand that capital punishment be imposed when justified and expanded to cover terrible crimes in addition to murder.

Eric M. Freedman  **NO**

The Case Against the Death Penalty

On Sept. 1, 1995, New York rejoined the ranks of states imposing capital punishment. Although the first death sentence has yet to be imposed, an overwhelming factual record from around the country makes the consequence of this action easily predictable: New Yorkers will get less crime control than they had before.

Anyone whose public policy goals are to provide a criminal justice system that delivers swift, accurate, and evenhanded results—and to reduce the number of crimes that actually threaten most people in their daily lives—should be a death penalty opponent. The reason is simple: The death penalty not only is useless in itself, but counterproductive to achieving those goals. It wastes enormous resources—fiscal and moral—on a tiny handful of cases, to the detriment of measures that might have a significant impact in improving public safety.

Those who believe the death penalty somehow is an emotionally satisfying response to horrific crimes should ask themselves whether they wish to adhere to that initial reaction in light of the well-documented facts:

Fact: The death penalty does not reduce crime.

Capital punishment proponents sometimes assert that it simply is logical to think that the death penalty is a deterrent. Whether or not the idea is logical, it is not true, an example of the reality that many intuitively obvious propositions—*e.g.*, that a heavy ball will fall faster if dropped from the Leaning Tower of Pisa than a light one—are factually false.

People who commit capital murders generally do not engage in probability analysis concerning the likelihood of getting the death penalty if they are caught. They may be severely mentally disturbed people like Ted Bundy, who chose Florida for his final crimes *because* it had a death penalty.

Whether one chooses to obtain data from scholarly studies, the evidence of long-term experience, or accounts of knowledgeable individuals, he or she will search in vain for empirical support for the proposition that imposing the death penalty cuts the crime rate. Instead, that person will find:

- The question of the supposed deterrent effect of capital punishment is perhaps the single most studied issue in the social sciences. The results are as unanimous as scholarly studies can be in finding the death penalty not to be a deterrent.

From Eric M. Freedman, "The Case Against the Death Penalty," *USA Today Magazine* (March 1997). Copyright © 1997 by The Society for the Advancement of Education. Reprinted by permission.

- Eighteen of the 20 states with the highest murder rates have and use the death penalty. Of the nation's 20 big cities with the highest murder rates, 17 are in death penalty jurisdictions. Between 1975 and 1985, almost twice as many law enforcement officers were killed in death penalty states as in non-death penalty states. Over nearly two decades, the neighboring states of Michigan, with no death penalty, and Indiana, which regularly imposes death sentences and carries out executions, have had virtually indistinguishable homicide rates.
- Myron Love, the presiding judge in Harris County, Tex. (which includes Houston), the county responsible for 10% of all executions in the entire country since 1976, admits that "We are not getting what I think we should be wanting and that is to deter crime. . . . In fact, the result is the opposite. We're having more violence, more crime."

Fact: The death penalty is extraordinarily expensive.

Contrary to popular intuition, a system with a death penalty is vastly more expensive than one where the maximum penalty is keeping murderers in prison for life. A 1982 New York study estimated the death penalty cost conservatively at three times that of life imprisonment, the ratio that Texas (with a system that is on the brink of collapse due to underfunding) has experienced. In Florida, each execution runs the state $3,200,000—six times the expense of life imprisonment. California has succeeded in executing just two defendants (one a volunteer) since 1976, but could save about $90,000,000 *per year* by abolishing the death penalty and re-sentencing all of its Death Row inmates to life.

In response, it often is proposed to reduce the costs by eliminating "all those endless appeals in death penalty cases." This is not a new idea. In recent years, numerous efforts have been made on the state and Federal levels to do precisely that. Their failure reflects some simple truths:

- Most of the extra costs of the death penalty are incurred prior to and at trial, not in postconviction, proceedings. Trials are far more likely under a death penalty system (since there is so little incentive to plea-bargain). They have two separate phases (unlike other trials) and typically are preceded by special motions and extra jury selection questioning—steps that, if not taken before trial, most likely will result in the eventual reversal of the conviction.
- Much more investigation usually is done in capital cases, particularly by the prosecution. In New York, for instance, the office of the State Attorney General (which generally does not participate in local criminal prosecutions) is creating a new multi-lawyer unit to provide support to county district attorneys in capital cases.
- These expenses are incurred even though the outcome of most such trials is a sentence other than death and even though up to 50% of the death verdicts that are returned are reversed on the constitutionally required first appeal. Thus, the taxpayers foot the bill for all the extra costs of capital pretrial and trial proceedings and then must pay either for incarcerating the prisoner for life or the expenses of a retrial, which itself often leads to a life sentence. In short, even if all post-conviction proceedings following the first appeal were abolished, the death penalty system still would be more expensive than the alternative.

In fact, the concept of making such an extreme change in the justice system enjoys virtually no support in any political quarter. The writ of *habeas corpus* to protect against illegal imprisonment is available to every defendant in any criminal case, whether he or she is charged with being a petty thief or looting an S&L. It justly is considered a cornerstone of the American system of civil liberties. To eliminate all those "endless appeals" either would require weakening the system for everyone or differentially with respect to death penalty cases.

Giving less due process in capital cases is the opposite of what common sense and elementary justice call for and eventually could lead to innocent people being executed. Since the rate of constitutional violations is far greater in capital cases than in others—capital defendants seeking Federal *habeas corpus* relief succeed some 40% of the time, compared to a success rate of less than five percent for non-capital defendants—the idea of providing less searching review in death penalty cases is perverse.

Considering that the vast majority of post-conviction death penalty appeals arise from the inadequacies of appointed trial counsel, the most cost-effective and just way of decreasing the number of years devoted to capital proceedings, other than the best way—not enacting the death penalty—would be to provide adequate funding to the defense at the beginning of the process. Such a system, although more expensive than one without capital punishment, at least would result in some predictability. The innocent would be acquitted speedily; the less culpable would be sentenced promptly to lesser punishments; and the results of the trials of those defendants convicted and sentenced to death ordinarily would be final.

Instead, as matters now stand, there is roughly a 70% chance that a defendant sentenced to death eventually will succeed in getting the outcome set aside. The fault for this situation—which is unacceptable to the defense and prosecution bars alike—lies squarely with the states. It is they that have created the endless appeals by attempting to avoid the ineluctable monetary costs of death penalty systems and to run them on the cheap by refusing to provide adequate funding for defense counsel.

Fact: The death penalty actually reduces public safety.

The costs of the death penalty go far beyond the tens of millions of dollars wasted in the pursuit of a chimera. The reality is that, in a time of fixed or declining budgets, those dollars are taken away from a range of programs that would be beneficial. For example:

- New York State, due to financial constraints, can not provide bullet-proof vests for every peace officer—a project that, unlike the death penalty, certainly would save law enforcement lives.
- According to FBI statistics, the rate at which murders are solved has dropped to an all-time low. Yet, empirical studies consistently demonstrate that, as with other crimes, the murder rate decreases as the probability of detection increases. Putting money into investigative resources, rather than wasting it on the death penalty, could have a significant effect on crime.

- Despite the large percentage of ordinary street crimes that are narcotics-related, the states lack the funding to permit drug treatment on demand. The result is that people who are motivated to cure their own addictions are relegated to supporting themselves through crime, while the money that could fund treatment programs is poured down the death penalty drain.

Fact: The death penalty is arbitrary in operation.

Any reasonably conscientious supporter of the death penalty surely would agree with the proposition that, before someone is executed by the state, he or she first should receive the benefits of a judicial process that is as fair as humanly possible.

However, the one thing that is clear about the death penalty system that actually exists—as opposed to the idealized one some capital punishment proponents assume to exist—is that it does not provide a level of fairness which comes even close to equaling the gravity of the irreversible sanction being imposed. This failure of the system to function even reasonably well when it should be performing excellently breeds public cynicism as to how satisfactorily the system runs in ordinary, non-capital cases.

That reaction, although destructive, is understandable, because the factors that are significant in determining whether or not a particular defendant receives a death sentence have nothing at all to do with the seriousness of his or her crime. The key variables, rather, are:

- Racial discrimination in death-sentencing, which has been documented repeatedly. For instance, in the five-year period following their re-institution of the death penalty, the sentencing patterns in Georgia and Florida were as follows: when black kills white—Georgia, 20.1% (32 of 159 cases) and Florida, 13.7% (34 of 249); white kills white—Georgia, 5.7% (35 of 614) and Florida, 5.2% (80 of 1,547); white kills black—Georgia, 2.9% (one of 34) and Florida, 4.3% (three of 69); black kills black—Georgia, 0.8% (11 of 1,310) and Florida, 0.7% (three of 69).

  A fair objection may be that these statistics are too stark because they fail to take into account other neutral variables—*e.g.*, the brutality of the crime and the number and age of the victims. Nevertheless, many subsequent studies, whose validity has been confirmed in a major analysis for Congress by the General Accounting Office, have addressed these issues. They uniformly have found that, even when all other factors are held constant, the races of the victim and defendant are critical variables in determining who is sentenced to death.

  Thus, black citizens are the victim of double discrimination. From initial charging decisions to plea bargaining to jury sentencing, they are treated more harshly when they are defendants, but their lives are given less value when they are victims. Moreover, all-white or virtually all-white juries still are commonplace in many places.

  One common reaction to this evidence is not to deny it, but to attempt to evade the facts by taking refuge in the assertion that any effective system for guarding against racial discrimination would mean the end of the death penalty. Such a statement is a powerful admission that governments are incapable of running racially neutral capital punishment systems. The response of any fair-minded person should be that, if such is the case, governments should not be running capital punishment systems.

- Income discrimination. Most capital defendants can not afford an attorney, so the court must appoint counsel. Every major study of this issue, including those of the Powell Commission appointed by Chief Justice William Rehnquist, the American Bar Association, the Association of the Bar of the City of New York, and innumerable scholarly journals, has found that the quality of defense representation in capital murder trials generally is far lower than in felony cases.

    The field is a highly specialized one, and since the states have failed to pay the amounts necessary to attract competent counsel, there is an overwhelming record of poor people being subjected to convictions and death sentences that equally or more culpable—but more affluent—defendants would not have suffered.

- Mental disability. Jurors are more likely to sentence to death people who seem different from themselves than individuals who seem similar to themselves. That is the reality underlying the stark fact that those with mental disabilities are sentenced to death at a rate far higher than can be justified by any neutral explanation. This reflects prejudice, pure and simple.

Fact: Capital punishment inevitably will be inflicted on the innocent.

It is ironic that, just as New York was reinstating the death penalty, it was in the midst of a convulsive scandal involving the widespread fabrication of evidence by the New York State Police that had led to scores of people—including some innocent ones—being convicted and sentenced to prison terms. Miscarriages of justice unquestionably will occur in any human system, but the death penalty presents two special problems in this regard:

- The arbitrary factors discussed above have an enormous negative impact on accuracy. In combination with the emotional atmosphere generally surrounding capital cases, they lead to a situation where the truth-finding process in capital cases is *less* reliable than in others. Indeed, a 1993 House of Representatives subcommittee report found 48 instances over the previous two decades in which innocent people had been sentenced to death.
- The stark reality is that death is final. A mistake can not be corrected if the defendant has been executed.

How often innocent people have been executed is difficult to quantify; once a defendant has been executed, few resources generally are devoted to the continued investigation of the case. Nonetheless, within the past few years, independent investigations by major news organizations have uncovered three cases, two in Florida and one in Mississippi, where people were put to death for crimes they did not commit. Over time, others doubtless will come to light (while still others will remain undiscovered), but it will be too late.

The fact that the system sometimes works—for those who are lucky enough to obtain somehow the legal and investigative resources or media attention necessary to vindicate their claims of innocence—does not mean that most innocent people on Death Row are equally fortunate. Moreover, many Death Row inmates who have been exonerated would have been executed if the legal system had moved more quickly, as would occur if, as those now in power in Congress have proposed, Federal *habeas corpus* is eviscerated.

The death penalty is not just useless—it is positively harmful and diverts resources from genuine crime control measures. Arbitrarily selecting out for execution not the worst criminals, but a racially determined handful of the poorest, most badly represented, least mentally healthy, and unluckiest defendants—some of whom are innocent—breeds cynicism about the entire criminal justice system.

Thus, the Criminal Justice Section of the New York State Bar Association—which includes prosecutors, judges, and defense attorneys—opposed reinstitution of the death penalty because of "the enormous cost associated with such a measure, and the serious negative impact on the delivery of prosecution and defense services throughout the state that will result." Meanwhile, Chief Justice Dixon of the Louisiana Supreme Court put it starkly: "Capital punishment is destroying the system."

POSTSCRIPT

Is Capital Punishment Justified?

Robert W. Lee and Eric M. Freedman cite some of the same facts and figures, but come to opposite conclusions. Both note how expensive it is to keep prisoners on death row for so many years while appeals continue. Lee believes that appeals should be limited, while Freedman concludes that it costs taxpayers less to keep a felon in prison for life than to execute him.

However, the most divisive questions transcend cost. Is the death sentence moral? Does it serve a basic human need to apply the most severe penalty for those found guilty of the most severe crimes? Does it deter the future commission of murder by others? Lee does not rest his case for capital punishment on deterrence. He calls deterrence a "bonus" but not a primary justification. What really counts is whether or not the convicted persons deserves the death penalty.

Does the death penalty brutalize society by applying a standard of a life for a life? Is it applied unequally in dealing with convicted whites and non-whites, and with those who can afford adequate defense counsel and those who cannot? Freedman and others conclude that it fails these tests and therefore fails to be an acceptable punishment.

Capital punishment is reserved in many countries for premeditated murder, espionage, or treason. It is also employed as punishment for the military crimes of desertion and mutiny. In some countries that lack a democratic tradition, the death penalty may be imposed for the sexual crimes of adultery and sodomy, drug trafficking and apostasy (the abandonment of the state religion). The worldwide trend in recent decades has been in favor of its abolition. Three decades ago, only sixteen countries had abolished the death penalty. By the end of 2005, 122 countries had ended capital punishment.

The United States and Japan are the only two industrial democracies that allow the death penalty. It was outlawed in most of western Europe in the mid-twentieth century, although The Netherlands banned it as early as 1870. It is still employed as punishment for a wide variety of crimes in China, South Korea, the Middle East, and other countries. Advocates of capital punishment argue that European experience is not relevant, because the American murder rate is four times greater than Europe's. Critics will counter that the murder rate has not increased in states that have abolished capital punishment.

Although capital punishment has existed throughout human history, the methods of execution have changed. In the United States, electrocution and the gas chamber were justified in the twentieth century as more humane than hanging, and more recently they have been replaced by lethal injection. Critics maintain that this newest method is too painful.

Despite the protest of former Attorney General Edwin Meese III that "if a person is innocent of a crime, then he is not a suspect," innocent people have been suspected and convicted. Their convictions may have been based upon false evidence, the suppression of information that would have led to acquittal, or inadequate legal defense. This criticism received dramatic support when thirteen first-degree murder convictions were overturned in Illinois between 1987 and 2000, leading Governor George Ryan to declare a moratorium on executions until the system could be reformed to reduce the likelihood of future miscarriages of justice.

Barry Scheck, Peter Neufeld, and Jim Dwyer discuss cases in which this has occurred in *Actual Innocence: Five Days to Execution and Other Dispatches from the Wrongly Convicted* (Doubleday, 2000). After examining many cases in which innocent persons were convicted and many sentenced to death, the authors list reforms to protect the innocent, including restrictions on admissible eyewitness testimony, reducing the risk of false testimony from jailhouse inmates, and requiring the admission of relevant DNA evidence. The recent use of DNA evidence to confirm or overturn convictions has inspired increased confidence in cases involving sexual assault, but it is of little or no use in most murder cases.

In *The Death Penalty: An American History* (Harvard University Press, 2000), Stuart Banner has provided an overview of American attitudes toward capital punishment from the seventeenth century to the present. Capital punishment is considered in the broader context of the American criminal justice system in Lawrence M. Friedman, *Crime and Punishment in American History* (Basic Books, 1993). Louis Pojman and Jeffrey Reiman engage in a lengthy debate in *The Death Penalty: For and Against* (Rowman and Littlefield, 1998).

Another problem in assessing capital punishment is that the determination to apply it is made by juries that often do not understand and often disregard the judge's instructions as to when to choose between a death sentence and a prison sentence. In some states there is no capital punishment. In most states, there is, although it is rarely applied in most. In 2005, two or more executions were performed in ten states, one in six, and none in 34. Within a state in cases that are virtually identical some juries will prescribe a death sentence and others will not. As author and attorney Scott Turow has put it, "Ambivalence about the death penalty is an American tradition." Given the extreme unlikelihood that the U.S. Supreme Court will reverse its judgment that execution is not "cruel and unusual punishment" barred by the Eighth Amendment, the issue will continue to arouse opposing passions.

ISSUE 10

Does Affirmative Action Advance Racial Equality?

YES: Glenn C. Loury, from *The Anatomy of Racial Inequality* (Harvard University Press, 2002)

NO: Walter E. Williams, from "Affirmative Action Can't Be Mended," in David Boaz, ed., *Toward Liberty: The Idea That Is Changing the World* (Cato Institute, 2002)

ISSUE SUMMARY

YES: Political scientist Glenn Loury argues that the prudent use of "race-sighted" policies is essential to reducing the deleterious effects of race stigmatization, especially the sense of "racial otherness," which still remain in America.

NO: Economist Walter Williams argues that the use of racial preferences sets up a zero-sum game that reverses the gains of the civil rights movement, penalizes innocent people, and ends up harming those they are intended to help.

We didn't land on Plymouth Rock, my brothers and sisters—Plymouth Rock landed on *us!*" Malcolm X's observation is borne out by the facts of American history. Snatched from their native land, transported thousands of miles—in a nightmare of disease and death—and sold into slavery, blacks were reduced to the legal status of farm animals. Even after emancipation, blacks were segregated from whites—in some states by law, and by social practice almost everywhere. American apartheid continued for another century.

In 1954 the Supreme Court declared state-compelled segregation in schools unconstitutional, and it followed up that decision with others that struck down many forms of official segregation. Still, discrimination survived, and in most southern states blacks were either discouraged or prohibited from exercising their right to vote. Not until the 1960s was compulsory segregation finally and effectively challenged. Between 1964 and 1968 Congress passed the most sweeping civil rights legislation since the end of the Civil War.

But is that enough? Equality of condition between blacks and whites seems as elusive as ever. The black unemployment rate is double that of whites, and the percentage of black families living in poverty is nearly four times that of whites. Only a small percentage of blacks ever make it into medical school or law school.

Advocates of affirmative action have focused upon these *de facto* differences to bolster their argument that it is no longer enough just to stop discrimination. The damage done by three centuries of racism now has to be remedied, they argue, and effective remediation requires a policy of "affirmative action." At the heart of affirmative action is the use of "numerical goals." Opponents call them "racial quotas." Whatever the name, what they imply is the setting aside of a certain number of jobs or positions for blacks or other historically oppressed groups. Opponents charge that affirmative action penalizes innocent people simply because they are white, that it often results in unqualified appointments, and that it ends up harming instead of helping blacks.

Affirmative action has had an uneven history in U.S. federal courts. In *Regents of the University of California v. Allan Bakke* (1978), which marked the first time the Supreme Court directly dealt with the merits of affirmative action, a 5–4 majority ruled that a white applicant to a medical school had been wrongly excluded due to the school's affirmative action policy; yet the majority also agreed that "race-conscious" policies may be used in admitting candidates—as long as they do not amount to fixed quotas. Since *Bakke,* other Supreme Court decisions have tipped toward one side or the other, depending on the circumstances of the case and the shifting line-up of Justices. Notable among these were two cases decided by the Court on the same day in 2003, *Gratz v. Bollinger* and *Grutter v. Bollinger.* Both involved affirmative action programs at the University of Michigan, *Gratz* pertaining to undergraduate admissions and *Grutter* to the law school. The court struck down the undergraduate program in *Gratz* on grounds that it was not "narrowly tailored" enough; it awarded every black and other protected minority an extra twenty points out of a one-hundred point scale—which, the court said, amounted to a "quota." But the law school admissions criteria in *Grutter* were more flexible, using race as only one criterion among others, and so the Court refused to strike them down.

The most radical popular challenge to affirmative action was the ballot initiative endorsed by California voters in 1996. Proposition 209 banned any state program based upon racial or gender "preferences." Among the effects of this ban was a sharp decline in the numbers of non-Asian minorities admitted to the elite campuses of the state's university system, especially Berkeley and UCLA. (Asian admissions to the elite campuses either stayed the same or increased, and non-Asian minority admissions to some of the less-prestigious branches increased.)

In the following selections, political scientist Glenn Loury argues that the prudent use of "race-sighted" policies is essential to reducing the deleterious effects of race stigmatization, while economist Walter Williams contends that racial preferences reverse the gains of the civil rights movement and end up harming those they are intended to help.

YES

Glenn C. Loury

The Anatomy of Racial Inequality
(Harvard, 2002)

Affirmative Action and the Poverty of Proceduralism

The current policy debate over racial preferences in higher education, while not the most significant racial justice question facing the nation today, is nonetheless worth considering here. I incline toward the view that the affirmative action debate receives too much attention in public discourses about racial inequality, obscuring as much as it clarifies. However, by exploring some aspects of this hotly contested public question, I hope to illustrate more incisively the conceptual distinctions that drive my larger argument. . . .

The deep question here are these: When should we explicitly undertake to reduce racial disparities, and what are the means most appropriately employed in pursuit of that end? My argument asserts an ordering of moral concerns, racial justice before race-blindness. I hold that departures from "blindness" undertaken to promote racial equality ought not be barred as a matter of principle. Instead, race-sighted policies should be undertaken, or not, as the result of prudential judgments made on a case-by-case basis. The broad acceptance of this view in U.S. society would have profound consequences. When prestigious institutions use affirmative action to ration access to their ranks, they tacitly and publicly confirm this ordering of moral priorities, in a salient and powerful way. This confirmation is the key civic lesson projected into American national life by these disputed policies. At bottom, what the argument over racial preference, in college admissions and elsewhere, is really about is this struggle for priority among competing public ideals. This is a struggle of crucial importance to the overall discourse on race and social justice in the United States.

Fundamentally, it is because these elite institutions are not "indifferent" to the racial effects of their policies that they have opted not to be "blind" to the racial identities of their applicants. If forced to be race-blind, they can pursue their race-egalitarian goals by other (in all likelihood, less efficient) means. Ought they to do so? Anyone interested in racial justice needs to answer this question. Liberal individualism provides little useful guidance here.

The priority of concerns I am asserting has far-reaching consequences. It implies, for example, that an end to formal discrimination against blacks in this post–civil rights era should in no way foreclose a vigorous public discussion about racial justice. More subtly, elevating racial equality above race-blindness as a normative concern inclines us to think critically, and with greater nuance, about the value of race-blindness. It reminds us that the demand for race-blindness—our moral queasiness about using race in public decisions—has arisen for historically specific reasons, namely slavery and enforced racial segregation over several centuries. These reasons involved the caste-like subordination of blacks—a phenomenon whose effects still linger, and one that was certainly not symmetrical as between the races. As such, taking account of race while trying to mitigate the effects of this subordination, though perhaps ill-advised or unworkable in specific cases, cannot plausibly be seen as the moral equivalent of the discrimination that produced the subjugation of blacks in the first place. To see it that way would be to mire oneself in ahistorical, procedural formalism.

Yet this is precisely what some critics of affirmative action have done, putting forward as their fundamental moral principle the procedural requirement that admissions policies be race-blind. "America, A Race-Free Zone," screams the headline from a recent article by Ward Connerly, who led the successful 1996 ballot campaign against affirmative action in California and is now at the helm of a national organization working to promote similar initiatives in other jurisdictions. Mr. Connerly wants to rid the nation of what he calls "those disgusting little boxes"—the ones applicants check to indicate their racial identities. He and his associates see the affirmative action dispute as an argument between people like themselves, who seek simply to eliminate discrimination, and people like the authors of *The Shape of the River*, who want permission to discriminate if doing so helps the right groups.

This way of casting the question is very misleading. *It obscures from view the most vital matter at stake in the contemporary debate on race and social equity—whether public purposes formulated explicitly in racial terms (that is, violating race-indifference) are morally legitimate, or even morally required.* Anti-preference advocates suggest not, arguing from the premise that an individual's race has no moral relevance to the race-indifferent conclusion that it is either wrong or unnecessary to formulate public purposes in racial terms. But this argument is a *non sequitur.* Moral irrelevance does not imply instrumental irrelevance. Nor does the conviction that an individual's race is irrelevant to an assessment of that individual's worth require the conclusion that patterns of unequal racial representation in important public venues are irrelevant to an assessment of the moral health of our society.

The failure to make these distinctions is dangerous, for it leads inexorably to doubts about the validity of discussing social justice issues in the United States in racial terms at all. Or, more precisely, it reduces such a discussion to the narrow ground of assessing whether or not certain policies are race-blind. Whatever the anti-preference crusaders may intend, and however desirable in the abstract may be their colorblind ideal, their campaign is having the effect of devaluing our collective and still unfinished efforts to achieve greater equality between the races. Americans are now engaged in deciding whether the pursuit of racial equality will continue in the century ahead to be a legitimate and vitally important purpose in our public life. Increasingly, doubts are being expressed about this. *Fervency for race-blindness has left some observers simply blind to a basic fact of American public life: We have pressing moral dilemmas in our society that can be fully grasped only when viewed against the backdrop of our unlovely racial history.*

"Figment of the Pigment" or "Enigma of the Stigma"?

Consider the stubborn social reality of race-consciousness in U.S. society. A standard concern about racial preferences in college admissions is that they promote an unhealthy fixation on racial identity among students. By classifying by race, it is said, we distance ourselves further from the goal of achieving a race-blind society. Many proponents of race-blindness as the primary moral ideal come close to equating the use of racial information in administrative practices with the continued awareness of racial identity in the broad society. They come close, that is, to collapsing the distinction between racial *information* and racial *identity*. Yet consciousness of race in the society at large is a matter of subjective states of mind, involving how people understand themselves and how they perceive others. It concerns the extent to which race is taken into account in the intimate, social lives of citizens. The implicit assumption of advocates of race-blindness is that, if we would just stop putting people into these boxes, they would oblige us by not thinking of themselves in these terms. But this assumption is patently false. Anti-preference advocates like to declare that we cannot get beyond race while taking race into account—as if someone has proven a theorem to this effect. But no such demonstration is possible.

The conservative scholars Stephen and Abigail Thernstrom, in their influential study *America in Black and White*, provide an example of this tendency of thought. They blame race-conscious public policies for what they take to be an excess of racial awareness among blacks. Affirmative action, they argue, induces blacks to seek political benefits from racial solidarity. This, in turn, encourages a belief by blacks in what they call "the figment of the pigment"—the conviction that, for African Americans, race is a trait that is inexorably and irrevocably different from European or Asian ethnicity. This gets it exactly backwards, in my view. It is not the use of race as a criterion of public action that causes blacks to nurture a sense of racial otherness. Rather, it is the historical fact and the specific nature of blacks' racial otherness that causes affirmative action—when undertaken to benefit blacks—to be so fiercely contested in contemporary American politics.

To see what I am getting at here, consider the following thought experiment. Few people, upon entering a shop with the sign "Smith and Sons" in the window to encounter a youngish proprietor at the counter, will begin to worry that they are about to be served by an unqualified beneficiary of nepotism. But I venture that a great many people, upon seeing a black as part of their treatment team at a top-flight hospital, may be led to consider the possibility that, because of affirmative action in medical school admissions, they are about to be treated by an unqualified doctor. Yet supposing that some preference had, in fact, been given in both cases and bearing in mind the incentives created by the threat of a malpractice suit, the objective probability that a customer will receive lower-quality service in the former situation is likely to be greater than the chance that a patient will receive lower-quality treatment in the latter. This difference between reality and perception has little to do with political principles, and everything to do with racial stigma.

Moreover, the ongoing experience of racial stigma is what causes many blacks to see racial solidarity as an existential necessity. Perhaps I could put it this way: It's not *the figment of the pigment,* it is *the enigma of the stigma* that causes race to be so salient for blacks today. Now mind you, I have already stipulated (in Axioms 1 and 2) that, at the most fundamental level, the "pigment" is a "figment." I have rejected racial essentialism. But I also have argued that, not withstanding the arbitrariness of racial markers, the classifying of persons on the basis of such markers is an inescapable social-cognitive activity. And I have suggested that such markers could be invested with powerful social meanings—that meaning-hungry agents could build elaborate structures of self-definition around them.

So after centuries of intensive racial classification we are now confronted with raced subjects demanding to be recognized as such. Here are selves endogenous to the historical and cultural flow, who see their social world partly through the lens of their "pigment," and the best some critics can do by way of a response is to dismiss them as deluded, confused believers in a "figment." ("Why are they so obsessed with race? Can't they see it was all a big mistake?") Would-be moralists, even some blacks, are puzzled and disturbed at the specter of African Americans being proud of the accomplishments, and ashamed of the failures, of their co-racialists. And those to whom the "wages of whiteness" flow like manna from heaven, who have a race but never have to think about it, can blithely declare, "It's time to move on."

This is simplistic social ethics and sophomoric social psychology, it seems to me. And it is an especially odd position for a liberal individualist to take. I have always supposed that the core idea of liberalism is to credit the dignity of human beings. Yet when those subjected to racial stigma, having managed to construct a more or less dignified self-concept out of the brute facts of an imposed categorization, confront us with their "true" selves—perhaps as believers in the need to carry forward a tradition of racial struggle inherited from their forebears, or as proponents of a program of racial self-help—they are written off as benighted adherents of a discredited creed. We would never tell the antagonists in a society divided by religion that the way to move forward is for the group in the minority to desist from worshiping their false god. But this, in effect, is what many critics today are saying to black Americans who simply refuse to "get over it."

The basic point needing emphasis here is this: The use of race-based instruments is typically the result, rather than the cause, of the wider awareness of racial identity in society. This is why race-blindness is such a superficial moral ideal: To forgo cognizance of race, out of fear that others will be encouraged to think in racial terms, is a bit like closing the barn door after the horses have gone. One cannot grasp the workings of the social order in which we are embedded in the United States without making use of racial categories, because these socially constructed categories are etched in the consciousness of the individuals with whom we must reckon. Because they use race to articulate their self-understandings, we must be mindful of race as we conduct our public affairs. This is a *cognitive,* not a *normative* point. One can agree with the liberal individualist claim that race is irrelevant to an individual's moral worth, that individuals and not groups are the bearers of rights, and nevertheless affirm that, to deal effectively with these autonomous individuals, account must be taken of the categories of thought in which they understand themselves.

Indeed, it is easy to produce compelling examples in which the failure to take race into account serves to exacerbate racial awareness. Consider the extent to which our public institutions are regarded as legitimate by all the people. When a public executive (like the hypothetical governor considered earlier) recognizes the link between the perceived legitimacy of institutions and their degree of racial representation, and acts on that recognition, he or she is acting so as to *inhibit,* not to *heighten,* the salience of race in public life. When the leaders of elite educational philanthropies attempt to bring a larger number of black youngsters into their ranks, so as to increase the numbers of their graduates from these communities, they are acting in a similar fashion. *To acknowledge that institutional legitimacy can turn on matters of racial representation is to recognize a basic historical fact about the American national community, not to make a moral error.* The U.S. Army has long understood this. It is absurd to hold that this situation derives from the existence of selection rules—in colleges and universities, in the military, or anywhere else—that take account of race.

So much may seem too obvious to warrant stating but, sadly, it is not. In the 5th U.S. Circuit Court of Appeals *Hopwood* opinion, Judge Smith questions the diversity rationale for using racial preferences in higher education admissions. He argues that, because a college or university exists to promote the exchange of ideas, defining diversity in racial terms necessarily entails the pernicious belief that blacks think one way, whites another. But this argument is fallacious for reasons just stated. Suppose one begins with the contrary premise, that there is no "black" or "white" way of thinking. Suppose further that conveying this view to one's students is a high pedagogic goal. The students being keenly aware of their respective racial identities, some racial diversity may be required to achieve the pedagogic goal. Teaching that "not all blacks think alike" will be much easier when there are enough blacks around to show their diversity of thought.

Walter E. Williams  **NO**

Affirmative Action Can't Be Mended

For the last several decades, affirmative action has been the basic component of the civil rights agenda. But affirmative action, in the form of racial preferences, has worn out its political welcome. In Gallup Polls, between 1987 and 1990, people were asked if they agreed with the statement: "We should make every effort to improve the position of blacks and other minorities even if it means giving them preferential treatment." More than 70 percent of the respondents opposed preferential treatment while only 24 percent supported it. Among blacks, 66 percent opposed preferential treatment and 32 percent supported it.

The rejection of racial preferences by the broad public and increasingly by the Supreme Court has been partially recognized by even supporters of affirmative action. While they have not forsaken their goals, they have begun to distance themselves from some of the language of affirmative action. Thus, many business, government, and university affirmative action offices have been renamed "equity offices." Racial preferences are increasingly referred to a "diversity multiculturalisn." What is it about affirmative action that gives rise to its contentiousness?

For the most part, post-World War II America has supported civil rights for blacks. Indeed, if we stick to the uncorrupted concept of civil rights, we can safely say that the civil rights struggle for blacks is over and won. Civil rights properly refer to rights, held simultaneously among individuals, to be treated equally in the eyes of the law, make contracts, sue and be sued, give evidence, associate and travel freely, and vote. There was a time when blacks did not fully enjoy those rights. With the yeoman-like work of civil rights organizations and decent Americans, both black and white, who fought lengthy court, legislative, and street battles, civil rights have been successfully secured for blacks. No small part of that success was due to a morally compelling appeal to America's civil libertarian tradition of private property, rule of law, and limited government.

Today's corrupted vision of civil rights attacks that civil libertarian tradition. Principles of private property rights, rule of law, freedom of association, and limited government are greeted with contempt. As such, the agenda of today's civil tights organizations conceptually differs little from yesteryear's restrictions that were the targets of the earlier civil rights struggle. Yesteryear civil rights organizations fought *against* the use of race in hiring, access to

From *Cato Journal,* vol. 17, no. 1, Spring/Summer 1997, pp. 1–9. Copyright © 1997 by Cato Institute. Reprinted by permission.

public schools, and university admissions. Today, civil rights organizations fight *for* the use of race in hiring, access to public schools, and university admissions. Yesteryear, civil rights organizations fought *against* restricted association in the forms of racially segregated schools, libraries, and private organizations. Today, they fight *for* restricted associations. They use state power, not unlike the racists they fought, to enforce racial associations they deem desirable. They protest that blacks should be a certain percentage of a company's workforce or clientele, a certain percentage of a student body, and even a certain percentage of an advertiser's models.

Civil rights organizations, in their successful struggle against state-sanctioned segregation, have lost sight of what it means to be truly committed to liberty, especially the freedom of association. The true test of that commitment does not come when we allow people to be free to associate in ways we deem appropriate. The true test is when we allow people to form those voluntary associations we deem offensive. It is the same principle we apply to our commitment to free speech. What tests our commitment to free speech is our willingness to permit people the freedom to say things we find offensive.

Zero-Sum Games

The tragedy of America's civil rights movement is that it has substituted today's government-backed racial favoritism in the allocation of resources for yesterday's legal and extralegal racial favoritism. In doing so, civil rights leaders fail to realize that government allocation of resources produces the kind of conflict that does not arise with market allocation of resources. Part of the reason is that any government allocation of resources, including racial preferential treatment, is a zero-sum game.

A zero-sum game is defined as any transaction where one person's gain necessarily results in another person's loss. The simplest example of a zero-sum game is poker. A winner's gain is matched precisely by the losses of one or more persons. In this respect, the only essential difference between affirmative action and poker is that in poker participation is voluntary. Another difference is the loser is readily identifiable, a point to which I will return later.

The University of California, Berkeley's affirmative action program for blacks captures the essence of a zero-sum game. Blacks are admitted with considerably lower average SAT scores (952) than the typical white (1232) and Asian student (1254).* Between UCLA and UC Berkeley, more than 2,000 white and Asian straight A students are turned away in order to provide spaces for black and Hispanic students. The admissions gains by blacks are exactly matched by admissions losses by white and Asian students. Thus, any preferential treatment program results in a zero-sum game almost by definition.

More generally, government allocation of resources is a zero-sum game primarily because government has no resources of its very own. When government gives some citizens food stamps, crop subsidies, or disaster relief payments, the recipients of the largesse gain. Losers are identified by asking: where does

---

*This practice was outlawed in California in 1996 with the passage of proposition 209. [*Editors*]

government acquire the resources to confer the largesse? In order fix government to give to some citizens, it must through intimidation, threats, and coercion take from other citizens. Those who lose the rights to their earnings, to finance government largesse, are the losers.

Government-mandated racial preferential treatment programs produce a similar result. When government creates a special advantage for one ethnic group, it necessarily comes at the expense of other ethnic groups for whom government simultaneously creates a special disadvantage in the form of reduced alternatives. If a college or employer has X amount of positions, and R of them have been set aside for blacks or some other group, that necessarily means there are $(X - R)$ fewer positions for which other ethnic groups might compete. At a time when there were restrictions against blacks, that operated in favor of whites, those restrictions translated into a reduced opportunity set for blacks. It is a zero-sum game independent of the race or ethnicity of the winners and losers.

Our courts have a blind-sided vision of the zero-sum game. They have upheld discriminatory racial preferences in hiring but have resisted discriminatory racial preferences in job layoffs. An example is the U.S. Supreme Court's ruling in *Wygant v. Jackson Board of Education* (1986), where a teacher union's collective-bargaining agreement protected black teachers from job layoffs in order to maintain racial balance. Subsequently, as a result of that agreement, the Jackson County School Board laid off white teachers having greater seniority while black teachers with less seniority were retained.

A lower court upheld the constitutionality of the collective bargaining agreement by finding that racial preferences in layoffs were a permissible means to remedy societal discrimination. White teachers petitioned the U.S. Supreme Court, claiming their constitutional rights under the Equal Protection clause were violated. The Court found in their favor. Justice Lewis F. Powell delivered the opinion saying, "While hiring goals impose a diffuse burden, only closing one of several opportunities, layoffs impose the entire burden of achieving racial equity on particular individuals, often resulting in serious disruption of their lives. The burden is too intrusive."

In *Wygant*, the Supreme Court recognized the illegitimacy of creating a special privilege for one citizen (a black teacher) that comes at the expense and disadvantage of another citizen (a white teacher). However, the Court made a false distinction when it stated that "hiring goals impose a diffuse burden [while] . . . layoffs impose the entire burden . . . on particular individuals."

There is no conceptual distinction in the outcome of the zero-sum game whether it is played on the layoff or the hiring side of the labor market. If a company plans to lay off X amount of workers and decides that R of them will have their jobs protected because of race, that means the group of workers that may be laid off have $(X - R)$ fewer job retention opportunities. The diffuseness to which Justice Powell refers is not diffuseness at all. It is simply that the victims of hiring preferencas are less visible than victims of layoff preferences as in the case of *Wygant*. The petitioners in *Wygant* were identifiable people who could not be covered up as "society." That differs from the cases of hiring and college admissions racial preferences where those who face a reduced opportunity set tend to be unidentifiable to the courts, other people, and even to themselves. Since they are invisible victims, the Supreme Court and others can blithely say racial hiring goals (and admission goals) impose a diffuse burden.

Tentative Victim Identification

In California, voters passed the California Civil Rights Initiative of 1996 (CCRI) that says: "The state shall not discriminate against, or grant preferential treatment to, any individual or group on the basis of race, sex, color, ethnicity, or national origin in the operation of public employment, public education, or public contracting." Therefore, California public universities can no longer have preferential admission policies that include race as a factor in deciding whom to admit. As a result, the UCLA School of Law reported accepting only 21 black applicants for its fall 1997 class—a drop of 80 percent from the previous year, in which 108 black applicants were accepted. At the UC Berkeley Boalt Hall School of Law, only 14 of the 792 students accepted for the fall 1997 class are black, down from 75 the previous year. At the UCLA School of Law, white enrollment increased by 14 percent for the fall 1997 term and Asian enrollment rose by 7 percent. At UC Berkeley, enrollment of white law students increased by 12 percent and Asian law students increased by 18 percent.

For illustrative purposes, let us pretend that CCRI had not been adopted and the UCLA School of Law accepted 108 black students as it had in 1996 and UC Berkeley accepted 75. That being the cace, 83 more blacks would be accepted to UCLA Law School for the 1997–98 academic year and 61 more blacks would be accepted to UC Berkeley's Law School. Clearly, the preferential admissions program, at least in terms of being accepted to these law schools, benefits blacks. However, that benefit is not without costs. With preferential admission programs in place, both UCLA and UC Berkeley law schools would have had to turn away 144 white and Asian students, with higher academic credentials, in order to have room for black students.

In the case of UC Berkeley's preferential admissions for blacks, those whites and Asians who have significantly higher SAT scores and grades than the admitted blacks are victims of reverse discrimination. However, in the eyes of the courts, others, and possibly themselves, they are invisible victims. In other words, no one can tell for sure who among those turned away would have gained entry to UC Berkeley were it not for the preferential treatment given to blacks.

The basic problem of zero-sum games (those of an involuntary nature) is that they are politically and socially unstable. In the case of UCLA and UC Berkeley, two of California's most prestigious universities, one would not expect parents to permanently tolerate seeing their children work hard to meet the university's admission standards only to be denied admission because of racial preference programs. Since the University of California is a taxpayer-subsidized system, one suspects that sooner or later parents and others would begin to register complaints and seek termination of racial preferences in admissions. That is precisely much of the political motivation behind Proposition 209.

Affirmative Action and Supply

An important focus of affirmative action is statistical underrepresentation of different racial and ethnic groups on college and university campuses. If the percentages of blacks and Mexican-Americans, for example, are not at a level deemed appropriate by a court, administrative agency, or university administrator, racial preference programs are instituted. The inference made from the underrepresentation argument is that, in the absence of racial discrimination, groups would be represented on college campuses in proportion to their numbers in the relevant population. In making that argument, little attention is paid to the supply issue—that is, to the pool of students available that meet the standards or qualifications of the university in question.

In 1985, fewer than 1,032 blacks scored 600 and above on the verbal portion of the SAT and 1,907 scored 600 and above on the quantitative portion of the examination. There are roughly 58 elite colleges and universities with student body average composite SAT scores of 1200 and above. If blacks scoring 600 or higher on the quantitative portion of the SAT (assuming their performance on the verbal portion of the examination gave them a composite SAT score of 1200 or higher) were recruited to elite colleges and universities, there would be less than 33 black students available per university. At none of those universities would blacks be represented according to their numbers in the population.

There is no evidence that suggests that university admissions offices practice racial discrimination by turning away blacks with SAT scores of 1200 or higher. In reality, there are not enough blacks to be admitted to leading colleges and universities on the same terms as other students, such that their numbers in the campus population bear any resemblance to their numbers in the general population.

Attempts by affirmative action programs to increase the percent of blacks admitted to top schools, regardless of whether blacks match the academic characteristics of the general student body, often produce disastrous results. In order to meet affirmative action guidelines, leading colleges and universities recruit and admit black students whose academic qualifications are well below the norm for other students. For example, of the 317 black students admitted to UC Berkeley in 1985, all were admitted under affirmative action criteria rather than academic qualifications. Those students had an average SAT score of 952 compared to the national average of 900 among all students. However, their SAT scores were well below UC Berkeley's average of nearly 1200. More than 70 percent of the black students failed to graduate from UC Berkeley.

Not far from UC Berkeley is San Jose State University, not one of the top-tier colleges, but nonetheless respectable. More than 70 percent of its black students fail to graduate. The black students who might have been successful at San Jose State University have been recruited to UC Berkeley and elsewhere where they have been made artificial failures. This pattern is one of the consequences of trying to use racial preferences to make a student body reflect the relative importance of different ethnic groups in the general population. There is a mismatch between black student qualifications and those of other students when the wrong students are recruited to the wrong universities.

There is no question that preferential admissions is unjust to both white and Asian students who may be qualified but are turned away to make room for less-qualified students in the "right" ethnic group. However, viewed from a solely black self-interest point of view, the question should be asked whether such affirmative action programs serve the best interests of blacks. Is there such an abundance of black students who score above the national average on the SAT, such as those admitted to UC Berkeley, that blacks as a group can afford to have those students turned into artificial failures in the name of diversity, multiculturalism, or racial justice? The affirmative action debate needs to go beyond simply an issue of whether blacks are benefited at the expense of whites. Whites and Asians who are turned away to accommodate blacks are still better off than the blacks who were admitted. After all, graduating from the university of one's second choice is preferable to flunking out of the university of one's first choice.

To the extent racial preferences in admission produce an academic mismatch of students, the critics of California's Proposition 209 may be unnecessarily alarmed, assuming their concern is with black students actually graduating from college. If black students, who score 952 on the SAT, are not admitted to UC Berkeley, that does not mean that they cannot gain admittance to one of America's 3,000 other colleges. It means that they will gain admittance to some other college where their academic characteristics will be more similar to those of their peers. There will not be as much of an academic mismatch. To the extent this is true, we may see an *increase* in black graduation rates. Moreover, if black students find themselves more similar to their white peers in terms of college grades and graduation honors, they are less likely to feel academically isolated and harbor feelings of low self-esteem.

Affirmative Action and Justice

Aside from any other question, we might ask what case can be made for the morality or justice of turning away more highly credentialed white and Asian students so as to be able to admit more blacks? Clearly, blacks as a group have suffered past injustices, including discrimination in college and university admissions. However, that fact does not spontaneously yield sensible policy proposals for today. The fact is that a special privilege cannot be created for one person without creating a special disadvantage for another. In the case of preferential admissions at UCLA and UC Berkeley, a special privilege for black students translates into a special disadvantage for white and Asian students. Thus, we must ask what have those individual white and Asian students done to deserve punishment? Were they at all responsible for the injustices, either in the past or present, suffered by blacks? If, as so often is the case, the justification for preferential treatment is to redress past grievances, how just is it to have a policy where a black of today is helped by punishing a white of today for what a white of yesterday did to a black of yesterday? Such an idea becomes even more questionable in light of the fact that so many whites and

Asians cannot trace the American part of their ancestry back as much as two or three generations.

Affirmative Action and Racial Resentment

In addition to the injustices that are a result of preferential treatment, such treatment has given rise to racial resentment where it otherwise might not exist. While few people support racial resentment and its manifestations, if one sees some of affirmative action's flagrant attacks on fairness and equality before the law, one can readily understand why resentment is on the rise.

In the summer of 1995, the Federal Aviation Administration (FAA) published a "diversity handbook" that said, "The merit promotion process is but one means of filling vacancies, which need not be utilized if it will not promote your diversity goals." In that spirit, one FAA job announcement said, "Applicants who meet the qualification requirements . . . cannot be considered for this position. . . . Only those applicants who do not meet the Office of Personnel Management requirements . . . will be eligible to compete."

According to a General Accounting Office report that evaluated complaints of discrimination by Asian-Americans, prestigious universities such as UCLA, UC Berkeley, MIT, and the University of Wisconsin have engaged in systematic discrimination in the failure to admit highly qualified Asian students in order to admit relatively unqualified black and Hispanic students.

In Memphis, Tennessee, a white police officer ranked 59th out of 209 applicants for 75 available positions as police sergeant, but he did not get promoted. Black officers, with lower overall test scores than he, were moved ahead of him and promoted to sergeant. Over a two-year period, 43 candidates with lower scores were moved ahead of him and made sergeant.

There is little need to recite the litany of racial preference instances that are clear violations of commonly agreed upon standards of justice and fair play. But the dangers of racial preferences go beyond matters of justice and fair play. They lead to increased group polarization ranging from political backlash to mob violence and civil war as seen in other countries. The difference between the United States and those countries is that racial preferences have not produced the same level of violence. However, they have produced polarization and resentment.

Affirmative action proponents cling to the notion that racial discrimination satisfactorily explains black/white socioeconomic differences. While every vestige of racial discrimination has not been eliminated in our society, current social discrimination cannot begin to explain all that affirmative action proponents purport it explains. Rather than focusing our attention on discrimination, a higher payoff can be realized by focusing on real factors such as fraudulent education, family disintegration, and hostile economic climates in black neighborhoods. Even if affirmative action was not a violation of justice and fair play, was not a zero-sum game, was not racially polarizing, it is a poor cover-up for the real work that needs to be done.

POSTSCRIPT

Does Affirmative Action Advance Racial Equality?

Much of the argument between Loury and Williams turns on the question of "color blindness." To what extent should our laws be color-blind? During the 1950s and early 1960s, civil rights leaders were virtually unanimous on this point. Martin Luther King, Jr., in a speech given at a civil rights march on Washington, said, "I have a dream that my four little children will one day live in a nation where they will not be judged by the color of their skin but by the content of their character." This was the consensus view in 1963, but today it may need to be qualified: In order to *bring about* color blindness, it may be necessary to become temporarily color-conscious. But for how long? And is there a danger that this temporary color consciousness may become a permanent policy?

Linda Chavez, a columnist and president of the Center for Equal Opportunity, an organization opposing affirmative action, develops her argument against it in "Promoting Racial Harmony," an essay published in George E. Curry, ed., *The Affirmative Action Debate* (Perseus, 1996); Mary Francis Berry, former chair of the U.S. Civil Rights Commission, argues for it ("Affirmative Action: Why We Need It, Why It Is Under Attack") in the same volume. An article by Richard H. Sander in the November, 2004 *Stanford Law Review* caused a stir in legal education circles. Sander argued that reduced admission standards for blacks entering law school leads to their receiving" lower grades and less learning," which in turn produce "higher attrition rates, lower pass rates on the bar," and "problems in the job market." The following spring (May, 2005) the *Review* published four rebuttals to Sanders, together with Sander's reply. Columnist Jim Sleeper's *Liberal Racism* (Viking, 1997) is critical of affirmative action and other race-based programs, as is a book by *ABC News* reporter Bob Zelnick, *Backfire: A Reporter's Look at Affirmative Action* (Regnery, 1996). Barbara Bergmann supports affirmative action in *In Defense of Affirmative Action* (Basic Books, 1996), while Stephan Thernstrom and Abigail Thernstrom, in their comprehensive survey of racial progress in America entitled *America in Black and White: One Nation, Indivisible* (Simon & Schuster, 1997), argue that it is counterproductive. In *Collision Course: The Strange Convergence of Affirmative Action and Immigration Policy in America* (Oxford University Press, 2002), Hugh David Graham maintains that affirmative action is now at loggerheads with America's expanded immigration policies, in that employers use affirmative action to hire new immigrants at the expense of American blacks.

Affirmative action is one of those issues, like abortion, in which the opposing sides seem utterly intransigent. But there may be a large middle sector of opinion that is simply weary of the whole controversy and may be willing to support any expedient solution worked out by pragmatists in the executive and legislative branches of the government.

ISSUE 11

Is "Middle Eastern" Profiling Ever Justified?

YES: Daniel Pipes, from "Fighting Militant Islam, Without Bias," *City Journal* (November 2001)

NO: David A. Harris, from "'Flying While Arab,' Immigration Issues, and Lessons from the Racial Profiling Controversy," Testimony before the U.S. Commission on Civil Rights (October 12, 2001)

ISSUE SUMMARY

YES: Daniel Pipes, director of the Middle East Forum, argues that "heightened scrutiny" of Muslims and Middle Eastern–looking people is justified because, while not all Muslims are Islamic extremists, all Islamic extremists are Muslims.

NO: Law professor David A. Harris opposes profiling people of Middle Eastern appearance because, like racial profiling, it compromises civil liberties and actually damages our intelligence efforts.

The word "stereotype" was introduced into political and social discourse by journalist-philosopher Walter Lippmann in *Public Opinion,* a book he published in 1922. Lippmann called stereotypes the "pictures in our heads," images of reality that we have in our minds even before sense data arrive there. Often these *a priori* definitions produce hasty, distorted generalizations of what is "out there" in the real world. He gives as an example, news reports describing the appearance of "radical" gatherings:

> There is, of course, some connection between the scene outside and the mind through which we watch it, just as there are some long-haired men and short-haired women in radical gatherings. But to the hurried observer a slight connection is enough. If there are two bobbed heads and four beards in the audience, it will be a bobbed and bearded audience to the reporter who knows beforehand that such gatherings are composed of people with these tastes in the management of their hair.

A reporter who consistently brings these stereotypes into news coverage is doing the readers a disservice, but at least they are free to check the reports for accuracy by comparing them to those in another news source. The case is different, though, if the stereotyping is being done by a government official. Government has a monopoly of coercive powers, so when an official engages in stereotyping, a perfectly innocent man or woman may be forced to submit to heightened scrutiny, or humiliating searches, or long interrogations, simply because of the person's appearance. This raises serious issues about civil liberties and civil rights.

Yet the issues are not easy to resolve. We tend to think of stereotyping as invariably wrong, but that was not Lippmann's view. First of all, he insisted, stereotyping cannot be avoided. We do not innocently perceive all the "facts" around us—we decide *which* facts are relevant and then combine them in our own ways. "A report is the joint product of the knower and known, in which the role of the observer is always selective and usually creative." Secondly, he contended, stereotypes are essential if we are to make sense of our world. A stereotype, then, is not unlike a road map, providing a simplified, schematic picture of what is otherwise an impossibly complicated set of facts.

How might Lippmann's observations, made in 1922, apply to the case of Middle Eastern profiling in the twenty-first century? If Lippmann were right to say that stereotyping is inevitable and even necessary to make sense of the world, then perhaps a case can be made for such profiling. Should we require an 82-year-old grandmother to remove her shoes at the airline gate, simply because we just asked a 25-year-old single man from Yemen to do the same? Our stereotype tells us that she is far less likely to have a bomb in her shoe; our common sense tells us that we can more efficiently use resources by concentrating our attention on people like him.

Notice, however, that our stereotype is more complicated than it may seem at first. The Middle Easterner in this hypothetical case is also male, unmarried, and in his twenties. This invites us to complicate the picture a little more. Remembering that Timothy McVeigh, the Oklahoma City bomber, and John Walker Linde, who consorted with the Taliban in Afghanistan, were Caucasian Americans, suppose we compare an 82-year-old Middle Eastern grandmother to a young white American man who has just bought a one-way ticket and looks nervous and shifty-eyed. Which of the two passengers deserves closer scrutiny? If we agree that in this case it would be the American, then there would seem to be qualitative differences among stereotypes; some are better than others. That was Lippmann's view. We need to put "more inclusive patterns" in our stereotypes, and, realizing that they *are* only stereotypes, "to hold them lightly, to modify them gladly."

In these dangerous times, we must somehow strike a balance between liberty and security.

In the following selections, Daniel Pipes, director of the Middle East Forum, argues that in the post–9/11 world, "heightened scrutiny" of Muslims and Middle Eastern–looking people is justified because, while not all Muslims are Islamic extremists, all Islamic extremists are Muslims. Law professor David A. Harris opposes profiling people of Middle Eastern appearance because, like racial profiling, it compromises civil liberties and actually damages our intelligence efforts.

YES

Daniel Pipes

Fighting Militant Islam, Without Bias

The whole country, and New York especially, has to face an urgent question in the wake of the September 11 attacks, organized by a militant Islamic network and carried out by Arabic-speaking Muslims resident in North America: how should Americans now view and treat the Muslim populations living in their midst?

Initial reactions have differed widely. Elite opinion, as voiced by President Bush, rushed to deny any connection between the acts of war and the resident Muslim population. "Islam is peace," Bush assured Americans, adding, "we should not hold one who is a Muslim responsible for an act of terror." Attorney General Ashcroft, Governor Pataki, and Mayor Giuliani closely echoed these comments. Secretary of State Powell went further still, declaring that the attacks "should not be seen as something done by Arabs or Islamics; it is something that was done by terrorists"—as though Arabs and Muslims by definition can't be terrorists.

This approach may have made sense as a way to calm the public and prevent attacks against Muslims, but it clearly failed to convince everyone. Rep. John Cooksey (R-La.) told a radio interviewer that anyone wearing "a diaper on his head and a fan belt wrapped around the diaper" should be "pulled over" for extra questioning at airports. And survey research shows that Americans overwhelmingly tie Islam and Muslims to the horrifying events of September. One poll found that 68 percent of respondents approved of "randomly stopping people who may fit the profile of suspected terrorists." Another found that 83 percent of Americans favor stricter controls on Muslim entry into the country and 58 percent want tighter controls on Muslims traveling on planes or trains. Remarkably, 35 percent of New Yorkers favor establishing internment camps for "individuals who authorities identify as being sympathetic to terrorist causes." Nationally, 31 percent of Americans favor detention camps for Arab-Americans, "as a way to prevent terrorist attacks in the United States."

What in fact are the connections between the atrocities and the Muslim minority resident in the United States and Canada? And what policies can protect the country from attack while protecting the civil rights of Muslims?

The problem at hand is not the religion of Islam but the totalitarian ideology of Islamism. As a faith, Islam has meant very different things over

14 centuries and several continents. What we can call "traditional Islam," forged in the medieval period, has inspired Muslims to be bellicose and quiescent, noble and not: one can't generalize over such a large canvas. But one can note two common points: Islam is, more than any other major religion, deeply political, in the sense that it pushes its adherents to hold power; and once Muslims do gain power, they feel a strong impetus to apply the laws of Islam, the shari`a. So Islam does, in fact, contain elements that can justify conquest, theocracy, and intolerance.

In the course of the twentieth century, a new form of Islam arose, one that now has great appeal and power. Militant Islam (or Islamism—same thing) goes back to Egypt in the 1920s, when an organization called the Muslim Brethren first emerged, though there are other strains as well, including an Iranian one, largely formulated by Ayatollah Khomeini, and a Saudi one, to which the [formerly] ruling Taliban in Afghanistan and Usama bin Ladin both belong. Islamism differs in many ways from traditional Islam. It is faith turned into ideology, and radical ideology at that. When asked, "Do you consider yourself a revolutionary?" Sudanese Islamist politician Hasan al-Turabi replied, "Completely." Whereas traditional Islam places the responsibility on each believer to live according to God's will, Islamism makes this duty something for which the state is responsible. Islam is a personal belief system that focuses on the individual; Islamism is a state ideology that looks to the society. Islamists constitute a small but significant minority of Muslims in the U.S. and worldwide, perhaps 10 to 15 percent.

Apologists would tell us that Islamism is a distortion of Islam, or even that it has nothing to do with Islam, but that is not true; it emerges out of the religion, while taking features of it to a conclusion so extreme, so radical, and so megalomaniacal as to constitute something new. It adapts an age-old faith to the political requirements of our day, sharing some key premises of the earlier totalitarianisms, fascism and Marxism-Leninism. It is an Islamic-flavored version of radical utopianism. Individual *Islamists may* appear law-abiding and reasonable, but they are part of a totalitarian movement, and as such, all must be considered potential killers.

Traditional Muslims, generally the first victims of Islamism, understand this ideology for what it is and respond with fear and loathing, as some examples from northern Africa suggest. Naguib Mahfouz, Egypt's Nobel Prize—winning novelist, said to his country's prime minister and interior minister as they were suppressing Islamism: "You are fighting a battle for the sake of Islam." Other traditional Egyptian Muslims concur with Mahfouz, with one condemning Islamism as "the barbaric hand of terrorism" and another calling for all extremists to be "hanged in public squares." In Tunisia, Minister of Religion Ali Chebbi says that Islamists belong in the "garbage can." Algeria's interior minister, Abderrahmane Meziane-Cherif, likewise concludes: "You cannot talk to people who adopt violence as their credo; people who slit women's throats, rape them, and mutilate their breasts; people who kill innocent foreign guests." If Muslims feel this way, non-Muslims may join them without embarrassment: being against Islamism in no way implies being against Islam.

Islamists of all stripes have a virulent attitude toward non-Muslims and have a decades-long history of fighting with British and French colonial rulers, as well as with such non-Muslim governments as those of India, Israel, and the Philippines. They also have had long and bloody battles against Muslim governments that reject the Islamist program: in Egypt, Pakistan, Syria, Tunisia, and Turkey, for instance—and, most spectacularly, in Algeria, where 100,000 persons so far are estimated to have lost their lives in a decade of fighting.

Islamist violence is a global phenomenon. During the first week of April, [2001], for example, I counted up the following incidents, relying only on news agency stories, which are hardly exhaustive: deaths due to violent Islamist action occurred in Algeria (42 victims), Kashmir (17), the southern Philippines (3), Bangladesh (2), and the West Bank (1); assorted violence broke out in many other countries, including Afghanistan, Indonesia, Nigeria, and Sudan; courts handed down judgments against radical Muslims in France, Germany, Italy, Jordan, Turkey, the United States, and Yemen. Islamists are well organized: fully 11 of the 29 groups that the State Department calls "foreign terrorist organizations" are Islamist, as are 14 out of 21 groups outlawed by Britain's Home Office.

Starting in 1979, Islamists have felt confident enough to extend their fight against the West. The new militant Islamic government of Iran assaulted the U.S. embassy in Tehran at the end of that year and held nearly 60 Americans captive for 444 days. Eight American soldiers (the first casualties in this war) died in the failed U.S. rescue attempt in 1980. Violence against Americans began in earnest in 1983 with an attack on the U.S. embassy in Lebanon, killing 63. Then followed a long sequence of assaults on Americans in embassies, ships, planes, barracks, schools, and elsewhere.

Islamists have also committed at least eight lethal attacks on the soil of the United States prior to September 11, 2001: the July 1980 murder of an Iranian dissident in the Washington area; the January 1990 murder of an Egyptian Islamic freethinker in Tucson; the November 1990 assassination of Rabbi Meir Kahane in New York; the January 1993 assault on CIA personnel, killing two, outside the agency's Langley, Virginia, headquarters; the February 1993 World Trade Center bombing, killing six; the March 1994 shooting attack on a van full of Orthodox Jewish boys driving over the Brooklyn Bridge, killing one; the February 1997 murder of a Danish tourist at the top of the Empire State Building; and the deliberate October 1999 crash of an EgyptAir flight by the Egyptian pilot into the Atlantic near New York City, killing 217. All but one of these murders took place near or in New York City or Washington, D.C. This partial list doesn't include a number of fearsome near misses, including the "day of terror" planned for June 1993 that would have culminated with the simultaneous bombing of the United Nations and the Lincoln and Holland Tunnels, and a thwarted plot to disrupt Seattle's millennial celebrations.

In short, the massacre of upward of 6,000 Americans in September 2001 was not the start of something new but the intensification of an Islamist campaign of violence against the U.S. that has been raging for more than two decades.

No one knows exactly how many Muslims live in the United States—the estimates, prone to exaggeration, range widely—but their numbers clearly range in the several millions. The faithful divide into two main groups, immigrants and converts, with immigrants two to three times more numerous than converts. The immigrants come from all over the world, but especially from South Asia, Iran, and the Arabic-speaking countries; converts tend overwhelmingly to be African-American.

This community now faces a profound choice: either it can integrate within the United States or it can be Islamist and remain apart. It's a choice with major implications for both the U.S. and the Muslim world.

Integrationist Muslims—some pious, others not—can live simultaneously as patriotic Americans and as committed Muslims. Such Muslims have no problem giving their allegiance to a non-Muslim government. Integrationists believe that what American culture calls for—hard work, honesty, tolerance—is compatible with Islamic beliefs, and they even see Islam as reaffirming such classic American values. They accept that the United States is not a Muslim country, and they seek ways to live successfully within its Constitutional framework. Symbolic of this positive outlook, the Islamic Supreme Council of America proudly displays an American flag on its Internet home page.

American Muslims who go the Islamist route, however, reject American civilization, based as it is on a mix of Christian and Enlightenment values that they find anathema. Islamists believe that their ways are superior to America's, and they want to impose these on the entire country. In the short term, they promote Islam as the solution to the nation's social and moral ills. Over time, however, and much more radically, they want to transform the United States into a Muslim country run along strict Islamist lines. Giving expression to this radical view, Zaid Shakir, a former Muslim chaplain at Yale University, argues that Muslims cannot accept the legitimacy of the existing American order, since it "is against the orders and ordainments of Allah." "[T]he orientation of the Quran," he adds, "pushes us in the exact opposite direction." However outlandish a political goal this might seem, it is widely discussed in Islamist circles, and the events of September 11 should make clear just how seriously U.S. authorities must take this ambition.

The great debate among Islamists is, in fact, not over the desirability or plausibility of transforming the U.S. into a Muslim nation but whether to work toward this goal in a legal but slow way, through conversion, or by taking a riskier but swifter illegal path that would require violence. Shamim A. Siddiqi, a Pakistani immigrant, expects that vast numbers of Americans will peacefully convert to Islam in what he calls a "Rush-to-Islam." Omar Abdel Rahman, the blind sheikh behind the 1993 World Trade Center bombing, wants Muslims to "conquer the land of the infidels." These two approaches can and do overlap, with some pinstripe-suited lobbyists in Washington doing things that help terrorists, such as closing down the practice of profiling Middle Eastern–looking airline passengers.

Integrationists tend to be thankful to live in the United States, with its rule of law, democracy, and personal freedoms. Islamists despise these achievements and long to bring the ways of Iran or Afghanistan to America.

Integrationists seek to create an American Islam and can take part in American life. Islamists, who want an Islamic America, cannot.

The good news is that integrationists far outnumber Islamists. The bad news—and this poses a real and still largely unacknowledged problem for the United States—is that Islamists are much more active in Muslim affairs than integrationists and control nearly all of the nation's Muslim institutions: mosques, schools, community centers, publications, websites, and national organizations. It is the Islamists who receive invitations to the White House and the State Department. It was primarily Islamists with whom President Bush, in gestures intended to reassure American Muslims, met with twice after September 11.

What must Americans do to protect themselves from Islamists while safeguarding the civil rights of law-abiding Muslims? The first and most straightforward thing is not to allow any more Islamists into the country. Each Islamist who enters the United States, whether as a visitor or an immigrant, is one more enemy on the home front. Officials need to scrutinize the speech, associations, and activities of potential visitors or immigrants for any signs of Islamist allegiances and keep out anyone they suspect of such ties. Some civil libertarian purists will howl, as they once did over similar legislation designed to keep out Marxist-Leninists. But this is simply a matter of national self-protection.

Laws already on the books allow for such a policy, though excercising them these days is extremely difficult, requiring the direct involvement of the secretary of state. . . . Though written decades before Islamism appeared on the U.S. scene, for example, the 1952 McCarren-Walter Act permits the exclusion of anyone seeking to overthrow the U.S. government. Other regulations would keep out people suspected of terrorism or of committing other acts with "potentially serious adverse foreign policy consequences." U.S. officials need greater leeway to enforce these laws.

Keeping Islamists out of the country is an obvious first step, but it will be equally important to watch closely Islamists already living here as citizens or residents. Unfortunately, this means all Muslims must face heightened scrutiny. For the inescapable and painful fact is that, while anyone might become a fascist or communist, only Muslims find Islamism tempting. And if it is true that most Muslims aren't Islamists, it is no less true that all Islamists are Muslims. Muslims can expect that police searching for suspects after any new terrorist attack will not spend much time checking out churches, synagogues, or Hindu temples but will concentrate on mosques. Guards at government buildings will more likely question pedestrians who appear Middle Eastern or wear headscarves.

Because such measures have an admittedly prejudicial quality, authorities in the past have shown great reluctance to take them, an attitude Islamists and their apologists have reinforced, seeking to stifle any attempt to single out Muslims for scrutiny. When Muslims have committed crimes, officials have even bent over backward to disassociate their motives from militant Islam. For example, the Lebanese cabdriver who fired at a van full of Orthodox Jewish boys on the Brooklyn Bridge in 1994, leaving one child dead, had a well-documented fury at Israel and Jews—but the FBI ascribed his motive to "road rage." Only after a persistent campaign by the murdered boy's mother did the FBI finally classify the attack as "the crimes of a terrorist," almost seven years after the killing. Reluctance to come to terms with militant Islam might have been understandable before September 11—but no longer.

Heightened scrutiny of Muslims has become de rigueur at the nation's airports and must remain so. Airline security personnel used to look hard at Arabs and Muslims, but that was before the relevant lobbies raised so much fuss about "airline profiling" as a form of discrimination that the airlines effectively abandoned the practice. The absence of such a commonsense policy meant that 19 Muslim Arab hijackers could board four separate flights on September 11 with ease.

Greater scrutiny of Muslims also means watching out for Islamist "sleepers"—individuals who go quietly about their business until, one day, they receive the call from their controllers and spring into action as part of a terrorist operation. The four teams of September 11 hijackers show how deep deception can go. As one investigator, noting the length of time the 19 terrorists spent in the United States, explained, "These weren't people coming over the border just to attack quickly. . . . They cultivated friends, and blended into American society to further their ability to strike." Stopping sleepers before they are activated and strike will require greater vigilance at the nation's borders, good intelligence, and citizen watchfulness.

Resident Muslim aliens who reveal themselves to be Islamist should be immediately expelled from the country before they have a chance to act. Citizen Islamists will have to be watched very closely and without cease.

Even as the nation monitors the Muslim world within its borders more closely for signs of Islamism, it must continue, of course, to protect the civil rights of law-abiding American Muslims. Political leaders should regularly and publicly distinguish between Islam, the religion of Muslims, and Islamism, the totalitarian ideology. In addition, they should do everything in their power to make sure that individual Muslims, mosques, and other legal institutions continue to enjoy the full protection of the law. A time of crisis doesn't change the presumption of innocence at the core of our legal system. Police should provide extra protection for Muslims to prevent acts of vandalism against their property or their persons.

Thankfully, some American Muslims (and Arab-Americans, most of whom actually are Christian) understand that by accepting some personal inconvenience—and even, let's be honest, some degree of humiliation—they are helping to protect both the country and themselves. Tarek E. Masoud, a Yale graduate student, shows a good sense that many of his elders seem to lack: "How many thousands of lives would have been saved if people like me had been inconvenienced with having our bags searched and being made to answer questions?" he asks. "People say profiling makes them feel like criminals. It does—I know this firsthand. But would that I had been made to feel like a criminal a thousand times over than to live to see the grisly handiwork of real criminals in New York and Washington."

A third key task will be to combat the totalitarian ideology of militant Islam. That means isolating such noisy and vicious Islamist institutions as the

American Muslim Council, the Council on American-Islamic Relations, and the Muslim Public Affairs Council. Politicians, the press, corporations, voluntary organizations, and society as a whole—all must shun these groups and grant them not a shred of legitimacy. Tax authorities and law enforcement should watch them like hawks, much as they watch the Teamsters.

Fighting Islamist ideology will also require shutting down Internet sites that promote Islamist violence, recruit new members to the terrorist campaign against the West, and raise money for militant Islamic causes ("Donate money for the military Jihad," exhorts one such website). The federal government began to take action even before September 11, closing InfoCom, a Dallas-based host for many Islamist organizations, some of them funneling money to militant Islamic groups abroad.

Essential, too, in the struggle against Islamist ideology will be reaching out to moderate non-Islamist Muslims for help. These are the people unfairly tarred by Islamist excesses, after all, and so are eager to stop this extremist movement. Bringing them on board has several advantages: they can provide valuable advice, they can penetrate clandestine Islamist organizations, and their involvement in the effort against Islamism blunts the inevitable charges of "Islamophobia."

Further, experts on Islam and Muslims—academics, journalists, religious figures, and government officials—must be held to account for their views. For too long now, they have apologized for Islamism rather than interpreted it honestly. As such, they bear some responsibility for the unpreparedness that led to September's horror. The press and other media need to show greater objectivity in covering Islam. In the past, they have shamefully covered up for it. The recent PBS documentary *Islam: Empire of Faith* is a case in point, offering, as the *Wall Street Journal* sharply put it, an "uncritical adoration of Islam, more appropriate to a tract for true believers than a documentary purporting to give the American public a balanced account." Islamists in New York City celebrated the destruction on September 11 at their mosques, but journalists refused to report the story for fear of offending Muslims, effectively concealing this important information from the U.S. public.

Taking these three steps—keeping Islamists out, watching them within the nation's borders without violating the civil liberties of American Muslims, and delegitimating extremists—permits Americans to be fair toward the moderate majority of Muslims while fighting militant Islam. It will be a difficult balancing act, demanding sensitivity without succumbing to political correctness. But it is both essential and achievable.

David A. Harris  **NO**

"Flying while Arab," Immigration Issues, and Lessons from the Racial Profiling Controversy

What changes in the law might we see? We know that we are a nation of immigrants—that, in many ways, immigrants built our great nation. We know that the immigrant experience has, in many ways, been at the core of the American experience, and that the diversity that these people have brought to our country has been, and continues to be, our greatest strength. But we also know that we have sometimes dealt harshly and unfairly with them, especially in times of national emergency and crisis. Thus the Commission does exactly the right thing by inquiring into these issues now, even as new legislative proposals continue to unfold in the Congress. In short, we seek to understand what the implications will be of the changes that will surely come because of the events of September 11—changes in the very idea of what America is, and what it will be in the future.

History

I said earlier that our history gives us reason to feel concern at such a critical juncture. Any serious appraisal of American history during the some of the key periods of the twentieth century would counsel an abundance of caution; when we have faced other national security crises, we have sometimes overreacted—or at the very least acted more out of emotion than was wise. In the wake of World War I, the infamous Palmer Raids resulted in the rounding up of a considerable number of immigrants. These people were deported, often without so much as a scintilla of evidence. During the Second World War, tens of thousands of Japanese—immigrants and native born, citizens and legal residents—were interned in camps, their property confiscated and sold off at fire-sale prices. To its everlasting shame, the U.S. Supreme Court gave the internment of the Japanese its constitutional blessing in the infamous Korematsu case. It took the United States government decades, but eventually it apologized and paid reparations to the Japanese. And during the 1950s, the Red Scare resulted in the ruining of lives and careers and the jailing of citizens, because they had had the temerity to exercise their constitutionally protected rights to free association by becoming members of the Communist Party years before.

From Testimony before U.S. Commission on Civil Rights, October 12, 2001.

Categorical Thinking

We must hope that we have learned the lessons of this history—that the emotions of the moment, when we feel threatened, can cause us to damage our civil liberties and our fellow citizens, and that this is particularly true for our immigrant populations. And it is this legacy that should make us think now, even as we engage in a long and detailed investigation of the September 11 terror attacks. As we listen to accounts of that investigation, reports indicate that the investigation has been strongly focused on Arab Americans and Muslims. What's more, private citizens have made Middle Eastern appearance an important criterion in deciding how to react to those who look different around them. Many of these reports have involved treatment of persons of Middle Eastern descent in airports.

In itself, this is not really surprising. We face a situation in which there has been a catastrophic terrorist attack by a small group of suicidal hijackers, and as far as we know, all of those involved were Arabs and Muslims and had Arabic surnames. Some or all had entered the country recently. Given the incredibly high stakes, some Americans have reacted to Middle Easterners as a group, based on their appearance. In a way, this is understandable. We seldom have much information on any of the strangers around us, so we tend to think in broad categories. It is a natural human reaction to fear to make judgments concerning our safety based on these broad categories, and to avoid those who arouse fear in us. This may translate easily into a type of racial and ethnic profiling, in which—as has been reported in the last few weeks—passengers on airliners refuse to fly with other passengers who have a Middle Eastern appearance.

Use of Race and Ethnic Appearance in Law Enforcement

The far more worrying development, however, is the possibility that profiling of Arabs and Muslims will become standard procedure in law enforcement. Again, it is not hard to understand the impulse; we want to catch and stop these suicidal hijackers, every one of whom fits the description of Arab or Muslim. So we stop, question, and search more of these people because we believe it's a way to play the odds. If all the September 11 terrorists were Middle Easterners, then we get the biggest bang for the enforcement buck by questioning, searching, and screening as many Middle Easterners as possible. This should give us the best chance of finding those who helped the terrorists or those bent on creating further havoc.

But as we embark in this new world, a world changed so drastically by the events of September 11, we need to be conscious of some of the things that we have learned over the last few years in the ongoing racial profiling controversy. Using race or ethnic appearance as part of a *description* of particular suspects may indeed help an investigation; using race or ethnic appearance as a broad *predictor* of who is involved in crime or terrorism will likely hurt our investigative efforts. All the evidence indicates that profiling Arab

Americans or Muslims would be an ineffective waste of law enforcement resources that would damage our intelligence efforts while it compromises basic civil liberties. If we want to do everything we can to secure our country, we have to be smart about the steps we take.

As we think about the possible profiling of Arabs and Muslims, recall that much the same argument has been made for years about domestic efforts against drugs and crime. African Americans and Latinos are disproportionately involved in drug crime, the reasoning goes; therefore concentrate on them. Many state and local police agencies, led by the federal Drug Enforcement Administration, did exactly that from the late 1980s on. We now know that police departments in many jurisdictions used racial profiling, especially in efforts to get drugs and guns off the highways and out of the cities. But as we look back, what really stands out is how ineffective this profile-based law enforcement was. In departments that focused on African Americans, Latinos, and other minorities, the "hit rates"—the rates of successful searches—were actually *lower* for minorities than they were for whites, who were not apprehended by using a racial or ethnic profile. That's right: when these agencies used race or ethnic appearance as a factor— not as *the only* factor but *one factor among many*—they did not get the higher returns on their enforcement efforts that they were expecting.

This is because race and ethnic appearance are very poor predictors of behavior. Race and ethnicity describe people well, and there is absolutely nothing wrong with using skin color or other features to describe known suspects. But since only a very small percentage of African Americans and Latinos participate in the drug trade, race and ethnic appearance do a bad job identifying the *particular* African Americans and Latinos in whom police should be interested. Racial and ethnic profiling caused police to spread their enforcement net far too widely and indiscriminately.

The results of this misguided effort have been disastrous for law enforcement: constant efforts to stop, question, and search people who "look like" suspects, the vast majority of whom are hard working, tax paying citizens. This treatment has alienated African Americans, Latinos, and other minorities from the police—a critical strategic loss in the fight against crime, since police can only win this fight if they have the full cooperation and support of those they serve. And it is precisely this lesson we ought to think about now, as the cry goes up to use profiling and intensive searches against people who look Middle Eastern or Muslim.

Even if the hijackers share a particular ethnic appearance or background, subjecting *all* Middle Easterners to intrusive questioning, stops, or searches will have a perverse and unexpected effect: it will spread our enforcement and detection efforts over a huge pool of people who we would not otherwise think worthy of any police attention. Profiling will drain enforcement efforts and resources away from more worthy investigative efforts and tactics that focus on the close observation of behavior—like the buying of expensive one-way tickets with cash just a short time before takeoff, as some of the World Trade Center hijackers did. Focusing on race and ethnicity keeps police attention on a set of surface details that tell us very little, and draw officers' attention away from what is much more important and concrete: conduct.

At least as important, one of the most crucial tools we can use against terrorism is intelligence. And if we are concerned about terrorists of Middle Eastern origin, among the most fertile places from which to gather intelligence will the Arab American and Muslim communities. If we adopt a security policy that stigmatizes every member of these groups in airports and other public places with intrusive stops, questioning, and searches, we will alienate them from the enforcement efforts at precisely the time we need them most. And the larger the population we subject to this treatment, the greater the total amount of damage we inflict on law-abiding persons.

And of course the profiling of Arabs and Muslims assumes that we need worry about only one type of terrorist. We must not forget that, prior to the attacks on September 11, the most deadly terrorist attack on American soil was carried out not by Middle Easterners with Arabic names and accents, but by two very average American white men: Timothy McVeigh, a U.S. Army veteran from upstate New York, and Terry Nichols, a farmer from Michigan. Yet we were smart enough in the wake of McVeigh and Nichols' crime not to call for a profile emphasizing the fact that the perpetrators were white males. The unhappy truth is that we just don't know what the next group of terrorists might look like.

Treatment of Immigrants

The numbers from the 2000 census of our country's population tell us that the 1990s were a time of considerable immigration to the United States. Some of this immigration came from Asia and the Middle East. These immigrants helped many of our older cities make population gains not seen in some time, and helped the American economy to achieve unprecedented growth and prosperity. This was especially true in the high technology sector, which has become a crucial mainstay of growth over the last ten years despite a shortage of American workers to fill computer-oriented positions. Immigrants stepped into the breach for us, bolstering our high-tech labor force just when we needed it.

Yet under the antiterrorism proposal now circulating in the U.S. Senate, immigrants could suffer treatment that smacks strongly of racial profiling and associated practices. Popularly referred to as the USA Act, S. 1510 allows the unlimited detention of noncitizens whom the Attorney General moves to deport or charge criminally, when the Attorney General "reasonably believes" these noncitizens to be engaged in certain terrorist activities. If none of the specifically mentioned activities applies, the Attorney General can still detain the noncitizens based on his or her own determination that the noncitizen "is engaged in any other activity that endangers the national security of the United States." . . .

The Attorney General is empowered to hold these noncitizens even in the face of a court's determination that they are not terrorists. And if the government attempts to deport them and no nation will take them, the legislation appears to allow the Attorney General to detain them indefinitely. The slippery slope here is obvious; the dangers of abuse are easy to see. The basic structure of Section 412 allows the Attorney General to make the decision of who is a terrorist suspect, and to continue to detain these people even in the face of contrary judicial review. The checks and balances built into our basic system of government vanish under this scheme—a worrisome development under any circumstances.

Conclusion

The terrorist attacks in New York and Washington present us with many difficult choices that will test our resolve and our abilities. We must find effective ways to secure ourselves without giving up what is best about our country; the proper balance will often be difficult to discern. But we should not simply repeat the mistakes of the past as we take on this new challenge. Nobody would gain from that—except those who would destroy us.

POSTSCRIPT

Is "Middle Eastern" Profiling
Ever Justified?

Both David Harris and Daniel Pipes tend to use "Muslim" and Middle Eastern" interchangeably. This is understandable, since the Middle East is predominantly Muslim, but it conflates terms that are quite distinct. Muslim refers to a religion, that of Islam. In this case, the religion is relevant, since Al Qaeda and other terrorist groups claim to be acting in the name of it. But a person's religion (absent some religious insignia) is invisible to the eye, so the tendency is to shift one's attention into something connected with appearance, such as skin color or facial features. The result can be confusing—and unfair. There are tan-complexioned Catholics from the Middle East and blond Chechnyan Muslims. Who are more likely to be scrutinized at the airport?

In his testimony, Harris makes reference to his earlier book, *Profiles in Injustice: Why Racial Profiling Cannot Work* (New Press, 2003), an analysis of racial profiling, its uses, and, he believes, its ultimate failure in crime prevention. In Daniel Pipes' *Militant Islam Reaches America* (Norton, 2003), one of the dozen or so he has published on the Middle East and what he calls "Islamism," he portrays it as the greatest threat to the United States since the end of the Cold War. While not directly addressing the issue of profiling, Samuel P. Huntington's seminal *The Clash of Civilizations and the Remaking of the World Order* (Touchstone Books, 1998) still remains as a powerful challenge to those who hope that "modernization" will bring Western-style democracy to the Middle East. Bernard Lewis's *What Went Wrong: The Clash Between Islam and Modernity in the Middle East* (Perennial, 2003) and his more recent *From Babel to Dragomans; Interpreting the Middle East* (Oxford, 2004) reach back far into the history of the Middle East and attempt to demonstrate his long-held contention that Islam presents a formidable obstacle to modernization. Michael Wolfe, ed., *Taking Back Islam: American Muslims Reclaim Their Faith* (Rodale Press, 2002) is a collection of writings from several American Muslims, including Yusuf Islam (Cat Stevens) and newer voices such as Aasma Khan, all of whom claim to represent a silent majority of "progressive" Muslims determined to divest their religion of its associations with terrorism and sexism.

Brian L. Wuthrow's *Racial Profiling: From Rhetoric to Reason* (Prentice-Hall, 2005) is an attempt to take the issue of profiling beyond the super-heated exchanges one sees in the media; Wuthorw summarizes some of the conclusions of social science analysts on the subject. In a similar vein is *Racial Profiling: Issues, Data and Analysis,* edited by Steven J. Muffler (Nova Science Publications, 2006).

The arguments for and against profiling are likely to continue as long as the threat of terror remains, which would appear to be indefinitely. But perhaps some sort of compromise is possible between the contending points of view. The case of Richard Reid, the would-be "shoe bomber," is instructive. Reid's attempt to ignite the explosive charge in his shoe was first detected by a flight attendant, who smelled the sulfur from his burning match, and he was wrestled to the ground by quick-thinking passengers. The lesson is that suspicious *actions* may be a better indication of the potential for terrorism than anything having to do with appearance—though, judging from the menacing photos of Reid, it is possible to speculate that the flight attendant was already keeping an eye on him.

ISSUE 12

Should Abortion Be Restricted?

YES: Robert P. George, from *The Clash of Orthodoxies: Law, Religion, and Morality in Crisis* (ISI Books, 2001)

NO: Mary Gordon, from "A Moral Choice," *The Atlantic Monthly* (March 1990)

ISSUE SUMMARY

YES: Legal philosopher Robert P. George asserts that, since each of us was a human being from conception, abortion is a form of homicide and should be banned.

NO: Writer Mary Gordon maintains that having an abortion is a moral choice that women are capable of making for themselves, that aborting a fetus is not killing a person, and that antiabortionists fail to understand female sexuality.

Until 1973 the laws governing abortion were set by the states, most of which barred legal abortion except where pregnancy imperiled the life of the pregnant woman. In that year, the U.S. Supreme Court decided the controversial case *Roe v. Wade.* The *Roe* decision acknowledged both a woman's "fundamental right" to terminate a pregnancy before fetal viability and the state's legitimate interest in protecting both the woman's health and the "potential life" of the fetus. It prohibited states from banning abortion to protect the fetus before the third trimester of a pregnancy, and it ruled that even during that final trimester, a woman could obtain an abortion if she could prove that her life or health would be endangered by carrying to term. (In a companion case to *Roe,* decided on the same day, the Court defined *health* broadly enough to include "all factors—physical, emotional, psychological, familial, and the woman's age—relevant to the well-being of the patient.") These holdings, together with the requirement that state regulation of abortion had to survive "strict scrutiny" and demonstrate a "compelling state interest," resulting in later decisions striking down mandatory 24-hour waiting periods, requirements that abortions be performed in hospitals, and socalled informed consent laws.

The Supreme Court did uphold state laws requiring parental notification and consent for minors (though it provided that minors could seek permission from a judge if they feared notifying their parents). And federal courts have affirmed the right of Congress not to pay for abortions. Proabortion groups, proclaiming the "right to choose," have charged that this and similar action at the state level discriminates against poor women because it does not inhibit the ability of women who are able to pay for abortions to obtain them. Efforts to adopt a constitutional amendment or federal law barring abortion have failed, but antiabortion forces have influenced legislation in many states.

Can legislatures and courts establish the existence of a scientific fact? Opponents of abortion believe that it is a fact that life begins at conception and that the law must therefore uphold and enforce this concept. They argue that the human fetus is a live human being, and they note all the familiar signs of life displayed by the fetus: a beating heart, brain waves, thumb sucking, and so on. Those who defend abortion maintain that human life does not begin before the development of specifically human characteristics and possibly not until the birth of a child. As Justice Harry A. Blackmun put it in 1973, "There has always been strong support for the view that life does not begin until live birth."

Antiabortion forces sought a court case that might lead to the overturning of *Roe v. Wade.* Proabortion forces rallied to oppose new state laws limiting or prohibiting abortion. In *Webster v. Reproductive Health Services* (1989), with four new justices, the Supreme Court upheld a Missouri law that banned abortions in public hospitals and abortions that were performed by public employees (except to save a woman's life). The law also required that tests be performed on any fetus more than 20 weeks old to determine its viability. In the later decision of *Planned Parenthood v. Casey* (1992), however, the Court affirmed what it called the "essence" of the constitutional right to abortion while permitting some state restrictions, such as a 24-hour waiting period and parental notification in the case of minors.

In 2000, a five-to-four decision of the Supreme Court in *Stenberg v. Carhart* overturned a Nebraska law that outlawed "partial birth" abortions. The law defined "partial birth abortion" as a procedure in which the doctor "partially delivers vaginally a living child before killing" the child, further defining the process as "intentionally delivering into the vagina a living unborn child, or a substantial portion thereof, for the purpose of performing a procedure that the [abortionist] knows will kill the child." The Court's stated reason for striking down the law was that it lacked a "health" exception. Critics complained that the Court has defined "health" so broadly that it includes not only physical health but also "emotional, psychological," and "familial" health, and that the person the Court has authorized to make these judgments is the attendant physician, that is, the abortionist himself.

In the following selections, Robert P. George contends that, since each of us was a human being from conception, abortion is a form of homicide and should be banned. Mary Gordon asserts that the fetus removed in most abortions may not be considered a person and that women must retain the right to make decisions regarding their sexual lives.

YES

Robert P. George

God's Reasons

In his contributions to the February 1996 issue of *First Things* magazine—contributions in which what he has to say (particularly in his critique of liberalism) is far more often right than wrong—Stanley Fish of Duke University cites the dispute over abortion as an example of a case in which "incompatible first assumptions [or] articles of opposing faiths"—make the resolution of the dispute (other than by sheer political power) impossible. Here is how Fish presented the pro-life and pro-choice positions and the shape of the dispute between their respective defenders:

> A pro-life advocate sees abortion as a sin against God who infuses life at the moment of conception; a pro-choice advocate sees abortion as a decision to be made in accordance with the best scientific opinion as to when the beginning of life, as we know it, occurs. No conversation between them can ever get started because each of them starts from a different place and they could never agree as to what they were conversing *about.* A pro-lifer starts from a belief in the direct agency of a personal God, and this belief, this religious conviction, is not incidental to his position; it is his position, and determines its features in all their detail. The "content of a belief" is a *function* of its source, and the critiques of one will always be the critique of the other.

It is certainly true that the overwhelming majority of pro-life Americans are religious believers and that a great many pro-choice Americans are either unbelievers or less observant or less traditional in their beliefs and practice than their fellow citizens. Indeed, although most Americans believe in God, polling data consistently show that Protestants, Catholics, and Jews who do not regularly attend church or synagogue are less likely than their more observant co-religionists to oppose abortion. And religion is plainly salient politically when it comes to the issue of abortion. The more secularized a community, the more likely that community is to elect pro-choice politicians to legislative and executive offices.

Still, I don't think that Fish's presentation of the pro-life and pro-choice positions, or of the shape of the dispute over abortion, is accurate. True, inasmuch as most pro-life advocates are traditional religious believers who, as such, see gravely unjust or otherwise immoral acts as sins—and understand sins precisely as offenses against God—"a pro-life advocate sees abortion as a sin

From Robert P. George, *The Clash of Orthodoxies: Law, Religion, and Morality in Crisis* (ISI Books, 2001). Copyright © 2001 by Robert P. George. Reprinted by permission of ISI Books, an imprint of The Intercollegiate Studies Institute. Notes omitted.

against God." But most pro-life advocates see abortion as a sin against God *precisely because it is the unjust taking of innocent human life.* That is their reason for opposing abortion; and that is God's reason, as they see it, for opposing abortion and requiring that human communities protect their unborn members against it. And, they believe, as I do, that this reason can be identified and acted on even independently of God's revealing it. Indeed, they typically believe, as I do, that the precise content of what God reveals on the subject ("in they mother's womb I formed thee") cannot be known without the application of human intelligence, by way of philosophical and scientific inquiry, to the question.

Fish is mistaken, then, in *contrasting* the pro-life advocate with the pro-choice advocate by depicting (only) the latter as viewing abortion as "a decision to be made in accordance with the best scientific opinion as to when the beginning of life . . . occurs." First of all, supporters of the pro-choice position are increasingly willing to sanction the practice of abortion even where they concede that it constitutes the taking of innocent human life. Pro-choice writers from Naomi Wolfe to Judith Jarvis Thomson have advanced theories of abortion as "justifiable homicide." But, more to the point, people on the pro-life side *insist* that the central issue in the debate is the question "as to when the beginning of life occurs." And they insist with equal vigor that this question is not a "religious" or even "metaphysical" one: it is rather, as Fish says, "scientific." In response to this insistence, it is pro-choice advocates who typically want to transform the question into a "metaphysical" or "religious" one. It was Justice Harry Blackmun who claimed in his opinion for the Court legalizing abortion in *Roe v. Wade* (1973) that "at this point in man's knowledge" the scientific evidence was inconclusive and therefore could not determine the outcome of the case. And twenty years later, the influential pro-choice writer Ronald Dworkin went on record claiming that the question of abortion is inherently "religious." It is pro-choice advocates, such as Dworkin, who want to distinguish between when a human being comes into existence "in the biological sense and when a human being comes into existence" in the moral sense. It is they who want to distinguish a class of human beings "with rights" from pre- (or post-) conscious human beings who "don't have rights." And the reason for this, I submit, is that, short of defending abortion as "justifiable homicide," the pro-choice position collapses if the issue is to be settled purely on the basis of scientific inquiry into the question of when a new member of Homo sapiens comes into existence as a self-integrating organism whose unity, distinctiveness, and identity remain intact as it develops without substantial change from the point of its beginning through the various stages of its development and into adulthood.

All this was, I believe, made wonderfully clear at a debate at the 1997 meeting of the American Political Science Association between Jeffrey Reiman of American University, defending the pro-choice position, and John Finnis of Oxford and Notre Dame, defending the pro-life view. That debate was remarkable for the skill, intellectual honesty, and candor of the interlocutors. What is most relevant to our deliberations, however, is the fact that it truly was a debate Reiman and Finnis did not talk past each other. They did not proceed from "incompatible first assumptions." They *did* manage to agree as to what they were talking *about*—and it was not about whether or when life was infused by God. It was precisely about the *rational* (i.e., scientific and philosophical) grounds, if any, available for distinguishing a class of human beings "in the moral sense" (with rights) from a class of human beings "in the (merely) biological sense" (without rights). Finnis did not claim any special revelation to the effect that no such grounds existed. Nor did Reiman claim that Finnis's arguments against his view appealed implicitly (and illicitly) to some such putative revelation. Although Finnis is a Christian and, as such, believes that the new human life that begins at conception is in each and every case created by God in His image and likeness, his argument never invoked, much less did it "start from a belief in the direct agency of a personal God." It proceeded, rather, by way of point-by-point philosophical challenge to Reiman's philosophical arguments. Finnis marshaled the scientific facts of embryogenesis and intrauterine human development and defied Reiman to identify grounds, compatible with those facts, for denying a right to life to human beings in the embryonic and fetal stages of development.

Interestingly, Reiman began his remarks with a statement that would seem to support what Fish said in *First Things*. While allowing that debates over abortion were useful in clarifying people's thinking about the issue, Reiman remarked that they "never actually cause people to change their minds." It is true, I suppose, that people who are deeply committed emotionally to one side or the other are unlikely to have a road-to-Damascus type conversion after listening to a formal philosophical debate. Still, any open-minded person who sincerely wishes to settle his mind on the question of abortion—and there continue to be many such people, I believe—would find debates such as the one between Reiman and Finnis to be extremely helpful toward that end. Anyone willing to consider the *reasons* for and against abortion and its legal prohibition or permission would benefit from reading or hearing the accounts of these reasons proposed by capable and honest thinkers on both sides. Of course, when it comes to an issue like abortion, people can have powerful motives for clinging to a particular position even if they are presented with conclusive reasons for changing their minds. But that doesn't mean that such reasons do not exist.

I believe that the pro-life position is superior to the pro-choice position precisely because the scientific evidence, considered honestly and dispassionately, fully supports it. A human being is conceived when a human sperm containing twenty-three chromosomes fuses with a human egg also containing twenty-three chromosomes (albeit of a different kind) producing a single-cell human zygote containing, in the normal case, forty-six chromosomes that are mixed differently from the forty-six chromosomes as found in the mother or father. Unlike the gametes (that is, the sperm and egg), the zygote is genetically unique and distinct from its parents. Biologically, it is a separate organism. It produces, as the gametes do not, specifically human enzymes and proteins. It possesses, as they do not, the active capacity or potency to develop itself into a human embryo, fetus, infant, child, adolescent, and adult.

Assuming that it is not conceived *in vitro,* the zygote is, of course, in a state of dependence on its mother. But independence should not be confused with distinctness. From the beginning, the newly conceived human being, not its mother, directs its integral organic functioning. It takes in nourishment and converts it to energy. Given a hospitable environment, it will, as Dianne Nutwell Irving says, "develop continuously without any biological interruptions, or gaps, throughout the embryonic, fetal, neo-natal, childhood and adulthood stages—until the death of the organism."

⋅❀⋅

Some claim to find the logical implication of these facts—that is, that life begins at conception—to be "virtually unintelligible." A leading exponent of that point of view in the legal academy is Jed Rubenfeld of Yale Law School, author of an influential article entitled "On the Legal Status of the Proposition that 'Life Begins at Conception.'" Rubenfeld argues that, like the zygote, *every* cell in the human body is "genetically complete"; yet nobody supposes that every human cell is a distinct human being with a right to life. However, Rubenfeld misses the point that there comes into being at conception, not a mere clump of human cells, but a distinct, unified, self-integrating organism, which develops itself, truly himself or herself, in accord with its own genetic "blueprint." The significance of genetic completeness for the status of newly conceived human beings is that no outside genetic material is required to enable the zygote to mature into an embryo, the embryo into a fetus, the fetus into an infant, the infant into a child, the child into an adolescent, the adolescent into an adult. What the zygote needs to function as a distinct self-integrating human organism, a human being, it already possesses.

At no point in embryogenesis, therefore, does the distinct organism that came into being when it was conceived undergo what is technically called "substantial change" (or a change of natures). It is human and will remain human. This is the point of Justice Byron White's remark in his dissenting opinion in *Thornburgh v. American College of Obstetricians & Gynecologists* that "there is no non-arbitrary line separating a fetus from a child." Rubenfeld attacks White's point, which he calls "[t]he argument based on the gradualness of gestation," by pointing out that, "[n]o non-arbitrary line separates the hues of green and red. Shall we conclude that green is red?"

White's point, however, was *not* that fetal development is "gradual," but that it is *continuous* and is the (continuous) development of a single lasting (fully human) being. The human zygote that actively develops itself is, as I have pointed out, a genetically complete organism directing its own integral organic functioning. As it matures, *in utero* and *ex utero,* it does not "become" a human being, for it is a human being *already,* albeit an immature human being, just as a newborn infant is an immature human being who will undergo quite dramatic growth and development over time.

These considerations undermine the familiar argument, recited by Rubenfeld, that "the potential" of an *unfertilized* ovum to develop into a whole human being does not make it into "a person." The fact is, though, that an ovum is not a whole human being. It is, rather, a part of another human being (the woman whose ovum it is) with merely the potential to give rise to, in interaction with a part of yet another human being (a man's sperm cell), a new and whole human being. Unlike the zygote, it lacks both genetic distinctness and completeness, as well as the active capacity to develop itself into an adult member of the human species. It is living human cellular material, but, left to itself, it will never become a human being, however hospitable its environment may be. It will "die" as a human ovum, just as countless skin cells "die" daily as nothing more than skin cells. If successfully fertilized by a human sperm, which, like the ovum (but dramatically unlike the zygote), lacks the active potential to develop into an adult member of the human species, then *substantial* change (that is, a change of *natures*) will occur. There will no longer be merely an egg, which was part of the mother, sharing her genetic composition, and a sperm, which was part of the father, sharing his genetic composition; instead, there will be a genetically complete, distinct, unified, self-integrating human organism, whose nature differs from that of the gametes—not mere human material, but a human being.

These considerations also make clear that it is incorrect to argue (as some pro-choice advocates have argued) that, just as "I" was never a week-old sperm or ovum, "I" was likewise never a week-old embryo. It truly makes no sense to say that "I" was once a sperm (or an unfertilized egg) that matured into an adult. Conception was the occasion of substantial change (that is, change from one complete individual entity to another) that brought into being a distinct self-integrating organism with a specifically human nature. By contrast, it makes every bit as much sense to say that I was once a week-old embryo as to say that I was once a week-old infant or a ten-year-old child. It was the new organism created at conception that, without itself undergoing any change of substance, matured into a week-old embryo, a fetus, an infant, a child, an adolescent, and, finally, an adult.

But Rubenfeld has another argument: "Cloning processes give to non-zygotic cells the potential for development into distinct, self-integrating human beings; thus to recognize the zygote as a human being is to recognize all human cells as human beings, which is absurd."

It is true that a distinct, self-integrating human organism that came into being by a process of cloning would be, like a human organism that comes into being as a monozygotic twin, a human being. That being, no less than human beings conceived by the union of sperm and egg, would possess a human nature and the active potential to mature as a human being. However, even assuming the possibility of cloning human beings from non-zygotic human cells, the non-zygotic cell must be activated by a process that effects substantial change and not mere development or maturation. Left to itself, apart from an activation process capable of effecting a change of substance or natures, the cell will mature and die as a human cell, not as a human being.

❧

The scientific evidence establishes the fact that each of us was, from conception, a human being. Science, not religion, vindicates this crucial premise of the pro-life claim. From it, there is no avoiding the conclusion that deliberate feticide is a form of homicide. The only real questions remaining are moral and political, not scientific: Although I will not go into the matter here, I do not see how direct abortion can even be considered a matter of "justified homicide." It is important to recognize, however, as traditional moralists always have recognized, that not all procedures that foreseeably result in fetal death are, properly speaking, abortions. Although any procedure whose precise objective is the destruction of fetal life is certainly an abortion, and cannot be justified, some procedures result in fetal death as an unintended, albeit foreseen and accepted, side effect. Where procedures of the latter sort are done for very grave reasons, they may be justifiable. For example, traditional morality recognizes that a surgical operation to remove a life-threateningly cancerous uterus, even in a woman whose pregnancy is not far enough along to enable the child to be removed from her womb and sustained by a life support system, is ordinarily morally permissible. Of course, there are in this area of moral reflection, as in others, "borderline" cases that are difficult to classify and evaluate. Mercifully, modern medical technology has made such cases exceptionally rare in real life. Only in the most extraordinary circumstances today do women and their families and physicians find it necessary to consider a procedure that will result in fetal death as the only way of preserving maternal life. In any event, the political debate about abortion is not, in reality, about cases of this sort; it is about "elective" or "social indication" abortions, viz., the deliberate destruction of unborn human life for nontherapeutic reasons.

A final point: In my own experience, conversion from the pro-choice to the pro-life cause is often (though certainly not always) a partial cause of religious conversion rather than an effect. Frequently, people who are not religious, or who are only weakly so, begin to have doubts about the moral defensibility of deliberate feticide. Although most of their friends are pro-choice, they find that position increasingly difficult to defend or live with. They perceive practical inconsistencies in their, and their friends', attitudes toward the unborn depending on whether the child is "wanted" or not. Perhaps they find themselves arrested by sonographic (or other even more sophisticated) images of the child's life in the womb. So the doubts begin creeping in. For the first time, they are really prepared to listen to the pro-life argument (often despite their negative attitude toward people—or "the kind of people"—who are pro-life); and somehow, it sounds more compelling than it did before. Gradually, as they become firmly pro-life, they find themselves questioning the whole philosophy of life—in a word, secularism—associated with their former view. They begin to understand the reasons that led them out of the pro-choice and into the pro-life camp as God's reasons, too.

 **NO**

A Moral Choice

I am having lunch with six women. What is unusual is that four of them are in their seventies, two of them widowed, the other two living with husbands beside whom they've lived for decades. All of them have had children. Had they been men, they would have published books and hung their paintings on the walls of important galleries. But they are women of a certain generation, and their lives were shaped around their families and personal relations. They are women you go to for help and support. We begin talking about the latest legislative act that makes abortion more difficult for poor women to obtain. An extraordinary thing happens. Each of them talks about the illegal abortions she had during her young womanhood. Not one of them was spared the experience. Any of them could have died on the table of whatever person (not a doctor in any case) she was forced to approach, in secrecy and in terror, to end a pregnancy that she felt would blight her life.

I mention this incident for two reasons: first as a reminder that all kinds of women have always had abortions; second because it is essential that we remember that an abortion is performed on a living woman who has a life in which a terminated pregnancy is only a small part. Morally speaking, the decision to have an abortion doesn't take place in a vacuum. It is connected to other choices that a woman makes in the course of an adult life.

Anti-choice propagandists paint pictures of women who choose to have abortions as types of moral callousness, selfishness, or irresponsibility. The woman choosing to abort is the dressed-for-success yuppie who gets rid of her baby so that she won't miss her Caribbean vacation or her chance for promotion. Or she is the feckless, promiscuous ghetto teenager who couldn't bring herself to just say no to sex. A third, purportedly kinder, gentler picture has recently begun to be drawn. The woman in the abortion clinic is there because she is misinformed about the nature of the world. She is having an abortion because society does not provide for mothers and their children, and she mistakenly thinks that another mouth to feed will be the ruin of her family, not understanding that the temporary truth of family unhappiness doesn't stack up beside the eternal verity that abortion is murder. Or she is the dupe of her husband or boyfriend, who talks her into having an abortion because a child will be a drag on his life-style. None of these pictures created by the anti-choice movement assumes that the decision to have an abortion is made responsibly, in the context of a morally lived life, by a free and responsible moral agent.

The Ontology of the Fetus

How would a woman who habitually makes choices in moral terms come to the decision to have an abortion? The moral discussion of abortion centers on the issue of whether or not abortion is an act of murder. At first glance it would seem that the answer should follow directly upon two questions: Is the fetus human? and Is it alive? It would be absurd to deny that a fetus is alive or that it is human. What would our other options be—to say that it is inanimate or belongs to another species? But we habitually use the terms "human" and "live" to refer to parts of our body—"human hair," for example, or "live red-blood cells"—and we are clear in our understanding that the nature of these objects does not rank equally with an entire personal existence. It then seems important to consider whether the fetus, this alive human thing, is a *person,* to whom the term "murder" could sensibly be applied. How would anyone come to a decision about something so impalpable as personhood? Philosophers have struggled with the issue of personhood, but in language that is so abstract that it is unhelpful to ordinary people making decisions in the course of their lives. It might be more productive to begin thinking about the status of the fetus by examining the language and customs that surround it. This approach will encourage us to focus on the choosing, acting woman, rather than the act of abortion—as if the act were performed by abstract forces without bodies, histories, attachments.

This focus on the acting woman is useful because a pregnant woman has an identifiable, consistent ontology, and a fetus takes on different ontological identities over time. But common sense, experience, and linguistic usage point clearly to the fact that we habitually consider, for example, a seven-week-old fetus to be different from a seven-month-old one. We can tell this by the way we respond to the involuntary loss of one as against the other. We have different language for the experience of the involuntary expulsion of the fetus from the womb depending upon the point of gestation at which the experience occurs. If it occurs early in the pregnancy, we call it a miscarriage; if late, we call it a stillbirth.

We would have an extreme reaction to the reversal of those terms. If a woman referred to a miscarriage at seven weeks as a stillbirth, we would be alarmed. It would shock our sense of propriety; it would make us uneasy; we would find it disturbing, misplaced—as we do when a bag lady sits down in a restaurant and starts shouting, or an octogenarian arrives at our door in a sailor suit. In short, we would suspect that the speaker was mad. Similarly, if a doctor or a nurse referred to the loss of a seven-month-old fetus as a miscarriage, we would be shocked by that person's insensitivity: could she or he not understand that a fetus that age is not what it was months before?

Our ritual and religious practices underscore the fact that we make distinctions among fetuses. If a woman took the bloody matter—indistinguishable from a heavy period—of an early miscarriage and insisted upon putting it in a tiny coffin and marking its grave, we would have serious concerns about her mental health. By the same token, we would feel squeamish about flushing a seven-month-old fetus down the toilet—something we would quite normally do with an early miscarriage. There are no prayers for the matter of a miscarriage, nor do we feel there should be. Even a Catholic priest would not baptize the issue of an early miscarriage.

The difficulties stem, of course, from the odd situation of a fetus's ontology: a complicated, differentiated, and nuanced response is required when we are dealing with an entity that changes over time. Yet we are in the habit of making distinctions like this. At one point we know that a child is no longer a child but an adult. That this question is vexed and problematic is clear from our difficulty in determining who is a juvenile offender and who is an adult criminal and at what age sexual intercourse ceases to be known as statutory rape. So at what point, if any, do we on the pro-choice side say that the developing fetus is a person, with rights equal to its mother's?

The anti-choice people have one advantage over us; their monolithic position gives them unity on this question. For myself, I am made uneasy by third-trimester abortions, which take place when the fetus could live outside the mother's body, but I also know that these are extremely rare and often performed on very young girls who have had difficulty comprehending the realities of pregnancy. It seems to me that the question of late abortions should be decided case by case, and that fixation on this issue is a deflection from what is most important: keeping early abortions, which are in the majority by far, safe and legal. I am also politically realistic enough to suspect that bills restricting late abortions are not good-faith attempts to make distinctions about the nature of fetal life. They are, rather, the cynical embodiments of the hope among anti-choice partisans that technology will be on their side and that medical science's ability to create situations in which younger fetuses are viable outside their mothers' bodies will increase dramatically in the next few years. Ironically, medical science will probably make the issue of abortion a minor one in the near future. The RU-486 pill, which can induce abortion early on, exists, and whether or not it is legally available (it is not on the market here, because of pressure from anti-choice groups), women will begin to obtain it. If abortion can occur through chemical rather than physical means, in the privacy of one's home, most people not directly involved will lose interest in it. As abortion is transformed from a public into a private issue, it will cease to be perceived as political; it will be called personal instead.

An Equivocal Good

But because abortion will always deal with what it is to create and sustain life, it will always be a moral issue. And whether we like it or not, our moral thinking about abortion is rooted in the shifting soil of perception. In an age in which much of our perception is manipulated by media that specialize in the sound bite and the photo op, the anti-choice partisans have a twofold advantage over us on the pro-choice side. The pro-choice moral position is more complex, and the experience we defend is physically repellent to contemplate. None of us in the pro-choice movement would suggest that abortion is not a regrettable occurrence. Anti-choice proponents can offer pastel photographs of babies in buntings, their eyes peaceful in the camera's gaze. In answer, we can't offer the material of an early abortion, bloody, amorphous in a paper cup, to prove that what has just been removed from the woman's body is not a child, not in the same category of being as the adorable bundle in an adoptive mother's arms. It is not a pleasure to look at the physical evidence of abortion, and most of us don't get the opportunity to do so.

The theologian Daniel Maguire, uncomfortable with the fact that most theological arguments about the nature of abortion are made by men who have never been anywhere near an actual abortion, decided to visit a clinic and observe abortions being performed. He didn't find the experience easy, but he knew that before he could in good conscience make a moral judgment on abortion, he needed to experience through his senses what an aborted fetus is like: he needed to look at and touch the controversial entity. He held in his hand the bloody fetal stuff; the eight-week-old fetus fit in the palm of his hand, and it certainly bore no resemblance to either of his two children when he had held them moments after their birth. He knew at that point what women who have experienced early abortions and miscarriages know: that some event occurred, possibly even a dramatic one, but it was not the death of a child.

Because issues of pregnancy and birth are both physical and metaphorical, we must constantly step back and forth between ways of perceiving the world. When we speak of gestation, we are often talking in terms of potential, about events and objects to which we attach our hopes, fears, dreams, and ideals. A mother can speak to the fetus in her uterus and name it; she and her mate may decorate a nursery according to their vision of the good life; they may choose for an embryo a college, a profession, a dwelling. But those of us who are trying to think morally about pregnancy and birth must remember that these feelings are our own projections onto what is in reality an inappropriate object. However charmed we may be by an expectant father's buying a little football for something inside his wife's belly, we shouldn't make public policy based on such actions, nor should we force others to live their lives conforming to our fantasies.

As a society, we are making decisions that pit the complicated future of a complex adult against the fate of a mass of cells lacking cortical development. The moral pressure should be on distinguishing the true from the false, the real suffering of living persons from our individual and often idiosyncratic dreams and fears. We must make decisions on abortion based on an understanding of how people really do live. We must be able to say that poverty is worse than not being poor, that having dignified and meaningful work is better than working in conditions of degradation, that raising a child one loves and has desired is better than raising a child in resentment and rage, that it is better for a twelve-year-old not to endure the trauma of having a child when she is herself a child.

When we put these ideas against the ideas of "child" or "baby," we seem to be making a horrifying choice of life-style over life. But in fact we are telling the truth of what it means to bear a child, and what the experience of abortion really is. This is extremely difficult, for the object of the discussion is hidden, changing, potential. We make our decisions on the basis of approximate and inadequate language, often on the basis of fantasies and fears. It will always be crucial to try to separate genuine moral concern from phobia, punitiveness, superstition, anxiety, a desperate search for certainty in an uncertain world.

One of the certainties that is removed if we accept the consequences of the pro-choice position is the belief that the birth of a child is an unequivocal good. In real life we act knowing that the birth of a child is not always a good thing: people are sometimes depressed, angry, rejecting, at the birth of a child. But this is a difficult truth to tell; we don't like to say it, and one of the fears preyed on by anti-choice proponents is that if we cannot look at the birth of a child as an unequivocal good, then there is nothing to look toward. The desire for security of the imagination, for typological fixity, particularly in the area of "the good," is an understandable desire. It must seem to some anti-choice people that we on the pro-choice side are not only murdering innocent children but also murdering hope. Those of us who have experienced the birth of a desired child and felt the joy of that moment can be tempted into believing that it was the physical experience of the birth itself that was the joy. But it is crucial to remember that the birth of a child itself is a neutral occurrence emotionally: the charge it takes on is invested in it by the people experiencing or observing it.

The Fear of Sexual Autonomy

These uncertainties can lead to another set of fears, not only about abortion but about its implications. Many anti-choice people fear that to support abortion is to cast one's lot with the cold and technological rather than with the warm and natural, to head down the slippery slope toward a brave new world where handicapped children are left on mountains to starve and the old are put out in the snow. But if we look at the history of abortion, we don't see the embodiment of what the anti-choice proponents fear. On the contrary, excepting the grotesque counterexample of the People's Republic of China (which practices forced abortion), there seems to be a real link between repressive anti-abortion stances and repressive governments. Abortion was banned in Fascist Italy and Nazi Germany; it is illegal in South Africa and in Chile. It is paid for by the governments of Denmark, England, and the Netherlands, which have national health and welfare systems that foster the health and well-being of mothers, children, the old, and the handicapped.

Advocates of outlawing abortion often refer to women seeking abortion as self-indulgent and materialistic. In fact these accusations mask a discomfort with female sexuality, sexual pleasure, and sexual autonomy. It is possible for a woman to have a sexual life unriddled by fear only if she can be confident that she need not pay for a failure of technology or judgment (and who among us has never once been swept away in the heat of a sexual moment?) by taking upon herself the crushing burden of unchosen motherhood.

It is no accident, therefore, that the increased appeal of measures to restrict maternal conduct during pregnancy—and a new focus on the physical autonomy of the pregnant woman—have come into public discourse at precisely the time when women are achieving unprecedented levels of economic and political autonomy. What has surprised me is that some of this new anti-autonomy talk comes to us from the left. An example of this new discourse is an article by Christopher Hitchens that appeared in *The Nation* last April, in which the author asserts his discomfort with abortion. Hitchens's tone is impeccably British: arch, light, we're men of the left.

> Anyone who has ever seen a sonogram or has spent even an hour with a textbook on embryology knows that the emotions are not the deciding factor. In order to terminate a pregnancy, you have to still a heartbeat, switch off a developing brain, and whatever the method, break some bones and rupture some organs. As to whether this involves pain on the "Silent Scream" scale, I have no idea. The "right to life" leadership, again, has cheapened everything it touches. ["Silent Scream" refers to Dr. Bernard Nathanson's widely debated antiabortion film *The Silent Scream*, in which an abortion on a 12-week-old fetus is shown from inside the uterus.—Eds.]

"It is a pity," Hitchens goes on to say, "that . . . the majority of feminists and their allies have stuck to the dead ground of 'Me Decade' possessive individualism, an ideology that has more in common than it admits with the prehistoric right, which it claims to oppose but has in fact encouraged." Hitchens proposes, as an alternative, a program of social reform that would make contraception free and support a national adoption service. In his opinion, it would seem, women have abortions for only two reasons: because they are selfish or because they are poor. If the state will take care of the economic problems and the bureaucratic messiness around adoption, it remains only for the possessive individualists to get their act together and walk with their babies into the communal utopia of the future. Hitchens would allow victims of rape or incest to have free abortions, on the grounds that since they didn't choose to have sex, the women should not be forced to have the babies. This would seem to put the issue of volition in a wrong and telling place. To Hitchens's mind, it would appear, if a woman chooses to have sex, she can't choose whether or not to have a baby. The implications of this are clear. If a woman is consciously and volitionally sexual, she should be prepared to take her medicine. And what medicine must the consciously sexual male take? Does Hitchens really believe, or want us to believe, that every male who has unintentionally impregnated a woman will be involved in the lifelong responsibility for the upbringing of the engendered child? Can he honestly say that he has observed this behavior—or, indeed, would want to see it observed—in the world in which he lives?

Real Choices

It is essential for a moral decision about abortion to be made in an atmosphere of open, critical thinking. We on the pro-choice side must accept that there are indeed anti-choice activists who take their position in good faith. I believe, however, that they are people for whom childbirth is an emotionally overladen topic, people who are susceptible to unclear thinking because of their unrealistic hopes and fears. It is important for us in the pro-choice movement to be open in discussing those areas involving abortion which are nebulous and unclear. But we must not forget that there are some things that we know to be undeniably true. There are some undeniable bad consequences of a woman's being forced to bear a child against her will. First is the trauma of going through a pregnancy and giving birth to a child who is not desired, a trauma more long-lasting than that experienced by some (only some) women who experience an early abortion. The grief of giving up a child at its birth—and at nine months it is a child whom one has felt move inside one's body—is underestimated both by anti-choice partisans and by those for whom access to adoptable children is important. This grief should not be forced on any woman—or, indeed, encouraged by public policy.

We must be realistic about the impact on society of millions of unwanted children in an overpopulated world. Most of the time, human beings have sex not because they want to make babies. Yet throughout history sex has resulted in unwanted pregnancies. And women have always aborted. One thing that is not hidden, mysterious, or debatable is that making abortion illegal will result in the deaths of women, as it has always done. Is our historical memory so short that none of us remember aunts, sisters, friends, or mothers who were killed or rendered sterile by septic abortions? Does no one in the anti-choice movement remember stories or actual experiences of midnight drives to filthy rooms from which aborted women were sent out, bleeding, to their fate? Can anyone genuinely say that it would be a moral good for us as a society to return to those conditions?

Thinking about abortion, then, forces us to take moral positions as adults who understand the complexities of the world and the realities of human suffering, to make decisions based on how people actually live and choose, and not on our fears, prejudices, and anxieties about sex and society, life and death.

POSTSCRIPT

Should Abortion Be Restricted?

The real issue dividing George and Gordon is whether or not the fetus is fully human, in the sense of being entitled to the treatment that civilized society gives to human beings. Their respective arguments use different methods of proof. George reasons from the biological premise that sperm and egg, each with 23 chromosomes, produce a fertilized human organism with the human's full 46 chromosomes; what occurs after that is simply human growth, which no one has the right to interrupt. Gordon reasons from the appearance of the fetus and how people normally react to it. Since even pro-lifers do not conduct funeral services and memorials for the "bloody matter" resulting from an early miscarriage, Gordon reasons, the Supreme Court was right to exclude early fetuses from legal protection. Such reactions, in George's view, proceed from emotion rather than reason.

Robert M. Baird and Stuart E. Rosenbaum, eds., *The Ethics of Abortion: Pro-Life v. Pro-Choice,* rev. ed. (Prometheus Books, 1993) contains a wide variety of views on the abortion controversy. Barbara Hinkson Craig and David M. O'Brien, *Abortion and American Politics* (Chatham House, 1993) is a historical treatment of the abortion controversy in America. An interesting examination of the political factors that have influenced the abortion debate can be found in William Saletan, *Bearing Right: How Conservatives Won the Abortion War* (University of California Press, 2000). Saletan concludes that, although abortion remains legal, anti-abortion forces have largely won by eliminating most public financing of anything related to abortion or family planning. Peter Charles Hoffer, ed., *The Abortion Rights Controversy in America: A Legal Reader* (University of North Carolina Press, 2004) brings together a wide variety of legal briefs, oral arguments, court opinions, newspaper reports, and contemporary essays. In *What* Roe v. Wade *Should Have Said,* edited by Jack M. Balkin (New York University Press, 2005), eleven leading constitutional scholars of varying viewpoints have rewritten the opinions in *Roe v. Wade* with the insights acquired by three decades of experience.

President Clinton twice vetoed federal bills outlawing "partial-birth" abortions, but President Bush signed a nearly similar bill in 2003. In February of 2006 the Supreme Court agreed to hear arguments on its constitutionality. In the meantime, President Bush had appointed two new members of the Court, Chief Justice John Roberts and Justice Samuel Alito, the latter replacing Justice Sandra Day O'Connor, who had voted to strike down the earlier Nebraska ban on that procedure. Perhaps anticipating a friendlier reception by the Court to legislative bans on abortion, South Dakota in 2006 passed a law outlawing all abortions except where the woman's life is endangered.

ISSUE 13

Are Tax Cuts Good for America?

YES: Amity Shlaes, from *The Greedy Hand: How Taxes Drive Americans Crazy and What to Do About It* (Random House, 1999)

NO: Paul Krugman, from "The Tax-Cut Con," *The New York Times Magazine* (September 14, 2003)

ISSUE SUMMARY

YES: *Wall Street Journal* editorial writer Amity Shlaes maintains that the federal income tax is too high, too complex, and biased against high-income earners who invest in economic growth.

NO: Economist Paul Krugman believes that the Bush tax cuts increase economic inequality, contribute to a huge budget deficit, and endanger the future of Medicare and Social Security.

Benjamin Franklin is credited with having first said, "In this world nothing is certain but death and taxes." That does not mean that we have to look forward to either one. When the colonists confronted the collection of taxes by Great Britain, they proclaimed "No taxation without representation" and moved toward revolution and the creation of the United States.

In 1912 the Sixteenth Amendment to the Constitution was adopted, enabling the federal government to levy taxes directly on income. The following year Congress adopted a graduated income tax, ranging from a 1 percent tax on individuals and businesses earning over $4,000 (most Americans did not earn that much) up to 6 percent on incomes over $500,000. Since then, tax rates have gone up and down, but some measure of progressivity—higher rates for higher incomes—has been retained. However, every change in the tax code has produced new deductions, concessions, and loopholes that benefit some groups to the disadvantage of others, lengthen and complicate the law, and stimulate a major tax-filing occupation for accountants and tax lawyers.

No one likes taxes, but upon reflection most Americans are likely to agree with Supreme Court Justice Oliver Wendell Holmes, Jr., that "taxes are what we pay for civilized society." No other way has been devised to pay for such essential services as public education, police and fire protection, roads and public transport, and the military defense of the nation. So the question is not whether or not Americans should be taxed but how and how much.

By the standards of other nations, American taxes are low. In fact, every other industrial nation has higher rates of taxation, except Japan, whose tax rate is about the same as that of the United States. Nevertheless, Americans appear to respond more favorably than citizens of other countries to proposals to lower taxes. When presidential candidate George Bush in 1988 said, "Read my lips: No new taxes," he enhanced his prospects for election. But when then–president Bush ran for reelection in 1992, his broken promise contributed to his defeat.

President George W. Bush secured the enactment of substantial tax cuts in 2001, 2002, and 2003. Bush argued that these would result in new investments that would revive a declining economy after the end of the Internet boom of the 1990s. His critics maintained that the tax cuts were of significant benefit only for the wealthiest Americans and blamed them, in part, for the nation's half-trillion dollar deficit.

President Bush sought the elimination, and achieved the reduction, of the estate tax. The estate tax is imposed on the inheritances left by the wealthiest Americans. Opponents of this tax characterized it as a death tax that taxes for a second time money that had been taxed when it was initially earned. Defenders of the tax argued that only a small number of the wealthiest Americans are subject to the tax, which would raise hundreds of billions of dollars within two decades. Warren Buffett, the second wealthiest person in America (Bill Gates, founder of Microsoft, is the first) commented: "All those people who think that food stamps are debilitating and lead to a cycle of poverty are the same ones who want to leave a ton of money to their kids."

Almost all critics of federal taxation, apart from anarchists who oppose all government and extreme libertarians who oppose almost all government, acknowledge that government has an essential role in protecting national security, creating trade policy, preserving the environment, and continuing specific social welfare policies, such as Social Security and Medicare. Disagreement arises over how much government should do, how much it should tax, and how the tax burden should be shared.

In the following selections, Amity Shlaes argues that the American tax rate is too high, too complex, unfair in withholding income from wage earners, and biased against high-income earners. Paul Krugman believes that cutting taxes doesn't benefit the middle class, doesn't create jobs or growth, and will create a severe fiscal crisis that will lower the quality of education and health care for Americans of modest means.

The Greedy Hand

The father of the modern American state was a pipe-puffing executive at R. H. Macy & Co. named Beardsley Ruml. Ruml, the department store's treasurer, also served as chairman of the board of directors of the Federal Reserve Bank of New York and advisor to President Franklin Roosevelt during World War II. In those years Washington was busy marshaling the forces of the American economy to halt Japan and Germany. In 1942, not long after Pearl Harbor, lawmakers raised income taxes radically, with rates that aimed to capture twice as much revenue as in the previous year. They also imposed the income tax on tens of millions of Americans who had never been acquainted with the levy before. The change was so dramatic that the chroniclers of that period have coined a phrase to describe it. They say that the "class tax" became a "mass tax."

The new rates were law. But Americans were ill-prepared to face a new and giant tax bill. A Gallup poll from the period showed that only some 5 million of the 34 million people who were subject to the tax for the first time were saving to make their payment. In those days, March 15, not April 15, was the nation's annual tax deadline.

The Treasury nervously launched a huge public relations campaign to remind Americans of their new duties. A Treasury Department poster exhorted citizens: "You are one of 50,000,000 Americans who must fill out an income tax form by March 15. DO IT NOW!" For wartime theatergoers, Disney had prepared an animated short film featuring citizen Donald Duck laboring over his tax return beside a bottle of aspirin. Donald claimed exemptions and dependent credits for Huey, Dewey, and Louie.

As March 15,1943 neared, though, it became clear that many citizens still were not filing returns. Henry Morgenthau, the Treasury secretary, confronted colleagues about the nightmarish prospect of mass tax evasion: "Suppose we have to go out and try to arrest five million people?"

The Macy's Model

Enter Ruml, man of ideas. At Macy's, he had observed that customers didn't like big bills. They preferred making payments bit by bit, in the installment plan, even if they had to pay for the pleasure with interest. So Ruml devised a plan, which he unfolded to his colleagues at the Federal Reserve and to anyone in Washington who would listen. The government would get business to do its work, collecting taxes for it. Employers would retain a percentage of taxes from workers every week—say, 20 percent—and forward it directly to Washington's war chest. This would hide the size of the new taxes from the worker. No longer would the worker ever have to look his tax bill square in the eye. Workers need never even see the money they were forgoing. Withholding as we know it today was born.

This was more than change, it was transformation. Government would put its hand into the taxpayer's pocket and grab its share of tax—without asking.

Ruml hadn't invented withholding. His genius was to make its introduction palatable by adding a powerful sweetener: the federal government would offer a tax amnesty for the previous year, allowing confused and indebted citizens to start on new footing. It was the most ambitious bait-and-switch plan in America's history.

Ruml advertised his project as a humane effort to smooth life in the disruption of the war. He noted it was a way to help taxpayers out of the habit of carrying income tax debt, debt that he characterized as "a pernicious fungus permeating the structure of things." The move was also patriotic. At Macy's, executives had found that a "young man in the comptroller's office who was making $75 or $100 [a week was] called into the navy at a salary of $2,600 and we had to get together and take care of his income tax for him." The young man, Ruml saw, would face a tax bill for a higher income at a time when he was earning less money in the service of his country. This Ruml deemed "an impossible situation."

Ruml had several reasons for wagering that his project would work. One was that Americans, smarting from the Japanese assault, were now willing to sacrifice more than at any other point in memory. The second was that the federal government would be able to administer withholding—six successful years of Social Security showed that the government, for the first time ever, was able to handle such a mass program of revenue collection. The third was packaging. He called his program not "collection at source" or "withholding," two technical terms for what he was doing. Instead he chose a zippier name: "pay as you go." And most important of all, there was the lure of the tax amnesty.

The policy thinkers of the day embraced the Ruml arrangement. This was an era in which John Maynard Keynes dominated the world of economics. The Keynesians placed enormous faith in government. The only thing they liked about the war was that it demonstrated to the world all the miracles that Big Government could work. The Ruml plan would give them the wherewithal to have their projects even, they sensed, after the war ended. Keynesianism also said high taxes were crucial to controlling inflation. The Keynesians saw withholding as the right tool for getting those necessary high taxes.

Conservatives played their part in the drama. Among withholding's backers was the man who was later to become the world's leading free-market economist, Milton Friedman. Decades after the war, Friedman called for the abolition of the withholding system. In his memoirs he wrote that "we concentrated single-mindedly on promoting the war effort. We gave next to no consideration to any longer-run consequences. It never occurred to me at the time that I was helping to develop machinery that would make possible a government that I would come to criticize severely as too large, too intrusive, too destructive of freedom. Yet, that was precisely what I was doing." With an almost audible sigh, Friedman added: "There is an important lesson here. It is far easier to introduce a government program than to get rid of it."

Such questions, though, had no place in the mind of a nation under attack. At the moment what seemed most important was that voters accepted the Ruml plan. Randolph Paul, a Treasury Department official and Ruml critic, wrote resignedly that "his plan had political appeal. Though he conceived the plan as getting people out of debt to the government, the public thought that Ruml had found a very white rabbit"—a magic trick—"which would somehow lighten their tax load."

⋅⟨◉⟩⋅

. . . Adam Smith described the "invisible hand," the hand of free commerce that brings magic order and harmony to our lives. Thomas Paine wrote of another hand, all too visible and intrusive: "the greedy hand of government, thrusting itself into every corner and crevice of industry." Today the invisible hand is a very busy one. Markets are wider and freer than ever, and we profit from that by living better than before. But the "greedy hand of government" is also at work. Indeed, in relative terms, the greedy hand has grown faster than the invisible hand. In the late 1990s, economists noted with astonishment that federal taxes made up one-fifth of the economy, a rate higher than at any time in American history outside of war. We cannot assign the blame for changes of such magnitude to Beardsley Ruml, who was, after all, not much more than a New Deal package man. The real force here is not even withholding, whatever its power. Behind Ruml's withholding lurks Paine's greedy hand.

. . . Today, more than half of the budget goes to social transfers mandated by expensive programs whose value many Americans question. Working citizens sense that someone is getting something, but that someone is often not they.

The avid tax haters who pop up occasionally in the news are the expression of this national unease. Their froth-mouthed manifestos strike us as extreme—how many of us truly want to "kill the IRS"?—but they reflect something that all Americans feel to some degree. Even the most moderate of us often feel a tick of sympathy when we hear the shouts of the tax haters. We think of our forefathers who felt compelled to rebel against the Crown for "imposing Taxes on us without our consent." We know we live in a democracy, and so must have chosen this arrangement. Yet nowadays we too find ourselves feeling that taxes are imposed on us "without our consent."

Washington doesn't necessarily recognize the totality of this tax frustration. The purview of the House Ways and Means Committee is limited to federal taxes, and so the committee writes tax law as if the federal income tax were the only tax in the country. The commissions that monitor Social Security concern themselves only with the solvency of Social Security, and so ignore the consequences of raising payroll taxes, or taxing pensions, at a time when income taxes are already high. Old programs with outdated aims stay in place. Newer ones, added piecemeal, often conflict with the old.

"Rube Goldberg machine," "unstoppable contraption"—none of the stock phrases adequately captures the complication that is our tax structure. As William E. Simon, a former Treasury secretary, once said, "The nation should have a tax system which looks like someone designed it on purpose." . . .

⋅⚬⟩⋅

Americans today are more prosperous than we have ever been. As a nation, we have come very far, so far that even our past is beginning to look different. In the 1960s, 1970s, and even the 1980s, we took Big Government America, the America of the postwar period, to be the only America, an America that permanently supplanted something antiquated. This conviction strengthened when we considered the enormous troubles that plagued us in those decades. Who else but government could end the underclass, right the wrongs of Vietnam, combat inflation?

We can see now that in those years we had a foreshortened view of history. From the heights of our new achievement, we recognize that the Great Society, for all its ideals, was something of an aberration. It is clear now that the self-doubt and gray misgivings of the Vietnam period were, in their way, just a momentary interruption. The inflation of the 1970s was an acute and terrible problem but a short-lived one. Our famous deficit agony—which so many commentators and foreigners alleged would bring us down—has, at least for the moment, receded. Today we are in many ways more like the America of Andrew Jackson or even Thomas Jefferson than we are like the America of Jimmy Carter.

This change was the result of enormous and serious work. We developed microchips and computers that secured our global economic dominance. We started the welfare state and then, when we saw it wasn't working, successfully ended it. We grew a stock market that will provide pensions for the baby boom and beyond. Serious challenges loom ahead. Unpredictable rogue states threaten our national security; the economy will not always live up to its 1990s boom. But we understand now that the key to sustaining our prosperity is recognizing that we are our own best providers. Thinkers from left, center, and right agree: we don't need a nanny state.

This American confidence is not new. It is simply a homecoming to older ideals, ideals that we held through most of our history. Self-reliance is the ultimate American tradition. Even through a good part of the Depression "no handouts" was Americans' self-imposed rule. We are coming to a new appreciation of what Tocqueville admiringly called "self-interest, rightly understood."

Yet we are still saddled with our tax structure, the unwieldy artifact of an irrelevant era.

Unburdening ourselves is not easy, but it is something we have in our power to do. Our impasse, in fact, contains the outline of its own solution, if only we allow ourselves to look at it clearly. What, exactly, does our long struggle with Paine's greedy hand tell us?

Taxes have to be visible. Beardsley Ruml's trap worked because it made taxes invisible. No one today Willingly gives a third or a half of his income into a strange hand; we only pay our taxes now because the trap locked shut long ago. We never see our tax bill in its entirety except during the madness of filing season.

When we rewrite our arrangement with government, we need to write into it a tax structure that is clear and comprehensible, whose outlines we can see and consider whenever we choose.

Taxes have to be simple. The tax code is a monster of complexity, but it doesn't have to be. When rules are added to rules, the change may benefit certain classes, but they hurt the rest of us. The best thing is to settle on one system, even if someone shouts that it's not "fair" to everyone.

Taxes are for revenue. For fifty years we have used taxes to steer behavior. Indeed, politicians often used the argument that they were promoting social good through the tax code as window dressing for their real aim: getting at the revenue. None of us likes the result. We are responsible for our own fate; let government take what we choose to give it and then retreat.

Taxes have to be lower. We have managed to achieve prosperity notwithstanding high taxes. But that prosperity would have been greater without those taxes. The microchip, in its way, has allowed us to postpone our date with tax reform.

But epochal transformations like the computer revolution, or the Industrial Revolution for that matter, cannot be counted on to come every decade. Taxes will slow our economy if we don't bring them down to rates that allow us to sustain desirable growth.

We don't have to load extra taxes on the rich. We've learned that a tax system that punishes the rich also punishes the rest of us. Those who have money should pay taxes like everyone else. In fact the rich already carry more of the tax burden than any other income group. Yet history—the history of the 1980s in particular—has shown an amazing thing—that lower rates on the rich produce more revenue from them.

Progressivity has had its day. Let us move on to a tax system that is more worthy of us, one that makes sense for the country.

It's time to privatize Social Security. Many of the core tax problems we face today are in reality Social Security problems. Markets have taught us that they can do a better job than government in providing public pensions. We should privatize a portion of Social Security—at least three of the percentage points that individuals carry.

The only thing to guard against is a privatization that is not a true privatization. When government enters the stock market on behalf of citizens, as many advocates of Social Security privatization would like, that is not privatization. That is expanding the public sector at the cost of the private sector. An office in government that invests on behalf of citizens, as many are proposing, is an office open to enormous moral hazard. To understand this you need only to consider what would happen if the chairman of the Securities and Exchange Commission directly controlled a few hundred million shares of blue-chip stocks.

Individuals need to control their own accounts, just as they control the rest of their money. Government guarantees of returns are also guarantees of disaster. One need only look to our recent history with savings and loans to see that. Raising the ceiling on federal insurance of S & L accounts led to that disaster by giving S & L directors license without accountability. The cost ran into the hundreds of billions, but it was far lower than the cost a government guarantee on privatized Social Security would be.

Local is good.   The enduring lesson of our schools crisis is that centralizing school finance to the state and federal level has not given us the equity or the academic performance we hoped for. These results have ramifications far beyond schools. The federal government cannot solve everything. Many problems—from school to health care to welfare—are better handled lower down. A wise tax reform is a tax reform that leaves much of the nation's work to the people and the officials they know. Trying to write a federal tax law that addresses all our national problems is a recipe for a repeat of the current trouble.

We must lock in change.   In the 1980s, through tremendous political and social exertion, the nation joined together to lower tax rates and prune out many of the code's absurdities. Within a few years, Washington had destroyed its own child. This time we must fix our change so the fiddlers can't get at it. . . .

Most Americans are not fire-breathing radicals or Ruby Ridge survivalists. They don't want to "kill the IRS." They just want a common-sense change in the system. And that is what they are telling lawmakers. When Steve LaTourette, a Republican congressman from Ohio, surveyed his constituents, he found that just about half wanted the IRS abolished. But a full three quarters wanted to see the tax code itself abolished. They saw that the code, not the bureaucrats, was the problem.

The second part of the program is to make the change truly permanent through a constitutional amendment. Our nation's last experience of trying to pass a significant-seeming constitutional amendment—the Equal Rights Amendment—was a bitter one. It soured Washington on amendments in general. Hesitation over amendments goes a long way toward explaining the current Republican foundering.

A constitutional amendment that calls for limiting federal taxes, including Social Security, to 25 percent of our income, or even a lower share, would be an important first step out of the logjam. For one thing, states would have to ratify the change, and that would allow us to have a much needed national discussion about taxes. Citizens would have to consider what lawmakers were proposing. This would give voters a chance to get around the lobbies and politicians who have kept the tax debate to themselves. It would get us all back into the discussion.

The third step is to realize that as a people we want to pay taxes. Roosevelt called taxes "the dues we pay for organized society." We still feel that way.

But people want a tax system that doesn't intrude on our private lives while it collects those dues; and we want those dues to be spent in a reasonable, limited way. We want a tax code that, to quote former Treasury secretary William Simon again, looks as if somebody designed it on purpose. Not a giant machine that collects our money merely to feed the monster.

Paul Krugman

 **NO**

The Tax-Cut Con

1. The Cartoon and the Reality

Bruce Tinsley's comic strip, "Mallard Fillmore," is, he says, "for the average person out there: the forgotten American taxpayer who's sick of the liberal media." In June, that forgotten taxpayer made an appearance in the strip, attacking his TV set with a baseball bat and yelling: "I can't afford to send my kids to college, or even take 'em out of their substandard public school, because the federal, state and local governments take more than 50 percent of my income in taxes. And then the guy on the news asks with a straight face whether or not we can 'afford' tax cuts."

But that's just a cartoon. Meanwhile, Bob Riley has to face the reality.

Riley knows all about substandard public schools. He's the governor of Alabama, which ranks near the bottom of the nation in both spending per pupil and educational achievement. The state has also neglected other public services—for example, 28,000 inmates are held in a prison system built for 12,000. And thanks in part to a lack of health care, it has the second-highest infant mortality in the nation.

When he was a member of Congress, Riley, a Republican, was a staunch supporter of tax cuts. Faced with a fiscal crisis in his state, however, he seems to have had an epiphany. He decided that it was impossible to balance Alabama's budget without a significant tax increase. And that, apparently, led him to reconsider everything. "The largest tax increase in state history just to maintain the status quo?" he asked. "I don't think so." Instead, Riley proposed a wholesale restructuring of the state's tax system: reducing taxes on the poor and middle class while raising them on corporations and the rich and increasing overall tax receipts enough to pay for a big increase in education spending. You might call it a New Deal for Alabama.

Nobody likes paying taxes, and no doubt some Americans are as angry about their taxes as Tinsley's imaginary character. But most Americans also care a lot about the things taxes pay for. All politicians say they're for public education; almost all of them also say they support a strong national defense, maintaining Social Security and, if anything, expanding the coverage of Medicare. When the "guy on the news" asks whether we can afford a tax cut, he's asking whether, after yet another tax cut goes through, there will be enough money to pay for those things. And the answer is no.

But it's very difficult to get that answer across in modern American politics, which has been dominated for 25 years by a crusade against taxes.

I don't use the word "crusade" lightly. The advocates of tax cuts are relentless, even fanatical. An indication of the movement's fervor—and of its political power—came during the Iraq war. War is expensive and is almost always accompanied by tax increases. But not in 2003. "Nothing is more important in the face of a war," declared Tom DeLay, the House majority leader, "than cutting taxes." And sure enough, taxes were cut, not just in a time of war but also in the face of record budget deficits. Nor will it be easy to reverse those tax cuts: the tax-cut movement has convinced many Americans—like Tinsley—that everybody still pays far too much in taxes.

A result of the tax-cut crusade is that there is now a fundamental mismatch between the benefits Americans expect to receive from the government and the revenues government collect. This mismatch is already having profound effects at the state and local levels: teachers and policemen are being laid off and children are being denied health insurance. The federal government can mask its problems for a while, by running huge budget deficits, but it, too, will eventually have to decide whether to cut services or raise taxes. And we are not talking about minor policy adjustments. If taxes stay as low as they are now, government as we know it cannot be maintained. In particular, Social Security will have to become far less generous; Medicare will no longer be able to guarantee comprehensive medical care to older Americans; Medicaid will no longer provide basic medical care to the poor.

How did we reach this point? What are the origins of the antitax crusade? And where is it taking us? To answer these questions, we will have to look both at who the antitax crusaders are and at the evidence on what tax cuts do to the budget and the economy. But first, let's set the stage by taking a look at the current state of taxation in America.

2. How High Are Our Taxes?

The reason Tinsley's comic strip about the angry taxpayer caught my eye was, of course, that the numbers were all wrong. Very few Americans pay as much as 50 percent of their income in taxes; on average, families near the middle of the income distribution pay only about half that percentage in federal, state and local taxes combined.

In fact, though most Americans feel that they pay too much in taxes, they get off quite lightly compared with the citizens of other advanced countries. Furthermore, for most Americans tax rates probably haven't risen for a generation. And a few Americans—namely those with high incomes—face much lower taxes than they did a generation ago.

To assess trends in the overall level of taxes and to compare taxation across countries, economists usually look first at the ratio of taxes to gross domestic product, the total value of output produced in the country. In the United States, all taxes—federal, state and local—reached a peak of 29.6 percent of G.D.P. in 2000. That number was, however, swollen by taxes on capital gains during the stock-market bubble.

By 2002, the tax take was down to 26.3 percent of G.D.P., and all indications are that it will be lower still this year and next.

This is a low number compared with almost every other advanced country. In 1999, Canada collected 38.2 percent of G.D.P. in taxes, France collected 45.8 percent and Sweden, 52.2 percent.

Still, aren't taxes much higher than they used to be? Not if we're looking back over the past 30 years. As a share of G.D.P., federal taxes are currently at their lowest point since the Eisenhower administration. State and local taxes rose substantially between 1960 and the early 1970's, but have been roughly stable since then. Aside from the capital gains taxes paid during the bubble years, the share of income Americans pay in taxes has been flat since Richard Nixon was president.

Of course, overall levels of taxation don't necessarily tell you how heavily particular individuals and families are taxed. As it turns out, however, middle-income Americans, like the country as a whole, haven't seen much change in their overall taxes over the past 30 years. On average, families in the middle of the income distribution find themselves paying about 26 percent of their income in taxes today. This number hasn't changed significantly since 1989, and though hard data are lacking, it probably hasn't changed much since 1970.

Meanwhile, wealthy Americans have seen a sharp drop in their tax burden. The top tax rate—the income-tax rate on the highest bracket—is now 35 percent, half what it was in the 1970's. With the exception of a brief period between 1988 and 1993, that's the lowest rate since 1932. Other taxes that, directly or indirectly, bear mainly on the very affluent have also been cut sharply. The effective tax rate on corporate profits has been cut in half since the 1960's. The 2001 tax cut phases out the inheritance tax, which is overwhelmingly a tax on the very wealthy: in 1999, only 2 percent of estates paid any tax, and half the tax was paid by only 3,300 estates worth more than $5 million. The 2003 tax act sharply cuts taxes on dividend income, another boon to the very well off. By the time the Bush tax cuts have taken full effect, people with really high incomes will face their lowest average tax rate since the Hoover administration.

So here's the picture: Americans pay low taxes by international standards. Most people's taxes haven't gone up in the past generation; the wealthy have had their taxes cut to levels not seen since before the New Deal. Even before the latest round of tax cuts, when compared with citizens of other advanced nations or compared with Americans a generation ago, we had nothing to complain about—and those with high incomes now have a lot to celebrate. Yet a significant number of Americans rage against taxes, and the party that controls all three branches of the federal government has made tax cuts its supreme priority. Why?

3. Supply-Siders, Starve-the-Beasters and Lucky Duckies

It is often hard to pin down what antitax crusaders are trying to achieve. The reason is not, or not only, that they are disingenuous about their motives—though as we will see, disingenuity has become a hallmark of the movement in recent years. Rather, the fuzziness comes from the fact that today's antitax movement moves back and forth between two doctrines. Both doctrines favor the same thing: big tax cuts for people with high incomes. But they favor it for different reasons.

One of those doctrines has become famous under the name "supply-side economics." It's the view that the government can cut taxes without severe cuts in public spending. The other doctrine is often referred to as "starving the beast," a phrase coined by David Stockman, Ronald Reagan's budget director. It's the view that taxes should be cut precisely in order to force severe cuts in public spending. Supply-side economics is the friendly, attractive face of the tax-cut movement. But starve-the-beast is where the power lies.

The starting point of supply-side economics is an assertion that no economist would dispute: taxes reduce the incentive to work, save and invest. A businessman who knows that 70 cents of every extra dollar he makes will go to the I.R.S. is less willing to make the effort to earn that extra dollar than if he knows that the I.R.S. will take only 35 cents. So reducing tax rates will, other things being the same, spur the economy.

This much isn't controversial. But the government must pay its bills. So the standard view of economists is that if you want to reduce the burden of taxes, you must explain what government programs you want to cut as part of the deal. There's no free lunch.

What the supply-siders argued, however, was that there was a free lunch. Cutting marginal rates, they insisted, would lead to such a large increase in gross domestic product that it wouldn't be necessary to come up with offsetting spending cuts. What supply-side economists say, in other words, is, "Don't worry, be happy and cut taxes." And when they say cut taxes, they mean taxes on the affluent: reducing the top marginal rate means that the biggest tax cuts go to people in the highest tax brackets.

The other camp in the tax-cut crusade actually welcomes the revenue losses from tax cuts. Its most visible spokesman today is Grover Norquist, president of Americans for Tax Reform, who once told National Public Radio: "I don't want to abolish government. I simply want to reduce it to the size where I can drag it into the bathroom and drown it in the bathtub." And the way to get it down to that size is to starve it of revenue. "The goal is reducing the size and scope of government by draining its lifeblood," Norquist told U.S. News & World Report.

What does "reducing the size and scope of government" mean? Tax-cut proponents are usually vague about the details. But the Heritage Foundation, ideological headquarters for the movement, has made it pretty clear. Edwin Feulner, the foundation's president, uses "New Deal" and "Great Society" as terms of abuse, implying that he and his organization want to do away with the institutions Franklin Roosevelt and Lyndon Johnson created. That means Social Security, Medicare, Medicaid—most of what gives citizens of the United States a safety net against economic misfortune.

The starve-the-beast doctrine is now firmly within the conservative mainstream. George W. Bush himself seemed to endorse the doctrine as the budget surplus evaporated: in August 2001 he called the disappearing surplus "incredibly positive news" because it would put Congress in a "fiscal straitjacket."

Like supply-siders, starve-the-beasters favor tax cuts mainly for people with high incomes. That is partly because, like supply-siders, they emphasize the incentive effects of cutting the top marginal rate; they just don't believe that those incentive effects are big enough that tax cuts pay for themselves. But they have another reason for cutting taxes mainly on the rich, which has become known as the "lucky ducky" argument.

Here's how the argument runs: to starve the beast, you must not only deny funds to the government; you must make voters hate the government. There's a danger that working-class families might see government as their friend: because their incomes are low, they don't pay much in taxes, while they benefit from public spending. So in starving the beast, you must take care not to cut taxes on these "lucky duckies." (Yes, that's what The Wall Street Journal called them in a famous editorial.) In fact, if possible, you must *raise* taxes on working-class Americans in order, as The Journal said, to get their "blood boiling with tax rage."

So the tax-cut crusade has two faces. Smiling supply-siders say that tax cuts are all gain, no pain; scowling starve-the-beasters believe that inflicting pain is not just necessary but also desirable. Is the alliance between these two groups a marriage of convenience? Not exactly. It would be more accurate to say that the starve-the-beasters hired the supply-siders—indeed, created them—because they found their naive optimism useful.

A look at who the supply-siders are and how they came to prominence tells the story.

The supply-side movement likes to present itself as a school of economic thought like Keynesianism or monetarism—that is, as a set of scholarly ideas that made their way, as such ideas do, into political discussion. But the reality is quite different. Supply-side economics was a political doctrine from Day 1; it emerged in the pages of political magazines, not professional economics journals.

That is not to deny that many professional economists favor tax cuts. But they almost always turn out to be starve-the-beasters, not supply-siders. And they often secretly—or sometimes not so secretly—hold supply-siders in contempt. N. Gregory Mankiw, now chairman of George W. Bush's Council of Economic Advisers, is definitely a friend to tax cuts; but in the first edition of his economic-principles textbook, he described Ronald Reagan's supply-side advisers as "charlatans and cranks."

It is not that the professionals refuse to consider supply-side ideas; rather, they have looked at them and found them wanting. A conspicuous example came earlier this year when the Congressional Budget Office tried to evaluate the growth effects of the Bush administration's proposed tax cuts. The budget office's new head, Douglas Holtz-Eakin, is a conservative economist who was handpicked for his job by the administration. But his conclusion was that unless the revenue losses from the proposed tax cuts were offset by spending cuts, the resulting deficits would be a drag on growth, quite likely to outweigh any supply-side effects.

But if the professionals regard the supply-siders with disdain, who employs these people? The answer is that since the 1970's almost all of the prominent supply-siders have been aides to conservative politicians, writers at conservative publications like National Review, fellows at conservative policy centers like Heritage or economists at private companies with strong Republican connections. Loosely speaking, that is, supply-siders work for the vast right-wing conspiracy. What gives supply-side economics influence is its connection with a powerful network of institutions that want to shrink the government and see tax cuts as a way to achieve that goal. Supply-side economics is a feel-good cover story for a political movement with a much harder-nosed agenda.

This isn't just speculation. Irving Kristol, in his role as co-editor of The Public Interest, was arguably the single most important proponent of supply-side economics. But years later, he suggested that he himself wasn't all that persuaded by the doctrine: "I was not certain of its economic merits but quickly saw its political possibilities." Writing in 1995, he explained that his real aim was to shrink the government and that tax cuts were a means to that end: "The task, as I saw it, was to create a new majority, which evidently would mean a conservative majority, which came to mean, in turn, a Republican majority—so political effectiveness was the priority, not the accounting deficiencies of government."

In effect, what Kristol said in 1995 was that he and his associates set out to deceive the American public. They sold tax cuts on the pretense that they would be painless, when they themselves believed that it would be necessary to slash public spending in order to make room for those cuts.

But one supposes that the response would be that the end justified the means—that the tax cuts did benefit all Americans because they led to faster economic growth. Did they?

4. From Reaganomics to Clintonomics

Ronald Reagan put supply-side theory into practice with his 1981 tax cut. The tax cuts were modest for middle-class families but very large for the well-off. Between 1979 and 1983, according to Congressional Budget Office estimates, the average federal tax rate on the top 1 percent of families fell from 37 to 27.7 percent.

So did the tax cuts promote economic growth? You might think that all we have to do is look at how the economy performed. But it's not that simple, because different observers read different things from Reagan's economic record.

Here's how tax-cut advocates look at it: after a deep slump between 1979 and 1982, the U.S. economy began growing rapidly. Between 1982 and 1989 (the first year of the first George Bush's presidency), the economy grew at an average annual rate of 4.2 percent. That's a lot better than the growth rate of the economy in the late 1970's, and supply-siders claim that these "Seven Fat Years" (the title of a book by Robert L. Bartley, the longtime editor of The Wall Street Journal's editorial page) prove the success of Reagan's 1981 tax cut.

But skeptics say that rapid growth after 1982 proves nothing: a severe recession is usually followed by a period of fast growth, as unemployed workers and factories are brought back on line. The test of tax cuts as a spur to economic growth is whether they produced more than an ordinary business cycle recovery. Once the economy was back to full employment, was it bigger than you would otherwise have expected? And there Reagan fails the test: between 1979, when the big slump began, and 1989, when the economy finally achieved more or less full employment again, the growth rate was 3 percent, the same as the growth rate between the two previous business cycle peaks in 1973 and 1979. Or to put it another way, by the late 1980's the U.S. economy was about where you would have expected it to be, given the trend in the 1970's. Nothing in the data suggests a supply-side revolution.

Does this mean that the Reagan tax cuts had no effect? Of course not. Those tax cuts, combined with increased military spending, provided a good old-fashioned Keynesian boost to demand. And this boost was one factor in the rapid recovery from recession that developed at the end of 1982, though probably not as important as the rapid expansion of the money supply that began in the summer of that year. But the supposed supply-side effects are invisible in the data.

While the Reagan tax cuts didn't produce any visible supply-side gains, they did lead to large budget deficits. From the point of view of most economists, this was a bad thing. But for starve-the-beast tax-cutters, deficits are potentially a good thing, because they force the government to shrink. So did Reagan's deficits shrink the beast?

A casual glance at the data might suggest not: federal spending as a share of gross domestic product was actually slightly higher at the end of the 1980's than it was at the end of the 1970's. But that number includes both defense spending and "entitlements," mainly Social Security and Medicare, whose growth is automatic unless Congress votes to cut benefits. What's left is a grab bag known as domestic discretionary spending, including everything from courts and national parks to environmental cleanups and education. And domestic discretionary spending fell from 4.5 percent of G.D.P. in 1981 to 3.2 percent in 1988.

But that's probably about as far as any president can shrink domestic discretionary spending. And because Reagan couldn't shrink the belly of the beast, entitlements, he couldn't find enough domestic spending cuts to offset his military spending increases and tax cuts. The federal budget went into persistent, alarming, deficit. In response to these deficits, George Bush the elder went back on his "read my lips" pledge and raised taxes. Bill Clinton raised them further. And thereby hangs a tale.

For Clinton did exactly the opposite of what supply-side economics said you should do: he raised the marginal rate on high-income taxpayers. In 1989, the top 1 percent of families paid, on average, only 28.9 percent of their income in federal taxes; by 1995, that share was up to 36.1 percent.

Conservatives confidently awaited a disaster—but it failed to materialize. In fact, the economy grew at a reasonable pace through Clinton's first term, while the deficit and the unemployment rate went steadily down. And then the news got even better: unemployment fell to its lowest level in decades without causing inflation, while productivity growth accelerated to rates not seen since the 1960's. And the budget deficit turned into an impressive surplus.

Tax-cut advocates had claimed the Reagan years as proof of their doctrine's correctness; as we have seen, those claims wilt under close examination. But the Clinton years posed a much greater challenge: here was a president who sharply raised the marginal tax rate on high-income taxpayers, the very rate that the tax-cut movement cares most about. And instead of presiding over an economic disaster, he presided over an economic miracle.

Let's be clear: very few economists think that Clinton's policies were primarily responsible for that miracle. For the most part, the Clinton-era surge probably reflected the maturing of information technology: businesses finally figured out how to make effective use of computers, and the resulting surge in productivity drove the economy forward. But the fact that America's best growth in a generation took place after the government did exactly the opposite of what tax-cutters advocate was a body blow to their doctrine.

They tried to make the best of the situation. The good economy of the late 1990's, ardent tax-cutters insisted, was caused by the 1981 tax cut. Early in 2000, Lawrence Kudlow and Stephen Moore, prominent supply-siders, published an article titled "It's the Reagan Economy, Stupid."

But anyone who thought about the lags involved found this implausible—indeed, hilarious. If the tax-cut movement attributed the booming economy of 1999 to a tax cut Reagan pushed through 18 years earlier, why didn't they attribute the economic boom of 1983 and 1984—Reagan's "morning in America"—to whatever Lyndon Johnson was doing in 1965 and 1966?

By the end of the 1990's, in other words, supply-side economics had become something of a laughingstock, and the whole case for tax cuts as a route to economic growth was looking pretty shaky. But the tax-cut crusade was nonetheless, it turned out, poised for its biggest political victories yet. How did that happen?

5. Second Wind: The Bush Tax Cuts

As the economic success of the United States under Bill Clinton became impossible to deny, there was a gradual shift in the sales strategy for tax cuts. The supposed economic benefits of tax cuts received less emphasis; the populist rationale—you, personally, pay too much in taxes—was played up.

I began this article with an example of this campaign's success: the creator of Mallard Fillmore apparently believes that typical families pay twice as much in taxes as they in fact do. But the most striking example of what skillful marketing can accomplish is the campaign for repeal of the estate tax.

As demonstrated, the estate tax is a tax on the very, very well off. Yet advocates of repeal began portraying it as a terrible burden on the little guy. They renamed it the "death tax" and put out reports decrying its impact on struggling farmers and businessmen—reports that never provided real-world examples because actual cases of family farms or small businesses broken up to pay estate taxes are almost impossible to find. This campaign succeeded in creating a public perception that the estate tax falls broadly on the population.

Earlier this year, a poll found that 49 percent of Americans believed that most families had to pay the estate tax, while only 33 percent gave the right answer that only a few families had to pay.

Still, while an insistent marketing campaign has convinced many Americans that they are overtaxed, it hasn't succeeded in making the issue a top priority with the public. Polls consistently show that voters regard safeguarding Social Security and Medicare as much more important than tax cuts.

Nonetheless, George W. Bush has pushed through tax cuts in each year of his presidency. Why did he push for these tax cuts, and how did he get them through?

You might think that you could turn to the administration's own pronouncements to learn why it has been so determined to cut taxes. But even if you try to take the administration at its word, there's a problem: the public rationale for tax cuts has shifted repeatedly over the past three years.

During the 2000 campaign and the initial selling of the 2001 tax cut, the Bush team insisted that the federal government was running an excessive budget surplus, which should be returned to taxpayers. By the summer of 2001, as it became clear that the projected budget surpluses would not materialize, the administration shifted to touting the tax cuts as a form of demand-side economic stimulus: by putting more money in consumers' pockets, the tax cuts would stimulate spending and help pull the economy out of recession. By 2003, the rationale had changed again: the administration argued that reducing taxes on dividend income, the core of its plan, would improve incentives and hence long-run growth—that is, it had turned to a supply-side argument.

These shifting rationales had one thing in common: none of them were credible. It was obvious to independent observers even in 2001 that the budget projections used to justify that year's tax cut exaggerated future revenues and understated future costs. It was similarly obvious that the 2001 tax cut was poorly designed as a demand stimulus. And we have already seen that the supply-side rationale for the 2003 tax cut was tested and found wanting by the Congressional Budget Office.

So what were the Bush tax cuts really about? The best answer seems to be that they were about securing a key part of the Republican base. Wealthy campaign contributors have a lot to gain from lower taxes, and since they aren't very likely to depend on Medicare, Social Security or Medicaid, they won't suffer if the beast gets starved. Equally important was the support of the party's intelligentsia, nurtured by policy centers like Heritage and professionally committed to the tax-cut crusade. The original Bush tax-cut proposal was devised in late 1999 not to win votes in the national election but to fend off a primary challenge from the supply-sider Steve Forbes, the presumptive favorite of that part of the base.

This brings us to the next question: how have these cuts been sold?

At this point, one must be blunt: the selling of the tax cuts has depended heavily on chicanery. The administration has used accounting trickery to hide the true budget impact of its proposals, and it has used misleading presentations to conceal the extent to which its tax cuts are tilted toward families with very high income.

The most important tool of accounting trickery, though not the only one, is the use of "sunset clauses" to understate the long-term budget impact of tax cuts. To keep the official 10-year cost of the 2001 tax cut down, the administration's Congressional allies wrote the law so that tax rates revert to their 2000 levels in 2011. But, of course, nobody expects the sunset to occur: when 2011 rolls around, Congress will be under immense pressure to extend the tax cuts.

The same strategy was used to hide the cost of the 2003 tax cut. Thanks to sunset clauses, its headline cost over the next decade was only $350 billion, but if the sunsets are canceled—as the president proposed in a speech early this month—the cost will be at least $800 billion.

Meanwhile, the administration has carried out a very successful campaign to portray these tax cuts as mainly aimed at middle-class families. This campaign is similar in spirit to the selling of estate-tax repeal as a populist measure, but considerably more sophisticated.

The reality is that the core measures of both the 2001 and 2003 tax cuts mainly benefit the very affluent. The centerpieces of the 2001 act were a reduction in the top income-tax rate and elimination of the estate tax—the first, by definition, benefiting only people with high incomes; the second benefiting only heirs to large estates. The core of the 2003 tax cut was a reduction in the tax rate on dividend income. This benefit, too, is concentrated on very high-income families.

According to estimates by the Tax Policy Center—a liberal-oriented institution, but one with a reputation for scrupulous accuracy—the 2001 tax cut, once fully phased in, will deliver 42 percent of its benefits to the top 1 percent of the income distribution. (Roughly speaking, that means families earning more than $330,000 per year.) The 2003 tax cut delivers a somewhat smaller share to the top 1 percent, 29.1 percent, but within that concentrates its benefits on the really, really rich. Families with incomes over $1 million a year—a mere 0.13 percent of the population—will receive 17.3 percent of this year's tax cut, more than the total received by the bottom 70 percent of American families. Indeed, the 2003 tax cut has already proved a major boon to some of America's wealthiest people: corporations in which executives or a single family hold a large fraction of stocks are suddenly paying much bigger dividends, which are now taxed at only 15 percent no matter how high the income of their recipient.

It might seem impossible to put a populist gloss on tax cuts this skewed toward the rich, but the administration has been remarkably successful in doing just that.

One technique involves exploiting the public's lack of statistical sophistication. In the selling of the 2003 tax cut, the catch phrase used by administration spokesmen was "92 million Americans will receive an average tax cut of $1,083." That sounded, and was intended to sound, as if every American family would get $1,083. Needless to say, that wasn't true.

Yet the catch phrase wasn't technically a lie: the Tax Policy Center estimates that 89 million people will receive tax cuts this year and that the total tax cut will be $99 billion, or about $1,100 for each of those 89 million people. But this calculation carefully leaves out the 50 million taxpayers who received no tax cut at all. And even among those who did get a tax cut, most got a lot less than $1,000, a number inflated by the very big tax cuts received by a few wealthy people. About half of American families received a tax cut of less than $100; the great majority, a tax cut of less than $500.

But the most original, you might say brilliant, aspect of the Bush administration's approach to tax cuts has involved the way the tax cuts themselves are structured.

David Stockman famously admitted that Reagan's middle-class tax cuts were a "Trojan horse" that allowed him to smuggle in what he really wanted, a cut in the top marginal rate. The Bush administration similarly follows a Trojan horse strategy, but an even cleverer one. The core measures in Bush's tax cuts benefit only the wealthy, but there are additional features that provide significant benefits to some—but only some—middle-class families. For example, the 2001 tax cut included a $400 child credit and also created a new 10 percent tax bracket, the so-called cutout. These measures had the effect of creating a "sweet spot" that could be exploited for political purposes. If a couple had multiple children, if the children were all still under 18 and if the couple's income was just high enough to allow it to take full advantage of the child credit, it could get a tax cut of as much as 4 percent of pretax income. Hence the couple with two children and an income of $40,000, receiving a tax cut of $1,600, who played such a large role in the administration's rhetoric. But while most couples have children, at any given time only a small minority of families contains two or more children under 18—and many of these families have income too low to take full advantage of the child tax credit. So that "typical" family wasn't typical at all. Last year, the actual tax break for families in the middle of the income distribution averaged $469, not $1,600.

So that's the story of the tax-cut offensive under the Bush administration: through a combination of hardball politics, deceptive budget arithmetic and systematic misrepresentation of who benefits, Bush's team has achieved a major reduction of taxes, especially for people with very high incomes.

But where does that leave the country?

6. A Planned Crisis

Right now, much of the public discussion of the Bush tax cuts focuses on their short-run impact. Critics say that the 2.7 million jobs lost since March 2001 prove that the administration's policies have failed, while the administration says that things would have been even worse without the tax cuts and that a solid recovery is just around the corner.

But this is the wrong debate. Even in the short run, the right question to ask isn't whether the tax cuts were better than nothing; they probably were. The right question is whether some other economic-stimulus plan could have achieved better results at a lower budget cost. And it is hard to deny that, on a jobs-per-dollar basis, the Bush tax cuts have been extremely ineffective. According to the Congressional Budget Office, half of this year's $400 billion budget deficit is due to Bush tax cuts. Now $200 billion is a lot of money; it is equivalent to the salaries of four million average workers. Even the administration doesn't claim its policies have created four million jobs. Surely some other policy—aid to state and local governments, tax breaks for the poor and middle class rather than the rich, maybe even W.P.A.-style public works—would have been more successful at getting the country back to work.

Meanwhile, the tax cuts are designed to remain in place even after the economy has recovered. Where will they leave us?

Here's the basic fact: partly, though not entirely, as a result of the tax cuts of the last three years, the government of the United States faces a fundamental fiscal shortfall. That is, the revenue it collects falls well short of the sums it needs to pay for existing programs. Even the U.S. government must, eventually, pay its bills, so something will have to give.

The numbers tell the tale. This year and next, the federal government will run budget deficits of more than $400 billion. Deficits may fall a bit, at least as a share of gross domestic product, when the economy recovers. But the relief will be modest and temporary. As Peter Fisher, under secretary of the treasury for domestic finance, puts it, the federal government is "a gigantic insurance company with a sideline business in defense and homeland security." And about a decade from now, this insurance company's policyholders will begin making a lot of claims. As the baby boomers retire, spending on Social Security benefits and Medicare will steadily rise, as will spending on Medicaid (because of rising medical costs). Eventually, unless there are sharp cuts in benefits, these three programs alone will consume a larger share of G.D.P. than the federal government currently collects in taxes.

Alan Auerbach, William Gale and Peter Orszag, fiscal experts at the Brookings Institution, have estimated the size of the "fiscal gap"—the increase in revenues or reduction in spending that would be needed to make the nation's finances sustainable in the long run. If you define the long run as 75 years, this gap turns out to be 4.5 percent of G.D.P. Or to put it another way, the gap is equal to 30 percent of what the federal government spends on all domestic programs. Of that gap, about 60 percent is the result of the Bush tax cuts. We would have faced a serious fiscal problem even if those tax cuts had never happened. But we face a much nastier problem now that they are in place. And more broadly, the tax-cut crusade will make it very hard for any future politicians to raise taxes.

So how will this gap be closed? The crucial point is that it cannot be closed without either fundamentally redefining the role of government or sharply raising taxes.

Politicians will, of course, promise to eliminate wasteful spending. But take out Social Security, Medicare, defense, Medicaid, government pensions, homeland security, interest on the public debt and veterans' benefits—none of them what people who complain about waste usually have in mind—and you are left with spending equal to about 3 percent of gross domestic product. And most of that goes for courts, highways, education and other useful things. Any savings from elimination of waste and fraud will amount to little more than a rounding-off error.

So let's put a few things back on the table. Let's assume that interest on the public debt will be paid, that spending on defense and homeland security will not be compromised and that the regular operations of government will continue to be financed. What we are left with, then, are the New Deal and Great Society programs: Social Security, Medicare, Medicaid and unemployment insurance. And to close the fiscal gap, spending on these programs would have to be cut by around 40 percent.

It's impossible to know how such spending cuts might unfold, but cuts of that magnitude would require drastic changes in the system. It goes almost without saying that the age at which Americans become eligible for retirement benefits would rise, that Social Security payments would fall sharply compared with average incomes, that Medicare patients would be forced to pay much more of their expenses out of pocket—or do without. And that would be only a start.

All this sounds politically impossible. In fact, politicians of both parties have been scrambling to expand, not reduce, Medicare benefits by adding prescription drug coverage. It's hard to imagine a situation under which the entitlement programs would be rolled back sufficiently to close the fiscal gap.

Yet closing the fiscal gap by raising taxes would mean rolling back all of the Bush tax cuts, and then some. And that also sounds politically impossible.

For the time being, there is a third alternative: borrow the difference between what we insist on spending and what we're willing to collect in taxes. That works as long as lenders believe that someday, somehow, we're going to get our fiscal act together. But this can't go on indefinitely. Eventually—I think within a decade, though not everyone agrees—the bond market will tell us that we have to make a choice.

In short, everything is going according to plan.

For the looming fiscal crisis doesn't represent a defeat for the leaders of the tax-cut crusade or a miscalculation on their part. Some supporters of President Bush may have really believed that his tax cuts were consistent with his promises to protect Social Security and expand Medicare; some people may still believe that the wondrous supply-side effects of tax cuts will make the budget deficit disappear. But for starve-the-beast tax-cutters, the coming crunch is exactly what they had in mind.

7. What Kind of Country?

The astonishing political success of the antitax crusade has, more or less deliberately, set the United States up for a fiscal crisis. How we respond to that crisis will determine what kind of country we become.

If Grover Norquist is right—and he has been right about a lot—the coming crisis will allow conservatives to move the nation a long way back toward the kind of limited government we had before Franklin Roosevelt. Lack of revenue, he says, will make it possible for conservative politicians—in the name of fiscal necessity—to dismantle immensely popular government programs that would otherwise have been untouchable.

In Norquist's vision, America a couple of decades from now will be a place in which elderly people make up a disproportionate share of the poor, as they did before Social Security. It will also be a country in which even middle-class elderly Americans are, in many cases, unable to afford expensive medical procedures or prescription drugs and in which poor Americans generally go without even basic health care. And it may well be a place in which only those who can afford expensive private schools can give their children a decent education.

But as Governor Riley of Alabama reminds us, that's a choice, not a necessity. The tax-cut crusade has created a situation in which something must give. But what gives—whether we decide that the New Deal and the Great Society must go or that taxes aren't such a bad thing after all—is up to us. The American people must decide what kind of a country we want to be.

POSTSCRIPT

Are Tax Cuts Good for America?

There is an obvious conflict between wanting to keep (and perhaps extend) most of the services and benefits that government provides and simultaneously wanting to lower taxes. Americans are increasingly skeptical about the uses to which their tax money is put. They do not understand how taxes are imposed, and they suspect that somebody else is getting a tax cut at their expense.

The consequences will likely be debated for many years. Do these tax cuts increase incentives for investment and spending, thus bolstering the economy and increasing tax revenues in the long run? Or do they unfairly reward upper-income earners, re-create federal deficits, and make it more difficult for Congress to adopt costly reforms that would benefit lower- and middle-income citizens?

The significant tax reductions that were adopted in 2001, 2002, and 2003 have contributed to the replacement of an anticipated federal surplus by a huge deficit in federal income.

John Podhoretz, *Bush Country: How Dubya Became a Great President While Driving Liberals Insane* (St. Martin's Press, 2004) defends the tax cuts and other fiscal policies as essential elements of the strategic policies of the Bush administration in reversing economic slowdown, encouraging business investment, and supporting the new expenditures for the war in Iraq and the war on terrorism. Current articles in *The Weekly Standard* and *National Review* make the case for eliminating dividend and estate taxes and reducing the cost of non-essential government services.

The title of David Cay Johnston's book criticizing tax policies of the second Bush administration clearly indicates its point of view: *Perfectly Legal: The Covert Campaign to Rig Our Tax System to Benefit the Super Rich—and Cheat Everybody Else* (Portfolio, 2003). Johnston believes that the tax code perpetuates a widening gulf between the super-rich and everyone else. Charles Lewis and Bill Allison, in *The Cheating of America: How Tax Avoidance and Evasion by the Super Rich Are Costing the Country Billions and What You Can Do About It* (William Morrow, 2001), are persuaded that the problem is not that Americans are taxed too much but that too many get away with paying too little.

John O. Fox, *If Americans Really Understood the Income Tax: Uncovering Our Most Expensive Ignorance* (Westview Press, 2001), cannot be characterized as favoring more or less taxation, but urges tax reform by eliminating special tax benefits and instituting lower taxes rate across the board.

ISSUE 14

Is America Becoming More Unequal?

YES: Jeff Madrick, from "Inequality and Democracy," in George Packer, ed., *The Fight Is for Democracy* (Perennial, 2003)

NO: Christopher C. DeMuth, from "The New Wealth of Nations," *Commentary* (October 1997)

ISSUE SUMMARY

YES: Editor and author Jeff Madrick maintains that the striking recent increase in income and wealth inequality reflects increasing inequality of opportunity and threatens the civil and political rights of less wealthy Americans.

NO: American Enterprise Institute president Christopher C. DeMuth asserts that Americans have achieved an impressive level of wealth and equality and that a changing economy ensures even more opportunities.

There has always been a wide range in real income in the United States. In the first three decades after the end of World War II, family incomes doubled, income inequality narrowed slightly, and poverty rates declined. Prosperity declined in the mid-1970s, when back-to-back recessions produced falling average incomes, greater inequality, and higher poverty levels. Between the mid-1980s and the late 1990s, sustained economic recovery resulted in a modest average growth in income, but high poverty rates continued.

Defenders of the social system maintain that, over the long run, poverty has declined. Many improvements in social conditions benefit virtually all people and, thus, make us more equal. The increase in longevity (attributable in large measure to advances in medicine, nutrition, and sanitation) affects all social classes. In a significant sense, the U.S. economy is far fairer now than at any time in the past. In the preindustrial era, when land was the primary measure of wealth, those without land had no way to improve their circumstances. In the industrial era, when people of modest means needed physical strength and stamina to engage in difficult and hazardous labor in mines, mills, and factories, those who were too weak, handicapped, or too old stood little chance of gaining or keeping reasonable jobs.

In the postindustrial era, many of the manufactured goods that were once "Made in U.S.A.," ranging from clothing to electronics, are now made by cheaper foreign labor. Despite this loss, America achieved virtually full employment in the 1990s, largely because of the enormous growth of the information and service industries. Intelligence, ambition, and hard work—qualities that cut across social classes—are likely to be the determinants of success.

In the view of the defenders of the American economic system, the sharp increase in the nation's gross domestic product has resulted in greater prosperity for most Americans. Although the number of superrich has grown, so has the number of prosperous small business owners, middle-level executives, engineers, computer programmers, lawyers, doctors, entertainers, sports stars, and others who have gained greatly from the longest sustained economic growth in American history. For example, successful young pioneers in the new technology and the entrepreneurs whose capital supported their ventures have prospered, and so have the technicians and other workers whom they hired. Any change that mandated more nearly equal income would greatly diminish the incentives for invention, discovery, and risk-taking enterprises. As a result, the standard of living would be much lower and rise much more slowly, and individual freedom would be curtailed by the degree of state interference in people's private lives.

None of these objections satisfies those who deplore what they characterize as an increasing disparity in the distribution of income and wealth. In 2002 the U.S. Census Bureau concluded that the relative prosperity of the 1990s left poverty virtually unchanged, with 8 percent of American families earning less than $17,600, the income level below which a family of four is considered to be living in poverty. One in five households was broke, with nothing to tide them over when confronted with unemployment or a health crisis—not to mention being unable to save for college or retirement. Contrary to the popular cliché, a rising tide does not lift all boats; it does not lift the leaky boats or those who have no boat. *Business Week* reported that the pay gap between top executives and production workers in the 362 largest U.S. companies soared from a ratio of 42 to 1 to 475 to 1 in 1989. The financial wealth of the top 1 percent of households now exceeds the combined household financial wealth of the bottom 98 percent.

Advocates of more nearly equal income argue that a reduced pay gap would lead to less social conflict, less crime, more economic security, and better and more universal social services. Also, more nearly egalitarian societies (Scandinavia and Western Europe, for example) offer more nearly equal access to education, medical treatment, and legal defense. What happens to democracy, some ask, when more money means better access to those who write and administer the laws and to the very offices of political power themselves?

In the following selections, Jeff Madrick examines the causes and consequences of income and wealth inequality, while Christopher C. DeMuth outlines a number of forces that have reduced inequality.

YES

Jeff Madrick

Inequality and Democracy

When I was a boy in the 1950s, "equality" was central to the public discourse. The word was seemingly everywhere. Equality before the law was widely thought of as an unquestioned good, charged with positive associations. Equality was an unquestioned component of American greatness, and of its democracy. We experienced it directly. Almost all of us went to public schools, drove on free and quite extraordinary public highways, and got our federally subsidized polio shots. Our GI parents went to college on the government dole and our teachers got federal subsidies for their education after Russia launched Sputnik.

Not all was ideal. Inequality of health care was never adequately or objectively discussed. That millions of African Americans were originally, and for a long time thereafter, excluded from this equality was still the nation's stunning hypocrisy. But in the 1950s, America was at least beginning to address this central tragedy more directly. "Separate but equal," the prevailing idea that justified legalizing school segregation, was disturbing because it clearly meant separate but unequal to a nation committed in its traditions to equality as a principle. Without that tradition, legal racism would have had an even more extended life.

But if equal rights before the law was an accepted principle of democracy, what can we say about economic equality and democracy? In this period, political and economic equality unmistakably went hand in hand. In fact, the association between political and economic equality made the very idea of equality fine and noble for us. In the 1950s, for example, civil rights clearly implied equality of economic opportunity, and equal economic opportunity implied a middle class life. It was a glorious time for the economy. Incomes grew for all levels of workers on average in America in these years, and the income distribution, which narrowed significantly during World War II, remained that way and even improved slightly for the next twenty-five years. The benefits of this most rapid period of growth in American history—at the least, on a par with the more uneven growth of the late 1800s—accrued to a new middle class.

Naïveté still abounded about how widespread prosperity was. In 1962 Michael Harrington's landmark book, *The Other America,* awakened the nation to convincing evidence that a large proportion of the population was still poor. Much of the nation was in truth appalled precisely because equality was a central American value. With the rise of a counterculture and eventual antagonism toward the prosecution of the Vietnam War, America was no longer thought blemish-free, and the fight for equality, or at least rough fairness, became imperative in many spheres. Relatively few disputed that poverty implied unequal opportunity. The majority increasingly favored programs that were outright grants to the poor, which went against the grain of much of American history. In the past, we typically (with a few exceptions) only gave money to those who already worked or sacrificed for their country—Social Security, unemployment insurance, and war veterans. Now, there were new programs, such as expanded welfare and Medicaid, that simply handed out money with relatively few qualifications. The commitment to equality in these years extended to the new feminists, marked by a threshold book, *The Feminine Mystique,* and it was again not confined to matters of civil rights for women. The wide gap in pay for the same work became a key issue in the struggle for equality.

Times are entirely different today, and regrettably so. Political discussion about economic equality has essentially become a taboo. Social Security is no longer the third rail of politics; equality is. Congressmen and senators are cautioned against discussing it because it sounds like class warfare to the public. A wide range of people believe they are put at an unfair disadvantage by affirmative action, welfare, a minimum wage, and other social programs designed to level the playing field. Ironically, the aversion to discussing equality intensified as inequality of incomes and wealth increased over twenty years to levels not seen since the 1920s.

Where does income and wealth inequality start to impinge on civil and political rights, and on America's long commitment to equality of economic opportunity? Where does it both reflect a failure of democracy and contribute to its weakening? There is a good argument to be made that we are already there.

The past few decades are not the first period in which the nation devalued equality. In the second half of the 1800s and in the 1920s, economic inequality rose rapidly. It was accompanied by a contraction of American ideology that limited the nation's focus to the individualistic components and excluded the egalitarian aspects of the national character. Social Darwinism was the simplistic individualistic philosophy of the day in the late 1800s. Survival of the fittest was a natural law with which government should not interfere, its advocates argued. In the 1920s, there was again a momentary return to rough individualism. Rates for the relatively new income tax were slashed, for example.

In the national mythology, if Americans are left to their own devices, to fall and rise according to their talents, the simple values of early America will reassert themselves and all will be well. If there is more inequality as a result, that merely reflects the abilities and tenacity of individuals, not a failure of the nation. The dominant ideological tenet of the time held that, left to their own devices, most Americans would do well.

Was this ever true? There was plenty of poverty in early America, a strong landed plutocracy, and by any modern standards, times were difficult for most. But compared to conditions in the Old World, the romantic notions about opportunity in early America were based in a large measure of fact. Equal rights did mean in the 1700s and early 1800s, to a greater extent than ever before, equal economic opportunity, even if mere self-sufficiency for most. And self-sufficiency meant political independence that was entirely new for most whites. Many people today fail to realize that equality was a reigning principle of the early 1800s and even the colonial years. . . .

Today, . . . America accepts its growing inequality equably. Yet the increase in income and wealth inequality since the late 1970s is striking. In 1979 the top 5 percent of earners made eleven times more than those in the bottom 20 percent. Now they earn nineteen times what the bottom quintile earns. The top 10 percent earn 40 percent of total income in America: They earned only about 30 percent from the 1940s to the late 1970s. We are now back to the income-distribution levels of the 1920s. In terms of wealth—homes and financial assets such as stocks and bonds (less debt)—the top 1 percent have 40 percent of all assets, again about the same as in the 1920s.

Some of the skewing toward the wealthy has been the result of capital gains on stocks during the extraordinary bull market of the late 1990s, which are temporary. If we include only wages, salaries, government payments, rent, dividends, and interest, however, we find that income became highly unequal, anyway. Families in the top 20 percent earned ten and a half times what families in the bottom quintile earned in the 1970s.

Forbes magazine's four hundred richest Americans were almost ten times richer in 2002, on average, even after the market crash, than the four hundred richest were in 1982. The economy grew by only three times over this period, and typical family incomes only doubled. In 1982, when the list was started, it required only $50 million to make it; in 2002, it required $550 million. The average net worth was almost $2.2 billion. Kevin Phillips, author most recently of *Wealth and Democracy*, figures that ten thousand families in 2000, at the height of the market, were worth $65 million. A quarter of a million may have been worth $10 million or more.

The CEOs, of course, ate their cake and had it, too. In the late 1970s, the average CEO made twenty-five times what the average worker made each year. By 1988, that ratio had soared with the stock market and the enormous Reagan tax cuts. The CEO now made nearly one hundred times what the typical worker made. By 2000, with stock options and a bull market like no other, the CEO made five hundred times on average what the typical worker made.

Phillips and others point out that the last twenty years or so are a period much like the late 1800s, the era of the robber barons. But, in fact, there is a disturbing difference. When such fabulous wealth accrued in the past, such as in the late 1880s and the 1920s, the economy grew rapidly. Wages on average rose handsomely, even if unevenly, over these years for most levels of workers. So did the typical family's net worth. Rising revenues enabled the nation to afford a federal government that ultimately minimized worker abuses and established new regulations for trade and markets. A case could at least be made that rising inequality was a price worth paying for rapid economic growth—a case I nevertheless think is wrong. Had incomes been more equal and abuse less prevalent, I believe that the economy would have grown still faster.

Since the rise of inequality in the recent era, however, the economy grew unusually slowly with the exception of the late 1990s. Even including the rise in wages in the late 1990s, average wages in 2002 were still only slightly higher than they were in 1973. Male workers bore the brunt of this decline. As they grew older and more experienced, nearly half of them lost ground over twenty years and another 10 percent made almost no gain—an extraordinary failure unprecedented in American history over so long a period of time. Women, by contrast, experienced fairly rapid wage increases, but they were still earning less than men, often when they were doing the same job. Businesses clearly substituted lower-wage women for men in these years. But this did not explain the decline in the average wage for all workers. And, even with so many spouses working, family income rose at an unusually slow rate. It could no longer be argued that rising inequality was worth the price, as it could have been argued in the late 1800s and the 1920s, because the economy raised the standard of living for all others. In the last quarter century, this was not true.

Arguably, the accrual of individual wealth in this period was as extreme as in the Gilded Age, although comparisons are difficult to draw. By the late 1990s, the great fortunes were surely much larger than they were, comparatively speaking, in the 1920s or 1960s when the American economy as a whole did far better. When we analyze the data further, we find more disheartening news. Average retirement wealth rose over this period, but highly unequally. The economist Edward Wolff calculates that retirement wealth actually fell between 1983 and 1998 for well more than half of America's families. Childhood poverty rates are simply alarming. Every way they can be calculated, whether in absolute terms or by comparison to median or high incomes, a higher proportion of children live in poverty in America than in any other developed nation. Nearly one out of five children grow up in poverty in America, compared to one in twelve in much of Europe. Moreover, the gap between better off and poor children, according to economist Timothy Smeeding, was significantly wider in America than almost everywhere else in comparably advanced nations. Only British children were almost as disadvantaged.

The pressures of inequality are by now quite severe. The strain on working people and on family life, as spouses have gone to work in dramatic numbers, has become significant. VCRs and television sets are cheap, but higher education, health care, public transportation, drugs, housing, and cars have risen faster in price than typical family incomes and in many cases, such as higher education, health care, and drugs, much faster. Life has grown neither calm nor secure for most Americans, by any means. Only in the late 1990s did all levels of workers do well, but they still had not compensated for falling behind in the prior twenty-odd years.

Some argue that Americans did better all along than the data indicated. For a while, some even argued that inequality did not rise, a claim now totally discredited. But the data are clear and, furthermore, anecdotal evidence vastly supports the stagnating economic indicators.

Yet most Americans have accepted slow-growing or stagnating wages and widening inequality with little complaint about the economy, business, or the traditional guarantees of equal opportunity before the law. A key question is: *Why?*

There are a few possible explanations. By the 1970s, America was exhausted by the modern liberal social policies of Presidents Kennedy and Johnson, even though they worked better than was recognized. Welfare programs created dependencies, but poverty was dramatically reduced, racism was seriously circumscribed, good education was made widely available, Medicare was created, and under President Nixon, Social Security was seriously enhanced. Incomes had become much more equal over these early post–World War II decades.

The bigger source of moral exhaustion was probably the Vietnam War, a mostly liberal venture. By the time it ended, the nation seemed tired of government. And the prosecution of the war was not equal. As noted, it fell largely on young working-class men to fight. The educated easily escaped the draft.

But set against this moral political exhaustion, I think it was mostly slow economic growth, high inflation and interest rates, and lost jobs that turned the nation against its long-standing progressive attitudes. The nation had to apportion a pie that was growing much more slowly—that was simply much smaller than Americans had come to expect it would be, based on their history and traditions. Government was now easily portrayed as the cause of, not the solution to, economically tightened conditions. To many, equality now meant taking from those who worked to give to those who didn't, taking from the working class who were not disposed to higher education to give to those advantaged young people who were, helping people of color at the expense of people who were white. In the past, equality meant that most people's opportunities were expanded. But working people were now suffering, and they needed a scapegoat or two. Business escaped blame partly because government had dominated the previous period. We were tired of government. It did indeed wage an unpopular war and develop expensive new social programs. Moreover, businesspeople were not making fortunes in the 1970s. Profits in general were poor. The stock market stagnated at 1960s levels. There was less obvious cause to direct anger at them.

Ultimately, financially straitened workers did not want to pay more taxes; to the contrary, they wanted to pay less. Beginning in the difficult 1970s, victimized by both high inflation and deep recession, and before Ronald Reagan's large tax cut of 1981, the electorate rewarded politicians who promised tax cuts. . . .

A fundamental question for Americans is whether the inequality in outcomes since the 1980s reflected an inequality in opportunity in these decades. In other words, did it amount to a direct challenge to one of our basic ideals? I think it did. What stands out most is childhood poverty. When one out of five children is so disadvantaged, and another one in five is nearly poor, one simply cannot argue that opportunity is equal in America. The parents of these children are typically at work, they do not get decent childcare, and early education is out of the question. Their standard primary schools are almost always below average. Measures of education quality across America are not as bad as they are often reported to be. But there are huge pockets of inadequate education in poorer and working-class neighborhoods. Some other economies also produce large numbers of poor children. In France, for example, as high a proportion of children are poor as in America. But their significant government social programs raise the lower levels to acceptable standards. Because schools are financed locally in America, poverty and poor education have become a vicious circle. Money matters. As the Nobel Prize–winning economist George Akerlof points out, the evidence is considerable that money spent in these schools has productive results.

Further, as economies become more complex and change in other ways, burdens on people change as well, and they fall on them unequally. Not only the poor, but those in the middle now bear these burdens, and slow-growing incomes for the wide middle of America make opportunity unequal. In recent times, the so-called New Economy of the 1990s placed even more emphasis on education. This economy has created greater need for public childcare because spouses have to go to work. Its demand for worker flexibility means that as workers lose jobs, they also lose pension and health-care benefits. These are all "dis-equalizing" circumstances to which the government should respond but has not.

To the contrary, it has gone energetically in the other direction, creating inequalities rather than ameliorating them. Consider the litany. The rise of defined-contribution pension plans, which supplanted old-style defined-benefits plans, helped corporations reduce their contributions but, it turns out, only the better-off were better off with them. The middle- and lower-income workers did worse. If Social Security is privatized, elderly incomes will become significantly more unequal. The march toward deregulation and privatization—partly, but only partly, necessary—often favored the well-off at the expense of middle- and lower-income workers. The nation in these years steadfastly refused to raise the minimum wage until relatively recently. America did not seriously enforce worker-safety regulations. It did not support laws to enable labor unions to organize. It found no way to provide health insurance for the nearly 20 percent of people who were not covered. It did not strengthen accounting regulations, even when the Securities and Exchange Commission tried to, beaten back by angry legislators who were lectured to by their investment-banking and accounting-industry campaign supporters. CEOs took tens of millions of dollars, workers lost their savings. The government did not adopt new protective regulations, even after the debacle of Long-Term Capital Management. It wholeheartedly supported regulation-free capital flows around the world, even when they were a primary cause of the Asian financial crisis. It reduced the coverage of unemployment insurance significantly. It reduced tax rates dramatically for upper-income workers. In general, as noted, it allowed a financial movement on Wall Street to emphasize job cuts as the best path to profitability; taking on debt was not discouraged. Many economists exalted the restraint on wages but said nothing about over-investment in high technology and telecommunications and absurdly romantic securities speculation. The Federal Reserve under Alan Greenspan was far more concerned about wage increases than about a stock-market bubble.

Let me be clear that some of these changes were necessary. Profits were probably too low in the 1960s and '70s, wages too high. Some federal programs were poorly thought out. Private business had become more sophisticated and government direction and sometimes even oversight were often no longer necessary. Some social programs will inevitably get more expensive, especially as the population ages, and therefore the nation has to deal with how to pay for them. International competition had toughened, and required leaner and more flexible companies. In general, tax revenues no longer grow as rapidly because the economy grows more slowly, so ultimately we can afford less. But the movement was carried too far, and government's role as a protector of equal opportunity and equal rights was often abandoned. The results showed up in falling wages, slow-growing family incomes, and rising inequality. It is not just the bottom 10 percent who have fared poorly. The lower 50 percent have, and in some ways, even the lower three-quarters are more strained than at any time in the post–World War II era. International competition from low-wage nations, a more sophisticated workplace, and slow growth all contributed to inequality. But government did not perform its traditional role of a counterforce to balance these other factors, and often exacerbated inequality in the name of self-reliance and limiting regulation in general.

What, then, is the case for equality in a democracy? Equal political rights may remain the most important issue. They are an end in themselves. But in practice, fairly equal economic outcomes have helped guarantee equal political rights. Nowhere has this been more true than in the American experience. The original source of political equality was not a simple social contract arrived at through agreement or revolution. Of course, John Locke's ideas mattered, and the European Enlightenment emboldened the Western world and valued the individual and his or her rights. But in America, the primary source of political equality was access to land. It was not an accident that Jefferson promised land to the thousandth generation when he purchased the Louisiana Territory. Land was not an issue of wealth to him but an issue of spreading political power.

Our current acceptance of inequality is dangerous for at least four reasons. First, it is unjust socially and may eventually generate spreading, if unarticulated, discontent, which will seek further scapegoats. Second, contrary to much conventional wisdom, inequality undermines economic growth because it limits the strength of demand, the optimism of a nation, and the capacity for people to educate themselves. Even now, only 60 percent of families own a PC; in contrast, by 1955, 90 percent of families had a television set, which was relatively much more expensive then. Wages were not sufficient to support booming demand in the late 1990s; consumers borrowed at record levels. Contrary to conventional wisdom of the moment, high levels of inequality imply generally low wages, and low-wage economies are generally inimical to growth. They do not create an internal market for goods and services on a sufficient scale to make production efficient. In *Why Economies Grow,* I argue that, historically, growing internal markets are a major source of economic growth, and perhaps the most important source. In fact, almost all economies that have taken off historically, such as those of the Netherlands in the 1600s or Britain in the 1700s, have been more egalitarian than those of their competitors. These domestic markets are themselves often the most important stimulants to capital investment and technological innovation. As British economic historian J.H. Habakkuk argued long ago, low wages do not provide incentives for business to invest in modern equipment or to train and provide private services for their workers. America's South, as economist Gavin Wright has shown time and again, beginning with his book *Old South, New South,* is still dominated by low-wage industries. Slow growth, in turn, invariably hurts lower-level workers more than the rest.

Third, unequal incomes can in themselves mean unequal opportunity. Poor families and even median-income families often cannot afford to live in neighborhoods that will provide their children with a decent education; they cannot get quality childcare when they have to work, and they cannot get adequate health care for the family. Costs of being middle class today—the costs of health care, education, transportation, and housing—have far outrun the incomes of the typical family, not merely those of the poor. Serious inequality of incomes and wealth already reflect unequal opportunity. Today, more than ever before, opportunity means a competitive education, and typically a decent higher education. But America probably has the most unequal education system in the developed world, supported by local tax revenues that reflect the incomes of the community. Vouchers are typical of the current response: They will save a few and discourage many, and on balance, will lead to more inequality. Those in the bottom half of America also cannot afford the best health care. They have jobs that do not provide health benefits. Poor health undermines equality of opportunity as well.

Fourth, inequality can lead to a skewing of political power toward elite interests. The congressional turn toward deregulation and lower taxes, many observers argue, is a function of the growing importance of money in politics. New well-financed think tanks supported by conservatives spread an ideology about the unimportance of equality and the dangers of government. Reforms, even of accounting principles, are beaten back by aggressive lobbyists with millions of dollars of campaign funds. Rightist foundations spend tens of millions of dollars to fight ideological battles. Most distressing, the growing numbers of those who do not vote in America are dominated by the least well off.

In my view, inequality means exclusion, and the nation needs something like a new social contract that emphasizes both inclusiveness and change. New programs should include a higher minimum wage, a still more expansive earned income tax credit, and serious savings subsidies for college. Efforts to universalize health care are critical, yet hardly addressed. Serious public investment must be directed toward equalizing education locally. Ideally, open discussion of how a high-wage economy can promote rather than impede growth will begin to change social norms about the expendability of workers. Campaign-finance reform should be enacted to minimize the growing political power of rich people and corporations.

The nation must also recognize that times change. Americans used to look forward, not backward. We built canals, railroads, primary and then high schools, public universities, vast public health systems to sanitize cities; we regulated business and put down a vast highway system. In retrospect, we think all this was inevitable, that the decisions made were obvious. But they were all reactions to change by an open and optimistic society. Now we scorn government responses to change. We look back, unwilling to risk. If we confronted change, we would emphasize new ideas. This means family-friendly policies like flexible hours and high quality day care. In a changing economy, with an increasingly expendable labor force, corporate benefits should be made portable.

A new New Deal? Of sorts, yes. Can we afford it? There are limits. But such programs can enhance economic growth, while reinforcing our long-held beliefs in equality. After a period of soaring income for the wealthy, higher progressive rates on very high incomes are entirely in order to pay for part of what we need. The preponderance of economic research suggests high marginal rates do not impede economic growth by undermining incentives for the wealthy.

But none of this is politically possible without a reinvigoration of fundamental principles. Our democracy is no longer working as it should. The influence of moneyed corporations has never been higher. But the most vigorous democracies are essentially about equality—in the case of America, about equality of civil rights and equality of economic opportunity in a complex and changing environment. Democracy is not about making economic outcomes equal. Americans want everyone and anyone to be able to make a fortune. But when outcomes are as skewed as they have been, it is clear that something in the process is badly wrong. Sustaining democracy may now depend on maintaining a vibrant spirit of national equality. If equality—let's call it inclusion, because that is what it is—were again the passion of the people, as it was two centuries ago, we might accomplish what is necessary. I doubt there is any true democracy without such a passion.

Christopher C. DeMuth  **NO**

The New Wealth of Nations

The Nations of North America, Western Europe, Australia, and Japan are wealthier today than they have ever been, wealthier than any others on the planet, wealthier by far than any societies in human history. Yet their governments appear to be impoverished—saddled with large accumulated debts and facing annual deficits that will grow explosively over the coming decades. As a result, government spending programs, especially the big social-insurance programs like Social Security and Medicare in the United States, are facing drastic cuts in order to avert looming insolvency (and, in France and some other European nations, in order to meet the Maastricht treaty's criteria of fiscal rectitude). American politics has been dominated for several years now by contentious negotiations over deficit reduction between the Clinton administration and the Republican Congress. This past June, first at the European Community summit in Amsterdam and then at the Group of Eight meeting in Denver, most of the talk was of hardship and constraint and the need for governmental austerity ("Economic Unease Looms Over Talks at Denver Summit," read the *New York Times* headline).

These bloodless problems of governmental accounting are said, moreover, to reflect real social ills: growing economic inequality in the United States; high unemployment in Europe; an aging, burdensome, and medically needy population everywhere; and the globalization of commerce, which is destroying jobs and national autonomy and forcing bitter measures to keep up with the bruising demands of international competitiveness.

How can it be that societies so surpassingly wealthy have governments whose core domestic-welfare programs are on the verge of bankruptcy? The answer is as paradoxical as the question. We have become not only the richest but also the freest and most egalitarian societies that have ever existed, and it is our very wealth, freedom, and equality that are causing the welfare state to unravel.

⚬

That we have become very rich is clear enough in the aggregate. That we have become very equal in the enjoyment of our riches is an idea strongly resisted by many. Certainly there has been a profusion of reports in the media and political speeches about increasing income inequality: the rich, it is said, are getting richer, the poor are getting poorer, and the middle and working classes are under the relentless pressure of disappearing jobs in manufacturing and middle management.

Although these claims have been greatly exaggerated, and some have been disproved by events, it is true that, by some measures, there has been a recent increase in income inequality in the United States. But it is a very small tick in the massive and unprecedented leveling of material circumstances that has been proceeding now for almost three centuries and in this century has accelerated dramatically. In fact, the much-noticed increase in measured-income inequality is in part a result of the increase in real social equality. Here are a few pieces of this important but neglected story.

• First, progress in agriculture, construction, manufacturing, and other key sectors of economic production has made the material necessities of life—food, shelter, and clothing—available to essentially everyone. To be sure, many people, including the seriously handicapped and the mentally incompetent, remain dependent on the public purse for their necessities. And many people continue to live in terrible squalor. But the problem of poverty, defined as material scarcity, has been solved. If poverty today remains a serious problem, it is a problem of individual behavior, social organization, and public policy. This was not so 50 years ago, or ever before.

• Second, progress in public health, in nutrition, and in the biological sciences and medical arts has produced dramatic improvements in longevity, health, and physical well-being. Many of these improvements—resulting, for example, from better public sanitation and water supplies, the conquest of dread diseases, and the abundance of nutritious food—have affected entire populations, producing an equalization of real personal welfare more powerful than any government redistribution of income.

The Nobel prize-winning economist Robert Fogel has focused on our improved mastery of the biological environment—leading over the past 300 years to a doubling of the average human life span and to large gains in physical stature, strength, and energy—as the key to what he calls "the egalitarian revolution of the 20th century." He considers this so profound an advance as to constitute a distinct new level of human evolution. Gains in stature, health, and longevity are continuing today and even accelerating. Their outward effects may be observed, in evolutionary fast-forward, in the booming nations of Asia (where, for example, the physical difference between older and younger South Koreans is strikingly evident on the streets of Seoul).

• Third, the critical *source* of social wealth has shifted over the last few hundred years from land (at the end of the 18th century) to physical capital (at the end of the 19th) to, today, human capital—education and cognitive ability. This development is not an unmixed gain from the standpoint of economic equality. The ability to acquire and deploy human capital is a function of intelligence, and intelligence is not only unequally distributed but also, to a significant degree, heritable. As Charles Murray and the late Richard J. Herrnstein argue in *The Bell Curve,* an economy that rewards sheer brainpower replaces one old source of inequality, socioeconomic advantage with a new one, cognitive advantage.

But an economy that rewards human capital also tears down far more artificial barriers than it erects. For most people who inhabit the vast middle range of the bell curve, intelligence is much more equally distributed than land or physical capital ever was. Most people, that is, possess ample intelligence to pursue all but a handful of specialized callings. If in the past many were held back by lack of education and closed social institutions, the opportunities to use one's human capital have blossomed with the advent of universal education and the erosion of social barriers.

Furthermore, the material benefits of the knowledge-based economy are by no means limited to those whom Murray and Herrnstein call the cognitive elite. Many of the newest industries, from fast food to finance to communications, have succeeded in part by opening up employment opportunities for those of modest ability and training—occupations much less arduous and physically much less risky than those they have replaced. And these new industries have created enormous, widely shared economic benefits in consumption; I will return to this subject below.

• Fourth, recent decades have seen a dramatic reduction in one of the greatest historical sources of inequality: the social and economic inequality of the sexes. Today, younger cohorts of working men and women with comparable education and job tenure earn essentially the same incomes. The popular view would have it that the entry of women into the workforce has been driven by falling male earnings and the need "to make ends meet" in middle-class families. But the popular view is largely mistaken. Among married women (as the economist Chinhui Juhn has demonstrated), it is wives of men with high incomes who have been responsible for most of the recent growth in employment.

• Fifth, in the wealthy Western democracies, material needs and desires have been so thoroughly fulfilled for so many people that, for the first time in history, we are seeing large-scale voluntary reductions in the amount of time spent at paid employment. This development manifests itself in different forms: longer periods of education and training for the young; earlier retirement despite longer life spans; and, in between, many more hours devoted to leisure, recreation, entertainment, family, community and religious activities, charitable and other nonremunerative pursuits, and so forth. The dramatic growth of the sports, entertainment, and travel industries captures only a small slice of what has happened. In Fogel's estimation, the time devoted to nonwork activities by the average male head of household has grown from 10.5 hours per week in 1880 to 40 hours today, while time per week at work has fallen from 61.6 hours to 33.6 hours. Among women, the reduction in work (including not only outside employment but also household work, food preparation, childbearing and attendant health problems, and child rearing) and the growth in nonwork have been still greater.

There is a tendency to overlook these momentous developments because of the often frenetic pace of modern life. But our busy-ness actually demonstrates the point: time, and not material things, has become the scarce and valued commodity in modern society.

One implication of these trends is that in very wealthy societies, income has become a less useful gauge of economic welfare and hence of economic equality. When income becomes to some degree discretionary, and when many peoples' incomes change from year to year for reasons unrelated to their life circumstances, *consumption* becomes a better measure of material welfare. And by this measure, welfare appears much more evenly distributed: people of higher income spend progressively smaller shares on consumption, while in the bottom ranges, annual consumption often exceeds income. (In fact, government statistics suggest that in the bottom 20 percent of the income scale, average annual consumption is about twice annual income—probably a reflection of a substantial underreporting of earnings in this group.) According to the economist Daniel Slesnick, the distribution of consumption, unlike the distribution of reported income, has become measurably *more* equal in recent decades.

If we include leisure-time pursuits as a form of consumption, the distribution of material welfare appears flatter still. Many such activities, being informal by definition, are difficult to track, but Dora Costa of MIT has recently studied one measurable aspect—expenditures on recreation—and found that these have become strikingly more equal as people of lower income have increased the amount of time and money they devote to entertainment, reading, sports, and related enjoyments.

Television, videocassettes, CD's, and home computers have brought musical, theatrical, and other entertainments (both high and low) to everyone, and have enormously narrowed the differences in cultural opportunities between wealthy urban centers and everywhere else. Formerly upper-crust sports like golf, tennis, skiing, and boating have become mass pursuits (boosted by increased public spending on parks and other recreational facilities as well as on environmental quality), and health clubs and full-line book stores have become as plentiful as gas stations. As some of the best things in life become free or nearly so, the price of pursuing them becomes, to that extent, the "opportunity cost" of time itself.

The substitution of leisure activities for income-producing work even appears to have become significant enough to be contributing to the recently much-lamented increase in inequality in measured income. In a new AEI study, Robert Haveman finds that most of the increase in earnings inequality among U.S. males since the mid-1970's can be attributed not to changing labor-market opportunities but to voluntary choice—to the free pursuit of nonwork activities at the expense of income-producing work.

Most of us can see this trend in our own families and communities. A major factor in income inequality in a wealthy knowledge economy is age—many people whose earnings put them at the top of the income curve in their late fifties were well down the curve in their twenties, when they were just getting out of school and beginning their working careers. Fogel again: today the average household in the top 10 percent might consist of a professor or accountant married to a nurse or secretary, both in their peak years of earning. As for the stratospheric top 1 percent, it includes not only very rich people like Bill Cosby but also people like Cosby's fictional Huxtable family: an obstetrician married to a corporate lawyer. All these individuals would have appeared well down the income distribution as young singles, and that is where their young counterparts appear today.

That more young people are spending more time in college or graduate school, taking time off for travel and "finding themselves," and pursuing interesting but low- or non-paying jobs or apprenticeships before knuckling down to lifelong careers is a significant factor in "income inequality" measured in the aggregate. But this form of economic inequality is in fact the social equality of the modern age. It is progress, not regress, to be cherished and celebrated, not feared and fretted over.

꿰

Which brings me back to my contention that it is our very wealth and equality that are the undoing of the welfare state. Western government today largely consists of two functions. One is income transfers from the wages of those who are working to those who are not working: mainly social-security payments to older people who have chosen to retire rather than go on working and education subsidies for younger people who have chosen to extend their schooling before beginning work. The other is direct and indirect expenditures on medical care, also financed by levies on the wages of those who are working. It is precisely these aspects of life—nonwork and expenditures on medical care and physical well-being—that are the booming sectors of modern, wealthy, technologically advanced society.

When the Social Security program began in America in the 1930's, retirement was still a novel idea: most men worked until they dropped, and they dropped much earlier than they do today. Even in the face of our approaching demographic crunch, produced by the baby boom followed by the baby bust, we could solve the financial problems of the Social Security program in a flash by returning to the days when people worked longer and died younger. Similarly, a world without elaborate diagnostic techniques, replaceable body parts, and potent pharmaceutical and other means of curing or ameliorating disease—a world where medical care consisted largely of bed rest and hand-holding—would present scant fiscal challenge to government as a provider of health insurance.

Our big government-entitlement programs truly are, as conservatives like to call them, obsolete. They are obsolete not because they were terrible ideas to begin with, though some of them were, but because of the astounding growth in social wealth and equality and because of the technological and economic developments which have propelled that growth. When Social Security was introduced, not only was retirement a tiny part of most people's lives but people of modest means had limited ability to save and invest for the future. Today, anyone can mail off a few hundred dollars to a good mutual fund and hire the best investment management American finance has to offer.

In these circumstances it is preposterous to argue, as President Clinton has done, that privatizing Social Security (replacing the current system of income transfers from workers to retirees with one of individually invested retirement savings) would be good for Warren Buffett but bad for the little guy. Private savings—through pension plans, mutual funds, and personal investments in housing and other durables—are *already* a larger source of retirement income than Social Security transfers. Moreover, although there is much talk nowadays about the riskiness of tying retirement income to the performance of financial markets, the social developments I have described suggest that the greater risk lies in the opposite direction. The current Social Security program ties retirement income to the growth of wage earners' pay-rolls; that growth is bound to be less than the growth of the economy as a whole, as reflected in the financial markets.

Similarly, Medicare is today a backwater of old-fashioned fee-for-service medicine, hopelessly distorted by a profusion of inefficient and self-defeating price-and-service controls. Over the past dozen years, a revolution has been carried out in the private financing and organization of medical care. The changes have not been unmixed blessings; nor could they be, so long as the tax code encourages people to overinsure for routine medical care. Yet substantial improvements in cost control and quality of service are now evident throughout the health-care sector—except under Medicare. These innovations have not been greeted by riots or strikes at the thousands of private organizations that have introduced them. Nor will there be riots in the streets if, in place of the lame-brained proposals for Medicare "spending cuts" and still more ineffective price controls currently in fashion in Washington, similar market-based innovations are introduced to Medicare.

❦

In sum, George Bush's famous statement in his inaugural address that "we have more will than wallet" was exactly backward. Our wallets are bulging; the problems we face are increasingly problems not of necessity, but of will. The political class in Washington is still marching to the tune of economic redistribution and, to a degree, "class warfare." But Washington is a lagging indicator of social change. In time, the progress of technology and the growth of private markets and private wealth will generate the political will to transform radically the redistributive welfare state we have inherited from an earlier and more socially balkanized age.

There are signs, indeed, that the Progressive-era and New Deal programs of social insurance, economic regulation, and subsidies and protections for farming, banking, labor organization, and other activities are already crumbling, with salutary effects along every point of the economic spectrum. Anyone who has been a business traveler since the late 1970's, for example, has seen firsthand how deregulation has democratized air travel. Low fares and mass marketing have brought such luxuries as foreign travel, weekend getaways to remote locales, and reunions of far-flung families—just twenty years ago, pursuits of the wealthy—to people of relatively modest means. Coming reforms, including the privatization of Social Security and, most of all, the dismantling of the public-school monopoly in elementary and secondary education, will similarly benefit the less well-off disproportionately, providing them with opportunities enjoyed today primarily by those with high incomes.

I venture a prediction: just as airline deregulation was championed by Edward Kennedy and Jimmy Carter before Ronald Reagan finished the job, so the coming reforms will be a bipartisan enterprise. When the political class catches on (as Prime Minister Tony Blair has already done in England), the Left will compete vigorously and often successfully with the Right for the allegiance of the vast new privileged middle class. This may sound implausible at a moment when the Clinton administration has become an energetic agent of traditional unionism and has secured the enactment of several new redistributive tax provisions and spending programs. But the watershed event of the Clinton years will almost certainly be seen to be not any of these things but rather the defeat of the President's national health-insurance plan in the face of widespread popular opposition.

The lesson of that episode is that Americans no longer wish to have the things they care about socialized. What has traditionally attracted voters to government as a provider of insurance and other services is not that government does the job better or more efficiently or at a lower cost than private markets; it is the prospect of securing those services through taxes paid by others. That is why today's advocates of expanding the welfare state are still trying to convince voters to think of themselves as members of distinct groups that are net beneficiaries of government: students, teachers, women, racial minorities, union members, struggling young families, retirees, and so forth. But as the material circumstances of the majority become more equal, and as the proficiency and social reach of private markets increasingly outstrip what government can provide, the possibilities for effective redistribution diminish. The members of an egalitarian, middle-class electorate cannot improve their lot by subsidizing one another, and they know it.

With the prospects dimming for further, broad-based socialization along the lines of the Clinton health-care plan, the private supply of important social services will continue to exist and, in general, to flourish alongside government programs. Defenders of the welfare state will thus likely be reduced to asserting that private markets and personal choice may be fine for the well-off, but government services are more appropriate for those of modest means. This is the essence of President Clinton's objection to privatizing Social Security and of the arguments against school choice for parents of students in public elementary and high schools. But "capitalism for the rich, socialism for the poor" is a highly unpromising banner for liberals to be marching under in an era in which capitalism has itself become a profound egalitarian force.

꧁◉꧂

Where, then, will the battlegrounds be for the political allegiance of the new middle class? Increasingly, that allegiance will turn on policies involving little or no redistributive cachet but rather society-wide benefits in the form of personal amenity, autonomy, and safety: environmental quality and parks, medical and other scientific research, transportation and communications infrastructure, defense against terrorism, and the like. The old welfare-state debates between Left and Right will be transformed into debates over piecemeal incursions into private markets that compete with or replace government services. Should private insurers be required to cover annual mammograms for women in their forties? Should retirement accounts be permitted to invest in tobacco companies? Should parents be permitted to use vouchers to send their children to religious schools? Thus transformed, these debates, too, will tend to turn on considerations of general social advantage rather than on the considerations of social justice and economic desert that animated the growth of the welfare state.

Political allegiance will also turn increasingly on issues that are entirely nonmaterial. I recently bumped into a colleague, a noted political analyst, just after I had read the morning papers, and asked him to confirm my impression that at least half the major political stories of the past few years had something to do with sex. He smiled and replied, "Peace and prosperity."

What my colleague may have had in mind is that grave crises make all other issues secondary: President Roosevelt's private life received less scrutiny than has President Clinton's, and General Eisenhower's private life received less scrutiny than did that of General Ralston (whose nomination to become chairman of the Joint Chiefs of Staff was torpedoed by allegations of an extramarital affair). There is, however, another, deeper truth in his observation. The stupendous wealth, technological mastery, and autonomy of modern life have freed man not just for worthy, admirable, and self-improving pursuits but also for idleness and unworthy and self-destructive pursuits that are no less a part of his nature.

And so we live in an age of astounding rates of divorce and family breakup, of illegitimacy, of single teenage motherhood, of drug use and crime, of violent and degrading popular entertainments, and of the "culture of narcissism"—and also in an age of vibrant religiosity, of elite universities where madrigal singing and ballroom dancing are all the rage and rampant student careerism is a major faculty concern, and of the Promise Keepers, over a million men of all incomes and races who have packed sports stadiums around the United States to declare their determination to be better husbands, fathers, citizens, and Christians. Ours is an age in which obesity has become a serious public-health problem—and in which dieting, fitness, environmentalism, and self-improvement have become major industries.

It is true, of course, that the heartening developments are in part responses to the disheartening ones. But it is also true that *both* are the results of the economic trends I have described here. In a society as rich and therefore as free as ours has become, the big question, in our personal lives and also in our politics, is: what is our freedom for?

POSTSCRIPT

Is America Becoming More Unequal?

Almost from the day of its publication, *The Bell Curve: Intelligence and Class Structure in American Life* by Richard J. Herrnstein and Charles Murray (Free Press, 1994) became the basic text against equality in America. Murray insists that the book is about intelligence; his critics say that it is about race. It is about both, but above all it is about equality, why it does not exist (people are very unequal intellectually), why it cannot exist (intelligence is largely a product of inheritance), and why we should reconcile ourselves to its absence (because income differences and intermarriage among intelligent people will widen the gap).

The enormous publicity and sales generated by *The Bell Curve* led to the publication of books and essays rejecting its thesis. A large number of critical essays (by biologist Stephen Jay Gould, philosopher Alan Ryan, educator Howard Gardner, psychologist Leon J. Kamin, and others) purporting to refute what the authors call the unwarranted premises, shaky statistics, and pseudoscience of *The Bell Curve* have been gathered together in Russell Jacoby and Naomi Glauberman, eds., *The Bell Curve Debate: History, Documents, Opinions* (Times Books, 1995).

In an effort to deal with educational inequality and its later economic and social consequences, the No Child Left Behind Act of 2001 required that every public school abolish social class differences in achievement, but that hope is contradicted by a U.S. Department of Education study that sees a close correlation between socioeconomic status and educational achievement in most countries including the United States, according to Richard Rothstein, *Class and Schools: Using Social, Economic, and Educational Reform to Close the Black-White Achievement Gap* (The Economic Policy Institute and Teachers College Press, 2004). A "culture of underachievement" is fostered and enforced by the absence of a literate and conversational family environment, peer pressure, and discrimination in school and workplace.

Kevin Phillips, in *Wealth and Democracy: A Political History of the American Rich* (Broadway Books, 2002), states that, between 1989 and 1997, the top one percent of income earners received 42 percent of the stock market gains, and the top ten percent took 86 percent. Phillips argues that American wealth owes as much to government and influence as to free markets and free competition. He concludes that "the imbalance of wealth and democracy in the United States is unsustainable."

The central question that Madrick an DeMuth consider remains. How much and what kinds of equality—educational, income, and legal—are necessary for democracy to exist and thrive?

ISSUE 15

Does the Patriot Act Abridge
Essential Freedom?

YES: Nat Hentoff, from *The War on the Bill of Rights and the Gathering Resistance* (Seven Stories Press, 2003)

NO: Heather Mac Donald, from "Straight Talk on Homeland Security," *City Journal* (Summer 2003)

ISSUE SUMMARY

YES: *Village Voice* columnist Nat Hentoff opposes the Patriot Act as an unjustified invasion of private belief and behavior, in the conviction that the sacrifice of liberty for security will result in the loss of both.

NO: Manhattan Institute fellow Heather Mac Donald believes that, since the new terrorism poses an unprecedented threat to America's survival, the Patriot Act is an appropriate response and contains adequate protection of fundamental liberties.

Ten days before the Declaration of Independence was adopted, the Continental Congress recommended that all colonies adopt laws punishing as treasonous persons those who levy war on the colonies or adhere to the king of Great Britain and other enemies. When independence was won, treason was the only crime against the nation mentioned in the Constitution, and it was defined as providing "aid and comfort" to an enemy.

Eleven years later, the threat of war with France led Congress to adopt and President John Adams to support the Sedition Act, which punished "whoever shall by word or act support or favor the cause of any country with which the United States is at war or by word or act oppose the cause of the United States therein." In 1918, when the United States was engaged in the First World War, another Sedition Act punished anyone who would "willfully utter, print, write or publish any disloyal, profane, scurrilous, or abusive language" about our form of government. The Second World War and the Cold War waged against the Soviet Union led to the passage of the Internal Security Act and Communist Control Act, which reacted in similar ways to perceived threats to national security. All of these measures were accompanied by efforts to punish, intern, or expel suspected aliens.

Wars inspire a response to strengthen internal security, and the declaration of a war against terrorism is no different. The most far-reaching reaction to the 9/11 attack on the United States was the quick passage of the USA Patriot Act. (The official title is The Uniting and Strengthening America by Providing Appropriate Tools Required to Intercept and Obstruct Terrorism Act.) The USA Patriot Act permits tracking Web sites and e-mails if the law enforcement agency certifies that it relates to an ongoing investigation; searching a business or residence with a warrant but without notifying the owner that the search has been conducted until some later time; installing wiretaps to be granted against individuals, instead of a particular phone, allowing government wiretaps of public phones used by suspected persons; seizing voice-mail messages under a warrant; detaining non-citizens without a hearing; denying entry to non-citizens based on their speech or deportation based on support of a terrorist group, even if that support is unrelated to terrorist activity, and a variety of other measures.

Less controversially, the Act encourages the exchange of information among the FBI, the CIA, and other law enforcement groups. Many critics had blamed the poor communications between the FBI and CIA for America's failure to put together pieces of information that might have alerted the nation to the terrorist threat before 9/11.

To its critics, the very title of the USA Patriot Act implicitly suggests that those who oppose it are less than patriotic, or at least are dangerously foolish. As proof, they cite this statement of Attorney General John Ashcroft: "To those who pit Americans against immigrants, citizens against non-citizens, to those who scare peace-loving people with phantoms of lost liberty, my message is this: Your tactics only aid terrorists for they erode our national unity and diminish our resolve. They give ammunition to America's enemies and pause to America's friends. They encourage people of good will to remain silent in the face of evil." They oppose the law's increase in the surveillance and investigative powers of law enforcement because they believe that it sacrifices the checks and balances vital to safeguarding civil liberties.

To its defenders, the Patriot Act is essential to the nation's security. The 9/11 acts were part of a war against the United States unlike any fought before. The enemy, bent upon the mass slaughter of civilians, is hidden on American soil and must be ferreted out—for which the techniques used for catching bank robbers and other traditional criminals are totally inadequate. From the perspective of its defenders, then, the Patriot Act is a modest step toward dealing with the new reality of massive terrorist strikes within this country. But what of the dangers the Patriot Act poses to civil liberties? Its defenders charge that the critics ignore the many safeguards for civil liberties built into the law, such as the fact that before FBI agents can demand records of any citizen they must first obtain judicial approval.

In the following selections, Nat Hentoff deplores the fact that, under this law, there is no need to show probable cause that a crime has been or is about to be committed, and that there is no effective check upon the executive power. Heather Mac Donald believes that civil liberties have been safeguarded, but that terrorist "acts of war" require new weapons in dealing with unidentified combatants within the United States.

YES

Nat Hentoff

How We Began to Lose Our Liberties

Two nights after the September 11 attack, the Senate swiftly, by voice vote after thirty minutes of debate, attached to a previously written appropriations bill an amendment making it much easier for the government to wiretap computers of terrorism suspects without having to go to various courts to get multiple search warrants. The bipartisan bill was introduced by Senators Orrin Hatch, Republican of Utah, and Dianne Feinstein, Democrat of California. "Terrorism" was not defined.

That was the beginning of the steamroller. Attorney General John Ashcroft then got his way with his originally titled Anti-Terrorism Act of 2001, which coolly contradicted the earnest assertions of the president and the secretary of defense that necessary security measures would not violate our fundamental liberties because our freedom is what we are fighting for. The final legislation passed the Senate on October 25 by a vote of 98 to 1, with only Russ Feingold, Democrat of Wisconsin, dissenting. In the House, the bill passed 356 to 66.

The law permits government agents to search a suspect's home without immediately notifying the object of the search. In J. Edgar Hoover's day, this was known as a "black bag job." The FBI then never bothered to get a search warrant for such operations. Now, a warrant would be required, but very few judges would turn a government investigator down in this time of fear. Ashcroft's "secret searches" provision can now extend to *all* criminal cases and can include taking photographs, the contents of your hard drive, and other property. This is now a permanent part of the law, not subject to any "sunset" review by Congress.

Ashcroft also asked for roving wiretaps—a single warrant for a suspect's telephone must include any and all types of phones he or she uses in any and all locations, including pay phones. If a suspect uses a relative's phone or your phone, that owner becomes part of the investigative database. So does anyone using the same pay phone or any pay phone in the area.

Ashcroft neglected to tell us, however, that roving wiretaps already became law under the Clinton Administration in 1998. At that time, only Congressman Bob Barr, Republican of Georgia, spoke against it in Congress, while the media paid little attention to this revision of the Fourth Amendment.

But Ashcroft demanded and received a radical extension of these roving wiretaps: a one-stop *national* warrant for wiretapping these peripatetic phones. Until now, a wiretap warrant was valid only in the jurisdiction in which it was issued. But now, the government won't have to waste time by having to keep going to court to provide a basis for each warrant in each locale.

The expansion of wiretapping to computers, and thereby the Internet, makes a mockery of Internet champion John Perry Barlow's 1996 "Declaration of the Independence of Cyberspace":

> Governments of the industrial world, on behalf of the future, I ask you of the past to leave us alone. . . . You have no sovereignty where we gather . . . nor do you possess any methods of enforcement we have true reason to fear. Cyberspace does not lie within your borders.

This government invasion of cyberspace fulfills the prophecy of Justice Louis Brandeis, who warned, in his dissent in the first wiretapping case before the Supreme Court, *Olmstead v. United States* (1928), "Ways may some day be developed by which the Government, without removing papers from secret drawers, can reproduce them in court, and by which it will be enabled to expose to a jury the most intimate occurrences of the home."

This has come to pass. The government now has access to bank records, credit card purchases, what has been searched for on the Internet, and a great deal more data from those who have "supported," or are suspected of, terrorism.

Moreover, as Brandon Koerner, a fellow at the New America Foundation, has pointed out in the *Village Voice,* the bill that Congress passed so hastily on the night of September 13—and that is now part of the law—"lowers the legal standards necessary for the FBI to deploy its infamous Carnivore surveillance system." Without showing—as the Fourth Amendment requires—probable cause that a crime has been committed or is about to be committed, the government invades your privacy through Carnivore.

The fearful name "Carnivore" disturbed some folks, and so it has been renamed DCS1000. Carnivore, Koerner notes, is "a computer that the Feds attach to an Internet service provider. Once in place, it scans e-mail traffic for 'suspicious' subjects which, in the current climate, could be something as innocent as a message with the word 'Allah' in the header." Or maybe: "SAVE THE FOURTH AMENDMENT FROM TYRANTS!" Carnivore also records other electronic communications.

There was resistance to the assault on the Bill of Rights. In Congress, such previously unlikely alliances between Maxine Waters and Bob Barr, Barney Frank and Dick Armey, helped hold back Ashcroft's rush to enact his antiterrorism weapons within a week, as he had demanded. In the Senate, Patrick Leahy, chairman of the Judiciary Committee, also tried to allow some deliberation, but Majority Leader Tom Daschle usurped and undermined Leahy's authority. Leahy ultimately caved and declared the law signed by Bush on October 26 "a good bill that protects our liberties."

The House Judiciary Committee did pass by a 36-to-0 vote a bipartisan bill that restored some mention of the Bill of Rights to Ashcroft's proposals. But, late at night, that bill was scuttled behind closed doors by Speaker of the House Dennis Hastert and other Republican leaders, along with emissaries from the White House.

As a result, on October 12, the House, 337 to 39, approved a harsh bill that most of its members had not had time even to read. David Dreier, chairman of the Committee on Rules, often seen being smoothly disingenuous on television, said casually that it was hardly the first time bills had been passed that House members had not read.

Democrat David Obey of Wisconsin accurately described the maneuver as "a back-room quick fix."

And Barney Frank made the grim point that this subversion of representative government was "the least democratic process for debating questions fundamental to democracy I have ever seen. A bill drafted by a handful of people in secret, subject to no committee process, comes before us immune from amendment."

Among those voting against the final bill were Barney Frank, John Conyers, David Bonior, Barbara Lee, Cynthia McKinney, John Dingell, Jesse Jackson Jr., Jerrold Nadler, Melvin Watt, and Maxine Waters. Unaccountably, Bob Barr voted for the bill.

But House Judiciary Committee Chairman James Sensenbrenner, as reported on National Public Radio, assured us all that this steamrolled bill did not diminish the freedom of "innocent citizens."

Providing, of course, that the presumption of innocence holds. (Sensenbrenner was later to change his mind.)

Also late at night, on October 11, the Senate, in a closed-door session attended only by Senate leaders and members of the Administration, created a similar, expansive antiterrorism bill that the Senate went on to pass by a vote of ninety-six to one. Only Russ Feingold, a Wisconsin Democrat, had the truly patriotic courage to vote against this attack on the Bill of Rights that the president and the secretaries of state and defense have said we are fighting for.

As Feingold had said while the Senate was allegedly deliberating the bill, "It is crucial that civil liberties in this country be preserved. Otherwise I'm afraid terror will win this battle without firing a shot."

In essence, the new law will, as the *Wall Street Journal* noted, "make it easier for government agents to track e-mail sent and Web sites visited by someone involved in an investigation; to collect call records for phones such a person might use; and to share information between the Federal Bureau of Investigation and the Central Intelligence Agency."

Until now, the CIA was not legally allowed to spy on Americans. Also, previously secret grand jury proceedings will now be shared among law enforcement and intelligence agencies.

In addition, the new law subverts the Fourth Amendment's standards of reasonable searches and seizures by allowing antiterrorism investigations to obtain a warrant not on the basis of previously defined "probable cause," as has been required in domestic criminal probes, but on the much looser basis that the information is "relevant to an ongoing criminal investigation" somehow linked to alleged terrorism.

The new law has a "sunset clause," requiring it to be reviewed in December 2005, to determine if these stringent measures are still needed. But before this collusion in reducing our liberties was effected, George W. Bush had assured us that the war on worldwide terrorism will be of indeterminate length. A Congress that so overwhelmingly passed this antiterrorism bill is hardly likely to expunge parts of it unless there is rising citizen resistance. And even if it did, evidence gathered in the first four years could be used in prosecutions after that. Moreover, not every part of the PATRIOT ACT is subject to the sunset clause. There are sections that are now part of our permanent laws.

In self-defense, all of us should be interested in how terrorism is defined in this historic legislation. As summarized by the ACLU, the language in the final bill said: A person "commits the crime of domestic terrorism if within the U.S., activity is engaged in that involves acts dangerous to human life that violate the laws of the United States or any State, and appear to be intended to: (1) intimidate or coerce a civilian population; (2) influence the policy of a government by intimidation or coercion; or (3) affect the conduct of the government by mass destruction, assassination, or kidnapping." (Note the words: "appear to be intended to" and "intimidate.")

Considering the loose language of the first two provisions, the ACLU points out that "this over-broad terrorism definition would sweep in people who engage in acts of political protest if those acts were dangerous to human life. People associated with organizations such as Operation Rescue and the Environmental Liberation Front, and the World Trade Organization protesters, have engaged in activities that should subject them to prosecution as terrorists."

Furthermore, "once the government decides that conduct is 'domestic terrorism,' law enforcement agents have the authority to charge anyone who provides assistance to that person, even if the assistance is an act as minor as providing lodging. They would have the authority to wiretap the home of anyone who is providing assistance."

"Assistance" includes "support." So, contributions to any group later charged with domestic terrorism—even if the donor was unaware of its range of activities—could lead to an investigation of those giving "support."

As Judge Learned Hand once said, "Liberty lies in the hearts of men and women; when it dies there, no constitution, no law, no court can even do much to help it. While it lies there, it needs no constitution, no law, no court to save it."

We and the Constitution have survived the contempt for the Bill of Rights in the Alien and Sedition Acts of 1798; Abraham Lincoln's suspension of *habeas corpus*, and the jailing of editors and other dissenters during the Civil War; Woodrow Wilson's near annihilation of the First Amendment in the First World War; and the Red Scares of 1919 and the early 1920s when Attorney General A. Mitchell Palmer and his enthusiastic aide, J. Edgar Hoover, rounded up hundreds of "radicals," "subversives," and "Bolsheviks" in thirty-three cities and summarily deported many of them. And we also survived Joe McCarthy. But will liberty still survive "in the hearts" of Americans?

This will be one of our severest tests yet to rescue the Constitution from our government. Benjamin Franklin has been quoted a lot since the USA PATRIOT Act and its progeny. "They that can give up essential liberty to obtain a little temporary safety deserve neither liberty nor safety."

On October 11, 2001, Senator Russ Feingold, dissenting to the PATRIOT Act, said on the floor of the Senate:

> There is no doubt that if we lived in a police state, it would be easier to catch terrorists. If we lived in a country where the police were allowed to search your home at any time for any reason; if we lived in a country where the government is entitled to open your mail, eavesdrop on your phone conversations, or intercept our e-mail communications; if we lived in a country where people could be held in jail indefinitely based on what they write or think, or based on mere suspicion that they are up to no good, the government would probably, discover and arrest more terrorists or would-be terrorists, just as it would find more lawbreakers generally.
>
> But that wouldn't be a country in which we would want to live, and it wouldn't be a country for which we could, in good conscience, ask our young people to fight and die. In short, that country wouldn't be America.
>
> I think it is important to remember that the Constitution was written in 1789 by men who had recently won the Revolutionary War . . . They wrote the Constitution and the Bill of Rights to protect individual liberties in times of war as well as in times of peace.
>
> There have been periods in our nation's history when civil liberties have taken a back seat to what appeared at the time to be legitimate exigencies of war. Our national consciousness still bears the stain and the scars of those events.
>
> We must not allow this piece of our past to become prologue. Preserving our freedom is the reason we are now engaged in this new war on terrorism. We will lose that war without a shot being fired if we sacrifice the liberties of the American people in the belief that by doing so we will stop the terrorists.

Russ Feingold predicted much of what was to come.

During the fierce debates in the new America on whether the Constitution, written in 1787, should be ratified, there was fear among the dissenters that a national federal government would be too powerful. During that debate, the proposed Constitution, which did not yet have a Bill of Rights, was attacked by Robert Yates, writing under the pseudonym "Brutus."

In Bernard Bailyn's *To Begin the World Anew* (Knopf, 2003), Brutus, much concerned with the new government's power to tax, predicted that this federal government "will introduce itself into every corner of the city and country. It [the national government] will wait upon the ladies at their toilett, and will not leave them in any of their domestic concerns; it will accompany them to the ball, the play, the assembly . . . it will enter the house of every gentlemen . . . it will take cognizance of the professional man in his office, or his study . . . it will follow the mechanic to his shop, and in his work, and will haunt him in his family, in his bed . . . it will penetrate into the most obscure cottage; and finally, it will light upon the head of every person in the United States."

It was as if "Brutus" could have foreseen beyond the power to tax, Admiral John Poindexter's Terrorism Information Awareness System in the Pentagon, or the ever increasing electronic surveillance of the citizenry by John Ashcroft. Soon after the hasty passage of the USA PATRIOT Act in the immediate wake of 9/11, Mindy Tucker, then the spokesperson for the Justice Department, promised: "This is just the first step. There will be additional items to come." . . .

In the April 11, 2003, issue of *The Chronicle of Higher Education*, the authoritative source of news and analysis concerning college and university affairs, Judith Grant, an associate professor of political science and women's studies at the University of Southern California, wrote in an article titled "Uncle Sam Over My Shoulder":

> I am now experiencing what American legal scholars call 'a chilling effect,' and I was indeed aware of it as a sort of chill running up my spine—a half-second of anxiety, almost subconscious, the moment I heard that the [USA PATRIOT] Act had been passed.
>
> I feel that chill again when I realize that I now pause a moment before I write almost anything. I think about how a government official might read my writing if he or she were trying to build a (completely unjustified) case against me. I worried even while I wrote that last sentence, then I worried about my worry. Might someone in the Justice Department ask: "Why would she be worried if she were doing nothing wrong?"

In the April 20, 2003, Letters section of the *New York Times*, Tina Rosan of Cambridge, Massachusetts, comments on a previous *Times* story, "Muslims Hesitating on Gifts as U.S. Scrutinizes Charities":

> Of course Muslims in the United States are "hesitating" to give money to charities because they are afraid . . . Many have been detained without trial. Given this environment, Muslims are trying to stay under the radar. They don't want a contribution to a charity to put them on a suspect list or cause them to end up in jail. Unfortunately the news media have not been paying attention to the severe violation of civil liberties at home. The real truth is much deeper and darker.

In the April 21, 2003, *Newsday*, columnist Sheryl McCarthy told of a twenty-six-year-old mechanical engineer, Daniel Ueda, and twenty-eight-year-old Carey Larsen, who were arrested in a demonstration "outside the offices of The Carlyle Group, a private investment house with holdings in the defense industry":

> At police headquarters both Ueda and Larsen were asked questions that seemed strange, considering the minor offenses with which they were charged. Questions like: how man protests had they participated in, what groups were they affiliated with, how they heard about the demonstrations . . . how they felt about the war with Iraq and whether they thought the United States should have entered World War II. Yes, really.
>
> When they balked at answering the political questions, they were warned they'd be held longer if they didn't cooperate.

When *New York Times* columnist Joyce Purnick (April 21) asked the New York City Police Department if the information obtained from such questioning could be used to infiltrate political groups, the Police Department's chief spokesman, Michael O'Looney, said: "I'm going to leave it with that." He refused to answer the question that brought back my memories of the days of J. Edgar Hoover's COINTELPRO, when the FBI, at will, infiltrated and disrupted entirely lawful groups.

Donna Lieberman, executive director of the New York Civil Liberties Union, is aware of the history of COINTELPRO, and she told Joyce Purnick: "When people are asked about their political affiliations, it's intimidation. It's discouraging people from exercising their fundamental right to criticize government."

So when Judith Grant feels "a chilling effect" when she writes for *The Chronicle of Higher Education,* she may not be entirely without reason to be somewhat intimidated by the environment that John Ashcroft has created.

Sam Adams, the eighteenth-century patriot, once said of this new sweet land of liberty: "Driven from every other corner of the earth, freedom of thought and the right of private judgement in matters of conscience, direct their course to this happy country as their last asylum."

Like "Brutus," Sam Adams did not foresee the Bush-Ashcroft omnivorous surveillance of the residents of this "last asylum."

Sam Adams was overly sanguine about the future of freedom of conscience here. In 1858, Abraham Lincoln, speaking in Edwardsville, Illinois—before assuming the powers of the presidency—spoke to a truth that George W. Bush would do well to keep in mind:

> What constitutes the bulwark of our own liberty and independence? It is not our frowning battlements, our bristling seacoasts, our army and navy. These are not our reliance against tyranny . . . Our reliance is the love of liberty . . . Destroy this spirit and you have planted the seeds of despotism at your door.

This was the same Abraham Lincoln who suspended *habeas corpus,* imprisoned many Americans who dissented from his policies, and set up military tribunals to dispose of citizens of contrary views—even though the civilian courts were still open.

Then there was Franklin Delano Roosevelt, who earnestly told the nation:

> We must scrupulously guard the civil liberties of all citizens, whatever their background. We must remember that any oppression, any injustice, any hatred, is a wedge designed to attack our civilization.

It was the same Franklin Delano Roosevelt who signed Executive Order No. 9066 that sent Japanese-Americans into detention camps, which they rightly regarded as concentration camps.

When, in August 2002, Federal Judge Damon J. Keith, writing for the Sixth Circuit Court of Appeals, ruled against the Bush administration's closing of all deportation hearings to the press and the public, though the Third Circuit voted the other way, he emphasized:

> Democracies die behind closed doors. The only safeguard on this extraordinary government power is in the public, deputizing the press as the guardians of their liberty. An informed public is the most potent of all restraints on government . . . the First Amendment, through a free press, protects the people's right to know that their government acts fairly, lawfully, and accurately.

But veteran journalist Jack Nelson, retired Washington bureau chief of the *Los Angeles Times,* told a First Amendment Center conference on March 12, 2003:

> President Bush has gone beyond just being extremely secretive about the conduct of the government's business. In the name of fighting terrorism, he has amassed powers and wrapped them in a cloak of resilience to normal oversight by Congress and the judiciary. *No president since I've been a reporter has so tried to change the very structure of government to foster secrecy.* (Emphasis added.)

Even the Fourth Circuit Court of Appeals—the most conservative Federal appellate court in the country—rebuked the Bush administration in the case of Zacarias Moussaoui, accused of involvement in a terrorist conspiracy. Reported the April 2, 2003, *Washington Post:*

> The court chided the government for "simultaneously prosecuting the defendant and attempting to restrict his ability to use information [in court] that he feels is necessary to defend himself against the prosecution . . .
>
> Courts must not be remiss in protecting a defendant's right to a full and meaningful presentation of his claim to innocence."

Concerning this case, Donald Rehkopf, chairman of the Military Law Committee of the National Association of Criminal Defense Lawyers, accused the government of "inventing the law as they go along. The Constitution," he reminded the administration—echoing the Supreme Court in the 1866 *Milligan* case—"is not suspended, even during time of war."

And when the government proposed, in "Patriot Act II," to strip Americans of their citizenship if they give "support" to an organization cited by the administration as implicated in terrorism—even if the accused American is unaware of that part of the group's activities—human rights attorney Joanne Mariner noted in an article on www.findlaw.com ("Patriot II's Attack on Citizenship", March 3, 2003) how Ashcroft and Bush also invent the law in proposing to take away the most essential of all American rights, our citizenship. Professor Mariner wrote:

> If you help fund an orphanage administered by one of the three Chechen separatist groups that the government has labeled as terrorist, or if you give pharmaceutical supplies to a medical outpost run by the East Turkestan Islamic Movement, or if you are on the wrong side of any of a number of other political conflicts in the world, you are vulnerable to the loss of your citizenship.

Although you "would be able to challenge this determination in court," she continued, you would "not necessarily succeed." Particularly, if during the limitless war on terrorism, our courts keep deferring to the government, bypassing the separation of powers in the Constitution.

Through the years, I have often quoted a warning by Supreme Court Justice Louis Brandeis that resonates throughout a study of American history. It is especially relevant now:

> Experience should teach us to be most on our guard to protect liberty when the government's purposes are beneficent. Men born to freedom are naturally alert to repel invasion of their liberty by evil-minded rulers. The greatest dangers to liberty lurk in insidious encroachment by men of zeal, well-meaning but without understanding.

Brandeis's warning was part of his dissent in the first wiretapping case, *Olmstead v. the United States* (1928). The year before, in a less often quoted but even more profound definition of the spirit that has enabled this country to remain the freest in the world—despite severe misunderstandings of the Constitution by past administrations—Justice Brandeis again spoke to us now.

The case, *Whitney v. California*, concerned the prosecution of Charlotte Anita Whitney for violating the Criminal Syndication Act of California. That law, as constitutional scholar Louis Fisher noted, penalized "efforts of trade union and industrial workers to gain control of production through general strikes, sabotage, violence, or other criminal means."

Whitney "was found guilty of having organized and participated in a group assembled to advocate, teach, aid, and abet criminal syndicalism." In 1919, at a convention in Oakland, California, held to organize a California branch of the Communist Labor Party, Charlotte Whitney, as a member of the Resolutions Committee, signed this statement: "The Communist Labor Party proclaims and insists that the capture of political power, locally or nationally by the revolutionary working class, can be of tremendous assistance to the workers in their struggle for emancipation."

The Supreme Court upheld California's Criminal Syndication Act. But, in a concurring opinion, which was really a dissent, Brandeis wrote:

> A State is ordinarily denied the power to prohibit the dissemination of social, economic, and political doctrine [even though] a vast majority of its citizens believes [it] to be false and fraught with evil consequence . . . It is . . . always open to Americans to challenge a law abridging free speech and assembly by showing that there was no emergency justifying [its abridgement.]

That is precisely what the continually growing number of Bill of Rights Defense Committees around the nation are doing in challenging the USA PATRIOT Act and the other violations of the Bill of Rights by Ashcroft and Bush. However, what Brandeis also said in *Whitney v. California* underlines this book's celebration of the gathering resistance to the war on the Bill of Rights:

> Those who won our independence . . . believed that the greatest menace to freedom is an inert people . . . They knew that order cannot be secured merely

through fear of punishment for its infraction . . . that fear breeds repression; that repression breeds hate; that hate menaces stable government . . .

Believing in the power of reason as applied through public discussion, they eschewed silence coerced by law—the argument of force in its worst form . . .

Fear of serious injury cannot alone justify suppression of free speech and assembly. Men feared witches and burnt women [as in the Salem witchcraft trials] . . .

Those who won our independence by revolution were not cowards . . . They did not exalt order at the cost of liberty. (Emphasis added.)

The challenge to Americans now is to act with the determination of those who won our independence because what we do now to recover the Bill of Rights will decide for years to come—as Justice William Brennan used to say—whether those words "will come off the page and into the very lives of the American people."

Heather Mac Donald  **NO**

Straight Talk on Homeland Security

The backlash against the Bush administration's War on Terror began on 9/11 and has not let up since. Left- and right-wing advocacy groups likened the Bush administration to fascists, murderers, apartheid ideologues, and usurpers of basic liberties. Over 120 cities and towns have declared themselves "civil liberties safe zones"; and the press has amplified at top volume a recent report by the Justice Department's inspector general denouncing the government's handling of suspects after 9/11. Even the nation's librarians are shredding documents to safeguard their patrons' privacy and foil government investigations.

The advocates' rhetoric is both false and dangerous. Lost in the blizzard of propaganda is any consciousness that 9/11 was an act of war against the U.S. by foreign enemies concealed within the nation's borders. If the media and political elites keep telling the public that the campaign against those terrorist enemies is just a racist power grab, the most essential weapon against terror cells—intelligence from ordinary civilians—will be jeopardized. A drumbeat of ACLU propaganda could discourage a tip that might be vital in exposing an al-Qaida plot.

It is crucial, therefore, to demolish the extravagant lies about the anti-terror initiatives. Close scrutiny of the charges and the reality that they misrepresent shows that civil liberties are fully intact. The majority of legal changes after September 11 simply brought the law into the twenty-first century. In those cases where the government has its powers—as is inevitable during a war—important judicial and statutory safeguards protect the rights of law-abiding citizens. And in the one hard case where a citizen's rights appear to have been curtailed—the detention of a suspected American al-Qaida operative without access to an attorney—that detention is fully justified under the laws of war.

The anti–War on Terror worldview found full expression only hours after the World Trade Center fell, in a remarkable e-mail that spread like wildfire over the Internet that very day. Sent out by Harvard Law School research fellow John Perry Barlow, founder of the cyber-libertarian Electronic Freedom Foundation, the message read: "Control freaks will dine on this day for the rest of our lives. Within a few hours, we will see beginning the most vigorous efforts to end what remains of freedom in America. . . . I beg you to begin NOW to do whatever you can . . . to prevent the spasm of control mania from destroying the dreams that far more have died for over the last two hundred twenty-five years than died this morning. Don't let the terrorists or (their natural allies) the fascists win. Remember that the goal of terrorism is to create increasingly paralytic totalitarianism in the government it attacks. Don't give them the satisfaction. . . . And, please, let us try to forgive those who have committed these appalling crimes. If we hate them, we will become them."

Barlow, a former lyricist for the Grateful Dead, epitomizes the rise of the sixties counterculture into today's opinion elite, for whom no foreign enemy could ever pose as great a threat to freedom as the U.S. For Barlow, the problem isn't the obvious evil of Islamic terrorism but the imputed evil of the American government—an inversion that would characterize the next two years of anti-administration jeremiads. In this spirit, critics would measure each legal change not against the threat it responded to, but in a vacuum. Their verdict: "increasingly paralytic totalitarianism."

Right-wing libertarians soon joined forces with the Left. A few months after the Twin Towers fell, the Rutherford Institute, a Christian think tank concerned with religious liberty, added the final piece to the anti-administration argument: the 9/11 attacks were not war but, at most, a crime. Rutherford president John Whitehead denounced the Bush administration's characterization of the terror strikes as "acts of war by foreign aggressors," without however offering a single argument to support his view. Since that characterization has produced, in Whitehead's view, growing "police statism" that is destroying Americans' freedom, the characterization must be false.

In fact, of course, the 9/11 bombings were classic decapitation strikes, designed to take out America's political and financial leadership. Had a state carried them out, no one could possibly deny that they were acts of war, as John Yoo and James Ho point out in a forthcoming *Virginia Journal of International Law* article. The aim of the 19 foreign terrorists and their backers was not criminal but ideological: to revenge U.S. policies in the Middle East with mass destruction.

Recognizing that the World Trade Center and Pentagon attacks were acts of war entails certain consequences. First, the campaign against al-Qaida and other Islamic terror organizations is really war, not a metaphor, like the "war on drugs." Second, it is a war unlike any the U.S. has ever fought. The enemy, mostly but not exclusively foreign, is hidden on American soil in the civilian population, with the intention of slaughtering as many innocent noncombatants as possible. The use of military force abroad, while necessary, is by no means sufficient: domestic counterterrorism efforts by the FBI and other domestic law enforcement agencies are at least as essential to defeating the enemy.

When these agencies are operating against Islamic terrorists, they are operating in an unprecedented war mode—but most of the rules that govern them were designed for crime fighting. The tension between the Justice Department's and FBI's traditional roles as law enforcement agencies and their new roles as terror warriors lies at the heart of the battle over the Bush administration's post-9/11 homeland-security policies: critics refuse to recognize the reality of the war and thus won't accept the need for expanded powers to prosecute it.

Most of the changes in the law that the Justice Department sought after 9/11 concern the department's ability to gather intelligence on terror strikes before they happen—its key responsibility in the terror war. Yet the libertarian lobby will not allow the department to budge from the crime paradigm, refusing to admit that surveillance and evidence-gathering rules designed to protect the rights of suspected car thieves and bank robbers may need modification when the goal is preventing a suitcase bomb from taking out JFK. But of course the libertarians rarely acknowledge that suitcase bombs and the like are central to this debate.

Ironically, none of the changes instituted by Attorney General Ashcroft comes anywhere near what the government *could* ask for in wartime, such as the suspension of *habeas corpus,* as Lincoln ordered during the Civil War. The changes preserve intact the entire criminal procedural framework governing normal FBI and police actions, and merely tinker around the edges. But the left and right civil libertarians are having none of it.

The charges they have brought against the War on Terror have been so numerous, impugning every single administration action since 9/11, that it would take hundreds of pages to refute them all. But the following analysis of only the main charges will amply illustrate the range of duplicitous strategies that the anti-government forces deploy.

Strategy #1: Hide the Judge

Jan O'Rourke, a librarian in Bucks County, Pennsylvania, is preparing for the inevitable post-9/11 assault: She is destroying all records of her patrons' book and Internet use and is advising other Bucks County libraries to do the same. The object of her fear? The U.S. government. O'Rourke is convinced that federal spooks will soon knock on her door to spy on her law-abiding clients' reading habits. So, like thousands of librarians across the country, she is making sure that when that knock comes, she will have nothing to show. "If we don't have the information, then they can't get it," she explains.

O'Rourke is suffering from Patriot Act hysteria, a malady approaching epidemic levels. The USA-PATRIOT Act, which President Bush signed in October 2001, is a complex measure to boost the federal government's ability to detect and prevent terrorism. Its most important provision relaxed a judge-made rule that, especially after Clinton administration strengthening, had prevented intelligence and law enforcement officials from sharing information and collaborating on investigations (see "Why the FBI Didn't Stop 9/11," Autumn 2002). But the act made many other needed changes too: updating surveillance law to take into account new communications technology, for instance, enhancing the Treasury Department's ability to disrupt terrorist financing networks, and modestly increasing the attorney general's power to detain and deport suspected terrorist aliens.

From the moment the administration proposed the legislation, defenders of the status quo started ringing the tyranny alarm. When the law passed, the Electronic Privacy Information Center depicted a tombstone on its website, captioned: "The Fourth Amendment: 1789–2001." The *Washington Post* denounced the bill as "panicky." And the ever touchy American Library Association decided that a particular provision of the Patriot Act—section 215—was a "present danger to the constitutional rights and privacy of library users," though the section says not a word about libraries.

The furor over section 215 is a case study in Patriot Act fear-mongering. Section 215 allows the FBI to seek business records in the hands of third parties—the enrollment application of a Saudi national in an American flight school, say—while investigating terrorism. The section broadens the categories of institutions whose records and other "tangible items" the government may seek in espionage and terror cases, on the post-9/11 recognition that lawmakers cannot anticipate what sorts of organizations terrorists may exploit. In the past, it may have been enough to get hotel bills or storage-locker contracts (two of the four categories of records covered in the narrower law that section 215 replaced) to trace the steps of a Soviet spy; today, however, gumshoes may find they need receipts from scuba-diving schools or farm-supply stores to piece together a plot to blow up the Golden Gate Bridge. Section 215 removed the requirement that the records must concern an "agent of a foreign power" (generally, a spy or terrorist), since, again, the scope of an anti-terror investigation is hard to predict in advance.

From this tiny acorn, Bush administration foes have conjured forth a mighty assault on the First Amendment. The ACLU warns that with section 215, "the FBI could spy on a person because they don't like the books she reads, or because they don't like the websites she visits. They could spy on her because she wrote a letter to the editor that criticized government policy." Stanford Law School dean Kathleen Sullivan calls section 215 "threatening." And librarians, certain that the section is all about them, are scaring library users with signs warning that the government may spy on their reading habits.

These charges are nonsense. Critics of section 215 deliberately ignore the fact that any request for items under the section requires judicial approval. An FBI agent cannot simply walk into a flight school or library and demand records. The bureau must first convince the court that oversees anti-terror investigations (the Foreign Intelligence Surveillance Act, or FISA, court) that the documents are relevant to protecting "against international terrorism on clandestine intelligence activities." The chance that the FISA court will approve a 215 order because the FBI "doesn't like the books [a person] reads . . . or because she wrote a letter to the editor that criticized government policy" is zero. If the bureau can show that someone using the Bucks County library computers to surf the web and send e-mails has traveled to Pakistan and was seen with other terror suspects in Virginia, on the other hand, then the court may well grant an order to get the library's Internet logs.

Moreover, before the FBI can even approach the FISA court with any kind of request, agents must have gone through multiple levels of bureaucratic review just to open an anti-terror investigation. And to investigate a U.S. citizen (rather than an alien) under FISA, the FBI must show that he is knowingly engaged in terrorism or espionage.

Ignoring the Patriot Act's strict judicial review requirements is the most common strategy of the act's critics. Time and again, the Cassandras will hold up a section from the bill as an example of rampaging executive power—without ever mentioning that the power in question is overseen by federal judges who will allow its use only if the FBI can prove its relevance to a bona fide terror (or sometimes criminal) investigation. By contrast, in the few cases where a law enforcement power does not require judicial review, the jack-boots-are-coming brigade screams for judges as the only trustworthy check on executive tyranny.

Strategy #2: Invent New Rights

A running theme of the campaign against section 215 and many other Patriot Act provisions is that they violate the Fourth Amendment right to privacy. But there is no Fourth Amendment privacy right in records or other items disclosed to third parties. A credit-card user, for example, reveals his purchases to the seller and to the credit-card company. He therefore has no privacy expectations in the record of those purchases that the Fourth Amendment would protect. As a result, the government, whether in a criminal case or a terror investigation, may seek his credit-card receipts without a traditional Fourth Amendment showing to a court that there is "probable cause" to believe that a crime has been or is about to be committed. Instead, terror investigators must convince the FISA court that the receipts are "relevant."

Despite librarians' fervent belief to the contrary, this analysis applies equally to library patrons' book borrowing or Internet use. The government may obtain those records without violating anyone's Fourth Amendment rights, because the patron has already revealed his borrowing and web browsing to library staff, other readers (in the days of handwritten book checkout cards), and Internet service providers. Tombstones declaring the death of the Fourth Amendment contain no truth whatsoever.

What's different in the section 215 provision is that libraries or other organizations can't challenge the FISA court's order and can't inform the target of the investigation, as they can in ordinary criminal proceedings. But that difference is crucial for the Justice Department's war-making function. The department wants to know if an al-Qaida suspect has consulted maps of the Croton reservoir and researched the toxic capacities of cyanide in the New York Public Library not in order to win a conviction for poisoning New York's water supply but to preempt the plot before it happens. The battleground is not the courtroom but the world beyond, where speed and secrecy can mean life or death.

Strategy #3: Demand Antiquated Laws

The librarians' crusade against section 215 has drawn wide media attention and triggered an ongoing congressional battle, led by Vermont socialist Bernie Sanders, to pass a law purporting to protect the "Freedom to Read." But the publicity that administration-hostile librarians were able to stir up pales in comparison to the clout of the Internet privacy lobby. The day the Patriot Act became law, the Center for Democracy and Technology sent around a warning that "privacy standards" had been "gutt[ed]." The Electronic Freedom Foundation declared that the "civil liberties of ordinary Americans have taken a tremendous blow." Jeffrey Rosen of *The New Republic* claimed that the law gave the government "essentially unlimited authority" to surveil Americans. The ACLU asserted that the FBI had suddenly gained "wide powers of phone and internet surveillance." And the Washington Post editorialized that the act made it "easier" to wiretap by "lowering the standard of judicial review."

The target of this ire? A section that merely updates existing law to modern technology. The government has long had the power to collect the numbers dialed from, or the incoming numbers to, a person's telephone by showing a court that the information is "relevant to an ongoing criminal investigation." Just as in section 215 of the Patriot Act, this legal standard is lower than traditional Fourth Amendment "probable cause," because the phone user has already forfeited any constitutional privacy rights he may have in his phone number or the number he calls by revealing them to the phone company.

A 1986 federal law tried to extend the procedures for collecting phone-number information to electronic communications, but it was so poorly drafted that its application to e-mail remained unclear. Section 216 of the Patriot Act resolves the ambiguity by making clear that the rules for obtaining phone numbers apply to incoming and outgoing e-mail addresses as well. The government can obtain e-mail headers—but not content—by showing a court that the information is "relevant to an ongoing criminal investigation." Contrary to cyber-libertarian howls, this is not a vast new power to spy but merely the logical extension of an existing power to a new form of communication. Nothing else has changed: the standard for obtaining information about the source or destination of a communication is the same as always.

Section 216 made one other change to communications surveillance law. When a court issues an order allowing the collection of phone numbers or e-mail headers, that order now applies nationally. Before, if a phone call was transmitted by a chain of phone companies headquartered in different states, investigators needed approval from a court in each of those states to track it. This time-consuming procedure could not be more dangerous in the age of terror. As Attorney General John Ashcroft testified in September 2001, the "ability of law enforcement officers to trace communications into different jurisdictions without obtaining an additional court order can be the difference between life and death for American citizens." Yet the ACLU has complained that issuing national warrants for phone and e-mail routing information marginalizes the judiciary and gives law enforcement unchecked power to search citizens.

The furor over this section of the Patriot Act employs the same deceptions as the furor over section 215 (the business records provision). In both cases, Patriot Act bashers ignore the fact that a court must approve the government's access to information. Despite the *Washington Post*'s assertion to the contrary, section 216 does not lower any standards of judicial review. Both the anti-216 and anti-215 campaigns fabricate privacy rights where none exists. And neither of these anti-government campaigns lets one iota of the reality of terrorism intrude into its analyses of fictional rights violations—the reality that communications technology is essential to an enemy that has no geographical locus, and whose combatants have mastered the Internet and every form of modern communications, along with methods to defeat surveillance, such as using and discarding multiple cell phones and communicating from Internet cafés. The anti–Patriot Act forces would keep anti-terror law enforcement in the world of Ma Bell and rotary phones, even as America's would-be destroyers use America's most sophisticated technology against it.

Strategy #4: Conceal Legal Precedent

Section 213 of the Patriot Act allows the FBI (with court approval) to delay notifying a property owner that his property will be or has been searched, if notice would have an "adverse result": if he might flee the country, for example, or destroy documents or intimidate witnesses before agents can acquire sufficient evidence to arrest him. In such cases, the court that issues the search warrant may grant a delay of notice for a "reasonable period" of time.

The advocates dubbed Section 213 the "sneak-and-peek" section and have portrayed it as one of the most outrageous new powers seized by Attorney General John Ashcroft. The ACLU's fund-raising pitches warn: "Now, the government can secretly enter your home while you're away . . . rifle through your personal belongings . . . download your computer files . . . and seize any items at will. . . . And, because of the Patriot Act, you may never know what the government has done." Richard Leone, president of the Century Foundation and editor of *The War on Our Freedoms: Civil Liberties in an Age of Terrorism*, cites the fact that the Patriot Act "allows the government to conduct secret searches without notification" to support his hyperbolic claim that the act is "arguably the most far-reaching and invasive legislation passed since the espionage act of 1917 and the sedition act of 1918."

These critics pretend not to know that, long before anyone imagined such a thing as Islamic terrorism, federal judges have been granting "sneak-and-peak" warrants in criminal cases under identical standards those of section 213. The possibility of seeking delayed notice is a long-standing law enforcement prerogative, sanctioned by numerous courts. Section 213 merely codified the case law to make the process uniform across different jurisdictions. Portraying section 213 as a new power is simple falsehood, and portraying it as an excessive and unnecessary power is extraordinarily ignorant. Delayed notice under life-threatening conditions is not just reasonable but absolutely imperative.

Strategy #5: Keep the FBI off the Web

In May 2002, Attorney General Ashcroft announced that FBI agents would for the first time be allowed to surf the web, just like hundreds of millions of people across the globe. Previously, the Internet was strictly off-limits to federal law enforcement, unless agents had already developed evidence that a crime was under way. In other words, although a 12-year-old could sit in on a *jihadi* chat room where members were praising Usama bin Ladin, visit sites teaching bombmaking, or track down the links for the production of anthrax—all information essential to mapping out the world of Islamic terrorists or finding out how much terrorists might know—intelligence officials couldn't inspect those same public sites until they had already discovered a terror plot. But for an FBI agent in Arizona to wait for specific information about a conspiracy before researching his local biochem lab to see if it might have any connection to the Washington anthrax attacks, or might be a target for sabotage, is not the best strategy for fighting terrorism.

But Ashcroft's critics say the bureau *should* wait. According to the Electronic Privacy Information Center, for instance, the new guidelines "threaten Fourth Amendment rights" because they permit the FBI to "engage in prospective searches without possessing any evidence of suspicious behavior." But there are no Fourth Amendment rights in the web. Far from expecting privacy on a website, its designers hope for the greatest possible exposure to all comers. The Internet is more public even than a newspaper, since it is free and unbound by geography; it is the most exhibitionistic communication medium yet designed. To require the FBI to be the one entity on earth that may not do general web searches, as the civil libertarians have demanded, makes no sense.

In fact, the new guidelines are unduly narrow. They prohibit searches by an individual's name—Usama bin Ladin, say—unless agents have cause to suspect him of involvement in a terror plot. But since millions of web users may conduct searches of Usama bin Ladin's name or of any other individual without violating anyone's privacy rights, it is hard to discern a basis for barring the government from also obtaining that information in preliminary criminal or terror investigations. Law enforcement agencies need to survey as much information as possible about Islamic terrorism before, not after, attacks happen, so that they can recognize an early warning sign or pattern in what an uninformed observer may see as an innocuous set of events.

Opening the web to the FBI, common sense for any criminal investigation, is particularly essential in fighting Islamic terrorism, because the web is the most powerful means of spreading jihad. Rohan Gunaratna, an al-Qaida expert at Scotland's Saint Andrews University, argues that unless the authorities shut down jihadist sites, "we will not able to end terrorism." But even if the U.S. can't shut down web pages celebrating mass destruction in the name of holy war, it should at least be able to visit them to learn what's out there.

The May guidelines also permit agents to attend public meetings for the first time since 1976 in order to "detect or prevent terrorist activities." Let's say a Moroccan imam at a Brooklyn mosque regularly preaches vengeance against America for its support of Israel. The imam was banished from Morocco for his agitation against the secular government. Visitors from Saudi Arabia known to associate with radical fundamentalists regularly visit.

Under previous guidelines, the FBI could not attend public worship at the mosque to learn more about the imam's activities unless it had actual evidence that he was planning to release sarin in the subways, say. But most of the preparations leading up to a terror attack—such as casing transportation systems, attending crop-dusting school, or buying fertilizer—are legal. Only intelligence gathering and analysis can link them to terrorist intent. To require evidence before permitting the intelligence gathering that would produce it is a suicidal Catch-22.

Yet the civil libertarian lobby would keep the FBI in the dark about public events until the last minute. The Electronic Privacy Information Center brands the public-meeting rule a "serious threat to the right of individuals to speak and assemble freely without the specter of government monitoring." But the First Amendment guarantees free speech and assembly, not freedom from government attendance at public meetings. Even so, the new guidelines narrow the government's power anyway, by allowing agents to participate in public meetings only for a terror investigation, not for criminal investigations.

Strategy #6: Exploit Hindsight

Early this June, anti–War on Terror advocates and journalists pulled out all the stops to publicize a report by the Justice Department's inspector general criticizing the department's detention of illegal immigrants suspected of terrorist ties. Headlines blared: DETAINEES ABUSED, CIVIL RIGHTS OF POST-SEPT. 11 DETAINEES VIOLATED, REPORT FINDS (*Washington Post*); U.S. FINDS ABUSES OF 9/11 DETAINEES; JUSTICE DEPT. INQUIRY REVEALS MANY VIOLATIONS OF IMMIGRANTS' RIGHTS (*Los Angeles Times*); THE ABUSIVE DETENTIONS OF SEPT. 11 (*New York Times* editorial). Advocacy groups declared full vindication of their crusade against the Bush administration.

These headlines exaggerated the report only modestly. To be sure, Inspector General Glenn Fine did not declare any rights violations in the Justice Department's policies or practices, but he did decry "significant problems in the way the 9/11 detainees were treated." He charged that the investigation and clearance of terror suspects took too long, that the Justice Department did not sufficiently differentiate moderately suspicious detainees from highly suspect ones, and that the conditions in one New York City detention center, where guards were charged with taunting detainees and slamming them against walls, were unduly.

Fine's report, however measured its language, is ultimately as much a misrepresentation of the government's post-9/11 actions as the shrillest press release from Amnesty International. While it pays lip service to the "difficult circumstances confronting the department in responding to the terror attacks," it fails utterly to understand the terrifying actuality of 9/11. Fine's cool and sensible recommendations—"timely clearance process, timely service of immigration charges, careful consideration of where to house detainees . . . ; better training of staff . . . ; and better oversight"—read, frankly, like a joke, in light of the circumstances at the time.

Recall what the Justice Department and FBI were facing on 9/11: an attack by an invisible, previously unsuspected enemy on a scale unprecedented in this country, with weapons never imagined. Utter uncertainty prevailed about what the next hour or day or week might bring: if these 19 men had remained undetected while plotting their assault with such precision, who else was ready to strike next, and with what weapons? In New York, the

FBI office, seven blocks from Ground Zero, had to evacuate on 9/11 to a temporary command center set up in a parking garage; the New York INS evacuated its processing center downtown as well. Electricity and other utilities were down, as was delivery and express mail service. One week after the attacks, 96,000 leads had flooded in to FBI offices around the country; tens of thousands more would soon follow, requiring round-the-clock operations at FBI headquarters, with thousands of agents following up the leads. Recriminations over the government's failure to prevent the catastrophe also flooded in: Why hadn't the intelligence community "connected the dots"? Why didn't the CIA and FBI communicate better? How had the State Department and INS let in foreign terrorists bent on destroying America?

Given the magnitude of the carnage and the depth of the uncertainty, the government would have failed in its duty had it not viewed suspects as serious risks. These were, possibly, enemy combatants, not car thieves or muggers. Justice Department officials declared that any suspect picked up in the course of a terror investigation, if an illegal immigrant, would be held in detention until the FBI cleared him of any possible terror connections. Moreover, if agents, following a lead, were looking for a particular individual and discovered half a dozen illegal immigrants at his apartment, all seven would be detained as suspects, since the FBI had no way of knowing who might be an accomplice of the wanted man. In another safeguard against letting a terrorist go, FBI headquarters ruled that it needed to sign off on all clearances, since only bureau brass possessed the full national picture of developing intelligence. Finally, the FBI mandated CIA background checks on all detainees.

These policies are eminently reasonable. That they ended up delaying clearance for an average of 80 days for the 762 illegal aliens detained after 9/11 does not discredit their initial rationale. (That delay is not unlawful, since the government can hold illegal aliens for an undefined period under emergency circumstances.) Justice Department officials expected to release innocent detainees in days, or at most several weeks, and they were concerned as the process stretched out; memos about the need to speed things up flew around the department daily. Officials worried about staying within the law and not violating anyone's rights (which they did not), but they also worried—and for good reason—about releasing even one deadly person. Even in retrospect, this calculus is unimpeachable: the costs of being legally held as an illegal alien and terror suspect for three months without ultimate conviction, while huge for the person held, pale in comparison to the costs of allowing terrorists to go free. (That some prison guards may have abused about 20 detainees is deplorable but does not invalidate the detention policy.)

The inspector general has plenty of good-government suggestions for how to make sure that, after the next terror attack, suspects are efficiently processed, but he is silent on the paramount questions that will face the government should a bomb go off in the nation's capital or a biological weapon in the subway at rush hour: how to find out who did it and who is waiting in the wings, and how to protect the country in the face of grossly inadequate knowledge. Should the country experience another attack on the scale of 9/11, the aftermath undoubtedly will not follow administrative law procedures perfectly. As long as the government does not deliberately or flagrantly abuse suspects' rights, it need have no apology for the slow functioning of bureaucracy through the crisis. . . .

Strategy #7: Treat War as a Continuation of Litigation by Other Means

The Bush bashers are correct that the Padilla case, with its serious liberty issues weighing against serious national peril, has pushed the law where it has never gone before. But that is because the threat the country is facing is without precedent, not because the administration is seizing unjustified power.

When the War on Terror's opponents intone, "We need not trade liberty for security," they are right—but not in the way they think. Contrary to their slogan's assumption, there is no zero-sum relationship between liberty and security. The government may expand its powers to detect terrorism without diminishing civil liberties one iota, as long as those powers remain subject to traditional restraints: statutory prerequisites for investigative action, judicial review, and political accountability. So far, these conditions have been met.

But the larger fallacy at the heart of the elites' liberty-versus-security formula is its blindness to all threats to freedom that do not emanate from the White House. Nothing the Bush administration has done comes close to causing the loss of freedom that Americans experienced after 9/11, when air travel shut down for days, and fear kept hundreds of thousands shut up in their homes. Should al-Qaida strike again, fear will once again paralyze the country far beyond the effects of any possible government restriction on civil rights. And that is what the government is trying to forestall, in the knowledge that preserving security is essential to preserving freedom.

POSTSCRIPT

Does the Patriot Act Abridge Essential Freedoms?

Those who deplore the USA Patriot Act are likely to share Nat Hentoff's conviction, expressed in quotations from Benjamin Franklin and Supreme Court Justice Louis Brandeis, that security cannot be obtained by the sacrifice of essential liberty. Defenders of the law will agree with Heather Mac Donald that liberty can be preserved while adopting new weapons in dealing with a new kind of threat to national security, and liberty will be lost if we do not respond effectively.

With the stakes so high and passions so great, it appears to be difficult for partisans on either side to retain civility in assessing the appropriate balance of civil liberty and national security. If we accept the accusations on both sides, rational discussion is impossible. Americans who favor the USA Patriot Act have been accused of being totalitarians who are enemies of civil liberty and individual privacy. Those who oppose many provisions of the law have been slandered in turn as implicitly unpatriotic and blind to all threats that do not originate with the American government.

Elaine Scarry, in "Resolving to Resist" (*Boston Review*, February–March 2004), sympathetically examines the opposition of more than 200 communities whose local governments have in different ways resolved not to assist the federal government in enforcing this law. A series of essays critical of the government's response to terrorism, largely but not exclusively focused on the USA Patriot Act, appear in the Winter 2002 issue of *Human Rights*, published by the American Bar Association. John Podesta, in "USA Patriot Act: The Good, the Bad, and the Sunset," acknowledges that some provisions are necessary, but others infringe on civil liberties and lack protective mechanisms to prevent abuse by the executive. Kate Martin, in "Intelligence, Terrorism, and Civil Liberties," concludes; "History has repeatedly demonstrated the dangers of allowing governments to secretly collect intelligence on their own people."

"The 2001 Patriot Act," in *The Federalist.com,* points out that defining domestic terrorism too narrow would allow terrorists to slip through loopholes. The Act "is a bold and timely piece of legislation, in keeping with the constitutional values of our nation's history, and essential to our nation's future." Robert H. Bork, in "Civil Liberties After 9/11" (*Commentary,* July–August 2003), points out that lawful prisoners of war are held without the right to a lawyer, and unlawful enemy combatants are entitled to even fewer rights. "A judicial system with rights of due process is crucial to a free society, but it is not designed for the protection of enemies engaged in armed conflict against us." Because some controversial features of the law are due to expire, debate will be vigorously renewed.

ISSUE 16

Stopping Illegal Immigration: Should Border Security Come First?

YES: **Mark Krikorian,** from "Comprehensive Immigration Reform II," Testimony Before Senate Committee on the Judiciary (October 18, 2005)

NO: **Frank Sharry,** from "Comprehensive Immigration Reform II," Testimony Before Senate Committee on the Judiciary (October 18, 2005)

ISSUE SUMMARY

YES: Mark Krikorian, executive director of the Center for Immigration Studies, argues that we have not seriously tried to enforce the laws against illegal aliens, and recommends shrinking the illegal population through consistent and equitable law enforcement.

NO: Frank Sharry, executive director of the National Immigration Forum, contends that the "enforcement only" approach ignores the fact that the United States has an increasingly integrated labor market with Latin America, and recommends a comprehensive approach combining border control with expanded legal channels.

In 1949 a delegation of Native Americans went to Washington to tell lawmakers about the plight of America's original occupants. After meeting with Vice President Alben Barkley, one old Sioux chief delivered a parting word to the vice president. "Young fellow," he said, "let me give you a little advice. Be careful with your immigration laws. We were careless with ours." As America prospered and offered the hope of opportunity and freedom, increasing numbers of immigrants came to the United States.

Between 1870 and 1920, more than 26 million people came to live in the United States. The National Origins Act was adopted in 1924 to restrict the number of new immigrants, ban East Asian immigration, and establish a European quota based on the population of the United States in 1890, when there had been far fewer new arrivals from eastern and southern Europe. In 1965 the national origins formula was abandoned, but strict limits on the number of immigrants were retained. The end of quotas spurred a dramatic increase of immigrants from Central and South America and Asia. Today, Mexico and the rest of Latin America account for the largest number of illegal immigrants. Approximately 57 percent of undocumented immigrants come from Mexico; the rest of Latin America (mainly Central America) accounts for just under 25 percent, while 10 percent come from Asia.

The growing number of illegal immigrants in the 1980s prompted congressional passage of the Immigration Reform and Control Act (IRCA) of 1986, which beefed up border controls, made it illegal for employers to hire undocumented immigrants, and required employers to confirm the legal status of their employees; at the same time, undocumented workers who had entered the United States before 1982 were granted immunity. It was hoped that IRCA's combination of carrots and sticks—tougher border controls, penalties for hiring illegal immigrants, and amnesty for those already here—would bring the illegals "out of the shadows," making them taxpayers and eventually citizens, while at the same time "de-magnifying" the United States as an attraction for further illegal immigration. Unfortunately, events didn't work out that way. At the time of IRCA's passage there were about 5 million illegal immigrants in the United States; today the figure is somewhere between 10 and 12 million.

What went wrong? It depends on whom you ask. For some, the main problem was the amnesty, which, they say, taught those already here that they could break the law with impunity and tempted others in the other side of the border to do the same. For other critics, however, the main problem was that IRCA never properly took account of the huge demand for low-skilled work in certain areas.

Both sides in this debate became increasingly vocal in 2005 and 2006 as Congress wrestled anew with the problem of illegal immigration. Everyone seemed to agree that border controls needed to be strengthened, but those supporting a route to legalization for the millions of undocumented immigrants already here argued that there also needed to be expanded legal channels for those seeking temporary employment in the United States, as well as some means of granting legal recognition for immigrants who had illegally crossed the border years earlier and were now living, working, and raising families in the United States. Critics of these latter proposals were quick to note that they sounded like the failed amnesty provisions of IRCA, but this was disputed by the proponents. They were not calling for *carte blanche* forgiveness, they said, but for fines, a requirement to learn English, and waiting periods of various length before the undocumented could become legalized.

Whatever the outcome of the congressional debate, neither of the clashing positions is likely to fade away any time soon. In the following selections, Mark Krikorian, Executive Director of the Center for Immigration Studies, argues that the best approach is to rigorously enforce the laws against illegal aliens and provide stiff punishments for employers who hire them, while Frank Sharry, Executive Director of the National Immigration Forum, contends that the "enforcement only" approach ignores the fact that the United States has an increasingly integrated labor market with Latin America; he recommends an expanded effort to keep illegal aliens out, together with expanded legal channels for those who are already here.

YES

Mark Krikorian

Comprehensive Immigration Reform II

There is broad dissatisfaction with the current state of our immigration policy. We have in our country 11 or 12 million illegal aliens among a total immigrant population of 35 million, the largest number in our nation's history and soon to be the largest percentage of the population in our history. Despite misleading reports to the contrary, the pace of immigration is not abating; in the past five years, eight million people from abroad have settled in the United States, about half of them illegally.

How should we deal with the illegal aliens who are here? How should we structure future immigration policy to prevent this situation from recurring? There are two major proposals before this house attempting to answer these questions, one by Senators Kyl and Cornyn, the other from Senators Kennedy and McCain. In addition, there are at least two comprehensive proposals before the other house. And, of course, the Administration has its own proposal. The plans differ widely, but most have some form of legalization (i.e., amnesty) for illegal aliens already here, plus provisions to import large numbers of foreign workers in the future, whether through guestworker programs or large increases in permanent immigration.

Rather than examine the minutiae of the various measures, I want to address some of the fallacies that pervade the discussion of immigration in general, and of amnesty and foreign-worker schemes in particular, in order to offer some principles by which to judge the soundness of the various proposals.

Immigration Is Not Inevitable

The bedrock assumption underlying most of the immigration plans being offered is that the flow of workers from Mexico and elsewhere is unstoppable—a natural phenomenon like the weather or the tides, which we are powerless to influence. Therefore, it is said, managing the flow in an orderly and lawful manner is preferable to the alternative.

On the surface, the flow of Mexican immigration may indeed seem inevitable; it is very large, rapidly growing, and spreading throughout the country. But a longer view shows that this flow has been created in large part by

Hearing on "Comprehensive Immigration Reform II," October 18, 2005. Senate Committee on the Judiciary.

government policies, both in the United States and Mexico. And, government policy having created the migration flows, government policy can interrupt the flows, though a social phenomenon like this is naturally more difficult to stop than to start.

Migration is often discussed in terms of pushes and pulls—poverty, corruption, oppression, and general societal dysfunction impel people to leave their homelands, while high wages and expanded economic and social opportunities attract people to this country. While true, this analysis is incomplete because it overlooks the connection between the sending country and the receiving country.

No one wakes up in Timbuktu and says, "Today I will move to Milwaukee!"—migration takes place by way of networks of relatives, friends, acquaintances, and fellow countrymen, and few people immigrate to a place where these connections are absent. Consider two countries on the other side of the planet—the Philippines and Indonesia. These neighbors both have large, poor populations and share many cultural similarities, yet there are more than one million Filipino immigrants in the United States and only a handful of Indonesians, and annual immigration from the Philippines is routinely 40–50 times greater than immigration from Indonesia. Why? Because the ties between the United States and the Philippines are numerous and deep, our having ruled the country for 50 years and maintained an extensive military presence there for another 50 years. On the other hand, the United States has very few ties to Indonesia, whose people tend to migrate to the Netherlands, its former colonial ruler.

At the end of the Mexican War in 1848, there were only a small number of Mexican colonists living in the Southwest, many of whom soon returned to Mexico with the Mexican government's assistance. The immigration of Mexican workers began in a small way with the construction of the railroads beginning in the 1870s and later with the expansion of other industries. But the process of mass migration northward to the United States, and the development of the networks which made further immigration possible, began in earnest during the Mexican Revolution of 1910–1920. The Cristero rebellion of the late 1920s was the last major armed conflict in Mexico and was centered in the states of west-central Mexico; partly to prevent further trouble, the newly consolidated Mexico City regime adopted a policy of encouraging emigration from these very states. The power of government-fostered migration networks is clear from the fact that even today these same states account for a disproportionate share of Mexican immigrants to the United States.

On the U.S. side, federal policies that established migration networks between the United States and Mexico arguably began in the 1920s, when Congress specifically excluded the Western Hemisphere from the newly enacted immigration caps so as not to limit the flow of Mexican immigrants. Then in 1942, the Bracero Program to import Mexican farmworkers was started under the cover of World War II, and it continued until 1964. About 4.6 million contracts were issued to Mexican workers (many were repeat contracts for workers who returned several times, so that an estimated one to two million individuals participated). By creating vast new networks connecting the United States and Mexico, the Bracero Program launched the mass illegal immigration we are still experiencing today. Illegal immigration networks were reinforced by the IRCA amnesty of 1986, which granted legal status to nearly three million illegal aliens, at least two-thirds of whom were Mexican. This new legal status conferred by the federal government generated even more immigration, legal and illegal, as confirmed by a 2000 INS report. And the federal government's effective abandonment of interior immigration enforcement has served to further promote immigration from Mexico.

As a result of this series of government decisions, the flow of Mexican immigration to the United States is very large. The Mexican immigrant population ballooned from less than 800,000 in 1970 to nearly eight million in 2000, and is more than 10 million today, most having arrived since 1990. This rapid growth has created a snowball effect through the reinforcement of old networks and the establishment of new ones. If present trends continue, within a few years Mexico will have sent more immigrants to the United States in 100 years than Germany (currently the leading historical source of immigrants) has in more than 300 years.

Far from being an inevitable process with deep historical roots, then, mass immigration from Mexico is a relatively recent phenomenon created by government policies. The same is true for most other sources of immigration to the United States, such as Cuba, India, Central America, Russia, Vietnam, and elsewhere.

We Have not Seriously Tried to Enforce the Law

A supporter of a guestworker/amnesty program might respond that while interrupting immigration flows may be possible in theory, it cannot be accomplished in practice, and the proof of that is that we have tried to enforce our immigration laws and failed.

We have done no such thing. Increases in immigration enforcement over the past decade have been confined almost exclusively to patrolling the border; as important as that is, enforcement of the immigration laws inside the country has declined precipitously, and without such a combined strategy, success is impossible. In particular, enforcement of the ban on hiring illegal aliens, the centerpiece of any effort to regain control of our chaotic immigration system, has been all but abandoned. We might date the abandonment from INS raids in Georgia during the Vidalia onion harvest in 1998, which caused large numbers of illegal aliens—knowingly hired by the farmers—to abandon the fields to avoid arrest. By the end of the week, both of the state's senators and three congressmen had sent an outraged letter to Washington complaining that the INS "does not understand the needs of America's farmers," and that was the end of that.

So, the INS tried out a "kinder, gentler" means of enforcing the law, which fared no better. Rather than conduct raids on individual employers, Operation Vanguard in 1998–99 sought to identify illegal workers at all meatpacking plants in Nebraska through audits of personnel records. The INS then asked to interview those employees who appeared to be unauthorized—and the illegals ran off. The procedure was remarkably successful, and was meant to be repeated every two or three months until the plants were weaned from their dependence on illegal labor.

Local law enforcement officials were very pleased with the results, but employers and politicians vociferously criticized the very idea of enforcing the immigration law. Gov. Mike Johanns organized a task force to oppose the operation; the meat packers and the ranchers hired former Gov. Ben Nelson to lobby on their behalf; and, in Washington, Sen. Chuck Hagel (R-Neb.) pressured the Justice Department to stop. They succeeded, the operation was ended, and the senior INS official who had thought it up in the first place was forced into early retirement.

The INS got the message and developed a new interior enforcement policy that gave up trying to actually control immigration and focused almost entirely on the important, but narrow, issues of criminal aliens and smugglers. As INS policy director Robert Bach told *The New York Times* in a March 9, 2000, story appropriately entitled "I.N.S. Is Looking the Other Way as Illegal Immigrants Fill Jobs": "It is just the market at work, drawing people to jobs, and the INS has chosen to concentrate its actions on aliens who are a danger to the community."

The enforcement statistics tell the story in a nutshell: According to the GAO, even in 1999, only 417 notices of intent to fine were levied against employers who knowingly hired illegal aliens; but in 2004, the number of employer fines was 3. That's "three". Nationwide.

Tony Blankley, the *Washington Times'* editorial-page editor, summed it up last year:

> I might agree with the president's proposals if they followed, rather than preceded, a failed Herculean, decades-long national effort to secure our borders. If, after such an effort, it was apparent that we simply could not control our borders, then, as a practical man I would try to make the best of a bad situation. But such an effort has not yet been made.

Amnesties and Foreign-Worker Programs Can't Stop Illegal Immigration

Even if it is possible to enforce the law, wouldn't accommodating the immigration flow through a guestworker program or increased issuance of green cards (plus an amnesty for those already here) be another way of eliminating illegal immigration?

No.

Putting aside their other effects, amnesties and increased immigration (whether permanent or "temporary") simply cannot eliminate illegal immigration. To begin with expansions in immigration: The sense seems to be that the economy demands a certain amount of foreign labor each year, but that the various legal channels only admit a portion of the needed flow, with the rest entering illegally. It would follow, then, that establishing a legal means for those foreign workers "forced" to come illegally would all but eliminate ordinary illegal immigration.

This represents a simplistic understanding of both the economy and of immigration. Immigration always creates more immigration and, as the discussion above about Bracero Program made clear, the proliferation of connections created by the arrival of workers from abroad will continually expand the pool of people who have the means to come here, leading to more immigration, legal and illegal. In fact, a large body of sociological research shows that one of the best predictors of a person's likelihood to immigrate to the United States illegally is whether he has legal immigrant family members already here.

This is why the momentum of immigration continues regardless of economic circumstances; the economy today no longer serves as a regulator of immigration levels. For instance, if we examine the four years before and after 2000, we see that the first period, 1996–2000, was a time of dramatic job growth and rapid expansion, while 2000–2004 saw slower economic growth and weaker labor demand. Immigrant unemployment grew significantly during that period, as did the number of unemployed immigrants. And yet immigration actually increased slightly, from 5.5 million arrivals during the first period and 6.1 million new immigrants during the second.

The experience with amnesties is no different. About 2.7 million people were legalized in the late 1980s and early 1990s as a result of the amnesties contained in the Immigration Reform and Control Act (IRCA) of 1986. But INS figures show that by the beginning of 1997 those former illegal aliens had been entirely replaced by new illegal aliens, and that the unauthorized population again stood at more than 5 million, just as before the amnesty.

In fact, INS estimates show that the 1986 amnesty almost certainly increased illegal immigration, as the relatives of newly legalized illegals came to the United States to join their family members. The flow of illegals grew dramatically during the years of the amnesty to more than 800,000 a year, before dropping back down to "only" 500,000 a year.

To sum up: If increased admission of foreign workers served to limit illegal immigration, how can it be that all three—legal immigration, "temporary" work visas, and illegal immigration—have all mushroomed together? In 1974, legal immigration was less than 400,000; in 2004, it was nearly 1 million. In 1981, about 45,000 "temporary workers and trainees" were admitted; in 2004, the number was 684,000. Twenty years ago, the illegal population was estimated to be 5 million; today it is 11–12 million, even after nearly 3 million illegals were amnestied.

Whatever other arguments might be made for them, neither amnesties nor foreign-worker programs are a solution to illegal immigration. . . .

No Amnesty or Foreign-Worker Program Is Administratively Feasible

In any large government program, plans on paper must translate into policies on the ground. Any amnesty or foreign-worker program would require extensive background checks as well as simple management of the program—processing applications, interviewing applicants, checking arrivals, tracking whether a worker is still employed, enforcing the departure of those who are supposed to leave. Supporters of the various amnesty and foreign-worker proposals have assumed that administering these programs would not be a problem.

But it is not explained how the immigration bureaus within the Department of Homeland Security, already choking on massive workloads, are supposed to be able to accomplish these goals. The GAO has reported that the backlog of pending immigration applications of various kinds was at 6.2 million at the end of FY 2003, up 59 percent from the beginning of FY 2001. It has since shrunk to "only" 4.1 million.

Because of the enormity of the backlog, the immigration service often issues work permits and travel documents to green-card applicants right when they submit their forms, knowing that it will be years before anyone actually reads the application. What's more, the immigration bureaus are trying to implement vast new tracking systems for foreign students and foreign visitors. The crush of work has been so severe, that many important statutory deadlines have been missed.

And the context for all this is a newly created Department of Homeland Security, which incorporates pieces of the old Immigration and Naturalization Service and many other agencies in various combinations. To add to DHS's well-known management problems, all three immigration bureaus are currently without a head.

The registration and screening and tracking of millions of additional aliens for amnesty or foreign-worker programs would result in complete institutional paralysis and breakdown. After all, the workload created by any such program would be larger than the total number of visas issued annually worldwide by the State Department (approximately 5 million), and many, many times larger than the total number of green cards issued each year by DHS (around 1 million). None of this is to pin blame on the bureaucrats charged with implementing congressional mandates. Rather, the immigration proposals themselves are the problem, because they are not based on any real-world assessment of the administrative capacity of the immigration agencies.

Massive Fraud Is a Security Threat

In addition to widespread paralysis, overloading administrative agencies with the vast and complicated new responsibilities of an amnesty and foreign-worker program would cause staggering levels of fraud, as overworked bureaucrats are pressured to rubber-stamp applications.

In fact, even without the tsunami of paperwork that new immigration programs would cause, fraud is already dangerously widespread. Stephen Dinan of *The Washington Times* reported earlier this month that internal investigators at U.S. Citizenship and Immigration Services (USCIS) have uncovered thousands of cases of misconduct, including bribery, exchanging immigration benefits for sex, and being influenced by foreign governments. And new charges are being added at the rate of 50 per week.

Nor is this a new development. A January 2002 GAO report addressed the consequences of such administrative overload. It found that the crush of work has created an organizational culture in the immigration services bureau where "staff are rewarded for the timely handling of petitions rather than for careful scrutiny of their merits." The pressure to move things through the system has led to "rampant" and "pervasive" fraud, with one official estimating that 20 to 30 percent of all applications involve fraud. The GAO concluded that "the goal of providing immigration benefits in a timely manner to those who are legally entitled to them may conflict with the goal of preserving the integrity of the legal immigration system."

This last point was reinforced in an especially lurid way by the last big amnesty program, which was part of the Immigration Reform and Control Act (IRCA) of 1986. As Paul Virtue, then general counsel of the INS, testified before Congress in 1999, "the provisions of IRCA were subject to widespread abuse, especially the Special Agricultural Worker (SAW) program." There were nearly 1.3 million applications for the SAW amnesty—double the total number of foreign farm workers usually employed in the United States in any given year, and up to six times as many applicants as congressional sponsors of the scheme assured skeptics would apply. INS officials told *The New York Times* that the majority of applicants in certain offices were clearly fraudulent, but that they were approved anyway, since the INS didn't have the means to prove the fraud. Some women came to interviews with long, painted nails, while others claimed to have picked strawberries off trees. One woman in New Jersey who owned a five-acre garden plot certified that more than 1,000 illegal aliens had worked on her land.

This is a problem not just because it offends our sensibilities but because ineligible people will get legal status—people like Mahmud Abouhalima, a cabbie in New York, who got amnesty as a farmworker under the 1986 law and went on to help lead the first World Trade Center attack. Having an illegal-alien terrorist in your country is bad; having one with legal status is far worse, since he can work and travel freely, as Abouhalima did, going to Afghanistan to receive terrorist training only after he got amnesty.

And we cannot safely assume that at least those illegal aliens who have snuck across the Mexican border are no threat, since they want only to wash our dishes. For example, Iraqi-born smuggler George Tajirian pled guilty in 2001 to forging an alliance with a Mexican immigration officer to smuggle "Palestinian, Jordanian, Syrian, Iraqi, Yemeni, and other illegal aliens through Mexico and into the United States." And in late 2003, the former Mexican consul in Beirut was arrested for her involvement in a similar enterprise.

Another amnesty or large foreign-worker program is guaranteed—guaranteed—to give legal residence to a future terrorist.

A Third Way—Neither Roundups Nor Amnesty

The final selling point for supporters of amnesty and foreign-worker programs is that there are only two options available to us—either massive roundups and a huge burst of deportations, or some form of legalization. And since it's clear there's no way we can remove 11 million people all at once, the only option available to us is amnesty, however it might be labeled or camouflaged.

But there is a third way that rejects this false choice, and it is the only approach that can actually work: Shrink the illegal population through consistent, across-the-board enforcement of the immigration law. By limiting the settlement of new illegals, by increasing deportations to the extent possible, and, most importantly, by increasing the number of illegals already here who give up and deport themselves, the United States can bring about an annual decrease in the illegal-alien population, rather than allowing it to continually increase. The result would be attrition of the illegal population, shrinking it over a period of several years to a manageable nuisance, rather than today's looming crisis. This is analogous to the approach a corporation might take to downsizing a bloated workforce: a hiring freeze, some layoffs, plus new incentives to encourage excess workers to leave on their own.

Churn in the illegal population. This strategy of attrition is not a pipe dream, or the idle imaginings of a policy wonk. The central insight is that there is already significant churn in the illegal population, which can be used to speed the decline in overall numbers. According to a 2003 report from the Immigration and Naturalization Service, thousands of people are subtracted from the illegal population each year. From 1995 to 1999, an average of 165,000 a year went back home on their own after residing here for at least a year; the same number got some kind of legal status, about 50,000 were deported, and 25,000 died, for a total of more than 400,000 people each year subtracted from the resident illegal population. The problem is that the average annual inflow of new illegal aliens over that same period was nearly 800,000, swamping the outflow and creating an average annual increase of close to 400,000.

A strategy of attrition would seek to reverse this relationship, so that the outflow from the illegal population is much larger than the number of new illegal settlers from abroad. This would be a measured approach to the problem, one that doesn't aspire to an immediate, magical solution to a long-brewing crisis, but also does not simply surrender, as the amnesty and foreign-worker proposals do.

There are a number of real-world examples of successful enforcement. During the first several years after the passage of the IRCA, illegal crossings from Mexico fell precipitously, as prospective illegals waited to see if we were serious. Apprehensions of aliens by the Border Patrol—an imperfect measure but the only one available—fell from more than 1.7 million in FY 1986 to under a million in 1989. But then the flow began to increase again as the deterrent effect of the hiring ban dissipated, when word got back that we were not serious about enforcement and that the system could be easily evaded through the use of inexpensive phony documents.

That showed that reducing new illegal immigration is possible; but what about increasing the number of illegals already here who give up and leave? That, too, has already been demonstrated. After the 9/11 attacks, immigration authorities undertook a "Special Registration" program for visitors from Islamic countries. The affected nation with the largest illegal-alien population was Pakistan, with an estimated 26,000 illegals here in 2000. Once it became clear that the government was getting more serious about enforcing the immigration law—at least with regard to Middle Easterners—Pakistani illegals started leaving on their own in large numbers. The Pakistani embassy estimated that more than 15,000 of its illegal aliens left the United States, and the *Washington Post* reported the "disquieting" fact that in Brooklyn's Little Pakistan the mosque was one-third empty, business was down, there were fewer want ads in the local Urdu-language paper, and "For Rent" signs sprouted everywhere.

And in an inadvertent enforcement initiative, the Social Security Administration in 2002 sent out almost a million "no-match" letters to employers who filed W-2s with information that was inconsistent with SSA's records. The intention was to clear up misspellings, name changes, and other mistakes that had caused a large amount of money paid into the system to go uncredited. But, of course, most of the problem was caused by illegal aliens lying to their employers, and thousands of illegals quit or were fired when they were found out. The effort was so successful at denying work to illegals that business and immigrant-rights groups organized to stop it and won a 90 percent reduction in the number of letters to be sent out.

A policy of attrition through enforcement would have two main components: an increase in conventional enforcement—arrests, prosecutions, deportations, asset seizures, etc.—plus expanded use of verification of legal status at a variety of important points, to make it as difficult and unpleasant as possible to live here illegally.

Conventional enforcement.   As to the first, the authorities—from the White House on down—need to make an unambiguous commitment to immigration enforcement. There must be an end to the climate of impunity for border-jumping, and illegal employment, and fake documents, and immigration fraud. To use only one example of the longstanding lack of commitment, aliens who repeatedly sneak across the border are supposed to be prosecuted and jailed, and the Border Patrol unveiled a new digital fingerprint system in the mid '90s to make tracking of repeat crossers possible. The problem is that short-staffed U.S. attorneys' offices kept increasing the number of apprehensions needed before they would prosecute, to avoid actually having to prosecute at all.

It would be hard to exaggerate the demoralizing effect that such disregard for the law has on immigration enforcement agents. Conversely, the morale of immigration workers would soar in the wake of a real commitment to law enforcement.

Among measures that would facilitate enforcement: hiring more U.S. Attorneys and judges in border areas, to allow for more prosecutions; expanding our laughably small Border Patrol which, even with recent increases, is barely one-quarter the size of the New York Police Department and is only able to deploy an average of one agent per mile along the Mexican border during any given shift; promoting enhanced cooperation between federal immigration authorities and state and local police; and seizing the assets, however modest, of apprehended illegal aliens; expanding detention capacity; streamlining the immigration appeals process to deport aliens more quickly.

Firewalls.   Even if we were somehow to increase deportations ten-fold, most of the decline in the illegal population would have to come through self-deportation, illegal aliens giving up and going home. Unlike at the visa office or the border crossing, once aliens are inside the United States, there's no physical site to exercise control, no choke point at which to examine whether someone should be admitted. The solution is to create "virtual choke points"—events that are necessary for life in a modern society but are infrequent enough not to bog down everyone's daily business. Another analogy for this concept is to firewalls in computer systems—filters that people could pass through only if their legal status is verified. The objective is not mainly to identify illegal aliens for arrest (though that will always be a tool) but rather to make it as difficult as possible for illegal aliens to live a normal life here.

This is the rationale for the prohibition against employing illegal aliens—people have to work, so requiring proof of legal status upon starting a job would serve as an important firewall. Congress instituted this firewall tactic in 1986 when in prohibited the employment of illegal aliens; but in the absence of a mandatory verification mechanism, such a system could not succeed. The immigration service has already developed a verification system which has proven both workable and popular with participating businesses (including my own Center for Immigration Studies). Building on this fledgling system, we need to find other instances in which legal status might be verified, and thus illegals barred, such as getting a driver's license, registering an automobile, opening a bank account, applying for a car loan or a mortgage, getting a business or occupational license, and obtaining government services of any kind.

An important element in this firewall tactic is secure documentation. By enacting the Real ID Act, Congress has already taken a step toward establishing uniform standards for state driver's licenses, which serve as our nation's de facto national identification system. At least as important is to formally prohibit acceptance of consular registration cards, chiefly Mexico's "matricula consular" card, which functions as an illegal-alien ID; when accepted by U.S. jurisdictions and companies as a valid ID, it enables illegal aliens to pass through many firewalls.

An important point about using verification of legal status as a way downsize the illegal population is that its effects would be felt gradually, rather than all at once. A new, functional verification system for employment, for instance, would be applied mainly to new hires (though employers should have the option of checking existing employees as well). The same is true for getting a driver's license or a mortgage—these are not things people do every day, so the effects of verifying legal status would unfold over a period of time.

Mr. Chairman, you and your colleagues should deliberate on immigration policy secure in the knowledge that reasserting control over immigration requires no land mines, no machine guns, no tattoos—none of the cartoonish images invoked by opponents of tight immigration controls. All that is needed is the consistent application of ordinary law-enforcement tools—plus a rejection of measures that would undermine enforcement, such as amnesties or expanded foreign-worker programs. I look forward to any questions you might have.

Frank Sharry  **NO**

Comprehensive Immigration Reform II

The American people are right to demand that Congress and the Administration take effective action to restore the rule of law to our nation's immigration system. The evidence of the system's dysfunction is all around us: young men and women die gruesome deaths in southwestern deserts as they attempt to enter the U.S. in search of work; fake document merchants and criminal smugglers turn huge profits in networks that one day might be exploited not by those seeking work in our economy but by those seeking to attack our nation; local community tensions simmer and sometimes explode as housing gets stretched, schools experience change, and language differences emerge; immigrant families remain divided for years, even decades, by restrictive admissions policies and inefficient processing; immigrant workers afraid of being discovered and deported are subject to abuse and exploitation by unscrupulous employers seeking to gain an unfair advantage over law-abiding competitors; meanwhile, public frustration mounts as the federal government seems incapable of mobilizing the political leadership and enacting the policy changes to fix the system once and for all.

Mr. Chairman, I urge you and the Committee to lead the way and take effective action in this Congress. The country is crying out for leadership on this issue and a solution to this problem. Immigration policy is fundamentally and constitutionally a matter for the federal government. States and local communities are understandably frustrated with the effects of a broken immigration system, but they cannot and do not set national immigration policy. It is up to Congress and the Administration to rise to the occasion. . . .

Fixing the broken immigration system requires sizing up its complexity and its dimensions. The numbers tell part of the story. Some 11 million undocumented immigrants now live and work in the United States. That means that almost one-third of all the immigrants in America lives here without government authorization. Fourteen million people, including some 5 million kids, live in households headed by an undocumented immigrant. One out of 20 workers in the nation's labor force is living and working here illegally. Two-thirds of them have arrived in the last decade. More than half are from Mexico. More than 80% are from Latin America and the Caribbean. America's backyard is showing up on America's front porch.

Hearing on "Comprehensive Immigration Reform II," October 18, 2005. Senate Committee on the Judiciary.

Illegal immigration is no longer a niche issue affecting a handful of gateway states and cities. It has gone nationwide. Consider the five states with the fastest growing populations of undocumented immigrants: North Carolina, Utah, Colorado, Arizona, and Idaho. In fact, a wide swath of the nation's heartland, from the old South stretching up through the Mountain states to the Northwest, is undergoing a remarkable demographic transformation with little to no recent experience to draw on to respond to it.

Moreover, most new undocumented immigrants appear to be here to stay. The vast majority no longer fit the stereotype of the migrant male on his own here to do temporary work before returning home. Today, 70% live with spouses and/or children. And only 3% work in agriculture. The vast majority are employed in year-round service sector jobs. After all, the jobs are plentiful. More than half the new jobs created in the American economy require hard work, not multiple diplomas. Meanwhile, young native-born workers are smaller in number, better educated than ever, and more interested in office work than manual labor. Consequently, much of the nation's demand for housekeepers, childcare workers, landscapers, protein processors, busboys, cooks, janitors, dry wallers, and construction workers is met by a steady flow of some 500,000 undocumented migrants who enter and settle in America each year.

Which begs the question: Since the U.S. has a legal immigration system, why don't these workers from Mexico and elsewhere simply wait in line and enter with legal visas? Answer: what legal visas? There are virtually none available for these workers. While the labor market demands an estimated 500,000 full-time low-skilled service jobs a year, our immigration laws supply just 5,000 permanent visas for workers to fill these jobs. And this tiny category is so backlogged it has been rendered useless. As the Immigration Policy Center recently pointed out, of the other 15 immigrant visa categories available for employment and training, only two are available to industries that require little or no formal training. These two categories (H2A and H2B) are small and seasonal. In addition to the enormous mismatch between labor market realities and our government's immigration policy, our family visa lines are so backlogged that it can take a decade for spouses to be reunited, legally. Not surprisingly, many stop waiting and cross the border illegally in order to reunite with their loved ones.

What to do? Some argue that the solution is to simply enforce the laws we already have on the books. And while we certainly need tighter, more targeted, and more effective enforcement as part of a comprehensive overhaul, the fact is that over the past two decades the "enforcement only" approach has failed miserably. . . . Since 1986 the border patrol budget has increased tenfold in value. This beefing up of border enforcement has been augmented by tough restrictions on immigrant access to employment, public services, and due process protections.

And yet this unprecedented increase in enforcement has coincided with an unprecedented increase in illegal immigration.

Why hasn't "enforcement only" worked to stem illegal immigration? Because our current approach to immigration and border security policy fails to recognize that the United States has an increasingly integrated labor market with Latin America. In much the same way that we used to see workers from rural areas in South migrate to the urban North to fill manufacturing jobs, we now see workers from rural areas south of the border migrating to all areas of the U.S. to fill service jobs. Our failure to account for this fact of life leads to a failure of policy. Instead of building a workable regulatory regime to govern what is essentially a market-driven labor migration, we keep legal channels severely restricted and then wonder why workers and their families have nowhere to go but into the clutches of a migration black market dominated by smugglers, fake document merchants, and unscrupulous employers.

Dan Griswold of the Cato Institute sums it up this way: "Demand for low-skilled labor continues to grow in the United States while the domestic supply of suitable workers inexorably declines—yet U.S. immigration law contains virtually no legal channel through which low-skilled immigrant workers can enter the country to fill that gap. The result is an illegal flow of workers characterized by more permanent and less circular migration, smuggling, document fraud, deaths at the border, artificially depressed wages, and threats to civil liberties." He adds, "American immigration laws are colliding with reality, and reality is winning."

Griswold is right. We will not be able to restore respect for the rule of law in our immigration system until we restore respect for the law of supply and demand. Instead of "enforcement only" or "enforcement first," we need an "enforcement plus" approach.

I recall the first time I came face to face with the reality of an integrated labor market and the futility of an "enforcement only" strategy. In the late 1990's I accompanied a delegation that visited Tixla ("Teesh-la"), a "sending community" located in Mexico. Most of its sons and daughters had left and migrated illegally to Chicago to fill available service jobs in construction, landscaping, hospitality, and childcare. Those left behind consisted mostly of women, children, and the elderly. The workers used to come back and forth, at least for visits, but this had mostly stopped due to the press of their multiple jobs up north and the risks associated with re-crossing the border illegally. The townspeople were proud to show us the new school and basketball court which had recently been built with pooled remittances. And there, right there in the middle of the basketball court, was a huge replica of the logo for the Chicago Bulls.

That's when it hit me. Tixla, a dusty, rural town south of Mexico City, is a bedroom community for Chicago. We may not think of it that way, but it is 21st century fact. The town produces the workers needed to fill newly-created service sector jobs in the Chicago area. There is plenty of work available just up the road, and these workers are willing to risk their lives to make the commute.

Needed: A New Perspective and a Comprehensive Strategy

Like so many other public policy debates, the highly-charged immigration debate is often polarized and paralyzed by an "either/or" framework. The tit-for-tat goes something like this: you are either for immigrants or for control;

you are either for higher levels or lower levels; you are either for closed borders or open borders; you are either for lax policies or tough policies. This narrow and lopsided framework is a trap that obscures realistic solutions.

What's needed is a "both/and" approach that recognizes the reality of an integrated labor market with Latin America and the legitimate U.S. demand for operational control of its borders in a post 9/11 world. Such an approach seeks to integrate seemingly contradictory elements into a comprehensive package; a package that combines expanded enforcement strategies and expanded legal channels for those entering the U.S. to work and join families and expanded pathways to legal status and citizenship for undocumented immigrants already living and working in the U.S. We need to change our immigration laws so that they are enforceable and enforce them effectively.

Senator Edward Kennedy put it this way in recent testimony before this Committee: "The past debate has long been polarized between those who want more enforcement and those who want more visas. But to repair what's broken, we need to combine increased enforcement and increased legality. Better border control and better treatment of immigrants are not inconsistent—they are two sides of the same coin."

This new perspective was first promoted and popularized by Presidents Bush and Fox in their 2001 migration negotiations. The two presidents imagined a system based on improved border security and widened legal channels. The idea was, and is, to recognize, regularize, and regulate the status of workers who are either coming from south of the border to jobs in the U.S. or already here working and contributing to our economy. The goal? Make the healthy, positive, and predictable movement of workers to available jobs safe, legal, and orderly.

The President deserves considerable credit for getting this "big idea" and sticking with it. In January 2004 he announced principles for immigration reform that, although somewhat vague and incomplete, captured this new perspective. And this vision of immigration reform has spawned two significant immigration reform proposals in the Senate. One is authored by Senators McCain and Kennedy. The other is authored by Senators Cornyn and Kyl. Both proposals are serious and go beyond an "enforcement only" approach. However, in our view only the McCain-Kennedy bill is both fully comprehensive and workable. That is why the organization I direct has joined with constituencies from across the political spectrum and across the country to endorse the Secure America and Orderly Immigration Act of 2005.

Secure America: A Cure for What Ails Us

Secure America is not perfect, but it is an excellent draft that should serve as the basis for fixing our broken immigration system. Specifically, the bill combines 1) enhanced enforcement to ensure the reformed immigration system is effectively policed; 2) widened legal channels for the future flow of workers and families; 3) a workable solution for the 11 million undocumented immigrants currently working and living in the United States; and 4) support for the successful integration of newcomers in the communities where they settle.

The key to effective enforcement is to augment our border enforcement efforts with a system that ensures that all workers hired in the United States are in our country legally. The bill accomplishes this by building an electronic worker verification system (the bill contemplates credit card swipe machines, but for social security cards, drivers' licenses, or immigration documents, and only at the point of hire) combined with tough sanctions for employers who attempt to end-run the new system. I predict that responsible employers will support it as long as the verification system is functional and the new system is combined with legal channels for workers here and those needed in the future. I predict that unscrupulous employers—those that benefit from the dysfunctional status quo—will oppose it.

The keys to making the admissions system realistic, controlled, and workable are a) to provide enough visas for the expected future flow of workers and families; and b) to avoid the exploitation and abuses of old-style guest worker programs. Secure America accomplishes the first by creating 400,000 worker visas a year and increasing family reunification visas so that the current illegal flow will be funneled into a legal one while being fair to those from around the world. It tackles the second by requiring employers to pay newly admitted workers the same wages as similarly-situated workers, and by mostly de-linking workers' status from employer say-so. For example, workers on temporary visas (three year visas, renewable) will be able to "vote with their feet" and change jobs without threatening their immigration status. After four years in the country, such workers will be able to self-petition for permanent residence—rather than having to ask for the blessing of a particular employer.

The key to putting migration on legal footing once and for all is finding a way for the 11 million or so undocumented immigrants to come out of the shadows voluntarily and transition to legal status. Secure America addresses this controversial issue head on. It offers incentives for undocumented immigrants already here to come forward, register with the government, submit to criminal, security, and health screenings, pay a hefty fine, study English and civics, and clear up their taxes as a way to eventually earn permanent residency. Immigrants who meet these requirements can apply for permanent residence after six years, and become eligible for citizenship in 11 years at the earliest. And this component interacts with the family reunification provisions such that those waiting in the queue outside the U.S. secure permanent residence before those previously undocumented immigrants who obtain temporary status.

Critics label this process of registration and earned legalization an "amnesty." Senator Kennedy rightly objects that "there is no free pass, no automatic pardon, no trip to the front of the line." The *Wall Street Journal* editorial page, which I suspect rarely lines up with the senior Massachusetts Senator, agrees: "This amnesty charge may be potent as a political slogan, but it becomes far less persuasive when you examine its real-world implications. If paying a fine isn't good enough for illegals already here, what are the restrictionists proposing? Mass arrests, raids on job-creating businesses, or deportations? . . . . Those who wave the 'no amnesty' flag are actually encouraging a larger underground illegal population. The only reform that has a chance to succeed is one that recognizes the reality that 10 or so million illegal aliens already work in the U.S. and are vital to the economy and their communities."

Finally, the bill promotes the successful integration of new immigrants into local communities. Immigration to America has worked throughout our history because newcomers have been encouraged to become new Americans. Secure America takes steps to renew this commitment by increasing English classes for adult immigrants, citizenship promotion and preparation, and the legal security immigrant workers need to move up the economic ladder. In fact, it's worth noting that when 3 million undocumented immigrants became legal immigrants some 20 years ago, their wages increased by 14% over 5 years—they were no longer afraid to speak up or change jobs—and their productivity increased dramatically—they studied English and improved their skills through training. The bill also deals with a longstanding and legitimate complaint from state and local governments by reimbursing costs related to health care and other public services.

The bill certainly has its faults and its critics. The immigration enforcement provisions are strong but will need to be strengthened if we are to ensure immigrant workers and families use widened legal channels and no others. Similarly, the bill aims to construct a temporary worker program that adequately protects both native and immigrant workers alike, but will probably need to be tweaked to fully realize this objective. After all, the goal of immigration reform should be nothing less than to restore the rule of law—both to our immigration system and to low-wage labor markets. And unfortunately, the bill does not adequately address the acknowledged long-term solution to the migration challenge: economic development in sending nations and communities. It is my hope that this session's immigration reform debate will serve as a stepping stone to, if not a venue for, a much-needed review of trade, aid, and development policies in the Americas.

Overall, though, the bill's premise is brilliant and its promise viable: take migration out of the black market and bring it under the rule of law; funnel the illegal flow into legal channels; increase the legality of the migration that is occurring, rather than increase the numbers of those who enter; get control of the flow so we get control of our border; bring undocumented immigrants out of the shadows and under the protection of our laws; know who is in our country and who is entering it; shift from repressing migration ineffectively to regulating migration intelligently; turn the broken status quo into a functioning, regulated system; drain the swamp of fake documents and criminal smugglers; vetted airport arrivals instead of deaths in the desert; families united rather than divided for decades; verification mechanisms that work and fake documents that don't; legal workers and an equal playing field for honest employers; equal labor rights for all rather than a race to the bottom for most. In sum, this bill represents a 21st century solution for a 21st century challenge.

The Cornyn-Kyl Bill: Right Direction, But Falls Short

The proposal introduced recently by Senators John Cornyn and Jon Kyl is a serious bill. And Senator Cornyn in particular has distinguished himself recently by his eloquent diagnosis of our broken immigration system. He has repeatedly said that the only way to solve the immigration dilemma is to combine tougher enforcement with a legal regime that deals realistically both with those entering our nation and those already here.

Unfortunately, the bill as introduced is not workable. Instead of offering carrots to draw the 11 million out of the shadows so they register with the government, submit to screenings, pay a fine, and get in line for eventual permanent residency, it presents mostly sticks that would end up with most undocumented immigrants opting to remain in the shadows. Instead of reuniting families in a more timely fashion and keeping nuclear families together, the bill fails to address existing backlogs and instead would most likely result in more families split between different countries for longer periods of time. Instead of ensuring that immigrant workers are treated equally so that both low-wage workers and law-abiding employers benefit, the bill would likely end up favoring employers who undercut their competitors by hiring short-term guest workers. Instead of providing for a stable workforce and promoting citizenship, the bill threatens to force workers out of the country or out of their jobs, and provides no meaningful path to citizenship.

Nevertheless, the authors have rightly steered clear of an "enforcement only" or "enforcement first" approach and have developed a number of ideas worthy of consideration and inclusion in a Senate Judiciary Committee bill. It is my hope and recommendation that this Committee, led by its Chairman, will start with the McCain-Kennedy template and include the best of the proposals before it in a way that builds momentum and support in the full Senate for workable comprehensive reform.

Final Remarks

We at the National Immigration Forum have been working on challenges related to immigration policy for more than 20 years. We understand how hard it is to fashion immigration reform that can pass Congress and work on the ground once enacted. We are fully prepared to support and fight for a combination of tough and smart enforcement measures if combined with simultaneous reforms to our admissions policies that bring undocumented immigrants out of the shadows and provide a sufficient number of worker and family reunification visas for the future flow. But we cannot and will not support proposals that have no realistic chance of working once implemented. Our stand is that we not only get it done, but that we get it done right.

But we are optimistic. We believe this is our generation's best shot at enacting workable reform. As a nation we seem poised to moved beyond the old debate—characterized by simplistic and shallow prescriptions of the past, the non-solution, sound bite-driven "get tough and be done with it" approach. The nation is ready to take part in a new debate, one that takes all of the moving parts into full consideration and at the same time. The old debate suggests that we have to choose between being a nation of immigrants or a nation of laws. The new debate recognizes that the only way to be either is to be both.

POSTSCRIPT

Stopping Illegal Immigration: Should Border Security Come First?

Few issues arouse such contradictory emotions as does immigration. Americans are proud of their immigrant past because they are all immigrants or the descendants of immigrants. Yet they are also concerned about how the newest immigrants, especially those who are coming here illegally, may affect American culture and values. Will their presence and growing numbers encourage others to break the law? Will they live in ethnic enclaves, finding it unnecessary to learn English or respect American traditions? Or will their experience parallel that of most immigrants in the last century, men and women who came to America to work hard, live decent lives, and raise their children to become good citizens?

In *Who Are We? The Challenges to America's National Identity* (Simon & Schuster, 2004), Samuel P. Huntington presents an alarming view of the new immigrants, particularly those from Mexico. He worries that they are forming their own trans-national culture in the United States, adversely affecting America's work ethnic and its sense of national identity. In a similar vein is Georgie Anne Geyer's *Americans No More* (Atantic Monthly Press, 1996). Geyer is not so much concerned about immigration per se but about the recent tendencies of even legal immigrants to resist assimilation. Her view is shared by Peter Brimlow, in *Alien Nation: Common Sense About America's Immigration Disaster* (Random House, 1995). Brimlow argues that no multi-cultural society has ever lasted very long. Opposing those views is Sanford J. Ungar's *In Fresh Blood: The New American Immigrants* (Simon & Schuster, 1995). "To be American," Ungar writes, "means being part of an ever more heterogeneous people and participating in the constant redefinition of a complex, evolving cultural fabric." Somewhere in between multiculturalists like Ungar and assimilationists like Brimelow and Geyer is Peter D. Salins. In *Assimilation, American Style* (Basic Books, 1997), Salins argues that the natu-ralization process is the best means for absorbing the flood of immigrants who arrive in America each year.

Often forgotten in these debates are the experiences of the immigrants themselves. Newer immigrants to America have recounted some of these experiences in recent books by and about them. In *Becoming American: Personal Essays by First Generation Immigrant Women* (Hyperion, 2000), Ghanaian American writer Meri Nana-Ama Danquah brings together the personal recol-lections and reflections by immigrant women from Europe, Latin America, Africa, Asia, and the Caribbean. In *American by Choice: The Remarkable Fulfill-ment of an Immigrant's Dreams* (Thomas Nelson, 1998), Sam Moore describes his rise in America from a poor Lebanese immigrant to president and CEO of

Thomas Nelson Publishers, a major religious publishing house. A more troubling account of the immigrant experience is that of Mary C. Waters, in *Black Identities: West Indian Immigrant Dreams and American Realities* (Harvard University Press, 2000). Waters finds that when West Indian immigrants first arrive, their skills, knowledge of English, and general optimism carry them forward, but later on, a variety of influences, from racial discrimination to low wages and poor working conditions, tend to erode their self-confidence.

Attitudes toward immigration change with time and circumstances. September 11, 2001, was one of those times. The terrorist attacks on the World Trade Center have increased the fear that many Americans have of all foreigners. Tamar Jacoby examines the changing circumstances in "Too Many Immigrants?" *Commentary* (April 2002).

The literature on immigration seems to grow as rapidly as immigration itself. Christopher Jencks has assessed this literature in two long essays entitled "Who Should Get In?" *New York Review of Books* (November 29 and December 20, 2001). Among the controversial issues that he examines is whether or not permanent status can be granted to illegal immigrants who are presently residing in the United States without encouraging the influx of many more and, if so, how. In 2004, President Bush proposed an amnesty program for illegal aliens. Mark Krikorian, in "Amnesty Again" (*The National Review*, January 26, 1994), criticizes the plan because it would lead to the permanent importation of thousands of new workers.

Americans confront a choice. On the one hand, there are the ethical and political consequences of restricting immigration into a country whose attraction to poor or persecuted people is as great as its borders are vast. On the other hand, there are the problems of absorbing new, generally non-English-speaking populations into an economy that may have to provide increasing public support and into a society whose traditions and values may clash with those of the newcomers.

On the Internet . . .

In addition to the Internet sites listed below, type in key words, such as "free trade," "Iraq," "Iraqi war," and "American world leadership," to find other listings.

U.S. State Department

View this site for understanding into the workings of a major U.S. executive branch department. Links explain exactly what the department does, what services it provides, and what it says about U.S. interests around the world, as well as provide other information.

http://www.state.gov

Marketplace of Political Ideas/University of Houston Libraries

Here is a valuable collection of links to campaign, conservative/liberal perspectives, and political party sites. There are general political sites, Democratic sites, Republican sites, third-party sites, and much more.

http://info.lib.uh.edu/politics/markind:htm

United States Senate Committee on Foreign Relations

This site is an excellent up-to-date resource for information about the United States' reaction to events regarding foreign policy.

http://www.senate.gov/~foreign/

Woodrow Wilson School of Public and International Affairs

This center of scholarship in public and international affairs, based at Princeton University, sponsors more than twenty research centers. Among its many links is the Princeton Center for Globalization and Governance, which explores the academic and policy dimensions of globalization and international governance.

http://www.wws.princeton.edu/mission/mission.html

American Diplomacy

American Diplomacy is an online journal of commentary, analysis, and research on U.S. foreign policy and its results around the world.

http://www.unc.edu/depts/diplomat/

Foreign Affairs

This page of the well-respected foreign policy journal *Foreign Affairs* is a valuable research tool. It allows users to search the journal's archives and provides Indexed access to the field's leading publications, documents, online resources, and so on. Link to dozens of other related Web sites from here too.

http://www.foreignaffairs.org

PART 4

America and the World

*A*t one time the United States could isolate itself from much of the world, and it did. That possibility disappeared long before the terrorist attack of September 11, 2001. Today America's unsurpassed wealth and military power mean that it cannot escape influencing and being influenced by world events. What are the advantages and risks of free trade for the American economy? To what extent should America rely on international bodies to help promote world peace and security? Does the world still need American leadership in these areas? What methods should America use in dealing with its enemies, and what moral limits should be in place? These are the kinds of issues that any serious student of American foreign policy must confront in the coming years.

- Is Free Trade Fair Trade?
- Does the War in Iraq Help the War Against Terrorism?
- Is the Use of Torture Against Terrorist Suspects Ever Justified?
- Does the United Nations Promote World Peace and Security?
- Must America Exercise World Leadership?

ISSUE 17

Is Free Trade Fair Trade?

YES: Douglas A. Irwin, from *Free Trade Under Fire* (Princeton University Press, 2002)

NO: David Morris, from "Free Trade: The Great Destroyer," in Jerry Mander and Edward Goldsmith, eds., *The Case Against the Global Economy: And for a Return to the Local* (Sierra Club Books, 1996)

ISSUE SUMMARY

YES: Professor of economics Douglas A. Irwin asserts that all countries benefit from free trade because it promotes efficiency, spurs production, and forces the least productive companies to reduce their output or shut down, resulting in better goods at lower prices.

NO: David Morris, vice president of the Institute for Local Self-Reliance, argues that free trade is unnecessary because gains in efficiency do not require large-scale multinational enterprises and that it is undesirable because it widens the standard-of-living gap between rich and poor nations.

An economic and cultural revolution like none before it has taken place over the past two decades. In centuries marked by Western imperialism, weak nations were ruled by powerful nations, and their raw and natural resources were expropriated for manufacture by the imperial powers. Now the owners are multinational corporations that know no national boundaries (although their principal owners are usually citizens of the industrial nations), and the manufacturing of the most highly sophisticated technological products takes place in the poorer nations, which achieve higher rates of employment, albeit for much lower wages than workers in the richer nations had earned.

This is globalization—a profound change in the ways in which large-scale business is conducted. Globalization is supported by technological breakthroughs, the new markets and profits that powerful corporations now pursue, and governments that subscribe to the changes it brings. For the underdeveloped nations, the advantages include training and employment for poor people and economic development support from international agencies. For the economically advanced nations, the advantages include cheaper manufactured goods and the profits that accrue to stockholders.

Globalization seems inescapable. Perhaps the most important and controversial characteristic of this change has been a movement toward free markets, or the removal of trade barriers and other constraints on doing business. Free trade is advocated because it fosters openness to new ideas and innovation, with a minimum degree of regulation, and, in the view of its supporters, it encourages the spread of democracy in societies that have not enjoyed political freedom.

Globalization and free trade are opposed by those who believe that the principal and perhaps only beneficiaries are the multinational corporations that sharply reduce their labor costs and even more sharply increase their profits. Opponents acknowledge that investors gain added value, but they maintain that highly skilled and well-paid workers in America and other advanced nations lose good jobs and that poorly paid workers in the underdeveloped countries are exploited. Furthermore, because the owners and most of the customers of industry do not live in the countries where the electronics, clothing, and other manufactured goods are produced, they have little or no concern for the consequences of their investments for those countries.

Thus, the critics charge, free trade is not fair trade. This protest comes from members of labor unions, who witness declining membership as their jobs are taken by workers in poor countries who will accept a fraction of the pay; environmentalists, who deplore deforestation, the pollution of rivers and the air by toxic chemicals, and other health hazards that accompany unregulated industry; and human rights groups, which oppose low wages that perpetuate poverty and exploitation. These groups organized the demonstrations at the 1999 World Trade Organization (WTO) ministerial meeting in Seattle, Washington, which have been repeated at subsequent meetings of the WTO and the World Bank.

The WTO denies that it advocates free trade at any cost. The organization maintains that countries must decide for themselves when, how, and how much to protect domestic producers from dumped or subsidized imports. However, agreements such as the North American Free Trade Agreement (NAFTA) permit foreign investors to sue a national government if their company's property assets, including the intangible property of expected profits, are damaged by that nation's laws, even if those laws were designed to protect the environment or public safety and health. Some advocates of free trade oppose NAFTA and other regional agreements on the grounds that they are preferential arrangements that compromise true free trade.

In the following selection, Douglas A. Irwin concludes that free trade is beneficial because countries that adopt it, improve their productivity and increase their per capita income. According to trade studies, says Irwin, the complete elimination of global barriers to trade brings gains to all nations. In the second selection, David Morris discusses the environmental harm and devastating effects in local communities that result from free trade.

YES

Douglas A. Irwin

The Case for Free Trade: Old Theories, New Evidence

For more than two centuries, economists have pointed out the benefits of free trade and the costs of trade restrictions. As Adam Smith argued more than two centuries ago, "All commerce that is carried on betwixt any two countries must necessarily be advantageous to both," and therefore "all duties, customs, and excise [on imports] should be abolished, and free commerce and liberty of exchange should be allowed with all nations." The economic case for free trade, however, is not based on outdated theories in musty old books. The classic insights into the nature of economic exchange between countries have been refined and updated over the years to retain their relevance to today's circumstances. More importantly, over the past decade economists have gathered extensive empirical evidence that contributes appreciably to our understanding of the free trade. This [selection] reviews the classic theories and examines the new evidence, noting as well the qualifications to the case for free trade.

Specialization and Trade

The traditional case for free trade is based on the gains from specialization and exchange. These gains are easily understood at the level of the individual. Most people do not produce for themselves even a fraction of the goods they consume. Rather, we earn an income by specializing in certain activities and then using our earnings to purchase various goods and services—food, clothing, shelter, health care—produced by others. In essence, we "export" the goods and services that we produce with our own labor and "import" the goods and services produced by others that we wish to consume. This division of labor enables us to increase our consumption beyond that which would be possible if we tried to be self-sufficient and produce everything for ourselves. Specialization allows us access to a greater variety and better quality of goods and services.

Trade between nations is simply the international extension of this division of labor. For example, the United States has specialized in the production of aircraft, industrial machinery, and agricultural commodities (particularly corn, soybeans, and wheat). In exchange for exports of these products, the United States purchases, among other things, imports of crude oil, clothing, and iron and steel mill products. Like individuals, countries benefit immensely from this division of labor and enjoy a higher real income than countries that forgo such trade. Just as there seems no obvious reason to limit the free exchange of goods within a country without a specific justification, there is no obvious reason why trade between countries should be limited in the absence of a compelling reason for doing so. . . .

Adam Smith, whose magnificent work *The Wealth of Nations* was first published in 1776, set out [the] case for free trade with a persuasive flair that still resonates today. Smith advocated the "obvious and simple system of natural liberty" in which individuals would be free to pursue their own interests, while the government provided the legal framework within which commerce would take place. With the government enforcing a system of justice and providing certain public goods (such as roads, in Smith's view), the private interests of individuals could be turned toward productive activities, namely, meeting the demands of the public as expressed in the marketplace. Smith envisioned a system that would give people the incentive to better themselves through economic activities, where they would create wealth by serving others through market exchange, rather than through political activities, where they might seek to redistribute existing wealth through, for example, legal restraints on competition. Under such a system, the powerful motivating force of self-interest could be channeled toward socially beneficial activities that would serve the general interest rather than socially unproductive activities that might advance the interests of a select few but would come at the expense of society as a whole.

Free trade is an important component of this system of economic liberty. Under a system of natural liberty in which domestic commerce is largely free from restraints on competition, though not necessarily free from government regulation, commerce would also be permitted to operate freely between countries. According to Smith, free trade would increase competition in the home market and curtail the power of domestic firms by checking their ability to exploit consumers through high prices and poor service. Moreover, the country would gain by exchanging exports of goods that are dear on the world market for imports of goods that are cheap on the world market. . . .

Comparative Advantage

In 1799, a successful London stockbroker named David Ricardo came across a copy of *The Wealth of Nations* while on vacation and quickly became engrossed in the book. Ricardo admired Smith's great achievement, but thought that many of the topics deserved further investigation. For example, Smith believed that a country would export goods that it produces most efficiently and import goods that other countries produce most efficiently. In this way, trade is a mutually beneficial way of increasing total world output and thus the consumption of every country. But, Ricardo asked, what if one country was the most efficient at producing everything? Would that country still benefit from trade? Would disadvantaged countries find themselves unable to export anything?

To overcome this problem, Ricardo arrived at a brilliant deduction that became known as the theory of comparative advantage. Comparative advantage implies that a country could find it advantageous to import some goods even if it could produce those same goods more efficiently than other countries. Conversely, a country would be able to export some goods even if other countries could produce them more efficiently. In either case, countries would be able to benefit from trade. Ricardo's conclusions about the benefits of trade were similar to Smith's, but his approach contains a deeper insight.

At first, the principle of comparative advantage seems counterintuitive. Why would a country ever import a good that it could produce more efficiently than another country? Yet comparative advantage is the key to understanding the pattern of international trade. For example, imagine a consulting firm hired to examine the factors explaining international trade in textiles. The consultants would probably start by examining the efficiency of textile production in various countries. If one country was found to be more efficient than another in producing textiles, the firm might conclude that this country would export textiles and other countries would import them. Yet because this single comparison is insufficient for determining the pattern of trade, this conclusion might well be wrong.

According to Ricardo and the other classical economists of the early nineteenth century, international trade is not driven by the *absolute* costs of production, but by the *opportunity* costs of production. The country most efficient at producing textiles might be even more efficient than other countries at producing other goods, such as shoes. In that case, the country would be best served by directing its labor to producing shoes, in which its margin of productive advantage is even greater than in textiles. As a result, despite its productivity advantage in textiles, the country would export shoes in exchange for imports of textiles. In the absence of other information, the absolute efficiency of one country's textile producers in comparison to another country's is insufficient to determine whether the country produces all of the textiles it consumes or imports some of them. . . .

The Gains From Trade

While the idea that all countries can benefit from international trade goes back to Smith and Ricardo, subsequent research has described the gains from trade in much greater detail. In the *Principles of Political Economy* (1848), John Stuart Mill, one of the leading economists of the nineteenth century, pointed to three principal gains from trade. First, there are what Mill called the "direct economical advantages of foreign trade." Second, there are "indirect effects" of trade, "which must be counted as benefits of a high order." Finally, Mill argued that the economical benefits of commerce are surpassed in importance by those of its effects which are intellectual and moral." What, specifically, are these three advantages of trade?

The "direct economical advantages" of trade are the standard gains that arise from specialization, as described by Smith and Ricardo. By exporting some of its domestically produced goods in exchange for imports, a country engages in mutually advantageous trade that enables it to use its limited productive resources (such as land, labor, and capital) more efficiently and therefore achieve a higher real national income than it could in the absence of trade. A higher real income translates into an ability to afford more of all goods and services than would be possible without trade.

These static gains from specialization are sizable. The classic illustration of the direct gains from trade comes from Japan's opening to the world economy. In 1858, as a result of American pressure, Japan opened its ports to international trade after decades of autarky (economic isolation). The gains from trade can be summarized by examining the prices of goods in Japan before and after the opening of trade. For example, the price of silk and tea was much higher on world markets than in Japan prior to the opening of trade, while the price of cotton and woolen goods was much lower on world markets. Japan therefore exported silk and tea in exchange for imports of clothing and other goods. With the introduction of trade, prices of those goods in Japan converged to the prices on the world market. Japan's terms of trade—the prices of the goods it exported relative to the prices of the goods it imported—improved by a factor of more than three and increased Japan's real income by as much as 65 percent.

Unlike nineteenth-century Japan, most countries have been open to some international trade for centuries, making it difficult to measure the overall gain from free trade. However, economists can estimate the gains from increased trade as a result of the reduction in trade barriers. Computable general equilibrium models, which are complex computational models used to simulate the impact of various trade policies on specific industries and the overall economy, calculate the gains that arise from shifting resources between various sectors of the economy. Specifically, these models examine the shift of labor and capital away from industries that compete against imports toward those in which the country has a comparative advantage as a result of changes in trade policy.

For example, one study showed that the agreements to reduce trade barriers reached under the Uruguay Round of multilateral trade negotiations in 1994 would result in an annual gain of $13 billion for the United States, about 0.2 percent of its GDP [gross domestic product], and about $96 billion in gains for the world, roughly 0.4 percent of world GDP. Another recent study suggests that the gains from further global liberalization are even larger. If a new trade round reduced the world's tariffs on agricultural and industrial goods and barriers on services trade by one third, the welfare gain for the United States would by $177 billion, or 1.95 percent of GDP. Most of this gain comes from liberalizing trade in services. The gain for the world amounts to $613 billion, or about 2 percent of world GDP.

As these examples indicate, the calculated welfare gains that emerge from these simulations are sometimes small as a percentage of GDP. Even some economists have interpreted these calculations to mean that trade liberalization is not especially valuable. But the small numbers arise partly because these agreements usually lead to modest policy changes for the United States. For example, what the United States undertook in signing the Uruguay Round or the North American Free Trade Agreement [NAFTA], essentially making already low import tariffs somewhat lower, cannot be compared to Japan's move from autarky to free trade. The numbers do not reflect the entire gains from trade, just the marginal gains from an additional increase in trade as a consequence of a partial reduction in trade barriers. A complete elimination of global barriers to trade in goods and services would bring much larger gains. According to the last study mentioned in the previous paragraph, removing all such barriers would generate $537 billion in gains for the United States (5.9 percent of GDP) and $1,857 billion in gains for the world (6.2 percent of world GDP).

More importantly, the reallocation of resources across industries as calculated in the simulation models does not take into account the other channels by which trade can improve economic performance. What are these other channels? One view is that greater openness to trade allows firms to sell in a potential larger market, and that firms are able to reduce their average costs of production by expanding the size of their output. The lower production costs resulting from these economies of scale are passed on to consumers and thereby generate additional gains from trade. In evaluating the impact of NAFTA through general equilibrium simulations, for example, moving from the assumption of constant returns to scale to increasing returns to scale boosted the calculated U.S. welfare gain from 1.67 percent of 2.55 percent of its GDP, Canadian welfare gain from 4.87 percent to 6.75 percent of its GDP, and Mexican welfare gain from 2.28 percent to 3.29 of its GDP, according to one study.

These numbers are more impressive, but there are also reasons to be skeptical. Evidence from both developed and developing economies suggests that economies of scale at the plant level for most manufacturing firms tend to be small relative to the size of the market. As a result, most plants have attained their minimum efficient scale. Average costs seem to be relatively unaffected by changes in output, so that a big increase in a firm's output does not lead to lower costs, and a big reduction in output does not lead to higher costs. For example, many firms are forced to reduce output as a result of competition from imports, but these firms' production costs rarely rise significantly. This suggests that the importance of scale economies may be overstated, and yet the simulation models sometimes include them.

There is much better, indeed overwhelming, evidence that free trade improves economic performance by increasing competition in the domestic market. This competition diminishes the market power of domestic firms and leads to a more efficient economic outcome. This benefit does not arise because foreign competition changes a domestic firm's costs through changes in the scale of output, as just noted. Rather, it comes through a change in the pricing behavior of imperfectly competitive domestic firms. Firms with market power tend to restrict output and raise prices, thereby harming consumers while increasing their own profits. With international competition, firms cannot get away with such conduct and are forced to behave more competitively. After Turkey's trade liberalization in the mid-1980s, for example, price-cost margins fell for most industries, consistent with a more competitive outcome. Numerous studies confirm this finding in other countries, providing powerful evidence that trade disciplines domestic firms with market power. Yet the beneficial effects of increasing competition are not always taken into account in simulation models because they frequently assume that perfect competition already exists. . . .

Productivity Gains

Trade improves economic performance not only by allocating a country's resources to their most efficient use, but by making those resources more productive in what they are doing. This is the second of John Stuart Mill's three gains from trade, the one he called "indirect effects." These indirect effects include "the tendency of every extension of the market to improve the processes of production. A country which produces for a larger market than its own can introduce a more extended division of labour, can make greater use of machinery, and is more likely to make inventions and improvements in the processes of production."

In other words, trade promotes productivity growth. The higher is an economy's productivity level, the higher is that country's standard of living. International trade contributes to productivity growth in at least two ways: it serves as a conduit for the transfer of foreign technologies that enhance productivity, and it increases competition in a way that stimulates industries to become more efficient and improve their productivity, often by forcing less productive firms out of business and allowing more productive firms to expand. After neglecting them for many decades, economists are finally beginning to study these productivity gains from trade more systematically.

The first channel, trade as a conduit for the transfer of foreign technologies, operates in several ways. One is through the importation of capital goods. Imported capital goods that embody technological advances can greatly enhance an economy's productivity. For example, the South Carolina textile magnate Roger Milliken (an active financier of anti-free-trade political groups) has bought textile machinery from Switzerland and Germany because domestically produced equipment is more costly and less sophisticated. This imported machinery has enabled his firms to increase productivity significantly. Between a quarter and half of growth in U.S. total factor productivity may be attributed to new technology embodied in capital equipment. To the extent that trade barriers raise the price of imported capital goods, countries are hindering their ability to benefit from technologies that could raise productivity. In fact, one study finds that about a quarter of the differences in productivity across countries can be attributed to differences in the price of capital equipment.

Advances in productivity are usually the result of investment in research and development, and the importation of foreign ideas can be a spur to productivity. Sometimes foreign research can be imported directly. For example, China has long been struggling against a devastating disease known as rice blast, which in the past destroyed millions of tons of rice a year, costing farmers billions of dollars. Recently, under the direction of an international team of scientists, farmers in China's Yunnan province started planting a mixture of two different types of rice in the same paddy. By this simple technique of biodiversity, farmers nearly eliminated rice blast and doubled their yield. Foreign R&D [research and development] enabled the Chinese farmers to increase yields of a staple commodity and to abandon the chemical fungicides they had previously used to fight the disease.

At other times, the benefits of foreign R&D are secured by importing goods that embody it. Countries more open to trade gain more from foreign R&D expenditures because trade in goods serves as a conduit for the spillovers of productive knowledge generated by that R&D. Several studies have found that a country's total factor productivity depends not only on its own R&D, but also on how much R&D is conducted in the countries that it trades with. Imports of specialized intermediate goods that embody new technologies, as well as reverse-engineering of such goods, are sources of R&D spillovers. Thus, developing countries, which do not conduct much R&D themselves, can benefit from R&D done elsewhere because trade makes the acquisition of new technology less costly. These examples illustrate Mill's observation that "whatever causes a greater quantity of anything to be produced in the same place, tends to the general increase of the productive powers of the world."

The second channel by which trade contributes to productivity is by forcing domestic industries to become more efficient. We have already seen that trade increases competition in the domestic market, diminishing the market power of any firm and forcing them to behave more competitively. Competition also stimulates firms to improve their efficiency; otherwise they risk going out of business. Over the past decade, study after study has documented this phenomenon. After the Côte d'Ivoire reformed its trade policies in 1985, overall productivity growth tripled, growing four times more rapidly in industries that became less sheltered from foreign competition. Industry productivity in Mexico increased significantly after its trade liberalization in 1985, especially in traded-goods sectors. Detailed studies of India's trade liberalization in 1991 and Korea's in the 1980s reached essentially the same conclusion: trade not only disciplines domestic firms and forces them to behave more like a competitive industry, but helps increase their productivity.

Competition can force individual firms to adopt more efficient production techniques. But international competition also affects the entry and exit decisions of firms in a way that helps raise the aggregate productivity of an industry. In any given industry, productivity is quite heterogeneous among firms: not all firms are equally efficient. Trade acts to promote high-productivity firms and demote low-productivity firms. On the export side, exposure to trade allows more productive firms to become experts and thereby expand their output. In the United States, plants with higher labor productivity within an industry tend to be the plants that export; in other words, more efficient firms are the ones that become exporters. The opportunity to trade, therefore, allows more efficient firms to grow.

On the import side, competition forces the least productive firms to reduce their output or shut down. For example, when Chile began opening up its economy to the world market in the 1970s, exiting plants were, on average, 8 percent less productive than plants that continued to produce. The productivity of plants in industries competing against imports grew 3 to 10 percent more than in non-traded-goods sectors. Protection had insulated less productive firms from foreign competition and allowed them to drag down overall productivity within an industry, whereas open trade weeded out inefficient firms and allowed more efficient firms to expand. Thus, trade brings about certain firm-level adjustments that increase average industry productivity in both export-oriented and import-competing industries.

The impact of the U.S.-Canada Free Trade Agreement on Canadian manufacturing is also suggestive. Tariff reductions helped boost labor productivity by a compounded rate of 0.6 percent per year in manufacturing as a whole and by 2.1 percent per year in the most affected (i.e., high tariff) industries. These are astoundingly large effects. This amounts to a 17 percent increase in productivity in the post-FTA period in the highly affected sectors, and a 5 percent increase for manufacturing overall. These productivity effects were not achieved through scale effects or capital investment, but rather due to a mix of plant turnover and rising technical efficiency within plants. By raising productivity, the FTA also helped increase the annual earnings of production workers, particularly in the most protected industries.

To sum up, traditional calculations of the gains from trade stress the benefits of shifting resources from protected industries to those with an international comparative advantage. But new evidence shows that, because large productivity differences exist between plants within any given industry, shifting resources between firms within an industry may be even more important. Trade may affect the allocation of resources among firms within an industry as much as, if not more than, it affects the allocation of resources among different industries. In doing so, trade helps improve productivity.

While difficult to quantify, these productivity effects of trade may be an order of magnitude more important than the standard gains. Countries that have embarked upon the course of trade liberalization over the past few decades, such as Chile, New Zealand, and Spain, have experienced more rapid grown in productivity than previously. Free trade contributes to a process by which a country can adopt better technology and exposes domestic industries to new competition that forces them to improve their productivity. As a consequence, trade helps raise per capita income and economic well-being more generally.

Free Trade: The Great Destroyer

Free trade is the religion of our age. With its heaven as the global economy, free trade comes complete with comprehensive analytical and philosophical underpinnings. Higher mathematics are used in stating its theorems. But in the final analysis, free trade is less an economic strategy than a moral doctrine. Although it pretends to be value-free, it is fundamentally value-driven. It assumes that the highest good is to shop. It assumes that mobility and change are synonymous with progress. The transport of capital, materials, goods, and people takes precedence over the autonomy, the sovereignty, and, indeed, the culture of local communities. Rather than promoting and sustaining the social relationships that create a vibrant community, the free trade theology relies on a narrow definition of efficiency to guide our conduct.

The Postulates of Free Trade

For most of us, after a generation of brain washing about its supposed benefits, the tenets of free trade appear almost self-evident:

- Competition spurs innovation, raises productivity, and lowers prices.
- The division of labor allows specialization, which raises productivity and lowers prices.
- The larger the production unit, the greater the division of labor and specialization, and thus the greater the benefits.

The adoration of bigness permeates all political persuasions. The Treasury Department proposes creating five to ten giant U.S. banks. "If we are going to be competitive in a globalized financial services world, we are going to have to change our views on the size of American institutions," it declares. The vice chair of Citicorp warns us against "preserving the heartwarming idea that 14,000 banks are wonderful for our country." The liberal *Harper's* magazine agrees: "True, farms have gotten bigger, as has nearly every other type of economic enterprise. They have done so in order to take advantage of the economies of scale offered by modern production techniques." Democratic presidential adviser Lester Thurow criticizes antitrust laws as an "old Democratic conception [that] is simply out of date." He argues that even IBM, with $50 billion in sales, is not big enough for the global marketplace. "Big companies do sometimes crush small companies,"

Thurow concedes, "but far better that small American companies be crushed by big American companies than that they be crushed by foreign companies." The magazine *In These Times,* which once called itself an independent socialist weekly, concluded, "Japanese steel companies have been able to outcompete American steel companies partly by building larger plants."

The infatuation with large-scale systems leads logically to the next postulate of free trade: the need for global markets. Anything that sets up barriers to ever-wider markets reduces the possibility of specialization and thus raises costs, making us less competitive.

The last pillar of free trade is the law of comparative advantage, which comes in two forms: absolute and relative. Absolute comparative advantage is easier to understand: Differences in climate and natural resources suggest that Guatemala should raise bananas and Minnesota should raise walleyed pike. Thus, by specializing in what they grow best, each region enjoys comparative advantage in that particular crop. Relative comparative advantage is a less intuitive, but ultimately more powerful concept. As the nineteenth-century British economist David Ricardo, the architect of free trade economics, explained: "Two men can both make shoes and hats and one is superior to the other in both employments; but in making hats he can only exceed his competitor by one-fifth or 20 percent, and in making shoes he can exceed him by one-third or 33 percent. Will it not be for the interest of both that the superior man should employ himself exclusively in making shoes and the inferior man in making hats?"

Thus, even if one community can make every product more efficiently than another, it should specialize only in those items it produces most efficiently, in relative terms, and trade for others. Each community, and ultimately each nation, should specialize in what it does best.

What are the implications of these tenets of free trade? That communities and nations abandon self-reliance and embrace dependence. That we abandon our capacity to produce many items and concentrate only on a few. That we import what we need and export what we produce.

Bigger is better. Competition is superior to cooperation. Material self-interest drives humanity. Dependence is better than independence. These are the pillars of free trade. In sum, we make a trade. We give up sovereignty over our affairs in return for a promise of more jobs, more goods, and a higher standard of living.

The economic arguments in favor of free trade are powerful. Yet for most of us it is not the soundness of its theory but the widely promoted idea that free trade is an inevitable development of our market system that makes us believers. We believe that economies, like natural organisms, evolve from the simple to the complex.

From the Dark Ages, to city-states, to nation-states, to the planetary economy, and, soon, to space manufacturing, history has systematically unfolded. Free trade supporters believe that trying to hold back economic evolution is like trying to hold back natural evolution. The suggestion that we choose another developmental path is viewed, at best, as an attempt to reverse history and, at worst, as an unnatural and even sinful act.

This kind of historical determinism has corollaries. We not only move from simple to complex economies. We move from integrated economies to segregated ones, separating the producer from the consumer, the farmer from the kitchen, the power plant from the appliance, the dump site from the garbage can, the banker from the depositor, and, inevitably, the government from the citizenry. In the process of development we separate authority and responsibility—those who make the decisions are not those who are affected by the decisions.

Just as *Homo sapiens* is nature's highest achievement, so the multinational and supranational corporation becomes our most highly evolved economic animal. The planetary economy demands planetary institutions. The nation-state itself begins to disappear, both as an object of our affection and identification and as a major actor in world affairs.

The planetary economy merges and submerges nations. Yoshitaka Sajima, vice president of Mitsui and Company, USA, asserts, "The U.S. and Japan are not just trading with each other anymore—they've become a part of each other." Lamar Alexander, former Republican Governor of Tennessee, agreed with Sajima's statement when he declared that the goal of his economic development strategy was "to get the Tennessee economy integrated with the Japanese economy."

In Europe, the Common Market has grown from six countries in the 1950s to ten in the 1970s to sixteen today, and barriers between these nations are rapidly being abolished. Increasingly, there are neither Italian nor French nor German companies, only European supracorporations. The U.S., Canadian, and Mexican governments formed NAFTA [North American Free Trade Agreement] to merge the countries of the North American continent economically.

Promotion of exports is now widely accepted as the foundation for a successful economic development program. Whether for a tiny country such as Singapore or a huge country such as the United States, exports are seen as essential to a nation's economic health.

Globalism commands our attention and our resources. Our principal task, we are told, is to nurture, extend, and manage emerging global systems. Trade talks are on the top of everybody's agenda, from Yeltsin to Clinton. Political leaders strive to devise stable systems for global financial markets and exchange rates. The best and the brightest of this generation use their ingenuity to establish the global financial and regulatory rules that will enable the greatest possible uninterrupted flow of resources among nations.

This emphasis on globalism rearranges our loyalties and loosens our neighborly ties. "The new order eschews loyalty to workers, products, corporate structure, businesses, factories, communities, even the nation," the *New York Times* announces. Martin S. Davis, chair of Gulf and Western, declares, "All such allegiances are viewed as expendable under the new rules. You cannot be emotionally bound to any particular asset."

We are now all assets.

Jettisoning loyalties isn't easy, but that is the price we believe we must pay to receive the benefits of the global village. Every community must achieve the lowest possible production cost, even when that means breaking whatever remains of its social contract and long-standing traditions.

The revised version of the American Dream is articulated by Stanley J. Mihelick, executive vice president for production at Goodyear: "Until we get real wage levels down much closer to those of the Brazils and Koreas, we cannot pass along productivity gains to wages and still be competitive."

Wage raises, environmental protection, national health insurance, and liability lawsuits—anything that raises the cost of production and makes a corporation less competitive—threatens our economy. We must abandon the good life to sustain the economy. We are in a global struggle for survival. We are hooked on free trade.

The Doctrine Falters

At this very moment in history, when the doctrines of free trade and globalism are so dominant, the absurdities of globalism are becoming more evident. Consider the case of the toothpick and the chopstick.

A few years ago I was eating at a Saint Paul, Minnesota, restaurant. After lunch, I picked up a toothpick wrapped in plastic. On the plastic was printed the word *Japan*. Japan has little wood and no oil; nevertheless, it has become efficient enough in our global economy to bring little pieces of wood and barrels of oil to Japan, wrap the one in the other and send the manufactured product to Minnesota. This toothpick may have traveled 50,000 miles. But never fear, we are now retaliating in kind. A Hibbing, Minnesota, factory now produces one billion disposable chopsticks a year for sale in Japan. In my mind's eye, I see two ships passing one another in the northern Pacific. One carries little pieces of Minnesota wood bound for Japan; the other carries little pieces of Japanese wood bound for Minnesota. Such is the logic of free trade.

Nowhere is the absurdity of free trade more evident than in the grim plight of the Third World. Developing nations were encouraged to borrow money to build an economic infrastructure in order to specialize in what they do best, (comparative advantage, once again) and thereby expand their export capacity. To repay the debts, Third World countries must increase their exports.

One result of these arrangements has been a dramatic shift in food production from internal consumption to export. Take the case of Brazil. Brazilian per capita production of basic foodstuffs (rice, black beans, manioc, and potatoes) fell 13 percent from 1977 to 1984. Per capita output of exportable food-stuffs (soybeans, oranges, cotton, peanuts, and tobacco) jumped 15 percent. Today, although some 50 percent of Brazil suffers malnutrition, one leading Brazilian agronomist still calls export promotion "a matter of national survival." In the global village, a nation survives by starving its people.

⌘

What about the purported benefits of free trade, such as higher standards of living?

It depends on whose standards of living are being considered. Inequality between and, in most cases, within countries has increased. Two centuries of trade has exacerbated disparaties in world living standards. According to economist Paul Bairoch, per capita GNP in 1750 was approximately the same in the developed countries as in the underdeveloped ones. In 1930, the ratio was about 4 to 1 in favor of the developed nations. Today it is 8 to 1.

Inequality is both a cause and an effect of globalism. Inequality within one country exacerbates globalism because it reduces the number of people with sufficient purchasing power; consequently, a producer must sell to wealthy people in many countries to achieve the scale of production necessary to produce goods at a relatively low cost. Inequality is an effect of globalism because export industries employ few workers, who earn disproportionately higher wages than their compatriots, and because developed countries tend to take out more capital from Third World countries than they invest in them.

Free trade was supposed to improve our standard of living. Yet even in the United States, the most developed of all nations, we find that living standards have been declining since 1980. More dramatically, according to several surveys, in 1988 U.S. workers worked almost half a day longer for lower real wages than they did in 1970. We who work in the United States have less leisure time in the 1990s than we had in the 1970s.

A New Way of Thinking

It is time to re-examine the validity of the doctrine of free trade and its creation, the planetary economy. To do so, we must begin by speaking of values. Human beings may be acquisitive and competitive, but we are also loving and cooperative. Several studies have found that the voluntary, unpaid economy may be as large and as productive as the paid economy. There is no question that we have converted more and more human relationships into commercial transactions, but there is a great deal of question as to whether this was a necessary or beneficial development.

We should not confuse change with progress. Bertrand Russell once described change as inevitable and progress as problematic. Change is scientific. Progress is ethical. We must decide which values we hold most dear and then design an economic system that reinforces those values.

Reassessing Free Trade's Assumptions

If price is to guide our buying, selling, and investing, then price should tell us something about efficiency. We might measure efficiency in terms of natural resources used in making products and the lack of waste produced in converting raw material into a consumer or industrial product. Traditionally, we have measured efficiency in human terms; that is, by measuring the amount of labor-hours spent in making a product.

But price is actually no measure of real efficiency. In fact, price is no reliable measure of anything. In the planetary economy, the prices of raw materials, labor, capital, transportation, and waste disposal are all heavily subsidized. For example, wage-rate inequities among comparably skilled work-forces can be as disparate as 30 to 1. This disparity overwhelms even the most productive worker. An American worker might produce twice as much per hour as a Mexican worker but is paid ten times as much.

In Taiwan, for example, strikes are illegal. In South Korea, unions cannot be organized without government permission. Many developing nations have no minimum wage, maximum hours, or environmental legislation. As economist Howard Wachtel notes, "Differences in product cost that are due to total-itarian political institutions or restrictions on economic rights reflect no natural or entrepreneurial advantage. Free trade has nothing to do with incomparable political economic institutions that protect individual rights in one country and deny them in another."

The price of goods in developed countries is also highly dependent on subsidies. For example, we in the United States decided early on that govern-ment should build the transportation systems of the country. The public, directly or indirectly, built our railroads, canals, ports, highways and airports.

Heavy trucks do not pay taxes sufficient to cover the damage they do to roads. California farmers buy water at as little as 5 percent of the going market rate; the other 95 percent is funded by huge direct subsidies to corporate farm-ers. In the United States, society as a whole picks up the costs of agricultural pollution. Having intervened in the production process in all these ways, we then discover it is cheaper to raise produce near the point of sale.

Prices don't provide accurate signals within nations; they are not the same as cost. *Price* is what an individual pays; cost is what the community as a whole pays. Most economic programs in the industrial world result in an enormous disparity between the price of a product or service to an individual and the cost of that same product or service to the society as a whole.

When a U.S. utility company wanted to send electricity across some-one's property, and that individual declined the honor, the private utility received governmental authority to seize the land needed. This is exactly what happened in western Minnesota in the late 1970s. Since larger power plants produced electricity more cheaply than smaller ones, it was therefore in the "public interest" to erect these power lines. If landowners' refusal to sell had been respected, the price of electricity would be higher today, but it would reflect the cost of that power more accurately.

Because the benefit of unrestricted air transportation takes precedence over any damage to public health and sanity, communities no longer have the authority to regulate flights and noise. As a consequence, airplanes awaken us or our children in the middle of the night. By one survey, some four million people in the United States suffer physical damage due to airport noise. If communities were given the authority to control noise levels by planes, as they already control noise levels from radios and motorcycles, the price of a plane ticket would increase significantly. Its price would be more aligned with its actual cost to society.

It is often hard to quantify social costs, but this doesn't mean they are insignificant. Remember urban renewal? In the 1950s and 1960s inner-city neighborhoods were leveled to assemble sufficient land area to rebuild our downtowns. Skyscrapers and shopping malls arose; the property tax base expanded; and we considered it a job well done. Later, sociologists, economists, and planners discovered that the seedy areas we destroyed were not fragmented, violence-prone slums but more often cohesive ethnic communities where generations had grown up and worked and where children went to school and played. If we were to put a dollar figure on the destruction of homes, the pain of broken lives, and the expense of relocation and re-creation of community life, we might find that the city as a whole actually lost money in the urban renewal process. If we had used a full-cost accounting system, we might never have undertaken urban renewal.

Our refusal to understand and count the social costs of certain kinds of development has caused suffering in rural and urban areas alike. In 1944, Walter Goldschmidt, working under contract with the Department of Agriculture [USDA], compared the economic and social characteristics of two rural California communities that were alike in all respects, except one. Dinuba was surrounded by family farms; Arvin by corporate farms. Goldschmidt found that Dinuba was more stable, had a higher standard of living, more small businesses, higher retail sales, better schools and other community facilities, and a higher degree of citizen participation in local affairs. The USDA invoked a clause in Goldschmidt's contract forbidding him to discuss his finding. The study was not made public for almost thirty years. Meanwhile, the USDA continued to promote research that rapidly transformed the Dinubas of our country into Arvins. The farm crisis we now suffer is a consequence of this process.

How should we deal with the price-versus-cost dilemma as a society? Ways do exist by which we can protect our life-style from encroachment by the global economy, achieve important social and economic goals, and pay about the same price for our goods and services. In some cases we might have to pay more, but we should remember that higher prices may be offset by the decline in overall costs. Consider the proposed Save the Family Farm legislation drafted by farmers and introduced in Congress several years ago by Iowa Senator Tom Harkin. It proposed that farmers limit production of farm goods nationwide at the same time as the nation establishes a minimum price for farm goods that is sufficient to cover operating and capital costs and provides farm families with an adequate living. The law's sponsors estimate that such a program would increase the retail cost of agricultural products by 3 to 5 percent, but the increase would be more than offset by dramatically reduced public tax expenditures spent on farm subsidies. And this doesn't take into consideration the cost benefits of a stable rural America: fewer people leaving farms that have been in their families for generations; less influx of jobless rural immigrants into already economically depressed urban areas; and fewer expenditures for medical bills, food stamps, and welfare.

Economists like to talk about externalities. The costs of job dislocation, rising family violence, community breakdown, environmental damage, and cultural collapse are all considered "external." External to what, one might ask?

The theory of comparative advantage itself is fast losing its credibility. Time was when technology spread slowly. Three hundred years ago in northern

Italy, stealing or disclosing the secrets of silk-spinning machinery was a crime punishable by death. At the beginning of the Industrial Revolution, Britain protected its supremacy in textile manufacturing by banning both the export of machines and the emigration of men who knew how to build and run them. A young British apprentice, Samuel Slater, brought the Industrial Revolution to the United States by memorizing the design of the spinning frame and migrating here in 1789.

Today, technology transfer is simple. According to Dataquest, a market research firm, it takes only three weeks after a new U.S.-made product is introduced before it is copied, manufactured, and shipped back to the U.S. from Asia. So much for comparative advantage.

The Efficiencies of Small Scale

This brings us to the issue of scale. There is no question that when I move production out of my basement and into a factory, the cost per item produced declines dramatically. But when the factory increases its output a hundredfold, production costs no longer decline proportionately. The vast majority of the cost decreases are captured at fairly modest production levels.

In agriculture, for example, the USDA studied the efficiency of farms and concluded, "Above about $40–50,000 in gross sales—the size that is at the bottom of the end of medium sized sales category—there are no greater efficiencies of scale." Another USDA report agreed: "Medium sized family farms are as efficient as the large farms."

Harvard Professor Joseph Bain's pioneering investigations in the 1950s found that plants far smaller than originally believed can be economically competitive. Further, it was found that the factory could be significantly reduced in size without requiring major price increases for its products. In other words, we might be able to produce shoes for a region rather than for a nation at about the same price per shoe. If we withdrew government subsidies to the transportation system, then locally produced and marketed shoes might actually be less expensive than those brought in from abroad.

Modern technology makes smaller production plants possible. For instance, traditional float glass plants produce 550 to 600 tons of glass daily, at an annual cost of $100 million. With only a $40 to 50 million investment, new miniplants can produce about 250 tons per day for a regional market at the same cost per ton as the large plants.

The advent of programmable machine tools may accelerate this tendency. In 1980, industrial engineers developed machine tools that could be programmed to reproduce a variety of shapes so that now a typical Japanese machine tool can make almost one hundred different parts from an individual block of material. What does this mean? Erich Bloch, director of the National Science Foundation, believes manufacturing "will be so flexible that it will be able to make the first copy of a product for little more than the cost of the thousandth." "So the ideal location for the factory of the future," says Patrick A. Toole, vice president for manufacturing at IBM, "is in the market where the products are consumed."

Conclusion

When we abandon our ability to produce for ourselves, when we separate authority from responsibility, when those affected by our decisions are not those who make the decisions, when the cost and the benefit of production or development processes are not part of the same equation, when price and cost are no longer in harmony, we jeopardize our security and our future.

You may argue that free trade is not the sole cause of all our ills. Agreed. But free trade as it is preached today nurtures and reinforces many of our worst problems. It is an ideological package that promotes ruinous policies. And, most tragically, as we move further down the road to giantism, globalism, and dependence, we make it harder and harder to back up and take another path. If we lose our skills, our productive base, our culture, our traditions, our natural resources; if we erode the bonds of personal and familial responsibility, it becomes ever more difficult to re-create community. It is very, very hard to put Humpty Dumpty back together again.

Which means we must act now. The unimpeded mobility of capital, labor, goods, and raw materials is not the highest social good. We need to challenge the postulates of free trade head on, to propose a different philosophy, to embrace a different strategy. There is another way. To make it the dominant way, we must change the rules; indeed, we must challenge our own behavior. And to do that requires not only that we challenge the emptiness of free trade but that we promote a new idea: economics as if community matters.

POSTSCRIPT

Is Free Trade Fair Trade?

In 2002, in order to overcome congressional objections based on the possible negative economic impact of foreign goods on particular districts, President George W. Bush imposed tariff barriers on steel imports to protect domestic manufacturers against cheaper or better imported steel. This is old-fashioned protectionism, the economic opposite of free trade. The president calculated that he could not get the trade power he sought without disarming some anti–free trade sentiment, so he made his concession to business owners, workers, and communities in which the steel industry is located. Underdeveloped nations, calling such concessions hypocritical, contend that they have more reasons to protect their weaker businesses but, unlike the United States, they are subject to the pressures of the international agencies that lend them invest-ment capital as well as of the multinational enterprises whose investment they want to get, keep, and enlarge.

Laissez-faire economics holds that if Asian countries can produce elec-tronic products better and less expensively than other nations, then those products will be sold throughout the world. Similarly, if the United States can produce movies that are more entertaining than those made elsewhere, then they will be seen throughout the world. According to Brink Lindsay, in *Against the Dead Hand: The Uncertain Struggle for Global Capitalism* (John Wiley, 2002), if these results have not yet followed in every economic area, it is because the economy has not yet gotten rid of state ownership, price con-trols, trade barriers, and other remnants of an earlier age. Protectionism has been discredited but it has not yet been banished, says Jagdish N. Bhagwati in *Free Trade Today* (Princeton University Press, 2002).

Critics of free trade argue that it is a deceptive term masking a conspir-acy by multinational corporations to expand their control over the global economy and, in so doing, undermine the safety, health, and environmental policies of nations while exploiting the impoverished peoples of third-world countries. One analysis presenting this view is in *The Race to the Bottom: Why a Worldwide Worker Surplus and Uncontrolled Free Trade are Sinking American Living Standards* by Alan Tonelson (Westview Press, 2002). In his quest for fair trade (as distinct from free trade), George Soros, one of the foremost American capitalist investors, advocates spending more money on global public goods and foreign aid in *Open Society: Reforming Global Capitalism* (Public Affairs, 2002).

The negotiation of new trade agreements and continuing criticism of the World Bank and the World Trade Organization make it clear that the issue remains unresolved. A global economy exists, what its impact will be on both industrially advanced and emerging economies has not been resolved.

ISSUE 18

Does the War in Iraq Help the War Against Terrorism?

YES: J. R. Dunn, from "Prospects of Terror," *The American Thinker* (March 21, 2006)

NO: Robert Jervis, from "Why the Bush Doctrine Cannot Be Sustained," *Political Science Quarterly* (Fall 2005)

ISSUE SUMMARY

YES: J. R. Dunn, a military editor and author, believes that the radical Islamists are losing the support of the Iraqi people, that Iraq is moving toward democracy, and that the war against terror is being won. In the same fashion, America and its allies will thwart Iran's quest for nuclear weapons.

NO: Robert Jervis, a professor of international relations, maintains that the war in Iraq distracted the United States from the war against terrorism, that preventive war risks grave errors of judgment, and that victory in Iraq will not necessarily result in more democracy or less terrorism.

On September 11, 2001, four commercial aircraft were hijacked after leaving New York and Boston airports on transcontinental flights. Two were directed into the World Trade Center, the two tallest buildings in New York City, one was directed into the Pentagon, the United States Defense Department headquarters in Washington, and a fourth crashed in a Pennsylvania field after passengers resisted the hijackers. All aboard the four planes and many of those in the struck buildings were killed. The continental United States had never suffered such a violent attack.

Since the end of the Gulf War in 1991, in which Iraq was driven out of Kuwait and United Nations forces defeated Iraq, Iraq was viewed as a potential breeding ground for terrorism directed against Western democracies, particularly the United States. Hostility toward Iraq was heightened by its failure to respond to United Nations' resolutions demanding an accounting of its weapons of mass destruction. Members of the administration of President Bush stated that there was a link between Saddam Hussein, the tyrannical head of the Iraqi government, and international terrorism, although fifteen of the nineteen hijackers came from Saudi Arabia and none from Iraq.

In 1998, the U.S. Congress appropriated funds to support a democratic opposition movement in Iraq. Later that year the United States and United Kingdom bombarded Iraq. In 2002, Congress authorized President George W. Bush to "use any means necessary" to "defend the national security of the United States against the continuing threat posed by Iraq." The success of the American invasion of Afghanistan, known to be the training ground for Al Qaeda, the Islamic radical group that had masterminded the attack of September 11, 2001 (now known simply as 9/11), inspired the invasion of Iraq on March 20, 2003 by the United States and Great Britain, which supplied 98 percent of the invading forces.

Smaller nations offered token forces, but France, Germany, Russia, and other major allies opposed the invasion. Despite the fact that Iraq had ignored United Nations' resolutions to reveal their weapons and weapons capacity, U.N. Secretary General Kofi Annan called the invasion "illegal." The military victory over the Iraqi armed forces was swift, but opposition by Iraqi insurgents to the American occupation, bolstered by the influx of anti-American terrorists, has not relented.

Saddam Hussein has been captured, free elections have been held, some terrorists have been killed or captured, and some vital services have been restored. But more than three years later, Osama bin Laden, the leader of Al Qaeda, is still at large, and no stockpiles of weapons of mass destruction have been found. In spring of 2006, after months of delay, a "unity government" was formed, but whether the actual unity of Sunnis, Shiites, and Kurds could be effected was by no means certain. The economy has not yet been restored and the military struggle continues, with two thousand Americans and an estimated tens of thousands of Iraqis among the fatalities.

President Bush maintains that Iraq can be reshaped as a democratic nation, that terrorism can be defeated, and that the two objectives are intimately intertwined. Foreign policy analysts and others who agree with the president believe that the democratization of Iraq will set an example in the Middle East, leading that troubled region to greater freedom and peaceful relations with other nations. Military historian J. R. Dunn states that America must take a long view, looking beyond temporary setbacks to recognize the inevitable defeat of the Islamic terrorists and the benefits this will bring to the United States and the free world.

Critics of the Bush administration, far from sharing this optimism, see the United States as having entered a morass from which it can extricate itself only at great cost. They believe that America's Iraqi policy has created wider distrust of government among citizens who feel deceived by government claims that have been disproved, as well as alienating public opinion among its natural allies. International relations professor Robert Jarvis is among those critics who believe that, far from combating terrorism, the invasion of Iraq resulted in the recruitment of more anti-American terrorists in Iraq and elsewhere.

YES

J. R. Dunn

Prospects of Terror

The first campaigns of the Long War are drawing to a close. The Jihadis have lost the opening rounds. What next?

There's an unconscious conviction that what happens next is . . . nothing. We go back to everyday life, the way things were before all that unpleasantness in lower Manhattan and Washington those long years ago. We shut out the harmful, hateful world once again, go our own way, and forget about jihads, and suicide belts, and dirty bombs, and beheadings, and all the other nightmares that have filled our days since 2001.

Unfortunately, that doesn't seem to be in the cards.

What happened on 9/11 was not an earthquake, over and done quickly, but a long, slow and complete reshuffling of the tectonic plates that comprise human civilization; something comparable to the deaths of empires and the passing of eras. Such events are not over in a day, or a year, or a decade. They take their time. And when it ends at last the world will be a different place, in ways that we now have no way of knowing. But the part we have played in it will, in some shape or form, match our position when it's all over, American or European or Arab, Muslim or Christian or Secular.

We are still amid early days, roughly the days of Midway and Guadalcanal and El Alamein in a previous great struggle. "Not the beginning of the end," as Churchill put it, "but the end of the beginning."

The Jihadis have lost Iraq and Afghanistan. It's true that fighting continues in both countries, but at this point it's effectively theater. It can't be repeated often enough that the type of war we are involved in is as much political as it is military. By any political measure, the Jihadis have been routed. Their only chance of prevailing was to appeal to the Iraqis and Afghans as a viable alternative to elected democratic governments. No such attempt was ever made. Instead, the Jihadis have relentlessly made the Iraqis and Afghans suffer. Their final chance in Iraq lay in derailing the political process last year. They failed at this, and now it is over. Not the violence—there will be car bombs going off in Iraq for years to come, unfortunately. But any opportunity of a Jihadi victory is gone.

(Skepticism on this point is understandable, considering the circumstances. Doubters are encouraged to read any of the myriad milblogs written by soldiers on the spot, or the recent reportage from Iraq by Victor Davis

Hanson and Ralph Peters. It's a sad comment on the nature of the times that anyone relying solely on the legacy media knows next to nothing of what's going on in Iraq, Afghanistan, or in truth most other areas of the world.)

The Islamists now have a choice of either changing or fading out the way the Anarchists did early in the last century. Like the Jihadis, the Anarchist followers of Bakunin and Galliani, no more than a vague memory today, were an international terror network bent on converting the world to their ideology. They had a good long run, set off a lot of bombs, and killed a lot of people, but they disappeared at last in the 1920s leaving behind only a legend far more romantic in tone that it deserves to be.

It's doubtful that the Jihadis will fade out yet, not after spending over twenty years organizing and laying the groundwork. They may be hurt, but they still have a punch. According to the Defense Department, at least eighteen distinct groups, active throughout the Islamic world, are currently operating under the Al-Queda umbrella. Organizing has been detected in Europe and elsewhere. Al-Queda has settled into Gaza (and probably the West Bank), and has been detected in Beirut. A lot of activity in a lot of places, in no way emblematic of a movement ready to give up.

But if the Jihadis want to continue, they'll need to adopt a strategy. Not modify the current one—they have never, up to this point, displayed the least signs of ever having one. Osama bin Laden's concept of action appears to have been to make his move, then sit back and wait for Allah to handle the rest. Allah has been disinclined to do any such thing. (In fact, if ObL actually believed that Allah's will is revealed in the course of events, he'd more than likely be devoting the rest of his days to prayer and repentance above all else.)

His followers and disciples have acted on the same principle, carrying out isolated actions in London, Madrid, or Bali, uncoordinated with each other and with a steadily decreasing effect. This randomness has been so striking as to lead some observers to postulate a deep and ornate plan beneath the surface irregularity. But after four years with no sign of such a thing, it's safe to say that a Jihadi uberplan does not exist.

This may change in the future. The intercepted letter from Ayman al-Zawahiri to Abu Musab al-Zarqawi suggests that deep thinking has been going on concerning the trend of Islamist fortunes. Many of the movement's wild men have been killed off by U.S. and Coalition action. The remainder will be more thoughtful, balanced, and cautious. Some will have had actual military training and experience. These last will be unwilling to take action only out of religious zeal, without a workable goal and a clear method of getting there—a strategy.

Actually, they would need three strategies, since their major targets—the Middle East, Europe, and the U.S.—differ so much as to require separate plans for each.

What follows is not a prediction, or advice, but something of the nature of what Einstein called a "thought experiment." An attempt to envision the strategies a Jihadi and his allies might choose for the Long War's next campaign, and what moves should be taken to counteract them.

I should mention here that you will find little concerning "4th Generation Warfare"—usually abbreviated to "4GW"—or "Asymmetrical Warfare."

Both have deteriorated into fads with more noise than content. 4GW has gotten a lot of mileage by claiming, on little evidence, that terrorism is something other than what it actually is. Asymmetrical Warfare addresses a real phenomenon but the term has in recent years been abused to the point of near meaninglessness.

The first campaign has been a complete, if not unqualified success for the West. But this war will continue for a long time, and to assure that the campaigns to come end the same way, we must be well prepared. Because the Islamists certainly will be.

> If you know the enemy and know yourself, you need not fear the result of a hundred battles. If you know yourself but not the enemy, for every victory gained you will suffer a defeat. If you know neither the enemy nor yourself, you will succumb in every battle.
>
> —Sun Tzu, *The Art of War*

The Iraq War has been a serious embarrassment for the Jihadis. They had two goals in Iraq: to hand the U.S. a Vietnam-style humiliation and to prevent the creation of a working government. They have failed at both.

The roots of this failure lie in the fact that terror is not a strategy. That, in a nutshell, is what went wrong with the Islamist effort in Iraq. If killing a lot of people in novel ways was a war-winning plan, the Jihadis would have prevailed. Fortunately, there's a little more to it.

Terror has its uses in the type of campaign being fought in Iraq. But it also has limitations, overlooked for many years, limitations that the Jihadi leadership, in particular Osama bin Laden and Abu Musab al-Zarqawi, have been slow to recognize.

Iraqi insurgents transferred the Palestinian Intifada model of random bombings intact to Iraq (Zarqawi himself is a Palestinian), evidently expecting similar results. But conditions in Iraq were not quite the same. Unlike helpless Israeli civilians, many of the targets in Iraq were able to shoot back, and the resulting losses to no effect forced a switch to the roadside bomb or IED, the Jihadi's single innovation.

The IED reduced Jihadi strategy to one of pure attrition. IEDs were effective at causing casualties but little else. They were not adaptable to any other role besides the booby trap, and despite occasional spectacular hits, were useless at maneuver, engaging the enemy, taking and holding territory, or anything else a military asset is expected to do. (Early attempts at ambushes and holding cities and neighborhoods were dropped after it became apparent that Jihadi forces could not stand up against conventional infantry.) Nor did the insurgents see anything wrong with this. They viewed warfare as a terror operation writ large. And there was no one, evidently, not even Saddam Hussein's ex-army officers, to tell them otherwise.

The Western media, as ignorant of military affairs as the Islamists, played a large role in Jihadi self-deception by covering each explosion as if it were Stalingrad in and of itself. By this time, the insurgents must know better. But it's too late to do anything about it. (The destruction of Samarra's Golden Mosque has all the qualities of a last-ditch desperation move, and may well turn out to be exactly that.) Dependence on the IED deprived the Jihadis of any opportunity of adapting their tactics to the actual situation.

Another drawback of relying on the Palestinian model involved the Jihadis' lack of a political goal. Ouster of the Israelis, by any means necessary, was a goal shared by virtually all Palestinians, creating a level of support that Zarqawi's gangs could only dream of. Al Fatah and Hamas could persuade anyone from fathers of young families to teenage schoolgirls to sacrifice themselves in suicide bombings. In contrast, the Baathists and Al-Queda were operating in an environment where support was a wasting asset, with each attack further eroding the trust of the populace. (Victor Davis Hanson points out that much of the "insurgent" violence occurring in Iraq actually originates with the 100,000 criminals released by Saddam Hussein just prior to his downfall. The fact that Zarqawi allowed Jihadi actions to become identified with criminal activity, to a point where no differentiation was possible, speaks volumes about Jihadi political judgment.)

What, precisely, could the Baathists and Al-Queda offer the Iraqi people? A return to Saddamist dictatorship, or a Taliban-style theocracy? The lack of a viable political program crippled the insurgency. Mao's theory of people's war, which formed the basis of every successful revolutionary movement of the late 20th century, emphasizes a struggle's political aspect over the military. A successful insurgency cultivates and holds on to popular support, as occurred in Algeria and Vietnam. Similar efforts were conspicuous in Iraq by their absence. (The Center for Combating Terrorism's report on Al-Queda states that since Zarqawi's aims were limited, he ". . . does not need to be as careful about whom [he] inflicts casualties upon." Clearly an error, in light of how the war has progressed.)

The U.S., on the other hand, was carrying out an exercise in grand strategy. What is the distinction between grand strategy and strategy *per se*? Grand strategy is the strategy of the long view, derived from national policy, involving a nation's long-term goals, its ideals, and its place in the world. As defined by B. H. Liddell-Hart, grand strategy involves

> the actual direction of military force, as distinct from the policy governing
> its employment, and combining it with other weapons: economic, political,
> psychological.

Grand strategy sets the goals; strategy fulfills them. Harry Truman was engaging in grand strategy with the Truman Doctrine, as was Ronald Reagan in his proactive campaign that finally defeated the USSR. George W. Bush's grand strategy for defeating terrorism is of the same order: to remake the region, replacing dictatorships with democracies in order to deprive terrorists of support—in Maoist terms, "drying up the water in which the insurgent fish swim."

It is a bold concept, as sweeping as anything that has occurred in the Middle East since the collapse of the Ottomans. Its execution will require years, if not decades—it's no accident that the administration has taken to calling the effort "the Long War."

This political goal set the agenda for the conduct of operations. The Coalition made few of the errors customary for a large army enmeshed in an insurgency—the mistakes of Vietnam were not repeated. Iraqis did not become "gooks"; their customs and culture remained respected. No free-fire zones were set up in the countryside. Apart from isolated imbecilities like Abu Ghraib, there was no brutality. Reprisals were avoided, as were deliberate attacks on civilians.

The Coalition displayed considerable adaptability once it became clear that insurgency was not simply gangs of stay-behinds but a broad and well-organized threat. Critics of the Coalition's performance in Iraq rarely mention that U.S. forces switched with no preparation or warning from a maneuver warfare campaign to a urban combat scenario (known by the unlovely acronym MOUT—Military Operations in Urbanized Terrain), and in truth one of the most difficult—battling an insurrection hiding among a friendly civilian population. The credit for this generally smooth transition goes to outstanding training and excellent commanders—the success of Gen. David Petraeus of the 101st Airborne in pacifying Mosul and that of Col. H. R. McMaster's 3rd Armored Combat Regiment in Tal Afar will be studied for years to come.

By locking himself into a strategy of attrition, Zarqawi enabled U.S. forces to vary their tactics in a search for what would work in the novel and complex Iraqi environment, an approach that might have been fatal against a nimbler opponent. Failed initiatives (e.g., the useless "Fallujah Brigade") were dropped, and the final strategy of "clear and hold," introduced in Fallujah in Novembe 2004, began to pay off in 2005 as the appearance of capable Iraqi troops enabled the Coalition to clean out the Euphrates corridor and its "ratlines" to Syria. The recent "sand berm" technique, in which isolated towns are surrounded by sand walls to prevent both infiltration and escape by Jihadi forces, is an fine example of adapting imaginative tactics to a novel environment.

The Jihadi response was an increase in bomb size and what the Germans call "*Schrecklicheit*" (frightfulness—literally, "shriekmaking"). The list of potential victims expanded to include children, hospital patients, and members of funeral processions. Men seeking to join the police or military became particular targets, and were murdered in batches of a hundred at a time.

As 2005 progressed, the operations of Al-Qaeda in Iraq took on a form chillingly suggestive of the "disorderly" phase of psychopathic breakdown, with killings occurring with no rhyme or reason, as if the sole purpose was to pile the bodies high. When Zarqawi's allies among the Sunnis began to distance themselves, he struck out at them as well, assassinating four respected sheiks in Anbar Province, his stronghold, along with others elsewhere, in the process triggering feuds that continue to this day. The bloody *walpurgisnacht* culminated in an inexplicable attack on three Jordanian hotels (one of which was hosting a wedding party), resulting in near-universal obloquy throughout the Middle East. Lost amid all the bloodshed was any sign of the strategy that many onlookers claimed to detect—an attempt to trigger a civil war between Sunni and Shi'ite factions.

Faced with a choice between men who killed children and men who built schools, the Iraqis made the rational decision. The triple votes—two elections and a constitutional referendum—comprising the Purple Revolution were carried out peacefully, on schedule, and with acceptable results. Territory and bases were turned over to the newly formed Iraqi military, and the police force, long the Achilles' heel of government efforts, began to come together. As 2006 opens, the Coalition's political program is achieving its goals, as revealed by the response to the Golden Mosque bombing, in which security forces stood firm and Sunnis, Shi'ites, and Kurds joined to halt a potential catastrophic break. (It's telling that even the thuggish Moqtada al-Sadr, whose militias were responsible for most of the killings that occurred, felt compelled to make overtures to his Sunni foes.) Recent reports tell of Sunni tribal fighters working with government troops to clean out the more troublesome provinces, which could well mean the end of Al-Queda in Iraq as a viable force. The Coalition effort has not been without errors and setbacks, but has been considerably more successful than critics are willing to grant.

Having failed in their two primary aims, the single Jihadi alternative is to roll back the Coalition program at any cost. What are their chances of bringing this off?

The Jihadis now face a serious dilemma. Their chosen weapon, the bomb, in its various manifestations, is losing effectiveness as Iraqi forces begin taking the lead. In short order, they'll be killing only Muslims, which is unacceptable to the Iraqi populace. (Recent polls among Iraqis reveal that up to 94% oppose attacks on Iraqi security forces while 97% oppose attacks on civilians. Oposition to attacks on foreigners is much lower.)

But fight on they must, or give up their dream of a new caliphate, of a return to a 'purified' Islam, of a world in which they are dominant. The Zawahiri letter touches gingerly on this problem. (How else would one reproach a man like Zarqawi?)

> "You know well," wrote Zawahiri, "that purity of faith and the correct way of living are not connected necessarily to success in the field unless you take into consideration the reasons and practices which events are guided by." The rest of Zawahiri's advice—some of which is excellent—can be summed up by the ancient saying that "tragedy in politics is when what is necessary is no longer possible."

So what possibilities are left? None open to the Jihadis acting on their own. Like guerillas, terrorists cannot prevail without intervention from an outside force. A coup or an invasion are the sole methods of destroying the budding Iraqi state (apart from the Iraqi's own errors). Both would require the cooperation of the Jihadis' local allies, and it's not at all certain that this would be forthcoming. The Baathist remnants almost certainly have a coup plan worked out and infiltrators in place within the government, army, and police, and Syria and Iran would both be eager to send troops across the border to rescue their lost Islamic brethren.

But Iraq will, for the foreseeable future, remain a protege of the United States, with a U.S. garrison maintained within the country's borders. Complete withdrawal is a fantasy—at least one base (and probably more) will remain, most likely in Kurdistan, with its America-loving population. Such a base would serve a large number of purposes that can't possibly be covered otherwise—air support and logistics, training of Iraqi forces, an intelligence window on Syria and Iran (and possibly a staging area for covert missions), and not the least, a barrier to prevent interference with the fledgling Iraqi state.

So the Jihadi problem may have no easy solution—which may explain why others in the region have been striking out on their own.

Two of the most surprising developments in the Middle East over the past year may well be responses to American success in Iraq.

The Iranian electoral system is one that fools a lot of people, almost all of whom are eager to claim that the election of Mahmoud Ahmadinejad "proves" something. In practice, a council of ayatollahs, answerable to no one, selects the candidates, using criteria known only to themselves. In Ahmadinejad's case, they went on to instruct local mullahs to order their flocks to vote for him. That may be an "election" in some sense of the term, but none that we recognize in this hemisphere.

The question remains as to why. The Iranian president is a figurehead, a mask for a theocratic despotism. Why go to such effort to elect a figurehead?

Iranian internal politics, the endless battles between "moderates" and "hard-liners," can't be ruled out. But we also can't overlook the Iranian view of international affairs. They have not forgotten the phrase "Axis of Evil," or the fact that Iran is number two on that list behind Saddam Hussein's Iraq. Everywhere they look, Kuwait, Dubai, Uzbekistan, Afghanistan, and Iraq, they find the U.S. military looking back. Under those circumstances, watching American forces at work in Axis Number One only a five-minute Tomahawk flight across the Persian Gulf must have been a sobering experience, particularly as Iraqi progress in 2005 began to free the most powerful land force in the world for potential duties elsewhere.

But the Iranians were also aware of the use to which Axis Number Three, North Korea (with which they had closely collaborated in the development of ballistic missiles), had put their nuclear weapons program. So they reached down into the country's political structure, plucked out the loudest, noisiest blusterer they could find (an ex-Revolutionary Guard and a "Twelver" to boot), one who could be depended on not to wilt under the spotlight, and threw him in front of the cameras.

It's interesting how closely the Iranian propaganda effort has matched that of North Korea's—the same stop and start activities with their nuclear programs, the same empty multinational negotiations, the same headline threats followed by back-door concessions. So far it has worked as well for Iran as it has for North Korea—Iran has become a problem, but, since the problem involves nuclear weapons, one that must be handled with caution.

Soviet premier Nikita Khrushchev did much the same thing in the 1950s, boasting that the Soviets were turning out nuclear-armed rockets "like sausages" and were simply blazing to fire some and see what they could do. This had results—it dampened any vague Western impulses toward aiding the Hungarian rebels in October 1956, and at the same time raised second thoughts concerning the Suez incursion.

It even had an effect on U.S. presidential politics, through the notorious "missile gap" that played a large role in the 1960 election.

But in the long run, it didn't work out well for the USSR—the U.S. response was a crash ICBM program, which succeeded in deploying over 1,000 missiles by the mid-60s. Something similar is likely for Iran. Ahmadinejad has succeeded in uniting not only the U.S. and Europe, but also, *mirabile dictu*, the UN. By any rational analysis, Iran is in a worse position than it held last year. But from the point of view of the Iranians, they have bought some time.

The other development is the Danish cartoon jihad. Despite inept mass media coverage, it's now widely understood that the scandal was a put-up job from first to last. But it's still unrecognized how broad-based the operation was. According to Amir Taheri, it involved the Arab League, the Muslim Brotherhood (the granddaddy of all Islamic terror organizations), the Islamic Liberation Party, the Movement of the Exiles, Al Jazeera, half a dozen Middle Eastern governments, and the Syrian and Iranian secret police. And the web may very well extend farther—Abu Laban, the Danish mullah who got the ball rolling, is an old associate of Ayman al Zawahiri.

This is an outlandishly large conspiracy for the sole purpose of embarrassing the mighty Danes. So the question arises once again: why? Why dig up a four-month-old provocation from a paper in Denmark, of all the innocuous places, and turn it into an international, umma-wide cause celebre? What got all these important figures involved? Why all the effort?

Taheri points out that the Syrians and Iranians had their reasons: Syria is under investigation for the Hariri assassination in Lebanon, while Denmark will be chairing the Security Council at the same time nuclear sanctions recommendations against Iran are making their way through the UN bureaucracy. But both were also late getting on the bandwagon. Iran originally dismissed Laban's troupe as Sunni pests, while Syria, these days, does nothing unless Iran moves first. Neither country got involved until the effort was well along.

A glance at the Middle Eastern timeline for late last year offers an explanation: what was the major event in the region between late September, when the cartoons first appeared to a universal yawn, and late January, when the mobs began howling? The answer: the December 15 parliamentary elections in Iraq, the keystone of U.S. efforts in the Middle East.

Clearly, the Danish cartoons are a pretext. Any other insult would have worked just as well. The actual target is the liberation of Iraq, and all that it portends for the region. The intended audience not the West, but the Muslim umma.

Viewed from that angle, it's no surprise that such heavy hitters became involved. American strategy embodies a threat to them all, Jihadis, religious throwbacks, and secular dictators alike. The advent of democracy marks the end of their way of doing business. What better method of forcing it back than to call on Muslim religious solidarity? Portraying the cartoons as an attack on Islam undercuts the attractions of democracy, drives an even wider wedge between Muslim states and the West, and characterizes the new Iraqi government as deluded servants of the Infidel, while the U.S. slips into its customary role as the Great Satan.

Several observers, among them Professor Sari Hanafi of American University in Beirut, concur, viewing the scandal as an attempt to limit the spread of democracy: ". . . you had regimes taking advantage saying, 'Look, this is the democracy they're talking about."

(The cartoon uproar scarcely registered in Iraq. The sole responses, some defiant talk from the minister of transport and a single demonstration in Baghdad, were instigated by Moqtadr al-Sadr, a man who would throw himself into a volcano if that would get him into the papers.)

There's an endless number of ways such campaigns can be played. More public scandals can be cooked up (or else pulled from the Western media—recall the Koran-in-the-toilet uproar, which may well have inspired Laban in the first place), each portraying democracy and the West at large as inveterate enemies of the Muslim umma, aided by the fact that Europe-based Muslims like Laban know exactly what buttons to push on both sides. The Iraqi insurrection can be characterized as a battle to save Iraqi Muslims from a depraved, secular West, with the Jihadis taking the role of defenders of Islam.

The sole drawbacks are that such campaigns are obviously a sign of Muslim weakness, not strength. It's also doubtful how far they can be taken—there's no such thing as keeping a population at constant fever pitch. Eventually the effort will reach a point of diminishing returns.

But these examples do suggest that the struggle in the Middle East has mutated, with the Islamists and their allies—the Arab nationalists and the old regimes—adapting a new strategy: the struggle to halt reform in the Middle East is no longer, for the moment, a military effort, but a political one.

A political attack requires a political response. Not that military efforts can be dropped—not while the Jihadis remain active in Iraq and the Iranians still present a threat. But the major effort for the near future will occur on the political plane. As for countermoves, three approaches suggest themselves.

The first is a more effective method of fighting public convulsions of the cartoon intifada type. The cartoon tempest was essentially a conspiracy involving individuals, NGOs, and governments. All of them can be targeted in one way or another, to clarify the point that any repetition will have a price. A first step would be the immediate expulsion of Abu Laban, who at last report was still roaming around Copenhagen. News comes today that Denmark has arrested Fadi Abdullatif for threatening the government for distributing a leaflet urging Muslims to "eliminate" rulers that prevent them from joining the Iraq insurgency.

Also advisable would be the defunding of Yusuf al Qaradawi, the popular mullah (he has his own show on Al Jazeera) who signed the fatwa against Denmark, and whose branch of the Muslim Brotherhood is financed by none other than the EU. (I have racked my brains for some rational explanation for this, and have come up with nothing.)

Above all, the response must be consistent. This was not a conspiracy against Denmark, but against the West and all its values. The only way to face such provocations is with a united front. European attitudes toward such matters—the mixture of frivolity, fatalism, and avarice that has marked all their recent dealings with the Middle East—must in particular be brought up short. This may in fact be occurring in response to events.

The second approach should be engagement of Middle Eastern governments and ruling classes to persuade them that democracy is coming, that it cannot be stopped, and that it is not a threat. Apart from the mullahs, these people are the major roadblock to serious reform. They view democracy with deep suspicion, and with some reason. The shabby fate of the Hindu nobility, who willingly gave up their ancestral holdings to the Indian government only to have the promised subsidies cut off a few years later, must always be before their eyes. But other examples do exist: buried in the uproar elsewhere in the Gulf is the fact that Bahrain became a constitutional monarchy in February 2002, thanks to a wise decision by King Hamad. Some people are prepared to take the step. On the other hand, Iranian ex-president Mohamed Khatami's recent call for democracy should be viewed with caution—it's doubtful that he means the same as we do in the West. (This is also true of the results of the Palestinian election, taken by many observers as evidence that the Bush strategy is empty. There is simply no rational way that a contest between two murderous terror organizations can be considered a "democratic election.")

The recently-released *Quadrennial Defense Review* envisions a second stage in the war against terror involving active undercutting of AQAM's (al-Qaeda and Affiliated Movements, the military term) appeal to the Muslim populace. Condeleezza Rice's "transformational diplomacy," in which crucial assets of the U.S. Foreign Service will be shifted to the Middle East from Europe, is aimed at implementing a democratic program. But it can't simply be left to the Defense and State Departments. (I keep trying to picture Joseph C. Wilson IV carrying out the assignment, but the image simply won't gel.) Such a campaign of influence and persuasion seems tailor-made for NGOs and trade associations in business, the sciences, and the arts and entertainment. It's dismaying to consider how few of this country's resources have actually been brought to bear against the terrorist threat. Many people would be willing to act but lack necessary direction. Some effort must be made to provide this.

The third and most difficult task involves getting through to the Muslim masses. To read the Middle Eastern media is an exercise in despair. Absolutely nothing of the Western or American case gets through. The Muslim worldview is a sad morass of conspiracy theories, ethnic and religious hatreds, and paranoia. (Only a handful of exceptions exist—the Saudi *Arab News* and the *Beirut Daily Star* among them.)

Last year's roadshow led by Karen Hughes was supposed to help correct this, but went nowhere. Which doesn't mean that it should not be reattempted, with more in the way of resources and imagination. There are plenty of successful, happy, and well-integrated American Muslims. We need to recruit from among them to speak to people of their own backgrounds about the America that they themselves know. More sophisticated approaches can be worked out by bringing together Western figures familiar with the culture and politics of the Middle East, such as Mansoor Ijaz, Salim Mansur, Amir Taheri, Fouad Ajami, Ayaan Hirsi Ali, Wafa Sultan, and for that matter, Bernard Lewis and David Pryce-Jones. The U.S. has a lot to tell the people of the Muslim world. Some, at least, will listen. Every one who does is one less supporter of jihad.

A political solution is necessary to secure the military victories already won. This strategy will require patience, understanding, and willingness to overcome setbacks. Things are going to happen that we do not like. There will be disappointments and failures. These are not products of policy, but aspects of the human condition. None of them will be any reason to turn back or abandon the effort. Errors can [be] corrected, failures can be overcome. And it should never be forgotten that, in the words of Churchill, the ongoing liberation of the Middle East remains "one of the great unsordid acts of history."

As it stands, there is little likelihood that the Jihadis will turn back U.S. gains. Al-Qaeda and it allies are paying the price of a flawed strategy. The Jihadis went into this war convinced that terror would carry all before it—a thesis disproven for all time. There is no practical action they can take to recover. (They might begin by replacing Zarqawi, but who would volunteer to bell that cat?) A nuclear-armed Iran would open new vistas, but that's the very reason, among many others, that Iran will not be allowed to procure them in the first place. The Iranian situation is an example of the type that Curtis LeMay used to dismiss with the words, "No alternative, so no problem."

Paradoxically, the Jihadi field of action is more constricted in their own backyard, the Middle East, than elsewhere. Iraq has been a trap for the Islamist cause, costing them well over 50,000 casualties and prisoners. It's difficult to conceive a set of circumstances where it will ever be anything else. The Jihadis, and their allies, are always going to be in a position where resistance will cost them more than they're able to pay. And that's the way you want a war to go.

And besides, there are better targets elsewhere.

Robert Jervis

 **NO**

Why the Bush Doctrine Cannot Be Sustained

With the reelection of George W. Bush, the apparent progress of democracy in Iraq and other countries in the Middle East, and the agreement of allies that Iran and North Korea should not be permitted to gain nuclear weapons, the prospects for what can be called the Bush Doctrine seem bright. I believe this impression is misleading, however, and politics within the United States and abroad is more likely to conspire against the course that Bush has set.

The Bush Doctrine, set out in numerous speeches by the President and other high-level officials and summarized in the September 2002 "National Security Strategy of the United States," consists of four elements. First and perhaps most importantly, democracies are inherently peaceful and have common interests in building a benign international environment that is congenial to American interests and ideals. This means that the current era is one of great opportunity because there is almost universal agreement on the virtues of democracy. Second, this is also a time of great threat from terrorists, especially when linked to tyrannical regimes and weapons of mass destruction (WMD). A third major element of the Bush Doctrine is that deterrence and even defense are not fully adequate to deal with these dangers and so the United States must be prepared to take preventive actions, including war, if need be. In part because it is difficult to get consensus on such actions, and in part because the United States is so much stronger than its allies, the United States must be prepared to act unilaterally. Thus the fourth element of the Doctrine is that although the widest possible support should be sought, others cannot have a veto on American action. . . .

The Bush Doctrine combines a war on terrorism with the strong assertion of American hegemony. Although elements arguably reinforced each other in the overthrow of the Taliban, it is far from clear that this will be the case in the future. Rooting out terrorist cells throughout the world calls for excellent information, and this requires the cooperation of intelligence services in many countries. American power allows it to deploy major incentives to induce cooperation, but there may come a point at which opposition to U.S. dominance will hamper joint efforts. The basic unilateralism of the U.S. behavior that goes with assertive hegemony as exemplified by the war in Iraq has strained the alliance bonds in a way that can make fighting terrorism more difficult.

Iraq highlights a related tension in the Bush Doctrine. The administration argued that overthrowing Saddam Hussein was a part of the war on terrorism because of the danger that he would give WMD to terrorists. Bush calls Iraq the "the central front" in the counterterrorist effort, and he rhetorically asks, "If America were not fighting terrorists in Iraq, . . . what would these thousands of killers do, suddenly begin leading productive lives of service and charity?"

I join many observers in finding this line of argument implausible and in believing that the war was, at best, a distraction from the struggle against al Qaeda. To start with, diplomatic, military, and intelligence resources that could have been used to seek out terrorists, especially in Afghanistan, were redeployed against Iraq. In perhaps an extreme case, in June of 2002, the White House vetoed a plan to attack a leading terrorist and his poison laboratory in northern Iraq because it might have disturbed the efforts to build a domestic and international coalition to change the regime, and Abu Musab al-Zarqawi later emerged as the most important insurgent in Iraq and second only to Osama bin Laden on the overall most-wanted list. More generally, thanks to the war, the United States is now seen as a major threat to peace, and in many countries, George Bush is more disliked than bin Laden. Of course, foreign policy is not a popularity contest, but these views eventually will be reflected in reduced support for and cooperation with the United States. Finally and most importantly, if the United States is fighting terrorists in Iraq, the main reason is not that they have flocked to that country to try to kill Americans but that the occupation has recruited large numbers of people to the terrorist cause. Although evidence, let alone proof, is of course elusive, it is hard to avoid the inference that the war has created more terrorists than it has killed, has weakened the resolve of others to combat them, and has increased the chance of major attacks against the West.

Even without the stimulus of the American occupation of Iraq, the highly assertive American policy around the world may increase the probability that it will be the target of terrorist attacks, inasmuch as others attribute most of the world's ills to America. Whether terrorists seek vengeance, publicity, or specific changes in policy, the dominant state is likely to be the one they seek to attack. American power, then, produces American vulnerability. If the United States wanted to place priority on reducing its attractiveness as a target for terrorism, it could seek a reduced role in world politics. The real limits to what could be done here should not disguise the tension between protection from terror and hegemony.

The Bush Doctrine argues that combatting terrorism and limiting proliferation go hand in hand. They obviously do in some cases. The danger that a rogue state could provide terrorists with WMD, although implausible in the case of Iraq, is not fictitious, and controlling the spread of nuclear weapons and nuclear material contributes to American security. But this does not mean that there are no trade-offs between nonproliferation and rooting out terrorism. Most obviously, Iraq's drain on American military resources, time and energy, and on the support from the international community means that the ability to deal with Iran and North Korea has been reduced. These two countries figured prominently in administration fears before September 11 and are more dangerous and perhaps more likely to provide weapons to terrorists than was Iraq. But the way the Bush administration interpreted the war on terror has hindered its ability to deal with these threats, and, in an added irony, if Iran gets nuclear weapons, the United States may be forced to provide a security guarantee for Iraq or permit that country to develop its own arsenal. Furthermore, even if better conceived, combating terrorism can call for alliances with regimes that seek or even spread nuclear weapons. The obvious example is Pakistan, a vital American ally that has been the greatest facilitator of proliferation. The United States eventually uncovered A. Q. Kahn's network and forced President Pervez Musharraf to cooperate in rolling it up, but it might have moved more quickly and strongly had it not needed Pakistan's support against al Qaeda. This compromise is not likely to be the last, and the need to choose between these goals will continue to erode the Bush Doctrine's coherence.

Despite its *realpolitik* stress on the importance of force, the Bush Doctrine also rests on idealistic foundations—the claim for the centrality of universal values represented by America, the expected power of positive example, the belief in the possibility of progress. What is important is that these have power through their acceptance by others, not through their imposition by American might. They require that others change not only their behavior but their outlook, if not their values, as well. For this to happen, the United States has to be seen as well-motivated and exemplifying shared ideals. America's success in the Cold War derived in part from its openness to allied voices, its articulation of a common vision, and a sense of common interest. Although we should not idealize this past or underestimate the degree to which allies, let alone neutrals, distrusted U.S. power and motives, neither should we neglect the ways that enabled influence to be exercised relatively cheaply and allowed the West to gain a much greater degree of unity and cooperation than many contemporary observers had believed possible.

Then, as now, the United States needed not only joint understandings but also multilateral institutions to provide for cooperation on a wide range of issues, especially economic ones. Perhaps the United States can ignore or diminish them in the security area without affecting those such as the World Trade Organization (WTO) on which it wants to continue to rely, but the possibility of undesired spillovers is not to be dismissed. If others do not expect the United States to respect limits that rules might place on it, they are less apt to see it as a trustworthy partner.

Just as the means employed by the Bush Doctrine contradict its ends, so also the latter, by being so ambitious, invite failure. Not only is it extremely unlikely that terror can ever be eradicated, let alone the world be rid of evil, but the fact that Saddam lost the war in Iraq does not mean that the United States won it. Ousting his regime was less important in itself than as a means to other objectives: reducing terrorism, bringing democracy to Iraq, transforming the Middle East, and establishing the correctness and the legitimacy of the Bush Doctrine. Although the effects of the invasion have not yet fully played out, it is hard to see it as a success in these terms. Indeed, despite the fact that the January 2005 elections in Iraq were relatively successful, the political outlook for the country is not good. Ironically, the dramatic and disabling insurgency has distracted American if not Iraqi attention from what is probably the even less-tractable problem of establishing a political settlement among those who have not (yet) resorted to arms. Overly ambitious goals invite not only defeat, but disillusion; if the experiment in Iraq does not yield satisfactory results, it will be hard to sustain support for the Doctrine in the future.

Finally, the Bush Doctrine is vulnerable because although it rests on the ability to deploy massive force, its army, despite being capable of great military feats, is not large enough to simultaneously garrison a major country and attack another adversary, and may not even be sufficient for the former task over a prolonged period. Thanks to the occupation of Iraq, the United States could not now use ground force against Iran or North Korea, and, indeed, the occupation appears to be gravely damaging the system of a volunteer-army, reserves, and national guard that has proven so successful since the draft was abolished more than a quarter-century ago. . . .

Public opinion, the structure of the U.S. government, and domestic politics make it difficult to sustain the Bush Doctrine or any other clear policy. "It seems that the United States was a very difficult country to govern," Charles de Gaulle is said to have told British Prime Minister Harold Macmillan when explaining why it was hard to count on the United States. The General was correct: democracies, and especially the United States, do not find it easy to sustain a clear line of policy when the external environment is not compelling. Domestic priorities ordinarily loom large, and few Americans think of their country as having an imperial mission. Wilsonianism may provide a temporary substitute for the older European ideologies of a *mission civilisatrice* and "the white man's burden," but because it rests on the assumption that its role will be not only noble but also popular, I am skeptical that it will endure if it meets much opposition from those who are supposed to benefit from it. . . .

At first glance, it would seem that much as the experts criticize the Bush Doctrine for its unilateralism, on this score, at least, it rests on secure domestic foundations. The line that drew the most applause in the President's 2004 State of the Union address was: "America will never seek a permission slip to defend the security of our country." In fact, the public is, sensibly, ambivalent. Although few would argue that the lack of international support should stop the United States from acting when a failure to do so would endanger the country, polls taken in the run-up to the war in Iraq indicated that international endorsement would have added as much as 20 percentage points to support for attacking. Even in a country with a strong tradition of unilateralism, people realize that international support translates into a reduced burden on the United States and increased legitimacy that can both aid the specific endeavor at hand and strengthen the patterns of cooperation that serve American interests. Furthermore, many people take endorsement by allies as an indication that the American policy is sensible. This is a great deal of the reason why Tony Blair's support for Bush was so important domestically, and this means that the Bush Doctrine is particularly vulnerable to British defection.

In summary, although the combination of Bush's preferences and the attack of September 11 have produced a coherent doctrine, domestic support is likely to erode. Congress will become increasingly assertive as the war continues, especially if it does not go well; the Democrats, although lacking a consistent policy of their own, have not accepted the validity of Bush's strategy; and although the public is united in its desire to oppose terrorism, the way to do so is disputed. The United States remains a very difficult country to govern.

It is particularly difficult for the Bush Doctrine to maintain public support, because preventive wars require more-accurate assessment of the international environment than intelligence can provide. The basic idea of nipping threats in the bud, of acting when there is still time, implies a willingness to accept false positives in order to avoid more-costly false negatives. That is, the United States must act on the basis of far from complete information, because if it hesitates until the threat is entirely clear, it will be too late: it cannot afford to wait until the smoking gun is a mushroom cloud, to use the phrase the administration favored before the Iraq war. In principle, this is quite reasonable. The costs of a WMD attack are so high that a preventive war could be rational even if retrospect were to reveal that it was not actually necessary.

Even if this approach is intellectually defensible, however, it is not likely to succeed politically. The very nature of a preventive war means that the evidence is ambiguous and the supporting arguments are subject to rebuttal. If Britain and France had gone to war with Germany before 1939, large segments of the public would have believed that the war was not necessary. If the war had gone well, public opinion might still have questioned its wisdom; had it gone badly, the public would have been inclined to sue for peace. At least as much today, the cost of a war that is believed to be unnecessary will be high in terms of both international and domestic opinion and will sap the support for the policy. (Indeed, in the case of Iraq, the administration chose not to admit that the war was not forced on it despite the clear evidence that the central claims used to justify it were incorrect.) Even if the public does not judge that the administration should be turned out of power for its mistake, it is not likely to want the adventure to be repeated.

Preventive war, then, asks a great deal of intelligence. It does not bode well for the Bush Doctrine that not only did the war in Iraq involve a massive intelligence failure concerning WMD (which is different from saying that it was caused by this failure), but also the United States started the war two days ahead of schedule because agents incorrectly claimed to know the whereabouts of Saddam Hussein and his sons. The amazing accuracy of the munitions that destroyed the location only underlined the falsity of the information.

The case for preventive war against Iraq turned on the claim that it had active WMD programs, and so, in retrospect, the question is often posed as to whether the intelligence was faulty or whether the Bush administration distorted it. I think the former was dominant but the latter should not be ignored. . . .

Despite the fact that the United States has more room to maneuver now that it does not have to worry about a new regime allying with a major enemy state, there appears to be a great deal of continuity between the U.S. policy during the Cold War, what it did in the first decade after it, and Bush's actions. While the United States hopes to replace hostile dictatorships with democracies, only rarely does it push for democracy when doing so could destabilize friendly regimes. It would be tiresome to recount the sorry but perhaps sensible history of U.S. policies toward Egypt, Pakistan, and Saudi Arabia, and I will just note that when the latter arrested reformers who had called for a constitutional monarchy and independent human rights monitoring, Colin Powell said that "each nation has to find its own path and follow that path at its own speed." Over the past year, Bush and his colleagues have taken a somewhat stronger position, but the depth of the American commitment still remains unclear.

Ironically, the war on terrorism, although accompanied by greater stress on the value of democracy, has increased the costs of acting accordingly by increasing the American need for allies throughout the globe. Without the war, the United States might have put more pressure on the nondemocratic states of the former Soviet Union, or at least not supported them. But the need for bases in Central Asia has led the United States to embrace a particularly unsavory set of regimes. The pressure to democratize Pakistan is similarly minimal, in part because of the fear that greater responsiveness to public opinion would lead to an unacceptable Islamic regime. This danger, and that of any kind of instability, is magnified because of Pakistan's nuclear arsenal. Although Egypt lacks nuclear weapons, instability in such a powerful and centrally placed country is also greatly to be feared. In other parts of the Middle East and areas such as the Caspian basin, it is the need for a secure flow of oil that leads the United States to support nondemocratic regimes. . . .

Furthermore, the Bush administration appears to be driven more by the politics of the regimes it is dealing with than by an abstract commitment to democracy, as is shown by its stance toward if not its role in the opposition (constitutional or otherwise) to, Hugo Chavez in Venezuela and Jean-Bertrand Aristide in Haiti. In a continuation of the Cold War pattern, leftist governments are seen as dangerous and authoritarian regimes of the right are acceptable. On other occasions, it is the specific policies of a leader that make him unacceptable despite his popular approval. The American refusal to treat Yasser Arafat as the Palestinians' leader was rooted in the belief that he was unwilling to stop terrorism, not in his inability to win an election, and the United States withdrew its recognition of President Rauf Denktash in Turkish Cyprus when he opposed proposals for reunifying the island.

But even vigorous support for democracy might not produce that outcome. The fate of Iraq may not yet be determined, and, at this writing, anything appears to be possible, from a partially democratic regime to a civil war to the return of a national strongman to the loss of national unity. But it is hard to believe that the foreseeable future will see a full-fledged democracy, with extensive rule of law, open competition, a free press, and checks and balances. The best that can be hoped for would be a sort of semi-democracy, such as we see in Russia or Nigeria, to take two quite different countries.

The Bush administration's position is much more optimistic, however, arguing that for democracy to flourish, all that is needed is for repression to be struck down. With a bit of support, all countries can become democratic; far from being the product of unusually propitious circumstances, a free and pluralist system is the "natural order" that will prevail unless something special intervenes. President Bush devoted a full speech to this subject, saying: "Time after time, observers have questioned whether this country, or that people, or this group, are 'ready' for democracy—as if freedom were a prize you win for meeting our own Western standards of progress. In fact, the daily work of democracy is itself the path of progress." This means that for him, the prospects for Iraq are bright. In his view, although it is true that you cannot force people to be democratic, this is not necessary. All that is needed is to allow people to be democratic.

We would all like this vision to be true, but it probably is not. Even if there are no conditions that are literally necessary for the establishment of democracy, this form of government is not equally likely to flourish under all conditions. Poverty, deep divisions, the fusion of secular and religious authority, militaristic traditions and institutions, and a paucity of attractive careers for defeated politicians all inhibit democracy. Although Bush is at least partly right in arguing that some of these conditions arise out of authoritarian regimes, they are causes as well and there is no reason to expect the United States to be able to make most countries democratic even if it were to bend all its efforts to this end. Indeed, movements for reform and democracy may suffer if they are seen as excessively beholden to the United States. As Colin Powell noted after one American attempt of this type had to be abandoned in the face of cries of U.S. bullying, "I think we are now getting a better understanding with the Arab nations that it has to be something that comes from them. If you don't want us to help, you don't want us to help."

Is it even true that the world would be safer and the United States better off if many more countries were democratic? The best-established claim that democracies rarely, if ever, fight each other is not entirely secure, and the more sophisticated versions of this theory stress that joint democracy will not necessarily produce peace unless other factors, especially economic interdependence and a commitment to human rights, are present as well. This makes sense, because democracy is compatible with irreconcilable conflicts of interest. Furthermore, even if well-established democracies do not fight each other, states that are undergoing transitions to democracy do not appear to be similarly pacifistic. Putting these problems aside, there is no reason to expect democracies to be able to get along well with nondemocracies, which means that establishing democracy in Iraq or in any other country will not make the world more peaceful unless its neighbors are similarly transformed.

The Bush administration has also argued that other countries are much more likely to support American foreign policy objectives if they are democratic. The basic point that democracies limit the power of rulers has much to be said for it, but it is far from clear how far this will translate into shared foreign policy goals. After all, at bottom, democracy means that a state's policy will at least roughly reflect the objectives and values of the population, and there is no reason to believe that these should be compatible between one country and another. Why would a democratic Iraq share American views on the Arab–Israeli dispute, for example? Would a democratic Iran be a closer ally than the Shah's regime was? If Pakistan were truly democratic, would it oppose Islamic terrorism? In many cases, if other countries become more responsive to public opinion, they will become more anti-American. In the key Arab states of Jordan, Egypt, and Saudi Arabia, cooperation with the United States could not be sustained if the public had greater influence; the elections in Pakistan in September of 2002 reduced the regime's stability and complicated the efforts to combat al Qaeda, results that would have been magnified had the elections been truly free; in Europe, the public is even more critical of the United States than are the leaders. . . .

Turning to what is already clear from events since September 11, the Bush Doctrine and the war in Iraq have weakened Western unity and called into question the potency of deterrence by claiming that the United States could not have contained a nuclear-armed Saddam. I think this belief was incorrect, but because deterrence rests on potential challengers' understanding that the defender is confident of its deterrent threats, the American demonstration of its lack of faith in this instrument will diminish its utility. Even if future administrations adopt a different stance and affirm the role of deterrence, some damage may be permanent.

The largely unilateral overthrow of Saddam has set in motion even more important irreversible changes in relations with allies. Before Bush came to power, the emerging consensus was that the United States was committed to multilateralism. This is not to say that it would never act without the consent of its leading allies, but that on major issues, it would consult fully, listen carefully, and give significant weight to allied views. International institutions, deeply ingrained habits, the sense of shared values and interests, close connections at the bureaucratic levels, public support for this way of proceeding, and the understanding that long-run cooperation was possible only if the allies had faith that the United States would not exploit its superior power position all led to a structure that inhibited American unilateralism. This partial world order, it was argued, served American interests as well as those of its partners, because it induced the latter to cooperate with each other and with the United States, reduced needless frictions, and laid the foundations for prosperity and joint measures to solve common problems. This way of doing business had such deep roots that it could absorb exogenous shocks and the election of new leaders.

Recent events have shown that although the argument may have been correct normatively, it was not correct empirically. It is quite possibly true that it would have been wise for the United States to have continued on the multilateral path, to have maintained a broad coalition, and to have given its allies more influence over the way it fought terrorism. But we can now see that it was wrong to conclude that the international system and U.S. policy had evolved to a point that compelled this approach.

This does not mean that the United States is now firmly set on a new course. Indeed, I do not think that the Bush Doctrine can be sustained. Bush's domestic support rests on the belief that he is making the United States safer, not on an endorsement of a wider transformationist agenda. Especially in the absence of a clear political victory in Iraq, support for assertive hegemony is limited at best. But if Bush is forced to retract, he will not revert to the sort of coalitionbuilding that Clinton favored. Of course there will be a new president elected in 2008, but even if he or she wanted to pick up where Clinton left off, this will not be possible. Although allies would meet the United States more than halfway in their relief that policy had changed, they would realize that the permanence of the new American policy could not be guaranteed. The familiar role of anarchy in limiting the ability of states to bind themselves has been highlighted by Bush's behavior and will not be forgotten.

The United States and others, then, face a difficult task. The collapse of the Bush foreign policy will not leave clear ground on which to build: new policies and forms of cooperation will have to be jury-rigged above the rubble of the recent past. The Bush administration having asserted the right (and the duty) to maintain order and provide what it believes to be collective goods, an American retraction will be greeted with initial relief by many, but it is also likely to produce disorder, unpredictability, and opportunities for others.

Machiavelli famously asked whether it is better to be feared or to be loved. The problem for the United States is that it is likely to be neither. Bush's unilateralism and perceived bellicosity have weakened ties to allies, dissipated much of the sympathy that the United States had garnered after September 11, and convinced many people that America was seeking an empire with little room for their interests or values. It will be very hard for any future administration to regain the territory that has been lost. At best, the policy is a gigantic gamble that a stable and decent regime can be established in Iraq and that this can produce reform in the other countries and a settlement between Israel and the Palestinians. In this case, the United States might gain much more support and approval, if not love. But anything less will leave the United States looking neither strong nor benign, and we may find that the only thing worse than a successful hegemon is a failed one. We are headed for a difficult world, one that is not likely to fit any of our ideologies or simple theories.

POSTSCRIPT

Does the War in Iraq Help the War Against Terrorism?

Whether the prosecution of the war in Iraq helps to defeat the war against terrorism or results in an increase in terrorist activity is bound to be a critical question—perhaps the decisive question—in the presidential election of 2008. Some of the almost-certain themes in that election are sounded in the preceding selections by J. R. Dunn and Robert Jervis.

Two of the most prominent essayists supporting the war in Iraq and the war on terror are William Kristol, editor of *The Weekly Standard,* and Robert Kagan, senior associate at the Carnegie Endowment for International Peace. Separately and together, they have written many books and articles dealing with America's role in the world. In a book they co-edited, *Present Dangers: Crisis and Opportunity in America's Foreign and Defense Policy* (Encounter Books, 2000), Kristol and Kagan call for a foreign policy of "benevolent hegemony" in order to secure peace and advance American ideals throughout the world. In their essay in that volume, "National Interest and Global Responsibility," they maintain that it would be dangerous and less congenial to democracy and liberty to share world dominance with other nations.

Norman Podhoretz, editor of *Commentary,* in which other defenses of the Bush doctrine have appeared, has written "The Panic Over Iraq," (*Commentary,* January 2006), in which he provides support for both the invasion of Iraq and the war on terror. James Fallows deplores what he called "Bush's Lost Year," *The Atlantic Monthly,* October 2004, because the president did not reconstruct Afghanistan, did not deal with the threats posed by North Korea and Iran, and did not wage an effective war on terror.

William Blum has compiled his harshly critical essays in *Freeing the World to Death: Essays on the American Empire* (Common Courage Press, 2005). Blum maintains that the United States vastly understates the resistance of ordinary Iraqi citizens who are not terrorists, but oppose being invaded, bombed, occupied, and humiliated by an invading power. We are losing the war on terror, according to Daniel Benjamin and Steven Simon, both former staff members of the National Security Council. In their book, *The Next Attack: The Failure of the War on Terror and a Strategy for Getting It Right* (Henry Holt, 2005), they argue that the invasion of Iraq radicalized large numbers of Iraqis and other Muslims. On the contrary, Richard A. Falkenrath asserts in "Grading the War on Terrorism," in *Foreign Affairs,* January/February 2006, Iraq has been more of a burial ground than a breeding ground for Islamic terrorists.

Richard A. Clarke, who was the National Security Council's antiterrorism chief under Presidents Clinton and Bush, wrote *Against All Enemies: Inside*

America's War on Terror (Free Press, 2004), in which he charges that he could not persuade National Security Advisor Condoleezza Rice to schedule meetings to plan how to deal with Al Qaeda and that President Bush himself urged Clarke to find a relationship between Iraq and the 9/11 attack on the United States.

The Council on Foreign Relations has published a transcript of a 2005 debate on *The Law of War in the War on Terrorism: A Council on Foreign Relations Debate*. The participants were University of California, Berkeley law professor John Yoo, defending the Bush administration's anti-terror policy, and Human Right Watch executive director Kenneth Roth, opposing that policy.

ISSUE 19

Is the Use of Torture Against Terrorist Suspects Ever Justified?

YES: Charles Krauthammer, from "The Truth About Torture," *The Weekly Standard* (December 5, 2005)

NO: Andrew Sullivan, from "The Abolition of Torture," *New Republic* (December 19, 2005)

ISSUE SUMMARY

YES: Charles Krauthammer argues that the legal protections for prisoners of war and civilians do not apply to terrorist suspects captured abroad, and in certain extreme cases torture may be used to extract information from them.

NO: Andrew Sullivan contends that any nation that uses torture infects itself with the virus of totalitarianism, belies its claim of moral superiority to the terrorists, and damages its chances of persuading the Arab world to adopt Western-style democracy.

Under Saddam Hussein, Iraq's former dictator, Abu Ghraib prison was a place where tens of thousands were routinely subjected to torture and execution. After the fall of the dictatorship following the invasion of Iraq, it was turned into a U.S. military prison. In December 2003, after hearing complaints about the treatment of prisoners at Abu Ghraib, the Army launched a major investigation. At its conclusion in February, 2004, the chief investigator's confidential report—later leaked to journalists—charged that numerous instances of "sadistic, blatant, and wanton criminal abuses" had occurred at Abu Ghraib. A few months later, photographs taken by some of those engaged in the abuses began circulating through the Internet, and some were shown on CBS's "60 Minutes." Soon the pictures were repeatedly shown throughout worldwide media. They have become iconic representations of abuse and oppression by Americans who were sent to liberate a country from abuse and oppression.

The Army and the Defense Department attributed these abuses largely to criminal behavior by a few low-level G.I.s and dereliction of duty by the officers in charge. Nevertheless, critics charge that constant demands by officials in the Defense Department and the C.I.A. for fresh information set the stage for the abuses, and the aggressive interrogating procedures used by the Army at Guantanamo Bay, Cuba, set an example that needed only a slight degree of amplification to become full-fledged torture.

What is torture? The 1994 U.N. Convention Against Torture, of which the United States is a signatory, defines it as "any act by which severe pain, whether physical or mental, is intentionally inflicted" to gain information. But since people have different thresholds of pain, it is hard to get the subjectivity out of this definition. The 1949 Geneva Conventions (also signed by the United States) require prisoners to be "treated humanely" and outlaw acts such as "violence to life and person," "mutilation, cruel treatment," and "outrages upon personal dignity." But the Geneva Conventions were meant to apply to uniformed soldiers captured in war and noncombatant civilians; whether they should be extended to suspected terrorists remains in dispute.

Shortly after 9/11 a team of Justice Department lawyers sought to formulate an unambiguous definition of "torture," but their attempt stirred controversy when it was publicized. To constitute "torture," they wrote, an act "must inflict pain that is difficult to endure"; it must be "equivalent in intensity to the pain accompanying serious physical injury, such as organ failure, impairment of bodily functions, or even death." Once this "torture memo," as some of its critics called it, came to light, the Bush administration distanced itself from it. Through various spokesmen, including the President himself, the administration has repeatedly condemned the use of torture. "Torture anywhere is an affront to human dignity anywhere," Bush stated in 2003. "Freedom from torture is an inalienable human right." Yet some critics contend that the administration has permitted and even facilitated practices that have culminated in torture, citing in particular the policy of "rendition," in which terrorist suspects apprehended in Western Europe are sent to other countries for interrogation. The policy of rendition began in the mid-1990s, during the Clinton administration, but since 9/11, according to some reports, it has come into more frequent use. A probe by a committee of the European Parliament has not found any human rights violations, and the Bush administration has neither confirmed nor denied the policy of rendition. The facts behind the rendition controversy thus remain murky. At some point, probably, the full truth will emerge, but uncovering it may require a few more drafts of history.

Whatever the validity of the charges, the larger question haunting Americans in the present era is not an empirical but a moral one: Are there *any* circumstances in which it could be morally permissible to apply pain or other extreme measures to prisoners in order to extract information from them? The immediate, almost reflexive answer of decent people is "no, never." But what of circumstances, say, in which an Al Qaeda prisoner knows that a nuclear device will soon go off somewhere in Manhattan but refuses to say where? The "ticking time bomb" has become the classic defense of torture, and in the following selections columnist and commentator Charles Krauthammer elaborates upon it. Opposing him is Andrew Sullivan, also a columnist and commentator, who argues against the legitimacy of torture even in extreme circumstances.

YES

Charles Krauthammer

The Truth about Torture

During the last few weeks in Washington the pieties about torture have lain so thick in the air that it has been impossible to have a reasoned discussion. The McCain amendment that would ban "cruel, inhuman, or degrading" treatment of any prisoner by any agent of the United States sailed through the Senate by a vote of 90–9. The Washington establishment remains stunned that nine such retrograde, morally inert persons—let alone senators—could be found in this noble capital.

Now, John McCain has great moral authority on this issue, having heroically borne torture at the hands of the North Vietnamese. McCain has made fine arguments in defense of his position. And McCain is acting out of the deep and honorable conviction that what he is proposing is not only right but is in the best interest of the United States. His position deserves respect. But that does not mean, as seems to be the assumption in Washington today, that a critical analysis of his "no torture, ever" policy is beyond the pale.

Let's begin with a few analytic distinctions. For the purpose of torture and prisoner maltreatment, there are three kinds of war prisoners: First, there is the ordinary soldier caught on the field of battle. There is no question that he is entitled to humane treatment. Indeed, we have no right to disturb a hair on his head. His detention has but a single purpose: to keep him *hors de combat*. The proof of that proposition is that if there were a better way to keep him off the battlefield that did not require his detention, we would let him go. Indeed, during one year of the Civil War, the two sides did try an alternative. They mutually "paroled" captured enemy soldiers, i.e., released them to return home on the pledge that they would not take up arms again. (The experiment failed for a foreseeable reason: cheating. Grant found that some paroled Confederates had reenlisted.)

Because the only purpose of detention in these circumstances is to prevent the prisoner from becoming a combatant again, he is entitled to all the protections and dignity of an ordinary domestic prisoner—indeed, more privileges, because, unlike the domestic prisoner, he has committed no crime. He merely had the misfortune to enlist on the other side of a legitimate war. He is therefore entitled to many of the privileges enjoyed by an ordinary citizen—the right to send correspondence, to engage in athletic activity and intellectual pursuits, to receive allowances from relatives—except, of course, for the freedom to leave the prison.

Second, there is the captured terrorist. A terrorist is by profession, indeed by definition, an unlawful combatant: He lives outside the laws of war because he does not wear a uniform, he hides among civilians, and he deliberately targets innocents. He is entitled to no protections whatsoever. People seem to think that the postwar Geneva Conventions were written only to protect detainees. In fact, their deeper purpose was to provide a deterrent to the kind of barbaric treatment of civilians that had become so horribly apparent during the first half of the 20th century, and in particular, during the Second World War. The idea was to deter the abuse of civilians by promising combatants who treated noncombatants well that they themselves would be treated according to a code of dignity if captured—and, crucially, that they would be denied the protections of that code if they broke the laws of war and abused civilians themselves.

Breaking the laws of war and abusing civilians are what, to understate the matter vastly, terrorists do for a living. They are entitled, therefore, to nothing. Anyone who blows up a car bomb in a market deserves to spend the rest of his life roasting on a spit over an open fire. But we don't do that because we do not descend to the level of our enemy. We don't do that because, unlike him, we are civilized. Even though terrorists are entitled to no humane treatment, we give it to them because it is in our nature as a moral and humane people. And when on rare occasions we fail to do that, as has occurred in several of the fronts of the war on terror, we are duly disgraced.

The norm, however, is how the majority of prisoners at Guantanamo have been treated. We give them three meals a day, superior medical care, and provision to pray five times a day. Our scrupulousness extends even to providing them with their own Korans, which is the only reason alleged abuses of the Koran at Guantanamo ever became an issue. That we should have provided those who kill innocents in the name of Islam with precisely the document that inspires their barbarism is a sign of the absurd lengths to which we often go in extending undeserved humanity to terrorist prisoners.

Third, there is the terrorist with information. Here the issue of torture gets complicated and the easy pieties don't so easily apply. Let's take the textbook case. Ethics 101: A terrorist has planted a nuclear bomb in New York City. It will go off in one hour. A million people will die. You capture the terrorist. He knows where it is. He's not talking.

Question: If you have the slightest belief that hanging this man by his thumbs will get you the information to save a million people, are you permitted to do it? Now, on most issues regarding torture, I confess tentativeness and uncertainty. But on this issue, there can be no uncertainty: Not only is it permissible to hang this miscreant by his thumbs. It is a moral duty. Yes, you say, but that's an extreme and very hypothetical case. Well, not as hypothetical as you think. Sure, the (nuclear) scale is hypothetical, but in the age of the car-and suicide-bomber, terrorists are often captured who have just set a car bomb to go off or sent a suicide bomber out to a coffee shop, and you only have minutes to find out where the attack is to take place. This "hypothetical" is common enough that the Israelis have a term for precisely that situation: the ticking time bomb problem.

And even if the example I gave were entirely hypothetical, the conclusion—yes, in this case even torture is permissible—is telling because it establishes the principle: Torture is not always impermissible. However rare the cases, there are circumstances in which, by any rational moral calculus, torture not only would be permissible but would be required (to acquire life-saving information). And once you've established the principle, to paraphrase George Bernard Shaw, all that's left to haggle about is the price. In the case of torture, that means that the argument is not *whether* torture is ever permissible, but *when*—i.e., under what obviously stringent circumstances: how big, how imminent, how preventable the ticking time bomb. That is why the McCain amendment, which by mandating "torture never" refuses even to recognize the legitimacy of any moral calculus, cannot be right. There must be exceptions. The real argument should be over what constitutes a legitimate exception.

Let's take an example that is far from hypothetical. You capture Khalid Sheikh Mohammed in Pakistan. He not only has already killed innocents, he is deeply involved in the planning for the present and future killing of innocents. He not only was the architect of the 9/11 attack that killed nearly three thousand people in one day, most of them dying a terrible, agonizing, indeed tortured death. But as the top al Qaeda planner and logistical expert he also knows a lot about terror attacks to come. He knows plans, identities, contacts, materials, cell locations, safe houses, cased targets, etc. What do you do with him?

We have recently learned that since 9/11 the United States has maintained a series of "black sites" around the world, secret detention centers where presumably high-level terrorists like Khalid Sheikh Mohammed have been imprisoned. The world is scandalized. Black sites? Secret detention? Jimmy Carter calls this "a profound and radical change in the . . . moral values of our country." The Council of Europe demands an investigation, calling the claims "extremely worrying." Its human rights commissioner declares "such practices" to constitute "a serious human rights violation, and further proof of the crisis of values" that has engulfed the war on terror. The gnashing of teeth and rending of garments has been considerable.

I myself have not gnashed a single tooth. My garments remain entirely unrent. Indeed, I feel reassured. It would be a gross dereliction of duty for any government *not* to keep Khalid Sheikh Mohammed isolated, disoriented, alone, despairing, cold and sleepless, in some godforsaken hidden location in order to find out what he knew about plans for future mass murder. What are we supposed to do? Give him a nice cell in a warm Manhattan prison, complete with Miranda rights, a mellifluent lawyer, and his own website? Are not those the kinds of courtesies we extended to the 1993 World Trade Center bombers, then congratulated ourselves on how we "brought to justice" those responsible for an attack that barely failed to kill tens of thousands of Americans, only to discover a decade later that we had accomplished nothing—indeed, that some of the disclosures at the trial had helped Osama bin Laden avoid U.S. surveillance?

Have we learned nothing from 9/11? Are we prepared to go back with complete amnesia to the domestic-crime model of dealing with terrorists, which allowed us to sleepwalk through the nineties while al Qaeda incubated and grew and metastasized unmolested until on 9/11 it finished what the first World Trade Center bombers had begun?

Let's assume (and hope) that Khalid Sheikh Mohammed has been kept in one of these black sites, say, a cell somewhere in Romania, held entirely incommunicado and subjected to the kind of "coercive interrogation" that I described above. McCain has been going around praising the Israelis as the model of how to deal with terrorism and prevent terrorist attacks. He does so because in 1999 the Israeli Supreme Court outlawed all torture in the course of interrogation. But in reality, the Israeli case is far more complicated. And the complications reflect precisely the dilemmas regarding all coercive interrogation, the weighing of the lesser of two evils: the undeniable inhumanity of torture versus the abdication of the duty to protect the victims of a potentially preventable mass murder.

In a summary of Israel's policies, Glenn Frankel of the *Washington Post* noted that the 1999 Supreme Court ruling struck down secret guidelines established 12 years earlier that allowed interrogators to use the kind of physical and psychological pressure I described in imagining how KSM might be treated in America's "black sites."

"But after the second Palestinian uprising broke out a year later, and especially after a devastating series of suicide bombings of passenger buses, cafes and other civilian targets," writes Frankel, citing human rights lawyers and detainees, "Israel's internal security service, known as the Shin Bet or the Shabak, returned to physical coercion as a standard practice." Not only do the techniques used "command widespread support from the Israeli public," but "Israeli prime ministers and justice ministers with a variety of political views," including the most conciliatory and liberal, have defended these techniques "as a last resort in preventing terrorist attacks."

Which makes McCain's position on torture incoherent. If this kind of coercive interrogation were imposed on any inmate in the American prison system, it would immediately be declared cruel and unusual, and outlawed. How can he oppose these practices, which the Israelis use, and yet hold up Israel as a model for dealing with terrorists? Or does he countenance this kind of interrogation in extreme circumstances—in which case, what is left of his categorical opposition to inhuman treatment of any kind?

But let us push further into even more unpleasant territory, the territory that lies beyond mere coercive interrogation and beyond McCain's self-contradictions. How far are we willing to go? This "going beyond" need not be cinematic and ghoulish. (Jay Leno once suggested "duct tape" for Khalid Sheikh Mohammed.) Consider, for example, injection with sodium pentathol. (Colloquially known as "truth serum," it is nothing of the sort. It is a barbiturate whose purpose is to sedate. Its effects are much like that of alcohol: disinhibiting the higher brain centers to make someone more likely to disclose information or thoughts that might otherwise be guarded.) Forcible sedation is a clear violation of bodily integrity. In a civilian context it would be considered assault. It is certainly impermissible under any prohibition of cruel, inhuman, or degrading treatment.

Let's posit that during the interrogation of Khalid Sheikh Mohammed, perhaps early on, we got intelligence about an imminent al Qaeda attack. And we had a very good reason to believe he knew about it. And if we knew what he knew, we could stop it. If we thought we could glean a critical piece of information by use of sodium pentathol, would we be permitted to do so?

Less hypothetically, there is waterboarding, a terrifying and deeply shocking torture technique in which the prisoner has his face exposed to water in a way that gives the feeling of drowning. According to CIA sources cited by ABC News, Khalid Sheikh Mohammed "was able to last between 2 and 2 1/2 minutes before begging to confess." Should we regret having done that? Should we abolish by law that practice, so that it could never be used on the next Khalid Sheikh Mohammed having thus gotten his confession?

And what if he possessed information with less imminent implications? Say we had information about a cell that he had helped found or direct, and that cell was planning some major attack and we needed information about the identity and location of its members. A rational moral calculus might not permit measures as extreme as the nuke-in-Manhattan scenario, but would surely permit measures beyond mere psychological pressure.

Such a determination would not be made with an untroubled conscience. It would be troubled because there is no denying the monstrous evil that is any form of torture. And there is no denying how corrupting it can be to the individuals and society that practice it. But elected leaders, responsible above all for the protection of their citizens, have the obligation to tolerate their own sleepless nights by doing what is necessary—and only what is necessary, nothing more—to get information that could prevent mass murder.

Given the gravity of the decision, if we indeed cross the Rubicon—as we must—we need rules. The problem with the McCain amendment is that once you have gone public with a blanket ban on all forms of coercion, it is going to be very difficult to publicly carve out exceptions. The Bush administration is to be faulted for having attempted such a codification with the kind of secrecy, lack of coherence, and lack of strict enforcement that led us to the McCain reaction.

What to do at this late date? Begin, as McCain does, by banning all forms of coercion or inhuman treatment by anyone serving in the military—an absolute ban on torture by all military personnel everywhere. We do not want a private somewhere making these fine distinctions about ticking and slow-fuse time bombs. We don't even want colonels or generals making them. It would be best for the morale, discipline, and honor of the Armed Forces for the United States to maintain an absolute prohibition, both to simplify their task in making decisions and to offer them whatever reciprocal treatment they might receive from those who capture them—although I have no illusion that any anti-torture provision will soften the heart of a single jihadist holding a knife to the throat of a captured American soldier. We would impose this restriction on ourselves for our own reasons of military discipline and military honor.

Outside the military, however, I would propose, contra McCain, a ban against all forms of torture, coercive interrogation, and inhuman treatment, except in two contingencies: (1) the ticking time bomb and (2) the slower-fuse high-level terrorist (such as KSM). Each contingency would have its own set of rules. In the case of the ticking time bomb, the rules would be relatively simple: Nothing rationally related to getting accurate information would be ruled out. The case of the high-value suspect with slow-fuse information is more complicated. The principle would be that the level of inhumanity of the measures used (moral honesty is essential here—we would be using measures that are by definition inhumane) would be proportional to the need and value of the information. Interrogators would be constrained to use the least inhumane treatment necessary relative to the magnitude and imminence of the evil being prevented and the importance of the knowledge being obtained.

These exceptions to the no-torture rule would not be granted to just any nonmilitary interrogators, or anyone with CIA credentials. They would be reserved for highly specialized agents who are experts and experienced in interrogation, and who are known not to abuse it for the satisfaction of a kind of sick sadomasochism Lynndie England and her cohorts indulged in at Abu Ghraib. Nor would they be acting on their own. They would be required to obtain written permission for such interrogations from the highest political authorities in the country (cabinet level) or from a quasi-judicial body modeled on the Foreign Intelligence Surveillance Court (which permits what would ordinarily be illegal searches and seizures in the war on terror). Or, if the bomb was truly ticking and there was no time, the interrogators would be allowed to act on their own, but would require post facto authorization within, say, 24 hours of their interrogation, so that they knew that whatever they did would be subject to review by others and be justified only under the most stringent terms.

One of the purposes of these justifications would be to establish that whatever extreme measures are used are for reasons of nothing but information. Historically, the torture of prisoners has been done for a variety of reasons apart from information, most prominently reasons of justice or revenge. We do not do that. We should not do that. Ever. Khalid Sheikh Mohammed, murderer of 2,973 innocents, is surely deserving of the most extreme suffering day and night for the rest of his life. But it is neither our role nor our right to be the agents of that suffering. Vengeance is mine, sayeth the Lord. His, not ours. Torture is a terrible and monstrous thing, as degrading and morally corrupting to those who practice it as any conceivable human activity including its moral twin, capital punishment.

If Khalid Sheikh Mohammed knew nothing, or if we had reached the point where his knowledge had been exhausted, I'd be perfectly prepared to throw him into a nice, comfortable Manhattan cell and give him a trial to determine what would be fit and just punishment. But as long as he had useful information, things would be different.

Very different. And it simply will not do to take refuge in the claim that all of the above discussion is superfluous because torture never works anyway. Would that this were true. Unfortunately, on its face, this is nonsense. Is one to believe that in the entire history of human warfare, no combatant has ever received useful information by the use of pressure, torture, or any other kind of inhuman treatment? It may indeed be true that torture is not a reliable tool. But that is very different from saying that it is *never* useful.

The monstrous thing about torture is that sometimes it does work. In 1994, 19-year-old Israeli corporal Nachshon Waxman was kidnapped by Palestinian terrorists. The Israelis captured the driver of the car used in the kidnapping and tortured him in order to find where Waxman was being held. Yitzhak Rabin, prime minister and peacemaker, admitted that they tortured him in a way that went even beyond the '87 guidelines for "coercive interrogation" later struck down by the Israeli Supreme Court as too harsh. The driver talked. His information was accurate. The Israelis found Waxman. "If we'd been so careful to follow the ['87] Landau Commission [which *allowed* coercive interrogation]," explained Rabin, "we would never have found out where Waxman was being held."

In the Waxman case, I would have done precisely what Rabin did. (The fact that Waxman's Palestinian captors killed him during the Israeli rescue raid makes the case doubly tragic, but changes nothing of the moral calculus.) Faced with a similar choice, an American president would have a similar obligation. To do otherwise—to give up the chance to find your soldier lest you sully yourself by authorizing torture of the person who possesses potentially lifesaving information—is a deeply immoral betrayal of a soldier and countryman. Not as cosmically immoral as permitting a city of one's countrymen to perish, as in the Ethics 101 case. But it remains, nonetheless, a case of moral abdication—of a kind rather parallel to that of the principled pacifist. There is much to admire in those who refuse on principle ever to take up arms under any conditions. But that does not make pure pacifism, like no-torture absolutism, any less a form of moral foolishness, tinged with moral vanity. Not reprehensible, only deeply reproachable and supremely impracticable. People who hold such beliefs are deserving of a certain respect. But they are not to be put in positions of authority. One should be grateful for the saintly among us. And one should be vigilant that they not get to make the decisions upon which the lives of others depend.

Which brings us to the greatest irony of all in the torture debate. I have just made what will be characterized as the pro-torture case contra McCain by proposing two major exceptions carved out of any no-torture rule: the ticking time bomb and the slow-fuse high-value terrorist. McCain supposedly is being hailed for defending all that is good and right and just in America by standing foursquare against any inhuman treatment. Or is he?

According to *Newsweek*, in the ticking time bomb case McCain says that the president should disobey the very law that McCain seeks to pass—under the justification that "you do what you have to do. But you take responsibility for it." But if torturing the ticking time bomb suspect is "what you have to do," then why has McCain been going around arguing that such things must never be done?

As for exception number two, the high-level terrorist with slow-fuse information, Stuart Taylor, the superb legal correspondent for *National Journal*, argues that with appropriate legal interpretation, the "cruel, inhuman, or degrading" standard, "though vague, is said by experts to codify . . . the commonsense principle that the toughness of interrogation techniques should be calibrated to the importance and urgency of the information likely to be obtained." That would permit "some very aggressive techniques . . . on that small percentage of detainees who seem especially likely to have potentially life-saving information." Or as Evan Thomas and Michael Hirsh put it in the *Newsweek* report on McCain and torture, the McCain standard would "presumably allow for a sliding scale" of torture or torture-lite or other coercive techniques, thus permitting "for a very small percentage—those High Value Targets like Khalid Sheikh Mohammed—some pretty rough treatment."

But if that is the case, then McCain embraces the same exceptions I do, but prefers to pretend he does not. If that is the case, then his much-touted and endlessly repeated absolutism on inhumane treatment is merely for show. If that is the case, then the moral preening and the phony arguments can stop now, and we can all agree that in this real world of astonishingly murderous enemies, in two very circumscribed circumstances, we must all be prepared to torture. Having established that, we can then begin to work together to codify rules of interrogation for the two very unpleasant but very real cases in which we are morally permitted—indeed morally compelled—to do terrible things.

Andrew Sullivan

 **NO**

The Abolition of Torture

Why is torture wrong? It may seem like an obvious question, or even one beneath discussion. But it is now inescapably before us, with the introduction of the McCain Amendment banning all "cruel, inhuman, and degrading treatment" of detainees by American soldiers and CIA operatives anywhere in the world. The amendment lies in legislative limbo. It passed the Senate in October by a vote of 90 to nine, but President Bush has vowed to veto any such blanket ban on torture or abuse; Vice President Cheney has prevailed upon enough senators and congressmen to prevent the amendment—and the defense appropriations bill to which it is attached—from moving out of conference; and my friend Charles Krauthammer, one of the most respected conservative intellectuals in Washington (and a *New Republic* contributing editor) has written a widely praised cover essay for *The Weekly Standard* endorsing the legalization of full-fledged torture by the United States under strictly curtailed conditions. We stand on the brink of an enormously important choice—one that is critical, morally as well as strategically, to get right.

This debate takes place after three years in which the Bush administration has defined "torture" in the narrowest terms and has permitted coercive, physical abuse of enemy combatants if "military necessity" demands it. It comes also after several internal Pentagon reports found widespread and severe abuse of detainees in Afghanistan, Iraq, and elsewhere that has led to at least two dozen deaths during interrogation. Journalistic accounts and reports by the International Committee of the Red Cross paint an even darker picture of secret torture sites in Eastern Europe and innocent detainees being murdered. Behind all this, the grim images of Abu Ghraib—the worst of which have yet to be released—linger in the public consciousness.

In this inevitably emotional debate, perhaps the greatest failing of those of us who have been arguing against all torture and "cruel, inhuman, and degrading treatment" of detainees is that we have assumed the reasons why torture is always a moral evil, rather than explicating them. But, when you fully ponder them, I think it becomes clearer why, contrary to Krauthammer's argument, torture, in any form and under any circumstances, is both antithetical to the most basic principles for which the United States stands and a profound impediment to winning a wider war that we cannot afford to lose.

❧

Torture is the polar opposite of freedom. It is the banishment of all freedom from a human body and soul, insofar as that is possible. As human beings, we all inhabit bodies and have minds, souls, and reflexes that are designed in part to protect those bodies: to resist or flinch from pain, to protect the psyche from disintegration, and to maintain a sense of selfhood that is the basis for the concept of personal liberty. What torture does is use these involuntary, self-protective, self-defining resources of human beings against the integrity of the human being himself. It takes what is most involuntary in a person and uses it to break that person's will. It takes what is animal in us and deploys it against what makes us human. As an American commander wrote in an August 2003 e-mail about his instructions to torture prisoners at Abu Ghraib, "The gloves are coming off gentlemen regarding these detainees, Col. Boltz has made it clear that we want these individuals broken."

What does it mean to "break" an individual? As the French essayist Michel de Montaigne once commented, and Shakespeare echoed, even the greatest philosophers have difficulty thinking clearly when they have a toothache. These wise men were describing the inescapable frailty of the human experience, mocking the claims of some seers to be above basic human feelings and bodily needs. If that frailty is exposed by a toothache, it is beyond dispute in the case of torture. The infliction of physical pain on a person with no means of defending himself is designed to render that person completely subservient to his torturers. It is designed to extirpate his autonomy as a human being, to render his control as an individual beyond his own reach. That is why the term "break" is instructive. Something broken can be put back together, but it will never regain the status of being unbroken—of having integrity. When you break a human being, you turn him into something subhuman. You enslave him. This is why the Romans reserved torture for slaves, not citizens, and why slavery and torture were inextricably linked in the antebellum South.

What you see in the relationship between torturer and tortured is the absolute darkness of totalitarianism. You see one individual granted the most complete power he can ever hold over another. Not just confinement of his mobility—the abolition of his very agency. Torture uses a person's body to remove from his own control his conscience, his thoughts, his faith, his selfhood. The CIA's definition of "waterboarding"—recently leaked to ABC News— describes that process in plain English: "The prisoner is bound to an inclined board, feet raised and head slightly below the feet. Cellophane is wrapped over the prisoner's face and water is poured over him. Unavoidably, the gag reflex kicks in and a terrifying fear of drowning leads to almost instant pleas to bring the treatment to a halt." The ABC report then noted, "According to the sources, CIA officers who subjected themselves to the waterboarding technique lasted an average of 14 seconds before caving in. They said Al Qaeda's toughest prisoner, Khalid Sheikh Mohammed, won the admiration of interrogators when he was able to last between two and two and a half minutes before begging to confess."

Before the Bush administration, two documented cases of the U.S. Armed Forces using "waterboarding" resulted in courts-martial for the soldiers implicated. In Donald Rumsfeld's post–September 11 Pentagon, the technique is approved and, we recently learned, has been used on at least eleven detainees, possibly many more. What you see here is the deployment of a very basic and inescapable human reflex—the desire not to drown and suffocate—in order to destroy a person's autonomy. Even the most hardened fanatic can only endure two and a half minutes. After that, he is indeed "broken."

⚜

The entire structure of Western freedom grew in part out of the searing experience of state-sanctioned torture. The use of torture in Europe's religious wars of the sixteenth and seventeenth centuries is still etched in our communal consciousness, as it should be. Then, governments deployed torture not only to uncover perceived threats to their faith-based autocracies, but also to "save" the victim's soul. Torturers understood that religious conversion was a difficult thing, because it necessitated a shift in the deepest recesses of the human soul. The only way to reach those depths was to deploy physical terror in the hopes of completely destroying the heretic's autonomy. They would, in other words, destroy a human being's soul in order to save it. That is what burning at the stake was—an indescribably agonizing act of torture that could be ended at a moment's notice if the victim recanted. In a state where theological doctrine always trumped individual liberty, this was a natural tactic.

Indeed, the very concept of Western liberty sprung in part from an understanding that, if the state has the power to reach that deep into a person's soul and can do that much damage to a human being's person, then the state has extinguished all oxygen necessary for freedom to survive. That is why, in George Orwell's totalitarian nightmare, the final ordeal is, of course, torture. Any polity that endorses torture has incorporated into its own DNA a totalitarian mutation. If the point of the U.S. Constitution is the preservation of liberty, the formal incorporation into U.S. law of the state's right to torture—by legally codifying physical coercion, abuse, and even, in Krauthammer's case, full-fledged torture of detainees by the CIA—would effectively end the American experiment of a political society based on inalienable human freedom protected not by the good graces of the executive, but by the rule of law.

The founders understood this argument. Its preeminent proponent was George Washington himself. As historian David Hackett Fischer memorably recounts in his 2004 book, *Washington's Crossing:* "Always some dark spirits wished to visit the same cruelties on the British and Hessians that had been inflicted on American captives. But Washington's example carried growing weight, more so than his written orders and prohibitions. He often reminded his men that they were an army of liberty and freedom, and that the rights of humanity for which they were fighting should extend even to their enemies. . . . Even in the most urgent moments of the war, these men were concerned about ethical questions in the Revolution."

Krauthammer has described Washington's convictions concerning torture as "pieties" that can be dispensed with today. He doesn't argue that torture is not evil. Indeed, he denounces it in unequivocal moral terms: "[T]orture is a terrible and monstrous thing, as degrading and morally corrupting to those who practice it as any conceivable human activity including its moral twin, capital punishment." But he maintains that the nature of the Islamofascist enemy after September 11 radically altered our interrogative options and that we are now not only permitted, but actually "morally compelled," to torture.

This is a radical and daring idea: that we must extinguish human freedom in a few cases in order to maintain it for everyone else. It goes beyond even the Bush administration's own formal position, which states that the United States will not endorse torture but merely "coercive interrogation techniques." (Such techniques, in the administration's elaborate definition, are those that employ physical force short of threatening immediate death or major organ failure.) And it is based on a premise that deserves further examination: that our enemies actually *deserve* torture; that some human beings are so depraved that, in Krauthammer's words, they "are entitled to no humane treatment."

Let me state for the record that I am second to none in decrying, loathing, and desiring to defeat those who wish to replace freedom with religious tyranny of the most brutal kind—and who have murdered countless innocent civilians in cold blood. Their acts are monstrous and barbaric. But I differ from Krauthammer by believing that monsters remain human beings. In fact, to reduce them to a subhuman level is to exonerate them of their acts of terrorism and mass murder—just as animals are not deemed morally responsible for killing. Insisting on the humanity of terrorists is, in fact, critical to maintaining their profound responsibility for the evil they commit.

And, if they are human, then they must necessarily not be treated in an inhuman fashion. You cannot lower the moral baseline of a terrorist to the subhuman without betraying a fundamental value. That is why the Geneva Conventions have a very basic ban on "cruel treatment and torture," and "outrages upon personal dignity, in particular humiliating and degrading treatment"—even when dealing with illegal combatants like terrorists. That is why the Declaration of Independence did not restrict its endorsement of freedom merely to those lucky enough to find themselves on U.S. soil—but extended it to all human beings, wherever they are in the world, simply because they are human.

⟿❦⟾

Nevertheless, it is important to address Krauthammer's practical points. He is asking us to steel ourselves and accept that, whether we like it or not, torture and abuse may be essential in a war where our very survival may be at stake. He presents two scenarios in which he believes torture is permissible. The first is the "ticking bomb" scenario, a hypothetical rarity in which the following conditions apply: a) a terrorist cell has planted a nuclear weapon or something nearly as devastating in a major city; b) we have captured someone in this cell; c) we know for a fact that he knows where the bomb is. In practice, of course, the likelihood of such a scenario is extraordinarily remote. Uncovering a terrorist plot is hard enough; capturing a conspirator involved in that plot is even harder; and realizing in advance that the person knows the whereabouts of the bomb is nearly impossible. (Remember, in the war on terrorism, we have already detained—and even killed—many innocents. Pentagon reports have acknowledged that up to 90 percent of the prisoners at Abu Ghraib, many of whom were abused and tortured, were not guilty of anything.) But let us assume, for the sake of argument, that all of Krauthammer's conditions apply. Do we have a right to torture our hypothetical detainee?

According to Krauthammer, *of course* we do. No responsible public official put in that position would refuse to sanction torture if he believed it could save thousands of lives. And, if it's necessary, Krauthammer argues, it should be made legal. If you have conceded that torture may be justified in one case, Krauthammer believes, you have conceded that it may be justified in many more. In his words, "Once you've established the principle, to paraphrase George Bernard Shaw, all that's left to haggle about is the price."

But this is too easy and too glib a formulation. It is possible to concede that, in an extremely rare circumstance, torture may be used without conceding that it should be legalized. One imperfect but instructive analogy is civil disobedience. In that case, laws are indeed broken, but that does not establish that the laws should be broken. In fact, civil disobedience implies precisely that laws should *not* be broken, and protesters who engage in it present themselves promptly for imprisonment and legal sanction on exactly those grounds. They do so for demonstrative reasons. They are not saying that laws don't matter. They are saying that laws do matter, that they should be enforced, but that their conscience in this instance demands that they disobey them.

In extremis, a rough parallel can be drawn for a president faced with the kind of horrendous decision on which Krauthammer rests his entire case. What should a president do? The answer is simple: He may have to break the law. In the Krauthammer scenario, a president might well decide that, if the survival of the nation is at stake, he must make an exception. At the same time, he must subject himself—and so must those assigned to conduct the torture—to the consequences of an illegal act. Those guilty of torturing another human being must be punished—or pardoned ex-post-facto. If the torture is revealed to be useless, if the tortured man is shown to have been innocent or ignorant of the information he was tortured to reveal, then those responsible must face the full brunt of the law for, in Krauthammer's words, such a "terrible and monstrous thing." In Michael Walzer's formulation, if we are to have dirty hands, it is essential that we show them to be dirty.

What Krauthammer is proposing, however, is not this compromise, which allows us to retain our soul as a free republic while protecting us from catastrophe in an extremely rare case. He is proposing something very different: that our "dirty hands" be wiped legally clean before and after the fact. That is a Rubicon we should not cross, because it marks the boundary between a free country and an unfree one.

Krauthammer, moreover, misses a key lesson learned these past few years. What the hundreds of abuse and torture incidents have shown is that, once you permit torture for someone somewhere, it has a habit of spreading. Remember that torture was originally sanctioned in administration memos only for use against illegal combatants in rare cases. Within months of that decision, abuse and torture had become endemic throughout Iraq, a theater of war in which, even Bush officials agree, the Geneva Conventions apply. The extremely coercive interrogation tactics used at Guantánamo Bay "migrated" to Abu Ghraib. In fact, General Geoffrey Miller was sent to Abu Ghraib specifically to replicate Guantánamo's techniques. According to former Brigadier General Janis Karpinski, who had original responsibility for the prison, Miller ordered her to treat all detainees "like dogs." When Captain Ian Fishback, a West Point graduate and member of the 82nd Airborne, witnessed routine beatings and abuse of detainees at detention facilities in Iraq and Afghanistan, often for sport, he tried to stop it. It took him a year and a half to get any response from the military command, and he had to go to Senator John McCain to make his case.

In short, what was originally supposed to be safe, sanctioned, and rare became endemic, disorganized, and brutal. The lesson is that it is impossible to quarantine torture in a hermetic box; it will inevitably contaminate the military as a whole. Once you have declared that some enemies are subhuman, you have told every soldier that every potential detainee he comes across might be exactly that kind of prisoner—and that anything can therefore be done to him. That is what the disgrace at Abu Ghraib proved. And Abu Ghraib produced a tiny fraction of the number of abuse, torture, and murder cases that have been subsequently revealed. The only way to control torture is to ban it outright. Everywhere. Even then, in wartime, some "bad apples" will always commit abuse. But at least we will have done all we can to constrain it.

Krauthammer's second case for torture is equally unpersuasive. For "slow-fuse" detainees—high-level prisoners like Khalid Sheikh Mohammed with potentially, if not immediately, useful intelligence—Krauthammer again takes the most extreme case and uses it to establish a general rule. He concedes that torture, according to almost every careful student and expert, yields highly unreliable information. Anyone can see that. If you are screaming for relief after a few seconds of waterboarding, you're likely to tell your captors anything, true or untrue, to stop the agony and terror. But Krauthammer then argues that, unless you can prove that torture *never* works, it should always be retained as an option. "It may indeed be true that torture is not a reliable tool," he argues. "But that is very different from saying that it is *never* useful." And if it cannot be deemed always useless, it must be permitted—even when an imminent threat is not in the picture.

The problem here is an obvious one. You have made the extreme exception the basis for a new rule. You have said that, if you cannot absolutely rule out torture as effective in every single case, it should be ruled in as an option for many. Moreover, if allowing torture even in the "ticking bomb" scenario makes the migration of torture throughout the military likely, this loophole blows the doors wide open. And how do we tell good intelligence from bad intelligence in such torture-infested interrogation? The short answer is: We cannot. By allowing torture for "slow-fuse" detainees, you sacrifice a vital principle for intelligence that is uniformly corrupted at best and useless at worst.

In fact, the use of torture and coercive interrogation by U.S. forces in this war may have contributed to a profound worsening of our actionable intelligence. The key to intelligence in Iraq and, indeed, in Muslim enclaves in the West, is gaining the support and trust of those who give terrorists cover but who are not terrorists themselves. We need human intelligence from Muslims and Arabs prepared to spy on and inform on their neighbors and friends and even family and tribe members. The only way they will do that is if they perceive the gains of America's intervention as greater than the costs, if they see clearly that cooperating with the West will lead to a better life and a freer world rather than more of the same.

What our practical endorsement of torture has done is to remove that clear boundary between the Islamists and the West and make the two equivalent in the Muslim mind. Saddam Hussein used Abu Ghraib to torture innocents; so did the Americans. Yes, what Saddam did was exponentially worse. But, in doing what we did, we blurred the critical, bright line between the Arab past and what we are proposing as the Arab future. We gave Al Qaeda an enormous propaganda coup, as we have done with Guantánamo and Bagram, the "Salt Pit" torture chambers in Afghanistan, and the secret torture sites in Eastern Europe. In World War II, American soldiers were often tortured by the Japanese when captured. But FDR refused to reciprocate. Why? Because he knew that the goal of the war was not just Japan's defeat but Japan's transformation into a democracy. He knew that, if the beacon of democracy—the United States of America—had succumbed to the hallmark of totalitarianism, then the chance for democratization would be deeply compromised in the wake of victory.

No one should ever underestimate the profound impact that the conduct of American troops in World War II had on the citizens of the eventually defeated Axis powers. Germans saw the difference between being liberated by the Anglo-Americans and being liberated by the Red Army. If you saw an American or British uniform, you were safe. If you didn't, the terror would continue in different ways. Ask any German or Japanese of the generation that built democracy in those countries, and they will remind you of American values—not trumpeted by presidents in front of handpicked audiences, but *demonstrated* by the conduct of the U.S. military during occupation. I grew up in Great Britain, a country with similar memories. In the dark days of the cold war, I was taught that America, for all its faults, was still America. And that America did not, and constitutively could not, torture anyone.

If American conduct was important in Japan and Germany, how much more important is it in Iraq and Afghanistan. The entire point of the war on terrorism, according to the president, is to advance freedom and democracy in the Arab world. In Iraq, we had a chance not just to tell but to show the Iraqi people how a democracy acts. And, tragically, in one critical respect, we failed. That failure undoubtedly contributed to the increased legitimacy of the insurgency and illegitimacy of the occupation, and it made collaboration between informed Sunnis and U.S. forces far less likely. What minuscule intelligence we might have plausibly gained from torturing and abusing detainees is vastly outweighed by the intelligence we have forfeited by alienating many otherwise sympathetic Iraqis and Afghans, by deepening the divide between the democracies, and by sullying the West's reputation in the Middle East. Ask yourself: Why does Al Qaeda tell its detainees to claim torture regardless of what happens to them in U.S. custody? Because Al Qaeda knows that one of America's greatest weapons in this war is its reputation as a repository of freedom and decency. Our policy of permissible torture has handed Al Qaeda this weapon—to use against us. It is not just a moral tragedy. It is a pragmatic disaster. Why compound these crimes and errors by subsequently legalizing them, as Krauthammer (explicitly) and the president (implicitly) are proposing?

Will a ban on all "cruel, inhuman, and degrading treatment" render interrogations useless? By no means. There are many techniques for gaining intelligence from detainees other than using their bodies against their souls. You can start with the 17 that appear in the Army Field Manual, tested by decades of armed conflict only to be discarded by this administration with barely the blink of an eye. Isolation, psychological disorientation, intense questioning, and any number of other creative techniques are possible. Some of the most productive may well be those in which interrogators are so versed in Islamic theology and Islamist subcultures that they win the confidence of prisoners and pry information out of them—something the United States, with its dearth of Arabic speakers, is unfortunately ill-equipped to do.

Enemy combatants need not be accorded every privilege granted legitimate prisoners of war; but they must be treated as human beings. This means that, in addition to physical torture, wanton abuse of their religious faith is out of bounds. No human freedom is meaningful without religious freedom. The fact that Koran abuse has been documented at Guantánamo; that one prisoner at Abu Ghraib was forced to eat pork and drink liquor; that fake menstrual blood was used to disorient a strict Muslim prisoner at Guantánamo—these make winning the hearts and minds of moderate Muslims far harder. Such tactics have resulted in hunger strikes at Guantánamo—perhaps the ultimate sign that the coercive and abusive attempts to gain the cooperation of detainees has completely failed to achieve the desired results.

The war on terrorism is, after all, a religious war in many senses. It is a war to defend the separation of church and state as critical to the existence of freedom, including religious freedom. It is a war to persuade the silent majority of Muslims that the West offers a better way—more decency, freedom, and humanity than the autocracies they live under and the totalitarian theocracies waiting in the wings. By endorsing torture—on anyone, anywhere, for any reason—we help obliterate the very values we are trying to promote. You can see this contradiction in Krauthammer's own words: We are "morally compelled" to commit "a terrible and monstrous thing." We are obliged to destroy the village in order to save it. We have to extinguish the most basic principle that defines America in order to save America.

No, we don't. In order to retain fundamental American values, we have to banish from the United States the totalitarian impulse that is integral to every act of torture. We have to ensure that the virus of tyranny is never given an opening to infect the Constitution and replicate into something that corrupts as deeply as it wounds. We should mark the words of Ian Fishback, one of the heroes of this war: "Will we confront danger and adversity in order to preserve our ideals, or will our courage and commitment to individual rights wither at the prospect of sacrifice? My response is simple. If we abandon our ideals in the face of adversity and aggression, then those ideals were never really in our possession. I would rather die fighting than give up even the smallest part of the idea that is 'America.'" If we legalize torture, even under constrained conditions, we will have given up a large part of the idea that is America. We will have lost the war before we have given ourselves the chance to win it.

POSTSCRIPT

Is the Use of Torture Against Terrorist Suspects Ever Justified?

Despite their obvious disagreements, there is an *almost* meeting of the minds between Sullivan and Krauthammer. Krauthammer admits that torture is a "terrible and monstrous thing," which is the essence of Sullivan's objection to it. Sullivan, for his part, concedes that, "in an extremely rare circumstance, torture may be used," though he refuses to allow its legalization. He compares it to civil disobedience, in which a principled law-breaker accepts the penalty for breaking the law. And so with torture: the decision to do it would have to be personally approved by the President, and he "must" then suffer the legal consequences. But if a President "must" be punished for doing something that he "may" do, isn't that unfair? Without directly answering this question, Sullivan opens up a loophole for the President: he can always be pardoned *ex post facto*.

Seymour Hersh, famous for breaking the story twenty-four years earlier on the Mai Lai massacre by American soldiers in Vietnam, has written an account of the mistreatment of prisoners at Abu Ghraib, based largely on a copy of the Army's own confidential report. See his "Torture at Abu Ghraib," *The New Yorker,* May 10, 2004. In another *New Yorker* article Jane Mayer has written on the "rendition" program, claiming that it amounts to American complicity in torture. See "Outsourcing Torture," *The New Yorker,* February 14, 2005. In an online site, the late Susan Sontag argues that the abuses at Abu Ghraib are the inevitable culmination of the foreign and even domestic policies of the Bush administration. See "What Have We Done?," *Serendipity* May 24, 2004, www.serendipity.li/iraqwar/susan_sontag_what_have_ we_done.htn. In *Why Terrorism Works: Understanding the Threat, Responding to the Challenge* (Yale University Press, 2003) Alan M. Dershowitz offers a qualified defense of interrogation procedures ranging from sleep deprivation to the insertion of needles under fingernails (though he specifies that the needles must be sterile). Kenneth Roth is the editor of *Torture: Does it Make Us Safer? Is It Ever OK?: A Human Rights Perspective* (New Press, 2005). As the subtitle suggests, none of the contributors answers either of these questions in the affirmative. Alfred McCoy, in *A Question of Torture: CIA Interrogation, From the Cold War to the War on Terror* (Metropolitan Books, 2006), argues that the American use of torture during interrogations has been deliberate and systematic, not accidental.

On December 30, 2005 President Bush signed a law passed by Congress prohibiting "cruel, inhuman, or degrading treatment or punishment" of detainees. It specifies that no person held by the Defense Department "shall be subject to any treatment or technique of interrogation not authorized by and listed in the United States Army field manual on Intelligence Interrogation." The techniques listed in the 1992 Field Manual allow for 17 different methods of interrogation but prohibit "techniques such as brainwashing, physical or mental torture, or any form of mental coercion." Critics of the new law complained that terrorists could simply order a copy of the Field Manual through Amazon.com and thus prepare themselves to outwit the interrogators, but the chief sponsor of the new law, Senator John McCain (R-Ariz.) replied that an updated version with a classified addendum was being prepared. The President, meanwhile, issued a "signing statement" indicating that he viewed the new law's interrogation limits in the context of his broader powers to protect national security.

ISSUE 20

Does the United Nations Promote World Peace and Security?

YES: Madeleine K. Albright, from "Think Again: The United Nations," *Foreign Policy* (September/October 2003)

NO: Joshua Muravchik, from "The Case Against the UN," *Commentary* (November 2004)

ISSUE SUMMARY

YES: Former Secretary of State Madeleine Albright believes that the United Nations continues to perform peacekeeping and humanitarian tasks no nation or other group of nations can perform.

NO: International relations scholar Joshua Muravchik concludes that the United Nations has failed to either keep the peace or intervene to defend weaker victims from aggressive enemies.

The United Nations turned 60 in 2005. It is a tribute to the UN that it is still here. The predecessor League of Nations, established after the first World War, barely lasted 20 years before the outbreak of the second World War. The world has survived many smaller wars since, including the Cold War between the United States and the former Soviet Union. Nevertheless, it remains necessary to ask whether the UN performs a necessary purpose, whether it falls short because it is not strong enough, or whether it should be abandoned because it is irrelevant.

During the second World War, President Franklin D. Roosevelt referred to the United States and its allies as the United Nations, and that was the name adopted when the United Nations Charter was adopted in 1945. That Charter sought to create the machinery to maintain peace and security, but almost immediately the development of nuclear weapons led to the first resolution at the first meeting of the UN General Assembly in 1946 calling for "the elimination from national armaments of atomic weapons and of all other major weapons adaptable to mass destruction." This led to debate and resolutions on a nuclear test ban, outerspace arms control, efforts to ban chemical weapons, nuclear and conventional disarmament, nuclear weapons–free zones, reduction of military budgets, and measures to strengthen international security. The proliferation of nuclear, chemical, and biological weapons as well as the persistence of poverty, disease, and ethnic discrimination are reminders that, six decades later, the same issues confront the UN and the United States.

Originally composed of 51 nations, the UN now has 191 member nations, including all internationally recognized independent countries, with the exception of the Holy See (the Vatican), which is the only permanent observer state. Although Taiwan has *de facto* independence and some international diplomatic recognition, it is not a member.

The principle elements of the UN are the General Assembly, of which all nations are members with one vote; the Security Council, which has five permanent members (China, France, the United Kingdom, the Russian Federation, and the United States) and 10 members elected for two-year terms; a Trusteeship Council; a Secretariat, headed by the Secretary General, and the International Court of Justice. The Security Council clearly possesses the most influence and power. Substantive decisions of the Security Council require the approval of nine members, including the five permanent members. All other UN agencies recommend actions to national governments, but under the UN Charter, all nations are obligated to carry out the decisions of the Security Council. If any of the permanent members withholds support, the Council cannot act.

In addition to peacekeeping operations, the UN has provided food, drinking water, shelter, and other services to people suffering from famine, displaced by war, or affected by natural disasters. The UN takes credit for increasing awareness of human rights abuses, playing a role in the abolition of apartheid (racial segregation and discrimination) in South Africa, and having succeeded, through the World Health Organization, in eliminating smallpox.

Some charge that the UN has been ineffective, failing to act forcefully to prevent ethnic cleansing in Rwanda or Darfur and failing to deliver food to starving people in Somalia (ending with the humiliating withdrawal of UN forces). It has been criticized as hypocritical because Sudan, Libya, and Cuba—nations with abysmal human rights records—have been elected to the UN Commission on Human Rights. It has been criticized as mismanaged and corrupt because some UN officials played a role in illegal actions in the Iraqi Oil-for-Food program, resulting in benefits to Saddam Hussein.

The administration of President George W. Bush criticized the UN for failing to support the American-led invasion of Iraq, which was prompted by Iraq's defiance of UN mandates regarding weapons of mass destruction. Others criticized the American action or saw it as a demonstration of the weakness of the UN when opposed by the power of the United States.

The following essays briefly explore these issues. International relations scholar Joshua Muravchik concludes that the UN has failed both to defend the peace and to advance the cause of human rights. On the contrary, former Secretary of State Madeleine Albright argues the UN has made great advances in stopping AIDS, feeding the poor, helping refugees, fighting global crime, and curbing the spread of nuclear weapons.

YES

Madeleine K. Albright

Think Again: United Nations

Bureaucratic. Ineffective. Undemocratic. Anti-United States. And after the bitter debate over the use of force in Iraq, critics might add "useless" to the list of adjectives describing the United Nations. So why was the United Nations the first place the Bush administration went for approval after winning the war? Because for $1.25 billion a year—roughly what the Pentagon spends every 32 hours—the United Nations is still the best investment that the world can make in stopping AIDS and SARS, feeding the poor, helping refugees, and fighting global crime and the spread of nuclear weapons.

"The United Nations Has Become Irrelevant"

No. The second Gulf War battered the U.N. Security Council's already shaky prestige. Hawks condemned the council for failing to bless the war; opponents for failing to block it. Nevertheless, when major combat stopped, the United States and Great Britain rushed to seek council authorization for their joint occupation of Iraq, the lifting of sanctions, and the right to market Iraqi oil.

What lessons will emerge from the wrangle over Iraq? Will France, Russia, and China grudgingly concede U.S. dominance and cooperate sufficiently to keep the United States from routinely bypassing the Security Council? Or might they form an opposition bloc that paralyzes the body? Will the United States and United Kingdom proceed triumphantly? Or will they suffer so many headaches in Iraq that they conclude, in hindsight, that initiating the war without council support was a mistake?

Both sides have reason to move toward cooperation. The French, Russians, and Chinese all derive outsized influence from their status as permanent Security Council members; they see the panel as a means to mitigate U.S. hegemony and do not want the White House to pronounce it dead. And despite their unilateralist tendencies, Bush administration officials will welcome council support when battling terrorists and rogue states in the future. Although the council is not and never has been the preeminent arbiter of war and peace that its supporters wish it were, it remains the most widely accepted source of international legitimacy—and legitimacy still has meaning, even for empires. That is why U.S. President George W. Bush and U.S. Secretary of State Colin Powell both made their major prewar, pro-war presentations before a U.N. audience.

From *Foreign Policy,* September/October 2003, pp. 16–18, 20, 22, 24. Copyright © 2003 as conveyed via Copyright Clearance Center. Reprinted by permission. www.foreignpolicy.com

Beyond the council itself, the United Nations' ongoing relevance is evident in the work of the more than two dozen organizations comprising the U.N. system. In 2003 alone, the International Atomic Energy Agency reported that Iran had processed nuclear materials in violation of its Nuclear Nonproliferation Treaty obligations; the International Criminal Tribunal for the Former Yugoslavia tried deposed Yugoslav leader Slobodan Milosevic for genocide; and the World Health Organization successfully coordinated the global response to severe acute respiratory syndrome (SARS). Meanwhile, the World Food Programme has fed more than 70 million people annually for the last five years; the U.N. High Commissioner for Refugees maintains a life-line to the international homeless; the U.N. Children's Fund has launched a campaign to end forced childhood marriage; the Joint U.N. Programme on HIV/AIDS remains a focal point for global efforts to defeat HIV/AIDS; and the U.N. Population Fund helps families plan, mothers survive, and children grow up healthy in the most impoverished places on earth. The United Nations may seem useless to the self-satisfied, narrow-minded, and micro-hearted minority, but to most of the world's population, it remains highly relevant indeed.

"Relations Between the United States and the United Nations Are at an All-Time Low"

Not even close. One day before the U.N. General Assembly convened in 1952, Republican Sen. Joseph McCarthy of Wisconsin began hearings in New York on the loyalty of U.S. citizens employed by the United Nations. A federal grand jury then opened a competing inquiry in the same city on the same subject. (Some U.N. employees called to testify even invoked their constitutional right against self-incrimination.) The furor generated massive indignation and mutual U.S.-U.N. distrust. J.B. Mathews, chief investigator for the House Un-American Activities Committee, declared that the United Nations "could not be less of a cruel hoax if it had been organized in Hell for the sole purpose of aiding and abetting the destruction of the United States."

East-West and North-South tensions transformed the General Assembly into hostile territory through much of the 1970s and 1980s. U.S. ambassadors such as Daniel P. Moynihan and Jeane Kirkpatrick earned combat pay rebut- ting the verbal pyrotechnics of delegates in the throes of anti-Semitic passions and Marxist moonbeams. The low point was the passage in 1975 of a resolution equating Zionism with racism.

In the 1990s, supporters of the Contract With America, led by Republican Rep. Newt Gingrich of Georgia, lambasted U.N. peacekeeping, blocked payment of U.N. dues, and ridiculed U.N. programs. Similarly, Republican Sen. Jesse Helms of North Carolina spoke for many of the far-right-minded but wrong-headed when he termed the United Nations "the nemesis of millions of Americans."

Today according to the Pew Global Attitudes Project, U.S. citizens consider U.N. Secretary-General Kofi Annan the fourth most respected world leader (trailing, in order, British Prime Minister Tony Blair, U.S. President George W. Bush, and Israeli Prime Minister Ariel Sharon). The United States has paid back most of its acknowledged U.N. arrears. The United Nations' agenda and core U.S. security interests have gradually converged. For example, the U.N. Charter says nothing about the importance of elected government, yet U.N. missions routinely sponsor democratic transitions, monitor elections, and promote free institutions. The charter explicitly prohibits U.N. intervention in the internal affairs of any government (save for enforcement actions), yet the U.N. High Commissioner for Human Rights, created in 1993 at the United States' urging, exists solely to nudge governments to do the right thing by their own people. The United Nations' founders never mentioned terrorism, yet today the United Nations encourages governments to ratify antiterrorist conventions, freeze terrorist assets, and tighten security on land, in air, and at sea. Polls continue to show that a significant majority of U.S. citizens believe the United States should seek U.N. authorization before using force and should cooperate with other nations through the world body.

"The Bush Administration's Doctrine of Preemption Is Not Authorized by the U.N. Charter"

So? The charter calls upon states to attempt to settle disputes peacefully and, failing that, to refer matters to the Security Council for appropriate action. Article 51 provides that nothing in the charter "shall impair the inherent right of individual or collective self-defense if an armed attack occurs against a Member of the United Nations, until the Security Council has taken measures necessary to maintain international peace and security."

Compare that to this passage from President Bush's 2002 National Security Strategy: "Given the goals of rogue states and terrorists, the United States can no longer solely rely on a reactive posture as we have in the past. The inability to deter a potential attacker, the immediacy of today's threats, and the magnitude of potential harm that could be caused by our adversaries' choice of weapons, do not permit that option. We cannot let our enemies strike first."

The mystery here is not what the administration said, but rather why it chose to arouse global controversy by elevating what has always been a residual option into a highly publicized doctrine. In reality, no U.S. president would allow an international treaty to prevent actions genuinely necessary to deter or preempt imminent attack upon the United States. The notion that the United States has relied solely "on a reactive posture" in the past is not true. In the name of self-defense, U.S. administrations of both parties initiated actions during the Cold War that violated the sovereignty of other nations. In 1994, the Clinton administration considered military strikes against nuclear facilities in North Korea. In 1998, U.S. President Bill Clinton launched cruise missiles into Afghanistan and Sudan in retaliation for the terrorist bombing of two U.S. embassies in Africa and in an effort to prevent al Qaeda leader Osama bin Laden from striking again.

Whether tracking the language of Article 51 or not, the Bush administration's preemption doctrine will prove a departure from past practice only if it is implemented in a manner that is aggressive, indifferent to precedent, and careless of the information used to justify military action. Calibrated and effective actions taken against real enemies posing an imminent danger should not overturn the international legal apple cart. Measures wide of that standard would indeed raise troubling questions about whether the United States is setting itself above the law or tacitly acknowledging the right of every nation to act militarily against threats that are merely potential and suspected. The administration approached that line by invading Iraq, but the issue was blurred by the multiple rationales given for the conflict–enforcement of Security Council resolutions (relatively strong legal grounds), self-defense (in this case, shaky), and liberation (shakier still). The issue now is whether the administration intends to strike first against nuclear aspirants North Korea and Iran (and, if so, on what evidence) and whether it will exhaust other options first. Thus far, the administration is traveling the diplomatic route.

"Political Correctness Often Trumps Substance at the United Nations"

Correct. The Cold War and the rapid growth in U.N. membership following decolonization shaped the United Nations' civil service, requiring the distribution of jobs on the basis of geography rather than qualifications. The U.S. Congress did not help over the years by buying in to the notion that the United States was entitled to many jobs and then filling them with defeated politicians.

While at the United Nations, I used to joke that managing the global institution was like trying to run a business with 184 chief executive officers-each with a different language, a distinct set of priorities, and an unemployed brother-in-law seeking a paycheck. Secretary-General Kofi Annan has done about everything possible within the system to reward high achievers and improve recruitment, but the pressure to satisfy members from Afghanistan to Zimbabwe remains a management nightmare.

Another long-standing problem is that decisions on U.N. committee chairs and memberships are most often made on a regional and rotating basis, with equal weight given to, for example, South Africa and Swaziland. By tradition, these decisions are sacrosanct, leading to the recent spectacle of Libya chairing the U.N. Commission on Human Rights. To prevent such an outcome, one must be willing to break some diplomatic china. Former President Clinton did so in blocking the reelection of Secretary-General Boutros Boutros-Ghali in 1996 and defeating Sudan's regionally endorsed nomination for Security Council membership in 2000. Both initiatives prompted resentment toward the United States, but both enhanced the standing and credibility of the United Nations.

"U.N. Peacekeeping Has Failed"

Untrue. U.N. peacekeeping has maintained order in such diverse places as Namibia, El Salvador, Cambodia, eastern Slavonia, Mozambique, and Cyprus. The traditional U.N. mission is a confidence-building exercise, conducted in strict neutrality between parties that seek international help in preserving or implementing peace. U.N. peacemaking, however, is quite another matter. During my years as the U.S. permanent representative to the United Nations, the tragic experiences in Bosnia and Herzegovina, Somalia, and Rwanda showed that traditional U.N. peacekeepers lack the mandate, command structure, unity of purpose, and military might to succeed in the more urgent and nasty cases—where the fighting is hot, the innocent are dying, and the combatants oppose an international presence. Such weaknesses, sadly, are inherent in the voluntary and collective nature of the United Nations. When the going gets tough, the tough tend to go wherever they want, notwithstanding the wishes of U.N. commanders.

One possible solution: peace-enforcement missions authorized by the United Nations, in which the Security Council deputizes an appropriate major power to organize a coalition and enforce the world's collective will. The council sets the overall mandate, but the lead nation calls the shots—literaly and figuratively—necessary to achieve the mission. The U.S.-led intervention in Haiti (1994), the Australian-led rescue of East Timor (1999), and the British action in Sierra Leone (2000) were largely successful and provide a model for the future.

Peacemaking is a hard, dangerous, and often thankless task. To deter people with guns, other people with more and bigger guns are necessary, and finding such people is not easy. It is one thing to expect a soldier to risk life and limb defending his or her homeland. It is another to expect that same soldier to travel halfway around the world and perhaps to die while trying to quell a struggle over diamonds, oil, or ethnic dominance on someone else's home turf. Most people are simply not that altruistic, especially when they see many intervention forces blamed for what such forces fail to accomplish rather than credited for the burdens they assume. As a result, the world is left with an international system of crisis response that is pragmatic, episodic, and incremental rather than principled, reliable, and decisive.

Without any expectation of perfection or even consistency, the international community can nevertheless make the best of things by doing more to equip and train selected military units willing to volunteer in advance for peace enforcement; by recruiting personnel to fill the gap between lightly armed police and heavily armed conventional military; by prosecuting war criminals; and by attacking the roots of conflicts such as arms peddling and economic desperation.

"The U.N. Security Council Should Be Enlarged"

Indubitably, but don't hold your breath. Probably no U.N. issue has been studied more with less to show for the effort than Security Council enlargement.

To ensure the council's strength as a guardian of international security and peace, the United Nations' founders assigned permanent membership and veto authority to the five leading nations on the winning side of World War II: the United States, Great Britain, France, the Soviet Union, and China. (Other countries compete for election to fill the 10 remaining council seats, with the winners serving a two-year term.) Obviously, the world has changed a bit since 1945: U.N. membership has more than tripled, and three of the eight most populous nations in the world can now be found in South Asia. Despite an apparent consensus to enlarge the council, its members have been tied up in knots trying to decide now. Major debates include fair regional representation (if India deserves a permanent seat, what about Pakistan?) and reluctance to extend veto power to additional countries.

During my years at the United Nations in the mid-1990s, the United States supported expanding the council to no more than 21 members and granting permanent seats to Japan and Germany. This position outraged Italian Ambassador E Paolo Fulci, whose country opposed the addition of more permanent members. By that logic, he argued, if Japan and Germany joined the Security Council, Italy should be included as a permanent member, too. "After all," he argued, "Italians also lost World War II."

"The United Nations Is a Threat to the Sovereignty of the United States"

Balderdash. The United Nations' authority flows from its members; it is servant, not master. The United Nations has no armed forces of its own, no power of arrest, no authority to tax, no right to confiscate, no ability to regulate, no capacity to override treaties, and—despite the paranoia of some—no black helicopters poised to swoop down upon innocent homes in the middle of the night and steal lawn furniture. The U.N. General Assembly has little power, except to approve the U.N. budget, which it does by consensus. Meanwhile, the Security Council, which does have power, cannot act without the acquiescence of the United States and the other four permanent members. That means that no secretary-general can be elected, no U.N. peacekeeping operation initiated, and no U.N. tribunal established without the approval of the United States. Questions about the efficiency of the United Nations and many of its specific actions are legitimate, but worries about U.S. sovereignty are misplaced and appear to come primarily from people aggrieved to find the United Nations so full of foreigners. That, I am constrained to say, simply cannot be helped.

"The United Nations Is a Huge Bureaucracy"

Nope. A bureaucracy certainly, but not huge. The annual budget for core U.N. functions—based in New York City, Geneva, Nairobi, Vienna, and five regional commissions—is about $1.25 billion, or roughly what the Pentagon spends every 32 hours. The U.N. Secretariat has reduced its staff by just under 25 percent over the last 20 years and has had a zero-growth budget since 1996. The entire U.N. system, composed of the secretariat and 29 other organizations, employs a little more than 50,000 people, or just 2,000 more than work for the city of Stockholm. Total annual expenditures by all U.N. funds, programs, and specialized agencies equal about one fourth the municipal budget of New York City.

Joshua Muravchik

 **NO**

The Case Against the UN

Among the "excellencies" attending the 59th session of the UN General Assembly that opened in late September were 64 world presidents, 25 prime ministers, and no fewer than 86 foreign ministers. Such an extraordinary turnout, exulted Secretary General Kofi Annan in his welcoming remarks, attested to the fact "that in these difficult times, the United Nations is . . . the common and indispensable home of the human family."

The speeches that followed, however, were depressingly typical of the miasma of rhetoric for which this "home of the human family" is famous. . . .

Above the blather, two contrasting voices stood out. One of them was the Secretary General's. As the theme of his formal statement, Annan chose to focus on the rule of law, especially international law as represented in and laid down by the UN. His sharpest points were aimed, none too obliquely, at the United States. "Those who seek to restore legitimacy must themselves embody it," he scolded. "And those who invoke international law must themselves submit to it." That the United States was derelict on this score, Annan had made clear a week earlier when he reiterated a prior accusation that the 2003 invasion of Iraq by America and its allies had been "illegal."

The second voice was President Bush's. Speaking soon after Annan, he focused on the advancement of democracy and human rights, but his remarks also included a rejoinder to critics like Annan: "The Security Council promised serious consequences for [Saddam Hussein's] defiance. And the commitments we make must have meaning. When we say serious consequences, for the sake of peace there must be serious consequences."

The subject of the thrust and parry was Iraq. But Iraq is only a single act in a larger drama whose theme is the tangled relationship of the United States with its troubling offspring, the United Nations, at a time when the distribution of global power is so extraordinarily skewed toward a single country. Annan's deputy Shashi Tharoor has suggested that "the exercise of American power may well be the central issue in world politics today." Conversely, as our presidential campaign has underscored, the degree to which Washington chooses to look to the UN to fulfill its foreign policy objectives is a central issue of American politics.

From *Commentary*, November 2004, excerpted from pp. 36–42. Copyright © 2004 by Commentary. Reprinted by permission.

❧◈❧

In 1990, the world body broke free from 45 years of cold-war paralysis to respond to Iraq's absorption of Kuwait. President George H. W. Bush had opted to take the matter to the Security Council even before laying it before the U.S. Congress for a remarkable reason: once he concluded that the liberation of Kuwait would require the use of force, he knew it would be easier to win the assent of the Soviet Union, China, France, and Britain—the other permanent members of the Security Council—than of Democrats in Congress. Only with this endorsement in hand was he able to gain a narrow majority in the U.S. Senate.

It was no doubt as a result of this experience that the first Bush administration left office proclaiming high hopes for the UN, which it said had "been given a new lease on life, emerging as a central instrument for the . . . preservation of peace." Succeeding Bush, Bill Clinton took a still more hopeful view. Determined as he was to "focus like a laser" on the domestic economy, Clinton declared that, to handle international problems, he would rely more on the world body. His first UN ambassador, Madeleine Albright, envisioned "assertive multilateralism" as a cornerstone of both U.S. policy and world peace. Kofi Annan's predecessor, Boutros Boutros-Ghali of Egypt, saw in this post-cold-war American attitude an "extraordinary opportunity; to expand, adapt, and reinvigorate the work of the United Nations."

But within two years, Clinton's and Boutros-Ghali's hopes were dashed. In Somalia, Clinton had wanted to remove the American troops that were sent there by his predecessor to help stem a famine caused mostly by the depredations of rival warlords. Yielding to Boutros-Ghali's pleas, he left behind a substantial contingent as the backbone of a UN force undertaking to build a nation in that godforsaken land. This well-intentioned gesture turned to debacle in October 1993 when eighteen U.S. Army Rangers, and as many as 1,000 Somalis, died in a ferocious battle in Mogadishu later immortalized in the movie *Black Hawk Down*.

The American losses, at the hands of Somalis whom we were there only to help, put a lasting chill on this kind of mission and, by extension, others under a UN banner.

Somalia, however, turned out to be the least in a string of disasters for the U.S., the UN, and relations between the two. Hot on the heels of Mogadishu there unfolded the world's first indisputable case of genocide since the Holocaust. In the spring of 1994, even without the benefit of the Nazi technology of murder, Hutus in Rwanda slaughtered their Tutsi countrymen (along with moderate Hutus) at a pace that rivaled Hitler's killing of Jews.

Not only did the UN stand aside as these unspeakable events occurred, but a small UN force that was already on the scene to enforce an earlier peacekeeping agreement was pulled back lest anyone in a blue helmet perish alongside the intended victims. The U.S. government, determined to avoid anything that smacked of a replay of Mogadishu, did more than its share to block any action by the Security Council that could put an American soldier in harm's way. Years later, Bill Clinton offered the most grudging of apologies. "The international community," he said, "must bear its share of responsibility for this tragedy." He did not bring himself to acknowledge that, in this instance, "the international community" was first and foremost himself.

⋯◉⋯

If the U.S. bore blame for the Rwanda catastrophe, the UN covered itself in shame. Although it is often said that the UN is nothing more than the sum of its member states, this is but a partial truth. Collective or derivative bodies take on lives of their own. The Secretary General of the United Nations is a major world figure, commanding a budget of $3 billion and a staff of some 15,000. Key members of this formidable apparatus, it was eventually revealed, had been forewarned of the Rwanda genocide months before it began.

General Roméo Dallaire, the Canadian commander of the UN force stationed there, had relayed reports that Hutu extremists were stockpiling weapons and training for a campaign of "extermination." Dallaire proposed to seize the weapons in the hope of disrupting the plan. His message was received by the UN's Department of Peacekeeping Operations with alarm—not at the prospect of genocide, but at the prospect that Dallaire might do something risky to prevent it. Clear orders were dispatched vetoing Dallaire's proposed intervention. "The overriding consideration," they read, "is the need to avoid entering into a course of action that might lead to the use of force and unanticipated consequences."

Even after the killing began, Dallaire "could have easily stopped" it, he claimed, with the forces already at his disposal plus several hundred others who were readily accessible. But his orders remained otherwise. As recounted in a new book by Dore Gold, Israel's former ambassador to the world body, "the UN told Dallaire simply to focus on evacuating foreigners from Rwanda. Dallaire told officers that he had received orders from UN headquarters in New York that no Rwandans were to be rescued: 'Orders from New York: no locals.'"

Reprehensible as was the UN's part in the Rwanda calamity, it was still worse in the grim events that unfolded in Bosnia-Herzegovina from 1992 through 1995. Both the member states and the secretariat shared in the culpability. The Security Council responded to the first inkling of trouble by imposing an arms embargo. Although the embargo applied to both sides, its consequences were disparate. The Serbian aggressors who were out to "cleanse" Bosnia of its Muslim plurality were hardly affected; they had at their disposal the formidable arsenal of the Yugoslav army. Their victims, however, were short of weapons, and the embargo contributed to their helplessness. Adding insult to injury, Secretary General Boutros-Ghali dismissed their plight as a "rich man's war." . . .

⋯◉⋯

. . . By design, the organization, which grew out of the anti-Axis coalition of World War II, was supposed to take sides with victims against aggressors. But from the start, it has inveterately refused to do so.

The first tests came in 1948. One was the openly announced attack by the nations of the Arab League on the infant state of Israel, at whose birth the UN itself had played midwife. Although the aggression and its annihilating intent were undisguised, the UN did not condemn it. Rather, it called on "all persons and organizations in Palestine" to "cease all activities of military or para-military nature." A similarly painstaking evenhandedness informed the Security Council's response to the second test of 1948: India's complaint to the UN about a Muslim offensive in Kashmir spearheaded, it said, by infiltrated Pakistani troops.

These precedents of strict neutrality between attackers and defenders made nonsense of the principles on which the organization was founded. But it has been the norm of UN behavior ever since, while the 1991 resistance to the occupation of Kuwait—driven by the steely determination of President Bush and British Prime Minister Margaret Thatcher—has been the rare exception. . . .

Even if it proved unable to muster the military strength to become the bulwark of world order that its founders had envisioned, the UN could have stood as an inspiration, a beacon of right and wrong in the behavior of states. It has, alas, been nothing of the sort.

Exhibit A under this heading, as I and others have rehearsed in detail, is the UN's record in the field of human rights. The central dynamic is this: those governments that repress and abuse their subjects most viciously are often the most energetic in seeking election to the UN Commission on Human Rights, for the simple reason that membership will make it easier to shield themselves from criticism. Year after year, fully half of the governments that Freedom House cites as "the worst of the worst" human-rights violators secure seats on the body overseeing human-rights abuses. They include China, Cuba, Sudan, Syria, Saudi Arabia, and Libya, which recently held the chair.

At its annual meeting, the commission adopts resolutions of two types. Some are abstract, affirming every imaginable right for every conceivable demographic group. These pour forth in nearly endless profusion; they cost little and are worth little more. The other resolutions criticize specific countries or governments. Almost never does such criticism extend to any of those countries, no matter how brutal, that have won election to the commission.

This holds true for both Left and Right: neither China nor Saudi Arabia has ever suffered a word of censure. Usually, a dozen or so violators are subjected to admonishments that are in most cases mild. For example, on one of the rare occasions that the dictatorship of Fidel Castro has been mentioned, the commission "invited" the government of Cuba, whose "efforts to give effect to the social rights of the population despite an adverse international environment are to be recognized, to make efforts to achieve similar progress in respect of human, civil, and political rights."

❧❦❧

Exhibit B in the indictment of the UN's moral turpitude is the differential treatment accorded to Israel. The UN, according to its founding Charter, is "based on the principle of the sovereign equality of all its members." But, to paraphrase Orwell, some states are less equal than others. Until recently, Israel was excluded from membership in any regional caucus, which has meant (under UN rules) that it has also been uniquely excluded from eligibility for a seat on the Security Council or other committees. Even though the United States has now won admission for Israel to the catch-all Western group to which we, too, belong (the so-called Western Europe and Others Group), its membership is attenuated, valid for UN bodies based in New York but not in Geneva, and its eligibility for the Security Council has been deferred for several years.

At meetings of the Commission on Human Rights, where the world's dictators can expect at most a single limp rebuke, Israel is treated in a class by itself, occupying a special item on the agenda. It is the subject of five to eight separate resolutions each year, which castigate it in harsh terms applied to no one else. . . .

Finally, the overweening animus toward Israel has gone hand in hand with still another egregious moral failing—namely, the UN's complicity in legitimizing terrorism, not only against Israel but against the democratic West, especially the United States. Gold cites a 1970 resolution of the General Assembly in which the UN affirmed "its recognition of the legitimacy of the struggle of the colonial peoples and peoples under alien domination to exercise their right to self-determination and independence by all the necessary means at their disposal." He comments cogently:

> This was a historic shift . . . and it occurred at a time when international terrorism was on the rise, with the world facing a new wave of airplane hijackings. The UN's new position could only be understood by those who regarded themselves as "national-liberation movements" as a license to commit murder in the name of the cause of self-determination.

On subsequent occasions, the General Assembly reaffirmed this doctrine, and in recent years it has been endorsed annually by the Commission on Human Rights. Palestinian—and now, it would seem, Iraqi—suicide bombing is thus validated as nothing less than an exercise of human rights. So routine has this macabre affirmation become that an overwhelming majority of the European Union members that sit on the commission vote for it each year. In a like vein, when Kofi Annan managed to propose a new convention against terrorism in the wake of 9/11, his efforts were beaten back by the Organization of the Islamic Conference, which insisted it would condemn "terrorism" only if it were defined by the objectives of the perpetrator rather than by the nature of the act.

⁓⊙⁓

It was in the light of similarly gross derelictions of reason and decency during the years of the cold war that the late Daniel Patrick Moynihan, speaking soon after stepping down as U.S. ambassador to the UN nearly three decades years ago, described the body as a "squalid circus," and wondered aloud how long we could bear to remain a part of it. Now Gold brings us face to face with the reality that, even with the passing of the Soviet Union, the UN's moral failings have not much diminished.

Are there nevertheless grounds for hope? In December, the UN's own High-Level Panel on Threats, Challenges, and Change will bring forth its recommendations. In appointing the panel last year, Annan charged it with proposing reforms, even "radical reforms." But its composition, which includes Brent Scowcroft, former Russian Prime Minister Yevgeny Primakov, Arab League chief Amr Moussa, and other, similar venerables, makes it an unlikely vehicle for any such mission.

This is, indeed, the fifth major reform initiative since Annan became Secretary General in 1996. It follows by less than a year the appointment of a Panel of Eminent Persons on United Nations-Civil Society Relations. This in turn followed the Secretary General's own program of reform in 2002 and the Millennium Summit of September 2000, whose report was similarly concerned largely with reform. All of these were preceded by a 1997 program for reform proposed by Annan and adopted by the General Assembly in December of that year. Setting aside questions about Annan's personal devotion to the task, the reform process under his tenure has proved predictably ineffectual.

Nor did the process begin with Annan. His predecessor, Boutros-Ghali, sponsored at least two major reform panels. Indeed, as Edward Luck has pointed out, even "before the UN could hold its first meeting, a number of states were already calling for its reform." But then Luck, a leading academic authority on the UN and a former president of the United Nations Association, adds:

> Does the déjà-vu nature of UN reform suggest that nothing changes or that reform is bound to fail? Not at all; indeed it could be argued that change is one of the few constants in the UN system. It incessantly has to adapt to an evolving mosaic of demands, priorities, and initiatives. . . . And few institutions are so fond of producing or coopting fresh conceptual and doctrinal approaches to addressing the world's problems.

As against this cheery assessment, one must ask where the tangible gain from all the UN's "fresh conceptual and doctrinal approaches" is to be found. In what ways has the organization improved? Annan himself, however comfortably he may wear the mantle of reform, can legitimately be seen as a symbol of much that is wrong with the institution. He is, after all, the quintessential product of the UN bureaucracy, the first Secretary General to have risen to his post through the ranks rather than winning it for his political standing in his own country.

The UN system is secretive; mechanisms of accountability are few. The officers are beholden to no public constituency, and, thanks to diplomatic immunity, subject to few laws. Hence, advancement need not be predicated on success. Annan acceded to his current eminence from the position of head of the UN's office of peacekeeping during the calamitous 1990's. As Philip Gourevitch has summarized the record:

> [M]any of the newer missions were in countries where there was no real peace to keep: Cambodia, Somalia, the former Yugoslavia, and . . . Rwanda.

With the exception of the mission to Cambodia, which was able to claim a deeply compromised success before it withdrew, all of these operations would meet with catastrophe on Annan's watch, at the end of which he was elevated to Secretary General.

. . . As for the legality of America's war in Iraq, this is a subject about which reasonable people may differ; but Annan's own contribution to the events that led to the war ought to disqualify him for judgment. When, in 1998, Saddam Hussein first moved to eviscerate the UN programs inspecting his efforts on weapons of mass destruction, it was Annan who interceded by means of a personal mission to Baghdad to rescue the Iraqi dictator from military strikes that the Clinton administration was preparing. "I can do business with him," Annan said of Saddam then. At almost the same time, Annan secured a vast expansion of the UN's oil-for-food program, from which it now appears that Saddam skimmed some $10 billion and the UN itself reaped a hefty commission. Had Saddam's intransigence not been encouraged in these ways by Annan, there is at least a chance that war with Iraq might have been avoided.

If Annan himself is an improbable figure to cure what ails the UN, his High-Level Panel is unlikely even to address the subject. "The panel will almost certainly focus on a single issue: the composition of the Security Council, which many countries want expanded so that they will have more opportunity to sit on it. Germany, Japan, India, and Brazil are pushing to become permanent members, holding a power of veto like the current "permanent five." Whatever the merit in these demands, they all center on the wish of countries to gratify their own prestige. None of the formulas currently being discussed even pretends to address the utter failure of the Security Council to play its intended role of defending the peace. To the contrary, all of them, if enacted, are certain to make the problem more acute, since any expansion (especially with veto power added in) will make an already unwieldy body thoroughly paralytic.

Independent observers seeking to cure the UN have focused less on structure than on politics, urging the formation of a caucus of democracies within the UN; the idea boasts some supporters in the American government, including in Congress. Such a caucus might serve to overcome the rank hypocrisy with which the body addresses human rights, and it might conceivably weaken the stranglehold that the retrograde "Non-Aligned Movement" holds on the General Assembly and other bodies. For his part, Gold calls this proposal "only a partial solution." He urges a more radical step, namely, the creation of a Community of Democracies as a *substitute* for the UN rather than as a caucus within it.

Perhaps a community, of this kind would escape the pit-falls that have dogged the UN, but any move along these lines is a long way off. In any case, although other world democracies have been willing to attend large conferences of democracies, they have shown precious little interest in joining any

UN caucus that would take the place of sub-groups in which they already participate to their own parochial advantage.

In the here and now, the world is thus left to face the choice embodied in the two contrasting figures who stood out at the opening of this year's General Assembly. One offers the image of a world in which the United Nations acts as the supreme political arbiter, the other an image of a world shaped by American leadership.

In terms of the prospects for peace, the alternative is stark. For nearly 60 years, the UN has proved an abject failure at safeguarding "international peace and security" (in the words of the Charter). It has in fact scaled back its ambitions to mere "peacekeeping," a specialized term that refers narrowly to policing internal conflicts. And even this has been diminished to policing such conflicts only *after* they have already been resolved. As Annan himself has put it: "Peacekeepers must never again be deployed into an environment in which there is no cease-fire or peace agreement."

Still, the world has known a large degree of peace since 1945, which it owes not to the UN but in large measure to American action. Through NATO, Europe has been at peace. Thanks to America's alliances with Japan, Australia, South Korea, and Taiwan, there has also been a measure of peace in Asia. As for the Middle East, an obvious exception, it would have been even more turbulent had America not deterred aggressors from preying on Jordan, Israel, Saudi Arabia, or the weak but rich sheikdoms of the Persian Gulf. In Latin America, which has been mostly calm for reasons having little to do with the U.S., America has suppressed and constrained radical elements that have sought to roil the waters.

Only twice in these six decades has the UN acted to turn back a breach of the peace: Korea in 1950 and Kuwait in 1990–91. On both occasions, the Security Council acted not through the peace-enforcing machinery spelled out in the Charter but by giving the United States a writ of authority to do the job.

The implications of this are clear. A world left to the UN as supreme arbiter would not be the world of law of Kofi Annan's incantation. It would be the opposite: a world of lawlessness. Nor would a United States that had been induced to yield to the superior majesty of the UN be replaced by an equivalent force for good, and certainly not by the UN itself. Instead, the peace we have known since 1945 would crumble.

True, no UN rule or regime could stay America from defending its own territory and citizenry. But numerous weaker nations whose security America has linked to its own would pay dearly for the wistful dream of a parliament of man, a dream that the sordid reality of the UN has turned into a mockery. And for this, in the end, America would surely suffer as well.

POSTSCRIPT

Does the United Nations Promote World Peace and Security?

No defense of the United Nations can make the extravagant claim that has created a world of peace or universal acceptance of human rights. Similarly, no rejection of the UN is persuasive that does no more than demonstrate its failure to have achieved these visionary goals. Fairly phrased, the issue whether America's desire for world peace and national security benefit from the operation of the UN, or whether the UN is an obstacle (or even, as some critics believe, an opponent) of these objectives.

Muravchik has expanded his criticism into a full-length book: *The Future of the United Nations: Understanding the Past to Chart a Way Forward* (AEI Press, 2005). His criticism is telling if we accept his conclusion that the UN's peace-keeping efforts have had effect of aiding well-armed aggressors against ill-armed victims. Madeleine Albright's defense of American participation prevails if the UN has succeeded in preserving or restoring peace and security in situations where no alternative solution held out hope. If the threats confronting the world stem from tyrannical regimes, as Michael Soussan argues in "Can the UN Be Fixed?" (*Commentary*, April 2005), Soussan concludes that such tyrannies should be expelled from the organization. Shashi Tharoor, UN Undersecretary-General for Communications and Public Information, has been an eloquent supporter of the UN's role and America's partcipation in it. In "Why America Still Needs the United Nations" (*Foreign Affairs*, September/October 2003), Tharoor argues that the United States benefits greatly from the fact that the UN is a unique multilateral force in international politics. Ramesh Thakur and Carlyle A. Thayer, editors, *A Crisis of Expectations: UN Peacekeeping in the 1990s* (Westview Press, 1995), contains essays that emphasize the increasing impor-tance of the UN with the end of the Cold War. Edward Newman and Roland Rich, *The UN Role in Promoting Democracy: Between Ideals and Reality* (United Nations University Press, 2004), explores how the ideals of democracy interact with the realities of power, and how the UN succeeds. Jeb Babbin, *Inside the Asy-lum: Why the United Nations and Old Europe Are Worse Than You Think* (Regnery, 2004), concludes that the UN assists international terrorists and pursued other anti-American policies. Dore Gold, *Tower of Babble: How the United Nations Has Fueled Global Chaos* (Crown Publishers, 2004), urges the United States to act alone to champion ideals that are opposed by a majority of UN member states. Gold, the former Israeli ambassador to the United Nations, maintains that the UN is dominated by America's worst enemies: anti-Western force, dictatorships, and state sponsors of terrorism. Jeane Kirkpatrick, former American ambassador to the United Nations, has warmly endorsed this book. Tom DeWeese, "Time to Declare Our Independence from the United Nations" (*Capitalism Magazine on-line*, May 5, 2005), asserts that the UN is a criminal enterprise in which a moral nation should not participate.

In *Making War and Building Peace: United Nations Peace Operations* (Princeton University Press, 2006) Michael W. Doyle and Nicholas Sambanis evaluate U.N. peacekeeping before, during, and after civil wars in various countries, comparing situations where the U.N. was involved to those where it was not. On the whole, the authors conclude, the U.N. has not been effective in heading off or moderating civil wars but it has played a useful role in their aftermath.

In a speech to the UN General Assembly in 2003, Secretary General Kofi Annan acknowledged that the UN did not meet the needs of its members, including the United States. He said: "We have come to a fork in the road. This may be a moment no less decisive than 1945 itself, when the United Nations was founded. . . . I believe the time is ripe for a hard look at fundamental policy issues, and at the structural changes that may be needed in order to strengthen them." He went on to call for "radical reform."

Annan appointed what he called a High-Level Panel on Threats, Challenges, and Change. In 2005, it appeared that one conclusion of this panel was that the UN might be more aggressive in mounting military operations against forces that engaged in mass killings. This raises the question of whether the UN is capable of reform, as Albright suggests, or whether the structure is fatally flawed, as Muravchik indicates.

Dispute over the value of the UN has never abated in the United States, and intensified when President George W. Bush nominated John Bolton, Undersecretary of States for Arms Control and International Security, to be the American Ambassador to the United Nations. Bolton, an outspoken critic of the UN, has said in 1994, "There is no such thing as the United Nations. There is an international community that occasionally can be led by the only real power left in the world and that is the United States when it suits our interest and we can get others to go along." Bolton's blunt statement posed the decisive question: Does the United States go along with the UN, or does it dissent when it believes that America's best interests are opposed to it?

ISSUE 21

Must America Exercise World Leadership?

YES: Robert J. Lieber, from *The American Era: Power and Strategy for the 21st Century* (Cambridge University Press, 2005)

NO: Niall Ferguson, from "An Empire in Denial," *Harvard International Review* (Fall 2003)

ISSUE SUMMARY

YES: International relations professor Robert J. Lieber believes that the United States, as the world's sole superpower, is uniquely capable of providing leadership against the threats of terrorism and weapons of mass destruction, as well as extending the rule of law and democracy.

NO: Author Niall Ferguson maintains that despite America's military and economic dominance, it lacks both the long-term will and the capital and human investment that would be necessary to sustain its dominance.

For centuries, great empires conquered and exploited distant colonies. All this changed with World War II, from which the United States emerged as the greatest military and economic power the world had ever known, without creating a network of colonies.

How was that power to be employed, if it was to be used at all? Before 1940, the United States avoided involvement in international relations beyond the Americas. This sentiment went back to the warning in President Washington's farewell address to avoid "entangling alliances." As long as the United States felt separated from most of the rest of the world by two great oceans, it thought it was impregnable and remained out of the League of Nations. Isolation no longer seemed possible after World War II, and an international role became inescapable as a consequence of instant communications, rapid transportation, increasing dependence on international trade, and the development of weapons of mass destruction (WMD).

For forty-five years after World War II, the supremacy of the United States was challenged by the military expansionism of the Soviet Union.

Confronted by this threat, liberal internationalism took the place of isolationism as the world seemed to divide between two superpowers, both capable of building and employing nuclear and other WMDs. Only the prospect of what seemed the certainty of what was dubbed Mutual Assured Destruction (MAD) kept both nations from using these weapons. The United States relied on the doctrine of containment to confine communist power. This policy called for the participation of allies in multinational treaties, United Nations resolutions, the North Atlantic Treaty Organization (NATO), and other political and military alliances.

This liberal internationalism was identified with the advocacy of self-determination, democracy, and human rights. The United States sometimes fell short of such ideals when it embraced anti-communist regimes that were not democratic or overlooked gross abuses of human rights, but it never discarded its moral posture in opposition to what President Reagan called "the evil empire" of the Soviet Union. The disintegration of the Soviet empire as a threat to Western democracy left the United States as the sole superpower.

Since the 9/11 attack, the United States has assumed a mantle of world leadership. If America is a new empire (as both authors in the following selections agree), it is different from empires of the past, without vast colonies, but with unparalleled military and economic strength, as well as unprecedented cultural and technological impact. The clearest official statement of the Bush foreign policy is found in "The National Security Strategy of the United States of America," issued by the National Security Council in 2002 (available on the Internet), which proclaims America's world leadership in fighting terrorism, preempting threats, and spreading democracy, development, free markets, and free trade throughout the world.

Where this differs most significantly from that of previous administrations is in its unilateralism. The U.S. government proclaimed a commitment to act on behalf of America's best interests irrespective of the objections or reservations of its allies or the United Nations. Contrast the unwillingness of President George H. W. Bush in 1991 to have the American army enter Baghdad and overthrow the regime of Saddam Hussein, because it would alienate some of America's allies, with the determination of President George W. Bush in 2003 to engage in the second war against Iraq despite the failure of the United Nations or many nominal allies to support that action.

An unwillingness to compromise the American government's perception of its best interests led the second President Bush to reject treaties on land mines, nuclear proliferation, biological and chemical warfare, the International Criminal Court, and other international agreements, and to justify preemptive strikes in the absence of an attack upon the United States or a treaty ally.

The differences between Robert J. Lieber and others who are prepared to have America act alone and Niall Ferguson and others who insist on international cooperation are differences as to what needs to be done, what the United Nations can do, and whether the United States can long sustain responsibility for world peace and security.

YES

Robert J. Lieber

The American Era: Power and Strategy for the 21st Century

References to America's unmatched power have become common-place, not only among those who welcome it, but especially by those who disdain it. The assessment made some years ago by a former French foreign minister is worth quoting, the more so because he spent so much of his time trying to stimulate a counterbalancing coalition, "The United States of America today predominates on the economic level, on the monetary level, on the military level, on the technological level, and in the cultural area in the broad sense of the word. It is not comparable, in terms of power and influence, to anything known in modern history."

All the same, it is well worth contemplating what this preponderance means in practice. Consider, first, the military realm. In material terms, no other country or group of countries comes close to approaching America's capacity in warfare and in virtually every dimension of modern military technology. Nor does any other country have a comparable ability to project power and to deploy and sustain large and effective forces abroad.

Air power provides a compelling illustration. A single American aircraft carrier with its high technology and precision munitions is capable of striking 700 targets in a single day. There are few, if any, air forces in the world that can muster such power, yet the United States possesses not one but twelve of these carriers and their battle groups. Military spending, too, dwarfs that of any other country and is roughly equivalent to that of the rest of the world combined. Yet at slightly more than 4 percent of GDP annually, this defense burden ought to be relatively manageable compared with levels during the Cold War. (At the height of the Reagan defense buildup in the mid-1998s, the figure was 6.6%, and at times during the 1950s and 1960s it was more than 10%.) Paul Kennedy has previously referred to America's ability to sustain the costs of its world role by observing, "Being Number One at great cost is one thing; being the world's single superpower on the cheap is astonishing."

Other dimensions of American power are impressive in their own right. The most important of these is economic. The United States, with less than 5 percent of the world's population, accounts for more than 30 percent of world GDP. By contrast, in 1914 when Britain was widely regarded as the world's foremost imperial power, its economy amounted to approximately 8 percent of world GDP. In addition, the United States is responsible for more than 40 percent of the world's spending on research and development, and—with Singapore and Finland—is consistently ranked as one of the top three countries in terms of global competitiveness. Moreover, the United States possesses dozens of major research universities, produces the lion's share of Nobel prizewinners in science, medicine, and economics, and exerts a remarkable cultural influence that, for example, accounts for more than 80 percent of world movie box office receipts. The unique traits of American society make the United States adaptable, dynamic, and—despite the impact of post-9/11 visa regulations—a magnet for talented immigrants from around the world. In the words of the *Economist* magazine of London, "The clamour of Indians, Chinese, Guatemalans and millions more to go to America to work or be educated is not merely a mercenary reaction to its wealth. It is a reaction to the blend of opportunity, knowledge and freedom that America provides and that nowhere else comes close to matching."

All in all, American primacy is both robust and unlikely to be challenged in the near future. It is robust because it rests on preponderance across all the realms—military, economic, technological, wealth, and size—by which we measure power. And with the possible exception of China, no other country or group of countries is likely to emerge as an effective global competitor in the coming decades. This unique status is evident when we consider other possible contenders. . . .

After the end of the Cold War, the absence of a single, overarching, and unambiguous threat had the effect of relegating global concerns to a low priority for most Americans, thus making it harder for any administration to gain support for a coherent foreign policy or allocation of substantial resources for that purpose. Abroad, despite allied collaboration in the 1991 Gulf War against Iraq and ultimately in dealing with the civil war in Bosnia and ethnic cleansing in Kosovo, the collapse of the Soviet Union made cooperation more difficult because there no longer seemed to be an Imperative for collective action in the face of a common enemy.

It is no exaggeration to describe September 11, 2001, as the start of a new era in American strategic thinking. The attacks of that morning had an effect comparable to the Pearl Harbor attack on December 7, 1941, which propelled the United States into World War II. In an instant, the events of September 11 transformed the international security environment. The threats from terrorism and weapons of mass destruction that had seemed distant and hypothetical suddenly became a dominant reality, and responding to them necessitated a new grand strategy. Terrorism was no longer one among a number of assorted dangers to the United States but a fundamental threat to America, its way of life, and its vital interests. The al-Qaeda terrorists who masterminded the use of hijacked jumbo jets to attack the Pentagon and to destroy the twin towers of the World Trade Center were carrying out mass murder as a means of political intimidation.

The gravity of this danger was amplified by two additional factors. First, the cold-blooded willingness to slaughter thousands of innocent civilians without the slightest moral compunction raised fears about potential use of

WMD. Given the terrorists' conduct and statements by their leaders, as well as evidence that state sponsors of terrorism were seeking to acquire chemical, biological, and nuclear weapons, there was a risk that WMD might be used directly against the United States as well as its friends and allies abroad.

Second, in view of the fact that the nineteen terrorists in the four hijacked aircraft committed suicide in carrying out their attacks, the precepts of deterrence were now called into question. By contrast, even at the height of the Cold War, American strategists could make their calculations based on the assumed rationality of Soviet leaders and the knowledge that they would not willingly commit nuclear suicide by initiating a massive attack against the United States or its allies. September 11, however, undermined that key assumption. We thus live at a time when deterrence, which has often worked in confronting hostile states, cannot be relied on in facing non-state actors with millenarian aims and potentially equipped with devastating weapons. Though the threat had been developing for some time, 9/11 demonstrated that this peril is now quite real. Nor is the danger unique to America, as shown by the March 11, 2004, terrorist attack in Madrid—Spain's equivalent of 9/11. As a result there is good reason to act decisively against the most lethal threats, rather than to hope to be able to deter them or to retaliate following a mass casualty attack.

Mechanisms of international law and organization can at times be effective, but international law is not self-enforcing. We continue to live not in a world of global governance, but in a world of states—some of which are benign, others malevolent or even failed. In reality, neither the U.N. nor other international institutions including the European Union are capable of intervening quickly and effectively on life and death matters. Thus, in its own interest, but also in terms of sustaining wider values of liberal democracy and economic openness, the United States can neither allow itself to be subject to an international veto nor disengage from the wider world. Nor should Americans be apologetic about the necessity or capacity of the United States to act. . . .

The terrorism of 9/11 dramatically altered the sense of complacency that had prevailed during the 1990s and provided the impetus for a new grand strategy. In the wake of the attacks, President Bush and his administration were explicit in saying that the war against terror would not be completed quickly, and in January 2002, speaking to a joint session of Congress, Bush outlined what quickly became known as the Bush Doctrine:

> [W]e will shut down terrorist camps, disrupt terrorist plans and bring terrorists to justice. And . . . we must prevent the terrorists and regimes who seek chemical, biological, or nuclear weapons from threatening the United States and the world. . . .
> Yet time is not on our side. I will not wait on events while dangers gather. I will not stand by as peril draws closer and closer. *The United States of America will not permit the world's most dangerous regimes to threaten us with the world's most destructive weapons.*

Two elements were crucial to the doctrine. The first was a sense of urgency, reflected in the words that "time is not on our side." The second was that the unique danger created by weapons of mass destruction required the United States to be prepared to take swift, decisive, and preemptive action. Both of these imperatives reflected the calculation that whatever the risks of acting, the risks of *not* acting were more ominous. These features foreshadowed the elaboration of a grand strategy, published just over a year after the September 11 attacks.

The National Security Strategy of the United States of America (NSS) was released by the White House on September 17, 2002, and immediately attracted wide attention, including both praise as a determined and far-reaching response to the grave dangers America now faced and criticism as a radical and even dangerous departure from foreign policy tradition. In its thirty-two pages, the document provided a candid, ambitious, and far-reaching proclamation of national objectives. First, it called for preemptive military action against hostile states and terrorist groups seeking to develop weapons of mass destruction. Second, it announced that the United States would not allow its global military strength to be challenged by any hostile foreign power. Third, it expressed a commitment to multilateral international cooperation but made clear that the United States "will not hesitate to act alone, if necessary" to defend national interests and security. Fourth, it proclaimed the goal of spreading democracy and human rights around the globe, especially in the Muslim world. . . .

The Bush NSS was not just about power and security. It also committed the United States to spread democracy worldwide and to promote the development of "free and open societies on every continent." To this end, the document called for a comprehensive public information campaign—"a struggle of ideas"—to help foreigners, especially in the Muslim world, learn about and understand America and the core ideas it stands for.

This aspiration embodied deep-seated themes within American history and evoked ling-standing beliefs about foreign policy. In particular, the idea that the exercise of American power goes hand in hand with the promotion of democratic principles can be found in the policy pronouncements of U.S. Presidents from Woodrow Wilson to John F. Kennedy, Ronald Reagan, and Bill Clinton (whose 1993 inaugural address proclaimed, "Our hopes, our hearts, our hands, are with those on every continent who are building democracy and freedom. Their cause is America's"). This combination of values reflects both a belief in universal ideals ("The United States," the NSS declares, "must defend liberty and justice because these principles are right and true for all people everywhere") and a judgment that promoting these principles abroad not only benefits citizens of other countries, but also increases U.S. national security by making foreign conflicts less likely because democracies are unlikely to attack on another.

The National Security Strategy committed the United States to "actively work to bring the hope of democracy, development, free markets, and free trade to every corner of the world." This objective was driven by the belief that the fundamental cause of radical Islamic terrorism lies in the absence of democracy, the prevalence of authoritarianism, and the lack of freedom and opportunity in the Arab world. In the past, this idea might have been dismissed as political rhetoric. But after September 11, even the United Nations in its 2002 *Arab Human Development Report* and in subsequent reports in 2003 and 2005, defined the problem similarly and called for the extension of representative institutions and basic human freedoms to the Muslim Middle East. A Bush speech to the National Endowment for Democracy in November 2003 provided an elaboration that was both moral and strategic in its commitment to democratization, while criticizing half a century of policies that had failed to make this a priority: "Sixty years of Western nations excusing and accommodating the lack of freedom in the Middle East did nothing to make us safe, because in the long run stability cannot be purchased at the expense of liberty."

The commitment to democratization was Wilsonian in its scope and ambition, but the practicality of this aspiration was daunting. The difficulties of reconstruction and political stabilization in Afghanistan and Iraq were sobering, and the American emphasis on democratization in the wider Middle East drew extensive criticism from domestic and European critics, who saw these efforts as overly ambitious and potentially destabilizing, and from Arab authoritarian governments, who depicted the approach as an imperialistic imposition of American and Western values. Media criticisms in the Arab world often struck similar notes, but a smaller number of Arab authors and political figures did speak up—often at great personal risk—to defend such initiatives as a means of breaking the tenacious hold of authoritarian rule throughout the region. . . .

The commitment to spread democracy "to every corner of the world" does remain an ideal and a long-term goal, one reiterated by president Bush in his second inaugural address, in acknowledging that the "great objective of ending tyranny" is "the concentrated work of generations." Often, external encouragement of liberalization is likely to be the most feasible course of action, yet remarkable achievements have been evident in the Middle East, not only in countries where the United States has led military intervention, but elsewhere as well. In Afghanistan and Iraq, the first free elections have taken place, drawing large voter turnouts even in the face of violence and intimidation by those opposed to democratization. In Gaza and the West Bank, Palestinians voted to elect a president, and in Gaza they held genuinely free local elections. These are initial steps in the face of serious obstacles, but they are noteworthy achievements and there are signs of ferment elsewhere in the region, both on the part of those seeking change and by existing regimes feeling more pressure to liberalize.

꧁⟐꧂

The United States possesses the military and economic means to act assertively on a global basis, but *should* it do so, and if so, how? In short, if the United States conducts itself in this way, will the world be safer and more stable, and is such a role in America's national interest? Here, the anarchy problem is especially pertinent. The capacity of the United Nations to act, especially in coping with the most urgent and deadly problems, is severely limited, and in this sense, the demand for "global governance" far exceeds the supply. Since its inception in

1945, there have only been two occasions (Korea in 1950 and Kuwait in 1991) when the U.N. Security Council authorized the use of force, and in both instances the bulk of the forces were provided by the United States.

In the most serious cases, especially those involving international terror-ism, the proliferation of weapons of mass destruction, ethnic cleansing, civil war, and mass murder, if America does not take the lead, no other country or organization is willing or able to respond effectively. The deadly cases of Bosnia (1991–95) and Rwanda (1994) make this clear, in their own way, so did the dem-onstrations by the people of Liberia calling for American intervention to save them from the ravages of predatory militias in a failed state. And the weakness of the international reaction to ethnic cleansing, rape, and widespread killing in the Darfur region of Western Sudan provides a more recent example.

International society, as Michael Walzer has observed, does not function in any way comparable to domestic society, whether in the use of force, rule of law, or effectiveness of its common institutions. As cases in point, North Korean vio-lations of the Nuclear Non-Proliferation Treaty, the funding by former Liberian President Charles Taylor of guerrilla armies in Sierra Leone and the Ivory Coast, and Saddam Hussein's violations of the U.N. sanctions and weapons inspections regime did not meet with effective enforcement by the international community. All too often, meaningful responses to challenges of this kind require ad hoc efforts, and for the most part that means leadership by a major power. . . .

American preponderance is a fact of life by the criteria that are com-monly used in measuring national power. But could this primacy prove to be short-lived? After all, there have been other periods in which judgments about the relative strength or weakness of the United States have proved to be over-stated. For example, in the aftermath of the Cuban missile crisis of October 1962 and into the mid-1960s, foreign policymakers embraced overly ambitious notions of American power and influence. Conversely, during the late 1970s and early 1980s, in reaction to a series of adverse events (the loss of South Vietnam, fall of the American-supported Shah of Iran, Soviet advances in parts of Africa and in Afghanistan, energy crises, and lagging economic perfor-mance), talk of American decline became widespread but proved to be exag-gerated. Instead, the decade of the 1990s saw the collapse of the Soviet Union and provided comprehensive evidence of American strength.

One of the most common contemporary warnings concerns imperial over-extension, in which a great power finds that the cost of maintaining its foreign commitments increasingly exceeds its resources. The process has been described elsewhere, most notably by Paul Kennedy, in his work on the rise and fall of great powers. And Robert Jervis has cautioned, "Avoiding this imperial temptation will be the greatest challenge that the United States faces." Might this happen to the United States? Here it is worth pondering possibilities of military risk, entanglement in a foreign quagmire, erosion of domestic support, and economic decline. . . .

Other developments that are unpredictable but have the potential to weigh on the economy might include, for example, a severe and prolonged interruption of oil imports or terrorist attacks with WMD that result in serious economic disruption and loss of life. Possible longer term causes over the course of a genera-tion or more could include serious deterioration of public primary and secondary education, curtailment in the flow of foreign scientists, engineers, and students working or studying in the United States, difficulty in coping with the steeply rising costs of retirement, disability, and medical benefits, or an unexpected erosion in society's ability to absorb large immigrant populations. However, other than China, which has the potential to become a formidable challenger, the U.S. economy is likely to maintain its edge over Japan, Russia, and Europe, all of whom lag behind the United States in competitiveness and face far more serious demographic pressures involving low birth rates, aging populations, and a declining ratio of those in the active work force compared with retirees.

౼ఉ౿

How a grand strategy is put into practice can be as important as the substance of that strategy. Here, the interplay between power and diplomacy is crucial. As Stanley Hoffmann has observed, diplomacy without power is impotent, but power without diplomacy is blind. A wise choice of priorities is equally essential, since the range of possible foreign commitments is vast.

Critics of an assertive grand strategy incorporate varying assumptions. Realists overstate the likelihood of other countries effectively balancing against American power and are too sanguine about what would occur if the United States really did disengage from its principal foreign commitments. Liberal internationalists, on the other hand, often exaggerate the effectiveness and cohesion of international institutions and idealize the motives of other countries who actually seek to use international organizations to constrain the United States rather than to achieve collective goals. And ultimately, neither realists nor liberal internationalists give sufficient weight to the implications of 9/11 and the gravity of the threats to American national security that it represents.

All the same, the risks of over-commitment are real. In the mid-1960s, when both the power and purpose of the United States seemed unparalleled, the kennedy and Johnson administrations found themselves drawn into Vietnam. At the time, a sense of benign invincibility shaped foreign policy-making in an atmosphere where our purposes seemed noble and our capacity to achieve those purposes unlimited. Decisions about the American role in Indochina thus unfolded without sufficient regard to priorities and limits. In the end, the United States was unable to achieve its objectives and withdrew after costly expenditures of lives, material resources, political capital, and domestic consensus. This experience means not that intervention and the use of force must not be undertaken, but that decisions about these issues need to be prioritized, carefully weighed, and skillfully implemented.

The United States today possesses unique strengths, but its ability to achieve desired outcomes is not infinite. It is thus essential that the application of power, including political commitments and military engagement, be focused on those cases in which American national interest is most squarely at stake. This dictates a focus on those places where nuclear proliferation and radical Islamist terrorism pose particular threats, and hence American grand strategy must be framed with such compelling priorities in mind.

Niall Ferguson  **NO**

An Empire in Denial: The Limits of U.S. Imperialism

It used to be only foreigners and those on the fringes of US politics who referred to the "American Empire." Invariably, they did so in order to criticize the United States. Since the attack on the World Trade Center in September 2001, however, there has been a growing volume of more serious writing on the subject of an American empire. The phrase is now heard both in polite academic company and in mainstream public debate. The striking thing is that not all those who now openly use the term "empire" do so pejoratively. A number of commentators—notably Max Boot, Thomas Donnelly, Robert Kaplan, and Charles Krauthammer—seem to relish the idea of a US imperium. "Today there is only one empire." James Kurth of Swarthmore College declared in a recent article in the *National Interest,* "the global empire of the United States."

Officially, however, the United States remains an empire in denial. In the words of US President George Bush during his presidential election campaign in 2000: "America has never been an empire. We may be the only great power in history that had the chance, and refused—preferring greatness to power, and justice to glory." Freud defined denial as a primitive psychological defense mechanism against trauma. Perhaps it was therefore inevitable that, in the aftermath of the September 11 attacks, US citizens would deny their country's imperial character more vehemently than ever. It may nevertheless be therapeutic to determine the precise nature of this American Empire—since empire it is, in all but name.

Imperial denial may simply be a matter of semantics. Many post-war writers about US power have used words like "hegemon" to convey the idea that US overseas influence is great but not imperial. There are other useful alternatives to the term "empire," including "unipolarity," global "leadership," and "the only superpower." Define the term "empire" narrowly enough, and the United States can easily be excluded from the category. Suppose empire is taken to mean "the forcible military occupation and governance of territory whose citizens remain permanently excluded from political representation." By that definition, the American Empire is laughably small. The United States accounts for around 6.5 percent of the world's surface, but its 14 formal dependencies add up to a mere 0.007 percent. In demographic terms, the United States and its dependencies account for barely five percent of the world's population, whereas the British ruled between one-fifth and one-quarter of the world's population at the zenith of their empire.

Yet this narrow definition of empire is as simplistic as it is convenient. To begin with, the expansion of the original 13 US states westwards and southwards in the course of the 19th century was itself a quintessentially imperialist undertaking. In both the US and British empires, indigenous populations were vanquished, expropriated and marginalized. The people living in the newer states were all ultimately enfranchised, but so were the settler populations of large tracts of the British Empire: "responsible government" was, after all, granted to Canada, Australia, New Zealand, and South Africa. The only substantial difference between the two processes of white settlement was that the United States absorbed most of its new territories—even Alaska and Hawaii—into its federal system, whereas the British never did more than toy with the idea of imperial federation.

In any case, the US empire is—and can afford to be—much less concerned with the acquisition of large areas of overseas territory than Britain's was. The United States has few formal colonies, but it possesses a great many small areas of territory within notionally sovereign states that serve as bases for its armed services. Before the deployment of troops for the invasion of Iraq, the US military had around 752 military installations located in more than 130 countries. New wars have meant new bases, like Camp Bondsteel in Kosovo, acquired during the 1999 war against Yugoslavia, and the Bishkek airbase in Kyrgyzstan, an "asset" picked up during the war against the Taliban regime in Afghanistan.

When the full extent of US military presence overseas is made plain, then the claim that the United States is not an empire rings hollow indeed. Nor should it be forgotten what formidable military technology can be unleashed from these bases. Commentators like to point out that the Pentagon's budget equals the combined military expenditures of the next 12 to 15 states. Such fiscal measures nevertheless understate the quantitative and qualitative lead currently enjoyed by US armed forces. In military terms, the British Empire did not dominate the full spectrum of military capabilities, as the United States does today; it was never so far ahead of its imperial rivals. If military power is the *sine qua non* of an empire, then it is hard to deny the imperial character of the United States today. The US sphere of military influence is now quite literally global.

It is, of course, conventional wisdom that large-scale overseas military commitments can have deleterious economic effects. Yet the United States seems a very long way from the kind of "overstretch" Paul Kennedy warned against in the late 1980s. According to one estimate, "America's 31 percent share of world product (at market prices) is equal to the next four countries (Japan, Germany, Britain, and France) combined," which exceeds the highest share of global output ever achieved by Great Britain by a factor of three. In terms of raw resources, then, the United States is already a vastly more powerful empire than Britain ever was. The rapid growth of the US economy since the late 1980s partly explains how the United States has managed to achieve a unique revolution in military affairs while at the same time substantially reducing the share of defense expenditures as a proportion of gross domestic product (GDP). The Defense Department Green Paper published in March 2003 forecast total expenditure on national defense to remain at 3.5 percent of GDP for at least three years, compared with an average figure during the Cold War of seven percent. Bearing in mind Paul Kennedy's "formula" that "if a particular nation is allocating *over the long term* more than 10 percent of gross national product (GNP) to armaments, that is likely to limit its growth rate," there seems little danger of imminent "overstretch."

In short, in terms of military capability and economic resources the United States not only resembles the last great Anglophone empire but exceeds it. Nor are its goals so very different. In September 2002, the Office of the President produced a document on "National Security Strategy" that explicitly states that it is a goal of US foreign policy "to extend the benefits of freedom . . . to every corner of the world." There are those who argue that such altruism is quite different from the more self-serving aims of British imperialism, but this betrays an ignorance of the comparably liberal ethos of the Victorian Empire. In any case, the National Security Strategy also asserts that the United States reserves the right, if the President should deem it necessary, to take pre-emptive military action against any state perceived as a threat to US security. If the US population still refuses to acknowledge that they have become an empire, the doctrine of pre-emption suggests—by way of a compromise—a possible neologism. Perhaps the United States today should be characterized as a pre-empire.

City on a Hill

One argument sometimes advanced to distinguish US "hegemony" from British Empire is qualitative. US power, it is argued, consists not just of military and economic power but also of "soft" power. According to Joseph Nye, "A country may obtain the outcomes it wants in world politics because other countries want to follow it, admiring its values, emulating its example, aspiring to its level of prosperity and openness." Soft power, in other words, is getting what you want without sticks or carrots. In the case of the United States, "it comes from being a shining 'city upon a hill'"—an enticing New Jerusalem of economic and political liberty. Nye is not so naïve as to assume that the US way is inherently attractive to everyone, everywhere. But he does believe that making it attractive matters more than ever before because of the global spread of information technology. To put it simply, soft power can reach the parts of the world that hard power cannot.

But does this really make US power so very different from imperial power? On the contrary. If anything, it illustrates how very like the last Anglophone empire the United States has become. The British Empire, too, sought to make its values attractive to others, though initially the job had to be done by "men on the spot." British missionaries, businessmen, administrators, and schoolmasters fanned out across the globe to "entice and attract" people toward British values.

These foot-slogging efforts were eventually reinforced by technology. It was the advent of wireless radio—and specifically the creation of the British

Broadcasting Corporation (BBC)—which really ushered in the age of soft power in Nye's sense of the term. Within six years, the BBC had launched its first foreign language service—in Arabic, significantly—and, by the end of 1938, it was broadcasting around the world in all the major languages of continental Europe.

In some ways, the soft power that Britain could exert in the 1930s was greater than the soft power of the United States today. In a world of newspapers, radio receivers, and cinemas—where the number of content-supplying corporations (often national monopolies) was relatively small—the overseas broadcasts of the BBC could hope to reach a relatively large number of foreign ears. Yet whatever soft power Britain thereby wielded did nothing to halt the precipitous decline of British power after the 1930s.

This raises the question of how much US soft power really matters today. If the term is to denote anything more than cultural background music to more traditional forms of dominance, it surely needs to be demonstrated that the United States can secure what it wants from other countries without coercing or suborning them, but purely because its cultural exports are seductive. One reason for skepticism about the extent of US soft power today is the very nature of the channels of communication for US culture, the various electronic media through which US culture is currently transmitted tend to run from the United States to Western Europe, Japan, and in the case of television, Latin America. It would be too much to conclude that US soft power is abundant where it is least needed, for it may well be that a high level of exposure to US cinema and television is one of the reasons why Western Europe, Japan, and Latin America are on the whole less hostile to the United States than countries in the Middle East and Asia. But the fact remains that the *range* of US soft power in Nye's sense is more limited than is generally assumed.

One important qualification applies. Whatever the critics of the United States may say, the United States is indeed a very attractive place—and its attraction extends for beyond of range of AOL-TimeWarner and CNN. It is so attractive that millions of foreigners want either to visit the country or to

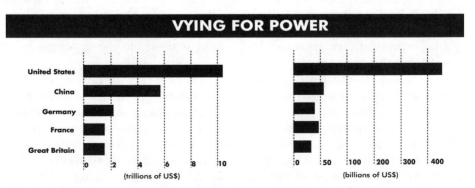

VYING FOR POWER

The graph on the left shows five selected countries with large gross domestic products (GDPs), derived from purchasing power parity calculations. The graph on the right depicts the military spending budgets of those countries. The graphs suggest that the United States is clearly the dominant economic and military power today, much like the British Empire at its height.

move here permanently. In 2000, for example, more than 50 million people visited the United States, making it the world's second most popular holiday destination (after France). That figure is more than double the approximately 20 million US citizens who traveled abroad on vacation. The United States also remains a popular destination for immigrants, with an annual net influx of around three people per thousand of population. Between 1974 and 1998, around 16.7 million foreigners came to live in the United States. About 26 million current US residents were born abroad, a number that vastly exceeds the four million US-born residents abroad. This is, of course, in marked contrast to the experience of Great Britain, which was a remarkable exporter of people throughout its imperial heyday. Between 1850 and 1950, nearly 18 million people left the British Isles.

But does this make the United States more or less powerful? Proponents of the "soft power" thesis argue that the very large numbers of foreign students who come to US universities act–unwittingly–as the agents of US empire when they return to their native lands, imbued with the distinctive value systems of the Harvard Business School or the Stanford Political Science Department. "The ability of the American empire to govern its domains," argues James Kurth, "will depend upon its success in producing this distinct kind of immigrant/emigrant to serve as its distinct kind of imperial civil official." There are two reasons why this seems over-optimistic. First, a substantial proportion of the foreign students simply never return home to spread the good news about US principles and practice. The second is that a very substantial number of the leading nationalists who opposed and ultimately supplanted British rule in both Asia and Africa were themselves the beneficiaries of British university education.

The United States, then, is an empire—but a peculiar kind of empire. It is militarily and economically peerless. It has great, though not unbounded, cultural reach. Yet it has distinctive limitations. It is an empire based not on colonization, but on net immigration. There are also important limits to the way in which its wealth can be deployed. First, there is good reason to fear that, in the foreseeable future, the costs of the US welfare system—specifically, the systems of Medicare and Social Security—will begin to outstrip tax revenues. According to one recent estimate, the difference between the present value of all the federal government's future liabilities and the present value of all its future tax receipts amounts to a staggering US$44 trillion. Only steep cuts in public expenditure or increases in taxation will enable the government to avoid a grave fiscal crisis.

Secondly, the prosperity of the United States has become heavily reliant on very large inflows of foreign capital. With the current account deficit rising above five percent of GDP last year, much (not least the exchange rate of the dollar) depends on the continued willingness of foreign investors to put their savings into dollar-denominated assets. Once again, the contrast between Britain in her imperial prime is pronounced. In the British case, net foreign investment was consistently positive between the mid 1870s and World War I, rising to a peak of nine percent of GDP in 1913. Moreover, the destinations of British overseas investment were very diverse: substantial shares flowed to those relatively poor countries in which Britain had a disproportionate strategic interest. By comparison, US citizens who invest abroad favor Europe (especially Britain) and the Pacific (especially Japan, Australia, and Hong Kong). Barely one percent of US Foreign Direct Investment goes to the Middle East, and even less (0.8 percent) goes to China. This is a far cry from the "dollar diplomacy" of the 1920s, when US loans to strategically important countries in Europe and Latin America played an important role in underpinning US foreign policy. Today, foreign investors are theoretically the ones who have leverage over the United States, since fully 40 percent of the federal debt in public hands is held by foreigners.

This is not to say that those pessimists are right who predict imminent relative decline for the United States. What it does mean is that the United States is not quite the *hyperpuissance* of French nightmares. And what it also means is that, in dealing with transnational threats such as terrorism, international crime, nuclear proliferation, and infectious diseases like AIDS or SARS—to say nothing of global warming—the United States can achieve relatively little by acting unilaterally. As surely as the continuation of international free trade depends on multilateral institutions, so too does the successful prosecution of the war against terrorism.

Does this mean that the United States is not, after all, an empire? On the contrary. As that great imperial statesman Lord Salisbury well understood, there was nothing more dangerous to a great empire than what he called, with heavy irony, "splendid isolation." Then as now, the great Anglophone empire needs perforce to work in concert with the lesser—but not negligible—great powers in order to achieve its objectives.

Consider just one example. It is becoming abundantly clear following the invasions of Afghanistan and Iraq that the United States is not capable of effective peacekeeping—that is to say, policing—without some foreign assistance. Peacekeeping is not what US soldiers are trained to do, nor do they have much appetite for it. It also seems reasonable to assume that the US electorate will not tolerate US soldiers' prolonged exposure to the unglamorous hazards of "low-intensity conflict," with suicide bombers at checkpoints, snipers down alleys, and missile grenade attacks on convoys. The obvious solution is to continue the now well established practice of delegating peacekeeping to the United Nations and, under its auspices, to the US European allies. According to figures published in *Foreign Policy* magazine, the EU states contributed more than twice as much on UN peacekeeping operations as the United States in the years 2000 and 2001.

It is also noteworthy the EU states also contributed three times as much in effective aid to poor countries. Those, like Robert Kagan, who dismiss the Europeans as Kant-reading Venusians—as opposed to America's macho Martians—overlook the crucial significance of Pluto in the process of "nation building." Without hefty investment in creating the rule of law and priming the pump of economic recovery, countries like Afghanistan and Iraq will stagnate, if not disintegrate altogether. Unless the United States radically alters its attitudes toward peacekeeping and aid, it will have little option but to cooperate with the more generous Europeans. Unilateralism, like isolation, is not so splendid after all. Indeed, it is seldom a realistic option for an empire.

Dangers of Denial

The Victorian historian J. R. Seeley famously joked that the British had "conquered and peopled half the world in a fit of absence of mind." In acquiring their empire, the United States has followed this example. Few Europeans today doubt the existence of a US empire. But as the German theologian Reinhold Niebuhr noted in 1960, Americans persist in "frantically avoiding recognition of the imperialism [they] in fact exercise."

Does it matter? The answer is yes. The problem with an empire that is in denial about its own imperial nature is that it tends to make two mistakes when it chooses to intervene in the affairs of lesser states. The first is to attempt economic and political transformation in an unrealistically short timeframe. The second is to allocate insufficient resources to the project. As I write, both of these mistakes are being made in Iraq and Afghanistan. By insisting that US forces will remain in Iraq until a democratic government can be established "and not a day longer," US spokesmen unintentionally create a powerful disincentive for local people to cooperate with them. Who in Iraq today can feel confident that, if he lends support to US initiatives, he will not simply lay himself open to the charge of collaboration when the US troops depart?

Moreover, who would wish to cooperate with an occupying force that spent all its resources on itself and devoted next to nothing to aid or reconstruction? A successful empire is seldom solely based on coercion; there must be some economic dividends for the ruled as well as the rulers, if only to buy the loyalty of indigenous elites. Yet in Iraq and Afghanistan the amounts of money the United States has made available to potential local partners have been paltry.

To put it bluntly, the United States is acting like a colossus with an attention deficit disorder engaged in cut-price colonization. And that is perhaps the reason why this vastly powerful economy, with its extraordinary military capability, has had such a very disappointing record when it has sought to bring about changes of regime abroad. According to one recent study, just four out of 16 US military interventions in foreign countries have been successful in establishing US-style institutions over the past century. The worst failures—in Haiti, Vietnam, Cuba, and Cambodia—might well be attributed to this fatal combination of a truncated time horizon and inadequate resources for non-military purposes.

There is no question, as we have seen, that the United States has the raw economic resources to take on the old British role as underwriter of a globalized, liberalized economic system. Nor is there any doubt that it has the military capability to do the job. On both scores, the United States is already a far more powerful empire than Britain's ever was. Perhaps—though I am less persuaded about this—its "soft power" is also greater. Yet the unspoken American Empire suffers from serious structural weaknesses. It imports rather than exports high quality human capital. It also imports more capital than it exports—and exports virtually none to pivotal regions like the Middle East. It underestimates the need to act in partnership with allied great powers. And its efforts at nation-building are both short-term and under-funded.

Some US neo-imperialists like to quote Kipling's "White Man's Burden," written in 1899 to encourage US President William McKinley's empire-building efforts in the Philippines. But Kipling wrote another poem, two years earlier, which they would also do well to remember. Entitled "Recessional," it was a somber intimation of mortality, perfectly crafted to temper late Victorian delusions of grandeur:

> Far-called our navies melt away—
> On dune and headland sinks the fire—
> Lo, all our pomp of yesterday
> Is one with Nineveh and Tyre!
> Judge of the Nations, spare us yet,
> Lest we forget—lest we forget!

POSTSCRIPT

Must America Exercise
World Leadership?

The disagreement between Robert J. Lieber and Niall Ferguson mirror the conflict between President Bush and those who fashioned the unilateralism of American foreign policy in the aftermath of 9/11 and the multilateralism that was dominant for decades after the end of the Second World War. The older policy depended upon the cooperation of leading nations allied with the United States in containing the Soviet Union and international aggression. The newer policy is premised on the view that the threat of terrorism and the potential use of weapons of mass destruction require the employment of preventive war (in anticipation of a future enemy attack) or even preemptive war (striking when an enemy attack is imminent).

Does support for the Bush doctrine require that America become the policeman of the world— or simply a prudent leader when emergency action is required? Does opposition to the Bush doctrine mean that the United States must never act in the absence of United Nations approval— or may it act to protect American interests when they are threatened? These and related questions are bound to surface in the coming years as Democrats and Republicans battle it out to win the hearts and minds of the American people.

The evolution of American international relations is related in Walter Russell Mead, *Special Providence: American Foreign Policy and How It Changed the World* (Alfred A. Knopf, 2001). Preemption is supported by John Lewis Gaddis, "A Grand Strategy of Transformation" (*Foreign Policy,* November–December 2002) who rhetorically asks: "Who would not have preempted Hitler or Milosevic [the Serbian leader who precipitated war in the former Yugoslavia] or Mohammed Atta [leader of the 9/11 terrorists], if given the chance?"

In the same spirit, Robert Kagan and William Kristol have defended America's "role as guarantor of national security in the Middle East," in "The Right War for the Right Reasons," in *The Weekly Standard,* February 23, 2004. America as the world leader is rejected by Clyde Prestowitz, *Rogue Nation: American Unilateralism and the Failure of Good Intentions* (Basic Books, 2003), and George Soros, "The Bubble of American Supremacy" (*The Atlantic Monthly,* December 2003). Ivo H. Daalder and James M. Lindsay, *America Unbound: The Bush Revolution in Foreign Policy* (Brookings Institution, 2003) conclude that "the fundamental premise of the Bush revolution—that America's security rested on an America unbound—was mistaken." Alan Curtis has edited a volume of essays that are highly critical of post-9/11 national policy in foreign and domestic affairs, *Patriotism, Democracy, and*

Common Sense: Restoring America's Promise at Home and Abroad (The Milton S. Eisenhower Foundation and Rowman & Littlefield Publishers, 2004).

The disagreement between Robert J. Lieber and Niall Ferguson is not likely to be soon resolved. On the contrary, it is likely that a major element in the outcome of the presidential election of 2008 will be how the American electorate perceives America's future role in the world.

Contributors to This Volume

EDITORS

GEORGE McKENNA is professor emeritus and former chair of the department of political science, City College of New York. His publications include *American Populism* (Putnam, 1974), *A Guide to the Constitution: That Delicate Balance* (Random House, 1984), and *The Drama of Democracy* (McGraw-Hill, 1998). He is currently writing a book on the Puritan origins of American patriotism.

STANLEY FEINGOLD, recently retired, held the Carl and Lily Pforzheimer Foundation Distinguished Chair for Business and Public Policy at Westchester Community College of the State University of New York. He received his bachelor's degree from the City College of New York, where he taught courses in American politics and political theory for 30 years, after completing his graduate education at Columbia University. He spent four years as Visiting Professor of Politics at the University of Leeds in Great Britain, and he has also taught American politics at Columbia University in New York and the University of California, Los Angeles. He is a frequent contributor to the *National Law Journal* and *Congress Monthly,* among other publications.

STAFF

Larry Loeppke	Managing Editor
Jill Peter	Senior Developmental Editor
Susan Brusch	Senior Developmental Editor
Beth Kundert	Production Manager
Jane Mohr	Project Manager
Tara McDermott	Design Coordinator
Nancy Meissner	Editorial Assistant
Julie Keck	Senior Marketing Manager
Mary Klein	Marketing Communications Specialist
Alice Link	Marketing Coordinator
Tracie Kammerude	Senior Marketing Assistant
Lori Church	Pemissions Coordinator

AUTHORS

MADELEINE ALBRIGHT served as Secretary of State in the administration of Bill Clinton. She is currently Mortana Distinguished Professor of Diplomacy at the Edmund A. Walsh School of Foreign Service at Georgetown University.

STEPHEN G. BREYER is associate justice of the United States Supreme Court.

GEORGE W. BUSH is the 43rd president of the United States.

CHRISTOPHER C. DeMUTH is president of the American Enterprise Institute for Public Policy Research. He has served in several administrative capacities in the executive branch of the federal government and on the faculty of the Kennedy School of Government at Harvard University.

J. R. DUNN is the former editor of the *International Military Encyclopedia* and a frequent contributor to *The American Thinker,* for which he recently wrote several articles entitled "Prospects of Terror: An Inquiry into Jihadi Alternatives."

GEORGE C. EDWARDS III is professor of political science at Texas A & M University and director of The Center for Presidential Studies. He is editor of the *Presidential Studies Quarterly* and the author of many books on the presidency. Edwards is the editor of *Readings in Presidential Politics* (Wadsworth Publishing, 2005).

NIALL FERGUSON has been a professor of modern European history at Oxford University and financial history at New York University. He is the author of *The Pity of War,* a history of the first World War, and *The Cash Nexus: Money and Power in the Modern World.* His book, *Empire: How Britain Made the Modern World,* was adapted for a television series. His most recent work is *Colossus: The Price of America's Empire.*

ERIC M. FREEDMAN is professor of law in the School of Law at Hofstra University. He chairs the Committee on Civil Rights of the Association of the Bar of the City of New York. He is coauthor, with Monroe H. Freedman, of *Group Defamation and Freedom of Speech: The Relationship Between Language and Violence* (Greenwood Press, 1995).

F. GREGORY GAUSE III is associate professor of political science at the University of Vermont and director of its Middle Eastern program.

ROBERT P. GEORGE is the McCormick Professor of Jurisprudence and director of the James Madison Program in American Ideals and Institutions at Princeton University. Recently, he was appointed by President George W. Bush to the President's Council on Bioethics. He previously served on the U.S. Commission on Civil Rights and as a judicial fellow at the Supreme Court of the United States.

BERNARD GOLDBERG is an Emmy-award winning broadcast journalist who worked for three decades as a television reporter and producer at the Columbia Broadcasting System (CBS). He is also the author of *Bias: A CBS Insider Exposes How the Media Distort the News* (Regnery, 2001).

MARY GORDON is a novelist and short-story writer. She is the author of *Penal Discipline: Female Prisoners* (Gordon Press, 1992), *The Rest of Life: Three Novellas* (Viking Penguin, 1993), and *The Other Side* (Wheeler, 1994).

AL GORE was the Vice President of the United States, 1993–2001, and the Democratic candidate for president in 2000. He is the author of two books on environmental issues: *Earth in the Balance: Ecology and the Human Spirit* (Plume Books, 1992) and *An Inconvenient Truth* (Rodale Books, 2006), and the narrator of a documentary film based on the latter book.

GARY L. GREGG is director of the Center for Political Leadership at the University of Louisville and editor of *Securing Democracy: Why We Have an Electoral College* (ISI Books, 2001) and, with Mark Rosell, *Considering the Bush Presidency* (Oxford University Press, 2003).

MARK GREEN is a political activist and frequent candidate who worked and wrote with consumer advocate Ralph Nader. He is co-editor, with Eric Alterman, of *The Book on Bush: How George W. (Mis)leads America* (Viking, 2004).

DAVID A. HARRIS is Balk Professor of Law and Values at University of Toledo College of Law and Soros Senior Justice Fellow. He is the author of *Profiles in Injustice: Why Racial Profiling Cannot Work* (New Press, 2002).

NAT HENTOFF writes a weekly column for *The Village Voice,* the leading New York alternative weekly. He has written novels, biographies, and books on civil liberties, including *Free Speech for Me and Not for Thee: How the American Left and Right Relentlessly Censor Each Other.* Among other publications, he has written for *The New Yorker,* the *Atlantic, New Republic, Commonweal,* and on jazz for *The Wall Street Journal.*

DOUGLAS A. IRWIN is professor of economics at Dartmouth College and research associate of the National Bureau of Economic Research. He is the author of *Against the Tide: An Intellectual History of Free Trade* (Princeton University Press, 1996) and *Managed Trade: The Case Against Import Targets* (AEI Press, 1994).

ROBERT JERVIS is professor of international relations at Columbia University. In addition to articles in leading international relations periodicals, he is the author of several books, including most recently *American Foreign Policy in a New Era* (Routledge, 2005).

ROBERT F. KENNEDY, JR. teaches environmental law at the Pace University School of Law and is co-director of the university's environmental litigation clinic. He also serves as a senior attorney for the Natural Resources Defense Council, a legal and lobbying firm that works to strengthen and enforce environmental laws.

CHARLES KRAUTHAMMER is a syndicated columnist whose articles appear in the *Washington Post, Time* magazine, and other publications.

MARK KRIKORIAN is executive director of the Center for Immigration Studies.

PAUL KRUGMAN is professor of economics and international affairs at Princeton University and an op-ed columnist for *The New York Times.* He is the author of many books and articles, including *The Great Unraveling: Losing Our Way in the New Century* (W.W. Norton, 2003), a collection of newspaper columns and essays.

ROBERT W. LEE is a contributing editor to *The New American* and the author of *The United Nations Conspiracy* (Western Islands, 1981).

ROBERT J. LIEBER is professor of government and international relations at Georgetown University, and the author or editor of thirteen books on international relations and U.S. foreign policy.

GLENN C. LOURY is university professor, professor of economics, and director of the Institute on Race and Social Division at Boston University.

JEFF MADRICK, editor of *Challenge* magazine, is a visiting professor at Cooper Union in New York. He is the author of several books, including *Why Economies Grow: The Forces That Shape Prosperity and How to Get Them Working Again* (Basic Books, 2002). His articles appear in *The American Prospect* and *The New York Review of Books*.

HEATHER MacDONALD is contributing editor of *City Journal* and a Fellow at the Manhattan Institute. She is the author of *The Burden of Bad Ideas: How Modern Intellectuals Misshape Our Society* and *Are Cops Racist?: How the War Against the Police Harms Black Americans*. She contributes frequently to the New York *Daily News,* the *New York Post,* and the *Weekly Standard.*

ANDREW C. McCARTHY was the U.S. attorney who led the 1995 terrorism prosecution that resulted in the conviction of Islamic militants for conducting urban terrorism, including the 1993 World Trade Center bombing. His essays have been published in *The Weekly Standard, Commentary, Middle East Quarterly,* and other publications.

WILFRED M. McCLAY holds the SunTrust Chair of Humanities at the University of Tennessee at Chattanooga.

DAVID MORRIS is cofounder and vice president of the Institute for Local Self-Reliance, director of its New Rules Project, and editor of the institute's publications, including *The New Rules* and *The Carbohydrate Economy.*

JOSHUA MURAVCHIK is a resident scholar at the American Enterprise Institute and an adjunct professor at the Institute of World Politics. He writes on Middle East politics, democracy, neoconservatism, and the history of socialism.

DANIEL PIPES is director of the Middle East Forum, a member of the presidentially appointed U.S. Institute for Peace, and a columnist for the *New York Sun* and the *Jerusalem Post.* His most recent book is *Miniatures: View of Islamic and Middle Eastern Politics* (Transaction Publishers, 2003).

WILLIAM H. REHNQUIST was appointed as an Associate Justice of the United States Supreme Court by President Richard Nixon in 1972, and then appointed as Chief Justice by President Ronald Reagan in 1986, in which position he served until shortly before his death in 2005. The Rehnquist Court was marked by increased conservatism in the court's leading opinions.

JOHN SAMPLES is the director of the CATO Institute Center for Representative Government. He is a frequent contributor to *The American Spectator* and other publications.

ANTONIN SCALIA is associate justice of the United States Supreme Court.

FRANK SHARRY is executive director of the National Immigration Forum.

AMITY SHLAES is an editorial writer on tax policy for *The Wall Street Journal.* She is the author of *Germany: The Empire Within* (Farrar, Straus & Giroux), and has been published in *Commentary* and *The New Yorker.*

ANDREW SULLIVAN is a journalist, blogger, and former editor of *The New Republic,* to which he frequently contributes.

WALTER E. WILLIAMS is the John M. Olin Distinguished Professor of Economics at George Mason University.

HOWARD ZINN, historian, playwright, and social activist, is best known for his book, *A People's History of the United States.* He has taught at Spelman College and Boston University, and has been a visiting professor at the University of Paris and the University of Bologna.

Index

0093592

TAKING SIDES

Clashing Views on

Political Issues

FIFTEENTH EDITION

Mc Graw Hill Contemporary Learning Series

A Division of The McGraw-Hill Companies